Lehrerhandbuch

Klasse! 2

Corinna Schicker
Sheila Brighten
Steve Williams

OXFORD
UNIVERSITY PRESS

Great Clarendon Street, Oxford OX2 6DP

Oxford University Press is a department of the University of Oxford. It furthers the University's objective of excellence in research, scholarship and education by publishing worldwide in

Oxford New York

Athens Auckland Bangkok Bogotá Buenos Aires Kolkata
Cape Town Chennai Dar es Salaam Delhi Florence
Hong Kong Istanbul Karachi Kuala Lumpur Madrid
Melbourne Mexico City Mumbai Nairobi Paris São Paulo
Shanghai Singapore Taipei Tokyo Toronto Warsaw
with associated companies in Berlin Ibadan

Oxford is a registered trade mark of Oxford University Press
in the UK and in certain other countries

First published 2001

ISBN 0 19 912274 1

Acknowledgements

The authors would like to thank the following people for their help and advice: Sharon Brien (course consultant), David Buckland, Marion Dill (language consultant), Kathryn Tate.

Designed and typeset by Herb Bowes Graphics, Oxford

Printed in Great Britain by Athenaeum Press, Gateshead

Contents

Symbols used in this Teacher's Book and in the Students' Book:

listening material on cassette or CD	
WB A	consolidation activities available in Workbook
C 10	copymaster materials available
AT 1.1	reference to National Curriculum attainment level
	pairwork activity
	groupwork activity

Summary of unit contents

Unit, Language contexts	Grammar	Skill focus	Pronunciation
Einheit 1 Wie waren die Ferien? Holidays; destinations; weather; activities; accommodation	Perfect tense of *haben* and *sein* Imperfect tense of *sein* *in* + dative case	Adapting a written text Making notes during listening activities	Pronouncing past participles
Einheit 2 Mein Alltag Daily routine; household chores; pocket money; part-time jobs	Reflexive verbs Inverted word order after a time phrase Separable verbs Accusative case: *den/die/das/die* *von* + dative *für* + accusative	Dictionary skills: reflexive verbs Expressing opinions	Inflections
Einheit 3 Freunde und Familie Appearance of people; best friends; your own character and other people's; relationships with parents; reasons for arguing; things you have to do and are not allowed to do	Possessive adjectives Nominative adjectives with and without endings *weil* and subordinate word order *müssen* and *dürfen*	Expressing opinions Dictionary skills: separable verbs	Pronunciation of –*b*, -*g*, -*t*
Einheit 4 Mode Clothes; likes and dislikes; school uniform; colours; favourite clothes	Plural nouns *dieser* and *welcher* Adjectival endings in the accusative after the indefinite article	Dictionary skills: plural nouns Correcting and redrafting written work Listening for detail	Vowels with and without an *Umlaut*
Einheit 5 Wie war die Party? Dates of birthdays and special events/celebrations; party invitations; accepting/refusing invitations; making excuses; saying where things are; birthday presents	*in* + dative *müssen* *auf, in, neben, unter* + dative	Letter-writing: dates Role-plays Identifying the meanings of unfamiliar words	Greetings
Einheit 6 Wir gehen in die Stadt Buildings/things to do in a town; meeting places; shops; lost property	*können* and *wollen* *in* + accusative/dative *an* and *vor* + dative Accusative of *mein/meine/mein*	Adapting language for different contexts	*ei* and *ie*
Einheit 7 Meine Umgebung Town and countryside; likes and dislikes; the environment	Adjective endings, accusative mixed declension, strong declension plural *weil* Comparative and superlative of adjectives	Expressing opinions Summarizing a spoken or written text	Pronunciation of long words
Einheit 8 Gesundes Leben Parts of the body; illnesses; remedies; healthy/unhealthy lifestyle	*seit* + present tense Imperative *sollen* Future tense	Meanings and genders of compound nouns Making a short presentation	Pronunciation of compound nouns
Einheit 9 Zukunft Plans for holidays; resolutions; comparing this year with next year; jobs; future plans	Future tense Review of perfect, present and future tenses Masculine and feminine forms of job titles *Ich möchte … werden* Review: *ich möchte*	Reading comprehension Recording a longer text	*ch* and *sch*

Introduction

The course

Welcome to **Klasse! 2.**

This is the second stage of a three-part course for learners of German. A nationwide survey identified the need for materials which provided coherent progression over the four or five years of foreign language learning, not only in terms of lexical items, but also in terms of grammar, pronunciation and skills development. Our response to this need is **Klasse!**, which provides a variety of lively learning materials, together with a systematic approach to the development of grammar, pronunciation, and linguistic and study skills. The course is clearly set out and easy to use.

Klasse! is a broad-ability course, designed for communicative language teaching. The focus in Stage 1 is on topics which are familiar to younger learners, e.g. personal identity, school, hobbies. Stage 2 builds on the personal language already met and deals with new areas, e.g. clothes, holidays, the environment. Stage 3 provides thorough preparation for the exam at 16+ within teenage-related contexts. Differentiated materials are integrated into the course to cater for a wide range of pupils, including all but the least able.

Rationale

The aims of **Klasse!** are:

- to present language in interesting and relevant contexts, expressing the kind of things young learners of German will want to be able to say
- to present and practise language via tasks with a clear purpose
- to promote language awareness, including a clear focus on pronunciation
- to provide a coherent approach to grammar in a communicative way
- to develop study skills, e.g. vocabulary learning strategies, dictionary skills, independent work
- to promote reading for pleasure, with a variety of reading material in every unit, including the *Thema im Fokus* pages
- to provide pupils with opportunities for regular revision, e.g. *Thema im Fokus* pages in each unit, copymasters, Workbook, ICT component, revision pages after every three units
- to encourage success by providing clear objectives and language summary sections for each unit
- to combine language in a project outcome at the end of each unit, giving pupils the opportunity to use new language and recycle other language in a new context
- to provide differentiated materials
- to maximize the use of German as the means of communication in the classroom
- to broaden pupils' awareness of life and culture in Germany and German-speaking countries
- to build confidence through a carefully structured approach which combines all aspects of language

learning, thus ensuring that pupils are able to progress coherently from dependent to more independent learners of German.

The components of Klasse! 2

Students' Book

Stage 2 ensures that pupils have appropriate activities for their second year of learning German, providing the necessary programme of teaching, practice, revision and reference materials. Throughout **Klasse!**, full attention has been given to the National Curriculum Programme of Study and SOED National Guidelines and full details of coverage are given in the grids that precede the notes on each unit in this book. A 160-page book in full colour, the Students' Book contains the following sections:

Die Klasse-Clique!

This introduces pupils to the four young people who feature throughout the book. Pupils who have been following Stage 1 will have met these characters already, but will find this summary useful.

Einheiten 1–9

There are nine twelve-page units on different topics. Each unit has been planned to be interesting and motivating, as well as providing a coherent and systematic approach to language development, e.g. grammar, pronunciation and study skills. An outline of the content of each unit is given on Teacher's Book page 4. For a detailed description of the features of a **Klasse!** unit, please refer to pages 7–8 of this book.

Wiederholung

After every three units, there is a page containing a range of revision activities across the four skills, aimed at providing consolidation and further practice of the language of the preceding units. Pupils can work on these activities independently, with a partner or as a whole class with their teacher. Some of the activities can also be done as homework activities.
The revision pages cannot cover all the language of the preceding units, but together with the assessment copymasters (*Kontrolle*), they provide the opportunity for pupils to demonstrate most of what they have learnt.

Noch mal!

A page of consolidation and reinforcement activities for each unit, placed at the back of the Students' Book, for those pupils who would benefit from further practice of some of the key language of the unit.

Extra!

A page of extension activities for each unit, at the back of the Students' Book, for motivated and more able learners who would benefit from some more challenging tasks.

Grammatik

This is a more detailed reference section which complements the explanations given within the body of the book. The grammar points are presented simply, but in a way which will help pupils to use other reference materials later on. The grammatical explanations in the units and grammar reference section are in English to ensure that all pupils can use them independently. An important feature of the **Klasse!** grammar section are the additional grammar practice activities, which are integrated in the appropriate grammatical explanation for pupils wishing to consolidate or revise further their grammatical knowledge. The answers for these activities are at the end of the grammar section in the Students' Book for self-checking.

Hilfreiche Ausdrücke

Following the grammar reference section, there is a small section containing useful general vocabulary for easy reference, including numbers, days, months, dates and countries.

Vokabular

A German–English glossary contains the words in the Students' Book for pupils' reference.

Workbook

The Workbook is an integral part of **Klasse!** It has been designed to provide reinforcement and extra practice for the Students' Book. Each Workbook activity is signposted at the most appropriate place in the Students' Book by a yellow and green arrow, providing a coherent path between Students' Book and Workbook.

In the Workbook there are ten pages per Students' Book unit, and activities provide consolidation of all key language and grammar in all four skills. The listening material is on cassette/CD 4, which can be duplicated for pupils to use for independent study, in class or as homework. *Du bist dran!* activities throughout the Workbook provide an opportunity for pupils to write down information about themselves. These can be used as a record of achievement and can be used for continuous assessment purposes. The songs from the Students' Book are reproduced in the Workbook and on cassette/CD 4 and a range of activities to exploit the song texts is provided.

At the end of each unit a checklist in English gives pupils the chance to assess their progress. The checklist is divided into the four attainment targets, providing a convenient resource for continuous assessment. A more comprehensive version in the Teacher's Book details which Students' Book activities can be used for assessment purposes for each objective, broken down by skill.

Teacher's Book

Detailed teaching notes are provided for each unit.

These notes include:

- ideas for presenting and practising new language
- detailed suggestions for using the material in the Students' Book
- ideas for additional differentiated activities
- some background information on the topics covered
- answers to all the activities
- suggestions for further activities to reinforce and extend the content of the Students' Book
- information about the Workbook and copymasters, including answers, for each unit
- transcripts for all recorded material
- answers and a mark scheme for the assessment activities
- scripts for the *Fun With Texts* ICT component and suggestions for using ICT.

Coursemaster

The Coursemaster provides teachers with an instant library of ready-made files for departmental planning and recording. The files are fully in line with the QCA Scheme of Work, and are referenced to the revised National Curriculum (September 2000). Four types of files are contained on the disk:

1. Unit overviews (one for each unit of the Students' Book) are ready-filled with information on new language, contexts, learning expectations and where the unit fits into the Scheme of Work as a whole.
2. Unit Scheme of Work files (one for every two-page spread of the Students' Book) are ready-filled with information on resources required, learning objectives, Attainment Target levels, Programme of Study, etc.
3. The Pupil Record of Progress can be issued to pupils in printed form and is broken down by Attainment Target.
4. The Class Record of Progress facilitates recording of continuous assessment and review tests, and provision is made for an overall level score per Attainment Target.

Cassettes/CDs

The cassettes/CDs provide the listening material to accompany the Students' Book, Workbook, copymasters and assessment material. The copymaster material for each unit follows the material for the corresponding Students' Book unit. The cassettes were recorded by native German speakers. The material is scripted and contains a range of types, including monologues, short dialogues, longer conversations and songs. All cassettes/CDs may be copied within the purchasing institution for use by teachers and pupils. Cassette/CD 4 contains the listening material for the Workbook, which can be duplicated for the pupils, for independent study.

Contents:
Cassette 1 side 1: Die Klasse-Clique, Unit 1, Unit 2 (up to *Extra!* page)
side 2: Unit 2 (copymasters), Unit 3, Revision and Assessment Units 1–3
Cassette 2 side 1: Unit 4, Unit 5 (up to *Extra!* page)
side 2: Unit 5 (copymasters), Unit 6, Revision and Assessment Units 4–6

Cassette 3 side 1: Unit 7, Unit 8 (up to p.105)
          side 2: Unit 8 (cont.), Unit 9, Revision and
                  Assessment Units 7–9
Cassette 4 side 1: Workbook, Units 1–5
          side 2: Workbook, Units 6–9

Copymasters

The copymasters are an integral part of **Klasse!** and
there are cross-references to them throughout the
Teacher's Book. Notes and transcripts for each unit's
copymasters are provided together at the end of each
unit's notes in the Teacher's Book. The copymasters
provide opportunities for further practice and extension
of the language of the unit.

Each unit has the following copymasters:

Visuals – two sheets of visuals for presenting and
practising new language (see pages 11–12 of this book
for suggestions)

Vokabular – summary of the key language of the unit for
learners to use as reference and for revision purposes.
Pupils should be encouraged to note any other useful
language of their own, either in a vocabulary book or on
the back of this copymaster

Hören – additional graded listening activities

Sprechen – further opportunities for speaking practice,
usually based on an information-gap activity

Lesen – additional graded reading activities

Schreiben – additional graded writing activities

Grammatik – thorough consolidation and practice of
grammatical points

Tipp – further practice of linguistic and study skills from
the unit

Kontrolle – assessment copymasters, for use after every
three units. There is one sheet for each of the four skill
areas (two sheets for reading).

The **Grammatik** and **Tipp** copymasters contain some
English for purposes such as grammatical explanations.
This is to ensure that pupils can work on these
copymasters independently.

Klasse! Informatik 2
This is **Klasse!**'s own ICT component. See detailed notes
on pages 14–27.

Teaching with Klasse! 2

Summary of main characters

The language of **Klasse!** in Stages 1 and 2 is set in the
context of the lives of four teenagers who live in Wesel.
The characters can be introduced using *Die Klasse!-
Clique* on page 7 of the Students' Book.

As pupils progress through the book, they learn more
about each of the characters. The four main characters
are: Jasmin, Sven, Annika and Atalay, who all appeared
in Stage 1. The characters feature in Stage 2 in the

context of an ongoing photo story at the start of each
unit.

Features of a Klasse! 2 unit

Die Klasse!-Clique
The opening spread for each unit contains an episode of
the soap opera *Die Klasse!-Clique*, set in the town of
Wesel and featuring the four main characters from
Klasse! 1. The episode is designed to provide an
introduction to the topic and the language of the unit
and to motivate pupils at the start of each new unit.
Activities to exploit the episode are provided on the page
and general suggestions for exploitation are given on
pages 10–11 of this book.

Songs
Most units contain a song, which is intended to provide
enjoyment, as well as to develop language skills. The
songs introduce some of the key language to be covered
in the unit and provide a fun way into the topic of the
unit. Where possible, pupils should be encouraged to
sing along with the cassette, as this will provide
additional pronunciation and intonation practice. Some
pupils will enjoy writing additional verses and more
musical pupils should be encouraged to compose other
songs to further practise the language of the unit.

Ideas for using songs:

- Start the lesson with a familiar song to give a German
  feel to the lesson
- Allow pupils to hear the whole song before working on
  it in smaller sections, perhaps starting with the chorus
  where applicable
- Don't worry if you're no good at singing – the songs
  can be used just as a listening activity if you prefer. All
  of the songs have activities in the Workbook.
- Use flashcards or visuals to provide support for a new
  song
- Encourage pupils to make up actions for a song if
  appropriate
- Split the class into two groups – who can sing the
  loudest? the most tunefully?
- Perform the songs (e.g. to another class, at an
  assembly, at an open evening)
- Get pupils to draw symbols or small pictures for each
  verse as they listen, or use the words of the song as a
  reading text for pupils to illustrate
- Ask pupils to memorize a verse or two for homework
- End the lesson with a song. Pupils will leave the
  classroom singing it or humming the tune!

Objectives
Each double-page spread of a unit has specific
objectives given in English, but supported by examples
in German.

The purpose of these frequent objectives is to ensure
that learners have a clear understanding of what they
are going to learn and are motivated by the speed of
their progress. The objectives are there to 'introduce' the
topic and offer the possibility of brainstorming-related
language learned in other contexts, and the examples in

German covered can be used by pupils for reference and revision.

Presentation and practice activities

New vocabulary is best introduced by the teacher using visuals. For specific notes on visuals, see page 11.

New language is presented in the Students' Book in a variety of ways, through the soap opera, other photos and illustrations. The soap opera conversations are provided on cassette and should be used for repetition by the pupils, as this will ensure the best possible pronunciation and intonation. Pupils will enjoy learning these short exchanges by heart and 'performing' them to the rest of the class. More able pupils can adapt the conversations by substituting phrases with other items of key language. Pupils should be encouraged to learn by heart on a regular basis, both items of vocabulary and short conversations. This will promote good language-learning habits and ensure that pupils are able to transfer language learned to new contexts.

Each topic is developed through a wide variety of mixed-skill practice, with activities to ensure language development from supported/guided to more open-ended activities. **Klasse!** intends each activity to have a purpose for learners, to ensure that they find the activities interesting as well as useful in terms of their linguistic development. The copymasters and the Workbook provide further consolidation and practice activities for each unit. Extension activities are provided both on the *Noch mal!* and *Extra!* pages at the end of the book and within each unit, whilst further grammar practice activities are provided in the grammar reference section at the end of the Students' Book.

Hilfe

The key language is summarized in these boxes on most spreads to provide support and reference for pupils. Pupils will find these sections useful for revision, and they may wish to copy this key language into their vocabulary books, although a summary of the key language for each unit is also provided on a copymaster for pupil reference and revision purposes.

Grammatik im Fokus

Grammar is included as a central part of each unit, as pupils need to understand how the language works from an early stage if they are to manipulate and use it successfully in other contexts. Pupils are exposed to examples that occur naturally in context in the units and are then encouraged to reflect on these and work out the rules. If teachers feel it is appropriate, pupils can be referred to the grammar reference section at the back of the book where a more in-depth explanation and practice activities are provided. The purple arrow on each grammar section indicates the relevant page number. Further practice is also provided in the Students' Book, in the Workbook, on the copymasters and on the revision pages.

An overview of the introduction and recycling of the grammatical points in **Klasse! 2** is given on page 4 of this

book. Please refer to the **Klasse! 1** Teacher's Book for a summary of grammatical points already covered.

Wiederholung

Grammar points already covered in Stage 1 or in an earlier unit of Stage 2 are flashed up where appropriate to act as a reminder to pupils, and as an aid to completing specific activities on the page where the panel appears.

Gut gesagt!

This regular feature encourages learners to focus on improving their pronunciation and intonation, enabling them to develop good habits in spoken German. Sounds which are traditionally more difficult for the English speaker are featured. This section should be made as much fun as possible in class, with whole-class repetition, followed by group- and individual work. Pupils who find pronunciation difficult should be given opportunities to further practise these sections on a regular basis, perhaps by recording them onto a separate cassette for independent use. An overview of all the pronunciation points for Stage 2 is provided in the Summary of contents grid on page 4 of this book.

Tipp

This regular feature promotes language-learning skills in a systematic way throughout **Klasse!** The skills are developed by means of practice activities on the corresponding copymasters for each unit. The development of language-learning skills is considered to be an integral part of the language-learning process and should be given sufficient time during whole-class work. Pupils who are given opportunities to practise these skills from the start will develop into effective independent language learners. For an overview of the language-learning skills of Stage 2, see page 4 of this book.

Kannst du ... ?

This checklist at the end of each unit summarizes the key language and grammatical content of the unit. This section corresponds to the objectives for the unit and the various *Grammatik im Fokus* sections. The checklist should be actively used by the teacher together with the pupils to help them review what they have learned in each unit. It should also be used by pupils to reflect on areas for further revision and practice. A full list of the key language for each unit is provided on the *Vokabular* copymasters. An English version of the checklist is provided at the end of each Workbook unit, providing pupils with a written record of their progress in each attainment target.

Thema im Fokus

Each of the nine units ends with a *Thema im Fokus* spread – a combined reading and project outcome for the unit. The spread combines the language of the whole unit and starts each time with a written text to act as a stimulus. The written texts take a variety of formats, ranging from tourist brochures and magazine extracts to articles giving background to cultural events. This offers pupils the chance to read items relating to the topic, but often in slightly diffferent contexts to those covered in the units themselves. Pupils should be encouraged to read the texts for pleasure and, to this end, only minimal comprehension tasks have been provided on the page. Teachers or foreign language assistants may wish to use these texts with the whole class, reading various items aloud for pupils to follow and repeat and by asking comprehension questions. Pupils should be given opportunities to read the items in pairs and groups, as this will encourage success. Dictionaries should be made available to pupils.

Pupils then build on what they have read to use the language they have learnt in the unit in a mini-project. A range of ideas and activities is suggested to encourage pupils to work imaginatively and creatively to produce work to the best of their ability. Pupils should be encouraged to use all available resources; computers, art equipment, cassette and video recorders, penfriends and link classes/schools, magazines and leaflets, dictionaries and information from the Internet. Each mini-project offers ample opportunity for pupils to work independently of the teacher and co-operatively in pairs and groups with others. Opportunities to work with a foreign language assistant would greatly enhance pupils' work on their project. It is not intended that every pupil will do every activity on the *Thema im Fokus* spread, but rather that pupils select an activity which interests them. However, teachers will need to ensure that able pupils are selecting sufficiently challenging activities, so that they can demonstrate what they have learned in the unit. Similarly, less able pupils may need to be guided to appropriate activities on the page to ensure that the outcome is successful. The activities on this page can be done/finished off as homework tasks. Much of the work produced for the mini-project could form the basis for displays and be used as evidence of pupils' achievements.

Target language

Klasse! aims to maximize the use of German as the means of communication in the classroom by providing rubrics and explanations in German. It is worth spending time on a regular basis revising classroom language, so that pupils are reminded of the key phrases and encouraged to use them.

Some suggestions for revising target language phrases:

– Play *Wie sagt man …?* at the start or end of the lesson. Two pupils come to the front of the class and the teacher asks a question (e.g. *Wie sagt man 'I haven't got a partner'?*). The winner is the first one to answer correctly. Another pupil then comes to the front to challenge the winner. Who can stay out at the front the longest? As pupils become more confident, greater emphasis should be placed on correct pronunciation and intonation. Some pupils will enjoy assuming the role of the teacher, too.
– The teacher or pupils choose an *Ausdruck der Woche* which is displayed at the front of the class. Every time a pupil uses the phrase in a relevant way a point is awarded. The points are added together at the end of

the week. Can the score be beaten by the phrase for the following week?
– Key target language phrases should be displayed in the classroom for pupils to refer to easily. To ensure that pupils don't rely on these phrases too much, cover up particular words (maybe using Post-it labels) on a rotational basis!
– Use brainstorming of target language phrases as a team game on a regular basis. Pupils work in pairs/teams to complete a phrase (e.g. *Ich habe kein/e/n …*) with as many possibilities as they can in three minutes. This could be varied to incorporate phrases for pairwork (*Schreib Sätze für Partnerarbeit auf*) or questions (*Schreib Fragen für deinen/deine Lehrer/in oder deinen/deine Partner/in auf*). Again, a time limit provides a useful element of competition.

A systematic and gradual introduction of key target language phrases will ensure that pupils recognize instructions quickly. Teachers should refer to their departmental policy for target language, but the following phrases might prove a useful starting point.

Setz dich/Setzt euch!
Steh/Steht auf, bitte!
Komm/Kommt bitte her!
Verstehst du/Versteht ihr?
Ruhe, bitte!

Hör/Hört die Kassette an.
Sieh/Seht …
Teil/Teilt die Hefte aus, bitte.
Sieh/Seht Seite X an.
Mach/Macht jetzt Übung X auf Seite X, bitte.
Schreib/Schreibt …
Mach/Macht jetzt die Übungen auf dem Arbeitsbogen.
Schreib/Schreibt die Tabelle in deinem Heft/euren Heften ab.
Notiere/Notiert jetzt deine/eure Hausaufgaben.
Bereite/Bereitet … vor.
Räume/Räumt deine/eure Sachen weg.

Partnerarbeit!/Arbeite/Arbeitet jetzt mit einem Partner/einer Partnerin.
Gruppenarbeit!/Arbeite/Arbeitet jetzt in einer Gruppe.
Dann ist Partner/Partnerin A/B dran.

Managing differentiation

There will be a broad range of pupils within any beginners' class. Ideas for consolidation and extension activities are given for each unit in the Teacher's Book.

There are particular features of **Klasse! 2** which will make it easier to differentiate work:

– Certain activities in the Students' Book have a *Noch mal!* and an *Extra!* activity. These are brief consolidation and extension activities for pupils to respond to at the level most appropriate for them.
– For each unit there is a *Noch mal!* and an *Extra!* page at the back of the book. The *Noch mal!* page provides

further practice of the core language of the unit. The *Extra!* page provides more challenging activities for more able pupils who could do the activities on this page when they complete other work quickly or as an alternative homework activity. For some of the activities, pupils will need a copy of the cassette/CD. The *Noch mal!* and *Extra!* pages could be done by pupils who finish the *Thema im Fokus* section and are ready for additional work on the topic.

- The *Thema im Fokus* spread suggests a variety of activities at different levels. Differentiation by outcome will be a major part of these activities, but pupils can be guided towards different activities according to their ability.
- The Workbook provides consolidation and reinforcement activities for less able pupils and useful extra practice for all abilities. These activities can be used in class or for homework, possibly while other pupils are working on the extension materials or practising grammar points in more detail.
- The copymasters provide differentiated activities. Activities are graded, and the final task may not always be appropriate for all learners.
- Within the teaching notes for individual activities, there are often suggestions for differentiation, e.g. varying the amount of support offered and adapting the tasks slightly to suit different pupils.

The following additional classroom management suggestions may help teachers wishing to further differentiate activities:

- Listening activities: individual copies of cassettes could be provided for less able pupils to work at their own pace, allowing them to play the cassette several times, possibly with the transcript. Able pupils who complete a listening task on the first hearing could be encouraged to note any other information they hear and check this against the transcript.
- Paired/group listening, reading and writing: pupils can usefully work together on many activities. Two weaker pupils working together will usually tackle a task with more success than one. A more able pupil working with a less able pupil will have the dual effect of helping one pupil, while consolidating language for the other.
- Writing activities: pupils should be encouraged to prepare a first draft of longer writing activities. This could then be improved in consultation with other pupils or the teacher. Basic errors could be eliminated in this way for less able pupils, and more able pupils could be encouraged to use a wider variety of vocabulary and structure.
- Groupwork lessons on a regular basis will make it easier to ensure that pupils are provided with appropriate consolidation and extension work. For example, a groupwork lesson towards the end of the topic might have some pupils revising basic vocabulary using the visuals (see page 12 of this book for ideas), some pupils working on copymaster or Workbook activities, and others working on the *Noch mal!* and *Extra!* pages. If a computer is available in the classroom, some pupils could be drafting some

written work or working on the *Klasse! Informatik* materials, too.

Independent learning

In the early stages of learning a new language, pupils are reasonably dependent on their teacher for presentation of new language. However, certain features of **Klasse!** are designed to encourage learner independence:

- After an initial presentation, the visuals provided on copymaster can be used by pupils to practise new vocabulary through a variety of games (see pages 12–13 of this book).
- Any of the copymasters can be used independently by pupils. Where appropriate, the *Tipp* and *Grammatik* copymasters include explanations in English. This is to ensure that pupils clearly understand the concepts, but also so that they can work on these copymasters independently of the teacher, either on their own or with a partner. The *Tipp* copymasters encourage pupils to reflect on how they learn, which is an important step towards independent learning.
- The emphasis on 'reading for pleasure' at the start of the *Thema im Fokus* pages provides an ideal opportunity for pupils to work independently. The mini-projects provide several suggested activities, and it is intended that pupils select an appropriate activity to work on, possibly with a partner or a small group.
- The *Noch mal!* and *Extra!* activities throughout the book plus the pages at the back of the Students' Book can be used in class or for independent work by more able pupils.
- The *Kannst du … ?* section at the end of the unit (and the corresponding English version in the Workbook) could be effectively used by pupils to review their progress and highlight any areas requiring further revision. This good habit will need to be established by the teacher over the first few units.
- The Workbook can be used by pupils for class work or independent work. It provides reinforcement activities for less able pupils and extra practice for all abilities. The *Can you …?* checklist at the end of each unit provides a summary in English of the key language and grammar in each unit. Pupils will find this useful for revision purposes.
- The grammar section at the back of the Students' Book provides full explanations of all the grammar points in English and also additional practice activities. Some pupils will find this invaluable when revising a unit's grammar points.
- The *Klasse! Informatik* component can be used in class or it can be made available for pupils to use independently on other occasions. Again, it encourages regular revision and recycling of previously learned language.

Using the soap opera: *Die Klasse!-Clique*

Each of the nine units in **Klasse! 2** begins with an episode of the soap opera, *Die Klasse!-Clique*, featuring four teenage friends. New language is introduced in the context of events in their lives, and the episode will motivate pupils by offering characters for them to identify with and a storyline to follow. There are activities on the page to help them cope with the unfamiliar and also to help develop their reading strategies.

A summary of the storyline for each episode is included in the teacher's notes.

There are many ways to approach using the story and you will need to select those most appropriate for your pupils. The following suggestions may be useful:

- In the Students' Book there are exploitation activities, the first of which is a pre-reading task. Your pupils might find this activity helpful before embarking on the actual episode.
- Introduce some of the new key vocabulary, e.g. clothes, using flashcards or visuals in the usual way, before reading and listening to the episode.
- Allow pupils to listen to the cassette/CD while reading. In this way, pupils will be encouraged to read for gist and won't have time to stop and worry about individual words at this stage. More detailed comprehension activities in the Students' Book will check their understanding more thoroughly later.
- Develop reading strategies with your pupils. For example, encourage pupils to deduce the meanings of new words which are cognates; ask pupils to look up a maximum of five words in the glossary and share their findings with a partner; ask pupils to pick out key words; ask pupils to make a list of any questions occuring in the soap opera, to ask a partner who can either answer from the story or give another appropriate answer.
- When pupils have listened to the episode and read it several times, you could divide the class into groups who each take one of the parts. Choral reading gives all pupils the opportunity to practise reading aloud, without putting any individual on the spot.
- More confident pupils could take a part each. Each pupil reads his/her part along with the cassette. This will encourage fluency as pupils try to keep up with the cassette. You could turn down the volume control every now and then, so that the pupils continue to speak unaccompanied, and then turn the volume back up again to see if they have managed to keep up with the cassette.
- Pupils might like to work in groups to act out each episode or record their own version on cassette or video.
- After each episode, write a brief summary of it on OHT with the help of the pupils. The OHT can then be shown at the start of the next unit to remind pupils of the storyline so far. For the first few units, you may have to prompt the summary with oral questions for the pupils to answer. Creating a summary in this collaborative way allows you to accept suggestions from the pupils, while at the same time correcting any inaccuracies and improving the quality of language as you write the suggestions onto OHT for the class to see. As they become more used to this process, some pupils might like to draft their own summary of the story.
- As you work through each unit, you can come back to the soap opera to look for examples of particular language/grammar points. You can also return to it at the end of a unit, to act it out now that pupils have much more familiarity with the language.

Grammar

One of the underlying principles of **Klasse!** is that all learners need to be presented with grammatical structures in a systematic and coherent way. A full overview of the introduction and recycling of grammar points in Stage 2 can be found in the Summary of contents grid on page 4 of this book. A measure of the importance attached to grammar is reflected in the numerous opportunities for consolidation and practice:

- the *Grammatik im Fokus* sections in the Students' Book
- the *Grammatik* copymaster for each unit
- some revision work on the *Wiederholung* pages and some additional work on the *Noch mal!* and *Extra!* pages
- grammar activities at a simple level in the Workbook
- additional practice activities (and answers) integrated into the grammar section at the back of the Students' Book.

Study skills

The authors of **Klasse!** consider that the gradual development of linguistic and study skills in a coherent way is essential if beginners are to move from being dependent to independent learners. Stage 2 builds on a wide range of skills (see Summary of contents grid on page 4 of this book), which are referred to in the Students' Book and then applied in a more detailed way on the *Tipp* copymasters. The importance of applying and practising these linguistic and study skills is one of the distinguishing features of **Klasse!** Teachers wishing to relate these skills to the National Curriculum Programme of Study (1 Acquiring knowledge and understanding of the target language; 2 Developing language skills; 3 Developing language-learning skills; 4 Developing cultural awareness; 5 Breadth of study) should refer to the grids that precede the notes on each unit in this book.

Visuals

A summary of the visuals provided on copymasters is supplied below. These can be enlarged or used on OHTs as flashcards.

Copymaster 1: Weather symbols: *Es war heiß. Es war kalt. Es war sonnig. Es hat geregnet. Es war neblig. Es hat geschneit. Es war windig. Es war wolkig. Es war schlecht. Es war schön.*

Copymaster 2: Holiday accommodation: *Hotel, Ferienwohnung, Wohnwagen, Zelt, Wohnmobil, Jugendherberge, Gastfamilie, bei Freunden, zu Hause*

Copymaster 10: Daily routine and household chores: *Ich stehe auf. Ich wasche mich. Ich ziehe mich an. Ich frühstücke. Ich gehe in die Schule. Ich gehe nach Hause. Ich ziehe mich aus. Ich gehe ins Bett. Ich räume mein Zimmer auf. Ich putze das Badezimmer. Ich sauge Staub. Ich wasche ab.*

Copymaster 11: Household chores and part-time jobs: *Ich füttere den Hund und die Katze. Ich decke den Tisch. Ich kaufe ein. Ich helfe zu Hause. Ich arbeite im Garten. Ich bin Babysitter(in). Ich führe den Hund aus. Ich wasche das Auto. Ich trage Zeitungen aus. Ich habe keinen Nebenjob. Ich bekomme Geld. Ich spare mein Geld.*

Copymaster 19: Physical appearance: *Er hat lange glatte Haare. Er hat kurze lockige Haare. Er trägt eine Brille. Er trägt einen Ohrring. Sie hat kurze glatte Haare. Sie hat lange lockige Haare. Sie trägt eine Brille. Sie trägt Ohrringe.*

Copymaster 20: Character: *nett, lustig, freundlich, launisch, ungeduldig, schüchtern, lieb, arrogant, gemein, streng, modern, altmodisch.*

Copymaster 28: Clothes: *T-Shirt, Bluse, Hemd, Jacke, Pullover, Hose, Rock, Rucksack, Schuhe, Jeans, Kleid, Mütze, Sweatshirt, Strumpfhose, Krawatte.*

Copymaster 29: Pictures of ill-fitting clothes and labels to match up with the pictures: *zu klein, zu kurz, zu groß, zu eng, zu lang, zu teuer.*

Copymaster 37: Party room items: *Kassettenrecorder, Kartoffelsalat, Apfelsaft, Luftballons, CD-Spieler, CDs, Limonade, Würstchen, Schreibtisch, Lampe, Regal, Bücher.*

Copymaster 38: Birthday presents: *Gutschein, Stofftier, Fußball, Buch, Computerspiel, Skateboard, Make-up, Geld, Schmuck, Handy, Pullover, Inline-Skates.*

Copymaster 46: Town buildings: *Fastfood-Restaurant, Café, Freizeitzentrum, Eisbahn, Schreibwarenladen, Apotheke, Drogerie, Post, Busbahnhof, Bushaltestelle, Eisdiele, Jugendzentrum.*

Copymaster 47: Shopping items: *Duschgel, Shampoo, Zahnpasta, Seife, Halstabletten, Asthmaspray, Federmappe, Buntstifte, Umschläge, Filzstifte, Briefmarken, Telefonkarte, Postkarten, Fahrplan, Monatskarte.*

Copymaster 55: Countryside items: *Bäume, Blumen, Seen, Vögel, Tiere, Frösche, Igel, Schmetterlinge, Schnecken, Eichhörnchen, Wald, Pflanzen.*

Copymaster 56: Town items: *Lärm, Müll, Verkehr, Fabriken, Zigaretten, Kraftwerke, Pestizide, großes Einkaufszentrum, Freizeitzentrum, neues Krankenhaus, schönes Park, interessanter Zoo.*

Copymaster 64: Parts of the body: *Kopf, Arm, Bauch, Fuß, Hals, Bein, Nase, Ohren, Zähne, Rücken, Hand, Knie.*

Copymaster 65: Illnesses and cures: *Grippe/Fieber, Husten, Schnupfen, Heuschnupfen, Tabletten, Tropfen, Lotion, Medikament, vor/nach dem Essen, mit Wasser.*

Copymaster 73: Jobs: *Polizist, Hausmann, Arzt, Krankenpfleger, Kellner, Sekretär, Lehrer, Postbote, Geschäftsmann, Informatiker, LKW-Fahrer, Büroarbeiter, Feuerwehrmann, Verkäufer, Mechaniker.*

Copymaster 74: Dreams for the future: *Ich möchte später gern um die Welt reisen, ein schönes Auto kaufen, viel Geld verdienen, eine große Wohnung kaufen, jeden Tag im Restaurant essen, Designermode tragen, viele Geschenke für meine Familie und Freunde kaufen, viele Popstars treffen, jedes Wochenende eine Party machen, im Lotto gewinnen, im Ausland arbeiten, Filmstar werden.*

Using visuals

Klasse! 2 provides extensive visual support for the purposes of presentation and practice. There are two copymasters of visuals for each unit. The variety of presentation visuals is intended to be stimulating for pupils and provide flexibility for teachers.

The illustrations provided on copymaster can be photocopied onto overhead projector transparencies (OHTs) or photocopied onto card for use in games (see below). If appropriate, the visuals can be enlarged using the photocopier for display or flashcard use.

General strategies for presenting new language with visuals:

– Introduce the new item of vocabulary and get pupils to repeat, e.g. *Das sind Hosen.* Organize new nouns into groups according to gender and introduce one set at a time. This helps to avoid confusion about gender. Make this repetition stage as interesting as possible by splitting the class into groups (e.g. boys only/right-hand side of room only), etc.
– Invite a physical response from pupils to check initial comprehension by sticking visuals around the room. As you say the word, pupils point to the relevant card. This is a particularly useful stage with more difficult vocabulary and with less able pupils.
– Check comprehension by asking alternative-type questions, e.g. *Sind das Hosen oder Jeans?* In the initial stages, it is a good idea to give the correct answer second, so that learners are able to copy the pronunciation more accurately.
– A final open-ended question will check whether learners have grasped the new vocabulary, e.g. *Was ist das?*
– With a mixed-ability group, use a mixture of alternative-type and open-ended questions, according to the ability of the pupils.

Games

Suggested games for practising language with visuals/flashcards:

Richtig oder falsch? This is an excellent game for helping pupils to concentrate. Hold up a flashcard or point to one of the visuals and make a statement, e.g. *Das sind Hosen.* If the pupils agree with the statement, they repeat it. If not, they remain silent.

Hold a collection of visuals facing yourself and hidden from the class, or put a collection of visuals onto the overhead projector (turned off) and point to one of the illustrations. If the visuals have been cut up, then a single item could be placed on the overhead projector. Say *Was ist das?* and pupils have to guess which flashcard is facing you or which visual is being pointed to. Pupils will suggest lots of vocabulary on the topic, which is excellent revision. The element of chance also ensures that it is not always the more able pupils who win. The winner is the pupil who guesses correctly. The winner could keep the card or come to the front and hide/select the next one.

This game can be adapted by placing the cards in an envelope. Slowly reveal one card from the envelope. The winner is the first pupil to correctly identify the picture.

Was fehlt? This suggestion works best with visuals on an overhead projector, but could be adapted to include a set of flashcards stuck on the board. Place a selection of visuals on the overhead projector. Give the class a limited amount of time to look at the visuals and then turn off the overhead projector and remove one item. As soon as the overhead projector is turned on again, the pupils have to try and guess which item is missing!

Spiel mit Nullen und Kreuzen: Flashcards stuck on the board or overhead projector visuals arranged in a grid can be used for playing Noughts and Crosses with the class divided into two teams. If a team gives the correct word for one of the illustrations, their symbol can be entered, either by removing the flashcard and writing it on the board, or by marking a small nought or cross on an overlay next to the illustration. This game can also be played in pairs or small groups.

Other suggestions for general language practice games using the visuals:

Gedächtnisspiel: The small visual cards lend themselves to Pelmanism games. Teachers will need to photocopy the visuals onto card twice. The cards are then cut up and pupils place them on the tables face downwards. In turn, the pupils turn over two cards and say what they are, e.g. *Das sind Hosen. Das sind Hemden.* The cards are then returned to their places on the table. If a pupil selects two identical cards, this pair is kept to one side. The winner is the pupil with the greatest number of pairs at the end of the game.

This game can be varied by providing one set of visuals and a piece of blank card. Pupils can then write the German for each of the visuals onto a small piece of card. The game is played in the same way, except a pair is made up of a visual and its matching written form. This variation should only be played when pupils are confident about pronouncing the German words from the written form. It is then a good means of revising spelling as well as vocabulary items.

Würfelspiel: Stick small pictures onto a large dice. Pupils throw the dice and make an appropriate statement.

Zwillinge: The small cards can be used for a traditional game of Snap. Pupils will need to repeat the items of vocabulary every time a card is turned over to ensure that they are revising the vocabulary and not just looking at the pictures, e.g. P1: *Ein Hemd.* P2: *Eine Hose.* P1: *Eine Hose! Zwillinge!*

Die richtige Reihenfolge: Pupils play this game in pairs. One pupil organizes a set of activities into a sequence, hidden from his/her partner. The partner then has to try and arrange his/her cards in the same order, by asking questions, e.g. *Stehst du auf? Gehst du in die Schule?*

Pupils can then check their answers. A correct set of visuals earns a point!

A variation on this game is to provide pupils with a grid for a Battleships game.

Lotto: Pupils play a game of Bingo in groups of four or five. One pupil is the 'caller'. One set of visuals can be cut up and used as the 'caller's' cards. The other pupils then draw five quick sketches of items for their own Bingo card. The 'caller' then selects cards at random. Any pupil with the item on their own card crosses it out.

Bingo cards for the players could be prepared in advance and pupils could cover up the picture with a counter when it is called out.

Useful language for playing games in German

It is worth spending time on a regular basis revising the necessary language to ensure that learners are able to play their games in the target language. Other useful expressions for playing games are listed below.

Fangen wir an?	*Shall we start?*
Ich fange an.	*I'll start.*
Du fängst an.	*You start.*
Mach doch.	*Go on.*
Einen Moment, bitte.	*Wait.*
Wo ist das Spielbrett?	*Where is the board?*
Ich habe keine Spielmarke.	*I haven't got a counter.*
Gib mir den Würfel, bitte.	*Give me the dice.*
Würfele.	*Throw the dice.*
Noch mal.	*Again.*
Wer ist dran?	*Whose turn is it?*
Ich bin dran.	*It's my turn.*
Du bist dran.	*It's your turn.*
Ein Feld vorwärts.	*Move forward one square.*
Zwei Felder zurück.	*Move back two squares.*
Hast du die Karten?	*Have you got the cards?*
Teil die Karten aus.	*Deal the cards.*
Nimm eine Karte.	*Take a card.*
Sieh die Karte nicht an.	*Don't look at the card.*
Die Karten nicht zeigen.	*Hide your cards.*
Leg eine Karte auf den Tisch.	*Put down a card.*
Halt.	*Stop.*
Mach weiter.	*Carry on.*
So.	*Like that.*
Nicht so.	*Not like that.*
Betrüger/Schummler/Falschspieler!	*Cheat!* (for a boy)
Betrügerin/Schummlerin/Falschspielerin!	*Cheat!* (for a girl)
Auf Deutsch!	*In German!*
Ich habe gewonnen.	*I've won.*
Wir sind fertig.	*We've finished.*

Teaching Klasse! 2 in England and Wales

National Curriculum information is provided in the detailed grids that precede the notes for each unit. In addition, the range of Programme of Study statements (1 Acquiring knowledge and understanding of the target language; 2 Developing language skills; 3 Developing language-learning skills; 4 Developing cultural awareness; 5 Breadth of study) covered in each double-page spread are outlined at the start of the teaching notes for that spread. Note that statement 5i ("working in a variety of contexts, including everyday activities, personal and social life, the world around us, the world of work and the international world") replaces the previous Areas of Experience. As this statement applies to every unit of *Klasse!*, teachers should refer to the 'Language Contexts' column of the Summary of unit contents grid on page 4 of this book for a listing of topic areas.

Levels are suggested for most activities for teachers to refer to as a guide, but these should be used in conjunction with the level descriptions in the National Curriculum document. Pupils' achievements will vary according to the amount of support given, reference materials used, the context of the activity, etc.

Teaching Klasse! 2 in Scotland

The Attainment Outcomes (listening, speaking, reading and writing) and their respective Strands as identified in the SOEID National Guidelines for Modern European Languages are all present in **Klasse! 2**. Pupils following **Klasse! 2** will mostly be working at Intermediate Level and Level E. In accordance with SOEID guidelines, most pupils should attain Level E in their second year of learning. **Klasse! 2** offers activities at Intermediate Level and Level E, and some Elementary Level.

To avoid confusion, level descriptions for specific tasks in **Klasse!** teaching notes are linked to those specified for England and Wales, but there is a broad correlation, so that, for example, a listening task referenced as level 1 is likely to be an Elementary level task, one at level 2 an Intermediate level task, etc. Nonetheless, the qualifications made above with regard to oversimplistic task labelling still apply, and it is assumed that departmental training will provide the safest guide to accurate assessment and recording.

Assessment

Regular assessment of pupil progress is an integral part of the learning process. **Klasse!** offers an approach to assessment in line with the National Curriculum and the SOEID National Guidelines. Clearly, almost every activity in the Students' Book and on the copymasters could be used for assessment purposes, but **Klasse!** also includes summative assessment material on copymasters after every three units. This is designed to coincide with the *Wiederholung* pages in the Students' Book after every three units. All the assessment material is in the target language. Answers and a mark scheme are provided for all assessment material, together with assessment criteria which offer guidance on attainment target levels. The assessment materials are graded, so you can easily select particular activities for some pupils, if this is felt to be appropriate.

Wesel

The main characters featured in Stages 1 and 2 of **Klasse!** live in Wesel, a medium-sized town on the Rhine. Situated in Nordrhein-Westfalen, north of Düsseldorf, Wesel has approximately 65,000 inhabitants,

and is a thriving Hansestadt with much to offer. It has a large shoppping area and Saturday market, excellent sporting and youth facilities, attractive parks, historical monuments such as the cathedral, and various museums including the regional museum of Prussian history.

Further information is available from the Stadtverwaltung in Wesel:

Amt für Stadtwerbung und Fremdenverkehrsförderung
Stadtverwaltung Wesel
Postfach 10 07 60
48467 Wesel
Tel: 00 49 281 203-555
Fax: 00 49 281 203-429

Klasse! 2 and ICT

There are various ways you can use ICT to support your pupils' learning in **Klasse!** Stage 2.

Checklist of ICT applications

If you are confident about using ICT, you may wish to devise your own ICT activities based on the applications described below.

Word-processing

The essential difference between word-processing and writing with pen and paper is that a word-processed text need never be a final product. It can be revised and improved at every stage.

Although writing can be a major stumbling block for the average learner, word-processing techniques can help improve both motivation and performance. Using word-processing, pupils can learn how to create a rough draft and edit it – alone, in collaboration with classmates or with guidance from you – until they reach the final perfect copy. Since errors can be easily corrected without spoiling the appearance of the work, writers gain the confidence to experiment as well as the motivation to take a more active interest in the language they are using.

You will of course need to provide clear guidelines and procedures for drafting and redrafting to help your pupils improve their work in terms of both accuracy and range of language.

By encouraging your pupils to learn how to redraft at this stage, you will provide them with an invaluable skill. Competence in redrafting is an essential tool for pupils hoping to fulfil the requirements of writing at GCSE and Standard Grade, for class work, coursework and for examinations.

Data handling

Data handling programmes (or databases) are used to collect, retrieve, analyse and present information stored in data files. By interrogating (and possibly creating) data files, learners can be given opportunities for using the target language actively and for a real purpose.

To be able to undertake these activities, you and your pupils will need to be familiar with basic data-handling terminology (e.g. file, record, field) as well as graphing techniques and searching routines, such as those involving the use of 'and'/'or' and 'includes'/'is equal to'. Another important aspect of these activities is the need for consistency and accuracy in data entry.

Presentation

Presentation software creates documents in which text and graphics can be combined. The user can experiment with layout by moving elements around the screen, and it is also possible to select from a range of type styles and sizes. Graphics can be found in the form of 'off the shelf' clip-art, artwork created by the learner him/herself, photos taken with a camera which saves images to disk rather than conventional film, or images copied by a scanner.

Learners can use this software to produce documents such as posters, booklets and leaflets for a range of purposes and audiences.

As with word-processing and data handling, it may be possible to give your pupils presentation tasks using skills they have already acquired in other curriculum areas.

Multimedia

Multimedia packages are the most sophisticated form of presentation software. These packages can be used to combine text, graphics, sound and even video images in a non-linear presentation made up of any number of screens. Such a process, which can be very time-consuming, would be inappropriate for language lessons. However, if some of your pupils have the relevant skills and access to resources, your support and guidance may help them to create exciting and interesting presentations.

The Internet

The Internet is a huge global network of computers providing a constantly growing and changing source of information. Most of this information is found in a huge Internet 'library' called the World Wide Web.

Materials from the Internet can provide a constant source of up-to-date and interesting information. They can also enrich the contexts in which language is taught and provide a major resource to support the development of reading skills whilst at the same time raising awareness of the life and culture of German-speaking countries.

Information on the Web can be found by using major MFL websites, such as Lingu@net (www.linguanet.org.uk) and search engines, such as Lycos (www.lycos.de) and Yahoo (de.yahoo.com). Search engines work by asking you to type in a key word, or a series of key words. A list of relevant websites is then listed for you to browse through.

If the school has access to the Internet, searching could be carried out by pupil volunteers or by the school librarian/manager of learning resources.

Text manipulation

Text manipulation software allows you to create short texts that are then transformed into one or a number of problem-solving activities, for example:

– reconstructing a text with all or some of the words and letters hidden
– gap filling
– unjumbling or decoding words
– putting lines in the right order
– predicting the next word

Imaginatively used, text manipulation programmes can help the learner to consolidate vocabulary and develop reading skills while at the same time practising patterns and structures.

A number of text manipulation programmes exist for language learners, and although each one presents a different set of possibilities, the following features are common to them all:

– a content-free framework that allows you to create and enter a text that will support the linguistic aims of the lesson/unit of work
– instant feedback each time a solution is attempted – a powerful source of motivation for pupils
– the security of being able to make (and learn from) mistakes in comparative privacy
– the opportunity for pupils to work independently and at their own pace. This frees you from the need to direct and manage whole-class activities, and gives you the opportunity to observe, prompt, explain and discuss with individuals and with groups.

In order to provide ongoing support to teachers planning for the use of ICT in MFL lessons, BECTA (the British Educational Communications and Technology Agency, Milburn Hill Road, Science Park, Coventry CV4 7JJ; tel: 024 7641 6994, fax: 024 7641 1418, e-mail: Becta@becta.org.uk, website: www.becta.org.uk) provides a constantly updated set of information sheets, some of which provide specific guidance and ideas related to the above applications.

The Klasse! Informatik 2 text manipulation package

To support the use of ICT to raise achievement, Stage 2 of **Klasse!** also features *Klasse! Informatik 2* – a bank of 54 integrated text manipulation files to be used in the programme *Fun With Texts*, published by Camsoft.

Software and hardware

The *Klasse! Informatik 2* textfiles can be obtained on disc direct from: Camsoft, 10 Wheatfield Close, Maidenhead, Berks SL6 3PS
tel: 01628 82 5206
fax: 01628 820431
e-mail: info@camsoftpartners.co.uk
website: www.camsoftpartners.co.uk

If you purchase *Klasse! Informatik 2*, you will also need either: Version 2 (MSDOS) of the *Fun With Texts* programme (for floppy disc, hard disc or network) or

Version 3 (Windows) of the Fun With Texts programme (for hard disc or network). These are also available from Camsoft.

N.B. If you are not sure which version of *Fun With Texts* to purchase, you should consult your school's ICT co-ordinator. You may also need to ask your ICT co-ordinator or computer manager to install the programme, following instructions in the *Fun With Texts* handbook.

To use the *Klasse! Informatik 2* text files, you will need to copy them into the *Fun With Texts* programme. Backup copies of the master discs should be made before this is done.

Camsoft have a Student Licence Scheme, which allows teachers to give students their own *Fun With Texts* discs to work on at home. If your school is interested in this facility, contact Camsoft at the address above.

Using Fun With Texts in the modern languages classroom

Fun With Texts can raise achievement and provide a powerful source of motivation by:

- allowing a text to be approached in a number of different ways
- providing opportunities for active, collaborative and independent learning
- providing feedback each time a solution is attempted
- allowing each learner to work at his/her own pace
- allowing learners to access clues and on-screen help
- freeing the teacher from the need to direct and correct
- helping learners realize that language is governed by rules
- showing new structures in a meaningful context
- stimulating learners to talk about language
- encouraging activities involving more than one discrete skill

Fun With Texts – required knowledge and understanding

It is assumed that users of *Klasse! Informatik 2* will already be familiar with the main features of *Fun With Texts*, which are described in detail in the handbook accompanying each copy of the programme.
For example, users will already know:

- how to call up a text
- the working of the different pupil options (e.g. Clozewrite)
- the scoring system used with each option
- how to obtain foreign accents
- how to print a text

Klasse! Informatik 2 – organization

The 54 text files have been organised as follows:
Each of the nine units of Klasse! 2 is supported by six text files.
The texts for unit 1 are named K2F1A (**K**lasse! **2** File **1A**), K2F1B, K2F1C, K2F1D, K2F1E and K2F1F.
The texts for unit 2 of the course are named K2F2A, K2F2B, K2F2C, K2F2D, K2F2E and K2F2F.

This pattern continues, so that the final text of unit 9 is named K2F9F.

Klasse! Informatik 2 – content

Each of the 54 files has been designed for pupils to work at either **word/sentence level**, **paragraph level** or **text level**.

Word / sentence level – texts with filenames ending in A and B

These consist mainly of word lists, phrases or simple sentences which, if understood and learnt, can later be used when working on longer texts.
For example, file K2F4A contains the names of different items of clothing, some of which reappear in a later conversation describing a shopping trip (file K2F4E).

Paragraph level – texts with filenames ending in C and D

Paragraph level files consist of short paragraphs or brief conversations incorporating essential vocabulary from the unit.
For example, file K2F3D, in which two people are talking about their friends, features a number of adjectives previously presented in the word / sentence level file K2F3A.

Text level – texts with filenames ending in E and F

These are mainly longer texts representing a model of what a good quality piece of pupil writing might look like at the end of a unit of work. Learners have the opportunity to work intensively on these models with a view to emulating them later in their own writing.

Using Klasse! Informatik 2 in lessons

Fun With Texts enables the learner to either:

- 'discover' an unknown text

or

- 'rebuild' a text that has already been seen

Both of these approaches could be used with the **Klasse! Informatik 2** text files.

Discovering Texts

Discovering texts with filenames ending in 'A' or 'B'
This approach could be used as a challenging and original way of presenting key items of new language in a particular unit. Pupils could:

- call up any of the 'A' and 'B' files in the **Copywrite Easy**, **Enigma** or **Scrambler** options
- choose to 'start without seeing the text'

and then reconstruct the text with the appropriate pages of the Students' Book to refer to. They could then work at pronouncing and checking the meaning of the new words or phrases.

Discovering texts with filenames ending in 'C', 'D', 'E' or 'F'
Fun With Texts offers a wide range of ways to discover continuous texts, and you may have devised particular approaches to suit the ability and experience of your pupils. However, the three scenarios described below could be particularly appropriate.

For each of these scenarios, you should begin by ensuring that your pupils are familiar with and competent in using all the vocabulary and grammar featured in the text. Prior to calling up the text, give them information about its subject matter (e.g. a girl is describing her best friend's appearance and character and is giving reasons as to why they get on well with one another) and help them to anticipate the items of language that they may encounter.

Scenario 1

Pupils call up the text in **Copywrite Easy**. Without previewing the text, they enter words for a specified amount of time - perhaps 5 minutes. During this time they are not allowed to use any of the 'help' options.

Then give them an allowance of 50 'help' points to 'spend'. It is up to them whether they choose 'expensive' options (e.g. reveal the whole text) or 'cheaper' options (e.g. reveal a single word or a single letter).

When pupils have completed the task, they call the text up again in **Prediction**, in which they must rebuild the text, a word at a time, from a choice of five possible words. This is a demanding option, but it is very useful for developing syntax.

Scenario 2

Pupils call up the text in **Clozewrite**, but do not preview it.

You or the pupils choose an appropriate gapping interval, e.g. between 4 and 6.

Pupils then work at restoring the text, using 'help' options and the text book as and when appropriate.

When pupils have completed the task, they call the text up again in **Enigma**.

Scenario 3

Pupils call up the text in **Copywrite Hard**, and, without previewing it, work at restoring the text.

Access to Students' Books is allowed. Pupils could also be given an 'allowance' of a small number of key words and 20 'help' points which may only be spent on the 'reveal one letter' help option.

When they have completed the task, they call up the text in **Copywrite Easy**.

Without previewing the text, they read it aloud, with just the first letter of each word visible on screen.

Rebuilding Texts

This approach involves pupils reconstructing a text that they have already previewed. The previewing could occur in an earlier lesson, during which a copy of the text is explored in detail (perhaps using an OHT), or using one of the programme's previewing options, namely:

- read the text for as long as you like
- see the text for 30 seconds
- see the text for 10 seconds

Fun With Texts offers a wide range of ways to rebuild texts, and you may have devised particular approaches to suit the ability and experience of your pupils.

However, the four scenarios described below could be particularly appropriate.

Rebuilding texts with filenames ending in 'A' or 'B'

Scenario 4

Pupils call up the text in **Copywrite Easy** and preview the text for as long as they like. Whilst previewing, pupils (who are working in pairs) read the text aloud to each other. You then draw attention to key items of meaning and/or spelling

Pupils end their preview and work at restoring the text, using 'help' keys or the Students' Book, if appropriate.

When they have completed the task they call the text up again in **Scrambler** or **Enigma**.

After completing this task, they call up the text again in **Copywrite Easy**. This time, they read it aloud, with just the first letter of each word visible on screen.

In this way pupils are able to use their memories to combine the skills of reading and speaking in a challenging way.

Rebuilding texts with filenames ending in 'C', 'D', 'E' or 'F'

Scenario 5

Pupils call up the text in **Clozewrite**, in which words are deleted at regular intervals. They preview the text for as long as they like.

You or the pupils choose an appropriate gapping interval – or you could let your pupils choose within a range, e.g. between 7 and 9.

Pupils work at restoring the text by typing in the missing words.

They use the 'help' facility as and when appropriate, to 'buy' letters.

When they have completed the task, pupils change to a more demanding gapping interval (e.g. between 4 and 6) and rebuild the text again.

Scenario 6

This scenario enables pupils to combine the skills of reading, listening and writing in a natural way whilst working on the text.

Pupils call up the text in **Copywrite Easy**, and preview the text for as long as they like. Whilst previewing, pupils (who are working in pairs) read the text aloud to each other. You then draw attention to key items of vocabulary and structure.

Pupils end their preview and work for about 5 minutes at restoring the text.

You then read the complete text aloud to the class whilst they watch their screens, following the text and looking for words that are still missing. (N.B. No typing allowed whilst the text is being read!)

Pupils return to their work, using 'help' keys as and when appropriate. You could also read the text aloud again to provide further support.

When pupils have completed the task, they call the text up again in **Clozewrite**, and gap every 7th, 8th or 9th word.

They could also call up the text in **Textsalad** or **Prediction**.

Helping less able pupils rebuild texts

Scenario 7

This scenario is often useful for less able pupils who are reluctant to use 'help' keys because of the negative effect they have on their score.

Give pupils a printout of the text, and let them study it for as long as they like.

They then put the printout aside and call up the text in **Copywrite Easy**, in which all letters, apart from the first letter of each word, are shown by dashes.

They work at restoring the text by typing in the missing letters.

If they get stuck, they can look at the printout, put it aside again and continue working – but do not let them type in words whilst they can see the printout.

When pupils have completed the task, they can call the text up again in **Enigma**, which features the text in code. This is a 'fun' option, which all pupils enjoy and complete quickly.

Please note that the above scenarios assume that the whole class is working together in a computer room and that pupils are working in pairs. (Pairwork is proven to improve pupils' enjoyment, perseverance, motivation and overall achievement.)

In an alternative situation (e.g. two pupils working together at a single computer in a classroom where a variety of activities are taking place) certain logical adjustments would need to be made; for example, instead of reading the text aloud (scenario 6) you could record it on tape for pupils to use independently.

In each of the seven given scenarios, pupils access the text in at least two different ways. The second (or third) activity is always a logical development from the previous one, enabling pupils to consolidate and reapply what they have already learnt. It also provides an immediate follow-up for pupils who quickly finish the first activity, simplifying issues of classroom management.

Klasse! Informatik 2 and the National Curriculum Programme of Study

Klasse! Informatik 2 will assist learners in realizing a number of the requirements of the National Curriculum (Modern Foreign Languages) Programme of Study, including:

Knowledge, skills and understanding

Acquiring knowledge and understanding of the target language

Pupils should be taught:

– the principles and interrelationship of sounds and writing in the target language
– the grammar of the target language and how to apply it

Developing language skills

Pupils should be taught:

– how to develop their independence in learning and using the target language

Breadth Of Study

During key stages 3 and 4, pupils should be taught the **Knowledge, skills and understanding** through:

– producing and responding to different types of spoken and written language, including texts produced using ICT
– using a range of resources, including ICT, for accessing and communicating information

Klasse! Informatik 2 and the National Curriculum Attainment Targets

According to the level of the task set and the quality of the response, pupils who have used *Klasse! Informatik 2* successfully will be likely to produce work showing characteristics of:

– AT3: reading and responding, levels 1-5
– AT4: writing, levels 1-6

Klasse! Informatik 2 and the Scottish 5–14 Guidelines

The 5–14 Guidelines state that 'All strands and their exemplification assume that where practicable, schools and teachers will choose to enhance learning and teaching activities in the modern languages classroom through the use of information and communications technology (ICT).' *Klasse! Informatik 2* can play a valuable role in this process.

Using *Klasse! Informatik 2* will help students achieve the following strands of the Attainment Outcomes:

Reading

– Reading for information and instructions
– Reading aloud

Writing

– Writing to exchange information and ideas
– Writing to establish and maintain personal contacts
– Writing imaginatively/to entertain

Knowing about language

Good practice before and after using Klasse! Informatik 2

You should always know which options you intend your pupils to use, and in what sequence. The different scenarios described in these notes have been written to help you make such decisions.

You should also decide whether to allow pupils access to reference/support materials.

After pupils have worked at the computer, you could spend some time during the following lesson, on rapid question-answer work related to the text. This could take the form of:

- asking pupils to spell words (not as a test, but to check how much has been retained)
- reading part of a sentence for pupils to predict the rest
- demonstrating good language use from a copy of the text on OHT (e.g. how two simple sentences are joined by *aber*, use of words such as *sehr* and *ziemlich* to qualify adjectives, use of different tenses)
- asking pupils to remember specific information (e.g. identify the different adjectives in the text)
- asking pupils to explain a point of language (e.g. why was *meine* spelt with an *e* at the end?)

It is invaluable to have clear strategies for encouraging pupils to emulate a model on which they have been working. For example, you could provide a 'parallel' text to the model (supported perhaps by key word/picture prompts) as well as clear guidance related to the use of support material.

Klasse! Informatik 2 text files

Please note:

Each text file is followed by a title that will appear

- as a file descriptor in the Files Menu of the MSDOS version of *Fun With Texts*
- on screen in the Windows version of *Fun With Texts*

In a number of texts, certain proper nouns (e.g. names of people, towns, films, pop groups) are automatically revealed. This ensures that the learner is not given problems that would be impossible to solve. In the texts printed below, these words are indicated by underlining.

K2F1A

Ich bin nach Spanien gefahren.
Ich habe meine Brieffreundin besucht.
Wir haben die Stadt besichtigt.
Wir haben einen Ausflug gemacht.
Wir haben Tennis gespielt.
Wir sind zum Freizeitpark gegangen.
Wir haben Paella gegessen.
Wir haben Limonade getrunken.
Wir sind in die Disco gegangen.
Ich habe Postkarten und Souvenirs gekauft.

K2F1B

Ich war in Frankreich.
Das Wetter war heiß.

Ich war in der Schweiz.
Es hat viel geschneit.

Ich war in Schottland.
Das Wetter war wolkig.

Ich habe in einem Hotel gewohnt.
Das Wetter war sonnig.

Ich habe in einer Ferienwohnung gewohnt.
Es hat viel geregnet.

Ich habe in einem Wohnwagen gewohnt.
Das Wetter war kalt.

K2F1C

Hallo, Jan!
Wohin bist du im Sommer gefahren?
Ich bin nach Italien geflogen. Mein Bruder ist nach Berlin gefahren – mit dem Zug. Und meine Eltern? Sie sind zu Hause geblieben.
Tschüs!   Anja

Hallo, Anja!
Ich bin mit Tom und Tobias nach Österreich gefahren. Wir haben Ferien in Wien gemacht. Meine Eltern sind nach Amerika geflogen. Sie haben New York und Boston besucht. Und meine Schwester? Sie hat bei ihrer Brieffreundin in Madrid gewohnt.
Dein   Jan

K2F1D

A: Wohin bist du im Sommer gefahren?
B: Ich bin nach England geflogen.
A: Und was hast du in England gemacht?
B: Ich habe Sehenswürdigkeiten besichtigt und ich habe Souvenirs gekauft.
A: Wo hast du gewohnt?
B: Ich habe in einer Jugendherberge gewohnt.
A: Wie war die Jugendherberge?
B: Sehr modern!
A: Das Wetter war gut?
B: Ja. Es war sehr sonnig. Es hat nie geregnet. Und du? Was hast du gemacht?
A: Ich bin zu Hause geblieben. Aber es war nie langweilig. Ich bin jeden Tag ins Schwimmbad gegangen und ich habe Fußball gespielt.

K2F1E

Hallo, Gabi!

Wie waren deine Sommerferien? Meine Familie und ich sind nach Wales gefahren, mit dem Auto. Wir haben in einem Zelt gewohnt. Das Zelt war sehr groß, aber nicht sehr modern!

Das Wetter war sehr schön. Es war immer sonnig und heiß und es hat nie geregnet! Also, wir haben sehr viel gemacht. Wir sind zum Strand gefahren und haben Tennis gespielt. Ich bin auch ins Schwimmbad gegangen und meine Schwester ist in die Disco gegangen.

Wir haben auch meine Tante besucht. Sie wohnt in Swansea. Dort haben wir Eis gegessen und viel Cola getrunken. Es war sehr heiß!

Und du? Wo warst du in den Ferien? Und was hast du gemacht?

Schreib bald wieder,
Anne

K2F1F

Ich war in Paris, in Frankreich. Ich habe dort bei Freunden gewohnt, am Stadtrand. Mein Zimmer war nicht sehr groß, aber es war sehr schön. Leider war das Wetter immer schlecht. Es hat viel geregnet und es war sehr kalt und windig. Aber wir haben die Stadt besichtigt und ich habe Souvenirs gekauft. Wir sind auch zum

Freizeitpark <u>Eurodisney</u> gefahren. Das war toll!
Martin

Ich bin in den Ferien zu Hause geblieben. Das war aber nicht schlecht! Meine Eltern und ich haben einen Ausflug nach <u>München</u> gemacht. Dort haben wir viele Sehenswürdigkeiten besichtigt. Wir sind auch ins Museum gegangen: Das war aber sehr langweilig! Ich habe auch in den Ferien viel Sport gemacht. Ich habe Fußball gespielt und ich bin ins Schwimmbad gegangen.
<u>Anja</u>

K2F2A

Um halb sieben stehe ich auf.
Um Viertel vor sieben wasche ich mich.
Um sieben Uhr ziehe ich mich an.
Um Viertel nach sieben frühstücke ich.
Um halb acht gehe ich in die Schule.
Um halb zwei gehe ich nach Hause.
Um drei Uhr mache ich Hausaufgaben.
Um acht Uhr sehe ich fern.
Um halb zehn ziehe ich mich aus.
Um zehn Uhr gehe ich ins Bett.

K2F2B

Ich habe einen Nebenjob.
Ich arbeite am Wochenende.
Ich arbeite am Samstag.
Ich arbeite jeden Tag.

Ich helfe zu Hause.
Ich arbeite im Garten.
Ich bin Babysitter.
Ich bin Babysitterin.
Ich führe den Hund aus.
Ich wasche Autos.
Ich trage Zeitungen aus.

Ich finde den Job toll.
Ich mag den Job nicht.

K2F2C

<u>Claudia</u> … Wie hilfst du zu Hause? Und wie oft?

Ich räume oft mein Zimmer auf, ich wasche jeden Tag ab und ich wasche einmal pro Woche das Auto.

Kaufst du ein?

Nein. Ich kaufe nie ein und ich putze selten das Badezimmer. Aber ich sauge oft Staub und ich füttere immer die Katze.

Und wie hilft dein Bruder?

Er putzt das Badezimmer, er füttert den Hund und er deckt oft den Tisch … aber er räumt nie sein Zimmer auf!

K2F2D

<u>Ulli</u>: <u>Alex</u>, wie viel Taschengeld bekommst du?
<u>Alex</u>: Ich bekomme pro Woche 12 Euro von meinen Eltern.
<u>Ulli</u>: Und was kaufst du mit deinem Taschengeld?
<u>Alex</u>: Süßigkeiten und Kleidung.

<u>Ulli</u>: Sparst du für etwas?
<u>Alex</u>: Ja, ich spare für ein Fahrrad. Und wie viel bekommst du?
<u>Ulli</u>: Ich bekomme pro Monat 35 Euro von meiner Mutter und 15 Euro von meinen Großeltern.
<u>Alex</u>: Kaufst du Kleidung?
<u>Ulli</u>: Ja, und auch Make-up und Zeitschriften.
<u>Alex</u>: Sparst du?
<u>Ulli</u>: Ja, ich spare pro Monat 15 Euro – für eine Stereoanlage.

K2F2E

A: <u>Heike</u>, wie ist dein Alltag? Was machst du wann?
B: Also, um sieben Uhr stehe ich auf und dann wasche ich mich.
A: Und wann gehst du in die Schule?
B: Ähm … um halb acht. Dann um ein Uhr gehe ich nach Hause.
A: Und hilfst du nachmittags zu Hause?
B: Hmm … nicht viel! Ich räume einmal pro Woche mein Zimmer auf, aber ich sauge selten Staub und ich putze nie das Badezimmer.
A: Und deine Haustiere?
B: Ach ja! Ich füttere jeden Tag den Hund und die Katze.
A: Und bekommst du Taschengeld?
B: Nicht viel – ich helfe nicht zu Hause!! Aber ich bekomme pro Woche 15 Euro von meiner Oma. Das finde ich toll!
A: Und was kaufst du davon? Oder sparst du das alles?
B: Nein, nein! Ich kaufe viele CDs und Süßigkeiten. Aber ich spare auch für einen Computer.

K2F2F

Lieber <u>Kai</u>,
ich habe jetzt einen Nebenjob. Ich trage jeden Morgen Zeitungen aus! Ich finde den Job nicht so gut, aber ich verdiene pro Woche 45 Euro! Das finde ich toll! Davon kaufe ich Kleidung und Computerspiele und ich spare auch für eine Stereoanlage.
Und du? Hast du einen Nebenjob? Wie viel verdienst du und was kaufst du davon?
Dein <u>Martin</u>

Lieber <u>Martin</u>,
leider habe ich keinen Nebenjob. Ich helfe aber oft zu Hause und ich bekomme ziemlich viel Taschengeld. Ich wasche jeden Tag ab und ich bekomme 2 Euro von meinem Vater. Ich arbeite einmal pro Woche im Garten und ich bekomme 10 Euro von meiner Mutter. Und ich decke jeden Abend den Tisch. Das macht keinen Spaß, aber ich bekomme noch 2 Euro!
Was ich davon kaufe? Computerzeitschriften, Jeans und CDs. Und ich spare pro Woche 10 Euro für ein Fahrrad.
Tschüs! <u>Kai</u>

K2F3A

Ich bin …
immer nett
oft lustig
manchmal launisch
nie gemein

Mein Vater ist …
immer sympathisch
oft freundlich
manchmal ungeduldig
nie arrogant

Meine Mutter ist …
immer lieb
oft schüchtern
manchmal altmodisch
nie unfreundlich

K2F3B

Ich muss …
jeden Tag abwaschen.
den Tisch decken.
um 21 Uhr zu Hause sein.
um 22 Uhr ins Bett gehen.
am Wochenende um 22 Uhr zu Hause sein.
jeden Abend lernen.
das Badezimmer putzen.

Ich darf …
Freunde nach Hause einladen.
in den Ferien arbeiten.
in meinem Zimmer fernsehen.
Fastfood essen.

Ich darf nicht in die Disco gehen.
Ich darf keine Musik im Wohnzimmer hören.

K2F3C

Ich habe blaue Augen und lange blonde glatte Haare. Ich trage Ohrringe. Meine Lieblingsmusik ist Reggae, meine Lieblingsfarbe ist Gelb und mein Lieblingsfilm ist Forrest Gump.

Meine Schwester heißt Inge. Ihre Haare sind rot und lockig und ihre Augen sind grün. Sie trägt eine Brille. Ihre Lieblingsfarbe ist Rot und ihre Lieblingsmusik ist Pop.

Das ist Tom, mein bester Freund. Toms Haare sind schwarz und kurz und er hat braune Augen. Er trägt einen Ohrring. Seine Lieblingsfarbe ist Blau und sein Lieblingsfilm ist Titanic.

K2F3D

Magst du Barbara?
Ja, ich mag sie, weil sie selten launisch ist.

Und Heide?
Ja, ich mag sie auch, weil sie immer nett und nie gemein ist.

Und Tobi? Magst du ihn?
Ja, ich mag Tobi, weil er immer sympathisch ist. Wir verstehen uns sehr gut.

Und Klaus?
Ach nein! Klaus ist manchmal unfreundlich. Und du? Magst du Klaus?

Ja. Klaus ist nicht unfreundlich. Er ist schüchtern! Ich mag ihn, weil er immer nett und nie arrogant ist. Wir streiten uns nie!

K2F3E

Meine beste Freundin heißt Nina. Sie hat lange braune Haare und grüne Augen. Sie trägt eine Brille, aber keine Ohrringe. Ninas Lieblingsfarbe ist Blau und ihr Lieblingsfilm ist Star Wars.

Wir verstehen uns sehr gut. Nina ist sehr lustig und sympathisch. Sie ist selten launisch und ich mag Nina, weil sie nie ungeduldig ist. Wir streiten uns aber manchmal: Meine Lieblingsgruppe ist The Beatles, aber Nina mag The Beatles gar nicht!

K2F3F

Liebe Gaby!

Ich habe ein Problem! Meine Mutter und ich verstehen uns nicht sehr gut. Wir streiten uns immer, weil ich nie zu Hause helfe. Ich räume mein Zimmer nicht auf, ich putze nie das Badezimmer und ich decke selten den Tisch. Meine Mutter sagt, ich bin faul und frech, aber das bin ich gar nicht!

Ich helfe nie zu Hause, weil ich kein Taschengeld bekomme. Also, ich darf keine CDs, keine Zeitschriften, keine Süßigkeiten kaufen. Ich darf auch nicht in den Ferien arbeiten und ich muss jeden Abend um 20 Uhr zu Hause sein. Das finde ich total ungerecht, weil ich auch keine Freunde nach Hause einladen darf. Meine Mutter ist gemein, finde ich. Hilfe, bitte!

Carsten

K2F4A

Was hast du gekauft?

Ich habe einen Ohrring gekauft.
Ich habe Schuhe gekauft.
Ich habe zwei T-Shirts gekauft.
Ich habe drei Pullover gekauft.
Ich habe vier Jeans gekauft!
Ich habe sechs Blusen gekauft!
Ich habe acht Jacken gekauft!
Ich habe zehn Taschen gekauft!
Ich habe elf Röcke gekauft!
Ich habe dreizehn Hemden gekauft!
Ich habe siebzehn Hosen gekauft!
Ich habe zwanzig Mützen gekauft!
Ich habe dreißig Rucksäcke gekauft!

K2F4B

Wie findest du deine Uniform?

Ich finde meine Uniform bequem.
Ich finde meine Uniform schlecht.

Meine Uniform ist gut.
Meine Uniform ist schrecklich.

Meine Uniform gefällt mir gut.
Meine Uniform gefällt mir gut, weil sie ganz altmodisch ist.

Meine Uniform gefällt mir nicht so gut.
Meine Uniform gefällt mir nicht so gut, weil sie sehr unbequem ist.

Meine Uniform gefällt mir gar nicht.
Meine Uniform gefällt mir gar nicht, weil sie hässlich ist.

K2F4C

A: Wie gefällt dir dieser Rock?
B: Er gefällt mir gut. Er ist schön und modern.

A: Wie gefällt dir dieses T-Shirt?
B: Es gefällt mir gut, aber es ist zu teuer.

A: Wie gefallen dir diese Schuhe?
B: Sie gefallen mir gar nicht. Sie sind zu klein. Aber diese Turnschuhe gefallen mir gut.

A: Welches Hemd gefällt dir?
B: Dieses.
A: Ja. Es sieht super aus.

A: Welche Hose gefällt dir?
B: Diese.
A: Ja. Sie ist sehr praktisch.
B: Und sie ist ziemlich billig.

K2F4D

A: Was trägst du gern?
B: Ich trage gern Kleider und Blusen. Ich trage nicht gern Sweatshirts.

C: Zur Schule trage ich ein weißes Hemd und eine graue Hose.
D: Wie findest du deine Uniform?
C: Sie gefällt mir gar nicht.

E: Was trägst du zur Schule?
F: Einen blauen Pullover und einen schwarzen Rock. Ich trage gern Röcke.
E: Trägst du gern Jeans?
F: Nein. Jeans gefallen mir nicht so gut.

G: Ich trage am liebsten eine schwarze Jacke, ein grünes Hemd, eine rote Krawatte, eine lila Hose und blaue Schuhe. Was trägst du am liebsten?
H: Ich trage am liebsten eine Jeans, ein Sweatshirt und ein T-Shirt. Jacken und Hemden gefallen mir gar nicht, weil sie sehr altmodisch sind!

K2F4E

A: Tag, Ina! Wie geht's?
B: Hallo, Britta! Gut, danke. Was hast du denn heute gemacht?
A: Du, ich bin in die Stadt gefahren! Ich habe viel Kleidung gekauft!
B: Ja? Was denn?
A: Also, ich bin zum Ausverkauf gegangen! Ich habe drei T-Shirts und zwei Hosen gekauft. Ach ja, und auch zwei Pullover!
B: He, Britta Cool! Schau mal!
A: Also, wie gefällt dir dieser Pullover?
B: Oh ja, toll! Und dieser auch!
A: Ja, aber welches T-Shirt gefällt dir?
B: Ähm ... dieses gefällt mir gar nicht!
A: Nein! Dieses ist für meinen Bruder!
B: Oh! Und dieses?
A: Nein, dieses ist zu klein! Es ist für meine kleine Schwester. Aber gefällt dir diese Hose?

B: Oh, ja! Sie ist schön! Trägst du die Hose heute Abend?
A: Aber natürlich!

K2F4F

Lieber Dieter,
was trägst du zur Schule? In Großbritannien muss ich eine Uniform tragen. Ich trage einen blauen Pullover, eine graue Jacke, eine rote Krawatte, eine graue Hose, ein weißes Hemd und schwarze Schuhe. Aber ich finde meine Uniform schlecht, weil sie sehr unbequem ist. Die Hose ist immer zu eng und die Jacke ist zu groß. Meine Uniform gefällt mir gar nicht!

Zu Hause trage ich aber keine Uniform! Ich trage lieber Jeans und Sweatshirts! Ich trage auch gern Turnschuhe. Und du? Was trägst du am liebsten?

K2F5A

Mein Geburtstag ist am elften Juli.
Ich habe am neunzehnten Januar Geburtstag.
Meine Mutter hat am achten März Geburtstag.
Mein Vater hat am zweiundzwanzigsten Dezember Geburtstag.

Ostern ist im Frühling
Fasching ist im Februar.
Id-ul-Fitr ist im Dezember.
Diwali ist im November.
Das Chinesische Neujahr ist im Januar oder Februar.

Weihnachten ist am 25. Dezember.
Sylvester ist am 31. Dezember.
Der Valentinstag ist am 14. Februar.

K2F5B

Wo ist die Zeitschrift?
Sie ist unter den Büchern.

Wo ist der CD-Spieler?
Er ist neben dem Fernseher.

Wo sind die CDs?
Sie sind auf dem Tisch.

Wo ist das Stofftier?
Es ist hinter dem Stuhl.

Wo ist die Limonade?
Sie ist neben der Lampe.

Wo sind die Würstchen?
Sie sind im Schreibtisch!

K2F5C

A: Ich habe am Wochenende Geburtstag. Wir machen eine Party. Kommst du?
B: Ja, gern. Und wann ist die Party?
A: Am Samstag um 20 Uhr.
B: Gut … und wo?
A: Zu Hause, im Garten.

C: Wir machen am Sonntag ein Picknick.
D: Wo?
C: Im Park, um 13 Uhr. Kommst du?
D: Ja, gern.

E: Wir machen eine Faschingsfete, im Partykeller. Kommst du?

F: Nein, ich kann leider nicht kommen. Ich muss Hausaufgaben machen, mein Zimmer aufräumen, die Katze füttern, im Garten helfen und das Badezimmer putzen!

K2F5D

Berlin, den 2. März
Lieber Daniel,
heute habe ich Geburtstag. Ich habe CDs, T-Shirts und ein Computerspiel bekommen. Um 19 Uhr mache ich eine Party – mit Tina, Heide, Tobias, Christina, Axel, Stefan, Anja und Barbara. Wir essen Pizza und wir trinken Cola.
Und du? Wie war deine Faschingsfete?
Dein   Jan

Hamburg, den 5. März
Hallo, Jan!
die Faschingsfete war toll! Ich habe Tanja und Gabi getroffen! Mehmet hat Gitarre gespielt und ich habe mit Amina getanzt. Sie ist sehr schön. Aber ich habe zu viel Limonade getrunken und Kartoffelsalat gegessen!
Schreib bald wieder,   Daniel

K2F5E

A: Hallo! Hier ist Marco. Peter, ich habe am 18. Mai Geburtstag und ich mache eine Party.
B: Toll! Wann ist die Party?
A: Am Abend – um 19 Uhr. Kommst du?
B: Ja, okay! Ich komme gern! Und wo ist die Party?
A: Zu Hause, im Partykeller.
B: Vielen Dank für die Einladung. Bis dann!

A: Hallo, Kati! Hier ist Marco.
C: Oh, Tag, Marco!
A: Kati, ich habe am 18. Mai Geburtstag und ich mache eine Party. Kommst du?
C: Am 18.? Oh nein! Ich kann leider nicht kommen. Ich muss meine Großeltern in Berlin besuchen.
A: Oh, schade.
C: Aber herzlichen Glückwunsch!
A: Ja, danke. Tschüs!
C: Tschüs!

K2F5F

A: Tag, Tanja! Komm herein!
B: Tag, Gabi! Na, wie war die Party?
A: Total super! Ich habe so viel gegessen und viel getanzt! Du, ich habe mit Tobi getanzt. Tobi aus der 10B! Und ich habe auch Timo und Karin gesehen. Und Tobi hat Gitarre gespielt!
B: Oh, Gabi! Das ist aber fantastisch! Und ich war nicht da! Und was hast du zum Geburtstag bekommen?
A: Oh, schau mal. Ich habe eine CD bekommen – von Tobi! Ich habe auch ein Computerspiel bekommen – von meinen Eltern. Ähm … und diesen Pullover von meiner Oma! Er gefällt mir aber nicht!
B: Schade.
A: Aber jetzt muss ich mein Zimmer aufräumen.
B: Ja? Ich mache mit! Wo ist denn alles?

A: Also, die Luftballons sind unter dem Tisch, die Chips sind auf dem Sofa …
B: Und die CDs sind unter dem Kleiderschrank. Ja, okay. Räumen wir das Zimmer auf!
A: Oh, danke, Tanja!

K2F6A

Was kann man in Berlin machen?

Man kann …
ins Kino gehen.
ein Picknick machen.
in die Eisdiele gehen.
ins Museum gehen.
Fußball spielen.
in die Disco gehen.
in den Park gehen.
ins Schwimmbad gehen.
Tennis spielen.
einen Einkaufsbummel machen.
ins Jugendzentrum gehen.
ins Popkonzert gehen.
ins Fastfood-Restaurant gehen.

K2F6B

Wo treffen wir uns?

Wir treffen uns …
vor der Eisbahn.
im Café.
neben dem Freizeitzentrum.
vor dem Bahnhof.
am Markt.
in der Eisdiele.
neben der Imbissstube.
an der Bushaltestelle.
vor dem Museum.
neben dem Kino.
an der Post.
neben dem Fastfood-Restaurant.
im Schwimmbad.

K2F6C

Kai …
Morgen will ich ins Schwimmbad gehen oder vielleicht einen Einkaufsbummel machen. Wir können auch ins Café gehen. Kommst du mit?
Dein E-Mail-Brieffreund Helmut

Helmut …
Vielen Dank für die E-Mail. Ja, ich will auch in die Stadt gehen, aber ich will nicht ins Schwimmbad gehen. Ich schwimme nicht gern! Aber ich will ins Jugendzentrum gehen.
Tschüs! Kai

Kai …
Ins Jugendzentrum? Gute Idee! Wann treffen wir uns?
Helmut

Helmut …
Um 18 Uhr 30, vor der Post.
Bis bald Kai

K2F6D

A: Guten Tag. Kann ich Ihnen helfen?
B: Ja, ich habe meine Tasche verloren.
A: Wie sieht sie aus?
B: Sie ist schwarz und aus Leder.
A: Ähm … ja, die haben wir!

C: Guten Tag. Kann ich dir helfen?
D: Ja, ich habe meinen Fotoapparat verloren.
C: Wann?
D: Gestern.
C: Wo?
D: Hier, im Museum.
C: Also … nein, das tut mir Leid. Wir haben keinen Fotoapparat. Du musst ins Fundbüro gehen.

K2F6E

A: Also, Kai. Was willst du heute machen?
B: Hmm … was kann man machen? Hier ist alles so langweilig!
A: Aber nein! Man kann sehr viel machen! Man kann in die Disco oder ins Kino gehen.
B: Ich tanze nicht gern. Und ich mag Filme nicht sehr gern.
A: Okay, willst du ins Schwimmbad gehen? Oder ins Freizeitzentrum?
B: Ähm … nein. Sport mag ich auch nicht sehr gern.
A: Okay, wollen wir dann einen Einkaufsbummel machen? Oder ein Picknick?
B: Einen Einkaufsbummel?! He, toll! Ja! Ich will einen Einkaufsbummel machen.
A: Und wir können auch in die Eisdiele gehen!
B: Okay. Und wo treffen wir uns?
A: Vor der Eisdiele? Um zwei Uhr?
B: Okay. Wir treffen uns um zwei Uhr vor der Eisdiele. Bis dann!
A: Ja, bis dann!

K2F6F

A: Hallo, Kai!
B: Tag! Also, was brauchst du in der Stadt?
A: Ich? Also, ich habe keine Buntstifte. Ich muss zum Schreibwarenladen gehen. Und du?
B: Ah, ich brauche viel!
A: Oh nein!
B: Ja, ich brauche eine Monatskarte.
A: Also, du musst zum Busbahnhof gehen.
B: Ja, und ich habe keine Briefmarken. Ich muss zur Post gehen.
A: Oh, ich brauche auch eine Telefonkarte. Ich muss auch zur Post gehen. Sonst noch etwas?
B: Duschgel. Ja, ich brauche Duschgel. Oh, und auch Shampoo.
A: Also, du musst zur Drogerie, zur Post und zum Busbahnhof gehen. Und ich muss auch zum Schreibwarenladen gehen.
B: Ja, und dann können wir in die Eisdiele gehen!
A: Super! Okay, gehen wir!

K2F7A

Wald
Wasser
Erde
Tiere
Luft
Pflanzen

Müll
Verkehr
Fabriken
Zigaretten
Kraftwerke
Lärm
Pestizide

K2F7B

Ich fahre mit dem Auto.
Ich bade jeden Tag.
Ich trenne meinen Müll nicht.
Ich nehme Plastiktüten.
Ich kaufe Cola in Dosen.

Ich trenne meinen Müll.
Ich kaufe Recyclingpapier.
Ich bringe Flaschen zum Altglascontainer.
Ich fahre mit dem Rad.
Ich nehme Tüten aus Stoff.
Ich bringe Altpapier zum Altpapiercontainer.
Ich kaufe Limonade in Recyclingflaschen.
Ich dusche jeden Morgen.
Ich gehe zu Fuß.

K2F7C

Ich wohne gern in der Stadt.
Es gibt viele Geschäfte.
Es gibt ein großes Einkaufszentrum.
Es gibt viel zu tun.

Ich wohne gern in der Stadt, weil es ein neues Krankenhaus, einen tollen Zoo und ein modernes Fußballstadion gibt.

Ich wohne nicht gern in der Stadt.
Es gibt zu viel Verkehr.
Es gibt keine Natur.
Es gibt Umweltverschmutzung.

Ich wohne nicht gern in der Stadt, weil es zu viele Autos und zu viel Lärm gibt.

K2F7D

Ich wohne gern auf dem Land.
Es ist sehr ruhig.
Es gibt Bäume, Blumen und Vögel.
Es gibt auch Schmetterlinge, Frösche und Igel. Das finde ich interessant.

Ich wohne gern auf dem Land, weil es keinen Lärm und keine Umweltverschmutzung gibt.

Ich wohne nicht gern auf dem Land.
Es ist zu ruhig.
Es gibt keine Disco, kein Kino, kein Jugendzentrum und kein Stadion. Das finde ich langweilig.

Ich wohne nicht gern auf dem Land, weil es Schnecken und Spinnen gibt und weil meine Freunde in der Stadt sind.

K2F7E

Ich heiße <u>Tanja</u> und ich bin 15 Jahre alt. Ich wohne in <u>Altberg</u> – das ist ein kleines Dorf in <u>Norddeutschland</u>. <u>Altberg</u> ist ganz auf dem Land – also, es gibt keine Umweltverschmuztung und nicht viele Gebäude. Es gibt ein Lebensmittelgeschäft und ein kleines Café, aber sonst nichts. Aber ich wohne sehr gern in <u>Altberg</u>, weil es so viel Natur gibt. Ich mag Tiere sehr gern und hier gibt es alles … Vögel, Igel, Schmetterlinge usw. Und ich wohne auch gern hier, weil ich jeden Tag einen Spaziergang auf dem Land machen kann. Hier ist es ganz ruhig, weil es nicht viel Verkehr gibt.

Ich heiße <u>Timo</u>. Ich bin <u>Tanjas</u> Bruder. Ich bin 19 und ich wohne in <u>Hamburg</u>. <u>Altberg</u> finde ich langweilig, weil es nichts zu tun gibt. Es gibt keine Disco und kein Kino usw. Es ist dort sehr ruhig: Es gibt nur Bäume, Blumen und Tiere. Nein, ich wohne lieber in <u>Hamburg</u> – das ist eine sehr große Stadt. <u>Hamburg</u> ist toll, weil es hier viel zu tun gibt. Es gibt hier viel Lärm und viele Menschen – das finde ich gut. Und ich wohne auch gern hier, weil es ein großes Fußballstadion gibt. Ich mag Fußball sehr gern! Ja, ich wohne lieber in der Stadt!

K2F7F

A: Willkommen in <u>Heutzutage</u>: Die Sendung für die Umwelt. Heute fragen wir … Was machst du für die Umwelt? Also, du, <u>Karo</u>, was machst du?

B: Also, ich trenne immer meinen Müll. Das ist ganz wichtig. Papier muss man zum Altpapiercontainer bringen und Flaschen zum Altglascontainer. Das können alle jede Woche machen.

A: Toll! Und du, <u>Arne</u>? Was machst du für die Umwelt?

C: Ich? Also, ich fahre immer mit dem Rad. Ich fahre nie mit dem Auto, weil das umweltfeindlich ist. Radfahren ist einfach umweltfreundlicher. Es gibt keine Umweltverschmutzung mit dem Rad!

A: Ja, stimmt! Und was ist denn das größte Problem für die Umwelt, glaubst du?

C: Fabriken und Kraftwerke, natürlich. Sie sind das größte Problem.

B: Aber nein! Ich denke, Lärm ist am schlimmsten. Lärm ist umweltfeindlicher als Fabriken!

C: Nein, nein! Fabriken und Kraftwerke sind am gefährlichsten! Sie sind viel gefährlicher als Lärm!

B: Ich glaube aber …

A: Okay, okay! Also, vielen Dank! Das war sehr interessant!

K2F8A

Mein Fuß tut weh!
Mein Hals tut weh!
Meine Nase tut weh!
Mein Bein tut weh!
Mein Arm tut weh!
Mein Rücken tut weh!
Meine Ohren tun weh!
Mein Kopf tut weh!
Meine Zähne tun weh!
Mein Bauch tut weh!

K2F8B

Ich mache viel für mein Gesundheit.

Ich esse Obst und Salat.
Ich trinke viel Wasser.
Ich esse viel Gemüse.
Ich rauche nicht.
Ich esse keine Süßigkeiten.
Ich esse kein Fastfood.
Ich trinke keinen Alkohol.
Ich gehe viel zu Fuß.
Ich kaufe keine Schokolade.
Ich esse jeden Tag Frühstück.
Ich gehe um 21 Uhr ins Bett.
Ich esse wenig Fleisch.
Ich schwimme jeden Tag.
Ich esse keinen Kuchen.

K2F8C

A: Ich habe seit zwei Wochen Husten.
B: Nimm dieses Medikament.
A: Und ich habe seit Mittwoch Grippe.
B: Nimm diese Tabletten vor dem Essen.

C: Ich habe seit gestern Fieber.
B: Nimm diese Tabletten mit Wasser.
C: Und ich habe seit einer Woche Heuschnupfen.
B: Nimm diese Tropfen zweimal täglich.

D: Ich habe seit Freitag Kopfschmerzen.
B: Nimm dieses Medikament nach dem Essen.
D: Und ich habe seit zwei Tagen Halsschmerzen.
B: Nimm diese Lotion dreimal täglich.

K2F8D

Ich esse gern Gemüse …
aber ich esse auch jeden Tag Schokolade!

Wir essen Obst und wir trinken Wasser …
aber wir essen auch viel Fleisch und Pizza!

Ich habe Müsli mit Bananen gegessen …
aber ich habe auch Alkohol getrunken!

Wir haben Mineralwasser getrunken …
aber wir haben auch viel Fastfood gegessen!

Ich werde jeden Tag Salat essen …
aber ich werde auch Cola trinken!

Wir werden keine Süßigkeiten essen …
aber wir werden auch jeden Tag rauchen!

K2F8E

A: Guten Tag! Was fehlt dir?
B: Ich habe Bauchschmerzen.
A: Bauchschmerzen? Ja, und seit wann?
B: Seit sechs Wochen, glaube ich.
A: Seit sechs Wochen? Das ist aber eine lange Zeit! Also, schauen wir mal … ich glaube, es ist nicht schlecht. Aber was isst du normalerweise jeden Tag? Isst du viel Fastfood?
B: Nein, nicht viel. Nur vier oder fünfmal pro Woche.

A: Fünfmal pro Woche? Nein!! Aber trinkst du viel Wasser?

B: Nein, Wasser mag ich gar nicht. Ich trinke lieber Cola oder Kaffee.

A: Das ist sehr ungesund. Isst du Obst und Gemüse?

B: Nein, auch nicht. Obst und Gemüse finde ich langweilig.

A: Ja, aber sie sind sehr gesund.

B: Oh, Entschuldigung! Doch! Ich esse viel Obst und Gemüse – ich esse sehr gern Pommes frites mit Ketchup. Also, ich esse Kartoffeln und Tomaten! Das ist sehr gesund, nicht wahr?

A: Nein! Das ist total ungesund! Geh nach Hause und trink viel Wasser! Iss keine Süßigkeiten und kein Fastfood! Und iss viel Obst und Gemüse!

K2F8F

Tag! Ich heiße Matthias. Ich wohne in Frankfurt, in der Stadtmitte. Ich wohne gern in Frankfurt, weil man viel Sport machen kann. Ich schwimme jeden Tag und ich spiele auch zweimal pro Woche Tennis. Das macht fit! Frankfurt ist auch sehr praktisch, weil ich jeden Tag zu Fuß zur Schule gehen kann.

Ich mache auch viel für meine Gesundheit. Ich rauche nicht und ich esse viel Obst und Gemüse – das soll man jeden Tag essen. Man soll auch keine Süßigkeiten essen und Alkohol ist auch nicht gut: Man soll lieber viel Wasser trinken.

Und was werde ich nächstes Jahr für meine Gesundheit machen? Ich esse oft Würstchen und auch Hamburger. Aber nächstes Jahr werde ich wenig Fleisch essen – und kein Fastfood! Das werde ich aber schwer finden!

K2F9A

Ich werde …
nach Los Angeles fliegen.

Meine Eltern werden …
einen Ausflug nach Frankreich machen.
eine Radtour machen.

Meine Schwester wird …
ins Popkonzert gehen.
faulenzen.

Wir werden …
Urlaub in Italien machen.
lange schlafen.

Du wirst …
zu Hause bleiben und Freunde besuchen.
jeden Tag ins Schwimmbad gehen.

K2F9B

Kellner
Kellnerin
Hausmann
Hausfrau
Polizist
Polizistin
Sekretär
Sekretärin
Krankenpfleger
Krankenschwester
Arzt
Ärztin
Lehrer
Lehrerin
Büroarbeiter
Büroarbeiterin
Verkäufer
Verkäuferin

K2F9C

Dieses Jahr habe ich zu viel Cola getrunken. Nächstes Jahr werde ich jeden Tag Mineralwasser trinken, Deutsch sprechen und um 7 Uhr aufstehen. Ich werde auch mein Taschengeld sparen, an meinen Brieffreund schreiben und nachmittags nicht fernsehen.

Dieses Jahr hat mein Bruder viel Fastfood gegessen. Nächstes Jahr wird er viel Obst und Gemüse essen und einen Kochkurs machen. Er wird auch jeden Tag zu Hause helfen, für ein Fahrrad sparen, Klavier lernen und nicht in seinem Zimmer essen.

Dieses Jahr sind meine Eltern zu Hause geblieben. Nächstes Jahr werden sie nach Amerika fahren und für ein neues Auto sparen. Sie werden auch um 11 Uhr ins Bett gehen, jede Woche ins Kino gehen und jeden Samstag im Garten arbeiten.

K2F9D

A: Was möchtest du später gern machen?

B: Ich möchte gern ein Auto haben und eine schöne Wohnung kaufen. Und du?

A: Ich möchte gesund sein, jeden Tag Tennis spielen und viel Geld verdienen.

A: Was möchte dein Freund später gern machen?

B: Er möchte im Lotto gewinnen, in Amerika wohnen und Popstar werden. Und deine Freundin?

A: Sie möchte Filmstar werden, Designermode tragen und jeden Tag eine Party machen

A: Möchtest du im Ausland arbeiten?

B: Ja, in England. Ich möchte Deutschlehrer werden und in London wohnen. Und du?

A: Ja. Ich möchte Ärztin in Paris werden. Ich möchte auch ein schönes modernes Haus haben – ein Haus mit Schwimmbad und Balkon.

K2F9E

Liebes Tagebuch!

Ich werde nächstes Jahr viel für die Schule machen. Ich werde jeden Tag um 7 Uhr aufstehen und meine Hausaufgaben vor der Schule machen. Ich werde auch viel Englisch sprechen und schreiben. Ich werde E-Mails an meine Brieffreundin in Amerika schreiben und jeden Tag mit meinem Bruder Englisch sprechen. Und was sonst … ?

Also, dieses Jahr habe ich einen Computerkurs gemacht. Das hat viel Spaß gemacht. Aber nächstes Jahr werde ich einen Kochkurs machen: Ich kann einfach nicht kochen

und das finde ich schrecklich! Und dieses Jahr habe ich
auch eine Theater-AG gewählt. Nächstes Jahr werde ich
also eine Umwelt-AG wählen. Ja, das wird interessant
sein, glaube ich. Na, und was sonst … ?

K2F9F

Lieber Dieter,
heute beginnen die Sommerferien und das macht viel
Spaß! Für zwei Monate keine Schule! Toll! Ich werde
jeden Morgen lange schlafen und jeden Tag faulenzen!
Aber ich werde auch Sport machen – ich bin nicht total
faul! Meine Schwester und ich werden eine Radtour
machen – nach Bayern. Das wird anstrengend sein, aber
auch sehr interessant. Und du? Was machst du in den
Ferien?
Dein   Karl

Hallo! Ich heiße Katrin und ich wohne mit meinen
Eltern in Bonn. Mein Vater ist Postbote und meine
Mutter ist Mechanikerin. Und was möchte ich später
werden? Also, ich möchte gern Tierärztin werden, glaube
ich. Ich mag Tiere sehr gern. Und was sonst? Also, ich
möchte später ein schönes Haus kaufen, ein Haus auf
dem Land. Und dann werde ich jedes Wochenende eine
Party mit meinen Freunden machen! Oh, und ich
möchte später auch gern um die Welt reisen – nach
Afrika und Asien. Ja, das wird toll sein! Aber jetzt muss
ich leider meine Hausaufgaben machen!

Willkommen!

Before starting unit 1 of the course, direct pupils' attention to the opening pages of the Students' Book where there is much useful material for them to refer to throughout the course.

Page 3 presents the regular features of *Klasse!* units. You may wish to go through these with pupils, to introduce to them the symbols and titles used in the book, or just direct their attention to what is here, so that they know where they can look them up.

Pages 4–5 contain a contents list, which may be particularly useful when pupils wish to find and revise specific topics.

Page 6 contains a list of instructions used in activities, with translations into English, in case pupils get stuck; and also some handy classroom phrases.

Page 7 reintroduces pupils who have used *Klasse! 1* to the characters they met there – Jasmin, Annika, Sven and Atalay – and gives pupils who are coming new to *Klasse! 2* a chance to get to know them before reading the first episode of the photo story in Unit 1. It is worth spending some time working with the information on this page to build up familiarity with these teenagers, while revising language related to personal information. See also the summary of the characters on page 7 of this book.

Suggestions for use:
- Ask pupils to read the bubbles and listen to the tape. This will allow them to get used to the characters' voices.
- Point to each photo and ask pupils: *Wer ist das? Wie alt ist er/sie? Wo wohnt er/sie? Hat er/sie Geschwister? Was sind seine/ihre Hobbys?*
- Ask pupils to read out a bubble without saying the person's name. The rest of the class must listen and guess who it is.
- Ask pupils to memorize what one of the characters says and to say it out loud, starting: *Ich heiße …* The rest of the class check in the book and stop the pupil with a noise each time he/she forgets something.
- Ask pupils to present themselves as the characters do here: *Ich heiße … , ich bin … Jahre alt, ich wohne in … , etc.*
- Pupils could then go on to manipulate this language, asking each other questions, predicting answers, recalling someone's answers from memory, etc.
- If copies of *Klasse! 1* are still available for pupils' use, you could ask them in groups, working on a character

each, to look through the book and pick up any other details they can find out about that character, in order to complete the picture.

Transcript   p 7, Die Klasse!-Clique

– Hallo! Ich heiße Jasmin. Ich bin 14 Jahre alt und ich wohne in Wesel. Ich habe eine Schwester und einen Bruder. Meine Hobbys sind Sport und Musikhören.

– Ich bin Annika. Ich bin 13 Jahre alt und ich komme aus Wesel. Ich bin Einzelkind, aber ich habe einen Hund und eine Katze. Mein Hund heißt Otto und meine Katze heißt Micki.

– Und ich heiße Sven. Ich bin 14 Jahre alt. Ich komme aus Chemnitz, aber ich wohne in Wesel – mit meinen Eltern. Ich habe zwei Brüder und drei Schwestern. Ich spiele gern Fußball und ich lese gern.

– Mein Name ist Atalay. Ich komme aus der Türkei und ich wohne in Wesel. Ich bin 14 Jahre alt. Ich habe keine Geschwister – leider! Aber ich habe einen Wellensittich – er heißt Bubu!

Einheit 1 Wie waren die Ferien?

					National Curriculum	
Pages	**Objectives**	**Grammar**	**Pronunciation, Skill focus**	**Key language**	**PoS**	**AT level**
8–9 Die Klasse!-Clique	Reading and listening for pleasure Familiarization with themes, structures and language of the unit	–	–		–	1.5, 3.3, 3.5
10–11 Wohin bist du gefahren?	Say where you went on holiday Ask others where they went on holiday	Perfect tense + *sein*	Pronouncing past participles	*Wohin bist du im Sommer gefahren?* *Ich bin/Wir sind nach ... gefahren/ geflogen.* *Ich bin/Wir sind zu Hause geblieben.* countries and towns/cities	1a, 1b, 1c, 2a, 2b, 2c, 2d, 2i, 5a, 5d, 5i	1.2–3, 2.2–3, 3.5, 4.2–3, 4.5
12–13 Was hast du in München gemacht?	Ask what someone did on holiday Say what you did on holiday	Perfect tense + *haben/sein*	Adapting a written text	*Was hast du in ... gemacht?* *Ich habe Tennis gespielt.* *Wir haben einen Ausflug gemacht.* *Wir haben Postkarten/souvenirs gekauft.* *Wir haben die Stadt/ Sehenswürdigkeiten besichtigt.* *Wir haben meinen Brieffreund/meine Brieffreundin/meine Großeltern besucht.* *Wir haben Paella/Curry/Kuchen gegessen.* *Wir haben Limonade getrunken.* *Ich bin in die Disco/ins Museum/in die Stadt/zum Freizeitpark gegangen.* *Wir sind zum Strand gefahren.*	1a, 1b, 1c, 2a, 2b, 2c, 2d, 2f, 5a, 5d, 5f, 5i	1.2–3, 2.3, 3.2, 4.3
14–15 Wie war das Wetter in Frankreich?	Ask where others went on holiday Say where you went on holiday Ask what the weather was like on holiday Say what the weather was like on holiday	Imperfect tense of *sein*	–	*Wo warst du (in den Ferien)?* *Ich war in ...* *Wie war das Wetter (in ...)?* *Es war sehr/gar nicht ...schön/ heiß/sonnig* *schlecht/kalt/windig/neblig/wolkig* *Es hat viel/nicht viel/nie/manchmal/ oft/immer geregnet/geschneit.*	1a, 1b, 1c, 2a, 2b, 2c, 2d, 2i, 3e, 5a, 5d, 5f, 5i	1.2–3, 2.4–5, 3.2, 4.5

Pages	Objectives	Grammar	Pronunciation, Skill focus	Key language	PoS	AT level
16–17 Wo hast du gewohnt?	Ask where someone stayed on holiday Say where you stayed on holiday Say what it was like	*in* + dative case	Making notes during listening activities	*Wo hast du gewohnt?* *Ich habe in einem Wohnwagen/einer Ferienwohnung/einer Jugendherberge/einem Hotel/einem Wohnmobil/einem Zelt gewohnt.* *Wir haben bei Freunden gewohnt.* *Wie war … ?* *Der Wohnwagen war sehr alt/modern.* *Die Ferienwohnung/Jugendherberge war sehr laut/nicht schön.* *Das Zimmer/Hotel/Wohnmobil/Zelt war sehr klein/groß.*	1a, 1b, 1c, 2a, 2b, 2c, 2d, 2i, 3e, 5a, 5c, 5d, 5f, 5i	1.2, 1.5, 2.3, 3.1–2, 4.2, 4.4–5
18–19 Thema im Fokus	Encourage reading for pleasure Use language from Unit 1 creatively Encourage independent, pair- and groupwork	–	–	–	1a, 1b, 1c, 2f, 2h, 2i, 3b, 3c, 3d, 3e, 5c, 5d, 5f, 5i	2.3–5, 3.5, 4.3–5

1 Wie waren die Ferien?

Aims of the unit
- To be able to talk about where you went on holiday
- To be able to talk about what you did on holiday
- To be able to talk about where you stayed and what it was like
- To be able to describe how the weather was

Die Klasse!-Clique
pages 8–9

Materials
- Students' Book pages 8–9
- Cassette 1 side A
- Workbook page 4

The first spread of each unit follows the same pattern, introducing the themes, structures and some of the key language of the unit in a light-hearted way without the need for overt grammar teaching. Each introductory spread features an instalment of the photo story, which concerns the adventures of the *Klasse!-Clique*: Jasmin, Annika, Atalay and Sven (the main characters from *Klasse! 1*). In this first episode, the members of the *Clique* meet up on the first day back at school and discuss their summer holiday experiences. Jasmin tells Annika that she has a new e-mail penfriend – Sascha. Could this be the beginning of a romance?

Preparatory work

Ask the pupils to look at the pictures. Can they remember which of the characters is which? Ask them if they can remember anything else about the characters.

AT 3.5 **1a** *Vor dem Lesen: Was meinst du – was passt? Finde die passenden Wörter.* In this pre-reading activity, pupils match the German words/phrases to their English translations. Encourage pupils to start with the items they recognize and work out the others by a process of elimination. Feed back the answers orally as a whole-class exercise.

Answers:

1 b; 2 e; 3 g; 4 f; 5 a; 6 c; 7 d

 1b *Ist alles richtig? Hör gut zu und lies mit.* Pupils listen
AT 1.5
AT 3.5 to the recording and follow the text in their books, locating the phrases from activity 1a. When pupils have listened to and read the text through once, ask them what they think the text is about. Point to the place names: it is about holidays and travel. Explain that this unit will be all about the summer holidays: where pupils went and what they did. You could then ask if pupils remember what form of the verb they use for talking about the past in German. (The perfect tense – *Klasse! 1*, Unit 9.) Ask if pupils can spot any examples of the perfect tense in the photo story.

Transcript   p 8, activity 1b

– Wohin bist du im Sommer gefahren, Annika?
  Ich bin nach Frankreich gefahren. Ich habe meine Brieffreundin Manon in Marseille besucht. Wir haben viel gemacht – Marseille ist toll!
– Und du, Sven?
– Ich bin nach Florida geflogen. Das Wetter war super! Wir sind jeden Tag zum Strand gefahren und ich habe Souvenirs gekauft.
– Und wir sind in die Schweiz gefahren – nach St. Gallen. Wir haben die Stadt besichtigt – und wir haben in einem Zelt gewohnt!

– Und du – was hast du gemacht, Jasmin?
– Ich? Ich bin zu Hause geblieben.
– Und wie war das Wetter?
– Es war schlecht – es hat jeden Tag geregnet! Aber es war nie langweilig – ich habe einen neuen Computer gekauft!
– He – fantastisch!
– Ja – ich surfe jetzt jeden Tag im Internet. Und ich schreibe E-Mails!

– Du Annika – ich habe einen E-Mail-Brieffreund! Er heißt Sascha und er wohnt hier in Wesel ...

AT3.3 **2** *Finde im Text.* Pupils scan the text for specific vocabulary items.

Answers:

1 Marseille, St. Gallen, Wesel; 2 Two of: toll, super, fantastisch; 3 Frankreich, die Schweiz; 4 schlecht, langweilig

AT 3.5 **3** *Wer ist das? Kopiere die Sätze und schreib die passenden Namen auf.* Pupils remind themselves of the word order and forms of the perfect tense by writing out the sentences, rather than just supplying the names.

Answers:

1 Sven; 2 Jasmin; 3 Annika; 4 Jasmin; 5 Atalay

Viel Spaß!

Spanien. The main aim of the songs in *Klasse! 2* is listening for pleasure, but the songs also act to consolidate the new language just presented in the photo story, and also to present other language to come in the unit. This song will help remind pupils of the forms of the perfect tense that they first learned in Unit 9 of *Klasse! 1*, and will enable them to assimilate the imperfect *war*. After listening to the song all the way through, pupils could sing along with a second playing. If pupils (or you) are reticent about singing, you could just use the song for listening practice.

Follow-up activities. Pupils could draw cartoons to illustrate the song. They could also write new versions of the verses, substituting single words or whole phrases.

Transcript   p 9, Viel Spaß!

Ich bin nach Spanien geflogen
Wohin bist du geflogen?
Ich bin nach Spanien geflogen
Und es war toll, toll, toll!

Sonne, Schwimmen, Sport und Strand,
Spanien ist mein Lieblingsland!

Ich bin zwei Wochen geblieben
Wie lange bist du geblieben?
Ich bin zwei Wochen geblieben
Und es war schön, schön, schön!

Refrain

Ich hab' Paella gegessen
Was hast du gegessen?
Ich hab' Paella gegessen
Und es war gut, gut, gut!

Refrain

Ich bin zum Strand gefahren
Wohin bist du gefahren?
Ich bin zum Strand gefahren
Und es war heiß, heiß, heiß!

Refrain

Ich bin nach Hause geflogen
Wohin bist du geflogen?
Ich bin nach Hause geflogen
Und es war schade, schade, schade!

Refrain

WB A   Workbook activity A exploits the song and provides an opportunity for students to familiarize themselves further with the perfect and imperfect tenses.

For the next lesson

Pupils could be invited to bring in holiday photos, postcards, brochure pictures or other visuals (e.g. souvenirs) relating to their summer holidays, or places they would like to go. Remember that this may be a sensitive issue, as not all families' economic situations permit them to take an expensive holiday.

Wohin bist du gefahren?
pages 10–11

Objectives

- Say where you went on holiday
- Ask others where they went on holiday

Key language

Wohin bist du im Sommer gefahren?
Ich bin/Wir sind nach … gefahren/geflogen.
Ich bin/Wir sind zu Hause geblieben.
countries and towns/cities

National Curriculum PoS

statements 1a, 1b, 1c, 2a, 2b, 2c, 2d, 2i, 5a, 5d, 5i

Materials

- Students' Book pages 10–11
- Cassette 1 side A
- Workbook pages 5–6
- Copymasters 4, 7, 8A

Preparatory work

Introduce *nach* + town/country by talking about your own summer holidays, using a photo, a brochure or another visual. T: *Schaut auf das Bild: das ist [Stadt/Land]. Ich bin im Sommer nach [Stadt/Land] gefahren.* Ask two or three pupils where they went. T: *Wohin bist du gefahren?* Supply the German place names as necessary. If they have brought photos or other visuals, they can show them to the class. Note the destinations on the board/OHT, being sure to add *nach* or *in die: nach Frankreich, nach Scarborough, in die Türkei,* etc.

1 *Hör gut zu und lies mit.* Pupils listen to the recording and follow the text in the book. After they have listened and read the text, you could ask them to find a form of *sein* and one other verb in each speech bubble. Write up the verb forms *ich bin … gefahren, wir sind … geflogen, wir sind … gefahren, ich bin … geblieben.* Ask pupils what they think these mean in English. T: *Ich bin gefahren. Was heißt das auf Englisch?*, etc. To help them, you could mime driving, flying and not moving (e.g. sitting still with arms crossed) whilst repeating the perfect tense forms. Once the meanings have been established, write up the infinitives *fahren, fliegen* and *bleiben.* Elicit from the pupils that these mean 'to travel/go', 'to fly' and 'to stay' respectively, again miming to give the pupils further help. T: *Was heißt „fahren" auf Englisch?*, etc.

Transcript   p 10, activity 1

1 – Ich bin nach Frankreich gefahren.
2 – Wir sind nach Afrika geflogen.
3 – Wir sind nach Tenby gefahren.
4 – Ich bin zu Hause geblieben.

2a *Wohin sind sie im Sommer gefahren? Hör gut zu und finde die passenden Namen, Länder, Kontinente und Städte.* Pupils listen to the recording and match the names to the destinations. On the first listening, ask pupils to note down the destinations they hear, referring to the map. On the second listening, pupils write the appropriate name next to each destination.

Answers can be checked as a whole-class activity afterwards. Write up the answers on the board/OHT in preparation for activity 2b.

Answers:

Anne: zu Hause (Deutschland); Matthias: Irland;
Mira: Pakistan (Asien); Kofi: Afrika (Ghana);
Heike: Griechenland; Tina: Schottland;
Alex: Italien (Rom); Susi: Australien (Sydney)

Transcript   p 10, activity 2a

– Hallo, Anne! Wohin bist du im Sommer gefahren?
– Tag, Matthias. Ich bin zu Hause geblieben. Berlin ist super im Sommer! Und du?
– Also, wir sind nach Irland gefahren.

– Hallo, Mira! Und wohin bist du im Sommer gefahren?
– Tag, Anne. Wir sind nach Asien geflogen. Meine Oma wohnt in Pakistan.

– Und du, Kofi? Wohin bist du gefahren?
– Ich bin nach Afrika geflogen. Ich komme aus Afrika – aus Ghana.

– Heike, wohin bist du im Sommer gefahren?
– Nach Griechenland – wir sind nach Griechenland gefahren.

– Tina, wohin bist du gefahren?
– Ich? Ich bin nach Schottland gefahren – mit dem Auto.

– Und du, Alex?
– Wir sind nach Italien gefahren – nach Rom.
– Nach Italien?
– Ja, mit dem Zug.

– Wohin bist du im Sommer gefahren, Susi?
– Ich bin nach Australien geflogen. Meine Brieffreundin wohnt in Sydney.

AT 2.2 **2b** *Ratespiel: Wer ist das? A fragt, B antwortet. Dann ist B dran.* Working in pairs, pupils take it in turns to be one of the characters from activity 2a, stating where they went on holiday. Their partners then say who they are. (They will need the correct answers from activity 2a for this.)

As a follow-up, pupils could take the pairwork activity one stage further and invite their partners to guess where they went, e.g.: P1: *Wohin bin ich gefahren?* P2: *Nach Italien?* P1: *Nein.* P2: *Nach Afrika?* P1: *Richtig!* P2: *Du bist Kofi! Wohin bin ich gefahren?*, etc.

C 4 Activity 1 on copymaster 4 provides further consolidation on this point.

WB B Workbook activity B could be used at this point for revision and further practice.

C 7 Activity 2 on copymaster 7 could be used to prepare pupils for activity 3 below.

AT 2.3 **3** *Mach eine Umfrage: „Wohin bist du im Sommer gefahren?"* Pupils carry out a class survey. They go round the class asking each other where they went in the summer holidays, recording their results initially in note form on paper. Draw pupils' attention to the sentences in the *Hilfe* panel. Point out that *Wohin*? is used to ask about travel to a place, not *Wo?*

Before beginning the activity, demonstrate with two or three pupils. T: *Marc. Wohin bist du im Sommer gefahren?* P1: *Ich bin nach Frankreich gefahren*, etc. Write up the structure *Ich bin nach … gefahren/geflogen.* on the board/OHT.

Review the results of the survey as a whole-class activity. T: *Wohin ist Gina im Sommer gefahren?* P1: *(Gina ist) nach Indien (gefahren)*, etc. This will give you the opportunity to provide the German names of any destinations not previously introduced.

AT 4.2 *Noch mal! Schreib die Namen und Länder auf.* This activity provides written reinforcement of activity 3. Pupils record their results in tabular form (name and destination) in their exercise books. Alternatively, the results could be presented on computer as a graph or bar-chart, or as a collage or poster (with postcards, photos and/or a map of the world).

AT 4.3 *Extra! Schreib die Resultate in Sätzen auf.* This activity provides a written extension of activity 3, practising the perfect with *sein*. Pupils write up their results in full sentences in their exercise books.

Grammatik im Fokus

Das Perfekt + sein This section focuses on the formation of the perfect tense with auxiliary *sein* for verbs of movement. Ask pupils whether they remember that some verbs form the perfect with *haben* and some with *sein* (*Klasse! 1*, Unit 9). Explain that the past participles of verbs which take *sein* are irregular – they have to be learnt by heart.

Remind pupils that *gehen* only means 'to go on foot': to illustrate the point, you could write *ich bin gegangen* and draw a footprint, and write *ich bin gefahren* and draw a car or train.

To help pupils familiarize themselves with the perfect forms, you could play a game. Draw a grid of three columns and four rows on a sheet of paper. In each of the squares, write one component of one of the past participles: *ge-fahr-en, ge-flog-en, ge-gang-en, ge-blieb-en*. Photocopy the sheet (half as many copies as pupils in the class) and cut out the squares, so that each sheet becomes 12 'cards', keeping each set of 12 cards together. Pupils work together in pairs, and each partner receives six cards. The object of the game is to use the cards to form past participles: the partner who uses up all of his/her cards first wins.

4 *bin, bist, ist oder sind? Füll die Lücken aus.* Pupils write out the sentences including the correct form of the auxiliary *sein*. Draw pupils' attention to the *Wiederholung* panel. Answers can be fed back orally afterwards. T: *Nummer 1 – wie heißt es richtig?* P1: *Ich bin nach Irland gefahren*, etc.

Answers: 1 bin; 2 ist; 3 sind; 4 sind; 5 bist

C 8A Activity 1 on copymaster 8A provides reinforcement of this point.

AT 3.5 **5a** *Lies Toms Brief und füll die Lücken aus.* Pupils write out the letter including the correct past participles. Rehearse the past participles as a whole-class activity first, perhaps as a chant. T: *fliegen!* Pupils: *geflogen!* T: *bleiben!* Pupils: *geblieben!*, etc.

Answers:

Hallo, Kathi!

Wohin bist du im Sommer **gefahren**? Ich bin nach Schottland **geflogen**. Meine Brüder Alex und Mark sind nach Griechenland **gefahren** – mit dem Auto. Und meine Eltern? Mein Vater ist zu Hause **geblieben** – und meine Mutter ist nach Wien **geflogen**!

AT 4.5 | **5b** *Schreib einen Antwortbrief für Kathi mit den Informationen unten.* Pupils write a letter on the model of activity 5a using the pictures as prompts, consolidating the perfect with *sein*. Check that pupils can identify the national flags. T: *Wohin ist Kathi gefahren?* P1: *Nach Frankreich*, etc. More able pupils can add an adverbial phrase for the mode of transport. Remind them that this phrase (= manner) should come before the destination (= place).

Suggested answers:

Hallo, Tom!

Ich bin im Sommer (mit dem Bus) nach Frankreich gefahren. Meine Schwester ist (mit dem Zug) nach Spanien gefahren. Mein Bruder ist nach Afrika geflogen. Und meine Eltern? Sie sind zu Hause geblieben!

WB C, D, E | Workbook activities C, D and E could be used at this point for revision and further practice.

Gut gesagt!

Perfekt-Partizipien. This section focuses on the pronunciation of the past participles.

 6a *Hör gut zu und lies mit.* Pupils listen to the past participles on the recording and relate the sounds to the written words.

Transcript	p 11, activity 6a
– gefahren	
– geflogen	
– gegangen	
– geblieben	

 6b *Hör gut zu und wiederhole.* Pupils listen to the sentences on the tape and repeat them. Explain that they should pay particular attention to intonation: the stress in the past participles lies on the second syllable (never on *ge-* or *-en*). The *-o-* in *geflogen* and the *-ah-* in *gefahren* are long vowels.

Transcript	p 11, activity 6b
– Ich bin nach Genf geflogen.	
– Gabi ist ins Geschäft gegangen.	
– Wir sind nach Gellen gefahren.	
– Und Günther ist zu Hause geblieben!	

Was hast du in München gemacht?
pages 12–13

Objectives

* Ask what someone did on holiday
* Say what you did on holiday

Key language

Was hast du in … gemacht?
Ich habe Tennis gespielt.
Wir haben einen Ausflug gemacht.
Wir haben Postkarten/Souvenirs gekauft.
Wir haben die Stadt/Sehenswürdigkeiten besichtigt.
Wir haben meinen Brieffreund/meine Brieffreundin/meine Großeltern besucht.
Wir haben Paella/Curry/Kuchen gegessen.
Wir haben Limonade getrunken.
Ich bin in die Disco/ins Museum/in die Stadt/zum Freizeitpark gegangen.
Wir sind zum Strand gefahren.

National Curriculum PoS

statements 1a, 1b, 1c, 2a, 2b, 2c, 2d, 2f, 5a, 5d, 5f, 5i

Materials

* Students' Book pages 12–13
* Cassette 1 side A
* Workbook pages 7–9
* Copymasters 4, 6, 8B, 9

Preparatory work

Introduce the new past participles by talking about your holidays, using visuals (e.g. postcards, brochure pictures, souvenirs) and/or acting out the activities. T: *Ich bin im Sommer nach … gefahren. Ich habe die Stadt besichtigt. Ich habe meine Freunde besucht. Ich habe … gegessen. Ich habe … getrunken.* Point out the difference between the two new verbs, *besichtigen* and *besuchen*. For *besichtigen*, you could mime looking around, taking photos, etc. For *besuchen*, you could mime visiting someone: ringing the doorbell, saying hello, shaking hands or kissing cheeks, etc. On the board/OHT, write up the perfect forms next to the present tense forms: *ich besichtige – ich habe besichtigt; ich besuche – ich habe besucht; ich esse – ich habe gegessen; ich trinke – ich habe getrunken.* Now ask pupils about their holidays. T: *Mary, was hast du besichtigt?*, etc. Allow single words/phrases in answer, rather than requiring full sentences using the perfect.

 | AT 1.2 | AT 3.2 | **1** *Hör gut zu und lies mit.* Pupils listen to the recording and follow the text in the book.

Transcript	p 12, activity 1
1 – Ich habe meine Großeltern besucht. Wir haben einen Ausflug gemacht.	
2 – Wir sind zum Strand gefahren. Wir haben Hamburger gegessen und wir haben Cola getrunken.	
3 – Ich habe die Stadt besichtigt – ich habe viele Sehenswürdigkeiten besichtigt!	

C 6 | Activity 2 on copymaster 6 could be used for consolidation before activity 2a below.

2a *Was haben Markus und Julia gemacht? Hör gut zu und finde die passenden Bilder.* Pupils listen to the recording and identify the activities mentioned by each speaker. Before playing the recording, ask the pupils to look at the pictures: can they describe them? T: *Was ist*

AT 1.3

Bild a? P: *Ein Schwimmbad,* etc. Write up key words for each picture on the board/OHT. (Pupils will find these helpful for activity 2b as well.)

Answers:

Markus: f, b, h, d; Julia: e, a, g, c

Transcript   p 12, activity 2a

– Was hast du im Sommer gemacht, Markus?
– Ich bin nach Frankreich gefahren – nach Lille. Also, Lille ist eine tolle Stadt!
– Und was hast du in Lille gemacht?
– Ich habe meinen Brieffreund Pascal besucht. Und was habe ich gemacht? Ich habe die Stadt besichtigt, und ich habe Sehenswürdigkeiten besichtigt. Wir sind auch ins Museum gegangen. Und wir sind mit dem Zug zum Euro Disney-Freizeitpark gefahren.

– Und du, Julia? Was hast du im Sommer gemacht?
– Also, ich bin nach Italien gefahren. Und ich habe viel gemacht! Ich bin sehr sportlich. Ich habe jeden Tag Fußball gespielt, und ich bin ins Schwimmbad gegangen. Wir – also meine Schwester Kathi und ich – wir sind auch in die Eisdiele gegangen, und wir haben Kakao getrunken und Eis gegessen. Ach ja, und wir sind in die Stadt gefahren, und ich habe viele CDs gekauft!

T 2.3 **2b** *A fragt: „Was hast du gemacht?", B antwortet. Macht Dialoge mit den Bildern (Übung 2a).* Pupils create their own dialogues, using the pictures from activity 2a as prompts. Draw their attention to the *Hilfe* box: can they find a sentence in the box to match each of the pictures?

C 4 Activity 2 on copymaster 4 provides further consolidation on this point.

F, G, H Workbook activities F, G and H could be used at this point.

Tipp

Einen Text adaptieren. This section focuses on adapting texts to pupils' own needs by substituting words and phrases. Write up the example text on the board/OHT. Now rub out the words/phrases which are green in the original, leaving gaps, and scribble over the phrases which are orange. Ask pupils for suggestions for each of the gaps. T: *„Hallo …".* Wer kennt einen Namen? P1: *Wayne.* T: Sehr gut. „Hallo Wayne! Ich war im Sommer …" Wer kennt ein Land?, etc.

AT 4.3 **3** *Schreib eine Postkarte an Julia – verändere die Wörter in Grün, lass die Wörter in Orange aus.* Pupils practise adapting a text, using the expressions in the *Hilfe* box. Do the first two or three examples with the whole class, asking them for suggestions.

C 9 Activity 1 on copymaster 9 provides further consolidation of this point.

Grammatik im Fokus

Das Perfekt. This section focuses on the perfect tense with auxiliary *haben,* including the formation of past participles for irregular (strong) verbs and verbs with inseparable prefixes. Explain that verbs which begin with *be-* do not take *ge-* in the past participle (because 'gebesucht' and 'gebesichtigt' would be difficult to say!).

4 *Was hast du gemacht? Schreib Sätze.* Pupils copy out the sentences and complete them with the correct past participles.

Answers:

1 Ich habe Limonade getrunken.
2 Wir haben Postkarten gekauft.
3 Ich habe die Stadt besichtigt.
4 Ich habe meine Großeltern besucht.
5 Wir haben Hamburger gegessen.

Wiederholung

Das Perfekt + sein. In this section, pupils are reminded that verbs of motion use auxiliary *sein* rather than auxiliary *haben* to form the perfect tense (see Students' Book page 11).

Refer more able pupils to *Grammatik* on page 150 of their books for the formation of the perfect with auxiliary *sein.*

C 6 Activity 3 on copymaster 6 could be used for further consolidation of the perfect tense at this point.

5 *sein oder haben? Lies Gabis Brief und füll die Lücken aus.* Pupils supply the correct perfect auxiliary, distinguishing between verbs which take *haben* and verbs which take *sein.*

As a follow-up activity, pupils could colour-code the completed text (as in activity 3 above) and adapt the text, adding their own details, to describe their own holiday experiences.

Answers:

Wir **sind** nach Spanien geflogen. Wir **haben** Tennis gespielt oder wir **sind** zum Strand gefahren. Wir **haben** auch einen Ausflug gemacht und ich **habe** Sehenswürdigkeiten besichtigt. Ich **habe** Paella gegessen und ich **bin** in die Disco gegangen.

WB I, J Workbook activities I and J could be used at this point.

C 8B Activity 1 on copymaster 8B provides further consolidation on this point.

Wie war das Wetter in Frankreich?
pages 14–15

Objectives
- Ask where others went on holiday
- Say where you went on holiday
- Ask what the weather was like on holiday
- Say what the weather was like on holiday

Key language
Wo warst du (in den Ferien)?
Ich war in …
Wie war das Wetter (in …)?
Es war sehr/gar nicht …
schön/heiß/sonnig

schlecht/kalt/windig/neblig/wolkig
Es hat viel/nicht viel/nie/manchmal/oft/immer
geregnet/geschneit.

National Curriculum PoS

statements 1a, 1b, 1c, 2a, 2b, 2c, 2d, 2i, 3e, 5a, 5d, 5f, 5i

Materials

- Students' Book pages 14–15
- Cassette 1 side A
- Workbook pages 9–10
- Copymasters 1, 6, 7, 8A

Preparatory work

| C 1 |

To introduce key weather vocabulary, use the pictures from copymaster 1 copied onto an OHT or as flashcards. Start off with the present tense: *Es ist heiß. Es regnet*, etc. (For general advice on using copymaster visuals, see page 12 of the introduction to this book.)

Explain that in this lesson pupils are going to learn to talk about what the weather was like over the summer holidays. To do this, they are going to use a new form of the verb *sein*: *war*, which means the same as 'was' in English.

| AT 1.2 |
| AT 3.2 |

1 *Hör gut zu und lies mit.* Pupils listen to the recording and follow the text in the book.

> **Transcript**   p 14, activity 1
>
> – Wie war das Wetter?
> – Es war schön.
> – Puuh – es war sehr heiß.
> – Es war sonnig.
> – Es war schlecht.
> – Brrr – es war immer kalt!
> – Es – war – windig!
> – Es war neblig.
> – Es war wolkig.
> – Es hat viel geregnet.
> – Es hat geschneit.

| C 6 |

Activity 1 on copymaster 6 provides further consolidation on this point.

| AT 1.3 |

2 *Wie war das Wetter? Hör gut zu und finde die passenden Bilder in Übung 1 für Stefan, Ruth und Erdal.* Pupils identify the weather experienced by each person, matching pictures to names.

Answers:

Stefan: b, a; Ruth: e, d, g; Erdal: c, b, h

> **Transcript**   p 14, activity 2
>
> – Hallo, Stefan!
> – Hallo, Andrea!
> – Hey, du bist ja total braun! Wo warst du in den Ferien?
> – Ich war in Schottland.
> – Wie war das Wetter in Schottland?
> – Es war sehr schön: es war sonnig und es war sehr heiß.

> – Ruth! Hallo, Ruth! Na, wie geht's?
> – Tag, Andrea! Schlecht! Ich war in Amerika, in Florida.
> – Wie war das Wetter? Gut?
> – Nein, schlecht! Es war sehr schlecht. Es war neblig und es war sehr windig. Und es hat viel geregnet!
>
> – Hallo, Andrea!
> – Tag, Erdal! Na, wie waren die Ferien?
> – Super! Ich war in Österreich – zum Skifahren.
> – Und wie war das Wetter?
> – Es war sehr kalt und es war manchmal sonnig. Und es hat viel geschneit.

| WB K, L |

Workbook activities K and L could be used at this point for revision and further practice.

| C 7 |

Activity 1 on copymaster 7 could be used for consolidation prior to activity 3 below.

| AT 2.4 |

3 *Wo warst du in den Ferien? Wie war das Wetter? Macht Dialoge mit den Informationen auf der Karte rechts.* Pupils work together in pairs, taking it in turns to ask each other where they were on holiday and what the weather was like. Work through one example with the class, making it clear that pupils should use the information in the map, rather than talking about their real holiday experiences. Draw pupils' attention to the form *warst*, explaining that this is the *du*-form of *war*.

| AT 4.3 |

Noch mal! Schreib einen Wetterbericht. This activity provides written consolidation of activity 3. For more variety, pupils could invent their own weather reports rather than using the map in the book. They could then draw a map to accompany their reports.

Answers:

Schottland: Es hat geschneit. Irland: Es war wolkig. England: Es war neblig. Frankreich: Es hat geregnet. Deutschland: Es war sonnig. Österreich: Es war kalt. Italien: Es war sehr heiß. Griechenland: Es war windig.

| AT 2.5 |
| AT 4.5 |

Extra! Du bist Reporter. Finde fünf Schüler/Schülerinnen. Frag: „Wo warst du in den Ferien? Wie war das Wetter?" und nimm die Interviews auf Kassette auf. Schreib dann fünf Postkarten mit den Informationen. In this extension activity, pupils work in groups of approximately six. They ask each other where they were in the summer holidays, recording their interviews on tape. (There is no need to use the map for this activity: pupils can discuss their real or imaginary holiday experiences.) One pupil takes the role of interviewer. Pupils then take notes individually from the recordings and write them up as postcards. They can add further details either at the speaking or the writing stage: activities (*wir haben die Stadt besichtigt*) and personal reactions (*es war langweilig/toll*), etc.

| WB M |

Workbook activity M could be used at this point for revision and further practice.

Grammatik im Fokus

Das Imperfekt. This section focuses on the imperfect tense of *sein*. Explain that *ich war, du warst*, etc. is the imperfect tense of *sein*. If pupils want to know why the imperfect is used, explain that this form of *sein* is more usual than the perfect (*ist … gewesen*) because it is much shorter, and *sein* is needed so often. (There is no need to introduce the imperfect of any other verbs in this unit.) Explain that, like the present tense of *sein*, the imperfect has to be learnt by heart.

C 8A Activity 2 on copymaster 8A provides further consolidation on this point.

4 *Lies Maltes Postkarte. Finde alle Sätze im Imperfekt und alle Sätze im Perfekt. Schreib die Sätze in zwei Listen auf.* Pupils practise identifying the perfect and the imperfect.

Answers:

Imperfect
wo warst du in den Ferien?
Ich war in Berlin.
Das Wetter war aber schlecht:
und es war nie heiß.
Es war immer kalt
Wie war das Wetter in Hamburg?

Perfect
Und was hast du gemacht?
Ich habe meinen Bruder besucht.
Ich habe einen Fußball gekauft
und wir haben Fußball gespielt.
Es hat immer geregnet
und es hat manchmal geschneit!

AT 4.5 **5** *Wo warst du in den Ferien? Wie war das Wetter? Schreib eine Postkarte mit den Informationen unten.* This is a guided writing activity using both the perfect and the imperfect. In preparation, present the adverbs of time *immer, oft, manchmal* and *nie*, which will be useful in completing activity 5. To demonstrate their meaning, you could draw up a rough diary page on the board/OHT with the days labelled *Montag, Dienstag*, etc. Demonstrate *immer* by drawing a raindrop against every day, saying *Es hat immer geregnet*; to demonstrate *oft*, rub out one or two of the raindrops and say *Es hat oft geregnet*; and so on for *manchmal* and *nie*.

As in Malte's postcard, pupils can add additional details about activities, etc. Less able pupils could adapt Malte's postcard from activity 4. As on page 12, they should first write out and colour code the original (green – to be changed; orange – to be left out) before writing their own version. This is an ideal activity for completing on computer.

AT 4.5 **6** *Du bist dran! Wie war das Wetter am Wochenende? Schreib Sätze.* Pupils can invent their own weather reports for this writing activity. Their report could have a local, a national, a European or a worldwide focus. This activity could be used for homework: ask pupils to watch the weather forecast or look it up on the Internet/in a newspaper and then write up a report.

WB N Workbook activity N could be used at this point for revision and further practice.

Wo hast du gewohnt?
pages 16–17

Objectives
- Ask where someone stayed on holiday
- Say where you stayed on holiday
- Say what it was like

Key language
Wo hast du gewohnt?
Ich habe in einem Wohnwagen/einer Ferienwohnung/einer Jugendherberge/einem Hotel/einem Wohnmobil/einem Zelt gewohnt.
Wir haben bei Freunden gewohnt.
Wie war … ?
Der Wohnwagen war sehr alt/modern.
Die Ferienwohnung/Jugendherberge war sehr laut/nicht schön.
Das Zimmer/Hotel/Wohnmobil/Zelt war sehr klein/groß.

National Curriculum PoS
statements 1a, 1b, 1c, 2a, 2b, 2c, 2d, 2i, 3e, 5a, 5c, 5d, 5f, 5i

Materials
- Students' Book pages 16–17
- Cassette 1 side A
- Workbook pages 11–13
- Copymasters 2, 4, 5, 7, 8B, 9

C 2 ## Preparatory work
To introduce key accommodation vocabulary, use the pictures from copymaster 2 copied onto an OHT or as flashcards. (For general advice on using copymaster visuals, see page 12 of the introduction to this book.) Remind pupils of *ich wohne in einem Bungalow/einer Wohnung/einem Dorf*, etc. (introduced in *Klasse! 1*, p. 53) before going on to introduce *ich habe in … gewohnt* in activity 1a.

AT 1.2 **AT 3.2** **1a** *Wo haben sie gewohnt? Hör gut zu und lies mit.* Pupils listen to the recording and follow the text in the book.

Transcript	p 16, activity 1a
a – Ich habe in einem Hotel gewohnt.	
b – Wir haben in einem Wohnwagen gewohnt.	
c – Ich habe in einem Wohnmobil gewohnt.	
d – Ich habe in einem Zelt gewohnt.	
e – Ich habe in einer Ferienwohnung gewohnt.	
f – Wir haben in einer Jugendherberge gewohnt.	
g – Ich habe bei einer Gastfamilie gewohnt.	
h – Ich habe bei Freunden gewohnt.	

AT 2.3 **1b** *Ratespiel: Wo hast du gewohnt? A fragt, B wählt ein Bild und antwortet. Dann ist B dran.* Working in pairs, pupils take it in turns to ask each other where they stayed, basing their answers on the pictures in activity 1a. Remind them of the structure i*ch habe … gewohnt* and encourage them to answer in full sentences.

WB 0, P Workbook activities O and P could be used at this point for revision and further practice.

Wiederholung

This section focuses on the dative with *in*. Remind pupils that *ein/eine/ein* take different endings when they follow the preposition *in* (*Klasse! 1*, p. 53), referring them to *Grammatik* on page 143 in their books. You may wish to explicitly introduce the concept of the dative at this stage, as a special form of *ein/eine/ein*, *der/die/das*, etc. which occurs after *in*. Alternatively, this could be left until Unit 2, where the accusative and dative are dealt with in depth.

| AT 4.2 | **2** *Wo hast du gewohnt? Schreib Sätze für die Bilder in Übung 1a.* This activity provides written consolidation of activity 1. Draw pupils' attention to the *Wiederholung* box.

| AT 3.1 | **3a** *Wie war ... ? Schau die Bilder an und finde die passenden Hilfe-Adjektive unten.* Pupils match the adjectives from the *Hilfe* box to the pictures.

Answers:

a laut; b groß/modern; c klein/alt; d schön; e modern

| AT 2.3 | **3b** *Wie war ... ? Macht Dialoge mit den Bildern (Übung 3a).* Using their answers to activity 3a, pupils work in pairs, asking each other questions about the various types of accommodation. Make sure that they understand that they are to answer in full sentences using *war*.

| WB Q, R | Workbook activities Q and R could be used at this point for revision and further practice.

Tipp

Hören: Notizen machen. This section gives suggestions for making notes during listening activities. Bear in mind that not all pupils will have the same facility in drawing pictures – for some this might take longer than recording the text verbatim!

Explain to pupils that they should find the way of note-taking which best suits them personally – they are the only ones who have to be able to understand the notes afterwards. The vital skill lies in quickly identifying which information is essential.

| C 4 | Activity 3 on copymaster 4 could be used at this point to prepare pupils for activity 4 below.

| AT 1.5 | **4** *Hör gut zu und mach Notizen.* Pupils practise note-taking, recording the holiday experiences of three speakers. Remind them that they should write down key words only.

> **Transcript**   p 17, activity 4
>
> – Nick, wohin bist du im Sommer gefahren?
> – Ich bin nach Spanien gefahren.
> – Und wo hast du gewohnt?
> – Ich habe in einer Ferienwohnung gewohnt. Die Ferienwohnung war aber nicht schön: sie war sehr klein und alt.
> – Und du? Katrin? Wohin bist du im Sommer gefahren?
> – Wir – also meine Klasse – wir sind nach London gefahren. Wir haben dort in einer Jugendherberge gewohnt.

> – Und wie war die Jugendherberge?
> – Na ja, sie war ziemlich modern, aber sie war auch sehr laut.
> – Und wohin bist du im Sommer gefahren, Timo?
> – Ich? Ich bin nach Frankreich gefahren.
> – Und wo hast du gewohnt? Bei einer Gastfamilie?
> – Nein, ich habe in einem Zelt gewohnt. Das Zelt war sehr alt, aber es war groß.

| C 5 | Activities 1 and 2 on copymaster 5 could be used at this point to provide additional speaking and note-taking practice.

| C 8B | Activity 2 on copymaster 8B provides further consolidation of perfect tense forms before *Noch mal!* or *Extra!* below.

| C 9 | Activity 2 on copymaster 9 provides extension material for more able pupils (accommodation and adjectives).

| AT 4.4 | *Noch mal! Lies deine Informationen von Übung 4. Schreib dann eine Postkarte für Nick, Katrin oder Timo..* Pupils write up their notes in postcard form. To make the activity a little more creative, they could invent further details. The activity could be done on computer or by hand, with photos added to make a class display.

| AT 4.5 | *Extra! Wohin bist du in den Ferien gefahren? Wo hast du gewohnt? Wie war ... ? Zeichne alles oder finde Fotos. Schreib dann ein ‚Ferientagebuch'.* This writing activity gives greater scope for imagination and creativity. Pupils could describe their ideal holiday or their 'holiday from hell' instead of a real experience. (For inspiration they could use the pictures from activity 1a or photos they or their classmates have brought in.) Remind them that the 'holiday diary' must be in the perfect and imperfect tenses – not in the present tense.

| C 7 | Activity 3 on copymaster 7 could be used as an alternative to *Extra!*

Thema im Fokus
pages 18–19

National Curriculum PoS
statements 1a, 1b, 1c, 2f, 2h, 2i, 3b, 3c, 3d, 3e, 5c, 5d, 5f, 5i

Materials
- Students' Book pages 18–19
- Cassette 1 side A
- Copymasters 3, 9

The final spread of each unit provides further reading practice, leading into a project outcome for the unit. See pages 8–9 of the introduction to this book for general notes on how to use these pages.

| AT 3.5 | **1** *Traumferien – wer war wo? Lies die Sprechblasen und finde die passenden Fotos für die Personen.* Before pupils attempt this reading activity, draw their attention to the *Tipp* box. Point out that they do not need to be able to understand every single word in order to complete the activity – they just need to be able to scan the text for clues which they can relate to the pictures.

Answers: 1 b; 2 c; 3 a

Tipp

Neue Wörter. This section provides three strategies for coping with unknown vocabulary: conjecture and inference, using reference materials and asking the teacher for help.

To practise tip 1: ask pupils to identify as many words as possible in activity 1 which are the same or similar in German and English.

To practise tip 2: ask pupils for one or two words from activity 1 which they do not know, and ask them to look them up in the *Vokabular* in the back of their books. Remind them to watch out for past participles and other verb forms which will not be listed separately.

C9 Activity 3 on copymaster 9 provides practice in dealing with unknown words.

4.3-5 **2** *Du bist dran! Beschreib deine Traumferien!* Pupils
2.3-5 describe their dream holiday as if they really went on it in the summer. The activity is broken down into five written stages, with a speaking activity as a final stage. The written work should be presented as a poster integrating all the components, with appropriate photos and/or illustrations. Note that pupils will need individual advice about how to present their material for the speaking activity, for example about how to present the menu as part of a coherent spoken report.

Kannst du ... ?

The end-of-unit summary is a checklist for pupils. See page 8 of the introduction to this book for ideas on how to use the checklist.

C3 Copymaster 3 provides a useful reference for pupils revising the language of this unit.

Noch mal!-Seite Einheit 1

page 122

National Curriculum PoS

statements **1a, 1b, 1c, 2a, 2b, 2c, 2h, 2i, 5a, 5d, 5f, 5i**

Materials

- Students' Book page 122
- Cassette 1 side A

This reinforcement page is intended for less able pupils. It consolidates the basic vocabulary and structures from the unit, and it can be used by pupils who experienced difficulty in completing some of the activities within the unit, or as alternative homework activities.

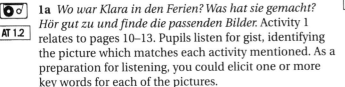
AT 1.2 **1a** *Wo war Klara in den Ferien? Was hat sie gemacht? Hör gut zu und finde die passenden Bilder.* Activity 1 relates to pages 10–13. Pupils listen for gist, identifying the picture which matches each activity mentioned. As a preparation for listening, you could elicit one or more key words for each of the pictures.

Answers: 1 b; 2 d; 3 f; 4 c; 5 a; 6 e

> **Transcript**   p 122, activity 1a
> 1 – Ich bin nach Frankreich geflogen.
> 2 – Wir haben in einem Wohnwagen gewohnt.
> 3 – Ich habe Sehenswürdigkeiten besichtigt.
> 4 – Wir haben Kaffee getrunken und Eis gegessen.
> 5 – Ich bin ins Schwimmbad gegangen.
> 6 – Das Wetter war schön: Es war heiß und sonnig.

AT 2.3 **1b** *Ist alles richtig? A wählt ein Bild, B antwortet. Dann ist B dran.* Pupils work together in pairs to create dialogues. Point out that different questions are needed according to which picture is chosen.

Answers:

a Was hast du gemacht? – Ich bin ins Schwimmbad gegangen.
b Was hast du gemacht? – Ich bin nach Frankreich geflogen.
c Was hast du gemacht? – Ich habe ein Eis gegessen/Kaffee getrunken.
d Wo hast du gewohnt? – Ich habe in einem Wohnwagen gewohnt.
e Wie war das Wetter? – Es war heiß und sonnig.
f Was hast du gemacht? – Ich habe Paris/Sehenswürdigkeiten besichtigt.

AT 3.5 **2a** *Lies die E-Mail. Finde:* Activity 2 relates to pages 10–17. Pupils identify the three past tense forms met in this unit: perfect + *haben*; perfect + *sein*; imperfect. For the purpose of the activity, each clause should be treated as a separate sentence.

Answers:

Perfect + *haben*:	Ich habe in einer Jugendherberge gewohnt. Ich habe viel in Aberdeen gemacht. Ich habe die Stadt besichtigt. Ich habe auch meine Brieffreundin besucht. Wir haben Haggis gegessen – lecker! Es hat viel geregnet.
Perfect + *sein*:	wohin bist du im Sommer gefahren? Ich bin nach Schottland geflogen, nach Aberdeen. Ich bin ins Museum gegangen.
Imperfect	Die Jugendherberge war sehr alt und sie war sehr laut! Das Wetter war aber nicht schön: ... es war ziemlich kalt.

AT 3.2 **2b** *Lies die E-Mail noch einmal. Lies dann Veras Sätze und finde die passenden Bilder.* Pupils read the text for gist and select the relevant picture from each pair.

Answers: 1 a; 2 b; 3 a; 4 b; 5 b

AT 4.5 **2c** *Du bist dran! Schreib eine E-Mail mit den anderen Bildern von Übung 2b.* Pupils write their own e-mails, using the remaining pictures from activity 2b as prompts, adding additional details if they wish. They will need the correct answers for activity 2b in order to do this activity.

Answers:

Ich war in Frankreich. Die Jugendherberge war modern. Ich bin ins Schwimmbad gegangen. Ich habe meine Großmutter besucht. Das Wetter war schön.

Extra!-Seite Einheit 1
page 123

National Curriculum PoS
statements 1a, 1b, 1c, 2a, 2b, 2c, 2d, 2f, 2i, 3e, 5a, 5c, 5d, 5f, 5i

Materials
- Students' Book page 123
- Cassette 1 side A

This extension page is intended for more able pupils. It contains slightly longer and more complex materials, and it can be used by pupils who have completed other activities quickly or as alternative homework activities.

AT 3.4
AT 4.5

1 *Lies Millis Tagebuch. Schreib dann einen Brief für sie im Perfekt/Imperfekt: Wohin ist sie gefahren? Was hat sie gemacht? Wie war das Wetter? usw.* Activity 1 relates to pages 10–17. Pupils transpose the sentences from the present tense into the perfect and imperfect. Before pupils attempt this activity, you could ask them to identify which verbs will be in the imperfect (*sein* only), which verbs take the perfect with *sein*, and which take the perfect with *haben*.

Remind pupils to provide the letter with an appropriate ending and close, e.g. *Liebe(r) … , Dein(e) …*

AT 1.5
AT 4.5

2a *Thorstens Brieffreund schreibt eine E-Mail. Hier sind seine Fragen. Thorsten schreibt einen Antwortbrief. Hör gut zu und beantworte die Fragen für Thorsten. (Schreib Sätze.)* Activity 2 relates to pages 10–17. Pupils listen to the recording and note down the information they need to answer the questions in the e-mail. Explain that they should read the e-mail first to get an idea of the sort of information which will be contained in the recording (destination, accommodation, etc.). They should make notes whilst listening, rather than try to formulate complete answers. After listening, pupils write up their notes into complete sentences in the perfect and imperfect.

Answers:

Wohin bist du gefahren?
Ich bin nach Austalien geflogen – nach Perth.
Wo hast du gewohnt?
Ich habe in einer Jugendherberge gewohnt.
Wie war das Zimmer usw.?
Die Jugendherberge war groß und modern.
Wie war das Wetter?
Das Wetter war super: Es hat nie geregnet und war heiß.
Was hast du gemacht?
Ich habe viel Eis gegessen und ich habe viel Wasser getrunken! Ich habe einen Ausflug zum ,Ayers Rock'

gemacht. Ich habe die Stadt besichtigt und ich bin zum Strand gefahren. Ich habe auch meinen Onkel besucht. Er wohnt in Adelaide.

Transcript   p 123, activity 2a

– Lieber Martin, ich bin nach Australien geflogen – nach Perth. Das Wetter war super: Es hat nie geregnet und es war heiß! Ich habe viel Eis gegessen und ich habe viel Wasser getrunken! Ich habe in einer Jugendherberge gewohnt. Sie war groß und modern. Was habe ich alles gemacht? Ich habe einen Ausflug zum ,Ayers Rock' gemacht. Ich habe die Stadt besichtigt und bin zum Strand gefahren. Ich habe auch meinen Onkel besucht. Er wohnt in Adelaide.

AT 4.5

2b *Du bist dran! Eine Radiosendung in Deutschland macht eine Umfrage. Das Thema ist ,Ferien'. Schreib einen Artikel über deine Sommerferien.* In this creative writing activity, pupils compose e-mails about their own (real or imaginary) activities during the recent summer holidays.

AT 2.5

2c *A ist Radioreporter und fragt, B antwortet. Dann ist B dran. Macht eine Kassette.* Pupils take it in turns to interview each other about their summer holidays. The 'reporter' should draw up a list of questions in advance of the interview, but should be prepared to ask other supplementary questions in reaction to the interviewee's responses, e.g. P1: *Was hast du gemacht?* P2: *Ich bin ins Museum gegangen.* P1: *Wie war das Museum?* P2: *Es war langweilig*, etc. Pupils should be encouraged to record the interview a number of times, improving their fluency and breaking down inhibitions about being recorded, rather than rehearsing the interview prior to recording.

AT 4.5

2d *Wo war dein Partner/deine Partnerin in den Ferien? Schreib einen Artikel mit den Informationen von Übung 2c.* Pupils use their recordings as the basis of a written report in the third person. This requires them to listen to the recording and take notes (they should not make a full transcript) before composing their report in full sentences. The report could be illustrated with photos (holiday snaps, brochure pictures or photos from tourism websites).

Workbook

Page 4
Use with page 9 in the Students' Book.

A1 *Hör gut zu und sing mit!* Singing the song is not only fun, it also helps pupils to memorize the past participles and other important vocabulary and structures. The class could be divided up into two groups: group A sings the first and third lines of each verse, group B sings the second line, and the whole class sings the fourth line and the chorus.

Transcript   W 4, activity A1

Ich bin nach Spanien geflogen
Wohin bist du geflogen?
Ich bin nach Spanien geflogen
Und es war toll, toll, toll!

Sonne, Schwimmen, Sport und Strand,
Spanien ist mein Lieblingsland!

Ich bin zwei Wochen geblieben
Wie lange bist du geblieben?
Ich bin zwei Wochen geblieben
Und es war schön, schön, schön!

Refrain

Ich hab' Paella gegessen
Was hast du gegessen?
Ich hab' Paella gegessen
Und es war gut, gut, gut!

Refrain

Ich bin zum Strand gefahren
Wohin bist du gefahren?
Ich bin zum Strand gefahren
Und es war heiß, heiß, heiß!

Refrain

Ich bin nach Hause geflogen
Wohin bist du geflogen?
Ich bin nach Hause geflogen
Und es war schade, schade, schade!

Refrain

AT 3.2 **A2** *Finde die passenden Bilder und Antworten.* Pupils
answer the multiple choice questions about the song
text. Most of the questions (except 3 and 4) can be
completed without knowledge of the perfect tense.

Answers: 1 b; 2 a; 3 a; 4 b; 5 a; 6 b

Pages 5–6
Use with pages 10–11 in the Students' Book.

AT 3.1 **B1** *Finde die Länder und Kontinente und schreib sie auf.*
This activity reinforces geographical names and may be
used in conjunction with activity 2 on page 10 of the
Students' Book. Pupils unscramble the letters to
discover the names of countries and continents (all of
them featured in the map in the Students' Book, page
10). Tell pupils they should start off with the ones they
find easiest, rather than getting 'stuck' on the difficult
ones – the latter can then be worked out by a process of
elimination, using the map.

Answers:

1 Frankreich; 2 England; 3 Asien; 4 Deutschland;
5 Australien; 6 Schottland; 7 Italien; 8 Afrika

AT 1.3 **B2** *Wer ist wohin gefahren? Hör gut zu und verbinde die
passenden Namen und Länder.* This activity provides
additional listening practice and reinforces geographical
names. It could be used after activity 2a on page 10 of
the Students' Book. Pupils match the names to the
destinations.

Answers:

Anne: Australien; Rajan: Schottland; Markus: Spanien;
Kathi: Amerika; Philipp: Irland; Leah: Österreich; Uwe:
zu Hause (Deutschland); Sandra: Indien

Transcript   W 5, activity B2

– Anne, wohin bist du im Sommer gefahren?
– Nach Australien – wir sind nach Australien geflogen.
  Meine Tante wohnt in Sydney.

– Und du, Rajan? Wohin bist du im Sommer gefahren?
– Ich? Ich bin nach Schottland gefahren – ja, nach
  Schottland.

– Und wohin bist du im Sommer gefahren, Markus?
– Nach Spanien – wir sind nach Spanien gefahren.

– Hallo, Kathi. Und wohin bist du gefahren?
– Also, wir sind nach Amerika geflogen – nach Florida!
  Florida ist super!

– Und du, Philipp? Wohin bist du im Sommer gefahren?
– Nach Irland – ja, ich bin nach Irland gefahren.

– Leah, und du? Wohin bist du gefahren?
– Ich? Meine Oma wohnt in Wien. Ich bin nach Österreich
  gefahren – nach Wien.

– Wohin bist du im Sommer gefahren, Uwe?
– Wir sind zu Hause geblieben – in Hamburg. Hamburg
  im Sommer ist toll!

– Und wohin bist du im Sommer gefahren, Sandra?
– Nach Indien! Ich bin nach Indien geflogen. Indien ist
  sehr interessant.

AT 4.2 **C** *Wohin sind sie im Sommer gefahren? Füll die
Sprechblasen aus.* This activity could be used as an
easier alternative or introduction to activity 5b on
page 11 of the Students' Book. Pupils use the picture
cues as prompts to complete the sentences.

Answers:

a Wir sind nach Amerika geflogen.
b Ich bin nach Spanien gefahren.
c Wir sind zu Hause geblieben.
d Ich bin nach Indien geflogen.

AT 2.3 **D** *Wohin bist du im Sommer gefahren? Macht Dialoge
mit den Bildern.* This activity could be used for
additional speaking practice in conjunction with activity
5b on page 11 of the Students' Book. Pupils work
together in pairs to create dialogues, using the picture
cues as prompts.

AT 4.3 **E** *Du bist dran! Wohin bist du im Sommer gefahren?*
This free writing activity could be used as a more
challenging alternative or extension to activity 5b on
page 11 of the Students' Book. Pupils write about their
own holiday experiences (real or imaginary). This
activity can form part of pupils' written records for
continuous assessment purposes. See the general notes
on pages 13–14 of the introduction to this book.

Pages 7–9

Use with pages 12–13 in the Students' Book.

AT 3.2 **F** *Was haben sie gemacht? Finde die Sätze.* This activity could be used as an introduction to activity 2a on page 12 of the Students' Book. Pupils choose the appropriate past participle to complete each sentence.

Answers: 1 c; 2 e; 3 a; 4 f; 5 d; 6 b

 AT 1.2 **G** *Was hat Jasmin in Marseille gemacht? Hör gut zu und finde die passenden Bilder.* This listening activity could be used to reinforce activities 1 and 2 on page 12 of the Students' Book. Pupils listen to the recording and match the pictures to the activities mentioned by Jasmin (one of the characters from the photo story).

Answers: 1 c; 2 e; 3 f; 4 b; 5 a; 6 d

Transcript   W 7, activity G

1 – Ich habe viele Sehenswürdigkeiten besichtigt.
2 – Wir sind ins Museum gegangen.
3 – Ich habe viele Croissants gegessen.
4 – Ich habe Schokolade gekauft.
5 – Wir haben einen Ausflug gemacht.
6 – Ich habe Kaffee getrunken.

AT 1.3 **H** *Was haben sie gemacht? Hör gut zu und kreuz die passenden Bilder an.* This activity could be used for further listening practice in conjunction with activity 2 on page 12 of the Students' Book. Pupils listen to the recording and complete the grid by matching the activities to the speakers.

Answers:

	🎾	👥	🎞	🍽	🎵	🏛	🧰	🍶
Tanja				✗	✗			
Alex						✗		✗
Silke		✗					✗	
Rainer	✗		✗					

Transcript   W 7, activity H

– Tanja, wohin bist du im Sommer gefahren?
– Ich bin nach Spanien gefahren.
– Und was hast du in Spanien gemacht?
– Also, ich habe Paella gegessen – Paella ist lecker! Ja, und ich bin in die Disco gegangen – jeden Abend.
– Und du, Alex?
– Wir sind nach Irland geflogen, nach Dublin. Wir haben viel gemacht: Wir haben die Stadt besichtigt und ich habe Limonade getrunken.
– Hallo, Silke. Wohin bist du im Sommer gefahren?
– Ich bin nach Österreich gefahren – ja, ich bin nach Wien gefahren.

– Und was hast du in Wien gemacht?
– Ich habe meine Großeltern besucht. Wir haben ein Picknick gemacht – ein Picknick im Wienerwald!

– Rainer, wohin bist du im Sommer gefahren?
– Ich bin nach Amerika geflogen – nach Florida. Ich habe Tennis gespielt. Ach ja, und ich habe Ansichtskarten gekauft.

AT 3.4 **I1** *Lies Maikes Postkarte und füll die Lücken aus.* This activity could be used in conjunction with activity 5 on page 13 of the Students' Book to give additional practice of forming the perfect tense. Pupils select the correct past participle to fill each of the gaps.

Answers:

Viele Grüße aus England. Ich bin am Samstag nach Manchester **gefahren**. Ich habe meine Brieffreundin Sarah **besucht**. Sarah ist sehr nett! Wir haben viel gemacht: Wir haben Fußball **gespielt** und wir haben auch einen Ausflug **gemacht**. Ich habe auch Fisch **gegessen** und viel Tee **getrunken**. Ich habe auch die Stadt **besichtigt** – Manchester ist sehr schön! Und ich habe Souvenirs **gekauft**. Am Sonntag sind wir ins Schwimmbad **gegangen**.

AT 4.4 **I2** *Du bist dran! Schreib eine Postkarte (so wie Maike) mit den Bildern und den Perfekt-Partizipien (Wörtern) von Übung I1.* This could be used as an extension activity after activity 5 on page 13 of the Students' Book. Pupils use the picture cues and the past participles from the previous activity to write their own postcards. This activity can form part of pupils' written records for continuous assessment purposes. See the general notes on pages 13–14 of the introduction to this book.

AT 2.5 **J** *Du bist dran! Was hast du in den Ferien gemacht? Nimm die Informationen auf Kassette auf.* This could be used as an extension activity after the previous activity, or after activity 5 on page 13 of the Students' Book. Pupils prepare an account of what they did in the summer holidays and record it on tape. Alternatively, this could be done as a pairwork activity, with one partner interviewing the other. The recording can form part of pupils' written records for continuous assessment purposes. See the general notes on pages 13–14 of the introduction to this book.

Pages 9–10

Use with pages 14–15 in the Students' Book.

AT 4.2 | **K** *Wetter-Worträtsel. Schreib die Sätze richtig auf.* This puzzle could be used to reinforce the weather expressions introduced in activities 1 and 2 on page 14 of the Students' Book and to ease the transition from recognition of the imperfect *war* to active use (activity 3 on page 15 of the Students' Book). Pupils decipher the 'word snake' to make sentences describing the weather, using the picture cues as additional hints.

Answers:

1 Es war sehr schlecht.
2 Es hat viel geschneit.
3 Es war sehr sonnig.
4 Es war immer wolkig.

AT 3.2 | **L** *Wie war das Wetter? Finde die passenden Bilder.* This activity offers further consolidation of the weather expressions introduced in activities 1 and 2 on page 14 of the Students' Book. Pupils match the weather symbols to the sentences.

Answers: 1 f; 2 a; 3 d; 4 b; 5 c; 6 e

AT 3.2 | **AT 4.2** | **M** *Schau die Wetterkarte an. Richtig oder falsch? Schreib* ✔ *oder* ✗ *und korrigiere dann die falschen Sätze.* This activity could be used as an introduction to activity 3 on page 15 of the Students' Book. Pupils compare the statements with the weather map and decide whether the statements are true or false, correcting the false ones.

Answers:

Stadt	Wetter	Richtig/Falsch?	Richtige Sätze
Hamburg	Es war sonnig.	✔	
Berlin	Es war heiß.	✗	Es hat geregnet.
Dresden	Es war neblig.	✗	Es war kalt.
Köln	Es war windig.	✔	
Stuttgart	Es hat geschneit.	✔	
München	Es war schön.	✗	Es war wolkig.

AT 2.4 | **N** *„Wo warst du – und wie war das Wetter?" Macht Dialoge mit den Bildern.* This activity could be used as a speaking extension to activity 6 on page 15 in the Students' Book. Pupils work together in pairs, using the picture cues as prompts for dialogues.

Pages 11–13

Use with pages 16–17 in the Students' Book.

AT 4.1 | **O** *Wo haben sie gewohnt? Schreib die passenden Wörter auf.* This activity could be used as an introduction to, or a consolidation of, activity 1 on page 16 of the Students' Book. Pupils use the picture cues to complete the crossword puzzle.

Answers:

AT 3.2 | **P1** *Wo haben sie gewohnt? Finde die passenden Bilder.* This activity could be used as consolidation of key vocabulary from activity 1 and preparation for activity 2 on page 16 of the Students' Book. Pupils match the pictures to the sentences.

Answers: 1 d; 2 c; 3 a; 4 b

AT 1.3 | **AT 4.1** | **P2** *Hör gut zu und füll die Lücken aus.* This activity could be used as preparation for activity 2 on page 16 of the Students' Book. Pupils listen to the recording and complete the sentences.

Answers:

Clemens: Wir haben in einem Wohnwagen gewohnt.
Hanna: Ich habe in einer Jugendherberge gewohnt.
Ulli: Ich habe in einem Zelt gewohnt.
Sabine: Wir haben bei einer Gastfamilie gewohnt.

Transcript   W 12, activity P2

– Clemens, wo hast du im Sommer gewohnt?
– Wir haben in einem Wohnwagen gewohnt.

– Und du, Hanna? Wo hast du gewohnt?
– Also, ich habe in einer Jugendherberge gewohnt – direkt in der Stadt.

– Und wo hast du gewohnt, Ulli?
– Ich? Ich habe in einem Zelt gewohnt. Das war super.

> – Sabine, wo hast du gewohnt?
> – Wir haben bei einer Gastfamilie gewohnt. Die Familie war sehr nett.

AT 4.3

Q *Wo hat Sven in Florida gewohnt? Wie war alles? Schreib Sprechblasen.* This activity could be used as an extension to activity 3 on page 17 of the Students' Book. It features Sven, one of the characters from the photo story. Pupils use the picture cues as prompts to write the speech bubbles.

Suggested answers:

Ich habe in einem Hotel gewohnt. Das Hotel war sehr laut.
Ich habe in einem Wohnmobil gewohnt. Das Wohnmobil war sehr groß.

Ich habe in einer Ferienwohnung gewohnt. Die Ferienwohnung war sehr modern.
Ich habe in einem Zelt gewohnt. Das Zelt war sehr klein.

AT 4.3

R *Du bist dran!* This activity could be used as an extension to activity 3b or as a simpler alternative to activity 4 *Extra!* on page 17 of the Students' Book. Pupils write about their summer holiday accommodation (real or imaginary). This activity can form part of pupils' written records for continuous assessment purposes. See the general notes on pages 13–14 of the introduction to this book.

Can you …?

The purpose of the checklist is to identify tasks in the Students' Book both by skill and by topic. Teachers may find this helpful in selecting specific tasks, as a record of pupils' achievements in an Attainment Target.

Einheit 1 Wie waren die Ferien?	AT 1 Listening	AT 2 Speaking	AT 3 Reading	AT 4 Writing
10–11 Wohin bist du gefahren?				
Say where you went on holiday	1, 2a	2b	1, 5a	4, 5a, 5b
Ask others where they went on holiday	–	3	–	Noch mal!, Extra!
12–13 Was hast du in München gemacht?				
Ask what someone did on holiday	–	2b	–	3
Say what you did on holiday	1, 2a	2b	1, 5	3, 4
14–15 Wie war das Wetter in Frankreich?				
Ask where others went on holiday	–	3, Extra!	–	–
Say where you went on holiday	–	3	–	–
Ask what the weather was like on holiday	–	3, Extra!	–	Extra!, 5
Say what the weather was like on holiday	1, 2	3	1, 4	Noch mal!, Extra!, 5, 6
16–17 Wo hast du gewohnt?				
Ask where someone stayed on holiday	–	1b	–	–
Say where you stayed on holiday	1a, 4	1b	1a	2, Noch mal!, Extra!
Say what it was like	4	3b	3a	Noch mal!, Extra!

Copymasters

For general advice about using the copymasters, see page 7 of the introduction to this book.

C 4

AT 1.2

Hören

1 *Hör gut zu und finde die passenden Länder.* Pupils match the countries to the speakers. Refer pupils to the world map on page 10 of the Students' Book if they need help identifying the country outlines.

Answers: 1 c; 2 d; 3 f; 4 b; 5 e; 6 a

Transcript	C 4, activity 1

1 – Wir sind nach Spanien gefahren.
2 – Ich bin nach China geflogen.
3 – Ich bin nach Amerika geflogen.
4 – Ich bin nach Frankreich gefahren.
5 – Wir sind nach Afrika geflogen.
6 – Wir sind nach Deutschland gefahren.

AT 1.4

2 *Anna hat eine Postkarte von ihrer Freundin Jasmin bekommen. Hör gut zu und kreuz die passenden Fotos an.* Pupils select the relevant picture from each pair.

Answers: 1 a; 2 b; 3 a; 4 a; 5 a; 6 a

U4 exam June '04

Transcript	C 4, activity 2

Oh, toll! Eine Postkarte von Jasmin! Was schreibt sie denn … ?
Liebe Anna!
Wie geht's?
Griechenland ist ganz toll!
Gestern sind wir zum Strand gefahren … und in die Disco gegangen.
Heute haben wir Tennis gespielt … und Eis gegessen.
Wir haben auch die Stadt besichtigt … und Postkarten gekauft.
Bis bald! Deine Jasmin

AT 1.5

3 *Hier sind Jakobs Ferienfotos. Hör gut zu und finde die richtige Reihenfolge.* Pupils listen to the recording and then put the pictures in the correct order.

Answers: c, a, e, d, f, b

U4 exam June '04

Transcript   C 4, activity 3

– Hallo, Jakob! Wie waren die Ferien?
– Sehr gut, danke! Schottland ist eigentlich sehr schön, aber das Wetter war schlecht. Es war jeden Tag windig und neblig. Aber das Hotel war toll – sehr groß und modern.
– Und wie war das Essen dort? Hast du auch mal ,Haggis' gegessen?
– Das Essen war lecker – nur das nicht!
– Und was hast du am Tag gemacht?
– Ja, wir sind ins Schwimmbad gegangen und haben Tennis gespielt. Wir sind auch nach Glasgow gefahren und haben die Sehenswürdigkeiten besichtigt.
– Schön. Ich möchte auch einmal nach Schottland fahren ...

Sprechen

AT 2.3 **1a** *Frag deinen Partner/deine Partnerin: „Wie war das Wetter in ... ?" Dein Partner/deine Partnerin antwortet.* Pupils work together in pairs to create dialogues, using the picture cues as prompts. Partner A asks the questions, Partner B responds.

AT 2.3 **1b** *Dein Partner/deine Partnerin fragt: „Wie war das Wetter in ... ?" Antworte mit den Informationen rechts.* This is the second part of the activity, with the roles reversed.

AT 2.5 **2a** *Beschreib deine letzten Sommerferien. Dein Partner/deine Partnerin macht Notizen.* Pupils work together in pairs. Partner A describes his/her holiday, and Partner B takes notes.

AT 2.5 **2b** *Dein Partner/deine Partnerin beschreibt seine/ihre letzten Sommerferien. Mach Notizen.* This is the second part of the activity, with the roles reversed.

Lesen

AT 3.2 **1** *Finde die passenden Bilder für die Sprechblasen.* Pupils match the pictures to the sentences.

Answers: 1 c; 2 f; 3 d; 4 b; 5 a; 6 e

AT 3.3 **2** *Was hat Tina in den Sommerferien gemacht? Finde die passenden Bilder.* Pupils select the picture from each pair which corresponds to Tina's notes in her diary.

Answers:

Samstag: plane; Sonntag: beach; Montag: trip to market; Dienstag: ice cream; Mittwoch: tennis; Donnerstag: postcards; Freitag: sightseeing in town; Samstag: home

AT 3.5 **3** *Lies Elisabeths Brief und finde die passenden Antworten.* Pupils read the letter and select the appropriate sentence ending from each pair.

Answers: 1 a; 2 b; 3 a; 4 a; 5 b

Schreiben

AT 4.2 **1** *Wie war das Wetter? Schreib die Sätze richtig auf.* Pupils re-order the words to form sentences.

Answers:
a Es hat immer geschneit.
b Es war nie kalt.
c Es war nicht schlecht.
d Es war gar nicht schön.
e Es war sehr sonnig.
f Es hat nicht viel geregnet.

AT 4.3 **2** *Wohin sind sie gefahren? Was sagen sie? Schreib Sprechblasen.* Pupils use the picture cues to write the speech bubbles.

Answers:

1 Ich bin nach Schottland gefahren.
2 Ich bin nach Spanien gefahren.
3 Ich bin nach Australien gefahren.
4 Ich bin nach Amerika gefahren.
5 Ich bin nach Frankreich gefahren.
6 Ich bin nach Afrika gefahren.

AT 4.5 **3** *Hier sind Leonards Ferienfotos. Er möchte eine Postkarte schreiben. Was schreibt er?* Pupils use the photos as prompts to write Leonard's postcard in the perfect and imperfect tenses.

Answers:

Ich bin nach Amerika geflogen. Ich habe in einem Hotel gewohnt. Das Hotel war groß und modern. Das Wetter war schön. Es war sonnig und sehr heiß. Ich habe Hamburger gegessen.

Ich bin zum Euro Disney-Freizeitpark gefahren, und ich habe Tennis gespielt und ins Schwimmbad gegangen.

Grammatik 1

This copymaster focuses on the perfect tense with auxiliary *sein* and the imperfect tense of *sein*.

1a *Füll die Lücken aus.* Pupils complete the sentences with the appropriate forms of sein.

Answers:

1 bin; 2 sind; 3 ist; 4 bist; 5 sind; 6 bin

1b *Füll die Lücken aus.* Pupils complete the sentences with the appropriate past participles.

Answers:

1 geflogen; 2 gefahren; 3 geblieben; 4 geflogen; 5 gefahren; 6 gegangen

2 *Füll die Lücken aus.* Pupils complete the sentences with the verb forms from the box. This requires them to know the complete conjugation of *sein* in the imperfect (except the *ihr* form).

Answers:

1 war; 2 waren; 3 war; 4 war/waren; 5 warst

Grammatik 2

This copymaster focuses on the perfect tense with auxiliary *haben*.

1a *Füll die Lücken aus.* Pupils complete the sentences with the appropriate forms of *haben*.

Answers:

1 habe; 2 hat; 3 hast; 4 haben; 5 haben; 6 habt

1b *Füll die Lücken aus.* Pupils complete the sentences with the appropriate past participles.

Answers:

1 gegessen; 2 besichtigt; 3 gemacht; 4 besucht; 5 gespielt; 6 getrunken

2 *Schreib die Sätze richtig auf. Es gibt mehrere Kombinationen.* Pupils use the jumbled words/phrases to construct sentences in the perfect tense. There are a number of possible solutions for each one.

Possible answers:

1 Ich habe im Restaurant gegessen/Fußball gespielt/die Stadt besichtigt.
2 Wir haben im Restaurant gegessen/Fußball gespielt/die Stadt besichtigt.
   Wir sind nach Holland gefahren/zu Hause geblieben/ins Museum gegangen.
3 Er hat im Restaurant gegessen/Fußball gespielt/die Stadt besichtigt.
   Er ist nach Holland gefahren/zu Hause geblieben/ins Museum gegangen.
4 Wir haben im Restaurant gegessen/Fußball gespielt/die Stadt besichtigt.
   Wir sind nach Holland gefahren/zu Hause geblieben/ins Museum gegangen.
5 Du bist nach Holland gefahren/zu Hause geblieben/ins Museum gegangen.
6 Tom hat im Restaurant gegessen/Fußball gespielt/die Stadt besichtigt.
   Tom ist nach Holland gefahren/zu Hause geblieben/ins Museum gegangen.

3 *Schreib Sätze für gestern. Sieh auch Lehrbuch, Seite 12–13. Erfinde dann weitere Beispiele.* Pupils put the sentences into the perfect tense, then make up some examples of their own.

Answers:

1 Wir haben die Stadt besichtigt. 2 Du hast Souvenirs gekauft. 3 Er ist zu Hause geblieben. 4 Ich bin nach Afrika geflogen. 5 Sie hat im Restaurant gegessen. 6 Er hat seine Oma besucht.

C9 **Tipp**

This copymaster focuses on the following skills: adapting a piece of written German; taking notes whilst listening; dealing with unknown vocabulary. It supplements and expands upon the *Tipp* sections on pages 12, 17 and 19 of the Students' Book. The advice in English will be helpful to all pupils, but less able pupils may have difficulty with some of the activities.

1 *Adaptiere diesen Brief mit den Informationen rechts.* Pupils adapt the text to fit the picture cues.

Answers:

1 Ich bin in den Ferien nach Paris geflogen. Gestern habe ich das Museum besichtigt und heute habe ich Fußball gespielt.
2 Ich bin in den Ferien nach London geflogen. Gestern habe ich die Stadt besichtigt und heute habe ich Postkarten gekauft.
3 Ich bin in den Ferien nach Amerika geflogen. Gestern bin ich ins Schwimmbad gegangen und heute habe ich Basketball gespielt.
4 Ich bin in den Ferien nach Australien geflogen. Gestern habe ich Freunde besucht und heute bin ich zum Strand gegangen.

 2a *Wie waren die Ferien für Agatha und Hannelore? Hör gut zu und schreib die Schlüsselwörter, Abkürzungen oder Bilder auf.* Pupils listen to the recorded conversation and take notes.

Answers:

Agatha	Hannelore
Hotel nicht schön – groß, laut	Zimmer schön
Essen schlecht – nur Pizza, Eis	keine Pizza, kein Eis
Wetter furchtbar, geregnet, kalt, windig	Wetter schön
Ausflüge – Stadt, Museum, zu viel	keine Ausflüge, zu Hause

U4 exam June '04

Transcript   C 9, activity 2a

– Wie waren denn die Ferien, Agatha?
– Die Ferien? Weißt du, das Hotel war nicht schön - zu groß und zu laut. Und das Essen! Ich habe die ganze Woche nur Pizza und Eis gegessen. Das esse ich gar nicht gern.
– Und das Wetter?
– Das Wetter! Furchtbar! Es hat immer geregnet und es war auch kalt und windig.
– Und was hast du dort gemacht?
– Ausflüge! Viele, viele Ausflüge! Wir haben die Stadt besichtigt ... Wir sind ins Museum gegangen ... Wir haben eigentlich viel zu viel gemacht. Aber wie waren deine Ferien, Hannelore?
– Ich ... ? Ich hatte eine sehr schöne Zeit. Mein Zimmer war sehr schön. Das Wetter auch. Keine Pizza. Kein Eis. Keine Ausflüge!
– Wieso denn?
– Ich bin zu Hause geblieben!

2b *Schreib dann Sätze mit deinen Informationen für Agatha und Hannelore.* Pupils use their notes to write sentences for Agatha and Hannelore.

3 *Was bedeuten diese Wörter?* Pupils look up the words in their dictionaries.

Answers:

Altglascontainer: bottle bank; Computerspiel: computer game; Eisbahn: ice rink; Ferienwohnung: holiday flat; Freizeitpark: leisure park; Gastfamilie: host family; Kartoffelsalat: potato salad; Krankenhaus: hospital;

Lieblingsgruppe: favourite group; Mineralwasser:
mineral water; Partykeller: 'party cellar';
Recyclingpapier: recycled paper; Schreibtisch: desk;
Schulfest: school function; Stadtmitte: town/city centre;
Taschengeld: pocket money; Telefonkarte: phone card;
Tomatensoße: tomato ketchup; Wohnwagen: caravan;
Zucker: sugar

Einheit 2 Mein Alltag

Pages	Objectives	Grammar	Pronunciation, Skill focus	Key language	PoS	AT level
20–21 Die Klasse!-Clique	Reading and listening for pleasure. Familiarization with themes, structures and language of the unit	–	–	–	–	1.3, 3.3–4
22–23 Was machst du heute?	Talk about your daily routine. Ask others about their daily routine	Reflexive verbs. Inverted word order after a time phrase	Dictionary skills: reflexive verbs	*Ich stehe auf.* *Ich wasche mich.* *Ich ziehe mich an.* *Ich frühstücke.* *Ich gehe in die Schule.* *Ich gehe nach Hause.* *Ich ziehe mich aus.* *Ich gehe ins Bett.* *Was machst du um …?* *Um …. Uhr stehe ich auf/wasche ich mich/ziehe ich mich an/frühstücke ich/gehe in die Schule/gehe ich nach Hause/ziehe ich mich aus/gehe ich ins Bett.*	1a, 1b, 1c, 2a, 2b, 2c, 3d, 3e, 5a, 5d, 5f, 5i	1.2–3, 2.3–4, 3.2, 4.3–4
24–25 Wie hilfst du zu Hause?	Talk about household chores. Ask someone about their household chores. Describe how often you help at home. Ask someone how often they help at home	Separable verbs. Accusative case, *den/die/das/die*	–	*Hilfst du zu Hause?* *Ich räume mein Zimmer auf.* *Ich kaufe ein.* *Ich wasche ab.* *Ich sauge Staub.* *Ich decke den Tisch.* *Ich putze das Badezimmer.* *Ich füttere den Hund/die Katze.* *Wie oft machst du das? immer/oft/selten/nie/jeden Tag/einmal pro Woche*	1a, 1b, 1c, 2a, 2b, 2c, 2e, 5a, 5f, 5i	1.2–3, 2.3–4, 3.2–3, 4.4
26–27 Wie viel Geld bekommst du?	Describe how much pocket money you get. Say from whom and how often you get it. Describe what you spend your pocket money on. Describe how much and why you save it	*von* + dative. *für* + accusative	–	*Wie viel Geld bekommst du?* *Ich bekomme pro Tag/Woche/Monat … von meinen Eltern/meinem Vater/meiner Oma, etc.* *Was kaufst du davon?* *Ich kaufe eine Jeans/ein Computerspiel/Kleidung/Make-up/ Süßigkeiten/Zeitschriften.* *Wofür sparst du?* *Ich spare für einen Computer/eine Stereoanlage/ein Fahrrad.*	1a, 1b, 1c, 2a, 2b, 2c, 3d, 3e, 5a, 5i	1.2–3, 2.4, 3.2–3, 4.4

National Curriculum

Pages	Objectives	Grammar	Pronunciation, Skill focus	Key language	PoS	AT level
28–29 Hast du einen Nebenjob?	Describe jobs you do to earn money Ask someone what jobs they do Say how much you earn Give your opinion on your job	–	Expressing opinions Pronunciation: inflections	*Hast du einen Nebenjob?* *Ich habe einen/keinen Nebenjob.* *Ich helfe zu Hause.* *Ich arbeite im Garten.* *Ich bin Babysitter/in.* *Ich führe den Hund aus.* *Ich wasche das Auto.* *Ich trage Zeitungen aus.* *Wie viel verdienst du?* *Ich verdiene/bekomme …* *Wie findest du den Job?* *Ich finde den Job super/toll/gut/langweilig/schrecklich/nicht so gut.* *Das macht (keinen) Spaß!* *Ich mag den Job sehr gern/gar nicht.*	1a, 1b, 1c, 2a, 2b, 2c, 2i, 3e, 5a, 5c, 5f, 5i	1.2–4, 2.3–4, 3.2–3, 4.2
30–31 Thema im Fokus	Encourage reading for pleasure Use language from Unit 2 creatively Encourage independent, pair- and groupwork	–	–	–	2c, 2e, 2h, 2j, 3d, 3e, 5a, 5c, 5d, 5e, 5f, 5i	1.4, 2.4, 3.4, 4.3–4

2 Mein Alltag

Aims of the unit

- To be able to talk about your daily routine
- To be able to talk about household chores
- To be able to talk about pocket money
- To be able to talk about jobs you do to earn money

Die Klasse!-Clique

pages 20–21

Materials

- Students' Book pages 20–21
- Cassette 1 side A
- Workbook page 14

The first spread of each unit follows the same pattern, introducing the themes, structures and some of the key language of the unit in a light-hearted way without the need for overt grammar teaching. For general advice on exploiting the photo story, see pages 10–11 of the introduction to this book.

In this episode of the photo story it is Saturday morning. Jasmin and Atalay want their friends to come swimming with them, but Annika and Sven have work to do: Sven has to finish his boring paper round, and Annika has a whole list of chores to do, including shopping in town for her mother. Later in the day, emerging from the supermarket, Annika finds that her bicycle has disappeared.

Preparatory work

Ask pupils to look at the photo story (without trying to read the text at this point). What do they think it might be about? (Point out the washing up, the newspapers and the supermarket: it is about jobs and chores.) Explain that this unit is all about daily routine and what pupils do to help at home and earn money.

AT 3.3

1 *Was meinst du? Vor dem Lesen: Rate!* In this pre-reading activity, pupils look at the pictures and then guess what is happening. Ask them to cover up the dialogue text for this activity, which could be done orally with the whole class.

Answers: 1 b; 2 a; 3 a; 4 a; 5 b

AT 1.3
AT 3.3

2 *Hör gut zu und lies mit. Wie heißt das auf Deutsch?* Pupils listen to the recording and follow the text in their books. They then find in the text the German equivalents of the English sentences. (Alternatively, this could be done as a pre-listening activity.) This draws pupils' attention to some of the key language for the unit, and could be done individually or in pairs. Answers could be checked as a whole-class activity. Point out that *bekommen* (question 5) is a 'false friend': it means 'to get, to receive', never 'to become'.

Answers:

1 Kommst du? 2 Ich füttere den Hund und die Katze.
3 Ich trage Zeitungen aus. 4 Wie findest du den Job?
5 Ich bekomme 30 Euro pro Woche.

Transcript   p 21, activity 2

– Morgen, Annika! Wir gehen um 11 Uhr ins Schwimmbad. Kommst du?
– Hallo, Jasmin! Nein, ich wasche ab und ich füttere den Hund und die Katze. Und dann fahre ich mit dem Rad in die Stadt – ich kaufe ein. Dafür bekomme ich 10 Euro von meiner Mutter!

– Sven! Sven! Wir gehen ins Schwimmbad!
– Und ich trage Zeitungen aus – leider!
– Wie findest du den Job?
– Er ist langweilig – aber ich bekomme 30 Euro pro Woche.

Später nach dem Einkaufen …
– Mein Rad!! Oh nein – wo ist mein Fahrrad??

AT 3.4

3 *Lies die Sätze. Sind sie richtig oder falsch?* Pupils read the questions and find out from the photo story whether they are true or false. They could complete this activity individually or in pairs.

Answers:

1 richtig; 2 falsch; 3 falsch; 4 richtig; 5 falsch; 6 richtig

Follow-up activity. Pupils could work together in groups to draw up their own list of true/false statements about the text and the pictures, which they could then challenge the rest of the class with (to be answered with books closed).

Viel Spaß!

Mein Tag beginnt. The main aim is listening for pleasure, but the song will help pupils to assimilate the forms of separable and reflexive verbs, as well as revising time expressions (*Klasse! 1*, Units 3 and 7). After listening to the song all the way through, pupils could sing along with a second playing. Alternatively, you could divide the class into two groups: one group sings while the other mimes the activities. For general advice on exploiting the songs in *Klasse! 2*, see page 7 of the introduction to this book.

Transcript   p 21, Viel Spaß!

Ich stehe auf!
Ich stehe auf!
Es ist sieben Uhr
Und ich steh' auf!

Ich wasche mich!
Ich wasche mich!
Es ist Viertel nach
Und ich wasche mich!

Ich ziehe mich an!
Ich ziehe mich an!
Es ist fast halb acht
Und ich zieh' mich an!

Ich esse Toast!
Ich esse Toast!
Es ist Viertel vor
Und ich esse Toast!

Ich trinke Milch!
Ich trinke Milch!
Es ist zehn vor acht
Und ich trinke Milch!

Mein Tag beginnt!
Mein Tag beginnt!
Es ist schon acht Uhr
Und mein Tag beginnt!

Follow-up activity. Some pupils may like to try writing additional verses for the song, either now or later in the unit when they have learned more language related to the topic.

WB A Workbook activity A could be used at this point for exploitation of the song text (daily routine, time expressions).

For the next lesson

Pupils could be encouraged to compile a collection of photos to illustrate their daily routine, chores and jobs, together with catalogue pictures or advertisements for any items they are saving for. These could be used to illustrate and enliven their written work throughout the unit.

Was machst du heute?
pages 22–23

Objectives
- Talk about your daily routine
- Ask others about their daily routine

Key language
Ich stehe auf.
Ich wasche mich.
Ich ziehe mich an.
Ich frühstücke.
Ich gehe in die Schule.
Ich gehe nach Hause.
Ich ziehe mich aus.
Ich gehe ins Bett.
Was machst du um … ?
Um … Uhr stehe ich auf/wasche ich mich/ziehe ich mich an/frühstücke ich/gehe ich in die Schule/gehe ich nach Hause/ziehe ich mich aus/gehe ich ins Bett.

National Curriculum PoS
statements 1a, 1b, 1c, 2a, 2b, 2c, 3d, 3e, 5a, 5d, 5f, 5i

Materials
- Students' Book pages 22–23
- Cassette 1 side A
- Workbook pages 15–16
- Copymasters 10, 13, 16, 17A
- dictionaries

C 10 ## Preparatory work

Use the relevant pictures from copymaster 10 copied onto an OHT or as flashcards to introduce language describing daily routine. (For general advice on using copymaster visuals, see page 12 of the introduction to this book.) Then talk about your daily routine, miming the actions. Elicit some of the expressions from the class. T: *Ich stehe auf.* (mime getting up) *Ich wasche mich.* (mime washing) *Was kommt jetzt?* (mime getting dressed), etc.

AT 1.2
AT 3.2 **1a** *Kai beschreibt seinen Alltag. Hör gut zu und lies mit.* Pupils listen to the recording and follow the text in the book.

> **Transcript** p 22, activity 1a
>
> a – Ich stehe auf.
> b – Ich wasche mich.
> c – Ich ziehe mich an.
> d – Ich frühstücke.
> e – Ich gehe in die Schule.
> f – Ich gehe nach Hause.
> g – Ich ziehe mich aus.
> h – Ich gehe ins Bett.

AT 2.3 **1b** *Wie ist dein Alltag? A wählt ein Bild, B antwortet. Dann ist B dran.* Pupils work together in pairs, taking it in turns to ask each other about the pictures. Encourage pupils to pronounce *frühstücke* correctly, with the stress on the first syllable and *ü* rather than *u*.

AT 1.3 **1c** *Hanna beschreibt ihren Alltag. Hör gut zu und finde die richtige Reihenfolge für die Sätze.* Pupils listen to the recording and identify the sentences 1–5 (still the same key language from activity 1a, but with more variations). On a second listening, pupils write down the order in which the sentences occur. Less able pupils could write out the sentences in their books, and then number them as they hear them.

Answers: 2, 4, 5, 3, 1

> **Transcript** p 22, activity 1c
>
> – Hallo! Ich heiße Hanna! Also, wie ist mein Alltag? Ähm … ich stehe auf. Dann frühstücke ich. Ähm … ich wasche mich. Und was dann? Ach, ja! Es ist Sonntag – prima! Ich gehe nicht in die Schule!

Follow-up activity. To consolidate the key language, pupils could play a guessing game. One pupil mimes an activity and says *Was mache ich?* while the rest of the class guesses. The pupil who guesses correctly is the next one to mime. P1: *Was mache ich?* P2: *Ich ziehe mich an.* P1: *Falsch.* P3: *Ich wasche mich.* P1: *Richtig. Du bist dran!*

WB B Workbook activity B could be used at this point for revision and further practice.

Grammatik im Fokus

Reflexivverben. This section focuses on reflexive verbs. Point out that *mich* means both 'myself' and 'me', and that in German you have to say 'I wash myself' – otherwise people would think that you were washing someone or something else! Ask pupils whether they can spot any other examples of reflexive verbs in activity 1a. (*Ich ziehe mich an. Ich ziehe mich aus.*)

At this point, you may want to introduce more able pupils to the reflexive pronouns *dich* ('yourself') and *sich* ('himself'/'herself') as well. Point out that *sich waschen* is irregular: *du wäschst dich*, etc.

2a *Schreib die Sätze richtig auf.* This activity focuses pupils' attention on the order of the verb and separable prefix/reflexive pronoun. Pupils write out the sentences in the correct order.

Answers:

1 Ich ziehe mich an. 2 Ich wasche mich. 3 Ich ziehe mich aus.

2b *Finde die passenden Bilder (Übung 1a) für die Sätze in Übung 2a.* This straightforward activity consolidates pupils' understanding of the key language. They find the pictures in activity 1a which match the sentences in activity 2a.

Answers: 1 c; 2 b; 3 g

WB C Workbook activity C could be used at this point for further practice of the three reflexive verbs *sich waschen*, *sich anziehen* and *sich ausziehen*.

C 16 Activity 2a on copymaster 16 could be used here as an extension activity on daily routine.

3 *Wann machst du das? Hör gut zu und finde die passenden Bilder für die Sätze.* This activity revises times (*Klasse! 1*, Units 3 and 7) as well as providing more exposure to the reflexive forms. The recording also revises inverted word order after a time phrase (see *Wiederholung* below). Pupils listen to the recording and follow the text in the book, before matching the clocks to the sentences. Check pupils' knowledge of time expressions before starting this activity. For example, you could draw up some clocks showing different times (including half-past the hour) on the board/OHT. T: *Wie viel Uhr ist es?* P1: *Es ist halb neun*, etc. T: (pointing to a clock) *Wann stehe ich auf?* P2: *Um sieben Uhr*, etc.

Answers: 1 b; 2 c; 3 a

Transcript p 23, activity 3

1 – Um sieben Uhr ziehe ich mich an.
2 – Um halb acht wasche ich mich.
3 – Um zweiundzwanzig Uhr ziehe ich mich aus.

C 13 Activity 1 on copymaster 13 could be used to reinforce the key language for describing daily routine and give more exposure to inverted word order after a time phrase in preparation for *Wiederholung* below.

Wiederholung

Wortstellung. This section revises inverted word order after a time phrase (*Klasse! 1*, p. 95), with the addition now of a reflexive pronoun. Start by writing *Ich wasche mich.* on the board/OHT. Now write *Um sieben Uhr* before *Ich* and draw an arrow from *Ich* to after *wasche*. Now write out the new sentence *Um sieben Uhr wasche ich mich.* Explain that the subject (*ich*) is 'pushed' to the other side of the verb by the time phrase; all the other elements stay in the same place. Draw pupils' attention to the position of the reflexive pronoun and the separable prefix in the example sentences. You could now do some more examples on the board/OHT with the whole class, eliciting the answers from pupils: *Ich dusche mich/Um Viertel nach sieben dusche ich mich; Ich ziehe mich an/Um Viertel nach sieben ziehe ich mich an*, etc.

4 *Schreib die Sätze richtig auf.* Pupils put the words into the correct order to form sentences which start with time phrases. They might find this activity easier if the words are written on separate pieces of paper which can be moved around until the correct position is found. Alternatively, you could put the sentences in a text file on computer, for pupils to cut and paste. More able pupils could add new jumbled sentences (being sure to keep a copy of the solutions in a separate file!) to challenge their classmates.

Answers:

1 Um sieben Uhr wasche ich mich. 2 Um 22 Uhr ziehe ich mich aus. 3 Um acht Uhr ziehe ich mich an.

WB D Workbook activity D could be used at this point for further listening practice with time phrases.

WB E Workbook activity E could be used at this point for more advanced written practice in preparation for activity 5 below.

Follow-up activity. Groups of pupils write their own sentences on sheets of paper. After you have corrected any mistakes, each group cuts up its sentence into individual words and gives the pieces to another group as a puzzle to solve. Alternatively, this activity could be done on computer.

AT 2.4 **5** *Du bist dran! Was machst du und wann? Macht Dialoge.* Pupils work in pairs to make up their own dialogues about their daily routine.

AT 4.3 *Noch mal! Was sagst du? Schreib Antworten.* Pupils write their own responses to the questions about their daily routine. Remind them that they should answer in full sentences beginning with a time phrase. This activity could be used for homework. Pupils could present it as a diary page, or as a photo story with captions, either drawn and written by hand, or as an ICT project with scanned/digital photos or illustrations. To make a more substantial piece of writing, they could complete a separate set of answers for each member of their family.

T 4.4 *Extra! Beschreib deinen Alltag: Was machst du und wann? Schreib acht Sätze.* Pupils write their own descriptions of their daily routine. This activity could be used for homework. Pupils could present it as a diary page, or as a photo story with captions, either prepared by hand or as an ICT project with scanned/digital photos. Rather than writing about themselves, they could write an account for a famous person or fictional character (e.g. Bart Simpson).

Tipp

Wörterbuchhilfe: Reflexivverben. This section focuses on dictionary skills, in particular how to recognize a reflexive verb in a dictionary or glossary. You may want to photocopy a relevant dictionary extract onto an OHT, as well as making sure that pupils have dictionaries to use in class. Point out that the information is recorded in different ways in the German–English and the English–German parts of the dictionary, and that it is good practice to look at both before deciding on the best translation. Introduce the reflexive pronoun *sich* if you have not already done so.

Explain that pupils need to familiarize themselves with their own particular dictionary and its abbreviations and symbols. There are some abbreviations which they don't need to worry about at this stage, but they should be able to recognize the abbreviations for a noun (masculine, feminine or neuter), a verb (including reflexive and separable) and an adjective. Ask pupils whether they can spot each of these abbreviations in their dictionary or on the OHT.

6a *Wie heißt das auf Englisch? Schau im Wörterbuch nach.* Pupils use their dictionaries to look up the English translations of reflexive verbs. Explain that verbs which are reflexive in German are very often not reflexive in English.

Answers:

1 to enjoy oneself/to have a good time; 2 to decide; 3 to feel; 4 to relax

6b *Und wie heißt das auf Deutsch?* Pupils use their dictionaries to look up the German translations of English verbs. Note that 'to get lost' and 'to make a mistake' may be difficult for them to find, and they may find a variety of translations – ask them to pick the reflexive ones. Suggest how they might find these expressions (e.g. look up 'to lose', 'lost' and 'to get'; look up 'mistake'). You could maybe do 'to get lost' with the whole class by way of demonstration. Help pupils with the pronunciation of the new words.

Answers:

1 sich verlaufen/sich verirren; 2 sich irren; 3 sich beeilen; 4 sich beschweren/sich beklagen

C 17A Activity 1 on copymaster 17A could be used here for consolidation of this aspect of dictionary work.

Wie hilfst du zu Hause?
pages 24–25

Objectives

- Talk about household chores
- Ask someone about their household chores
- Describe how often you help at home
- Ask someone how often they help at home

Key language

Hilfst du zu Hause?
Ich räume mein Zimmer auf.
Ich kaufe ein.
Ich wasche ab.
Ich sauge Staub.
Ich decke den Tisch.
Ich putze das Badezimmer.
Ich füttere den Hund/die Katze.
Wie oft machst du das?
immer/oft/selten/nie/jeden Tag/einmal pro Woche

National Curriculum PoS

statements **1a, 1b, 1c, 2a, 2b, 2c, 2e, 5a, 5f, 5i**

Materials

- Students' Book pages 24–25
- Cassette 1 side A
- Workbook pages 17–18
- Copymasters 10, 13, 15, 16, 17A, 17B

C 10 ### Preparatory work

Use the relevant pictures from copymaster 10 copied onto an OHT or as flashcards to introduce language describing household chores. (For general advice on using copymaster visuals, see page 12 of the introduction to this book.)

AT 1.2
AT 3.2
1 *Hör gut zu und lies mit.* Pupils listen to the recording and follow the text in the book. Draw their attention to the pronunciation of *räume* and *füttere*.

Transcript	p 24, activity 1
a – Ich räume mein Zimmer auf.	
b – Ich putze das Badezimmer.	
c – Ich sauge Staub.	
d – Ich füttere den Hund und die Katze.	
e – Ich wasche ab.	
f – Ich decke den Tisch.	
g – Ich kaufe ein.	

WB F Workbook activity F could be used at this point to consolidate the new language.

AT 1.3
2 *Wer macht was? Hör gut zu und finde die passenden Bilder von Übung 1.* Pupils listen to the recording and match the speakers to the pictures from activity 1. Play the recording at least three times. On the second listening, ask pupils to note down the names they hear. On the third listening, pupils write the letters of the relevant pictures next to each name. You could put the names on the board/OHT to avoid spelling problems.

Answers: Stefan: f, a; Atalay: g, a; Astrid: d, e; Sven: c, g

> **Transcript**   p 24, activity 2
>
> – Stefan, hilfst du zu Hause?
> – Ja, natürlich. Ich decke den Tisch und ich räume mein Zimmer auf.
> – Und du, Atalay?
> – Ja und nein. Ich kaufe ein und ich räume mein Zimmer auf aber ich decke den Tisch nicht!
> – Wie hilfst du, Astrid? Saugst du Staub?
> – Ich? Nein, das mache ich nicht aber ich füttere die Katze und ... ach ja, ich wasche ab. So ein Pech!
> – Hilfst du zu Hause, Sven?
> – Leider. Ich sauge Staub und ich kaufe ein. Ich putze aber nie das Badezimmer. Das mag ich nicht.

AT 2.3 **3** *Du bist dran! Wie hilfst du zu Hause? A fragt und B antwortet. Dann ist B dran.* Working together in pairs, pupils interview each other about the chores they do around the house. Initially, they should use only the sentences from the cartoon (activity 1). Once this vocabulary is thoroughly familiar, you may wish to allow variations (e.g. *ich trockne ab; ich mähe den Rasen*), supplying the necessary vocabulary in response to pupils' queries. Remind pupils that in *Klasse! 1* they learned other pet vocabulary (p. 26: *der Fisch, der Hamster, der Wellensittich, die Schildkröte, die Maus, das Meerschweinchen, das Kaninchen, das Pferd*) and other rooms of the house (p. 54: *der Garten, der Keller, die Dusche, die Garage, die Küche, das Esszimmer, das Wohnzimmer*) which they could substitute for the pets and rooms mentioned in activity 1. This additional vocabulary should be written on the board/OHT, as it will also be useful for activity 5b *Noch mal!* and *Extra!*

C 16 Activity 2b on copymaster 16 could be used at this point for extension work on household chores.

Grammatik im Fokus

Trennbare Verben. This section focuses on the use of separable verbs. Explain that verbs such as *ich stehe auf, ich kaufe ein, ich räume auf, ich wasche ab* are called separable verbs. Explain that this is because the *auf/ein/ab* prefix is usually separate from the main part of the verb (i.e. the verb is in second position whilst *auf/ein/ab* is at the end of the sentence), but in the infinitive (the dictionary form), it is joined to the front of the verb: *aufstehen, einkaufen, aufräumen, abwaschen.* So for example, German speakers don't say 'to tidy up', they say 'to uptidy', and they don't say 'I tidy up my room,' but 'I tidy my room up'. If you pronounce the 'German' versions in a suitably Germanic accent, this may help pupils to remember the pattern!

C 17A Activity 2 on copymaster 17A could be used at this point for further consolidation/extension work on separable verbs.

4 *Schreib die Sätze richtig auf.* Pupils put the words into the correct order to form sentences with separable

verbs. Point out that the main part of the verb must always be the second element in the sentence.

Answers:

1 Ich räume mein Zimmer auf. 2 Ich kaufe ein. 3 Ich stehe auf. 4 Ich wasche ab. 5 Ich sauge Staub.

WB G Workbook activity G could be used at this point to focus pupils' attention on the separable prefixes and how these modify the basic meaning of the verb.

5a *Wie oft machst du das? Hör gut zu und lies mit.*
AT 1.3
AT 3.3 Pupils listen to the recording and follow the text in the book. Draw their attention to the adverbs of frequency in the *Hilfe* box (some of which were introduced in Unit 1, p.14) in preparation for activity 5b below.

> **Transcript**   p 25, activity 5a
>
> – Ich sauge jeden Tag Staub. Ich räume immer mein Zimmer auf. Ich putze oft das Badezimmer.
> – Ich kaufe nie ein. Ich füttere selten den Hund. Ich decke einmal pro Woche den Tisch.

C 13 Activity 2 on copymaster 13 could be used for consolidation of the adverbs of frequency in preparation for activity 5b below.

AT 2.4 **5b** *Was machst du und wie oft?* Pupils work in small groups asking each other what chores they never, always, often do, etc. Encourage pupils to use the additional vocabulary you may have covered in activity 3, as well as the key language presented on this spread.

C 15 Activity 1 on copymaster 15 could be used for reinforcement of daily routine and the adverbs of frequency before *Noch mal!* below.

WB H Workbook activity H could be used at this point for consolidation of daily routine and adverbs of frequency before either *Noch mal!* or *Extra!* below.

AT 2.3 *Noch mal! Mach eine Umfrage in deiner Klasse. Frag: „Wie hilfst du zu Hause und wie oft machst du das?" Schreib die Resultate auf.* Pupils conduct a survey about what chores their classmates do, writing up the results in tabular form. This reinforces the key vocabulary without pupils having to worry about the correct placement of the adverbs of frequency.

AT 4.4 *Extra! Wie hilfst du zu Hause – und wie oft? Schreib Sätze.* Pupils write their own sentences about what chores they do and how often.

WB I Workbook activity I could be used in conjunction with *Extra!* or *Noch mal!* to contribute to a written record of pupils' achievement.

Grammatik im Fokus

Akkusativ (den/die/das/die). This section focuses on the use of the accusative case for the direct object of a verb, and the accusative forms of the definite article. (Pupils met the accusative of the indefinite and negative articles in *Klasse! 1*, p. 30.) Pupils may be uncertain about the term *Akkusativ* – even though they have been using the accusative all the way through *Klasse! 1.* You may want to introduce/revise the term *Akkusativ*/accusative and the idea of case at this point, before moving on to the dative case on page 26. Below we suggest one approach.

Explain that most sentences have a subject, a verb and an object: the subject is the 'doer' of the verb, and the object is the person or thing affected by the verb. Write up a simple sentence, e.g. *Ich füttere den Hund* and explain that the subject of the verb is *ich* (because I give the food) and the object is *den Hund* (because the dog gets fed). Explain that, in German, the object is said to be in the *Akkusativ* and the subject in the *Nominativ*.

Explain that all this means in practice is that the forms of *ein/eine/ein* and *der/die/das* change slightly: the masculine article changes from *der* to *den* and from *ein* to *einen*.

You could remind pupils at this point of the importance of knowing the gender of the noun. Colour coding may help them to remember it – for example if they highlight every masculine noun in their vocabulary lists (copymaster 3 for Unit 1, copymaster 12 for Unit 2) in blue, every feminine noun in red and every neuter noun in green. (See *Klasse! 1*, p. 26.)

6a *Finde die passenden Wörter.* Pupils choose the correct form of the definite article. You could help less able pupils by pointing out that *der* will always be wrong, since it does not occur in the second column of the table in *Grammatik im Fokus*. They can also colour code their answers as above.

Answers:

1 Ich decke den Tisch. 2 Ich putze das Badezimmer. 3 Ich füttere die Katze. 4 Ich wasche das Auto. 5 Ich räume die Zimmer auf. 6 Ich füttere den Hund.

C 17B Activity 1 on copymaster 17B could be used at this point for reinforcement of the accusative forms of the definite article.

6b *Füll die Lücken aus.* Pupils fill in the correct accusative form of the definite article. Less able pupils could colour code the nouns first.

Answers:

Wie hilfst du zu Hause? Ich decke jeden Tag **den** Tisch und räume oft **das/die** Zimmer auf. Zweimal pro Woche füttere ich **den** Hund und **die** Katze. Ich wasche einmal pro Woche **das** Auto, aber ich putze nie **das** Badezimmer. Das mag ich gar nicht!

WB J Workbook activity J could be set as homework at this point to consolidate household chores and the accusative of the definite article.

Wie viel Geld bekommst du?
pages 26–27

Objectives
- Describe how much pocket money you get
- Say from whom and how often you get it
- Describe what you spend your pocket money on
- Describe how much and why you save it

Key language

Wie viel Geld bekommst du?
Ich bekomme pro Tag/Woche/Monat … von meinen Eltern/meinem Vater/meiner Oma, etc.
Was kaufst du davon?
Ich kaufe eine Jeans/ein Computerspiel/Kleidung/Make-up/Süßigkeiten/Zeitschriften.
Wofür sparst du?
Ich spare für einen Computer/eine Stereoanlage/ein Fahrrad.

National Curriculum PoS
statements 1a, 1b, 1c, 2a, 2b, 2c, 3d, 3e, 5a, 5i

Materials
- Students' Book pages 26–27
- Cassette 1 side A
- Workbook pages 19–21
- Copymasters 13, 16, 17B

Preparatory work
Revise family vocabulary (*Klasse! 1*, pp. 24–25) by drawing a family tree on the board/OHT, with male and female stick figures representing the family members (three generations). Label one of the figures at the bottom of the tree as, for example 'Tom'. Now use the diagram to elicit the terms for the other family members with *mein/e*. T: (Points to Tom's father) *Tom sagt: „Das ist mein Vater."* (Points to Tom's mother) *Was sagt Tom?* P1: *Das ist meine Mutter.* T: *Richtig*, etc. Write up the forms *mein Vater, meine Mutter, mein Onkel*, etc. Bear in mind that this could be a sensitive subject with some pupils, and extend the diagram to illustrate the terms *meine Stiefmutter, mein Stiefvater*, etc.

AT 1.2
AT 3.2
1 *Hör gut zu und lies mit.* Pupils listen to the recording and follow the text in the book. Then ask the pupils to find terms for family members in the text. What do they notice about them in comparison to the ones you previously wrote up? Answer: the endings of *mein/meine* are different. Explain that this is because of *von*.

> **Transcript** p 26, activity 1
>
> – Ich bekomme pro Woche 5 Euro von meinem Stiefvater.
> – Ich bekomme pro Monat 8 Euro von meinen Eltern.
> – Ich bekomme kein Geld von meiner Mutter.

WB K Workbook activity K could be used at this point to practise the word order of these sentences and familiarize pupils with the expressions *von meinem Vater, von meinen Eltern*, etc.

Grammatik im Fokus

von + Dativ. This section focuses on the use of the dative case after the preposition *von*. Remind pupils how *eine Wohnung* becomes *in einer Wohnung, ein Bungalow* becomes *in einem Bungalow*, etc. (Unit 1, pp. 16–17). Explain that *von* does exactly the same thing as *in*, i.e. it makes *ein/eine/ein, mein/meine/mein* and *der/die/das* take a different set of endings, and that this set of endings is called the *Dativ/*'dative case'. Draw up a table on the board/OHT, colour-coded as follows:

[blue:]	mein Vater	von meinem Vater
[red:]	meine Mutter	von meiner Mutter
[green:]	mein Kaninchen	von meinem Kaninchen
[black/white:]	meine Eltern	von meinen Eltern

2 *Füll die Lücken aus.* Pupils fill in the correct form of *mein*. As a first step, they could write out the incomplete versions with the appropriate colour-coding (i.e. 1 and 5 blue, 2, 4 and 6 red, 3 black), before referring to the colour-coded table above and filling in the forms of *mein*.

Answers:

1 meinem; 2 meiner; 3 meinen; 4 meiner; 5 meinem; 6 meiner

WB L Workbook activity L could be used at this point for further practice of the dative endings of *mein*.

C 17B Activity 2 on copymaster 17B could be used at this point for consolidation (2a) and extension work (2b) using the dative of *mein*.

AT 2.4 **3a** *Mach eine Klassenumfrage. Wie viel bekommen die Schüler/Schülerinnen und von wem?* Pupils go around the class asking each other about pocket money, taking notes initially on pieces of paper. Draw their attention to the form *Von wem?* (i.e. not *Von wer?*). Remind pupils that there is no need to give true answers if they don't want to.

AT 4.4 **3b** *Schreib die Resultate auf.* Pupils write up their results in full sentences. Make sure that they state whom the money is from.

WB M Workbook activity M could be used at this point for further practice of this structure.

4 *Hör gut zu und lies mit.* Pupils listen to the recording and follow the text in the book. Encourage pupils to guess what *ich spare* might mean. It is obviously something to do with money, and it can't be 'to get' (= *bekommen*) or 'to buy' (= *kaufen*).

AT 1.3
AT 3.3

> **Transcript**   p 27, activity 4
>
> – Annika, was kaufst du von deinem Taschengeld?
> – Ähm … Zeitschriften, Make-up, Kleidung usw.
> – Und sparst du auch etwas?
> – Ja, ich spare pro Woche 2 Euro. Ich spare für eine Stereoanlage!

5 *Was kaufen sie und wofür sparen sie? Hör gut zu und finde die passenden Bilder.* Pupils listen to the recording and note down which items each person is saving for or buying. Before playing the recording, tell pupils that they should look at the pictures for clues about expressions which will come up. Can they match the pictures a–j to the vocabulary in the *Hilfe* box? Now play the recording. During the first listening, pupils should only note the names of the speakers. After listening, they should write *spart für* and *kauft* next to each name. During the second listening, they should note the letters of the objects mentioned, distinguishing between items which the speakers are going to buy and those which they are saving up for.

AT 1.3

Draw pupils' attention to the question word *Wofür?* explaining that this is used instead of *Für was?* Remind pupils that in German *Jeans* is feminine singular: *eine Jeans*.

Answers:

Annalise: spart für: d; kauft: f, e
Frank: spart für: b, h; kauft: i, f
Dominik: spart für: a; kauft c, g
Britta: spart für: j; kauft e, c

> **Transcript**   p 27, activity 5
>
> 1
> – Ich heiße Annalise. Ich bekomme pro Monat 10 Euro von meinen Eltern. Ich spare für ein Fahrrad, aber ich kaufe auch Süßigkeiten und Make-up.
>
> 2
> – Mein Name ist Frank. Ich bekomme pro Woche 5 Euro von meiner Mutter. Ich spare für einen Computer und auch neue Jeans. Ich kaufe Zeitschriften und Süßigkeiten.
>
> 3
> – Und du, Dominik?
> – Ich bekomme pro Woche 4 Euro. Ich höre gern Musik und ich spare für eine Stereoanlage. Ich kaufe Kleidung und Computerspiele.
>
> 4
> – Sparst du auch, Britta?
> – Ja, ich spare pro Monat 5 Euro für CDs und ich kaufe Make-up und Kleidung.

WB N Workbook activity N could be used at this point for consolidation of the new vocabulary.

WB O Workbook activity O could be used at this point as additional listening practice.

C 13 Activity 3 on copymaster 13 could be used at this point as additional listening practice.

C 16 Activity 1 on copymaster 16 could be used at this point to reinforce the key vocabulary (nouns) from activity 5 above.

Grammatik im Fokus

für + Akkusativ. This section focuses on the use of the accusative case after the preposition *für*. Remind pupils that only masculine nouns require new endings in the accusative case. Draw up a table on the board/OHT, colour-coded:

[blue:]	ein Computer	für einen Computer
[red:]	eine Stereoanlage	für eine Stereoanlage
[green:]	ein Fahrrad	für ein Fahrrad

6a *Wofür sparst du? Schreib drei Listen – für Maskulinum, Femininum und Neutrum.* Pupils look up the words in their dictionaries to establish their gender, then write them up in three lists. They could colour-code their lists (or write them on different coloured pieces of paper) for reinforcement of the genders. Check pupils' answers before they proceed to activity 6b.

Answers:

Maskulinum: Fernseher, Pullover
Femininum: Bluse, Jeans, Jacke
Neutrum: Hemd, Buch, T-Shirt, Computerspiel

6b *Schreib jetzt Sätze mit den Wörtern in Übung 6a.*
Pupils use the vocabulary from activity 6a to write
sentences. Ask them what they need to watch out for
(masculine nouns and the correct accusative forms of
ein/eine/ein).

Answers:

Ich spare für einen Fernseher. Ich spare für einen
Pullover. Ich spare für eine Bluse.

Ich spare für eine Jeans. Ich spare für eine Jacke. Ich
spare für ein Hemd.

Ich spare für ein Buch. Ich spare für ein T-Shirt. Ich
spare für ein Computerspiel.

| C 17B | Activity 3 on copymaster 17B could be used here for
reinforcement of the accusative after *für*.

*Noch mal! „Was kaufst du und wofür sparst du?" Frag
vier Freunde und schreib zwei Listen.* Pupils work
together in groups of approximately five and ask each
other what they are going to buy and what they are
saving for, writing up the results in tabular form.
Remind pupils that they should write the two lists in the
accusative as shown.

Extra! Gedächtnisspiel. Pupils work together in small
groups. The first pupil says that he/she is saving for an
item, the second pupil repeats the first pupil's words
and adds another item, and so on.

| WB P | Workbook activity P could be used at this point to
reinforce the accusative endings of the indefinite article.

| WB Q | Workbook activity Q could be used here as an additional
writing activity.

Hast du einen Nebenjob?
pages 28–29

Objectives
- Describe jobs you do to earn money
- Ask someone what jobs they do
- Say how much you earn
- Give your opinion on your job

Key language
Hast du einen Nebenjob?
Ich habe einen/keinen Nebenjob.
Ich helfe zu Hause.
Ich arbeite im Garten.
Ich bin Babysitter/in.
Ich führe den Hund aus.
Ich wasche das Auto.
Ich trage Zeitungen aus.
Wie viel verdienst du?
Ich verdiene/bekomme …
Wie findest du den Job?

Ich finde den Job
super/toll/gut/langweilig/schrecklich/nicht so gut.
Das macht (keinen) Spaß!
Ich mag den Job sehr gern/gar nicht.

National Curriculum PoS
statements 1a, 1b, 1c, 2a, 2b, 2c, 2i, 3e, 5a, 5c, 5f, 5i

Materials
- Students' Book pages 28–29
- Cassette 1 side A
- Workbook pages 21–23
- Copymasters 11, 14, 15

| C 11 | ### Preparatory work
Use the pictures from copymaster 11 copied onto an
OHT or as flashcards to introduce language describing
jobs. (For general advice on using copymaster visuals,
see page 12 of the introduction to this book.)

| AT 1.2 | AT 3.2 | **1a** *Hast du einen Nebenjob? Was sagen sie? Hör gut zu
und lies mit.* Pupils listen to the recording and follow the
text in the book.

Transcript	p 28, activity 1a
a – Ich helfe zu Hause.	
b – Ich arbeite im Garten.	
c – Ich bin Babysitter.	
d – Ich führe den Hund aus.	
e – Ich wasche das Auto.	
f – Ich trage Zeitungen aus.	

| AT 2.3 | **1b** *Ratespiel. A wählt ein Bild, B rät. Dann ist B dran.*
Pupils work together in pairs. One pupil describes a job
(i.e. reads out the appropriate caption) and the other
says which picture it is.

| WB R | Workbook activity R could be used at this point for
revision and further practice.

| AT 1.3 | AT 3.3 | **2a** *Hör gut zu und lies mit.* Pupils listen to the recording
and follow the text in the book.

Transcript	p 28, activity 2a
– Jasmin, hast du einen Nebenjob?	
– Ja, ich bin Babysitterin.	
– Und wie viel verdienst du?	
– Ich verdiene pro Abend 10 Euro.	

| AT 1.4 | **2b** *Was sagen Sven, Atalay, Annika und Katrin? Hör gut
zu und füll die Tabelle aus.* Pupils listen to the recording
and complete the table with Sven, Atalay, Annika and
Katrin's information. The answers should be fed back as
a whole-class activity so that all pupils have the
necessary information to attempt activities 2c and 2d.

Answers:

Sven	ich helfe zu Hause ich wasche das Auto	8 Euro
Atalay	ich bin Babysitter ich führe den Hund aus	5 Euro 50 Cent
Annika	ich trage Zeitungen aus ich arbeite im Garten	10 Euro 3 Euro
Katrin	ich führe die Hunde aus ich helfe zu Hause	9 Euro

Transcript p 28, activity 2b

– Hast du einen Nebenjob, Sven?
– Ja, ich helfe zu Hause und ich wasche das Auto.
– Und wie viel verdienst du?
– Ich bekomme 8 Euro von meinen Eltern.

– Und du, Atalay?
– Ich bin Babysitter für meine Tante und ich verdiene 5 Euro. Ich führe auch jeden Tag den Hund aus und ich bekomme 50 Cent von meiner Mutter.

– Arbeitest du, Annika?
– Ja. Ich trage montags und freitags Zeitungen aus und ich verdiene 10 Euro. Ich arbeite auch im Garten und bekomme 3 Euro.

– Hast du einen Nebenjob, Katrin?
– Ja, natürlich. Wir haben drei Hunde und ich führe die Hunde jeden Tag aus. Ich helfe auch zu Hause und bekomme 9 Euro.

AT 3.2
AT 4.2 **2c** *Richtig oder falsch? Korrigiere die falschen Sätze.* Pupils compare the statements with their information from activity 2b. For any statements which are incorrect, they provide the correct version.

Answers:

1 Ich bekomme pro Woche 5 Euro 50 Cent. 2 Ich führe den Hund aus. 3 Ich verdiene pro Woche 13 Euro. 4 Ich arbeite im Garten. 5 Ich führe die Hunde aus. 6 richtig

AT 2.4 **2d** *Macht Dialoge mit den Informationen von Übung 2b.* Pupils work together in pairs to create dialogues using their information from activity 2b.

WB S Workbook activity S could be used at this point for reinforcement and improvement of spoken fluency.

WB T Workbook activity T could be used at this point as a written extension activity which can form part of the pupil's written record of achievement.

C 14 Copymaster 14 could be used at this point as oral extension activities on jobs and money.

Tipp

Meinungen. This section focuses on methods of expressing opinions. The first text gives examples of negative opinions, while the second gives examples of positive opinions.

3a *Lies die Texte und finde alle Meinungs-Sätze. Welche sind positiv und welche sind negativ? Schreib zwei Listen.*

Pupils scan the texts for sentences which express positive and negative expressions, compiling two lists.

Answers:

Positiv: Das macht Spaß!
Ich finde den Job toll.
Ich mag den Hund sehr gern.
Das finde ich gut.
Negativ: Ich mag den Job nicht.
Das finde ich sehr langweilig.
Das finde ich nicht sehr freundlich.

3b *Hast du einen Job? Wie findest du den Job? Schreib Sätze auf Deutsch.* Pupils use the picture prompts to write sentences expressing opinions about various jobs.

3c *Was ist dein Nebenjob und wie findest du das? A macht eine Pantomime, die Gruppe rät.* Pupils work together in groups. One pupil mimes a job and his or her opinion of it (e.g. washing the car with an unhappy expression), while the other pupils try to guess the job. The job should be chosen from those already introduced. The pupil who guesses correctly is the next one to mime.

Noch mal! Wie findest du die Nebenjobs in Übung 1a? Schreib einen positiven oder einen negativen Satz. Pupils write their opinions of the jobs introduced in activity 1a.

Extra! Beschreib einen positiven und einen negativen Nebenjob wie Richard und Monika. Pupils write texts about two jobs, using the two reading texts as models.

WB U Workbook activity U could be used at this point for consolidation of the new language.

WB V Workbook activity V could be used at this point as a writing outcome for pages 28 and 29.

C 15 Activity 2 on copymaster 15 could be used at this point as a reading extension activity.

Gut gesagt!

Wortendungen.

 4a *Hör gut zu und lies mit.* Pupils listen to the articles and possessive adjectives on the recording and relate the sounds to the written words.

Transcript p 29, activity 4

– der, die, das, die
– den, die, das, die
– mein, meine, mein, meine
– meinen, meine, mein, meine

4b *Hör gut zu und wiederhole.* Pupils listen to the articles and possessive adjectives on the tape and repeat them. Explain that they should pay particular attention to the endings and pronounce them clearly: <maɪnen> etc. not <maɪnən>.

Thema im Fokus
pages 30–31

National Curriculum PoS
statements 2c, 2e, 2h, 2j, 3d, 3e, 5a, 5c, 5d, 5e, 5f, 5i

Materials
- Students' Book pages 30–31
- Cassette 1 side A

The final spread of each unit provides further reading practice, leading into a project outcome for the unit. See pages 8–9 of the introduction to this book for general notes on how to use these pages.

`AT 3.4` `AT 4.3` **1** *Welche Jobs findest du interessant und welche langweilig? Schreib zwei Listen und schreib auch warum.* Pupils give their personal reactions to the jobs, followed by a short statement of their reasons. The terms *die Haustiere, die Hausarbeit* and *das Babysitting* will be useful for pupils in formulating their responses. Remind them to review the language required for expressing positive and negative opinions from page 29.

`AT 4.4` **2** *Deine Oma/dein Opa braucht Hilfe zu Hause oder im Garten. Schreib eine Anzeige für sie oder ihn.* Pupils write their own advertisements using the texts from activity 1 as a model. They can write the advertisement as if they are *Oma/Opa*, or more able pupils can write in the third person (*Meine Oma braucht …*), although they may need some support with this. Point out that the advertisement should contain the following elements: description of the job/what you need doing; what times and how long for; pay; contact details. Tell pupils that they should look through the texts for useful expressions, but should be careful not to copy whole sentences. Less able pupils could be given a bank of sentences to mix and match and then copy out.

`AT 1.4` `AT 2.4` **3a** *Mach eine Umfrage in deiner Klasse.* Pupils conduct a detailed class survey about jobs – an activity which requires them to do some advance planning. Before they start, ask them how they are going to record their results, and how they are going to phrase the questions. Encourage them to anticipate likely replies and think about what information they need (see activity 3b): if their forms are well designed, it will be much easier for them to conduct the survey and to extract the information later. They may find it useful to write out the questions in full at the top of their sheet of paper, and then to divide up the rest of the sheet into equal columns with short headings, e.g. *Name, Nebenjob?, Wann?, Geld?, Kaufen?, Sparen?* with space in each column to record their results in note form.

`AT 4.3` **3b** *Schreib die Resultate auf.* Pupils present the results of their survey. Point out that presenting information from a survey always involves selection. The form of presentation should emphasize interesting information from the survey, e.g. male/female differences or the range of jobs (as in the examples in the Students' Book), or the range of earnings, hours worked, etc. First of all, pupils should look at the information they have gathered and see what interesting facts they notice. Is

the range of jobs wide or narrow? Do the earnings or the hours vary a great deal? This could be done as a discussion or brainstorming activity before pupils go away to work on their presentations individually.

Pupils can use the presentation ideas from the Students' Book (bar chart and pie chart), or any other ideas for graphic presentation they may have. This is an ideal ICT task: spreadsheet, presentation or word-processing software can be used to present statistics in a visually striking way, and pupils can experiment to find the clearest and most attractive way of presenting their results.

`AT 4.4` `AT 2.4` **4** *Schreibt einen Artikel für eine Klassenzeitung oder für eine Internet-Seite: ,Die Nebenjobs von Klasse …'.* Pupils collaborate to present the results of their survey as a magazine-style article or web page, using the text *Die Nebenjobs von Klasse 9B* as a stimulus. As in the example, each pupil could contribute a piece about his/her job, together with a photo or illustration. The graphics from activity 3b can be incorporated into the article/web page.

Kannst du … ?
The end-of-unit summary is a checklist for pupils. See page 8 of the introduction to this book for ideas on how to use the checklist.

Noch mal!-Seite Einheit 2
page 124

National Curriculum PoS
statements 1a, 1b, 1c, 2a, 2b, 5a, 5i

Materials
- Students' Book page 124
- Cassette 1 side A

This reinforcement page is intended for less able pupils. It consolidates the basic vocabulary and structures from the unit, and it can be used by pupils who experienced difficulty in completing some of the activities within the unit, or as alternative homework activities.

`AT 1.2` **1** *Hör gut zu und finde die richtige Reihenfolge für die Bilder.* Activity 1 relates to pages 22–23. Pupils listen to the recording and put the pictures into the correct sequence. Encourage pupils to look at the pictures before listening to the recording, and to identify what is happening in each picture. They could attempt to sequence the pictures at this stage, and note down key expressions they are likely to hear, e.g. *f – stehe auf; b – ziehe aus*, etc. Pupils then listen to the recording and check the actual sequence against their predictions.

Answers: f, e, c, d, b, a

Transcript	p 124, activity 1

– Um sieben Uhr stehe ich auf und dann wasche ich mich. Um halb acht frühstücke ich und ich gehe schnell in die Schule. Um neun Uhr ziehe ich mich aus und gehe ins Bett.

AT 2.2

2 *Gedächtnisspiel: Der Alltag. A beginnt, dann ist B dran.* Activity 2 relates to pages 22–23. Pupils play the memory game together in pairs. Demonstrate how the game works with the whole class first: the first player makes a statement about his/her daily routine, the second player repeats this statement and adds another, and so on. Appropriate sentences could be put on an OHT to help pupils if necessary.

AT 3.3

3 *Lies den Brief von Anja und füll die Lücken aus.* Activity 3 relates to pages 26–27. Pupils write out the letter and fill in the gaps with the appropriate forms of *mein/meine/mein* and the indefinite article (accusative and dative case). The activity could be broken down into three stages:

1 Pupils decide the gender/number of the noun after the gap
2 They look for case information in the words before the gap (is there *für* or *von*?; is the noun the object of a verb?)
3 They select the appropriate form from the box.

Answers:

Für **meinen** Geburtstag bekomme ich 10 Euro von **meinen** Großeltern. Das sind 5 Euro von **meiner** Oma und 5 Euro von **meinem** Opa. Ich bekomme auch 8 Euro von **meiner** Tante und 20 Euro von **meinen** Eltern. Was mache ich damit? Also, ich spare für **einen** Computer und auch **eine** Stereoanlage. Ich habe schon 250 Euro! Aber ich kaufe auch **ein** Buch und **eine** Jeans.

AT 2.3

4 *Macht Dialoge. A wählt und B antwortet. Dann ist B dran.* Activity 4 relates to pages 26–27. Pupils work together in pairs. Partner A says a letter and number combination (A–D and 1–4); partner B locates the appropriate sectors on the two discs and formulates a sentence. Before attempting the activity, pupils should look at the picture prompts and check that they can name the items (1 *Süßigkeiten und CDs*; 2 *Make-up und Zeitschriften*; 3 *Kleidung und Schokolade*; 4 *Jeans und Computerspiele*).

Extra!-Seite Einheit 2
page 125

National Curriculum PoS
statements 1a, 1b, 1c, 2a, 2b, 2e, 2j, 3e, 5d, 5e, 5f, 5i

Materials
- Students' Book page 125
- Cassette 1 side A

This extension page is intended for more able pupils. It contains slightly longer and more complex materials, and it can be used by pupils who have completed other activities quickly or as alternative homework activities.

AT 3.4

1a *Lies den Text. Was sagt Katrin? Sind die Sätze richtig oder falsch?* This activity relates to pages 24–29. Pupils read Katrin's plan and then decide which of the speech bubbles contain the same information as the plan.

Answers:

1 falsch; 2 falsch; 3 richtig; 4 richtig; 5 falsch; 6 falsch; 7 falsch; 8 falsch; 9 richtig; 10 richtig

AT 4.4

1b *Wofür sparst du? Schreib einen Plan wie Katrin.* This activity relates to pages 24–29. Pupils write their own plan, using Katrin's plan as a model.

AT 1.4

2a *Atalay sucht einen Nebenjob. Hör gut zu und beantworte die Fragen.* This activity relates to pages 28–29. Pupils listen to the recording and then answer the questions. Encourage pupils to read the questions before listening, in order to get an idea of the likely content of the recording. You could write up the expressions *morgens, abends* and *von … bis* on the board/OHT, as they will be useful for pupils in completing activity 2b.

Answers:

1 In einem Zeitungskiosk in der Stadtmitte. 2 Der Nebenjob ist für Jungen oder Mädchen. 3 Der Nebenjob ist für drei Stunden pro Tag. 4 Man verdient 50 Euro pro Woche. 5 Nein. 6 Frau Albrecht. 7 wie alt er ist, hat er zur Zeit einen Nebenjob (und wo), an welchen Tagen er arbeitet am liebsten.

Transcript   p 125, activity 2a

– Hallo! Und willkommen bei Radio-Wesel. Heute haben wir den Jobs-Slot. Viele Anzeigen für viele Jobs!
– Ich habe einen Zeitungskiosk in der Stadtmitte und ich suche einen Jungen oder ein Mädchen ab dreizehn Jahre alt. Der Nebenjob ist von sechs bis sieben Uhr morgens und von sechzehn bis achtzehn Uhr abends. Pro Tag ist das 8 Euro oder 50 Euro pro Woche von Montag bis Freitag. Schreib einen Brief an Frau Albrecht und beantworte die folgenden Fragen: Wie alt bist du? Hast du zur Zeit einen Nebenjob und wo? An welchen Tagen arbeitest du am liebsten?

AT 4.4
AT 2.4

2b *Schreib eine Anzeige für einen Nebenjob. Nimm die Anzeige auf Kassette auf. Sag:* This activity relates to pages 28–29. Pupils write their own radio advertisement for a job and record it on tape. Encourage them to make the tape recording as lively and authentic-sounding as possible.

As an additional activity, pupils could write a set of questions to go with their recording and set this as a listening comprehension for other pupils.

Workbook

Page 14
Use with page 21 in the Students' Book.

A1 *Hör gut zu und sing mit!* Singing this song will help pupils to memorize the key vocabulary for daily routine and revise time expressions. If your pupils are reticent about singing, you could still use the song to elicit key structures in the following way. After listening and following the text in their books, pupils close their books. Play the song again, but pause the tape before each verse and mime the activity, eliciting from pupils the first line of the verse. Then play the verse.

Transcript   W 14, activity A1

Ich stehe auf!
Ich stehe auf!
Es ist sieben Uhr
Und ich steh' auf!

Ich wasche mich!
Ich wasche mich!
Es ist Viertel nach
Und ich wasche mich!

Ich ziehe mich an!
Ich ziehe mich an!
Es ist fast halb acht
Und ich zieh' mich an!

Ich esse Toast!
Ich esse Toast!
Es ist Viertel vor
Und ich esse Toast!

Ich trinke Milch!
Ich trinke Milch!
Es ist zehn vor acht
Und ich trinke Milch!

Mein Tag beginnt!
Mein Tag beginnt!
Es ist schon acht Uhr
Und mein Tag beginnt!

AT 3.2 **A2** *Finde die passenden Bilder und Antworten.* This is a reading comprehension activity focusing on the key vocabulary and structures from the song (daily routine and time expressions). It encourages pupils to use their skills of dealing with unknown language to work out the meanings of new items of vocabulary.

Answers:

1 b; 2a 7:15, 2b 7:30; 3 b; 4 free answers; 5 a; 6 a

Pages 15–16

Use with pages 22–23 in the Students' Book.

AT 3.2 **B1** *Was machen sie? Finde die passenden Bilder.* Pupils match the pictures to the sentences. Activities B1–B3 consolidate the key vocabulary for describing daily routine.

Answers:

1 c; 2 f; 3 e; 4 b; 5 h; 6 d; 7 g; 8 a

B2 *Wer sagt was? Hör gut zu und finde die passenden Bilder in Übung B1.* Pupils listen to the recording and match the names to the pictures a–h from the previous activity. Clock times could be revised (in preparation for activities 3–5 on page 23 of the Students' Book) by asking pupils to write in the times mentioned next to the names (Uwe: 10 Uhr, Hanna: 7 Uhr; Monika: 1 Uhr).

Answers:

1 c; 2 a; 3 g; 4 f; 5 e; 6 b; 7 h; 8 d

Transcript   W 15, activity B2

– Peter, Peter, PETER!
– Ja, ja, Mutti. Ich stehe auf.

– Was machst du, Uwe?
– Es ist schon zehn Uhr. Ich gehe ins Bett.

– Und was machst du, Kai, bevor du ins Bett gehst?
– Ich ziehe mich natürlich aus.

– Anne, was machst du im Badezimmer?
– Mensch! Ich wasche mich natürlich!

– Philipp, wo bist du?
– Im Schlafzimmer! Ich ziehe mich an.

– Leah, wohin gehst du?
– Ich? Ich gehe in die Schule. Tschüs!

– Was machst du, Hanna?
– Ich gehe in die Küche und frühstücke. Es ist sieben Uhr.

– Wohin gehst du um ein Uhr, Monika?
– Ich gehe nach Hause.

AT 2.1 **AT 1.1** **B3** *A sagt einen Satz von Übung B1, B macht eine Pantomime.* Pupils work together in pairs. Partner A reads out a sentence from activity B1 above, and partner B mimes the appropriate action. B then reads out a sentence which A mimes, and so on.

AT 3.2 **C1** *Was fehlt? Füll die Lücken aus und finde die passenden Bilder.* Pupils complete the gap-fill task and match the sentences to the pictures. They will find the gap-fill task easier if they look at the pictures first.

Answers:

1 b Ich wasche mich.
2 c Ich ziehe mich an.
3 a Ich ziehe mich aus.

AT 2.2 **C2** *Ist alles richtig? A fragt, B antwortet. Dann ist B dran.* Pupils work together in pairs to practise the sentences from activity C1. More able pupils should be able to complete this activity without completing C1 first.

D *Wann machst du das? Hör gut zu und schreib die Namen unter die passenden Bilder.* Pupils listen to the recording and write the name of the relevant person beneath each clockface. Point out to pupils that they should listen for a name and a time in each dialogue and not be distracted by non-relevant information.

Answers: a Britta; b Angi; c Ralf; d Oma; e Martin

Transcript   W 16, activity D

– Tschüs, Mutti! Ich gehe in die Schule.
– Du gehst in die Schule? Warum?
– Aber, Mutti, es ist doch schon halb acht!
– Halb acht! Schon so spät! Auf Wiedersehen, Angi.

- Wie spät ist es, Peter?
- Zehn Uhr.
- Zehn Uhr und die Britta ist noch nicht da!
- Ah, Britta, endlich! Es ist schon zehn Uhr.
- Ja, es tut mir Leid – der Bus war nicht da!

- Oh! Ich bin müde!
- Oh, Martin. Wie spät ist es denn?
- Es ist elf Uhr.
- Elf Uhr? Dann geh ins Bett!

- Gute Nacht, ihr alle!
- Aber, Oma, wohin gehst du?
- Ich? Es ist schon neun Uhr und ich gehe ins Bett!
- Nein, Oma. Komm zurück. Es ist erst halb fünf!
- Oh!

- Ralf, wie spät ist es?
- Ich weiß nicht. Warte mal! … Ach ja, es ist acht Uhr.
- Ralf! Acht Uhr. Geh in die Schule!

Transcript   W 17, activity H1

- Martin, wie oft hilfst du zu Hause?
- Ähm … also … Am Abend decke ich den Tisch.
- Machst du das jeden Tag?
- Ja, ja – jeden Tag.
- Und was machst du sonst?
- Also, wir haben einen Hund und eine Katze und ich füttere sie jeden Tag.
- Aha … und putzen oder Staub saugen? Machst du auch das?
- Ich sauge einmal pro Woche Staub, aber ich putze selten das Badezimmer. Das mag ich nicht sehr gern.
- Und dein Zimmer? Räumst du dein Zimmer auf?
- Ja, ich räume mein Zimmer einmal pro Woche auf.
- Und kaufst du auch ein?
- Ähm, nein. Ich kaufe nie ein. Aber, ich wasche IMMER ab.

AT 4.3   **E** *Was machst du – und wann? Schreib Sätze.* Pupils use the picture prompts to write sentences about daily routine. This activity practises inverted word order after a time phrase.

Answers:

a Um halb sieben stehe ich auf. b Um sieben Uhr wasche ich mich. c Um acht Uhr frühstücke ich. d Um neun Uhr ziehe ich mich aus. e Um halb zwölf gehe ich ins Bett.

Pages 17–18

Use with pages 24–25 in the Students' Book.

AT 3.2   **F** *Wie hilfst du zu Hause? Füll die Lücken aus.* Pupils use the picture prompts to help them complete the gap-fill task.

Answers:

1 Ich sauge Staub. 2 Ich füttere den Hund und die Katze. 3 Ich räume mein Zimmer auf. 4 Ich putze das Badezimmer. 5 Ich decke den Tisch. 6 Ich kaufe ein. 7 Ich wasche ab.

AT 3.2   **G** *Finde die passenden Wörter und schreib die Sätze auf.* Pupils select the correct separable prefix and write out the sentences.

Answers: 1 b; 2 a; 3 e; 4 c; 5 d

H1 *Wie oft hilft Martin zu Hause? Hör gut zu und füll die Tabelle aus.* Pupils listen to the recording and complete the grid, using the appropriate symbol to show the frequency with which Martin does each chore. Pupils should look at the grid and the key before listening to get an idea of the language which is likely to occur in the recording.

AT 1.4

Answers:

shopping: ✗✗
hoovering: ✔
setting the table: ✔✔✔
cleaning the bathroom: ✗

tidying up: ✔
feeding pets: ✔✔✔
washing up: ✔✔✔✔

AT 4.3   **H2** *Schreib Sprechblasen für Martin. Was sagt er?* Pupils use their completed grids from activity H1 to reconstruct Martin's words.

Answers:

Ich decke jeden Tag den Tisch. Ich füttere jeden Tag den Hund und die Katze.
Ich sauge einmal pro Woche Staub. Ich putze selten das Badezimmer.
Ich räume mein Zimmer einmal pro Woche auf. Ich kaufe nie ein.
Ich wasche immer ab.

AT 4.4   **I** *Du bist dran! Wie hilfst du zu Hause? Wie oft machst du das?* Pupils write about the chores they do at home. This activity can form part of pupils' written records for continuous assessment purposes. See the general notes on pages 13–14 of the introduction to this book.

AT 3.2   **J** *Jasmin hilft zu Hause. Was fehlt? Füll die Lücken aus.* Pupils select the appropriate word to complete each sentence.

Answers:

1 Ich füttere die **Katze**. 2 Ich decke den **Tisch**. 3 Ich räume das **Zimmer** auf. 4 Ich putze das **Badezimmer**. 5 Ich füttere den **Hund**. 6 Ich wasche das **Auto**.

Page 19

Use with page 26 in the Students' Book.

AT 3.2   **K** *Was sagen sie? Schreib die Sätze richtig auf.* Pupils put the words into the correct order to form sentences. Less able pupils may find this easier if each word is written on a separate piece of paper.

Answers:

Peter: Ich bekomme pro Woche 7 Euro von meinem Vater.
Annika: Ich bekomme kein Geld von meinen Eltern.
Meike: Ich bekomme pro Woche 8 Euro von meinem Onkel.
Leon: Ich bekomme pro Monat 10 Euro von meinen Großeltern.

T3.2 **L** *Von wem bekommst du Geld? Füll die Lücken aus.* Pupils complete the forms of *mein/meine/mein* with the correct endings for the dative case.

Answers:

1 Von **meinen** Großeltern. 2 Von **meinem** Stiefvater. 3 Von **meiner** Oma. 4 Von **meinem** Opa. 5 Von **meiner** Tante. 6 Von **meinem** Onkel.

T4.3 **M** *Klaus hat eine Umfrage gemacht. Hier sind die Resultate. Was sagen die Schüler und Schülerinnen? Schreib Sprechblasen.* Pupils use the information from the grid to write sentences.

Answers:

a Ich bekomme pro Woche 5 Euro von meiner Tante.
b Ich bekomme pro Monat 30 Euro von meinen Eltern.
c Ich bekomme pro Tag 3 Euro von meinen Großeltern.
d Ich bekomme pro Monat 20 Euro von meiner Stiefmutter.
e Ich bekomme pro Tag 2 Euro von meinem Vater.

Page 20

Use with page 27 in the Students' Book.

AT3.1 **N** *Was kaufst du? Finde die passenden Wörter.* Pupils choose the correct words from the box and write them below the pictures. For further practice, they could write up their answers in complete sentences (*Ich kaufe eine Jeans*, etc.).

Answers:

a eine Jeans; b eine Stereoanlage; c Kleidung; d ein Computerspiel; e Zeitschriften; f Make-up; g ein Fahrrad; h einen Computer; i Süßigkeiten; j CDs

O1 *Hör gut zu und verbinde die Namen mit den passenden Bildern.* Pupils listen to the recording and then draw lines linking each name with a picture in each column. They should examine the pictures before listening and remind themselves of the German word for each item shown.

AT1.3

Answers: Ich kaufe …   Ich spare für …

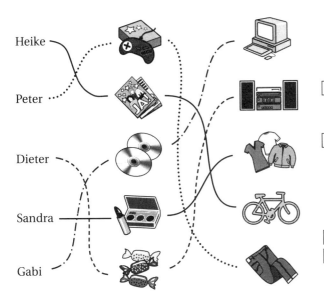

Heike

Peter

Dieter

Sandra

Gabi

Transcript   W 20, activity O1

– Hallo, Heike! Ich mache ein Interview. Was kaufst du mit deinem Geld?
– Ich kaufe Zeitschriften.
– Und wofür sparst du?
– Ich spare für ein neues Fahrrad.

– Und du, Peter?
– Ich? Ich kaufe ein Computerspiel, aber ich spare für eine neue Jeans. Ich bekomme nicht viel Taschengeld.

– Dieter, was kaufst du?
– Also, bei mir ist es so. Ich kaufe nur Süßigkeiten.
– Warum nur Süßigkeiten?
– Ich spare für eine neue Stereoanlage. Meine alte ist kaputt.
– Danke, Dieter.

– Und du, Sandra?
– Ich kaufe Make-up, aber ich spare für neue Kleidung.

– Gabi, kaufst du auch Make-up?
– Nein. Ich kaufe CDs und noch mehr CDs! Ich höre sehr gern Musik! Ich spare auch für einen Computer, aber ich habe nicht viel Geld.

AT4.3 **O2** *Was sagen sie in Übung O1? Schreib die Sätze auf.* Pupils use their answers to activity O1 to reconstruct the speakers' words.

Answers:

1 Ich kaufe Zeitschriften und ich spare für ein Fahrrad. 2 Ich kaufe ein Computerspiel und ich spare für eine Jeans. 3 Ich kaufe Süßigkeiten und ich spare für eine Stereoanlage. 4 Ich kaufe Make-up und ich spare für Kleidung. 5 Ich kaufe CDs und ich spare für einen Computer.

Page 21

Use with pages 27–28 in the Students' Book.

AT3.1 **P** *Wofür spart Tom? Füll die Lücken aus.* Pupils complete the sentences with the correct form (accusative) of the indefinite article.

Answers:

einen Computer; **ein** Computerspiel; **eine** Jeans; **ein** Buch; **ein** Fahrrad; **eine** Stereoanlage; **einen** Pullover; **ein** Auto

AT4.3 **Q** *Du bist dran!* Pupils write their own responses to the questions. This activity can form part of pupils' written records for continuous assessment purposes.

AT3.2 **R1** *Was für Nebenjobs haben Sven und Jasmin? Lies die Sätze und finde die passenden Bilder.* Pupils read the speech bubbles and then find a picture to match each of the sentences.

Answers: 1 d; 2 b; 3 e; 4 c; 5 a; 6 f

AT2.2 **R2** *„Hast du einen Nebenjob?" Mach eine Umfrage in* **AT4.2** *deiner Klasse und schreib die Resultate auf. Frag vier Schüler/Schülerinnen.* Pupils work together in groups of approximately five, asking each other whether they have a job. They should record the answers in note form and then write them up in whole sentences. Explain that pupils should choose one or more of the six jobs from the previous activity.

If you wish pupils in a more able class to go beyond the six jobs already introduced, in order to describe what they really do, prepare this with the whole class prior to the activity. Ask for a show of hands for each of the six jobs, before establishing who has a different job. T: *Wer hilft zu Hause? Wer arbeitet im Garten? (etc.) Wer hat einen anderen Nebenjob?* You can then supply the German translations for the new jobs.

Pages 22-23

Use with pages 28–29 in the Students' Book

AT 2.3 **S** *Würfelspiel: Wie viel verdienst du? Wie oft bekommst du das? A fragt, B antwortet. Dann ist B dran.* Pupils play the game in pairs; each pair needs two dice. Partner A asks *Wie viel verdienst du?* and partner B throws the dice and responds accordingly with an amount and a frequency.

AT 4.3 **T** *Du bist dran!* Pupils answer the questions about their jobs in full sentences. Encourage them to invent a job if they don't do one. This activity can form part of pupils' written records for continuous assessment purposes.

AT 3.2 **U1** *Was ist positiv und was ist negativ? Schreib zwei Listen.* Pupils sort the sentences into two lists for positive and negative reactions.

Answers:

Positiv:
Ich mag den Job.   Das finde ich gut.
Ich finde den Job toll.   Ich mag den Job sehr gern.
Das macht Spaß!
Der Job ist super.

Negativ:
Ich finde den Job langweilig.
Der Job ist schrecklich.
Das macht keinen Spaß!
Das mag ich gar nicht.
Der Manager ist sehr unfreundlich.
Ich finde den Job nicht so gut.

AT 2.4 **U2** *Positiv oder negativ – was ist deine Meinung? Macht Dialoge.* Pupils use the picture prompts and expressions to form dialogues. More able pupils can add further details and/or give their own jobs and reactions rather than using the prompts.

AT 4.4 **V** *Lies die Postkarte und schreib eine Antwort-Postkarte.* Pupils read the postcard and then use it as a model to construct their reply. Suggest that they put in something like *Danke für deine Postkarte.* This activity can be used as a written outcome for pages 28-29 of the Students' Book.

Can you ...?

The purpose of the checklist is to identify tasks in the Students' Book both by skill and by topic. Teachers may find this helpful in selecting specific tasks, as a record of pupils' achievements in an Attainment Target.

Einheit 2 Mein Alltag	AT 1 Listening	AT 2 Speaking	AT 3 Reading	AT 4 Writing
22–23 Was machst du heute?				
Talk about your daily routine	1a, 1c, 3	1b, 5	1a, 2b	2a, 4, Noch mal!, Extra!
Ask others about their daily routine	–	1b, 5	–	–
24–25 Wie hilfst du zu Hause?				
Talk about household chores	1, 2	3	1, 6b	4, 6a, Extra!
Ask someone about their household chores	–	3	–	–
Describe how often you help at home	5a	5b	5a, 6b	Noch mal!, Extra!
Ask someone how often they help at home	–	5b, Noch mal!	–	–
26–27 Wie viel Geld bekommst du?				
Describe how much pocket money you get	1	3a	1	3b
Say from whom and how often you get it	–	3a	–	2, 3b
Describe what you spend your pocket money on	4, 5	Noch mal!	4	Noch mal!
Describe how much and why you save it	5	Noch mal!, Extra!	–	6a, 6b, Noch mal!
28–29 Hast du einen Ne°benjob?				
Describe jobs you do to earn money	1a, 2a, 2b	1b, 2d, 3c	1a, 2a, 2b, 2c	2c, 3b
Ask someone what jobs they do	2a	2d	2a	–
Say how much you earn	2b, 2c	2d	2b, 2c	2c
Give your opinion on your job	–	3c	3a	3b, Noch mal!, Extra!

Copymasters

For general advice about using the copymasters, see page 7 of the introduction to this book.

`C 13` **Hören**

`AT 1.2`

1 *Hör gut zu und finde die passenden Bilder.* Pupils listen to the recording and then choose the appropriate picture for each speaker.

Answers: 1 c; 2 a; 3 e; 4 d; 5 b

> **Transcript** C 13, activity 1
>
> 1 – Um halb neun frühstücke ich.
> 2 – Um vier Uhr gehe ich nach Hause.
> 3 – Um halb acht stehe ich auf.
> 4 – Um neun Uhr ziehe ich mich aus.
> 5 – Um zehn Uhr gehe ich ins Bett.

`AT 1.3`

2 *Wie oft machen sie das? Hör gut zu und kreuz die Bilder richtig an.* Pupils listen to the recording and then put the appropriate number of ticks or crosses next to each picture.

Answers: 1 ✔✔✔✔; 2 ✘; 3 ✔; 4 ✔✔; 5 ✘✘; 6 ✔✔✔

> **Transcript** C 13, activity 2
>
> 1 – Ich sauge immer Staub. Staub saugen – das macht immer Spaß.
> 2 – Ja, Mutti! Nein, Mutti! Ich räume mein Zimmer selten auf. Ich bin zu faul.
> 3 – Ich kann keine Tasse finden und ich wasche einmal pro Woche ab. Das ist nicht fair!
> 4 – Hier, Bruno! Bruno hat immer Hunger! Ja, ich füttere oft meinen Hund.
> 5 – Nie, nie, ich meine nie ... ich putze nie das Badezimmer.
> 6 – Ich ... decke ... jeden ... Tag ... den ... Tisch ... Ja, ... wirklich ... jeden ... Tag!

`AT 1.4`

3 *Was kaufen sie und wofür sparen sie? Hör gut zu und füll die Tabelle aus.* Pupils listen to the recording and then complete the grid. Less able pupils can just supply the nouns, more able pupils should also fill in the correct forms of the indefinite article where appropriate. For further practice, pupils could write out their results in complete sentences.

Answers:

	kauft ...	spart für ...
Max	Süßigkeiten, ein Computerspiel	eine neue Jacke, Zeitschriften
Beate	Kleidung	einen Computer, einen Pullover
Pepi	Bücher, ein T-Shirt	einen Fernseher, eine Stereoanlage

> **Transcript** C 13, activity 3
>
> 1
> – Max, was kaufst du von deinem Taschengeld?
> – Ich kaufe Süßigkeiten und ein Computerspiel.
> – Und sparst du auch etwas?
> – Ja, natürlich. Ich spare pro Woche 4 Euro. Ich spare für eine neue Jacke und Zeitschriften.
>
> 2
> – Und du, Beate? Was kaufst du von deinem Taschengeld?
> – Ich kaufe oft nichts. Aber manchmal kaufe ich Kleidung.
> – Und sparst du etwas?
> – Ja, immer. Ich spare pro Monat 10 Euro – für einen Computer und auch einen Pullover.
>
> 3
> – Pepi, was machst du mit deinem Taschengeld?
> – Ich kaufe und ich spare.
> – Was kaufst du?
> – Ich kaufe Bücher und ein T-Shirt. Ich bekomme pro Woche 20 Euro von meinem Vater – also, ich spare für einen Fernseher und eine Stereoanlage.

`C 14` **Sprechen**

`AT 2.4`

1a *Dein Partner/deine Partnerin stellt Fragen. Wähle ein Bild (a–f) und beantworte die Fragen. Dein Partner/deine Partnerin findet das passende Bild.* Pupils work together in pairs to create dialogues. Partner A chooses one of the six pictures, without telling B which picture he/she has chosen, and then answers B's questions. On the basis of A's answers, B decides which picture A has chosen.

`AT 2.4`

1b *Stell die Fragen unten. Dein Partner/deine Partnerin antwortet. Finde das passende Bild in Übung 1a.* This is the second part of the activity, with the roles reversed.

`AT 2.5`

2 *Du bist dran! Mach weitere Dialoge mit den Fragen in Übung 1b.* This activity is suitable for more able pupils. Pupils continue to work in pairs, but now the 'interviewee' can give free responses about his or her own (real or imaginary) job, with the 'interviewer' asking the same questions as above. Then the roles are reversed. Pupils could record these dialogues on tape, where they could form part of pupils' records for continuous assessment purposes.

`C 15` **Lesen**

`AT 3.2`

1 *Wer sagt das? Anja oder Paul? Schreib A oder P in die Kästchen.* Pupils look at the pictures in the thought bubbles and complete the grid, by identifying who says what.

Answers: 1 A; 2 A; 3 P; 4 P; 5 A; 6 P

`AT 3.4`

2 *Peter ist Popstar. Lies den Text und die Sätze unten. Sind sie richtig oder falsch?* Pupils read the extended text and then decide whether the statements in the grid are true or false. Less able pupils will benefit from the text being read as a whole-class activity.

Answers:

1 richtig; 2 falsch; 3 falsch; 4 richtig; 5 richtig; 6 falsch;
7 falsch; 8 richtig

C 16   **Schreiben**

AT 4.1   **1**   *Was kaufst du und wofür sparst du? Schreib die Wörter richtig auf und finde die passenden Bilder.* Pupils re-order the letters to form the names of the objects and match the names to the pictures. Encourage less able pupils to do the easiest ones first. This should give them confidence to then go on and tackle the trickier examples.

Answers:

1: c, Computer; 2: e, Stereoanlage; 3: j, Jeans;
4: a, Fahrrad; 5: h, Computerspiel; 6: g, Fernseher;
7: i, Kleidung; 8: b, Make-up; 9: f, Süßigkeiten;
10: d, Zeitschriften

AT 4.3   **2a**   *Was machst du heute? Schreib Sätze.* Pupils use the picture prompts to construct sentences about daily routine.

Answers:

a Ich stehe auf und ich frühstücke. b Ich ziehe mich aus und ich gehe ins Bett. c Ich wasche mich und ich ziehe mich an. d Ich frühstücke und ich gehe in die Schule.

AT 4.3   **2b**   *Wie hilfst du zu Hause? Schreib Sätze.* Pupils use the picture prompts to construct sentences about household chores.

Answers:

a Ich räume mein Zimmer auf und ich sauge Staub.
b Ich wasche ab und ich decke den Tisch.
c Ich kaufe ein und ich füttere den Hund und die Katze.
d Ich putze das Badezimmer und ich wasche das Auto.

AT 4.4   **3**   *Du bist dran! Beantworte diese Fragen. Schreib ganze Sätze.* Pupils complete the questionnaire with their own responses about their daily routine, jobs and pocket money. This activity can form part of pupils' written records for continuous assessment purposes.

C 17A   **Grammatik 1**

This copymaster focuses on reflexive verbs and separable verbs.

1a   *Wie schreibt man ,to sunbathe' auf Deutsch?*
1b   *Wie schreibt man ,I sunbathe' auf Deutsch?*
1c   *Schreib Stufen 1a und 1b für die folgenden Verben.* Pupils read the 'Flashback' explanation and then look up the English verbs in their dictionaries to find the German translations, writing the infinitive and the first person singular form. Note that pupils will find more than one translation for several of the verbs, and less able pupils will need a lot of guidance in order to complete this activity. It may be preferable to provide simplified versions of the dictionary entries for less able pupils to use.

Answers:

1a sich sonnen
1b ich sonne mich
1c 1 sich beeilen – ich beeile mich; 2 sich beklagen – ich beklage mich/sich beschweren – ich beschwere mich; 3 (sich) duschen – ich dusche (mich); 4 sich fühlen – ich fühle mich; 5 sich rasieren – ich rasiere mich; 6 sich setzen – ich setze mich

2a   *Was sind die zwei Teile von diesen trennbaren Verben?* Pupils read the 'Flashback' explanation and then separate the separable verbs into prefix and verb.

Answers: auf + stehen; ab + waschen; ein + kaufen

2b   *Schreib Sätze mit den Verben in Übung 2a.* Pupils write sentences with the separable verbs from activity 2a.

2c   *Was sind die Infinitive von diesen Verben und wie heißen sie auf Englisch?* This activity is suitable for more able pupils. Pupils reconstruct the infinitives from the finite forms and look up the English translations in their dictionaries. Accept any correct alternative translations.

Answers:

1 ankommen – to arrive; 2 abfahren – to depart;
3 aufwachen – to wake up; 4 einschlafen – to go to sleep;
5 abtrocknen – to dry (the dishes); 6 zuhören – to listen

C 17B   **Grammatik 2**

This copymaster focuses on the accusative and dative cases.

1   *Füll die Lücken aus.* Pupils read the 'Flashback' and then complete the sentences with the correct (accusative) forms of the definite article.

Answers: 1 den; 2 das; 3 die; 4 die; 5 den

2a   *Füll die Lücken mit meinem, meiner, meinem oder meinen aus.* Pupils read the 'Flashback' and then complete the sentences with the correct (dative) forms of *mein/meine/mein*.

Answers:

1 meinem; 2 meiner; 3 meinen; 4 meinem; 5 meinen

2b   *Du bist dran! Erfinde weitere Beispiele.* Pupils write their own examples using different objects and different family members.

3   *Füll die Lücken aus.* Pupils read the 'Flashback' and then complete the sentences with the correct (accusative) forms of the indefinite article and *mein/meine/mein*.

Answers: 1 meine; 2 eine; 3 ein; 4 meinen; 5 einen

C 18   **Tipp**

1a   *Schreib zwei Listen mit 10 positiven und 10 negativen Adjektiven.* Pupils read the 'Flashback' and then compile their own lists of positive and negative adjectives, using the *Vokabular* at the back of the Students' Book as well as the adjectives presented in the 'Flashback'.

1b *Du bist dran! Schreib Sätze mit positiven und negativen Adjektiven über deine Schule.* Pupils write their own sentences about their school.

2a *Ergänze die Sätze mit den Adjektiven.* Pupils select appropriate adjectives to complete the sentences. They will need to look up *lieb* and *hässlich* in the *Vokabular* at the back of the Students' Book. There is scope for variation in the answers.

2b *Du bist dran! Beschreib einen Freund/eine Freundin.* Pupils describe a friend, using positive and negative adjectives.

3a *Wie hilfst du zu Hause? Wie findest du das alles? Schreib Sätze.* Pupils write about the chores they do and how they feel about them.

3b *Schreib positive und negative Sätze über die Nebenjobs unten.* Pupils write their own responses to the jobs in the pictures.

Einheit 3 Freunde und Familie

National Curriculum

Pages	Objectives	Grammar	Pronunciation, Skill focus	Key language	PoS	AT level
32–33 Die Klassel-Clique	Reading and listening for pleasure Familiarization with themes, structures and language of the unit	–	–	–	–	1.4, 3.2, 3.4
34–35 Wie siehst du aus?	Say what you look like Ask what someone else looks like Say what someone else looks like Talk about your best friend	Possessive adjectives, nominative adjectives with and without endings	–	*Wie siehst du aus?* *Wie sieht er/sie aus?* *Mein bester Freund/Meine beste Freundin ist/heißt …* *Ich habe/Er/Sie hat braune/blaue/grüne Augen.* *Meine/Seine/Ihre Augen sind braun/blau/grün.* *Ich habe/Er/Sie hat blonde/braune/schwarze/rote/lange/kurze/lockige/glatte Haare.* *Meine/Seine/Ihre Haare sind blond/braun/schwarz/rot/lang/kurz/lockig/glatt.* *Ich trage/Er/Sie trägt eine Brille/Ohrringe/einen Ohrring.* *Meine/Seine/Ihre Lieblingsfarbe/Lieblingsgruppe/Lieblingsmusik ist …* *Mein/Sein/Ihr Lieblingsfilm ist …*	1a, 1b, 1c, 2a, 2b, 2c, 2d, 3e, 5a, 5f, 5i	1.3–4, 2.4, 3.3, 4.3–4
36–37 Wie bist du?	Describe your own character Describe someone else's character Explain why you like your best friend Say how you get on with your best friend	*weil* and subordinate word order	–	*Wie bist du?/Wie ist er/sie?* *Ich bin/Er/Sie ist immer/oft/selten/nie nett/lustig/freundlich/unfreundlich/launisch/ungeduldig/sympathisch/schüchtern/lieb/arrogant/gemein/frech.* *Ich mag …, weil er/sie immer/oft/selten/nie … ist.* *Wir verstehen uns sehr gut/immer gut.* *Wir streiten uns nie/selten/manchmal/oft.*	1a, 1b, 1c, 2a, 2b, 2c, 2d, 3e, 5a, 5c, 5f, 5i	1.3–4, 2.3–4, 3.2–3, 4.3–4

Pages	Objectives	Grammar	Pronunciation, Skill focus	Key language	PoS	AT level
38–39 Meine Eltern sind zu streng!	Describe your parents Say how you get on with your parents Say why you argue	–	Expressing opinions Pronunciation of -b, -g, -t	*Meine Eltern sind/Meine Mutter/Mein Vater ist zu/sehr/oft/immer/manchmal/nie streng/lieb/ungeduldig.* *Wir verstehen uns gut/nicht gut, weil er/sie ... ist/sind.* *Wir streiten uns, weil ich zu wenig Taschengeld bekomme/kein eigenes Zimmer habe/nie/selten zu Hause helfe/mein Zimmer aufräume/das Badezimmer putze/den Tisch decke/zu viel fernsehe/Fastfood/Süßigkeiten esse/Zeitschriften/CDs kaufe.*	1a, 1b, 1c, 2a, 2b, 2c, 2d, 2e, 3e, 5a, 5c, 5d, 5f, 5i	1.2, 1.4, 2.3–4, 3.2, 3.4, 4.4
40–41 Ich muss immer zu Hause helfen!	Say what you have to do Say what you're not allowed to do	*müssen* and *dürfen*	Dictionary skills: separable verbs	*Ich muss jeden Tag abwaschen.* *Ich muss um 19 Uhr zu Hause sein.* *Ich muss um 21 Uhr ins Bett gehen.* *Ich muss am Wochenende um 21 Uhr zu Hause sein.* *Ich muss jeden Abend lernen.* *Ich darf nicht fernsehen.* *Ich darf keine Musik im Wohnzimmer hören.* *Ich darf in die Disco/in Konzerte gehen.* *Ich darf keine Freunde nach Hause einladen.* *Ich darf in den Ferien arbeiten.*	1a, 1b, 1c, 2a, 2b, 2c, 2d, 2f, 3d, 3e, 5a, 5c, 5d, 5f, 5i	1.2, 1.4, 2.3–4, 3.2, 4.4
42–43 Thema im Fokus	Encourage reading for pleasure Use language from Unit 3 creatively Encourage independent, pair- and groupwork	–	–	–	1c, 2c, 2e, 2f, 2i, 3d, 3e, 5a, 5c, 5d, 5e, 5f, 5i	1.3, 2.3–4, 3.4, 4.2–4

3 Freunde und Familie

Aims of the unit

- To be able to talk about someone's appearance
- To be able to talk about someone's character and preferences
- To be able to talk about your parents and how you get on with them
- To be able to talk about things you have to do and things you are not allowed to do

Die Klasse!-Clique
pages 32–33

Materials

- Students' Book pages 32–33
- Cassette 1 side B
- Workbook page 24

For general advice on exploiting the photo story, see pages 10–11 of the introduction to this book. In this episode it is still Saturday, and Jasmin is giving Atalay an enthusiastic account of her new e-mail penfriend Sascha. Sven is in low spirits, as he can't go to the disco with Jasmin and the others: his father is so strict that he won't allow Sven out after 8 p.m. In fact, things just aren't going Sven's way. Later that day, his father informs him that the family is moving back to Chemnitz in April – and Sven has to go with them. Sven is horrified.

AT 3.2 **1** *Vor dem Lesen: Was meinst du – was passt? Finde die passenden Adjektive.* In this pre-reading activity, pupils match the German adjectives to their English translations. Most of the words will be new to the pupils. Copy the activity onto the board/OHT and complete it with the whole class, starting with the cognate *blond* and with *kurz*, which pupils should know. Explain that for the other words they will have to look for clues, but fortunately, many German words are similar to English ones with similar meanings. For example, *altmodisch* begins with *alt*: can they find a match for this in the English column? For *gemein*, they could try taking off the *ge-*: can they see an English word which looks similar? *Streng* looks like 'strong': which word in the English column is closest to this in meaning? *Sympathisch* looks like 'sympathetic': what sort of person is sympathetic? *Ungeduldig* starts with the negative *un-*: can they find an English word with a negative prefix?

Answers:

1 c; 2 e; 3 f; 4 b; 5 g; 6 a; 7 d

 2 *Hör gut zu und lies mit. Wie heißt das auf Deutsch?*
AT 1.4
AT 3.4 Pupils listen to the recording and follow the text in their books. (Encourage them to listen/look out for the words from activity 1.) They then match the English sentences to their German equivalents in the text. The sentences contain new vocabulary: *aussehen, Augen, sich streiten, Heimat, mitkommen*; however, each sentence contains enough familiar words for pupils to be able to work out the answers by a process of elimination.

Having completed the activity, you could recap on the grammar of Unit 2 by asking pupils to find examples of separable verbs and reflexive verbs in the photo story. Answers: separable verbs: *aussehen, mitkommen, fernsehen*; reflexive verb: *sich streiten*. Ask pupils what other verbs they can remember in either of these categories.

Answers:

1 Wie sieht er aus? 2 Seine Augen sind blau. 3 Wir streiten uns immer. 4 Ich darf nicht fernsehen.
5 Chemnitz ist unsere Heimat. 6 Du kommst mit.

Transcript   p 33, activity 2

- Sascha ist super – er ist lustig und nett und er ist sehr sympathisch!
- Hast du ein Foto von Sascha?
- Nein, leider nicht.
- Wie sieht er aus – was meinst du?
- Also: Seine Augen sind blau und er hat kurze blonde Haare ...

- Hallo, Sven! Kommst du heute Abend in die Disco?
- Nein, mein Vater ist total altmodisch! Er ist zu streng: Ich muss jeden Abend um 20 Uhr zu Hause sein – wir streiten uns immer! Ich muss immer zu Hause helfen und ich darf nicht fernsehen! Und er ist immer ungeduldig! Das finde ich gemein!

Später zu Hause ...

- Sven, ich habe ein Haus in Chemnitz gekauft – wir gehen wieder nach Chemnitz!
- Was?? Wann? Nein!
- Sven! Chemnitz ist unsere Heimat!
- Aber ich wohne gern in Wesel! Alle meine Freunde wohnen hier!
- Du hast aber auch Freunde in Chemnitz, Sven!
- Wir fahren im April – und du kommst mit!

AT 3.4 **3** *Finde die richtige Reihenfolge für die Geschichte.* Pupils put the sentences into the correct order to construct a summary in German of the photo story. Ask pupils to tell you in German what is happening in each of the photos – who is talking to whom about what. T: *Bild eins. Wer ist das? Was sagen sie?*, etc. Then pupils could complete the activity individually or in pairs before the answers are checked with the whole class.

Now ask pupils to tell you in English what the unit is going to be about, judging by the photo story. Answers: friends and family – what they look like and their personalities; things you have to do/are not allowed to do at home.

Answers: e, b, d, c, f, a

Viel Spaß!

Mein bester Freund. The main aim is listening for pleasure, but the song also introduces vocabulary and structures for describing appearance and personality.

For general advice on exploiting the songs in *Klasse! 2*, see page 7 of the introduction to this book.

Transcript   p 33, Viel Spaß!

Lukas ist mein bester Freund
Bester Freund, bester Freund
Lukas ist der beste Freund
Der beste Freund der Welt

Er hat blaue Augen
Er hat blaue Augen
Er hat blaue Augen
Lukas ist so lieb

Refrain

Er hat rote Haare
Er hat rote Haare
Er hat rote Haare
Lukas ist so lieb

Refrain

Er trägt eine Brille
Er trägt eine Brille
Er trägt eine Brille
Lukas ist so lieb

Refrain

Er ist immer lustig
Er ist immer lustig
Er ist immer lustig
Lukas ist so lieb

Refrain

WB A Workbook activity A could be used at this point for exploitation of the song text (consolidation of expressions for describing appearance and personality).

For the next lesson

Ask pupils to bring in photos of themselves, their friends, their families, their favourite pop stars and groups, etc. These can be used as additional/alternative visual stimuli for speaking and writing activities throughout this unit.

Wie siehst du aus?
pages 34–35

Objectives

- Say what you look like
- Ask what someone else looks like
- Say what someone else looks like
- Talk about your best friend

Key language

Wie siehst du aus?
Wie sieht er/sie aus?
Mein bester Freund/Meine beste Freundin ist/heißt …
Ich habe/Er/Sie hat braune/blaue/grüne Augen.
Meine/Seine/Ihre Augen sind braun/blau/grün.
Ich habe/Er/Sie hat blonde/braune/schwarze/rote/lange/kurze/lockige/glatte

Haare.
Meine/Seine/Ihre Haare sind blond/braun/schwarz/rot/lang/kurz/lockig/glatt.
Ich trage/Er/Sie trägt eine Brille/Ohrringe/einen Ohrring.
Meine/Seine/Ihre Lieblingsfarbe/Lieblingsgruppe/Lieblingsmusik ist …
Mein/Sein/Ihr Lieblingsfilm ist …

National Curriculum PoS

statements 1a, 1b, 1c, 2a, 2b, 2c, 2d, 3e, 5a, 5f, 5i

Materials

- Students' Book pages 34–35
- Cassette 1 side B
- Workbook pages 25–28
- Copymasters 19, 22, 23, 25, 26

C 19 ### Preparatory work

Use the pictures from copymaster 19 copied onto an OHT or as flashcards to introduce language describing people's appearance: *Er/Sie hat lange/kurze/glatte/lockige Haare. Er/Sie trägt eine Brille/Ohrringe.* (For general advice on using copymaster visuals, see page 12 of the introduction to this book.) Once you have familiarized pupils with this vocabulary, you could ask questions with *oder* about photos of people, also recycling the basic expressions for describing people from *Klasse! 1* pp. 28–29: T: *Wie ist sie? Ist sie jung oder alt? Hat sie braune Haare oder hat sie blonde Haare?*, etc.

AT 1.3
AT 3.3
1 *Hör gut zu und lies mit.* Pupils listen to the recording and follow the text in the book.

Transcript   p 34, activity 1

– Ich heiße Eva. Ich habe lange lockige Haare und meine Augen sind blau. Ich trage Ohrringe.
Das ist Mark. Seine Haare sind schwarz und kurz und er hat braune Augen.
Und das ist Ina. Sie hat glatte rote Haare. Ihre Augen sind grün und sie trägt eine Brille.

C 22 Activity 1 on copymaster 22 (listening) could be used for consolidation of descriptions at this point.

AT 2.4
AT 1.4
2 *Klassen-Ratespiel: A beschreibt einen Schüler/eine Schülerin in der Klasse, die Klasse rät.* One pupil chooses another pupil in the class and describes him or her. The rest of the class tries to guess who is being described. The pupil who guesses correctly is the next one to give a description. In preparation for this activity, elicit eye and hair colours and hairstyles from the class and write these up on the board/OHT.

C 23 Activity 1 on copymaster 23 could be used here for additional speaking practice of descriptions.

C 25 Activity 1 on copymaster 25 could be used here for additional writing practice of descriptions.

WB B, C Workbook activities B and C could be used at this point to consolidate and reinforce structures and vocabulary for describing appearance (using adjectives both as attribute and as predicate).

AT 1.4

3a *Hör gut zu. Silke macht einen Wettbewerb. Kopiere den Steckbrief zweimal und schreib Antworten für Silke und Viola.* Pupils copy the 'identity card' twice and then listen to the recording before filling in the details for Silke and Viola. After the first playing, you could draw pupils' attention to the phrase *mein bester Freund/meine beste Freundin* and elicit from them that *Lieblings-* means 'favourite' (*Klasse! 1* p.68: *Lieblingsessen*; p.91: *Lieblingshobby*). Point out to pupils that in the expression *meine Lieblingsfarbe ist …*, the colour should have a capital letter, because it is used as a noun.

Answers:

Name:	Silke
Augen:	braun
Haare:	kurz, braun
Ich trage/sie trägt:	einen Ohrring
Lieblingsfarbe:	Gelb
Lieblingsgruppe:	‚Die Teenies'
Lieblingsfilm:	‚Die Skateboarders'
Name:	Viola
Augen:	blau
Haare:	lang, rot
Ich trage/sie trägt:	eine Brille
Lieblingsfarbe:	Schwarz
Lieblingsgruppe:	‚Sascha'
Lieblingsfilm:	‚Girlpower'

Transcript   p 34, activity 3a

– Oh, was ist das denn? „Macht mit beim Jugendmagazin-Wettbewerb: ‚Meine beste Freundin/mein bester Freund'. Es ist ganz einfach: beantwortet unsere Fragen – die Sieger gewinnen tolle Preise!" He, super! Ich mache mit – für Viola und mich!

– Also: Wie heißt du?
– Silke Kaiser.

– Wie heißt dein bester Freund oder deine beste Freundin?
– Meine beste Freundin heißt Viola – Viola Berger.

– Wie siehst du aus?
– Also: ich habe braune Augen und meine Haare sind kurz und braun. Und ich trage einen Ohrring.

– Wie sieht deine beste Freundin aus?
– Viola hat lange rote Haare und ihre Augen sind blau. Sie trägt eine Brille.

– Was ist deine Lieblingsfarbe?
– Gelb – meine Lieblingsfarbe ist Gelb.

– Was ist ihre Lieblingsfarbe?
– Ihre Lieblingsfarbe ist Rot … ach nein, ihre Lieblingsfarbe ist Schwarz.

– Also, weiter … Was ist deine Lieblingsgruppe?
– Also, meine Lieblingsgruppe sind ‚Die Teenies'!

– Und was ist ihre Lieblingsgruppe?
– Das ist einfach – ihre Lieblingsgruppe ist ‚Sascha'.

– Okay … Was ist dein Lieblingsfilm?
– Mein Lieblingsfilm ist ‚Die Skateboarders'.

– Und was ist ihr Lieblingsfilm?
– Ihr Lieblingsfilm ist ‚Girlpower'.

AT 4.3

3b *Du bist dran! Schreib einen Steckbrief für dich.* Pupils fill out an 'identity card' for themselves on the model of those in activity 3a. This could be completed on computer or by copying the headings into exercise books.

Follow-up activity. Pupils swap books and read out each other's identity cards, omitting the names, and the rest of the class tries to guess the identity of the person.

AT 2.4

3c *„Wie siehst du aus? Was ist dein(e) Lieblings … ?" A fragt, B antwortet.* Pupils work together in pairs, taking it in turns to ask each other about their appearance and preferences, using the headings from the 'identity cards'.

In preparation for this activity, you could look at the speech bubbles in activity 1 again with the pupils. Ask them to find adjectives, or just colours. Answers: *lange, lockige, blau, schwarz, kurz, braune, glatte, rote, grün*. Write the words up on the board/OHT, putting those with endings in one list and those without in another. Ask pupils what they notice about the two lists, aiming to elicit that the words in one list end in *-e*. Now write up a pair of example sentences, e.g. *Meine Augen sind blau. Ich habe blaue Augen.* Rub out *blau* and *blaue* and write *braun* and *braune* on another part of the board; elicit from the pupils which word should go in which gap. T: *Braun oder braune? Was meint ihr?* Repeat the process with *grün/grüne*, continuing with other colours until pupils can see the pattern.

WB D

Workbook activity D could be used at this point for consolidation of the vocabulary for physical descriptions and for favourites.

WB E

Workbook activity E is a creative writing activity using a photo as stimulus for a description, and could also be used at this point.

AT 4.3

Noch mal! Kopiere den Steckbrief von Übung 3a. Füll den Steckbrief aus – für deinen besten Freund/deine beste Freundin. Pupils copy the 'identity card' headings from activity 3a and use them to describe their best friend (real or imaginary).

C 25

Activity 2 on copymaster 25 (writing) offers a different format for this activity.

AT 4.4

Extra! Gedicht-Wettbewerb: ‚Mein bester Freund/meine beste Freundin'. Pupils write a poem about their best friend (real or imaginary). The term 'poem' can be interpreted very loosely for this activity. Pupils may wish to use additional vocabulary. Remind them that they can use vocabulary from Unit 2 of *Klasse! 1* (p. 29). The poems could be used for a classroom display, together with photos, and pupils could vote for the best/funniest/strangest poem.

Grammatik im Fokus

Possessivpronomen. This section focuses on possessive adjectives and their endings in the nominative case. Select three objects in the class which are respectively masculine, feminine and neuter in German, e.g. *Kuli, Tasche, Heft*. Show them to the class and write up *der Kuli, die Tasche, das Heft*. Now elicit from the class the indefinite article. T: *Kuli – ein oder eine?*, etc. Rub out *der, die, das* and insert *ein, eine, ein* as you go. Now demonstrate 'my pen', etc. by clutching the item possessively and elicit the appropriate possessive adjective. T: *Kuli – mein oder meine?*, etc. To give the plural, write *meine Sachen*. Repeat with the other possessive adjectives until you are sure that pupils understand the pattern.

4 *Finde die passenden Wörter.* Pupils select the correct possessive adjective to complete each sentence. Less able pupils may need to be reminded that they need to know the gender of the noun before they can select the correct possessive adjective.

Answers:

1 dein; 2 Mein; 3 Seine; 4 Mein; 5 ihre; 6 Ihre; 7 dein; 8 ihr

C 26 Activity 1 on copymaster 26 offers consolidation of possessive adjectives and could be used at this point.

T 4.4 **5a** *Beschreib Tom und Tina.* Pupils write short paragraphs describing Tom and Tina. Draw their attention to the *Hilfe* box, which contains structures they can use to complete this activity.

Suggested answers:

Mein bester Freund heißt Tom. Seine Haare sind kurz, blond und glatt. Seine Augen sind braun. Seine Lieblingsfarbe ist Grün. Seine Lieblingsgruppe ist ‚Sascha‘.

Meine beste Freundin heißt Tina. Ihre Haare sind lang, rot und lockig. Ihre Augen sind blau. Ihre Lieblingsfarbe ist Schwarz. Ihr Lieblingsfilm ist ‚Alien‘.

AT 4.4 **5b** *Du bist dran! Schreib eine Beschreibung für dich.* Using their descriptions of Tom and Tina as models, pupils write about themselves. The activity could be completed on computer with scanned photos for illustration. To make a more substantial piece of work, pupils could also write about their best friend. Activity 8 on page 37 could be added to the piece later. Alternatively, Workbook activity G (see below) could be used as a framework for this piece of work.

Grammatik im Fokus

Adjektive. This section focuses on adjectives with and without endings, a subject you may have broached before activity 3c above. Look at the two examples with the class and explain, or if possible elicit from the class, that when the adjective comes before a plural noun, it takes the ending *-e*; when it comes after the noun, it has no ending.

6 *Schreib neue Sätze mit Er/sie hat ...* Pupils rewrite the sentences with the adjectives as attribute rather than predicate, requiring them to add an adjective ending (*-e* in all instances).

Answers:

1 Sie hat rote Haare. 2 Er hat lange Haare. 3 Sie hat grüne Augen. 4 Er hat kurze Haare. 5 Sie hat braune Augen. 6 Er hat schwarze Haare.

C 26 Activity 2 on copymaster 26 could be used here for consolidation of adjective endings.

7 *Du bist dran! Wie siehst du aus? Kopiere den Text und füll die Lücken aus.* Pupils write a short physical description of themselves using the text provided as a template.

Follow-up activity. Pupils could construct a ‘wanted poster’, including either a drawing or an ‘identikit’ photo put together from features cut out of magazine photos, with a description of the person below.

WB F Workbook activity F could be used as homework to reinforce the new language introduced on this spread.

WB G Workbook activity G could be used as homework to form part of pupils’ written records for continuous assessment purposes.

Wie bist du?
pages 36–37

Objectives
- Describe your own character
- Describe someone else’s character
- Explain why you like your best friend
- Say how you get on with your best friend

Key language
Wie bist du?/Wie ist er/sie?
Ich bin/Er/Sie ist immer/oft/selten/nie nett/lustig/freundlich/unfreundlich/launisch/ungeduldig/sympathisch/ schüchtern/lieb/arrogant/gemein/frech.
Ich mag ... , weil er/sie immer/oft/selten/nie ... ist.
Wir verstehen uns sehr gut/immer gut.
Wir streiten uns nie/selten/manchmal/oft.

National Curriculum PoS
statements 1a, 1b, 1c, 2a, 2b, 2c, 2d, 3e, 5a, 5c, 5f, 5i

Materials
- Students’ Book pages 36–37
- Cassette 1 side B
- Workbook pages 28–31
- Copymasters 20, 22, 26

C 20 ### Preparatory work

Use the pictures from copymaster 20 copied onto an OHT or as flashcards to introduce language describing people’s character: *Er/Sie ist nett/lustig/freundlich/ launisch*, etc. (For general advice on using copymaster visuals, see page 12 of the introduction to this book.)

AT 3.2 **1** *Lies die Adjektive. Was ist positiv und was ist negativ? Schreib zwei Listen. (Du brauchst Hilfe? Schau im Wörterbuch nach.)* Pupils sort the adjectives into positive and negative attributes. If they are still uncertain of the precise meanings of some words, encourage them to look up the words in a dictionary or in the *Vokabular* at the back of the Students’ Book.

Answers:

Positive: freundlich, lieb, lustig, nett, sympathisch
Negative: arrogant, frech, gemein, launisch, schüchtern, unfreundlich, ungeduldig

Follow-up activity. You could play an acting game to consolidate the new vocabulary. T: *Wie bin ich?* (acting in a shy way) P1: *Unfreundlich?* T: *Nein.* P2: *Schüchtern?* T: *Richtig! Du bist dran!,* etc.

WB H Workbook activity H could be used at this point to consolidate the new vocabulary and practise dictionary skills.

AT 1.4 **2** *Jasmin, Annika, Atalay und Sven machen ein Quiz: ‚Wie bist du?' Wie sind sie (✔)? Wie sind sie nicht (✗)? Hör gut zu und mach Notizen.* Pupils listen to the recording and decide which adjectives apply to which of the characters from the *Klasse!-Clique.* Play the recording at least three times. On the second playing, pupils should write down the adjectives they hear next to the names of the characters. On the third playing, they should decide whether these adjectives are said to apply (✔) or not to apply (✗) to the character.

Answers:

Jasmin:	gemein ✗		Atalay:	sympathisch ✔
	launisch ✔			gemein ✗
	ungeduldig ✔			ungeduldig ✗
Annika:	lustig ✔		Sven:	lustig ✔
	schüchtern ✔			launisch ✗
	arrogant ✗			arrogant ✗

Transcript   p 36, activity 2

– Hallo!
– Jasmin! Wir machen ein Quiz – machst du mit?
– Ja, okay!
– Also, es geht los – hier ist die Frage Nummer eins: Wie bist du?
– Puuh, das ist schwer ... Also, ich bin nicht gemein! Ich bin manchmal launisch ... ja, und ich bin ungeduldig!
– Jasmin ... nicht gemein ... manchmal launisch ... und ungeduldig ... Und du, Annika? Wie bist du?
– Hmm ... ich bin immer lustig – aber ich bin auch schüchtern. Aber ich bin nicht arrogant.
– Annika: lustig ... schüchtern ... nicht arrogant ... Und wie bist du, Atalay?
– Na ja, Jasmin und Annika sagen: Ich bin sympathisch ... ja, ich bin sympathisch und ich bin nicht gemein. Und ich bin nicht ungeduldig.
– Okay, Atalay: sympathisch ... nicht gemein ... und nicht ungeduldig. So, du bist dran, Sven: Wie bist du?
– Also, wie bin ich? Ich bin lustig. Und wie bin ich nicht? Ich bin nicht launisch – und ich bin nicht arrogant!
– ... lustig ... nicht launisch ... nicht arrogant ... Okay, hier ist die Frage Nummer zwei ...

C 22 Activity 2 on copymaster 22 (listening) could be used here for further practice of adjectives describing character.

AT 2.4 **3** *Wie bist du (nicht)? Wie ist dein Partner/deine Partnerin (nicht)? Macht Dialoge.* Pupils work in pairs to interview each other about their personal attributes,

both positive and negative. Remind pupils of the adverbs of frequency *immer, oft, manchmal, selten* and *nie* from Unit 2, which they can use for this activity.

WB I Workbook activity I could be used at this point as a listening extension activity practising the adverbs of frequency with personal attributes.

WB J Workbook activity J could be used after activity I as writing and speaking extension material.

In Klasse! 1, (p. 29) pupils learned adjectives to describe personal attributes: *intelligent, ernst, faul, fleißig, sportlich, leise, laut, musikalisch.* You could reactivate some of this vocabulary for incorporation into the *Noch mal!* and *Extra!* activities below.

AT 2.3 *Noch mal! Gedächtnisspiel: Wie bist du?* Pupils work together in groups. Pupil A gives one adjective to describe him/herself, e.g. *Ich bin launisch.* Pupil B repeats what pupil A said and adds another adjective, e.g. *Ich bin launisch und nett,* and so on round the group. Any pupil who forgets an adjective, hesitates for too long or gets the order wrong loses a point, and the game starts again. Less able pupils may have difficulty in remembering sequences, but can participate in this game if permitted to write down the adjectives or to use adjectives written on card.

Follow-up activity. The cartoons from copymaster 20 could be used for a variation on this game, for use with groups of two to four pupils: the pictures are copied onto card or paper (one set for each group) and cut out to make cards. Each group shuffles its cards and lays them face down on the table. The first player turns over the top card and says the sentence appropriate to that card, e.g. *Ich bin sympathisch.* The next player turns over the next card and adds the appropriate adjective, e.g. *Ich bin sympathisch und freundlich.* If the player gets the sentence right, he/she keeps the card; if not, the card is put back on the bottom of the pile and the next player plays. The game ends when all the cards are taken, or nobody can remember the correct order. The winner is the player with the most cards.

AT 4.3 *Extra! Schreib ein ‚Adjektiv-ABC'. Schreib dann Sätze – für deine Freunde, Familie, Haustiere usw. (Du brauchst Hilfe? Schau im Wörterbuch nach.)* Pupils compile an alphabetical list of adjectives and use each to write a sentence about friends, family members or pets. To make this a shorter task, you may wish to assign a sequence of letters to each pupil (missing out difficult letters such as Q, X and Y), maybe asking pupils to illustrate their sentences. This could also be done as a group activity. Pupils can start off by using the *Vokabular* at the back of the Students' Book, but encourage them to use dictionaries to get a greater variety of adjectives. The ‘Adjektiv-ABCs' could be compiled into a poster to make a classroom display.

4 *Hör gut zu und lies mit.* Pupils listen to the recording and follow the text in the book. This short recording introduces the use of *weil* and subordinate clause word order.

AT 1.3
AT 3.3

> **Transcript** p 37, activity 4
>
> – Ich mag Ina, weil sie immer lustig ist! Wir verstehen uns sehr gut.
> – Und ich mag Susi, weil sie nie launisch ist! Wir streiten uns nie.

Grammatik im Fokus

weil. This section focuses on the conjunction *weil* and subordinate clause word order. Once you have read through the explanation with the class, you could try the following activity to consolidate this unfamiliar sentence structure.

Write each word of the following pair of sentences in large letters on a separate sheet of paper: *Ich mag Doro. Sie ist sehr nett.* The two full stops should also be on separate sheets of paper. Hand out one word per pupil and ask them to stand up in front of the class, holding their words in front of them. Write a comma and *weil* on two more sheets of paper. Hand these to two other pupils. Then ask the remaining pupils in the class to call out instructions in German (*Nach rechts! Nach links! Halt!*) to direct these two pupils to their correct places, making any other changes which are necessary (i.e. 'first full stop' leaves the line (*Setz dich!*), '*ist*' goes to the end (*Ans Ende!*) just before 'second full stop'. When they have completed their task, the pupils in the line return to their seats and hand their sheets of paper to other pupils, who now stand up and have to be directed to their correct places (first for the two simple sentences, then for the complex sentence) by the pupils who are sitting.

An alternative approach would be for pupils to create their own individual sentence/word chains, which they can cut up and then hand to another pupil to reconstruct. For less able pupils, you may wish to put jumbled sentences into the computer for them to rearrange.

5 *Oliver mag Paula. Füll die Lücken aus.* Pupils complete the subordinate clauses with the words in the box.

Answers:

1 ist; 2 manchmal; 3 sie; 4 launisch/arrogant; 5 ist; 6 arrogant/launisch

C 26 Activity 3 on copymaster 26 could be used at this point for consolidation of *weil* + subordinate clause.

6 *Lies Ankes Tagebuch. Schreib dann Sätze für sie mit Ich mag ..., weil ...* Pupils write complex sentences with *ich mag* and *weil*, based on the simple sentences given. Draw pupils' attention to the *Hilfe* box and remind them of the word order of the subordinate clause.

Answers:

1 Ich mag Ellen, weil sie nie frech ist.
2 Ich mag Daniel, weil er immer lieb ist.
3 Ich mag Christina, weil sie oft lustig ist.
4 Ich mag Tom, weil er immer nett ist.
5 Ich mag Sandra, weil sie selten unfreundlich ist.
6 Ich mag Markus, weil er nie gemein ist.

7 *„Ich mag ..., weil ...". Macht Dialoge mit den Informationen unten.* Pupils work together in pairs to create dialogues using the prompts. To help less able pupils, you could write up the structure on the board/OHT: *Ich mag [Name], weil er/sie (nicht) [Adjektiv] ist.*

AT 4.4 **8** *Beschreib deinen besten Freund/deine beste Freundin. Schreib Sätze mit Ich mag ..., weil ...* Pupils write about their own best friend (real or imaginary). Encourage them to think of several appropriate adjectives and write several sentences. The description can be humorous, and positive or negative.

Follow-up activity. Pupils could invent characters for a soap opera, giving details such as physical appearance, character, favourites and who likes/doesn't like whom. The 'cast' could be illustrated with photos taken from magazines – or with the photos of pupils, each of whom takes on a role in the soap.

WB K Workbook activity K could be used as homework to consolidate the word order of the subordinate clause after *weil*.

WB L Workbook activity L could be used as writing and speaking extension material on the topics covered in this spread.

Meine Eltern sind zu streng!
pages 38–39

Objectives

- Describe your parents
- Say how you get on with your parents
- Say why you argue

Key language

Meine Eltern sind/Meine Mutter/Mein Vater ist ... zu/sehr/oft/immer/manchmal/nie streng/lieb/ungeduldig. Wir verstehen uns gut/nicht gut, weil er/sie ... ist/sind. Wir streiten uns, weil ich zu wenig Taschengeld bekomme/kein eigenes Zimmer habe/nie/selten zu Hause helfe/mein Zimmer aufräume/das Badezimmer putze/den Tisch decke/zu viel fernsehe/Fastfood/Süßigkeiten esse/Zeitschriften/CDs kaufe.

National Curriculum PoS

statements 1a, 1b, 1c, 2a, 2b, 2c, 2d, 2e, 3e, 5a, 5c, 5d, 5f, 5i

Materials

- Students' Book pages 38–39
- Cassette 1 side B
- Workbook pages 31–32
- Copymaster 27

AT 3.4 **1a** *Lies die Briefe.* Pupils read the three letters to agony aunt Gaby. You could ask pupils to identify the adjectives contained in each letter and list each adjective with its English translation, or just categorize each as positive or negative.

AT 3.4 **1b** *Wer sagt ... ?* Pupils answer the comprehension questions, each of which summarizes the content of one of the letters. They will have the opportunity to check and correct their own answers when they do activity 1c.

Answers: 1 Jan; 2 Nadine; 3 Anne

AT 1.4 **1c** *Ist alles richtig? Hör gut zu.* Pupils listen to the recording and compare it with their answers to activity 1b. The sense of the recording is the same as that of the letters in 1a, but the speakers use sentences with *weil*.

Transcript   p 38, activity 1c

– Ich heiße Anne, und ich bin 15. Also, ich mag meine Eltern, ja. Aber wir verstehen uns nicht gut, weil mein Vater zu streng und selten freundlich ist. Und meine Mutter? Na ja, wir verstehen uns auch nicht gut, weil sie ungeduldig ist.

– Ich bin Jan, und ich bin 14 Jahre alt. Meine Eltern? Also, wir verstehen uns sehr gut, weil sie sehr lustig sind. Meine Mutter ist super, finde ich. Wir verstehen uns gut, weil sie immer freundlich ist. Und mein Vater? Wir verstehen uns auch gut, weil er nicht altmodisch ist!

– Ich heiße Nadine. Ich bin 14 Jahre alt. Meine Eltern und ich? Also, sie sind sehr nett. Aber wir verstehen uns nicht so gut, weil sie nicht tolerant sind. Und ich finde, mein Vater ist streng – ja, er ist manchmal streng. Aber meine Mutter und ich – wir verstehen uns gut, weil sie sehr lieb ist.

WB M Workbook activity M could be used at this point to provide additional listening practice.

AT 2.4 **2a** *Wie sind deine Eltern? Wie ist dein Vater/deine Mutter? Macht Dialoge.* Pupils work together in pairs to interview each other about their parents. Any male or female relative could be substituted if necessary.

AT 4.4 **2b** *Schreib einen Brief über deine Eltern. Benutze die Hilfe-Wörter rechts.* Pupils write letters using the ones in activity 1a as models. Draw pupils' attention to the *Hilfe* box. Encourage pupils to use *weil* at least once in their letters, as well as the other structures from the *Hilfe* box, and remind them to be tactful. Again, pupils could choose any relatives for this task.

Tipp

Deine Meinung sagen – mit Takt! This section focuses on register – specifically, on appropriate choice of words when criticizing someone. You could ask pupils for further examples of rude personal remarks and discuss moderate, tactful alternatives. You could look again at the letters in activity 1a and discuss with pupils whether Anne's and Nadine's letters are tactful or not, pointing out that it is more tactful to say *Das finde ich gemein/nicht nett* than *Mein Vater/Meine Mutter ist gemein/nicht nett*. *Manchmal* can also soften harsh criticism.

C 27 Activity 1 on copymaster 27 could be used in conjunction with the *Tipp* panel above.

Gut gesagt!

-b, -g, -t. This section focuses on the correct pronunciation of consonants in final position.

3a *Hör gut zu, lies mit und wiederhole.* Pupils listen to the recording and follow the text in their books, before repeating what they hear. Point out that *-b* sounds more like <p> than <b>, *-g* sounds more like <k> or <ç> than <g> (except in the combination *-ng*, pronounced <ŋ>). Encourage pupils to pronounce *-t* clearly – it is never swallowed or turned into a glottal stop as in some English accents.

Transcript   p 38, activity 3a

– lieb   gelb   halb
– streng   ungeduldig   lustig   jung
– nett   tolerant   alt   intelligent   laut

3b *Hör gut zu, lies mit und wiederhole.* Pupils listen to the recording and follow the text in their books, before repeating what they hear. This can also be done as a whole-class chanting exercise.

Transcript   p 38, activity 3b

Meine Familie ist nett und laut:
Vati ist lustig und jung,
Mutti ist tolerant und intelligent
Und mein Fisch ist lieb und gelb!

AT 3.2 **4a** *Finde die passenden Sätze unten für die Bilder.* Pupils match the sentences to the pictures. This activity brings in language from Unit 2 (household chores and adverbs of frequency; what pupils buy with their pocket money) and combines it with the current topic of character and the structure *weil* + subordinate clause. Pupils will have the opportunity to check and correct their own answers when they do activity 4b.

Answers: 1 b; 2 a; 3 h; 4 d; 5 g; 6 c; 7 f; 8 e

AT 1.2 **4b** *Ist alles richtig? Hör gut zu.* Pupils listen to the recording to check their own answers to activity 4a. For less able pupils, it would also be beneficial to write the correct version on the board/OHT.

Transcript   p 39, activity 4b

1 – Wir streiten uns, weil ich kein Taschengeld bekomme.
2 – Wir streiten uns, weil ich kein eigenes Zimmer habe.
3 – Wir streiten uns, weil ich nie mein Zimmer aufräume.
4 – Wir streiten uns, weil ich nie das Badezimmer putze.
5 – Wir streiten uns, weil ich selten den Tisch decke.
6 – Wir streiten uns, weil ich zu viel fernsehe.
7 – Wir streiten uns, weil ich zu viele CDs kaufe.
8 – Wir streiten uns, weil ich zu viele Süßigkeiten esse.

AT 2.3 **4c** *A wählt einen Satz, B antwortet mit Wir streiten uns, weil … Dann ist B dran.* Pupils work together in pairs. Pupil A makes a statement based on the sentences in activity 4a. Pupil B responds by transforming the sentence into one with *weil*. Both pupils are likely to find this quite a challenging activity to complete verbally. You may wish pupils to prepare the sentences derived from 4a in advance and write them down. Less able pupils could then do the activity with their books open, while more able pupils could do the activity with their books closed.

BN Workbook activity N could be used at this point for consolidation of the vocabulary and structures in activity 4.

3.4 **5a** *Lies Tanjas Brief und die Sätze unten. Sind die Sätze richtig oder falsch?* Pupils read Tanja's letter and decide whether the statements below it are true or false.

Answers:

1 richtig; 2 falsch; 3 falsch; 4 falsch; 5 falsch; 6 richtig

4.4 **5b** *Du bist dran! „Meine Eltern und ich – wir streiten uns, weil ..." Schreib einen Brief an ‚Liebe Gaby'.* Pupils write a letter to the agony aunt, using the letter in activity 5a as a model. This would be a good opportunity to remind pupils of the advice about adapting texts (Unit 1, p. 12). Less able pupils could copy and colour-code Tanja's letter as described in Unit 1 (green = adapt; orange = omit) before writing their own version.

WB O Workbook activity O provides an alternative framework for a writing activity along similar lines to activity 5b above. This activity can form part of pupils' written records for continuous assessment purposes.

Ich muss immer zu Hause helfen! ■
pages 40–41

Objectives

- Say what you have to do
- Say what you're not allowed to do

Key language

Ich muss jeden Tag abwaschen.
Ich muss um 19 Uhr zu Hause sein.
Ich muss um 21 Uhr ins Bett gehen.
Ich muss am Wochenende um 21 Uhr zu Hause sein.
Ich muss jeden Abend lernen.
Ich darf nicht fernsehen.
Ich darf keine Musik im Wohnzimmer hören.
Ich darf in die Disco/in Konzerte gehen.
Ich darf keine Freunde nach Hause einladen.
Ich darf in den Ferien arbeiten.

National Curriculum PoS

statements 1a, 1b, 1c, 2a, 2b, 2c, 2d, 2f, 3d, 3e, 5a, 5c, 5d, 5f, 5i

Materials

- Students' Book pages 40–41
- Cassette 1 side B
- Workbook pages 32–33
- Copymasters 22, 23, 24, 25, 26, 27
- Dictionaries

Preparatory work

Demonstrate the meaning of *ich muss* and *ich darf nicht* by inventing a daily routine for yourself. Write on the board, e.g. *8 Uhr: in die Schule gehen – nicht zu Hause bleiben! 12.30 Uhr: zu Mittag essen – keine Pizza!*, etc. Now talk about your daily routine using *ich muss* and *ich darf nicht*. T: *Es ist acht Uhr. Ich muss in die Schule gehen. Ich darf nicht zu Hause bleiben. Es ist halb eins. Ich muss zu Mittag essen. Ich darf keine Pizza essen! Ich muss Salat essen*, etc. Now ask the class what they think *ich muss* and *ich darf nicht* mean in English, illustrating the meaning, e.g. with a wagging finger for *ich muss* and by shaking your head for *ich darf nicht*.

AT 1.2 **AT 3.2** **1** *Oliver schreibt einen Brief an ‚Liebe Gaby'. Hör gut zu und lies mit.* Pupils listen to the recording and follow the text in their books. Note that *Freunde nach Hause einladen* will be unfamiliar to pupils; *in die Disco gehen* is also new, but should not present any problems. Check that pupils recognize *fernsehen* as *ich sehe fern*.

> **Transcript** p 40, activity 1
>
> Liebe Gaby, meine Eltern sind zu streng!
> Ich muss immer zu Hause helfen.
> Ich muss um 19 Uhr zu Hause sein.
> Ich muss jeden Abend lernen.
> Ich darf nicht fernsehen.
> Ich darf nicht in die Disco gehen.
> Ich darf keine Freunde nach Hause einladen. Das finde ich gemein!

AT 3.2 **2a** *Finde die passenden Bilder für die Sätze.* Pupils match the pictures to the sentences. Note that *in Konzerte gehen* is new: check that pupils recognize the cognate *Konzert–*'concert'. Check that pupils recognize *abwaschen* as *ich wasche ab*.

Answers: 1 d; 2 a; 3 e; 4 c; 5 b; 6 f

AT 1.4 **AT 3.2** **2b** *Hör gut zu und lies dann die Sätze von Übung 2a. Was sagt Hanna – und was sagt Thomas?* Pupils listen to the recording and select the appropriate sentences from activity 2a for each speaker. Note that the correct answers to this activity are required for activity 2c. The recording also offers the opportunity to look at the positive use of *ich darf* for things that you **are** allowed to do. After the activity is completed, you could draw pupils' attention to this aspect. T: *Hört noch mal zu: Was darf Hanna machen? Was darf Thomas machen?*

Answers:

Hanna: Ich muss jeden Tag abwaschen.
Ich darf nicht in Konzerte gehen.
Ich muss samstags um 20 Uhr zu Hause sein.

Thomas: Ich darf keine Musik im Wohnzimmer hören.
Ich muss um 21 Uhr ins Bett gehen.
Ich darf nicht in den Ferien arbeiten.

Transcript   p 40, activity 2b

– Hallo, Thomas!
– Hallo, Hanna! Wie geht's?
– Schlecht! Ich mag meine Eltern nicht! Sie sind zu streng – und zu altmodisch! Ich muss jeden Tag abwaschen – und mein Bruder? Mein Bruder sieht fern! Das ist ungerecht!
– Ja, ja – Eltern ... mein Vater ist auch zu streng – ich darf keine Musik im Wohnzimmer hören!
– Oh nein! Also, ich darf Musik im Wohnzimmer hören – aber ich darf nicht in Konzerte gehen. Aber mein Bruder geht jedes Wochenende in Konzerte!
– Das finde ich gemein! Du, und ich muss um 21 Uhr ins Bett gehen!
– Ach – Eltern!!! Ja, und ich muss samstags um 20 Uhr zu Hause sein – um 20 Uhr!! Das finde ich doof!
– Ja ... UND ich darf nicht in den Ferien arbeiten!
– Nein! Also, ich darf am Wochenende arbeiten – und in den Ferien ...
– Aber ich nicht! Ich spare für einen Computer – aber ich darf nicht arbeiten ... das finde ich ungerecht!

C 22   Activity 3 on copymaster 22 could be used at this point for extension work on *(nicht) dürfen*.

AT 2.3   **2c** *Ratespiel: Wer ist das? A fragt, B antwortet. Dann ist B dran.* Pupils work together in pairs. Partner A reads out a sentence from activity 2a, and partner B has to say whether Hanna or Thomas says this. The correct answers to activity 2b are required for this activity.

AT 2.4   **2d** *Du bist dran! Was musst du zu Hause machen? Was darfst du nicht machen? Macht weitere Dialoge.* Pupils work together in pairs to create their own dialogues. They should use the recording in activity 2b as a model, and keep to the sentences introduced in activities 1 and 2a. More able pupils could be encouraged to expand their answers to include other previously learnt language.

WB P   Workbook activity P could be used at this point for consolidation of the new structure: modal verb + infinitive at the end.

WB Q   Workbook activity Q could be used at this point for further listening comprehension on *ich darf nicht …* and *ich muss …*

Grammatik im Fokus

ich muss …, ich darf nicht/kein(e) … This section focuses on the modal verbs *müssen* and *dürfen* and how to use them in a sentence. Remind pupils that the infinitive is the dictionary form, and that separable verbs like *abwaschen* are joined together in this form (Unit 2, p. 24). After you have looked at the examples in the Students' Book with the class, you could construct some other examples as a whole class activity. For example, write up:

Ich decke den Tisch.
Ich sauge Staub.
Ich füttere die Katze.
Ich fahre in die Stadt.
Ich kaufe Süßigkeiten.

For each sentence in turn, invite the class to suggest a modal verb. T: *Ich decke den Tisch: ,muss' oder ,darf nicht'?* Write up whichever verb is suggested. Now invite the class to call out the new sentence word by word. Do not correct wrong suggestions immediately; let pupils discover them for themselves by posing questions such as *Ist das richtig?*

C 26   Activity 4 on copymaster 26 could be used in conjunction with the grammar panel.

3 *Schreib die Sätze richtig auf.* Pupils rearrange the words to form sentences using modal verbs.

Answers:

1 Ich darf nicht fernsehen! 2 Ich muss abwaschen! 3 Ich darf kein Fastfood essen! 4 Ich muss abends lernen!

C 23   Activity 2 on copymaster 23 (speaking) could be used here for extension work on *(nicht) dürfen*.

4a *Schreib neue Sätze mit Ich muss …* Pupils transform the sentences using the modal verb *müssen*. You may want to encourage less able pupils to break down the task into two stages: 1 replace the verb with *muss*; 2 put the infinitive of the verb at the end of the sentence. If necessary, remind them that the infinitive always ends in *-n*.

Answers:

1 Ich muss in die Schule gehen. 2 Ich muss den Tisch decken. 3 Ich muss das Badezimmer putzen. 4 Ich muss Hausaufgaben machen.

4b *Jetzt schreib neue Sätze mit Ich darf nicht/keine …* Pupils transform the sentences using the modal verb *dürfen*. Remind them that they have to decide whether to use *nicht* or *keine*.

Answers:

1 Ich darf nicht in die Disco gehen. 2 Ich darf keine Freunde einladen. 3 Ich darf nicht samstags arbeiten. 4 Ich darf keine Musik hören.

C 24   Activity 1 on copymaster 24 (reading) could be used here to introduce pupils to the positive use of *ich darf* as well as practising *ich muss*. Activity 2 could also be used at this point.

AT 4.4   **5** *Du bist dran! Was musst du/darfst du nicht zu Hause machen? Schreib einen Brief an ,Liebe Gaby'.* Pupils write their own letter complaining about what they have to/are not allowed to do. You could write up *Ich muss …* and *Ich darf nicht …* on the board/OHT and brainstorm ideas (which can be drawn from the previous two units or from *Klasse! 1*) before pupils complete the activity as a homework task.

WB R   Workbook activity R could be used at this point for reinforcement of the new structures introduced on this spread.

WB S   Workbook activity S could be used as a simpler alternative to activity 5 above, and could also form part of pupils' written records for continuous assessment.

25 Activity 3 on copymaster 25 (writing) brings together the main language from this unit in an activity suitable for more able pupils. This activity can form part of pupils' written records for continuous assessment purposes.

Tipp

Wörterbuchhilfe: Trennbare Verben. This section focuses on finding and recognizing separable verbs in a dictionary or glossary. You may want to photocopy a relevant dictionary extract onto an OHT, as well as making sure that pupils have dictionaries to use in class. Point out that only the German–English part of the dictionary shows whether a verb is separable or not.

Explain that pupils need to familiarize themselves with their own particular dictionary and the way it denotes separable verbs. Ask pupils whether they can spot examples of separable verbs in their dictionary or on the OHT.

27 Activity 2 on copymaster 27 could be used in conjunction with the *Tipp.*

6 *Finde die Infinitive für diese Verben.* Pupils locate the separable verbs in their dictionaries or the *Vokabular* at the back of the Students' Book. Less able pupils may find it helpful to copy the sentences onto paper before highlighting the verb and the prefix. Then they: 1 swap the two parts around; 2 join the prefix to the verb; 3 add -*n* to the end for the infinitive.

You could point out to more able pupils that two of the verbs are reflexive – although they will find them in a dictionary without knowing this, they will need to be aware that the verb is reflexive in order to choose the right definition. Ask them how reflexive verbs are denoted in their dictionary (Unit 2, p. 23).

Answers:

1 aufstehen; 2 aufräumen; 3 (sich) anziehen; 4 einkaufen; 5 fernsehen; 6 (sich) ausziehen

Thema im Fokus
pages 42–43

National Curriculum PoS
statements 1c, 2c, 2e, 2f, 2i, 3d, 3e, 5a, 5c, 5d, 5e, 5f, 5i

Materials
- Students' Book pages 42–43
- Cassette 1 side B
- Copymaster 21

The final spread of each unit provides further reading practice, leading into a project outcome for the unit. See pages 8–9 of the introduction to this book for general notes on how to use these pages.

T 3.4 **1a** *Lies die Problembriefe. Finde dann die passenden Überschriften.* Pupils read the letters to an agony uncle and then select the appropriate title for each letter. This only requires pupils to read the letters for gist, but the language in the letters should also be used in drawing up the questionnaire in activity 1b.

Answers: 1 b; 2 d; 3 c; 4 a

AT 4.3 **1b** *Mach eine Klassenumfrage: ‚Probleme mit den Eltern'. Schreib 5 Sätze.* Pupils draw up a questionnaire consisting of five questions to ask their classmates about problems with their parents. As a first step, pupils could look through the four letters in activity 1a for relevant language. Encourage pupils to construct at least one question using *Ich muss* and one using *Ich darf nicht.* As this may be a sensitive issue, teachers may prefer to put the focus on parents in general, rather than asking pupils to talk about their own parents.

AT 2.3 **1c** *Frag die Schüler/Schülerinnen: „Kein Taschengeld –*
AT 1.3 *ist das ein Problem?" usw. Notiere die Antworten.* Pupils now carry out the class survey using the questions they prepared in activity 1b.

AT 4.2 **1d** *Was ist das Problem Nummer eins? Schreib die Resultate auf (z. B. mit dem Computer).* Pupils write up the results of their survey in graphical form, using spreadsheet, presentation or word-processing software if possible to find the clearest and most visually attractive way of displaying the information. Pupils may wish to use a 3D pie chart or another format instead of the bar chart shown in the Students' Book. The graphic could be decorated with symbols (either originals or clip-art) representing, e.g. washing up, music, etc. You may wish pupils to write up their results without a computer or as homework. Pupils can experiment with various other attractive ways of presenting the information, e.g. a bar chart in which each of the bars is a symbol representing the particular problem (e.g. vacuum cleaner for *Ich muss zu Hause helfen*, banknote for *Ich bekomme kein Taschengeld.*).

AT 2.4 **1e** *Finde* 📻 . *Mach eine Kassette mit den Informationen für eine Radiosendung in Deutschland.* Pupils use their survey results as the basis of a spoken presentation in a journalistic style. They will probably need to write up their presentation beforehand, or at least make notes about what they are going to say. Encourage them to rehearse their presentations thoroughly, so that they can speak fluently into the microphone using only brief notes as a prompt.

AT 4.2–3 **2a** *Schreib einen Steckbrief für deinen Lieblingsstar (Musik, Fernsehen, Sport). Finde auch Fotos.* Using the example in the Students' Book, pupils write an ID card for their favourite actor, sportsperson, musician or other personality. Encourage them to be as creative as possible in their choice of subject. They do not have to know all the biographical details and can be inventive if they wish. This is an ideal activity for ICT.

AT 4.4 **2b** *Wie ist er/sie? Finde andere Adjektive im Englisch-Deutsch-Wörterbuch. Dann frag deinen Lehrer/deine Lehrerin: „Wie sagt man ‚cool'?" usw.* Pupils add more personal information to their *Steckbriefe.* Point out that the Internet is an excellent source of this kind of information. The information on hobbies and character should be based on fact/imagination, not just taken from the language used in this unit. Some individual vocabulary research will be required, using a dictionary and using the teacher as a resource. Depending on the resources available to pupils, you may wish to tailor pupils' selections from the outset. This can avoid disappointment or frustration on the part of the pupil, brought about by an inability to complete the task due to a lack of information. Once the *Steckbriefe* are completed, they could be displayed in the classroom and pupils could vote for the funniest, most unusual and most interesting *Steckbrief*, best photo, etc.

AT 4.4 **2c** *Schreib auch einen kurzen Artikel. (Tipp – der Artikel unten ist dein Modell – ändere nur die Wörter in Grau.)* Using the example given, pupils write an article based on their *Steckbrief*. More able pupils could be encouraged to be more independent of the structure of the example.

Kannst du ... ?

The end-of-unit summary is a checklist for pupils. See page 8 of the introduction to this book for ideas on how to use the checklist.

C 21 Copymaster 21 provides a useful reference for pupils revising the language of this unit.

Noch mal!-Seite Einheit 3
page 126

National Curriculum PoS
statements 1a, 1b, 1c, 2a, 2b, 2c, 5a, 5c

Materials
• Students' Book page 126
• Cassette 1 side B

This revision page is intended for less able pupils. It reinforces the basic vocabulary and structures from the unit, and it can be used by pupils who experienced difficulty in completing some of the activities within the unit, or as alternative homework activities.

AT 3.3 **1** *Lies die Beschreibungen. Wer ist das? Finde die passenden Bilder.* Activity 1 relates to pages 34–35. Pupils read the descriptions and match them to the pictures. There is no need for pupils to have mastered adjective endings for this activity.

Answers: 1 c; 2 a; 3 b

AT 1.3 **2a** *Wie sind Kathi und Matthias? Hör gut zu und finde die passenden Wörter.* Activity 2 relates to pages 36–37. Note that pupils need the correct answers from activity 2a in order to do activity 2b. Again, there is no need for pupils to have mastered adjective endings.

Answers:

Kathi: lieb, schüchtern, launisch, (selten) ungeduldig
Matthias: (selten) frech, unfreundlich, lustig, nett

> **Transcript**   p 126, activity 2a
>
> – Meine beste Freundin heißt Kathi. Also, wie ist Kathi? Sie ist immer lieb – das ist schön, finde ich. Aber sie ist oft schüchtern. Sie ist manchmal launisch, aber sie ist

> selten ungeduldig. Kathi ist nie gemein. Das finde ich super!
> – Mein bester Freund heißt Matthias. Und wie ist Matthias? Hmm ... Er ist nie arrogant – das finde ich gut. Er ist selten frech, aber er ist manchmal unfreundlich! Er ist oft lustig, und er ist immer nett.

AT 2.3 **2b** *Ratespiel: Wer ist das? A ist Kathi oder Matthias und sagt einen Satz, B rät. Dann ist B dran.* Pupils work together in pairs. Partner A says a sentence describing Kathi or Matthias (in the first person); partner B decides who is being described. Then the roles are exchanged. The correct answers from activity 2a are required for this activity.

AT 3.3 **3** *Finde die passenden Antworten.* Activity 3 relates to pages 36–39. Pupils choose the alternative that makes better sense to complete the *weil*-clause. This activity provides consolidation of the key language and reinforcement of the word order of subordinate clauses.

Answers: 1 b; 2 b; 3 a; 4 a; 5 b

AT 4.3 **4** *Ergänze die Sprechblasen.* Activity 4 relates to pages 40–41. Pupils complete the speech bubbles using the pictures as prompts. This activity reinforces the structure of sentences using modal auxiliaries. Remind pupils that the main verb goes to the end of the sentence. The activity could be broken down into four stages: 1 identify the expression suggested by the picture, e.g. *(ich) gehe ins Bett*; 2 put the verb in the infinitive form (here just add *-n*); 3 put the infinitive at the end; 4 insert the expression into the sentence after *Ich muss …*

Answers:

1 Ich muss um 20 Uhr ins Bett gehen. 2 Ich muss zu Hause helfen. 3 Ich darf keine Musik im Wohnzimmer hören. 4 Ich muss abends immer lernen. 5 Ich darf nicht in die Disco gehen. 6 Ich darf nicht fernsehen.

Extra!-Seite Einheit 3
page 127

National Curriculum PoS
statements 1a, 1b, 1c, 2a, 2b, 3e, 5a, 5c, 5i

Materials
• Students' Book page 127
• Cassette 1 side B

This extension page is intended for more able pupils. It contains slightly longer and more complex materials, and it can be used by pupils who have completed other activities quickly, or as alternative homework activities.

 AT 1.4 **1a** *Hör gut zu und beantworte die Fragen in Sätzen.* Activity 1 relates to pages 34–36. In activity 1a, pupils listen to the recording and answer the questions about appearance and character in complete sentences.

Answers:

1 Sie ist 14 Jahre alt.
2 Sie hat lange blonde Haare und ihre Augen sind blau.
  Sie trägt Ohrringe.
3 Sie ist immer lustig, aber sie ist manchmal launisch.
  Sie ist nie frech.
4 Daniel ist 13 Jahre alt.
5 Seine Haare sind braun und lockig und seine Augen
  sind grün. Er trägt eine Brille.
6 Er ist nie gemein, aber er ist manchmal ungeduldig.
  Er ist immer nett.

> **Transcript**   p 127, activity 1a
>
> – Ich heiße Ina und ich bin 14 Jahre alt. Ich habe lange
> blonde Haare und meine Augen sind blau. Ich trage
> Ohrringe. Ich bin immer lustig, aber ich bin auch
> manchmal launisch! Aber ich bin nie frech. Mein bester
> Freund heißt Daniel. Daniel ist 13 Jahre alt. Seine
> Haare sind braun und lockig und seine Augen sind
> grün. Er trägt eine Brille. Daniel ist nie gemein – das
> finde ich super. Aber er ist manchmal ungeduldig! Er ist
> aber immer nett – das ist toll.

AT 4.4 **1b** *Beantworte die Fragen für deinen besten Freund/deine beste Freundin.* Pupils now answer the questions from activity 1a for their own best friend. You could encourage them to research new vocabulary (e.g. adjectives describing appearance or character) using their dictionaries.

AT 2.4 **2** *Wie ist dein Vater/deine Mutter? Macht Dialoge mit Wir verstehen uns (nicht) gut, weil …* Activity 2 relates to pages 36–37. Pupils work together in pairs to create dialogues about how they get on with their parents, using the adjectives provided. Before they start the activity, you could remind them of the adverbs of frequency: *immer, oft, manchmal, selten, nie.* Stress the importance of correct word order: verb to the end after *weil.*

AT 4.4 **3a** *Was musst du zu Hause machen? Lies den Brief. Schreib dann einen Antwortbrief an Michael mit den Informationen unten.* Activity 3 relates to pages 40–41. In activity 3a, pupils read the letter and then construct a reply using the picture prompts. Point out that they can use Michael's letter as a model. Pupils could then add further details if they wish, using a dictionary to research new vocabulary.

AT 4.4 **3b** *Kathis Eltern sind super! Was darf Kathi alles machen? Schreib einen Brief an Michael.* Pupils now write a positive letter about what Kathi is allowed to do (in the first person, as if they are Kathi themselves), using the picture prompts. They could then add further details if they wish, using a dictionary to research new vocabulary.

Workbook

Page 24

Use with page 33 in the Students' Book.

 A1 *Hör gut zu und sing mit!* Singing this song will help pupils to memorize the key vocabulary for descriptions of appearance and character. Pupils might like to perform suitable actions while listening/singing, e.g. pointing to their eyes in the second verse, their hair in the third verse, miming glasses in the third verse, laughing in the fourth verse. You could gradually reduce the volume of the recording with each playing, until pupils are singing the verses in response to your mime prompts.

> **Transcript**   W 24, activity A1
>
> Lukas ist mein bester Freund
> Bester Freund, bester Freund
> Lukas ist der beste Freund
> Der beste Freund der Welt
>
> Er hat blaue Augen
> Er hat blaue Augen
> Er hat blaue Augen
> Lukas ist so lieb
>
> Refrain
>
> Er hat rote Haare
> Er hat rote Haare
> Er hat rote Haare
> Lukas ist so lieb
>
> Refrain
>
> Er trägt eine Brille
> Er trägt eine Brille
> Er trägt eine Brille
> Lukas ist so lieb
>
> Refrain
>
> Er ist immer lustig
> Er ist immer lustig
> Er ist immer lustig
> Lukas ist so lieb
>
> Refrain

AT 3.2 **A2** *Finde die passenden Antworten.* Pupils answer the comprehension questions on the song text and then draw a picture of Lukas. You could provide the feminine form [*Name*] *ist meine beste Freundin* as another useful expression for pupils to learn.

Answers: 1 a; 2 a; 3 b; 4 a

Pages 25–27

Use with pages 34–35 in the Students' Book.

AT 4.2 **B** *Schreib die Sätze richtig auf.* This activity consolidates the structures and vocabulary for describing appearance and can be used with activity 2 on page 34 of the Students' Book. Pupils put the words in the correct order to form sentences.

Answers:

1 Meine beste Freundin heißt Tanja. 2 Seine Haare sind braun. 3 Ich habe blaue Augen. 4 Wie siehst du aus? 5 Ich trage einen Ohrring. 6 Sie hat blonde Haare.

AT 3.2 **C** *Wer ist das? Finde die passenden Bilder.* Pupils find the picture which matches each personal description. This activity can be used as additional reading comprehension in conjunction with activities 1 and 2 on page 34 of the Students' Book.

Answers: 1 e; 2 b; 3 c; 4 a; 5 d

AT 1.3 **D1** *„Wie siehst du aus?" Hör gut zu und zeichne Lukas, Maja und Alexander. Schreib auch die passenden Farben für sie auf.* Activity D could be used for consolidation of physical descriptions and favourites in conjunction with activity 3 on page 34 in the Students' Book. In activity D1, pupils listen to the recording and then add the correct length and style of hair to the heads of the three characters, using the information they have heard. In addition, they write down the colour of each character's hair and eyes. Point out that they should write down the colour adjectives without endings, so if they hear for example *rote Haare*, they write down *rot*.

Answers:

Lukas: Haare: rot; Augen: blau
Maja: Haare: braun; Augen: grün
Alexander: Haare: blond; Augen: braun

Transcript   W 25 activity D1

– Lukas, wie siehst du aus?
– Ich habe rote Haare und meine Haare sind kurz. Ja, und meine Augen sind blau. Und ich trage eine Brille.

– Wie siehst du aus, Maja?
– Meine Haare sind braun. Und ich habe lockige Haare. Und meine Augen – meine Augen sind grün.

– Und du, Alexander? Wie siehst du aus?
– Also, ich habe braune Augen. Ich habe blonde Haare. Meine Haare sind lang und glatt. Ich trage auch einen Ohrring.

AT 2.2
AT 1.3 **D2** *Ratespiel – wer ist das? A wählt ein Bild und beschreibt es, B rät. Dann ist B dran.* Pupils work together in pairs in this speaking activity. Partner A describes one of his/her pictures from activity D1 (without letting partner B see the picture), and partner B decides whether the description is of Lukas, Maja or Alexander.

AT 1.3 **D3** *„Was ist deine Lieblings … ?" Was sagen Lukas, Maja und Alexander? Hör gut zu und schreib L, M oder A auf.* Pupils listen to the recording and then match the three speakers to the picture cues.

Answers: a L; b L; c M; d A; e A; f M

Transcript   W 26, activity D3

– Lukas, was ist deine Lieblingsfarbe?
– Meine Lieblingsfarbe? Meine Lieblingsfarbe ist Gelb – ja, Gelb.

– Und was ist deine Lieblingsgruppe?
– Also, meine Lieblingsgruppe ist ‚Die Mädchen'.

– Und du, Maja? Was ist deine Lieblingsfarbe?
– Grau! Meine Lieblingsfarbe ist Grau!
– Und was ist dein Lieblingsfilm?
– Mein Lieblingsfim ist ‚Karo die Katze'. Der Film ist total lustig!

– Und was ist deine Lieblingsfarbe, Alexander?
– Blau … oder Grün? Nein, meine Lieblingsfarbe ist Orange … ja, Orange. Und meine Lieblingsgruppe ist ‚Die Drei'. ‚Die Drei' sind super!

AT 4.3 **D4** *Was ist deine Lieblings … ? Schreib Sprechblasen für Lukas, Maja und Alexander.* Pupils use their information from activity D3 to write speech bubbles for the three characters about their favourite things.

Answers:

Lukas: Meine Lieblingsfarbe ist Gelb und meine Lieblingsgruppe ist ‚Die Mädchen'.
Maja: Meine Lieblingsfarbe ist Grau und mein Lieblingsfilm ist ‚Karo die Katze'.
Alexander: Meine Lieblingsfarbe ist Orange und meine Lieblingsgruppe ist ‚Die Drei'.

AT 4.4 **E** *Finde Fotos – z. B. von Freunden, Freundinnen, Film-, Pop- oder Sportstars usw. Wähle ein Foto und kleb es auf. Wie sieht die Person aus? Beschreib sie oder ihn.* This creative writing activity could be used after activity 3 on page 34 of the Students' Book. Pupils provide their own photo of their best friend/favourite filmstar, etc. and describe the person. They could research any new vocabulary they need using the *Vokabular* at the back of the Students' Book, their dictionaries and/or the teacher as a resource. Point out to pupils that the description should be written in the *er/sie*-form, not in the *ich*-form.

AT 3.4
AT 4.2 **F** *Lies Jans Brief und die Sätze unten. Sind sie richtig (✔) oder falsch (✘)? Korrigiere die falschen Sätze.* This activity could be used as homework to reinforce the new language introduced on pages 34–35 of the Students' Book. Pupils read the letter and then decide whether the statements in the table are true or false, correcting the false ones. They should modify the statements in the table, rather than copying sentences verbatim from the letter.

Answers:

1 falsch: Seine Haare sind braun und kurz. 2 falsch: Er hat lockige Haare. 3 falsch: Er hat blaue Augen. 4 falsch: Er trägt keinen Ohrring. (Er trägt eine Brille.) 5 falsch: Er mag Schwarz. 6 falsch: Er hört am liebsten Techno.

Page 28

Use with pages 35–36 of the Students' Book.

AT 4.4 **G** *Du bist dran! Wie siehst du aus? Was ist deine Lieblingsfarbe, -musik oder -gruppe? Was ist dein Lieblingsfilm? Finde ein Foto von dir und beschreib dich.* This creative writing activity could be used as homework after pages 34–35 of the Students' Book. This activity can form part of pupils' written records for continuous assessment purposes. See the general notes on pages 13–14 of the introduction to this book.

3.1 **H1** *Wie bist du? Finde 12 Adjektive und schreib sie unten auf Deutsch auf.* Activity H is a fun way to consolidate the new vocabulary introduced in activity 1 on page 36 of the Students' Book and to practise dictionary skills. Pupils look for 12 adjectives in the word puzzle. Pairs of pupils could collaborate to find all 12 against the clock or in competition with their classmates. Warn pupils that words may be horizontal or vertical and could read upwards or downwards.

Answers:

U	L	U	S	T	I	G	J	V
N	A	R	R	O	G	A	N	T
F	R	E	C	H	I	K	S	S
R	L	C	A	G	D	U	C	Y
E	A	L	P	A	L	F	H	M
U	U	K	R	Z	U	R	Ü	P
N	N	G	T	K	D	E	C	A
D	I	D	B	S	E	U	H	T
L	S	A	T	I	G	N	T	H
I	C	G	E	H	N	D	E	I
C	H	B	C	K	U	L	R	S
H	S	G	E	M	E	I	N	C
L	I	E	B	G	Y	C	R	H
N	E	T	T	I	S	H	H	N

H2 *Wie heißt das auf Englisch? Finde die passenden Wörter im Wörterbuch und schreib sie auf.* Pupils look up the 12 adjectives from activity H1 in the dictionary and write down their English translations. You could point out that they will also find adverbial forms for most of them (ending in -(i)ly), but should only write down the adjectives. Again, this activity could be completed by pairs of pupils working against the clock.

Answers:

unfreundlich unfriendly; arrogant arrogant; schüchtern shy; freundlich friendly; lustig funny; gemein mean, nasty; nett nice; sympathisch nice; frech cheeky; lieb kind, sweet; ungeduldig impatient; launisch moody

Pages 29–30

Use with pages 36–37 in the Students' Book.

 AT 1.3 **I1** *Wie sind Doro und Uwe? Hör gut zu und schreib die passenden Adjektive in Übung I2 auf.* Activity I is a listening activity practising the adverbs of frequency with personal attributes, extending the work done in activities 2 and 3 on page 36 of the Students' Book. Pupils listen to the recording, choose from the box the

adjectives they hear associated with each character, and write them down below activity I2.

AT 1.3 **I2** *Wie oft sind sie das? Hör noch einmal zu und schreib die passenden Buchstaben in die Kästchen.* Pupils listen again to the recording and select the appropriate frequency adverb for each adjective.

Answers:

Doro:		Uwe:	
sympathisch	a	schüchtern	e
freundlich	a	unfreundlich	e
lustig	b	gemein	d
ungeduldig	c	launisch	c
frech	d	lieb	b
arrogant	e	nett	a

> **Transcript** W 29, activities I1 and I2
>
> – Meine beste Freundin heißt Doro. Ja, wie ist Doro? Also, sie ist immer sehr sympathisch. Doro ist immer freundlich – das ist super, finde ich. Und sie ist oft lustig. Sie ist manchmal ungeduldig, aber sie ist selten frech. Doro ist nie arrogant. Das finde ich toll!
>
> – Mein bester Freund? Mein bester Freund heißt Uwe. Also, wie ist Uwe? Hmm … Er ist nie schüchtern und er ist nie unfreundlich – das finde ich gut. Er ist selten gemein, aber er ist manchmal launisch! Er ist oft lieb und er ist immer nett.

AT 4.4 **J1** *Lies noch einmal die Wörter in Übung I. Was meinst du – wie ist ein Superfreund/eine Superfreundin? Wie ist er/sie nicht? Schreib Sätze.* Activity J offers writing and speaking extension material for use in conjunction with activity 3, page 36 of the Students' Book. In activity J1, pupils use the adjectives from activity I to write about their ideal friend. They should write positive sentences, e.g. *Er/Sie ist immer …,* and also negative ones, e.g. *Er/Sie ist nie …* Encourage them also to use *oft, manchmal* and *selten.*

AT 2.4 **J2** *Ratespiel – wie ist dein Superfreund/deine Superfreundin? A fragt, B antwortet. Dann ist B dran.* Using their sentences from J1, pupils work together in pairs to guess what each other has written. Partner A tries to guess one of the attributes of B's ideal friend; B either confirms what A has said or corrects it.

K1 *„Ich mag …, weil …" Schreib die Sätze richtig auf.* Activity K could be used as homework to consolidate the word order of the subordinate clause after *weil.* In activity K1, pupils re-order the words in boxes to form subordinate clauses. Before pupils attempt the activity, elicit from them that *weil* will always be the first word after the comma, and that the verb will always be the last word before the full stop. Questions 5 and 6 are more difficult, as pupils have to construct the whole sentence, not just the *weil* clause.

Answers:

1 Ich mag Tom, weil er nett ist. 2 Ich mag Ina, weil sie sympathisch ist. 3 Ich mag Mark, weil er freundlich ist. 4 Ich mag Susi, weil sie lustig ist. 5 Ich mag Max, weil er schüchtern ist. 6 Ich mag Kathi, weil sie lieb ist.

K2 Schreib Sätze mit „Ich mag …, weil …" Pupils use the word prompts to write sentences containing subordinate clauses with *weil*.

Answers:

1 Ich mag Heiko, weil er nie launisch ist. 2 Ich mag Ulla, weil sie selten ungeduldig ist. 3 Ich mag Martin, weil er selten arrogant ist. 4 Ich mag Cora, weil sie nie unfreundlich ist. 5 Ich mag Ralf (nicht), weil er oft frech ist. 6 Ich mag Lola, weil sie nie gemein ist.

Page 31

Use with pages 37–39 in the Students' Book.

AT 4.4
AT 2.4

L *„Wie ist er/sie?" Schreibt Informationen, z.B. für Freunde, Popstars, Sportstars usw. Macht dann Dialoge mit „Ich mag …, weil …"* Activity L could be used as writing and speaking extension material on the topics covered on pages 36-37. Pupils write sentences about why they like particular people, and then work in pairs to create dialogues using the sentences they have prepared. You could encourage more able pupils to go beyond the range of adjectives which have been introduced in the Students' Book.

AT 1.4

M *Annika beschreibt ihre Eltern. Wie sind sie? Hör gut zu und kreuz die passenden Wörter an.* Activity M provides additional listening practice after activity 1 on page 38 of the Students' Book. Annika from the *Klasse!-Clique* describes her parents. Pupils listen to the recording and put crosses against the appropriate adjectives for each person. Remind pupils that if *nie* is used, the following adjective does not apply.

Answers:

Mutter: launisch, lieb, modern;
Stiefvater: nett, tolerant, ungeduldig;
Vater: lustig, streng, altmodisch

Transcript   W 31, activity M

– Annika, wo wohnst du?
– Also, meine Mutter, mein Stiefvater und ich – wir wohnen in Wesel. Aber mein Vater wohnt in Köln und ich fahre zweimal pro Monat nach Köln und wohne dann bei Vati.
– Und wie sind deine Eltern?
– Na ja , meine Mutter ist sehr lieb – wir verstehen uns gut. Aber sie ist auch manchmal launisch – das finde ich nicht gut. Aber sie ist ziemlich modern – das ist super.
– Und wie ist dein Stiefvater?
– Mein Stiefvater ist sehr nett. Wir verstehen uns gut, weil er tolerant ist – das finde ich super. Und er ist nie unfreundlich. Aber er ist oft ungeduldig. Das finde ich nicht gut.
– Und dein Vater? Wie ist dein Vater?
– Mein Vater ist ziemlich altmodisch – leider. Ja, wir verstehen uns nicht gut, weil er zu streng ist. Das finde ich gemein. Aber mein Vater ist manchmal lustig – das finde ich gut.

AT 1.3

N *Hör gut zu und finde die passenden Bilder.* This listening activity consolidates the vocabulary and

structures used in activity 4 on page 39 of the Students' Book. Pupils listen to the recording and then match the speakers to the pictures.

Answers: a 3; b 1; c 4; d 2; e 8; f 6; g 5; h 7

Transcript   W 31, activity N

1 – Mutti und ich – wir streiten uns, weil ich kein eigenes Zimmer habe. Das finde ich doof.
2 – Wir streiten uns, weil ich nie das Badezimmer putze. Das ist sooo langweilig!
3 – Meine Eltern sind total ungerecht! Wir streiten uns, weil ich kein Taschengeld bekomme.
4 – Mein Vater ist nicht tolerant. Also, wir streiten uns, weil ich nie mein Zimmer aufräume.
5 – Vati ist total altmodisch. Wir streiten uns, weil ich zu viele Zeitschriften kaufe.
6 – Meine Eltern und ich – wir streiten uns, weil ich zu viel fernsehe. Aber ich sehe gern fern!
7 – Also, wir streiten uns, weil ich zu viel Fastfood esse. Das finde ich nicht gut.
8 – Wir streiten uns, weil ich selten den Tisch decke. Das finde ich ungerecht.

Page 32

Use with pages 39–40 in the Students' Book.

AT 4.4

O *Du bist dran! Wie sind deine Eltern?* Pupils write about their own relationship with their parents (or other relatives), providing an alternative or additional piece of creative writing to activity 5b on page 39 of the Students' Book. This activity can form part of pupils' written records for continuous assessment purposes.

AT 3.2

P *Finde die passenden Wörter und schreib die Sätze richtig auf.* This activity reinforces the structure of sentences with a modal auxiliary and an infinitive, and could be used in conjunction with activity 2 on page 40 of the Students' Book. Pupils connect the sentence halves and then write up the sentences.

Answers: 1 f; 2 a; 3 d; 4 e; 5 b; 6 c

AT 1.4

Q *Was sagt Sven? Hör gut zu und finde die richtige Reihenfolge für die Bilder.* This activity provides further listening comprehension on *ich darf nicht …* and *ich muss …* following activity 2 on page 40 of the Students' Book. Pupils listen to the recording and then put the pictures in the order in which the activities are mentioned in the recording. The recording links with Sven's problems in the photo story on page 32 of the Students' Book.

Answers: a 6; b 3; c 2; d 4; e 1; f 5

Transcript   W 32, activity Q

– Hallo, Sven! Was ist los?
– Oh – meine Eltern! Wir streiten uns immer! Ich darf nicht fernsehen. Das finde ich ungerecht. Und ich darf keine Süßigkeiten essen!
– Oh nein!

> – Ja, und ich muss jeden Abend lernen. Und mein Vater ist so streng: Ich muss um 20 Uhr zu Hause sein!
> – Um 20 Uhr??
> – Ja – das ist total gemein! Und ich darf keine Musik im Wohnzimmer hören.
> – Und deine Mutter?
> – Meine Mutter ist total altmodisch: Ich darf nicht in die Disco gehen.

Page 33

Use with page 41 in the Students' Book.

4.3 **R1** *Schreib Sätze für die Bilder in Übung Q.* Activity R provides reinforcement of the new structures introduced on pages 40–41 of the Students' Book. In activity R1, pupils use the pictures from activity Q above as prompts to complete the sentences. The answers are checked by the pupils when they do activity R2.

Answers:

a Ich darf nicht in die Disco gehen. b Ich muss jeden Abend lernen. c Ich darf keine Süßigkeiten essen. d Ich muss um 20 Uhr zu Hause sein. e Ich darf nicht

fernsehen. f Ich darf keine Musik im Wohnzimmer hören.

AT 2.2 **R2** *Ist alles richtig? A wählt ein Bild in Übung Q, B antwortet. Dann ist B dran.* Pupils work together in pairs. Partner A chooses a picture from activity Q and partner B responds with the appropriate sentence from activity R1. Pupils can use this activity to check each other's answers to R1.

AT 4.4 **S** *Du bist dran! Was musst du/darfst du nicht zu Hause machen?* Activity S could be used as a simpler alternative to activity 5 on page 41 of the Students' Book. Pupils write about the rules and prohibitions which apply in their own family. This activity can form part of pupils' written records for continuous assessment purposes.

Can you ...?

The purpose of the checklist is to identify tasks in the Students' Book both by skill and by topic. Teachers may find this helpful in selecting specific tasks to be used as a record of pupils' achievements in an Attainment Target.

Einheit 3 Freunde und Familie	AT 1 Listening	AT 2 Speaking	AT 3 Reading	AT 4 Writing
34–35 Wie siehst du aus?				
Say what you look like	1, 3a	–	1	3b, 5b, 7
Ask what someone else looks like	–	3c	–	–
Say what someone else looks like	1, 3a	2	1	6
Talk about your best friend	–	–	–	Noch mal!, Extra!, 5a
36–37 Wie bist du?				
Describe your own character	2	3, Noch mal!	1	–
Describe someone else's character	–	–	1	Extra!
Explain why you like your best friend	4	7	4, 5	6, 8
38–39 Meine Eltern sind zu streng!				
Describe your parents	1c	2a	1a, 1b	2b
Say how you get on with your parents	1c	–	1a, 1b	2b
Say why you argue	4b	4c	4a, 5a	5b
40–41 Ich muss immer zu Hause helfen!				
Say what you have to do	1, 2b	2c, 2d	1, 2a, 2b	3, 4a, 5
Say what you're not allowed to do	1, 2b	2c, 2d	1, 2a, 2b	3, 4b, 5

Copymasters

For general advice about using the copymasters, see page 7 of the introduction to this book.

C 22 ### Hören

AT 1.2 **1** *Hör gut zu und finde die passenden Fotos.* This activity consolidates vocabulary for describing people. Pupils listen to the recording and match the 'photos' to the speakers.

Answers: a 3; b 4; c 2; d 6; e 1; f 5

Transcript	C 22, activity 1
1 – Ich habe kurze blonde lockige Haare.	
2 – Ich habe lange blonde lockige Haare.	
3 – Ich habe kurze schwarze glatte Haare.	
4 – Ich habe kurze blonde lockige Haare und ich trage einen Ohrring.	
5 – Ich habe lange glatte braune Haare und ich trage eine Brille.	
6 – Ich habe kurze braune lockige Haare und ich trage eine Brille.	

2 *Julia beschreibt ihre Klassenkameraden. Hör gut zu und finde die passenden Bilder.* This is a more challenging listening comprehension about character descriptions. Pupils listen to the recording and then decide which picture matches the description of which person. You may want to look at the pictures with the class first and elicit from them appropriate adjectives for describing the characters in the pictures.

Answers:

Andreas: c; Thomas: a; Marco: e; Lena: f; Claudia: d; Susie: b

---

Transcript   C 22, activity 2

– Also, das ist die Schule und hier ist deine neue Klasse!
– Meine neue Klasse! Wie sind sie alle ... ?
– Also, das ist Andreas. Er ist sehr nett und immer lustig. Und das ist Thomas. Er ist manchmal arrogant. Und das ist Marco. Er ist immer so ungeduldig.
– Und die Mädchen?
– Ja, die Mädchen. Schau mal. Es gibt hier Lena. Sie ist sehr nett und freundlich. Ja, sehr sympathisch. Und dann gibt es Claudia. Ja, die liebe Claudia! Sie ist sehr oft launisch. Und Susie. Susie ist immer lieb aber auch sehr schüchtern.
– Danke. Aber so viele Namen ...

3a *Was dürfen sie machen? (✔) Was dürfen sie nicht machen? (✗) Hör gut zu und füll die Tabelle aus.* This challenging listening comprehension focuses on *dürfen* and *nicht dürfen* and is suitable for more able pupils. Pupils should look at the pictures on the table first and note expressions likely to be used in describing each (e.g. *fernsehen, Musik hören, Fastfood essen*) before listening to the recording. Pause the cassette after each section (1–4) for pupils to fill in the table.

Answers:

Martina:	in die Disco gehen ✔, in Konzerte gehen ✔, Freunde einladen ✔
Christian:	Musik hören ✗, in Konzerte gehen ✗, Freunde einladen ✗
Sabina:	Fernsehen ✔, in die Disco gehen ✔, Freunde einladen ✔, in den Ferien arbeiten ✗
Markus:	Fast food essen ✗, CDs kaufen ✔, in die Disco gehen ✔, in den Ferien arbeiten ✔

Transcript   C 22, activities 3a and 3b

1
– Guten Morgen, liebe Zuhörer. Das Thema für heute ist: Teenager und ihre Eltern. Also, Martina. Wie sind deine Eltern?
– Meine Eltern sind sehr sympathisch und wir verstehen uns sehr gut. Ich darf in die Disco und in Konzerte gehen und ich darf auch Freunde nach Hause einladen. Meine Eltern sind immer sehr tolerant.
– Meine Eltern aber nicht!

2
– Ja, Christian?
– Meine Eltern sind sehr streng und wir streiten uns immer.
– Warum?
– Ich darf nichts machen! Ich darf keine Musik im Wohnzimmer hören, ich darf keine Freunde nach Hause einladen, ich darf in keine Konzerte gehen ... Das finde ich doof!

3
– Christian! Deine Eltern sind sehr lieb. Aber du ... ! Du hilfst nie zu Hause ... !
– Na, und ... Sabina?
– Meine Eltern und ich verstehen uns gut, weil sie sehr lieb sind, aber auch, weil ich immer zu Hause helfe! Ich habe meinen eigenen Fernseher im Schlafzimmer und darf dort fernsehen - nur bis neun Uhr. Ich darf Freunde nach Hause einladen und ich darf auch abends in die Disco gehen. Ich darf nur nicht in den Ferien arbeiten.

4
– Darfst du in den Ferien arbeiten, Markus?
– Ja, das darf ich machen. Ich bekomme nicht so viel Taschengeld. Also, in den Ferien arbeite ich im Supermarkt. Von dem Geld kaufe ich CDs oder ich gehe in die Disco. Ich darf nur kein Fastfood kaufen. Das finde ich gemein ...
– Vielen Dank! Und nächste Woche hören wir von den Eltern ...

3b *Hör noch einmal zu. Sind die Sätze richtig oder falsch? Schreib R oder F.* Pupils listen to the recording again before identifying whether the statements are true or false. You could ask the class to predict likely answers before playing the cassette for them to check their predictions. Pause the cassette after each section (1–4) to discuss the answers.

Answers: 1 F; 2 F; 3 F; 4 F

Sprechen

1a *Wähle ein Bild und beschreib es deinem Partner/deiner Partnerin. Dein Partner/deine Partnerin sucht dann das passende Bild.* Pupils work together in pairs to create dialogues. Partner A chooses one of the six pictures, without telling B which picture he/she has chosen, and then describes the picture. On the basis of A's description, B decides which picture A has chosen.

1b *Dein Partner/deine Partnerin beschreibt ein Bild. Finde das passende Bild in Übung 1a.* This is the second part of the activity, with the roles reversed.

2a *Frag deinen Partner/deine Partnerin: „Was darfst du machen?"* This activity is suitable for more able pupils. Pupils work together in pairs to create dialogues. In response to partner A's question, partner B says what he/she is and is not allowed to do, using the picture cues provided.

2b *Dein Partner/deine Partnerin fragt: „Was darfst du machen?" Antworte mit den Informationen unten.* This is the second part of the activity, with the roles reversed.

C 24 Lesen

AT 3.2 **1a** *Was passt zusammen? Verbinde die Wörter.* Pupils join the sentence halves together to make sentences using *ich muss* and *ich darf*. You could help less able pupils by pointing out that *ich darf* will be followed by something pleasant, while *ich muss* will be followed by something unpleasant!

Answers:

1 Ich muss jeden Abend lernen.
2 Ich darf in die Disco gehen.
3 Ich muss um 21 Uhr ins Bett gehen.
4 Ich darf keine Süßigkeiten essen.
5 Ich muss jeden Tag um 20 Uhr zu Hause sein.
6 Ich darf nicht fernsehen.

AT 3.2 **1b** *Wer sagt was? Finde die passenden Bilder für die Sätze in Übung 1a.* Pupils now match the pictures to the sentences they constructed in activity 1a.

Answers: 1 d; 2 e; 3 c; 4 b; 5 a; 6 f

AT 3.3 **2** *Lies Annas Brief und die Sätze. Sind sie richtig oder falsch? Schreib R oder F in die Kästchen.* This activity may be unsuitable for some less able pupils. Pupils read the letter and decide whether the statements in the table are true or false.

Answers: 1 F; 2 F; 3 R; 4 F; 5 F; 6 F

C 25 Schreiben

AT 4.2 **1** *Schreib Sätze.* Pupils write simple sentences to describe the pictures. Only one adjective is required per sentence. Accept alternative answers which correspond to the pictures. Help less able pupils by giving them the structure *Er/Sie hat … Haare*, pointing out that the adjectives will all have the ending -*e*, because they come before the noun.

Answers:

a Sie hat lange Haare. b Er hat schwarze Haare. c Sie hat lockige Haare. d Er hat kurze Haare. e Sie hat glatte Haare. f Er hat blonde Haare.

AT 4.3 **2** *Beantworte die Fragen in Sätzen.* Pupils give their own personal responses to the questions about their best friend.

AT 4.4 **3a** *Michael beschreibt seine Eltern. Beantworte die Fragen für Michael und schreib einen Brief.* This activity is suitable for more able pupils. Pupils use the pictures to answer the questions, then construct a letter from their answers. Note that some of the pictures (those concerning character) are open to various interpretations.

Answers:

The letter should contain the following information:
Vater: kurze schwarze/braune/dunkle Haare; streng/unfreundlich/ungeduldig
Mutter: lange blonde Haare; trägt Ohrringe; modern/tolerant/lieb/nett
Vater: wir streiten uns/verstehen uns nicht gut
Mutter: wir verstehen uns gut

Ich muss zu Hause helfen/abwaschen/mein Zimmer aufräumen
Ich darf keine Musik im Wohnzimmer hören.
Ich darf (im Schlafzimmer) fernsehen.
Ich darf in die Disco gehen.
Ich darf nicht in Konzerte gehen.

AT 4.4 **3b** *Du bist dran! Beschreib deine Eltern.* Pupils write their own independent piece on the model of their letter in activity 3a.

C 26 Grammatik

This copymaster focuses on possessive adjectives, adjectival endings, subordinate clauses with *weil*, and the modal verbs *müssen* and *dürfen*.

1 *Füll die Lücken aus.* Pupils read the 'Flashback' explanation and then fill in the correct forms of the possessive adjectives.

Answers:

1 mein; 2 meine; 3 meine; 4 deine; 5 seine; 6 ihr

2 *Schreib Sätze.* Pupils read the 'Flashback' explanation and then write sentences using attributive adjectives with the ending -*e*.

Answers:

1 Ich habe schwarze Haare. 2 Ich habe blaue Augen. 3 Ich habe lockige Haare. 4 Ich habe grüne Augen. 5 Ich habe lange glatte Haare. 6 Ich habe kurze braune Haare.

3 *Verbinde die Sätze mit weil.* Pupils read the 'Flashback' explanation and then rewrite each pair of sentences as a single sentence, turning the second sentence into a subordinate clause with *weil*.

Answers:

1 Ich mag Annika nicht, weil sie sehr laut ist. 2 Ich mag Martin, weil er freundlich ist. 3 Ich mag Tobias nicht, weil er sehr arrogant ist. 4 Ich mag Silke, weil sie sehr sympathisch ist. 5 Ich mag Sabine, weil wir uns nie streiten.

4 *Schreib neue Sätze.* Pupils read the 'Flashback' explanation and then rewrite the sentences to incorporate *müssen* or *dürfen*.

Answers:

1 Ich muss in die Schule gehen. 2 Ich darf in die Disco gehen. 3 Ich darf Süßigkeiten kaufen. 4 Ich muss den Tisch decken. 5 Ich darf in den Ferien arbeiten.

C 27 Tipp

This copymaster focuses on criticizing/giving opinions tactfully, and using separable verbs.

1 *Wie ist deine Familie? Wie versteht ihr euch? Schreib Sätze.* Pupils read the 'Flashback' and then write sentences about how they get on with their own families.

2 *Schreib Sätze mit den Verben.* Pupils read the 'Flashback' and then write sentences using the separable verbs. More able pupils may construct more complex/varied sentences. Note that not all of these separable verbs are used in this unit of the Students' Book.

Answers:

(Accept any grammatically correct alternatives.)
1 aufräumen – Ich räume auf. 2 sich anziehen – Ich ziehe mich an. 3 aufstehen – Ich stehe auf. 4 abfahren – Ich fahre ab. 5 ankommen – Ich komme an. 6 fernsehen – Ich sehe fern. 7 sich ausziehen – Ich ziehe mich aus. 8 einkaufen – Ich kaufe ein. 9 mitmachen – Ich mache mit. 10 abwaschen – Ich wasche ab.

Materials

- Students' Book pages 44–45
- Cassette 1 side B

This revision spread provides consolidation and further practice of language from Units 1–3. You can either take pupils through the activities as a whole class or they can work independently (at home or in school) or in pairs. The activities should help pupils prepare for the assessment for Units 1–3.

T 1.5 **1a** *Hör gut zu. Kai, Benedikt und Astrid beschreiben die Ferien. Kopiere die Tabelle und füll sie aus.* Activity 1 revises the material from Unit 1, pages 10–13. In activity 1a, pupils listen to the recording and then fill out the table in note form. Pupils may benefit from advice on note-taking and the form of notes required for this task.

Answers:

	Wohin?	Wie?	Was gemacht?
Kai	nach Irland	mit dem Auto	ins Schwimmbad gegangen, Rad gefahren
Benedikt	nach Stuttgart	mit dem Zug	Tante und Onkel besucht, einen Ausflug nach München gemacht, ein T-Shirt gekauft
Astrid	nach Indien	geflogen	in viele Museen gegangen, Großeltern besucht, Curry gegessen, Limonade getrunken

Transcript   p 44, activity 1a

– Hallo, Kai! Wohin bist du im Sommer gefahren?
– Ich? Ich bin mit meiner Familie nach Irland gefahren – mit dem Auto.
– Was hast du in Irland gemacht?
– Ich habe viel gemacht! Ich bin ins Schwimmbad gegangen und Rad gefahren. Es war toll.

– Und du, Benedikt? Bist du zu Hause geblieben?
– Ja und nein. Ich bin zu Hause geblieben und ich habe meine Tante und meinen Onkel in Stuttgart besucht. Ich bin mit dem Zug dorthin gefahren.
– Hast du viel gemacht?
– Ja. Wir haben einen Ausflug nach München gemacht und wir sind in die Stadt gefahren. Ich habe ein T-Shirt von Bayern-München gekauft!

– Astrid, was hast du im Sommer gemacht?
– Wir sind nach Indien geflogen. Also, meine Familie und ich sind in viele Museen gegangen und wir haben meine Großeltern besucht. Ich habe viel Curry gegessen und Limonade getrunken.

AT 2.5 **1b** *Ist alles richtig? Macht Dialoge.* Pupils use their answers to activity 1a as the basis for a dialogue, taking it in turns to be the interviewer and one of Kai, Benedikt and Astrid.

AT 3.5 **2a** *Lies die Postkarte von Katja und beantworte die Fragen.* Activity 2 revises the material from Unit 1, pages 10–17. Pupils read Katja's postcard and answer the

comprehension questions in full sentences. Pupils may benefit from a reminder of the basic rules for the perfect tense, or from answering the questions verbally in class, before writing up the answers.

Answers:

1 Sie ist nach Bangor in Wales gefahren. 2 Sie ist im Sommer gefahren. 3 Sie hat einen Ausflug gemacht, Eis gegessen und Cola getrunken. 4 Sie hat in einer Ferienwohnung gewohnt. 5 Es war windig, aber es war sehr heiß. 6 Es war toll.

AT 4.5 **2b** *Schreib zwei Postkarten (so wie Katja) mit den Informationen unten.* Pupils use Katja's postcard as a model for two postcards of their own, using the picture cues provided. Less able pupils may benefit from oral discussion of the task, before attempting to write out the postcards.

Answers:

a To include: nach Spanien gefahren/geflogen, in die Disco gegangen, in einem Hotel gewohnt, windig und sonnig, zum Strand gegangen.
b To include: nach Amerika gefahren/geflogen, Sehenswürdigkeiten besichtigt, Hamburger und Pommes frites gegessen, in einem Wohnmobil gewohnt, hat geregnet, war kalt

AT 2.5 **2c** *Nimm jetzt die Informationen auf Kassette auf.* Pupils now use their postcards as the basis for a recording. This could take the form of a monologue, with or without notes, or could be done by pairs of pupils as an interview.

AT 3.4 **3a** *Lies den Brief von Maja.* Activity 3 revises the material from Unit 2, pages 22–25. In activity 3a, pupils read Maja's letter. You may wish to ask some questions to check their comprehension, e.g. *Wann steht Maja auf? Hilft sie zu Hause? Wie oft räumt sie ihr Zimmer auf? Was macht sie abends?*

AT 4.4 **3b** *Du bist dran! Beschreib deinen Alltag wie Maja.* Pupils use Maja's letter as a model for their own descriptions of their daily routine. Point out that they should vary the sequence, as well as the times of the activities, and add or omit activities to individualize their work.

 AT 1.4 **4a** *Interview im Radio. Hör gut zu und lies die Sätze. Sind sie richtig oder falsch?* Activity 4 revises the material from Unit 2, pages 26–29. In activity 4a, pupils listen to

the recording and then decide whether the statements are true or false.

Answers:

1 falsch; 2 falsch; 3 richtig; 4 richtig; 5 richtig; 6 falsch; 7 richtig; 8 falsch

U4 exam June '04

Transcript   p 45, activities 4a and 4b

– Udo! Wie hilfst du zu Hause?
– Also, einmal pro Woche kaufe ich für meinen Vater ein und ich decke immer den Tisch. Aber ich räume nie mein Zimmer auf.
– Hast du auch einen Nebenjob?
– Ja, natürlich. Ich brauche das Geld. Ich bekomme kein Taschengeld von meinem Vater – also, ich habe einen Nebenjob.
– Was ist dein Nebenjob?
– Ich trage Zeitungen aus und ich arbeite auch im Garten.
– Wie findest du die Arbeit?
– Ich trage nicht gern Zeitungen aus und ich bekomme nur 25 Euro pro Woche. Ich finde den Job langweilig, aber ich arbeite gern im Garten – dafür bekomme ich jeden Samstag 10 Euro von meinen Großeltern.
– Was kaufst du mit dem Geld oder sparst du das alles?
– Ich spare nur 5 Euro pro Woche und ich kaufe CDs oder Schokolade.

 AT 1.4 **4b** *Hör noch einmal gut zu und korrigiere die falschen Sätze.* Pupils listen to the recording again and correct the false statements in activity 4a.

Answers:

1 Udo kauft einmal pro Woche ein. 2 Er räumt sein Zimmer nie auf. 6 Er arbeitet gern im Garten. 8 Er spart 5 Euro pro Woche.

AT 2.4 **4c** *Macht ein Interview so wie in Übung 4a.* Pupils use the recorded interview and the questions given as the basis for their own interviews, working in pairs. The interviews could be recorded.

AT 2.2 **5** *Ratespiel: A wählt einen Jungen und beschreibt ihn, B rät. Dann ist B dran.* This activity revises the material from Unit 3, pages 34–35. Pupils work together in pairs. Partner A chooses one of the three boys (without telling B which one he/she has chosen) and describes him. Partner B has to decide which boy is being described.

AT 3.4 **6a** *Lies Marks Brief.* Activity 6 revises the material from Unit 3, pages 36–41. In activity 6a, pupils read Mark's letter. You may wish to check their comprehension of the letter by asking questions, e.g. *Was darf Mark zu Hause nicht machen? Was muss er machen? Warum muss Mark jeden Abend lernen? Was darf Mark bei seinen Großeltern machen?*

AT 4.4 **6b** *Du bist dran! Wie sind deine Eltern/Großeltern? Schreib einen Antwortbrief an Mark.* Pupils reply to Mark, using his letter as a model for their own. Tell pupils that they can reply as Thomas or another person if they prefer.

AT 2.3 **7** *Gedächtnisspiel: Was darfst du nicht machen? Was musst du machen?* This game revises the material from Unit 3, pages 40–41. Pupils play in small groups, each player repeating what the previous player said and adding a sentence of his/her own. Each time a player forgets a sentence, hesitates or gets the sentences in the wrong order, the game starts again with the next player.

1-3 Kontrolle

Materials
- Copymasters 82–85
- Cassette 1 side B

Hören

1 *Warum streiten sich Angelika und ihre Eltern? Hör gut zu und finde die richtige Reihenfolge für die Bilder.* Pupils listen to the recording, in which Angelika talks about her relationship with her parents, and then put the pictures into the correct sequence.

Answers: b, d, e, c, a

Mark scheme:
2 marks for each correct answer (total 10)

Assessment criteria:
Pupils who can sequence the pictures correctly show evidence of performance at AT1 level 4. Pupils who have correctly identified some individual pictures but failed to comprehend the whole sequence may be awarded level 2 or 3 depending on the number of correct answers.

Transcript   C 82, activity 1

- Angelika, wie verstehst du dich mit deinen Eltern?
- Wir verstehen uns nicht sehr gut – wir streiten uns oft.
- Warum?
- Na ja, erstens, weil ich kein eigenes Zimmer habe. Ich teile mein Zimmer mit meiner Schwester und sie ist sehr laut und unfreundlich.
- Und sonst?
- Zweitens streiten wir uns, weil ich mein Zimmer immer aufräumen muss. Meine Mutter ist sehr ungeduldig und ich muss das jeden Tag machen.
- Und nummer drei?
- Also, ich sehe zu viel fern. Nach der Schule gibt es meine Lieblingssendungen und ich sehe meistens jeden Abend zwei Stunden fern!
- Sonst noch etwas?
- Oh, ja! Wir streiten uns auch, weil ich selten zu Hause helfe. Meine Mutter sagt, ich muss jeden Tag abwaschen, aber ich will fernsehen. Und ich habe auch so viele Hausaufgaben ...
- Und nummer fünf?
- Also, nummer fünf: Wir streiten uns, weil ich nicht viel Taschengeld bekomme. Ich bekomme pro Woche nur zwei Euro und das finde ich nicht fair!

---

2 *Wo haben Monika, Abi, Sven, Robert und Irene in den Ferien gewohnt? Wie waren die Leute? Hör gut zu und füll die Tabelle mit den passenden Wörtern aus.* Pupils listen to the recording, in which the speakers talk about their recent holiday experiences, and complete the table with the words provided in the two boxes.

Answers:

	Wo hat er/sie gewohnt?	Wie waren die Leute?
Monika	Ferienwohnung	launisch, gemein
Abi	Gastfamilie	lieb, tolerant, sympathisch
Sven	Wohnmobil	freundlich, nett
Robert	Jugendherberge	nett, geduldig, lustig
Irene	Freunde	freundlich, lieb, nie streng

Mark scheme:
1 mark for each word correctly located in the appropriate box, up to a total of 18. In order to encourage accuracy, a bonus of 2 marks can be awarded for correctly copying spelling and capital letters, etc. 1 mark can be awarded for each answer with minor errors (total 20).

Assessment criteria:
Due to the length, content and tense coverage of the text, pupils who score 14 or more marks show evidence of AT1 level 5. Pupils scoring 10 marks may be awarded a level 4.

Transcript   C 82, activity 2

- Tag, Monika! Warst du in Spanien?
- Ja, wir haben in einer Ferienwohnung in Malaga gewohnt. Die Wohnung war sehr groß. Malaga war prima, aber die Leute dort waren nicht so super. Die Leute in der nächsten Wohnung waren launisch und gemein.
- Oh, das tut mir wirklich Leid. Und du, Abi?
- Ich bin nach Italien geflogen. Wir haben bei einer Gastfamilie gewohnt.
- War die Familie nett?
- Meine Gastfamilie war wirklich lieb, sehr tolerant und sehr sympathisch.
- Warst du auch in Italien, Sven?
- Nein, ich bin nach Amerika geflogen. Wir haben in einem großen Wohnmobil gewohnt und das war einfach Klasse! Wir haben viele freundliche und nette Leute getroffen.
- Und du, Robert?
- Ich bin nach Frankreich gefahren.
- Wo in Frankreich?
- Ich bin nach Reims gefahren – mit meiner Klasse. Wir haben in einer Jugendherberge gewohnt.
- Wie war die Jugendherberge, Robert?
- Sie war ganz neu und die Leute waren so nett. Ich war ein bisschen schüchtern, aber sie waren sehr geduldig und auch lustig.
- Und wo warst du, Irene?
- Ich habe bei Freunden hier in Deutschland gewohnt. Sie wohnen in Bayern, in Süddeutschland. Ich mag meine Freunde sehr, weil sie so freundlich und lieb sind – und sie waren nie streng!

C 83 **Sprechen**

AT 2.4 **1a** *Frag deinen Partner/deine Partnerin:* Pupils work together in pairs to create dialogues. Partner A asks questions about a variety of topics (appearance, relationship with parents, pocket money, jobs, spending). Partner B responds with his/her own information (no cues are provided).

AT 2.4 **1b** *Dein Partner/deine Partnerin stellt Fragen. Du antwortest.* This is the second part of the activity with the roles reversed.

Mark scheme:
2 marks for each correct answer communicated. If the answer is partially communicated, or if the answer contains a significant grammatical error, 1 mark may be awarded. Up to 5 marks may be awarded for pronunciation (total 15).

Assessment criteria:
Pupils who communicate 4 answers correctly without significant error, show evidence of performance at AT2 level 3 or 4 depending on the length and quality of their response. If the answers are partially communicated or contain significant grammatical errors, 1 mark may be awarded and the performance would show evidence of AT2 levels 1 or 2.

AT 2.5 **2a** *Dein Partner/deine Partnerin stellt Fragen über deine Ferien. Schau das Bild rechts an und antworte.* Pupils work together in pairs to create dialogues. Partner B asks questions about Partner A's recent holidays (destination, accommodation, activities). Partner A responds with the information provided in his/her picture cues.

AT 2.5 **2b** *Frag deinen Partner/deine Partnerin:* This is the second part of the activity with the roles reversed.

Mark scheme:
2 marks for each correct answer fully and unambiguously communicated, including correct appropriate tense. (Note that question 3 contains 3 details: 2 marks per detail). If the answer is partially communicated, or if the answer contains significant grammatical error, 1 mark may be awarded. Up to 5 marks may be awarded for pronunciation (total 15).

Assessment criteria:
Pupils gaining 7 or more marks show evidence of performance at AT2 level 5. Pupils gaining 4 or more marks show evidence of performance at AT2 level 3 or 4.

C 84A **Lesen 1**

AT 3.2 **1** *Finde die passenden Bilder für die Sätze.* Pupils match the pictures to the sentences (house rules, holiday activities in the present and perfect tenses).

Answers: 1 c; 2 d; 3 b; 4 e; 5 a

Mark scheme:
2 marks for each correct answer (total 10)

Assessment criteria:
Pupils with 4 or more correct answers show evidence of performance at AT3 level 2.

AT 3.3 **2** *Finde die passenden Antworten für die Fragen.* Pupils match the responses to the questions (various topics in the present and imperfect tenses).

Answers: 1 b; 2 e; 3 d; 4 a; 5 c

Mark scheme:
2 marks for each correct answer (total 10)

Assessment criteria:
Pupils with 4 or more correct answers show evidence of performance at AT3 level 3.

C 84B **Lesen 2**

AT 3.5 **1** *Richard beschreibt seinen besten Freund Peter. Was findet er gut und nicht so gut? Lies den Brief und füll die Tabelle aus.* Pupils read the text, in which Richard describes his relationship with his best friend, and then complete the table.

Answers:

gut	nicht so gut
immer nett, nie launisch	manchmal ungeduldig
wir verstehen uns sehr gut	Eltern altmodisch – darf nicht fernsehen
Lieblingsgruppe – cool	kein Taschengeld – muss in den Ferien arbeiten
Lieblingsfarbe	
Ferien in Italien – hat viel Spaß gemacht	

Mark scheme:
Award up to 10 marks for answers in the *gut* and *nicht so gut* sections. A dash (–) indicates an alternative/additional answer, which may be awarded one mark (total 10).

Assessment criteria:
Pupils gaining 7 or more marks show evidence of performance at AT3 level 5. Teachers may award level 4 for pupils whose performance narrowly misses 7 marks.

Note that Copymasters 84A and 84B (*Lesen 1* and *Lesen 2*) should be treated as one assessment, totalling 30 marks.

C 85 **Schreiben**

AT 4.3 **1** *Wie ist Herr Schwarz? Schreib Sätze.* Pupils write sentences to describe Herr Schwarz, in response to the numbered picture cues.

Answers:

(Accept different formulations.)
1 Er hat lange, schwarze, lockige Haare./Seine Haare sind lang, schwarz und lockig.
2 Er trägt eine Brille.
(3 Er isst gern Hamburger und trinkt Cola.)
4 Er ist gemein.
5 Er trägt Ohrringe.
6 Er sieht gern fern./Sein Lieblingsfilm ist Star Wars.

Mark scheme:
2 marks for each correct description (total 10)

Assessment criteria:
Pupils gaining 7 or more marks show evidence of performance at AT4 level 3.

AT 4.4 **2** *Beschreib den Alltag von Hanna.* Pupils look at the cartoon strip and then describe Hanna's daily routine using the first person.

Answers:

(Pupils should convey the following information; formulations will vary:)
Um halb acht ziehe ich mich an und ich frühstücke.
Ich räume mein Zimmer auf und sauge Staub.
Ich bekomme Taschengeld (4 Euro) von meiner Mutter.
Ich kaufe Kleidung (eine Jeans und ein T-Shirt).
Ich trage Zeitungen aus.

Mark scheme:
2 marks for each complete description containing a key verb accurately communicated. 1 mark may be awarded for each complete description containing significant error (total 10).

Assessment criteria:
Pupils gaining 6 or more marks show evidence of performance at AT4 level 4. Teachers may award level 3 for pupils whose performance narrowly misses 6 marks.

AT 4.5 **3** *Wohin bist du im Sommer gefahren und wie war das Wetter? Schreib Sätze.* Pupils write sentences about their holidays (in the perfect and imperfect tenses) in response to the picture cues.

Answers:

(Accept different formulations which convey the same information.)
(1 Ich bin nach Spanien gefahren. Das Wetter war heiß und windig.)
 2 Ich bin nach Indien gefahren. Es hat geregnet und es war wolkig.
 3 Ich bin nach Amerika gefahren. Es hat geschneit.
 4 Ich bin nach Frankreich gefahren. Es war immer heiß.
 5 Ich bin nach Deutschland gefahren. Es war neblig und kalt.
 6 Ich bin nach Griechenland gefahren. Es war heiß und sonnig.

Mark scheme:
2 marks for each complete description accurately communicated, including details of the location and the weather. 1 mark may be awarded for each complete description containing significant error, or for accurate communication of one only of the location or the weather (total 10).

Assessment criteria:
Pupils gaining 8 or more marks show evidence of performance at AT4 level 5. Teachers may award level 4 for pupils whose performance narrowly misses 8 marks.

Einheit 4 Mode

Pages	Objectives	Grammar	Pronunciation, Skill focus	Key language	PoS	AT level
46–47 Die Klasse!- Clique	Reading and listening for pleasure. Familiarization with themes, structures and language of the unit	–	–	–	–	1.4, 3.2, 3.4
48–49 Was hast du gekauft?	Ask others what clothes they have bought. Say what clothes you have bought	Plural nouns	Pronunciation: vowels with and without an *Umlaut*. Dictionary skills: plural nouns	*Was hast du gekauft? Ich habe zwei/drei T-Shirts/Hemden/ Schuhe/Blusen/Pullover/Röcke/Jeans/ Hosen/Mützen/Rucksäcke gekauft.*	1a, 1b, 1c, 2a, 2b, 2c, 2d, 3d, 5a, 5f, 5i	1.2, 1.5, 2.2, 3.2, 4.3
50–51 Wie gefällt dir diese Jeans?	Ask others their opinion on items of clothes. Give your opinion on items of clothes	*dieser* and *welcher*	–	*Wie gefällt dir dieser Pullover/Rock? Wie gefällt dir diese Jacke/Hose/Jeans? Wie gefällt dir dieses Hemd/T-Shirt? Wie gefallen dir diese Schuhe? Welcher Pullover/Rock gefällt dir? Welche Bluse/Jacke gefällt dir? Welches Hemd/T-Shirt gefällt dir? Welche Schuhe gefallen dir? Er/Sie/Es gefällt mir (sehr) gut/nicht so gut/gar nicht. Sie gefallen mir (sehr) gut/nicht so gut/gar nicht. Er/Sie/Es ist zu klein/kurz/groß/eng/ lang/teuer.*	1a, 1b, 1c, 2a, 2b, 2c, 2d, 5a, 5c, 5f, 5i	1.2, 1.4, 2.3–4, 3.2, 4.4
52–53 Was trägst du zur Schule?		Adjectival endings in the accusative after the indefinite article	Correcting and redrafting written work	*Was trägst du zur Schule? Ich trage einen roten/grünen Pullover/Schlips/Rock. Ich trage eine gelbe/weiße Jacke/Bluse/Strumpfhose/Jeans/Hose. Ich trage ein braunes/graues/großes/ kurzes Hemd/T-Shirt/Kleid. Ich trage blaue/schwarze Schuhe.*	1a, 1b, 1c, 2a, 2b, 2c, 2d, 2j, 3e, 4c, 5a, 5d, 5f, 5i	1.3, 2.3, 3.2, 4.2, 4.4

National curriculum

Pages	Objectives	Grammar	Pronunciation, Skill focus	Key language	PoS	AT level
54–55 **Ich trage am liebsten eine Jeans!**	Ask others what they wear to school Say what you wear for school Describe colours Ask others what clothes they like Say what clothes you like and dislike Ask and say what your favourite clothes are Ask for and give opinions on school uniform	–	Listening for detail	*Was trägst du gern/nicht gern/am liebsten?* *Ich trage gern/nicht gern/am liebsten einen Pullover/Minirock; eine Jeansjacke/Bluse/Hose;* *ein Sweatshirt/Kleid/Hemd/T-Shirt; Turnschuhe/Socken.* *Ich trage nicht gern Uniform.* *Ich trage lieber Jeans.* *Wie findest du/Wie gefällt dir deine Uniform?* *Meine Uniform gefällt mir (nicht so) gut/gar nicht.* *Ich finde meine Uniform schön/ hässlich/schrecklich/bequem/ unbequem/altmodisch/modern/ praktisch.* *Meine Uniform ist gut/schlecht, weil sie … ist.*	1a, 1b, 1c, 2a, 2b, 2c, 2d, 3d, 4c, 5a, 5c, 5d, 5f, 5i	1.3–4, 2.3–4, 3.3, 4.3–4
56–57 **Thema im Fokus**	Encourage reading for pleasure Use language from Unit 4 creatively Encourage independent, pair- and groupwork	–	–	–	1c, 2b, 2e, 2h, 2j, 3e, 4a, 5c, 5d, 5f, 5i	2.4, 3.3–4, 4.3–4

 **Mode**

Aims of the unit

- To be able to talk about clothes you have bought
- To be able to give your opinion on items of clothing
- To be able to talk about what you wear for school
- To be able to say which clothes you like and dislike, and which are your favourites

Die Klasse!-Clique

pages 46–47

Materials

- Students' Book pages 46–47
- Cassette 2 side A
- Workbook page 34

For general advice on exploiting the photo story, see pages 10–11 of the introduction to this book.

In this episode we are introduced to Alexander, Annika's neighbour. Alexander brings round Annika's lost bicycle, which he found abandoned in town. This is the first time Jasmin has met Alexander, and it seems like love at first sight. Later in the day, Jasmin and Annika are hunting for clothes bargains in town when they see Alexander again, and Jasmin admits to Annika that she rather likes the look of him. Then the girls bump into Sven, who is looking very down. The girls are puzzled: what can be the cause of Sven's gloominess?

Unit 4 goes over reassuringly familiar ground: rather than introducing radically new structures, it focuses on accuracy in inflections – specifically plural noun endings, determiners and adjectival endings. Thus most of the vocabulary and structures from the photo story should be familiar to pupils: in *Klasse! 1* (p. 81) they were introduced to basic clothes vocabulary: *der Pullover, der Rock, die Bluse, die Jacke, die Jeans, das T-Shirt, das Hemd, die Schuhe*, while the perfect with auxiliary *haben* and *sein* was introduced in *Klasse! 1*, Unit 9 and revised in *Klasse! 2*, Unit 1.

AT 3.2 **1a** *Was meinst du? Vor dem Lesen: Rate!* Pre-reading activity: pupils look at the photos without reading the text, and predict what the content of the photo story will be, choosing the sentence ending they consider more likely from each pair given. The vocabulary and structures used in the questions should be familiar to pupils from Units 1–3. Do not give the pupils the answers yet: they will check them themselves in activity 1b.

Answers: 1 b; 2 a; 3 a; 4 b; 5 b

1b *Ist alles richtig? Hör gut zu und lies mit.* Pupils listen to the recording and follow the text in the book. Then they decide whether their predictions in activity 1a were correct or not. This could be done as a whole-class activity. Ask pupils for sentences from the text to back up their choices.

AT 1.4
AT 3.4

Transcript p 47, activity 1b

- Hallo, Annika! Ich glaube, das ist dein Fahrrad!
- Ja!! Oh, danke – vielen Dank! Wo hast du das gefunden?
- Ich war gestern in der Stadt und da war dein Fahrrad – am Markt!
- Oh, danke Alexander! Oh, Alexander, das ist Jasmin – Jasmin, das ist Alexander.
- Hallo!
- Tag, Alexander!
- Hmm ... Er ist so nett!

Später in der Stadt ...
- Annika, Annika! Dort drüben ... da ist Alexander!
- Wo? Wo?
- Dort links! Er trägt eine schwarze Jeans und ein graues Hemd ... Oh, er sieht super aus!
- Also ... gefällt dir Alexander, Jasmin?
- Ja!

- Hallo, Sven! Wie geht's?
- Bist du auch zum Ausverkauf gefahren? Was hast du gekauft? Ich habe zwei T-Shirts gekauft – und Annika hat drei Pullover gekauft!
- Was? Nein ... ich – ich muss nach Hause ...
- Was hat Sven? Er ist so ernst – und so traurig ...

AT 3.4 **2** *Finde im Text:* Pupils scan the text for specific information. *Traurig* will probably be unfamiliar to pupils: ask them for suggestions as to what it might mean, using the context. As a general point of comprehension, ask pupils what they think an *Ausverkauf* might be.

Answers:

1 Jeans, Hemd, T-Shirts, Pullover; 2 schwarz, grau; 3 nett, ernst, traurig

AT 3.4 **3** *Sind die Sätze richtig oder falsch?* Pupils re-read the text and decide whether the statements are true or false.

Answers:

1 richtig; 2 falsch; 3 falsch; 4 richtig; 5 richtig; 6 falsch

Follow-up activity. After completing the comprehension activities, pupils could work together in groups of approximately four (ideally, two male and two female pupils in each group) to read the parts of Alexander, Annika, Jasmin and Sven. Encourage the pupils to put as much expression into the parts as possible: Alexander can be a real hunk, Annika friendly and lively, Jasmin shy and lovestruck, and Sven gloomy and serious.

Viel Spaß!

Ausverkauf. The main aim is listening for pleasure, but the song also revises clothing vocabulary and introduces *dieser*. For general advice on exploiting the songs in *Klasse! 2*, see page 7 of the introduction to this book.

Transcript   p 47, Viel Spaß!

Junge Mode im Ausverkauf!
Junge Mode im Ausverkauf!

Ich kaufe dieses T-Shirt
Wie gefällt es dir?
Es gefällt mir leider nicht
Denn es ist viel zu klein!

Refrain

Ich kaufe diese Hose
Wie gefällt sie dir?
Sie gefällt mir leider nicht
Denn sie ist viel zu kurz!

Refrain

Ich kaufe diese Bluse
Wie gefällt sie dir?
Sie gefällt mir leider nicht
Denn sie ist viel zu eng!

Refrain

Ich kaufe diese Mütze
Wie gefällt sie dir?
Sie gefällt mir leider nicht
Denn sie ist viel zu gelb!

Refrain

WB A Workbook activity A could be used at this point for exploitation of the song text.

For the next lesson

Ask pupils to bring in pictures of their favourite clothing from catalogues, or pictures of their favourite personalities wearing fashionable clothes. These can be used as additional/alternative visual stimuli for speaking and writing activities throughout this unit.

Was hast du gekauft?
Pages 48–49

Objectives

• Ask others what clothes they have bought
• Say what clothes you have bought

Key language

Was hast du gekauft?
Ich habe zwei/drei T-Shirts/Hemden/Schuhe/Blusen/
Pullover/Röcke/Jeans/Hosen/Mützen/Rucksäcke gekauft.

National Curriculum PoS

statements 1a, 1b, 1c, 2a, 2b, 2c, 2d, 3d, 5a, 5f, 5i

Materials

• Students' Book pages 48–49
• Cassette 2 side A
• Workbook pages 35–37
• Copymasters 28, 31, 34, 35A

C 28 **Preparatory work**

Use the pictures from copymaster 28 copied onto an OHT or as flashcards to revise and extend pupils' clothing vocabulary. Use the pictures to elicit the singular forms from the class. T: *Was ist das?* P1: *Das ist ein Rock.* T: *Richtig!*, etc. (For general advice on using copymaster visuals, see page 12 of the introduction to this book.) Once pupils are confident about the singular forms, you can move on to activity 1a and plurals.

AT 3.2 **1a** *Jasmin ist in die Stadt gefahren. Es ist Ausverkauf – alles ist billig! Was hat sie gekauft? Finde die passenden Sätze für die Bilder.* This activity introduces the plural forms of some clothing items. Pupils match the speech bubbles to the pictures of clothes. They can check their own answers by doing activity 1b.

Answers: 1 c; 2 d; 3 b; 4 e; 5 a

1b *Ist alles richtig? Hör gut zu.* Pupils listen to the recording and check their answers to activity 1a against what they hear. If necessary, the answers could be fed back as a whole-class activity. Now you could elicit the plural forms from the class. T: *Ein Rock, zwei …* P1: *Röcke?* T: *Richtig!*, etc., checking pronunciation. Alternatively, you could wait until you are ready to do the *Grammatik im Fokus* section before asking pupils to produce the plural forms.

AT 1.2

Transcript   p 48, activity 1b

1 – Ich habe zwei T-Shirts gekauft.
2 – Ich habe zwei Pullover gekauft.
3 – Ich habe auch zwei Blusen gekauft.
4 – Ich habe zwei Röcke gekauft.
5 – Und ich habe Schuhe gekauft.

C 31 Activity 1 on copymaster 31 could be used at this point for additional listening comprehension on *ich habe … gekauft* and plural nouns.

1c *Sind die Sätze richtig oder falsch? Hör gut zu und korrigiere die falschen Sätze.* Pupils listen to the recording and then decide whether the statements are true or false. They then write true statements for the ones which are false.

AT 1.5

Answers:

1 falsch: Sie spart für einen Computer. 2 richtig; 3 falsch: Sie mag Schwarz./Schwarz ist ihre Lieblingsfarbe. 4 richtig; 5 falsch: Die Röcke sind sehr modern. 6 richtig

Transcript   p 48, activity 1c

– Hallo, Jasmin!
– Hi, Annika! Du bist auch in der Stadt! Bist du auch zum Ausverkauf gefahren?
– Nein, ich habe kein Geld! Ich spare für einen Computer … Aber du hast eins – zwei – drei – vier Taschen! Was hast du gekauft?
– Hier, schau mal – ich habe zwei T-Shirts gekauft – zwei T-Shirts in Schwarz. Schwarz ist meine Lieblingsfarbe!
– Oh, die T-Shirts sind sehr schön!
– Ja, und ich habe auch zwei Röcke gekauft – hier!

> – Toll! Ein Rock in Rot, und ein Rock in Blau – sehr modern!
> – Ja. Und ich habe Schuhe gekauft – Schuhe in Braun, für die Schule.
> – Aha ... Und was ist in der Tasche hier?
> – Pullover – ich habe auch zwei Pullover gekauft. Einen Pullover in Grün ...
> – ... und einen Pullover in Gelb – nicht schlecht! Ist das alles?
> – Nein, ich habe auch zwei Blusen gekauft – hier!
> – Hey, super! Eine Bluse in Weiß, und eine Bluse in Orange ...

WB B Workbook activity B could be used at this point to provide extension work on plural forms. Alternatively, you could leave this activity until the *Grammatik im Fokus* section has been completed and use it as consolidation.

WB C Workbook activity C provides listening comprehension on further plural forms and could also be used at this point, or after the *Grammatik im Fokus* section.

Gut gesagt!

Vokale und Umlaute. This section focuses on the correct pronunciation of vowels with and without an *Umlaut*. You could point out to the class that it is very important to make the distinction between the vowels with and without an *Umlaut* – they should think of them as completely different sounds, rather than regarding the *Umlaut* as an 'optional extra' which they don't really need to bother with! It may help to impress on pupils that an *Umlaut* may sometimes be the only thing that helps distinguish between one word and another.

2a *Hör gut zu und lies mit.* Pupils listen to the pronunciation of the vowels with and without an *Umlaut*. They could then practise making the individual vowel sounds themselves. Pronounce each pair of vowels for the class, asking them to observe and then copy the shape of your lips for each vowel. (You could treat *e* and *ä* as identical, since not all German dialects make a clear distinction.) Making the transition from the unmutated to the mutated vowel (*u–ü, o–ö, a–ä*) will be particularly helpful in increasing the accuracy of pupils' pronunciation. Encourage pupils to practise at home in front of a mirror – this will help them to get the lip shape right.

Transcript   p 48, activity 2a

– u   eine Bluse
– o   ein Rock
– i   ein Ohrring
– a   eine Jacke
– e   ein Hemd

– ü   eine Mütze
– ö   Röcke
– ä   Rucksäcke

2b *Hör gut zu und wiederhole.* Pupils practise the vowel sounds in connected speech. Encourage them to practise these little texts at home or elsewhere by themselves. They could record themselves on tape, listen critically and try to improve their pronunciation with every recording.

Transcript   p 48, activity 2b

Meine Hose ist rot,
meine Schuhe sind super!
Mein Pullover ist groß,
mein Hemd ist gelb!
Meine Tasche ist schwarz,
meine Mütze ist grün
und meine Röcke sind schön!

Grammatik im Fokus

Plural. This section focuses on the various types of plural formation in German. Before looking at the table, elicit plural forms from the pupils as suggested for activity 1b. Write up more plural forms (e.g. *Taschen, Mützen, Hosen*) and ask pupils whether they can see any patterns. For example, have they noticed that words which end in *-e* in the singular usually take the plural ending *-n*? How many of the words take the plural ending *-s*? You could point out to pupils that *-s* is one of the **least** common plural forms in German (*-e* is probably the most common, with or without an *Umlaut*), and is mostly used for words borrowed from English. So, if they don't know the plural, putting an *-s* on the end and hoping for the best is not a good policy!

C 35A Copymaster 35A gives additional information and advice about plurals.

3a *Was ist der Singular für diese Plural-Wörter? Schreib die Wörter auf.* Pupils find the singular forms of the nouns. If pupils have completed Workbook activities B and C they should be familiar with these forms. If not, more able pupils should be able to work them out from the patterns shown in the *Grammatik im Fokus* panel above.

Answers:

1 eine Jacke; 2 eine Hose; 3 ein Hemd; 4 eine Mütze;
5 ein Rucksack; 6 eine Jeans

3b *Ist alles richtig? A fragt, B antwortet. Dann ist B dran.* Pupils work together in pairs to check their answers to activity 3a. Partner A gives the plural form, partner B gives the singular form, then the roles are reversed.

Follow-up activity. Pupils could extend this activity to other fields of vocabulary they are familiar with, e.g. pets, items in their school bags, etc. Pupils could work individually or in teams to compile a list of ten plurals and then challenge their partners/other teams to provide the singular forms.

C 34 Activity 1 on copymaster 34 is a crossword puzzle on clothing items in the plural and could be used for consolidation at this point.

4 *Deine Schwestern haben Geburtstag. Du hast Kleidung usw. für sie gekauft. Was hast du gekauft? Schreib Sätze.* Pupils write sentences about the presents they have bought, based on the picture. Tell pupils that they have to treat both sisters equally, so they will have bought two of everything. Prepare for the activity by looking at the *Hilfe* box on page 48 with the class.

Answers:

Ich habe zwei Rucksäcke gekauft. Ich habe zwei Mützen gekauft. Ich habe zwei T-Shirts gekauft. Ich habe zwei Pullover gekauft. Ich habe zwei Röcke gekauft. Ich habe Schuhe gekauft.

WB D Workbook activity D is an information-gap activity to practise plurals, and could be done at this point.

T 2.2 **5** *Gedächtnisspiel: Was hast du gekauft?* Pupils play the game in small groups. Player A names something (always a pair of items, to practise the plural forms) he/she has bought, player B repeats this and adds another pair of items, and so on.

WB E Workbook activity E could be used as an extension writing task at this point.

AT 4.1 *Noch mal! Schau die Bilder auf Seite 48–49 an. Wie viele Kleidungsstücke siehst du? Schreib eine Liste.* Pupils list the items of clothing they can see on this spread.

AT 4.3 *Extra! Was hast du in deinem Kleiderschrank? Schreib eine Kleidungsliste.* Pupils list the items in their own wardrobes. Encourage them to think of items not featured on the spread and to look these up in their dictionaries. Pupils could invent their 'dream wardrobe' and illustrate it by cutting out photos of clothing from advertisements, etc. to make a collage. Spellings, singular and plural forms and correct articles are important in this activity.

Tipp

Wörterbuchhilfe: Plural. This section focuses on finding information about plurals in a dictionary. You may want to point out to pupils that dictionaries vary in the conventions they use, and many do not give information about plurals of German nouns in the English–German half. You could copy an appropriate dictionary extract onto an OHT, or use the school's dictionaries, and ask pupils to give the plurals of certain nouns. Encourage pupils to become familiar with the dictionary they use.

6 *Du hast Schreibwaren gekauft. Finde den Plural für die Wörter.* Pupils find the plurals of the nouns using a dictionary. Pupils could compete with each other in teams to find the plurals in the fastest time. They could then compile new lists of other singular nouns with which to challenge other teams.

Answers:

1 zwei Rechner; 2 zwei Hefte; 3 zwei Kulis; 4 zwei Taschen; 5 zwei Bücher; 6 zwei Lineale

C 35A Activities 1 and 2 on copymaster 35A could be used for more dictionary practice at this point.

Wie gefällt dir diese Jeans?
pages 50–51

Objectives
- Ask others their opinion on items of clothes
- Give your opinion on items of clothes

Key language
Wie gefällt dir dieser Pullover/Rock?
Wie gefällt dir diese Jacke/Hose/Jeans?
Wie gefällt dir dieses Hemd/T-Shirt?
Wie gefallen dir diese Schuhe?
Welcher Pullover/Rock gefällt dir?
Welche Bluse/Jacke gefällt dir?
Welches Hemd/T-Shirt gefällt dir?
Welche Schuhe gefallen dir?
Er/Sie/Es gefällt mir (sehr) gut/nicht so gut/gar nicht.
Sie gefallen mir (sehr) gut/nicht so gut/gar nicht.
Er/Sie/Es ist zu klein/kurz/groß/eng/lang/teuer.

National Curriculum PoS
statements 1a, 1b, 1c, 2a, 2b, 2c, 2d, 5a, 5c, 5f, 5i

Materials
- Students' Book pages 50–51
- Cassette 2 side A
- Workbook pages 37–39
- Copymasters 29, 31, 35B

Preparatory work
Use pictures cut out from a magazine to introduce *er/sie/es gefällt mir (nicht)*. For example, hold up a picture of a hideous pair of trousers, pull a face and say *Diese Hose gefällt mir nicht. Nein, sie gefällt mir gar nicht!* Hold up a picture of a nice sweatshirt, smile ecstatically and say *Dieses Sweatshirt gefällt mir. Es gefällt mir sehr gut!* and so on, making sure that masculine, feminine, neuter and plural nouns are covered. Pupils may benefit from seeing the positive and negative expressions on the board/OHT while you express your views. Now start to ask the pupils their opinions, e.g. T: *Lisa, wie gefällt dir dieser Rock?* P1: *Gut.* T: *Es gefällt dir gut?* P1: *Ja.* Do not insist that pupils produce the whole structure at this stage, unless they do so spontaneously.

1a *Hör gut zu und lies mit.* In this activity, the four characters introduce *dieser* and *welcher* as well as *er/sie/es gefällt mir (nicht)*. Pupils listen to the recording and read the speech bubbles in the book. Present *er/sie/es gefällt mir* and *sie gefallen mir* as set expressions.

AT 1.2
AT 3.2

Transcript	p 50, activity 1a

– Wie gefällt dir dieser Rock?
– Er gefällt mir gar nicht. Aber wie gefallen dir diese Schuhe? Sie gefallen mir sehr gut!

– Welche Jeans gefällt dir?
– Diese Jeans! Und welches T-Shirt gefällt dir?

AT 3.2 **1b** *Wer sagt was? Schreib die passenden Namen auf.* Pupils match the statements to the speakers in activity 1a.

Answers: 1 Annika; 2 Sven; 3 Annika

AT 2.3 **1c** *Du bist dran! Wie gefällt dir die Kleidung in den Fotos? Macht Dialoge.* Pupils work together in pairs to create dialogues about the clothes in the photos. In preparation, elicit from the class that it is *dieser Rock, diese Jeans, dieses T-Shirt* and *diese Schuhe.* T: *Rock – dieser, diese oder dieses?*, etc. Less able pupils will benefit from these being written up on the board/OHT as a point of reference.

AT 1.4 **2a** *Hör gut zu. Was sagen Leonie und Ingo – wie finden sie die Kleidung? Kopiere die Tabelle und schreib ✔ (gefällt mir)* oder ✘ *(gefällt mir nicht).* Pupils listen to the recording and fill in the table with Leonie and Ingo's likes and dislikes. As a follow-up activity, ask the class whether it is *dieser/diese/dieses Hemd, Hose, Jacke*, etc. More able pupils should already have grasped the pattern in activity 1, less able pupils may need to do this as an additional listening activity. Ask them to write *dieser/diese/dieses* above the items in the table – they will need this language for activity 2b.

Answers:

	Hemd	Hose	Jacke	Jeans	Pullover	Rock	Schuhe	T-Shirt
Leonie			✘	✘	✔	✘		
Ingo	✔	✔					✘	✘

Transcript   p 50, activity 2a

– Leonie, wo finde ich T-Shirts?
– Dort links. Hier, schau mal, Ingo – wie findest du dieses T-Shirt?
– Hmm – es gefällt mir nicht so gut. Aber wie gefällt dir dieser Pullover?
– Dieser Pullover in Rot? Er gefällt mir sehr gut – Rot ist meine Lieblingsfarbe! Du, wo sind die Röcke?
– Ach, hier. Oh schau mal, dieser Rock in Rot – wie gefällt dir dieser Rock?
– Er gefällt mir gar nicht! Und er ist sehr teuer! Aber hier sind Hosen – sie sind im Ausverkauf! Schau mal, Ingo, hier – welche Hose gefällt dir?
– Diese Hose hier – sie gefällt mir sehr gut! Sie ist super, finde ich. Und wie gefällt dir diese Jeans?
– Diese Jeans? Nein, sie gefällt mir nicht so gut. Wo sind Jacken?
– Dort rechts. Wie gefällt dir diese Jacke?
– Diese Jacke in Blau? Sie gefällt mir gar nicht – sie ist sehr altmodisch, finde ich. Aber schau mal, hier sind Hemden. Welches Hemd gefällt dir?
– Dieses Hemd in Grün! Es gefällt mir sehr gut. Leonie, wo sind die Schuhe? Ich muss Schuhe kaufen – für die Schule. Langweilig!
– Schuhe sind hier. Wie gefallen dir diese Schuhe?
– Sie gefallen mir gar nicht – nein!

AT 2.4 **2b** *Macht Dialoge für Leonie und Ingo.* Pupils work together in pairs to create dialogues on the basis of their answers to activity 2a. Draw pupils' attention to the *Hilfe* box. Less able pupils may benefit from an example written on the board/OHT.

WB F Workbook activity F provides further exposure to *dieser, welcher* and *gefallen* and could be used at this point.

WB G Workbook activity G could be used at this point for slightly more challenging oral work than activity 2b.

Grammatik im Fokus

dieser .../welcher ... ? This section focuses on the endings (nominative) of the determiners *dieser* and *welcher*. More able pupils may notice the similarity between the endings of *dieser* and *welcher* on the one hand and the definite article on the other. To help pupils to memorize the endings, you could make up a chant like this: T: *Der Pullover gefällt mir gut!* P: *Welcher Pullover?* T: *Dieser Pullover!*, etc., using as many examples as possible. Once pupils have got the idea, they can call out new nouns for you to use.

3a *Füll die Lücken mit dieser, diese und dieses aus.* Pupils complete the sentences with the correct form of *dieser.*

Answers:

1 Diese; 2 Dieser; 3 Diese; 4 Dieses; 5 Diese; 6 Diese; 7 Dieses; 8 Dieser

3b *Schreib Fragen mit welcher, welche und welches für die Sätze in Übung 3a.* Pupils turn their statements from activity 3a into questions with the correct form of *welcher.*

Answers:

1 Welche; 2 Welcher; 3 Welche; 4 Welches; 5 Welche; 6 Welche; 7 Welches; 8 Welcher

C 35B Copymaster 35B contains additional information about *dieser* and *welcher.* Activity 1 provides more practice of the endings.

WB H Workbook activity H could be used at this point to provide further practice of the endings of *dieser* and *welcher.*

AT 1.2 **AT 3.2** **4** *Hör gut zu und lies mit.* Pupils listen to the recording and read the text in their books. This activity provides further exposure to *dieser/diese/dieses* and introduces *zu klein/groß/teuer*, etc. Check that pupils have understood the texts with oral questions.

Transcript   p 51, activity 4

a – Dieses T-Shirt is zu klein!
b – Dieser Pullover ist zu groß!
c – Diese Schuhe sind zu teuer!
d – Dieses Hemd ist zu eng!
e – Diese Jeans ist zu kurz!
f – Dieser Rock ist zu lang!

C29 Copymaster 29 could be used at this point to reinforce *zu klein/groß/teuer*, etc. You could make one copy for each pair of pupils.

For less able pupils: Partner A holds the picture cards, partner B holds the word cards. Partner A lays down a picture card, and partner B lays down the appropriate word card as quickly as possible.

For more able pupils: Partner A has all the cards. He or she lays down a card (word or picture card) and partner B has to say an appropriate sentence as quickly as possible. For example: *Dieser Pullover ist zu groß*.

C31 Activity 2 on copymaster 31 could be used for further listening comprehension after activity 4 above.

T2.4 **5a** *Tom kauft Kleidung. Wie ist alles – was sagt er? Macht Dialoge*. Pupils work together in pairs to create dialogues about the clothing in the cartoon. Encourage pupils to put as much feeling into their complaints as possible. If they want to, they could also mime putting on short trousers, a huge cap, etc.

T4.4 **5b** *Zeichne andere Kleidung – so wie in Übung 5a. Schreib Sätze*. Pupils draw pictures of clothing and write sentences about them. Alternatively, they could cut pictures of clothing out of magazines, etc. and create a photo montage of themselves (or their least favourite sportsperson, popstar, actor, etc.) wearing a variety of ill-fitting garments.

WB I Workbook activity I provides further listening practice on items of clothing and *zu klein/groß/teuer*, etc.

Was trägst du zur Schule?
pages 52–53

Objectives
- Ask others what they wear to school
- Say what you wear for school
- Describe colours

Key language
Was trägst du zur Schule?
Ich trage einen roten/grünen Pullover/Schlips/Rock.
Ich trage eine gelbe/weiße Krawatte/Jacke/Bluse/ Strumpfhose/Jeans/Hose.
Ich trage ein braunes/graues/großes/kurzes Hemd/ T-Shirt/Kleid.
Ich trage blaue/schwarze Schuhe.

National Curriculum PoS
statements 1a, 1b, 1c, 2a, 2b, 2c, 2d, 2j, 3e, 4c, 5a, 5d, 5f, 5i

Materials
- Students' Book pages 52–53
- Cassette 2 side A
- Workbook pages 39–40
- Copymasters 34, 35B, 36

Preparatory work
Use magazine pictures of clothing to revise colours. Avoid using the inflected forms for now, but encourage pupils to give whole sentences in response to your questions about the pictures. T: *Welche Farbe hat dieser Rock?* P1: *Blau*. T: *Richtig! Wiederhole: Dieser Rock ist blau*, etc. Now you could use the same pictures to remind pupils of the concept of adjective endings which they met in Unit 3. T: *Hat diese Frau **rote** Haare oder **schwarze** Haare?* P1: *Sie hat schwarze Haare*. T: *Richtig! Sie hat **schwarze** Haare*. You could then start to add in attributive adjectives in the accusative after *einen/eine/ ein*, without explanation or requiring pupils to reproduce this structure. T: *Sie hat schwarze Haare und sie trägt **einen gelben** Rock*, etc.

AT 1.3 **AT 3.2** **1a** *Hör gut zu und lies mit*. Pupils listen to the recording and follow the text in the book. You could then ask questions about the colours of the clothes, e.g. T: *Welche Farbe hat dieser Rock?* (pointing to Tina) P1: *Dieser Rock ist rot*, etc. Encourage pupils to respond in full sentences, and correct any pupils who give you an incorrect inflected form of the adjective.

Transcript   p 52, activity 1a

1
– Was trägst du zur Schule, Tina?
– Ich trage eine weiße Bluse. Ich trage einen roten Rock und ich trage einen grauen Pullover.
2
– Und du, Markus? Was trägst du zur Schule?
– Also, ich trage eine blaue Jeans und ein grünes Sweatshirt. Und ich trage braune Schuhe.
3
– Anja, was trägst du zur Schule?
– Ich? Ich trage ein gelbes Kleid. Ich trage auch eine grüne Jacke und ich trage eine rote Strumpfhose.
4
– Tim, was trägst du zur Schule?
– Ich trage ein weißes Hemd und eine blaue Krawatte. Und ich trage eine schwarze Hose.

AT 2.3 **1b** *Ratespiel: Wer ist das? A wählt eine Person von Übung 1a, B rät. Dann ist B dran*. Pupils work together in pairs. Partner A chooses one of the four characters from activity 1a (without revealing his/her choice to partner B) and describes his/her clothing (in the first person: *Ich trage …*). Partner B decides who is being described. In this way, pupils familiarize themselves with the text of activity 1a and the forms of the attributive adjectives, without the need to produce them independently. (They can just read the captions verbatim.)

AT 4.2 **1c** *Zeichne deine Schuluniform (so wie in Übung 1a) und schreib die Wörter auf.* Pupils draw a picture of their school uniform and label it in German. Draw their attention to the colours in the *Wiederholung* box. They should just use the uninflected adjectives for now, instead of trying to construct full sentences on the model of those in activity 1a. Pupils could leave space to add the inflected sentence at a later date. Alternatively, you could go through the grammar explanation first, go through the *Hilfe* box with the class and then ask pupils to label their drawings with captions as in activity 1a. If you do this, make sure that pupils understand that *rosa, orange* and *lila* do not take endings.

WB J Workbook activity J could be used at this point to increase pupils' awareness of the adjective endings, or it could be left until after *Grammatik im Fokus* as consolidation/reinforcement.

Grammatik im Fokus

Ich trage einen/eine/ein + Adjektiv. This section focuses on adjectival endings in the accusative after the indefinite article. By now, pupils have been exposed to these endings quite a lot, and more able pupils will have grasped the pattern. After looking at the table of endings with the class, you could ask pupils to call out colours, writing these up on the board. Write up the example sentences from the table also. Now ask pupils to substitute the new colours for those given in the table.
T: (pointing to *'Ich trage einen blauen Rock'*) *Alice: rot.*
P1: *Ich trage einen roten Rock,* etc.

At this point you could give the pupils the paradigm of the verb *tragen* in the present tense (only the singular forms *ich trage, du trägst, er/sie trägt* are needed for this spread) and ask questions to consolidate the verb forms.
T: *Leah, was trage ich?* P1: *Du trägst eine blaue Hose.*
T: *Richtig! Ich trage eine blaue Hose. Alex, was trägst du?*
P1: *Ich trage ein weißes Hemd.* T: *Richtig! Du trägst ein weißes Hemd. Paula, was trägt Alex?* P3: *Er trägt ein weißes Hemd,* etc.

Background information

Explain to pupils that school uniform is not normally worn in German-speaking countries, but that there are basic rules about what is acceptable.

2a *Eine Schule in Deutschland macht eine Umfrage: Was trägst du zur Schule? Hier sind zwei Antworten. Kopiere die E-Mails und füll die Lücken aus.* Pupils fill in the adjectival endings. If they need additional help, you could draw their attention to the *Hilfe* box on page 52, which will provide them with many of the answers directly, and with the rest by substituting a different adjective but keeping the same ending. You should check the answers as a whole-class activity before pupils go on to complete activity 2b.

Answers:

Ich trage eine **weiße** Bluse. Ich trage auch eine **rote** Krawatte, einen **grauen** Rock und eine **schwarze** Strumpfhose.
Ich trage eine **blaue** Jeans und ein **rotes** T-Shirt. Ich trage auch ein **gelbes** Hemd und einen **schwarzen** Pullover.

C 35B Copymaster 35B contains additional information about adjective endings after *einen/eine/ein*. Activity 2 could be used for consolidation at this point.

AT 4.4 **2b** *Was sagen Sabine und Alex? Schreib zwei Antworten für sie.* Pupils write descriptions for the two pictures, using the e-mails in activity 2a as a model. Once pupils have written the first draft of their texts, you could go through the *Tipp* box with them, and they could then practise checking and correcting their own and each others' work before writing out a final version. Draw pupils' attention in particular to the accuracy of the adjective endings and articles in their written versions.

Answers:

Ich trage ein blaues Kleid, einen gelben Pullover, eine weiße Strumpfhose und weiße Schuhe.
Ich trage eine schwarze Hose, ein weißes Hemd, einen grünen Pullover und braune Schuhe.

WB K Workbook activity K could be used at this point to reinforce colours, clothes and adjective endings.

WB L Workbook activity L provides additional speaking practice to consolidate colours, clothes and adjective endings.

WB M Workbook activity M could be used at this point as an individual writing task to contribute to pupils' written records of achievement.

C 34 Activity 2 on copymaster 34 provides additional writing practice using the accusative of the indefinite article, and could be used here.

AT 4.2 *Noch mal! Was trägt dein Lieblingsstar? Finde Fotos und mach ein Poster.* Pupils find a picture of their favourite star (singer, sports personality, etc.) and label the items of clothing to create a fashion poster. If you want to make the linguistic aspect of the activity slightly more advanced, you could ask them to write a heading, e.g. *'Robbie Williams trägt ...'* and then have labels such as *eine schwarze Mütze, einen schwarzen Pullover,* etc. This activity could be done on computer.

AT 4.4 *Extra! Mach ein 'Junge Mode'-Poster. Finde Fotos und schreib dann Sprechblasen für die Jugendlichen. Und wie findest du alles? Schreib Sätze.* Pupils use photos to create a fashion poster with descriptions of clothes and opinions about them. Draw pupils' attention to the form *... gefällt mir sehr,* explaining that this is an alternative to *... gefällt mir sehr gut.*

Tipp

Einen Text entwerfen. This panel contains advice on correcting and redrafting written work. You could demonstrate this advice by putting a text on the board/OHT with deliberate mistakes and correcting and revising it with the class. Tell the class that it is important to be methodical when checking their work – they should make a list of points to check, and always check them in the same order. You could then give them a second text to correct and revise.

C 36 Copymaster 36 contains additional advice on this topic. Activity 1 could be used at this point to put the advice into practice.

Ich trage am liebsten eine Jeans! ■
pages 54–55

Objectives
- Ask others what clothes they like
- Say what clothes you like and dislike
- Ask and say what your favourite clothes are
- Ask for and give opinions on school uniform

Key language
Was trägst du gern/nicht gern/am liebsten?
Ich trage gern/nicht gern/am liebsten einen
Pullover/Minirock; eine Jeansjacke/Bluse/Hose; ein
Sweatshirt/Kleid/Hemd/T-Shirt; Turnschuhe/Socken.
Ich trage nicht gern Uniform.
Ich trage lieber Jeans.
Wie findest du/Wie gefällt dir deine Uniform?
Meine Uniform gefällt mir (nicht so) gut/gar nicht.
Ich finde meine Uniform schön/hässlich/schrecklich/
bequem/unbequem/altmodisch/modern/praktisch.
Meine Uniform ist gut/schlecht, weil sie ... ist.

National Curriculum PoS
statements 1a, 1b, 1c, 2a, 2b, 2c, 2d, 3d, 4c, 5a, 5c, 5d, 5f, 5i

Materials
- Students' Book pages 54–55
- Cassette 2 side A
- Workbook pages 40–43
- Copymasters 31, 32, 33, 34, 36

Preparatory work
Gern/nicht gern was introduced in Unit 5 of *Klasse! 1* (pp. 66–67) and consolidated in Unit 7, so pupils should be familiar with this structure as the way to express 'I like ...-ing' in German. *Am liebsten* was introduced in Unit 7 of *Klasse! 1.* You may want to take this opportunity to review the ways of expressing approval which pupils have learned so far: *ich* (verb) *gern; ich finde* (person or thing) *super/toll/gut*, etc.; *ich mag* (person); (thing or, in a romantic context, person – cf. Jasmin on p. 46) *gefällt mir (gut);* (person or thing) *ist mein Lieblings-; ich* (verb) *am liebsten.* You could practise these structures with the class by writing key words (e.g. *Fußball, Tina, lesen, Computerspiele, Pizza*) on the board and then using a thumbs-up or thumbs-down sign to elicit *ich finde Fußball langweilig/schlecht; ich mag Tina; ich lese nicht gern,* etc. from pupils.

AT 1.4
1a *Was trägst du am liebsten/gern/nicht gern? Was sagen Annika, Jasmin, Sven und Atalay? Hör gut zu und finde die passenden Bilder.* Pupils listen to the recording and select the appropriate pictures for each speaker, noting his/her preferences. In preparation for this activity, elicit the names of the items of clothing from the class. On the first playing, pupils write down the names in the order in which they occur; on the second playing, they note down the items of clothing they hear mentioned in each conversation, and on the third playing, they note down the speakers' reactions to the clothes mentioned. You

could feed back the answers as a whole-class activity in preparation for activity 1b.

Answers:

Annika: am liebsten – b; gern – a; nicht gern – c
Sven: am liebsten – l; gern – h; nicht gern – e
Jasmin: am liebsten – g; gern – d; nicht gern – k
Atalay: am liebsten – j; gern – i; nicht gern – f

> **Transcript**   p 54, activity 1a
>
> – Annika, was trägst du am liebsten?
> – Ich? Ich trage am liebsten Hosen – Hosen sind sehr modern! Ich trage auch gern Blusen.
> – Hosen und Blusen – und was trägst du nicht gern?
> – Kleider – ich trage nicht gern Kleider.
>
> – Und du, Sven? Was trägst du am liebsten?
> – Also, ich trage am liebsten T-Shirts – T-Shirts sind super. Und ich trage gern Hemden.
> – Und was trägst du nicht gern?
> – Ich trage nicht gern Jacken.
>
> – Jasmin, was trägst du nicht gern?
> – Also, ich trage nicht gern Strumpfhosen – Strumpfhosen sind furchtbar, weil sie total unbequem sind!
> – Aha ... und was trägst du gern?
> – Ich trage gern Jeans. Jeans gefallen mir gut.
> – Und was trägst du am liebsten?
> – Röcke – ich trage am liebsten Röcke!
>
> – Atalay, und du? Was trägst du am liebsten?
> – Hmm, was trage ich am liebsten? Ich bin sportlich – ich trage am liebsten Turnschuhe, und ich trage gern Sweatshirts.
> – Und was trägst du nicht gern?
> – Also, ich trage nicht gern Krawatten - Krawatten sind altmodisch, finde ich.

AT 2.3
1b *Wer ist das? A fragt, B antwortet. Dann ist B dran.* Pupils work together in pairs. A adopts the role of one of the speakers from activity 1a and makes a statement about his/her clothing preferences. B guesses who it is. Note that pupils need the correct answers to activity 1a for this. Draw pupils' attention to the *Wiederholung* box.

C 32
Activities 1 and 2 on copymaster 32 provide additional oral practice of the language points covered above, and could be used in preparation for the class survey below.

AT 2.4
2a *Mach eine Umfrage: „Was trägst du am liebsten? Was trägst du (nicht) gern?"* Pupils conduct a class survey about clothing preferences.

AT 4.3
2b *Schreib die Resultate für drei Schüler/Schülerinnen auf (z. B. mit dem Computer).* Pupils write up the results of their survey. This could be illustrated with photos of the pupils, or of the items of clothing they like/don't like. The *Hilfe* box contains a summary of useful structures and vocabulary for this activity. This activity is ideal for producing a class display using IT.

WB N
Workbook activity N provides reinforcement of *gern/nicht gern/am liebsten.*

WB O Workbook activity O could be used to provide individual writing practice at this point.

AT 3.3 **3a** *Lies die Sprechblasen. Wer ist Schüler/Schülerin in Deutschland – und wer ist Schüler/Schülerin in Großbritannien?* Pupils read the speech bubbles and decide which of the speakers is German and which is British. They check their answers by doing activity 3b.

Answers:

1 British (wears school uniform); 2 German (no school uniform)

AT 1.3 **3b** *Ist alles richtig? Hör gut zu.* Pupils listen to the recording and check their answers to activity 3a.

> **Transcript**   p 55, activity 3b
>
> 1
> – Anna, wo wohnst du?
> – Ich wohne in Schottland – in Glasgow.
> – Was trägst du zur Schule, Anna?
> – Also, ich trage eine Uniform. Ich trage einen schwarzen Rock, eine weiße Bluse und eine grüne Krawatte. Und ich trage eine graue Jacke.
> 2
> – Und du, Martin? Woher kommst du?
> – Ich komme aus Deutschland und ich wohne in Berlin.
> – Und was trägst du zur Schule? Eine Uniform?
> – Nein, ich trage keine Uniform! Ich trage Jeans und ein gelbes T-Shirt. Ich trage auch ein Sweatshirt und weiße Turnschuhe.

AT 3.3 **4a** *Wie findest du deine Uniform? Hier sind einige Adjektive. Was ist positiv und was ist negativ? Schreib zwei Listen. (Du brauchst Hilfe? Schau im Wörterbuch nach.)* Pupils sort the adjectives into positive and negative, using their dictionaries as necessary.

Answers:

Positive: bequem, modern, praktisch, schön, gut;
Negative: altmodisch, hässlich, schrecklich, unbequem, schlecht

AT 1.4 **4b** *Was sagen Sarah, James, David und Jessica? Hör gut zu und schreib die passenden Adjektive auf.* Pupils listen to the recording and write down the adjectives they hear for each speaker. In preparation, look at the *Tipp* box with the class and discuss with them how to apply the advice on listening for detail to this activity. Do the first conversation (Sarah) with the whole class.

Answers:

Sarah: praktisch, gut, bequem; James: schlecht, altmodisch, hässlich; David: modern, gut, schön; Jessica: schrecklich, schlecht, unbequem, zu klein, zu lang

> **Transcript**   p 55, activity 4b
>
> – Sarah, wie findest du deine Uniform?
> – Ich finde meine Uniform sehr praktisch.
> – Du findest deine Uniform gut?
> – Ja, meine Uniform ist gut, weil sie bequem ist.

> – Hallo, James! Wie gefällt dir deine Uniform?
> – Meine Uniform gefällt mir gar nicht! Ich finde meine Uniform schlecht, weil sie altmodisch ist. Meine Uniform ist hässlich!
>
> – Und wie findest du deine Uniform, David?
> – Also, meine Uniform ist modern – das finde ich gut. Ja, sie ist schön – meine Uniform gefällt mir gut.
>
> – Und du, Jessica? Wie gefällt dir deine Uniform?
> – Also, meine Uniform ist schrecklich! Sie gefällt mir gar nicht. Meine Uniform ist schlecht, weil sie unbequem ist: Mein Hemd ist zu klein und meine Hose ist zu lang!

WB P Workbook activity P could be used at this point for consolidation of the adjectives describing clothing.

C 31 Activity 3 on copymaster 31 could be used here for additional listening comprehension using the same group of adjectives.

C 34 Activity 3 on copymaster 34 could be used for additional writing practice at this point.

AT 2.4 **5** *Mach eine Umfrage. Frag: „Wie findest du deine Uniform?" Schreib die Resultate auf.* Pupils conduct a class survey about attitudes to the school uniform and write up the results. Draw their attention to the *Hilfe* box, which contains a summary of useful structures. Pupils could present the results in a graphical form, such as pie charts, etc., or could write speech bubbles for a classroom display.

AT 2.3 *Noch mal! Macht acht Adjektiv-Karten (sieh Übung 4a). A wählt eine Karte und beschreibt seine/ihre Uniform mit dem Adjektiv. Dann ist B dran.* This activity provides additional practice in giving opinions. Pupils make eight cards, each containing a single adjective applicable to school uniform. They then work in pairs, laying the cards face down on the desk and taking it in turns to turn over a card and make a sentence.

AT 4.4
AT 2.4 *Extra! Mach eine Kassette: ‚Schuluniformen in meiner Stadt'. Wie findest du die Uniformen? Mach eine ‚Uniform-Hitparade'!* Pupils compare the uniforms of various schools in their area, recording their presentation on cassette. Alternatively, the presentation could be written up as a web page with photos. Pupils could collaborate in groups, with one pupil acting as interviewer and presenter, the others giving their opinions as interviewees.

WB Q Workbook activity Q can be used as homework to revise *weil* (Unit 3) and to consolidate the language from this spread.

WB R Workbook activity R is an imaginative writing activity and could be set as homework at this point. It can form part of pupils' written records for continuous assessment purposes.

C 33 Activity 2 on copymaster 33 provides additional reading comprehension, bringing in many of the language points covered in this unit.

Tipp

Hören im Detail. This panel gives advice on listening for detail, focusing on pre-listening preparation, listening for non-verbal clues (tone of voice, etc.) and not being put off by unfamiliar words.

`C 36` Copymaster 36 contains additional advice about listening for detail. Activity 2 provides an opportunity to put this advice into practice.

Thema im Fokus
pages 56–57

National Curriculum PoS
statements 1c, 2b, 2e, 2h, 2j, 3e, 4a, 5c, 5d, 5f, 5i

Materials
- Students' Book pages 56–57
- Cassette 2 side A
- Copymaster 30

The final spread of each unit provides further reading practice, leading into a project outcome for the unit. See pages 8–9 of the introduction to this book for general notes on how to use these pages.

`3.3–4` **1** *Wie finden die Schüler/Schülerinnen die neue Kleidung für die Lehrer/die Lehrerinnen? Lies die Antworten.* Pupils read the article on page 56 and then the reactions from pupils. This only requires pupils to read the text for gist, but the language from the article and pupil reactions can be used in activity 2.

`4.3–4` **2** *JUMA macht einen Wettbewerb: Neue Kleidung für deine Lehrer/deine Lehrerinnen! Mach ein Poster: Zeichne Kleidung oder finde Fotos.* Pupils create posters using the article on page 56 as a model. Encourage them to think of other items of clothing and to look up the terms in their dictionaries (with guidance and further help as necessary). They should draw clothing, cut up photos or cut and paste images on computer to create composite pictures using photos of staff members.

`T 4.3–4` **3** *Was tragen sie? Schreib Sprechblasen für die Lehrer/Lehrerinnen.* Pupils write speech bubbles for each of the teachers featured in their poster, again following the model on page 56.

`T 4.3–4` **4** *JUMA fragt: „Wie gefällt dir die neue Kleidung für die Lehrer/die Lehrerinnen?" Schreib zwei oder drei Sätze für jeden Lehrer/jede Lehrerin – so wie in Übung 1.* Pupils write their own reactions to the teachers' 'new outfits'.

`AT 2.4` **5** *Finde* 🔊 *und mach eine Kassette mit den Informationen für JUMA.* Pupils record a spoken presentation based on their written work for activities 3 and 4 above. Discuss with them how best to present this, e.g. as interviews, or as a commentary on an imaginary fashion show, introducing the teachers and describing their clothes as if they were catwalk models.

`AT 2.4` **6** *Die Klasse liest die Poster und hört die Kassetten an. Welches Projekt ist die Nummer eins?* The whole class discusses the posters and recorded presentations and votes for the one they find best.

Kannst du … ?

The end-of-unit summary is a checklist for pupils. See page 8 of the introduction to this book for ideas on how to use the checklist.

`C 30` Copymaster 30 provides a useful reference for pupils revising the language of this unit.

Noch mal!-Seite Einheit 4
page 128

National Curriculum PoS
statements 1a, 1b, 1c, 2a, 2b, 2c, 2d, 5a, 5c, 5i

Materials
- Students' Book page 128
- Cassette 2 side A

This revision page is intended for less able pupils. It reinforces the basic vocabulary and structures from the unit, and it can be used by pupils who experienced difficulty in completing some of the activities within the unit, or as alternative homework activities.

`AT 4.5` **1a** *Was hat Tom gekauft? Schreib Sätze für ihn mit den Bildern rechts.* Activity 1 relates to pages 48–49. In activity 1a, pupils write sentences about what Tom has bought, based on the picture. Establish the pattern of *Ich habe … gekauft* with pupils before asking them to complete the task.

Answers:
(There will be variations in order.)
Ich habe Hemden gekauft. Ich habe Schuhe/Turnschuhe gekauft. Ich habe Hosen gekauft. Ich habe eine Jacke gekauft. Ich habe Mützen gekauft. Ich habe Rucksäcke gekauft.

`AT 4.5` **1b** *Du bist dran! Was hast du am Wochenende gekauft? Schreib Sätze.* Pupils write sentences about the clothes they bought at the weekend. Encourage them to be imaginative and to use as much of the vocabulary from pages 48–49 as possible. You may wish to set pupils a target, e.g. write at least six sentences.

`AT 3.2` **2a** *Was trägst du zur Schule? Finde die passenden Bilder.* Activity 2 relates to pages 52–53, with limited active practice of adjective endings. In activity 2a, pupils match the descriptions to the pictures.

Answers: 1 d; 2 b; 3 a; 4 c

`AT 1.3` **2b** *Hör gut zu. Was tragen Hannah und Martin zur Schule? Finde die passenden Bilder in Übung 2a.* Pupils listen to the recording and find the matching pictures in activity 2a.

Answers: Hannah: a; Martin: d

> **Transcript** p 128, activity 2b
>
> – Hannah, was trägst du zur Schule?
> – Also, ich trage eine Uniform. Ich trage eine weiße Bluse und einen grauen Rock. Und ich trage auch eine blaue Jacke und braune Schuhe.
> – Und du, Martin? Was trägst du zur Schule? Eine Uniform?
> – Ja, ich trage auch eine Uniform. Ich trage ein weißes Hemd, eine rote Krawatte und einen grünen Pullover. Und ich trage eine graue Hose.

AT 2.3 **2c** *Was trägst du zur Schule? A fragt, B wählt ein Bild von Übung 2a und antwortet. Dann ist A dran.* Pupils work together in pairs, taking it in turns to ask each other what they wear to school and to answer as one of the characters depicted in activity 2a. For more advanced practice, the pupil providing the description could cover up the written descriptions 1–4.

 3 *Was tragen Karla, Olaf und Maja am liebsten/nicht gern? Wer sagt was? Hör gut zu und finde die passenden Sätze.* Activity 3 relates to pages 54–55. Pupils listen to the recording and match the numbered sentences to the speakers.

AT 1.4

Answers: Karla: 6, 3; Olaf: 5, 2; Maja: 4, 1

> **Transcript** p 128, activity 3
>
> – Karla, was trägst du am liebsten?
> – Also, ich trage am liebsten Röcke. Röcke sind schön, finde ich.
> – Und was trägst du nicht gern?
> – Jeans – ich trage nicht gern Jeans.
> – Und was trägst du nicht gern, Olaf?
> – Ich trage nicht gern Krawatten. Krawatten sind unbequem!
> – Was trägst du am liebsten?
> – Ich trage am liebsten Sweatshirts. Die sind sehr praktisch.
> – Maja, und du? Was trägst du am liebsten?
> – Ich? Ich trage am liebsten Hemden – Hemden in Blau und Rot.
> – Und was trägst du nicht gern?
> – Also, ich trage nicht gern Strumpfhosen – ich finde Strumpfhosen schrecklich!

Extra!-Seite Einheit 4
page 129

National Curriculum PoS
statements 1b, 1c, 5a, 5c, 5d, 5f, 5i

Materials
- Students' Book page 129
- Cassette 2 side A

This extension page is intended for more able pupils. It contains slightly longer and more complex materials, and it can be used by pupils who have completed other activities quickly or as alternative homework activities.

AT 3.3 **1** *Finde die passenden Satzteile.* Activity 1 relates to pages 50–51. Pupils match up the sentence halves, using their knowledge of noun genders and the endings for *dieser* and *welcher*.

Answers: 1 b; 2 d; 3 e; 4 c; 5 f; 6 a

AT 4.4 **2a** *Schreib Sprechblasen für die Bilder.* Activity 2 relates to pages 50–51. In activity 2a, pupils write an appropriate speech bubble for each of the ill-fitting clothes items depicted.

Answers:

a Dieser Rock ist zu lang! b Dieser Pullover ist zu kurz/klein! c Diese Bluse ist zu eng/klein! d Diese Hose ist zu lang! e Diese Jacke ist zu teuer! f Diese Schuhe sind zu groß!

AT 2.3 **2b** *Ist alles richtig? Macht Dialoge.* Pupils work together in pairs to create dialogues, checking each other's answers to activity 2a.

AT 3.5 **3a** *Lies Saras E-Mail und beantworte die Fragen in ganzen Sätzen.* Activity 3 relates to pages 52–55. In activity 3a, pupils read the text and answer the comprehension questions in full sentences.

AT 4.5

Answers:

1 Sie hat zwei Blusen, ein Sweatshirt und einen Rock gekauft. Sie hat auch Schuhe, drei Hemden und eine braune Hose gekauft.
2 Sie trägt eine weiße Bluse, ein blaues Sweatshirt und einen schwarzen Rock.
3 Sie trägt nicht gern Röcke.
4 Sie trägt nicht gern Röcke, weil sie unbequem sind.
5 Sie trägt am liebsten Hosen.
6 Sie trägt am liebsten Hosen, weil sie praktisch und bequem sind.

AT 4.5 **3b** *Du bist dran! Schreib eine Antwort-E-Mail an Sara.* Pupils write a reply to Sara, telling her about their own clothing preferences, using the e-mail from activity 3a as a model. They could incorporate a photo of themselves wearing their favourite clothes.

Workbook

Page 34

Use with page 47 in the Students' Book.

A1 *Hör gut zu und sing mit!* Pupils listen to the song and then sing along. If your pupils are not keen on singing, you could try pausing the tape after the first two lines of every verse and inviting the pupils to call out the next two lines.

> **Transcript** W 34, activity A1
>
> Junge Mode im Ausverkauf!
> Junge Mode im Ausverkauf!
>
> Ich kaufe dieses T-Shirt
> Wie gefällt es dir?
> Es gefällt mir leider nicht
> Denn es ist viel zu klein!

> Refrain
>
> Ich kaufe diese Hose
> Wie gefällt sie dir?
> Sie gefällt mir leider nicht
> Denn sie ist viel zu kurz!
>
> Refrain
>
> Ich kaufe diese Bluse
> Wie gefällt sie dir?
> Sie gefällt mir leider nicht
> Denn sie ist viel zu eng!!
>
> Refrain
>
> Ich kaufe diese Mütze
> Wie gefällt sie dir?
> Sie gefällt mir leider nicht
> Denn sie ist viel zu gelb!
>
> Refrain

AT 3.2 **A2** *Finde die passenden Antworten.* Pupils use their deductive skills to answer the questions about the song text. This activity introduces *dieser* and *gefallen*, which will be looked at in depth later in the unit.

Answers: 1 a; 2 b

AT 3.4 **A3** *Finde die passenden Bilder für jede Strophe (verse).* Pupils match the pictures to the verses of the song. This activity introduces *zu groß/klein*, etc., which will feature later in the unit.

Answers: a 2; b 1; c 4; d 3

Page 35
Use with page 48 in the Students' Book.

AT 3.1 **B1** *Was hast du gekauft? Finde elf Plural-Wörter und schreib sie auf.* Pupils find 11 plural nouns in the wordsearch grid. Note that *Jacken, Hosen, Hemden, Mützen* and *Rucksäcke* are not introduced in activities 1a–1c in the Students' Book, but were introduced in Unit 6, *Klasse! 1* in their singular forms. More able pupils could approach this individually or in pairs as an extension task, consulting their dictionaries or the *Vokabular* at the back of their books to check the plurals once they have located recognizable singular forms. For less able pupils, introduce these new plural forms first. For example, make two copies of copymaster 28 and cut out the pictures to make individual cards. You can then use these as flashcards to introduce the new plural forms.

Answers:

T-Shirts, Jacken, Pullover, Blusen, Jeans, Hosen, Röcke, Hemden, Mützen, Schuhe, Rucksäcke

AT 4.1 **B2** *Schreib den Singular für die Plural-Wörter auf.* Pupils use their dictionaries to find out the singular forms of the 11 plural nouns from activity B1. You may prefer pupils to provide the definite article as well, to help them memorize the genders of the nouns.

Answers:

(das) T-Shirt, (die) Jacke, (der) Pullover, (die) Bluse, (die) Jeans, (die) Hose, (der) Rock, (das) Hemd, (die) Mütze, (der) Schuh, (der) Rucksack

AT 1.4 **C** *Alexander und seine Cousine Leah sind in der Stadt. Was haben sie gekauft? Hör gut zu und kreuz die passenden Bilder an.* Pupils listen to the recording and then complete the grid. Note that *Mützen, Hemden, Rucksäcke* and *Hosen* will be unfamiliar forms unless pupils have done activity B above; however, this should not impede comprehension if pupils are familiar with the singular forms.

Alexander	✗	✗				✗
Leah			✗	✗	✗	

> **Transcript** W 35, activity C
>
> – Alexander! Hallo, Alexander!
> – Hallo, Leah! Na, bist du auch zum Ausverkauf gefahren?
> – Ja – und ich habe viel gekauft! Schau mal: Ich habe zwei Jeans gekauft – eine Jeans in Weiß und eine Jeans in Schwarz. Und du – was hast du gekauft?
> – Also, ich habe drei Hemden gekauft – hier.
> – Oh, die Hemden sind sehr schön! Wo hast du die Hemden gekauft?
> – Im Kaufhaus. Und ich habe zwei Mützen gekauft – eine zum Skifahren und eine zum Skateboardfahren.
> – He, klasse! Die Mützen sind super! Hier, und ich habe zwei Rucksäcke gekauft.
> – Ein Rucksack in Blau und ein Rucksack in …
> – … Gelb! Was hast du noch gekauft?
> – Moment … ach ja – ich habe eine Hose gekauft – für die Schule.
> – Und ich habe Schuhe gekauft – auch für die Schule. Hier …

Page 36
Use with page 49 in the Students' Book.

AT 2.5 **D1** *„Was hast du gekauft?" A deckt Bs Bilder zu und fragt, B antwortet. A schreibt die Antwort auf. Dann ist B dran.* Pupils work together in pairs to create dialogues based on an information gap. Partner A covers up the pictures for partner B and asks *Was hast du gekauft?* B responds according to the cues in column B, e.g. *Ich habe zwei Jacken gekauft.* A writes down the number of items named by B next to the appropriate picture in column A, then it is B's turn to ask. At the end, A should have completed column A, and B should have completed column B, and their answers should be identical.

AT 2.5 **D2** *Was hat dein Partner/deine Partnerin gekauft? Macht Dialoge mit deinen Notizen von Übung D1.* Pupils again work in pairs to create dialogues using their answers to activity D1.

Page 37

Use with pages 49–50 in the Students' Book.

AT 4.4 **E** *Du bekommst 100 Euro von deiner Oma und gehst zum Ausverkauf. Was hast du gekauft? Schreib einen Danke-Brief an deine Oma.* In this extension activity, pupils use the information from the till receipt to write a thank you letter to their grandmother, describing what they bought. Prices do not need to be included: the focus of this activity should be the plural forms of the clothes items.

AT 3.2 **F** *Finde die passenden Bilder.* Pupils match the pictures to the speech bubbles. This activity can be used for reinforcing *dieser/welcher* and *gefallen*.

Answers: 1 b; 2 c; 3 d; 4 a

Page 38

Use with pages 50–51 in the Students' Book.

AT 2.3 **G** *„Wie gefällt dir … ?" Macht Dialoge mit den Bildern.* Pupils work together in pairs to create dialogues using the picture cues, providing further practice of *dieser/welcher* and *gefallen*.

H *Was sagen sie? Füll die Lücken aus.* Pupils fill in the endings for *dieser* and *welcher*.

Answers:

1 diese; 2 welches; 3 dieser; 4 welche; 5 dieses; 6 welcher

AT 1.2 **I1** *Jasmin und Annika kaufen Kleidung. Wie ist alles – was sagt Jasmin? Hör gut zu und finde die passenden Bilder.* Pupils listen to the recording and match each utterance to the appropriate picture. This activity provides additional practice of items of clothing and *zu lang/kurz*, etc.

Answers: a 6; b 2; c 5; d 3; e 1; f 4

Transcript W 38, activity I1

1 – Und?
 – Nein, dieses T-Shirt ist zu kurz!
2 – Diese Schuhe sind zu groß!
3 – Oh nein! Dieser Rock ist zu eng!
4 – Und diese Bluse ist zu lang!
5 – Nein, nein, nein! Diese Hose ist zu teuer!
6 – Ooohhh! Dieser Pullover ist zu klein!

Page 39

Use with pages 51–53 in the Students' Book.

AT 4.3 **I2** *Schreib dann Sprechblasen für die Bilder.* Pupils use the language they heard in activity I1 to write speech bubbles for the pictures.

Answers:

a Dieser Pullover ist zu klein! b Diese Schuhe sind zu groß! c Diese Hose ist zu teuer! d Oh nein! Dieser Rock ist zu eng! e Dieses T-Shirt ist zu kurz! f Diese Bluse ist zu lang!

AT 3.2 **J** *Worträtsel: „Was trägst du zur Schule?" Schreib den Satz richtig auf.* Pupils divide up the word snake to complete the sentence with colour adjectives and items of clothing. This simple and quick activity increases pupils' awareness of the adjective endings after *ein*.

Answers:

Ich trage ein grünes Sweatshirt, einen grauen Rock, eine schwarze Strumpfhose und braune Schuhe.

AT 1.3 **K1** *„Was trägst du zur Schule?" Hör gut zu und schreib die Farben auf. Male dann die Bilder aus.* Pupils note down the colours they hear on the recording and then colour in the pictures accordingly.

Answers:

1 a grau, b rot, c schwarz; 2 a grün, b gelb, c rot; 3 a blau, b grau, c braun; 4 a gelb, b schwarz, c blau

Transcript W 39, activity K1

1
 – Daniel, was trägst du zur Schule?
 – Ich? Ich trage ein graues Hemd und eine rote Krawatte. Und ich trage eine schwarze Hose.
2
 – Und du, Meike? Was trägst du zur Schule?
 – Also, ich trage ein grünes Kleid. Ich trage auch einen gelben Pullover und ich trage eine rote Strumpfhose.
3
 – Hallo, Philipp! Was trägst du zur Schule?
 – Ja, ich trage eine blaue Jeans und ein graues Sweatshirt. Und ich trage braune Schuhe.
4
 – Und was trägst du zur Schule, Hanna?
 – Ich trage eine gelbe Bluse. Ich trage einen schwarzen Rock und ich trage eine blaue Jacke.

Page 40

Use with pages 53–54 in the Students' Book.

AT 3.3 **K2** *Füll die Lücken aus und finde die passenden Bilder in Übung K1.* Pupils insert the adjective endings and match the speech bubbles to the pictures in activity K1. Oral practice may be of benefit to less able pupils before attempting this task.

Answers:

1 3: Ich trage eine **blaue** Jeans und ein **graues** Sweatshirt. Ich trage auch **braune** Schuhe.
2 1: Ich trage ein **graues** Hemd und eine **rote** Krawatte. Und ich trage eine **schwarze** Hose.
3 4: Ich trage eine **gelbe** Bluse. Ich trage einen **schwarzen** Rock. Ich trage auch eine **blaue** Jacke.
4 2: Ich trage ein **grünes** Kleid. Ich trage auch einen **gelben** Pullover und ich trage eine **rote** Strumpfhose.

AT 2.4 **L** *Was trägst du heute zur Schule? A fragt, B beschreibt alles. Dann ist B dran.* Pupils work together in pairs to interview each other about the clothes they are wearing. Emphasize the need for accuracy rather than speed in completing the task.

T 4.4 **M** *Du bist dran! Was trägst du zur Schule?* Pupils write about the clothes they wear to school. This activity can form part of pupils' written records for continuous assessment purposes. See the general notes on pages 13–14 of the introduction to this book.

 AT 1.4 **N1** „*Was trägst du am liebsten/gern/nicht gern?" Was sagen sie? Hör gut zu und füll die Tabelle aus.* Pupils listen to the recording and complete the table.

AT 4.4 **O** *Du bist dran! Was trägst du am liebsten/gern/nicht gern?* Pupils write about their own clothing preferences. This activity can form part of pupils' written records for continuous assessment purposes.

AT 3.1 **P1** *Wie findest du deine Uniform? Finde die Adjektive und schreib sie auf.* Pupils divide up the word snake to form a list of adjectives, consolidating the clothing adjectives given in activity 4a on page 55 of the Students' Book.

Uwe				✔✔				✗			✔	
Heike			✔✔			✗						✔
Martin		✔			✗		✔✔					
Steffi	✔✔								✔	✗		

Transcript — W 40, activity N1

– Hallo, Uwe! Was trägst du am liebsten?
– Ich trage am liebsten Pullover – Pullover in Schwarz. Schwarz ist meine Lieblingsfarbe! Und ich trage gern Hosen.
– Auch in Schwarz?
– Ja, Hosen in Schwarz. Aber ich trage nicht gern Krawatten – Krawatten sind furchtbar, finde ich!

– Heike, was trägst du am liebsten?
– Ich? Ich trage am liebsten Jeans – Jeans sind sehr bequem! Ich trage auch gerne T-Shirts – ja, Jeans und T-Shirts.
– Und was trägst du nicht gern?
– Was trage ich nicht gern? Röcke – ich trage nicht gern Röcke.

– Martin, was trägst du nicht gern?
– Also, was trage ich nicht gern? Ich weiß: Hemden – ich trage nicht gern Hemden, weil sie altmodisch sind.
– Und was trägst du gern?
– Ich trage gern Jacken. Jacken sind modern. Aber ich trage am liebsten Sweatshirts, weil sie sehr bequem sind.

– Und du, Steffi? Was trägst du am liebsten?
– Ich? Ich trage am liebsten Kleider, weil sie schön sind. Ich trage auch gerne Strumpfhosen – Strumpfhosen sind super, finde ich.
– Aha … und was trägst du nicht gern?
– Turnschuhe! Ich trage nicht gern Turnschuhe.

Page 41

Use with pages 54–55 in the Students' Book.

AT 2.3 **N2** *Ratespiel – „Was trägst du am liebsten/gern/nicht gern?" A wählt eine Person von Übung N1 und beschreibt die Kleidung, B rät.* Pupils work together in pairs to create dialogues using the information they have compiled in activity N1. Draw pupils' attention to the correct placement of *(nicht) gern/am liebsten*: it comes directly after the verb in statements, at the end in questions.

Answers:

schrecklich, hässlich, modern, schön, unbequem, altmodisch, praktisch, bequem, gut

Page 42

Use with page 55 in the Students' Book.

AT 2.2 **P2** „*Meine Uniform ist …" Macht Dialoge mit den Adjektiven in Übung P1.* Pupils work together in pairs to create dialogues about their uniform, using the adjectives from activity P1. Pupils could also be asked to make a written record of their dialogues.

AT 3.2 **Q1** *Finde die passenden Sätze für die Bilder.* Pupils match the speech bubbles to the pictures. This activity consolidates *zu groß/klein*, etc. and revises *weil* + subordinate clause from Unit 3.

Answers: a 2; b 3; c 1; d 4

Page 43

Use with page 55 in the Students' Book.

AT 4.4 **Q2** *Eine Austauschklasse in Deutschland fragt: „Wie findest du deine Uniform?" Schreib Sätze für diese Schüler/Schülerinnen mit „Meine Uniform ist gut/schlecht, weil …"* Pupils write sentences with *weil*, following the example.

Answers:

Meine Uniform ist schlecht, weil sie hässlich ist.
Meine Uniform ist gut, weil sie bequem ist.
Meine Uniform ist schlecht, weil sie schrecklich ist.
Meine Uniform ist gut, weil sie schön ist.

AT 4.4 **R** *Du bist dran! Zeichne deine Traumuniform! Was trägst du? Schreib die Wörter auf. Wie findest du deine Uniform? Schreib zwei Sätze.* Pupils describe their 'dream uniform'. This activity can form part of pupils' written records for continuous assessment purposes. You may wish to encourage pupils to write as much as they are able.

Can you ...?

The purpose of the checklist is to identify tasks in the Students' Book both by skill and by topic. Teachers may find this helpful in selecting specific tasks, as a record of pupils' achievements in an Attainment Target.

Einheit 4 Mode	AT 1 Listening	AT 2 Speaking	AT 3 Reading	AT 4 Writing
48–49 Was hast du gekauft?				
Say what clothes you have bought	1b, 1c	3b, 5	1a	3a, 4, Noch mal!, Extra!
50–51 Wie gefällt dir diese Jeans?				
Ask others their opinion on items of clothes	1a, 2a	2b	1a	3b
Give your opinion on items of clothes	1a, 2a, 4	1c, 2b, 5a	1a, 1b, 4	3a, 5b
52–53 Was trägst du zur Schule?				
Ask others what they wear to school	1a	–	1a	–
Say what you wear for school	1a	1b	1a	1c, 2a, 2b, Noch mal!, Extra!
Describe colours	1a	1b	1a	1c, 2a, 2b, Noch mal!, Extra!
54–55 Ich trage am liebsten eine Jeans!				
Ask others what clothes they like	–	2a	–	–
Say what clothes you like and dislike	1a	1b, 2a	–	2b
Ask and say what your favourite clothes are	1a	1b, 2a	–	2b
Ask for and give opinions on school uniform	3a, 3b, 4b	5, Noch mal!, Extra!	3a, 4a	5, Extra!

Copymasters

For general advice about using the copymasters, see page 7 of the introduction to this book.

  Hören

 1 *Was haben sie gekauft? Hör gut zu und finde die passenden Bilder.* Pupils listen to the recording and find the appropriate picture for each speaker.

Answers: a 3; b 1; c 4; d 5; e 2

> **Transcript**   C 31, activity 1
>
> 1 – Ich habe drei T-Shirts und eine neue Jacke gekauft.
> 2 – Ich habe einen Rock und zwei Blusen für die Schule gekauft.
> 3 – Ich habe eine Hose und einen Rucksack gekauft.
> 4 – Ich habe drei schöne Mützen gekauft.
> 5 – Ich habe neue Schuhe gekauft!

 2 *Hör gut zu und kreuz die passenden Bilder an.* Pupils listen to the recording and select the appropriate picture from each pair.

Answers: 1 b; 2 b; 3 a; 4 a; 5 a; 6 b

> **Transcript**   C 31, activity 2
>
> 1
> – Oh, Schade! Er ist viel zu lang.
> 2
> – Mutti! Hilfe! Er ist mir viel zu groß!
> 3
> – Zu eng. Das kann nicht sein!
> 4
> – Oh, nein! Das ist leider viel zu klein.
> 5
> – Hm ... Nicht schlecht ... Und was kostet sie? Sie kostet was?! Unglaublich! Das ist viel zu teuer!

> 6
> – Na, und? Wie geht's, mein Liebling?
> – Es geht nicht! Sie ist zu kurz!

 3 *Sechs deutsche Schüler und Schülerinnen besuchen eine englische Schule. Wie finden sie die Schuluniform? Hör gut zu und finde die passenden Wörter.* Pupils listen to the recording and select the adjective appropriate to each speaker's reaction.

Answers:

1 altmodisch; 2 schön; 3 praktisch; 4 hässlich; 5 bequem; 6 teuer

> **Transcript**   C 31, activity 3
>
> 1
> – Und wie habt ihr die Zeit bei uns in unserer Schule gefunden?
> – Prima, aber ...
> – Ja, Jürgen?
> – Nur die Uniform nicht. Ich finde sie sehr altmodisch.
> 2
> – Und du, Beate? Wie findest du die Uniform?
> – Ich finde sie wirklich schön.
> 3
> – Gefällt dir auch unsere Uniform, Johanna?
> – Ja, sehr. Ich finde sie sehr praktisch.
> 4
> – Was meinst du, Anna?
> – Ich? Ich finde die Uniform hässlich!
> 5
> – Und du, Jakob?
> – Mir gefällt sie ziemlich gut. Ich finde sie sehr bequem.
> 6
> – Und du, Markus? Was meinst du?
> – Ich finde sie auch gut – nur etwas teuer!
> – Teuer. Das stimmt! Danke. Das war sehr interessant ...

32 **Sprechen**

T2.4 **1a** *Wähle ein Bild (a–d). Dein Partner/deine Partnerin stellt Fragen. Beantworte die Fragen.* Pupils work together in pairs to create dialogues. Partner A chooses one of the four pictures, without telling B which picture he/she has chosen, and then answers B's questions. On the basis of A's answers, B decides which picture A has chosen.

T2.4 **1b** *Stell die Fragen unten. Dein Partner/deine Partnerin antwortet. Finde das passende Bild (a–d) in Übung 1a.* This is the second part of the activity, with the roles reversed.

T2.4 **2** *Du bist dran! Macht weitere Dialoge mit den Fragen in Übung 1b.* This activity is suitable for more able pupils. Pupils now go on to give their own answers to the questions from the previous activity.

C33 **Lesen**

T3.2 **1** *Wer spricht? Finde die passenden Bilder für die Sprechblasen.* Pupils match the pictures to the speech bubbles.

Answers: 1 e; 2 d; 3 a; 4 b; 5 c

T3.4 **2** *Lies dieses Interview mit Sabine Schön. Sind die Sätze unten richtig oder falsch?* This activity is suitable for more able pupils. Pupils read the text and decide whether the statements are true or false.

Answers:

	Richtig	Falsch
1 Sabine trägt gern schöne Kleidung.	✗	
2 Sie findet Mode langweilig.		✗
3 Sie kauft oft neue Schuhe.	✗	
4 Sie trägt am liebsten braune Kleidung.		✗
5 Sie trägt keine Uniform zur Schule.	✗	
6 Sie findet Strumpfhosen sehr bequem.		✗

C34 **Schreiben**

AT4.1 **1** *Kreuzworträtsel. Schreib die passenden Wörter auf.* This activity practises plurals of nouns for clothing. Pupils complete the crossword according to the picture clues.

Answers:

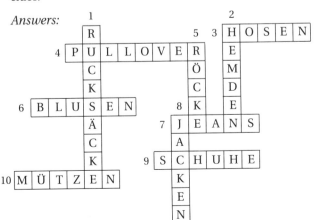

AT4.3 **2** *Was tragen sie zur Schule? Schreib Sätze.* This activity practises the accusative of the indefinite article and clothing vocabulary. Pupils write sentences describing the clothing each character is wearing.

Answers:

1 Ich trage einen Rock, eine Bluse, ein Sweatshirt, Schuhe und eine Strumpfhose.
2 Ich trage Jeans, Turnschuhe und ein Sweatshirt.
3 Ich trage ein Kleid, Socken und Schuhe.
4 Ich trage eine Mütze, eine Jacke, ein Hemd, eine Krawatte, eine Hose, einen Pullover und Schuhe.

AT4.4 **3** *Beantworte diese Fragen. Schreib Sätze.* Pupils give their own answers to the questions about their clothing preferences.

C35A **Grammatik 1**

This copymaster focuses on plural nouns and dictionary skills (finding the plurals of nouns).

1 *Finde den Plural für die Wörter unten.* Pupils read the 'Flashback' and then look up the plurals of the nouns in their dictionaries. Each pair of nouns has the same plural ending.

Answers:

die Tücher; die Taschentücher; die Katzen; die Kerzen; die Quittungen; die Wohnungen; die Fische; die Haifische

2 *Schau in deinem Wörterbuch nach und finde den Plural für diese Wörter.* Pupils read the 'Flashback' and then use their dictionaries to find the plural forms.

Answers:

1 die Hände; 2 die Beine; 3 die Arme; 4 die Augen; 5 die Zähne; 6 die Zehen; 7 die Ohren; 8 die Füße

C35B **Grammatik 2**

This copymaster focuses on *dieser* and *welcher* and adjective endings in the accusative after the indefinite article.

1 *Füll die Lücken aus.* Pupils read the 'Flashback' and then complete the sentences with the correct ending for *dieser* or *welcher*.

Answers:

1 **Dieses** T-Shirt? Nein, **dieses** T-Shirt. 2 **Welcher** Pullover? **Dieser** Pullover! 3 **Welche** Schuhe? **Diese**? Nein! **Diese** Schuhe hier. 4 **Welche** Mütze? **Diese** Mütze. 5 **Welche** Jacke? **Diese** Jacke hier.

2 *Füll die Lücken aus.* Pupils read the 'Flashback' and then complete the sentences with the correct adjective endings (accusative after the indefinite article).

Answers:

1 Ich kaufe eine **kleine** Mütze. 2 Ich kaufe einen **schwarzen** Rock. 3 Sie kauft ein **neues** T-Shirt. 4 Wir haben eine **schöne** Schuluniform. 5 Er trägt eine **neue** Jacke. 6 Ich trage einen **grünen** Pullover.

C 36 **Tipp**

This copymaster focuses on correcting and redrafting written work, and listening for specific details.

1a *Schreib einen kurzen Text auf Deutsch ohne Hilfe. Beantworte die Fragen:* Pupils write a short text in response to the questions.

1b *Schau die Checkliste oben an und überprüfe deinen Text. Schreib eine Liste der Fehler und verbessere dann den Text.* Pupils read the 'Flashback' and then correct and redraft their texts.

2a *Lies die Fragen und schau das Foto an.* Pre-listening activity. Pupils prepare for listening by reading the 'Flashback' and the questions and looking at the photo.

2b *Hör gut zu und notiere Schlüsselwörter.* Pupils listen to the recording and take notes which will help them to answer the questions in activity 3a.

> **Transcript** C 36, activities 3b and 3c
>
> Alexander ist neunzehn Jahre alt und wohnt in Bremen. Er hat kurze blonde Haare und blaue Augen und ist sehr lustig und freundlich. Er hat zwei Schwestern und einen Bruder. Sein Lieblingshobby ist Sport und er spielt besonders gern Tennis. Er geht sehr oft schwimmen und samstags spielt er Fußball. Er trägt gern Jeans und Turnschuhe und geht abends gern in die Disco.

 3c *Hör noch einmal zu und beantworte die Fragen.* Pupils listen to the recording again and write down their answers to the questions in activity 3a.

Answers:

1 Er ist neunzehn Jahre alt. 2 Er hat kurze blonde Haare und blaue Augen. 3 Ja, er hat zwei Schwestern und einen Bruder. 4 Er spielt sehr gern Tennis und er geht gern schwimmen und spielt gern Fußball. 5 Er trägt gern Jeans und Turnschuhe.

Einheit 5 Wie war die Party?

Pages	Objectives	Grammar	Pronunciation, Skill focus	Key language	National Curriculum PoS	National Curriculum AT level
58–59 Die Klasse!-Clique	Reading and listening for pleasure Familiarization with themes, structures and language of the unit	–	–	–	–	1.4, 3.2, 3.4
60–61 Wir feiern!	Say when your birthday is Ask and say when special events/celebrations are	–	Letter-writing: dates Pronunciation: greetings	Wann hast du Geburtstag? Mein Geburtstag ist am 8. April. Ich habe am 8. April Geburtstag. Weihnachten, Heiligabend, Silvester, Neujahr; Fasching, Ostern, Nikolaustag, Diwali, Id-ul-Fitr	1a, 1b, 1c, 2a, 2b, 2c, 2d, 4c, 4d, 5a, 5f, 5i	1.2–4, 2.2–3, 3.2, 4.2–3
62–63 Ich mache eine Party!	Invite others to a party Accept invitations Make excuses	in + dative müssen	Role-plays	Ich habe am Wochenende/Samstag/Sonntag Geburtstag. Ich mache eine Party. Ich mache am Wochenende/Samstag/Sonntag eine Faschingsfete. Wir machen am Sonntag ein Picknick. Meine Schule macht am Freitag ein Schulfest. Kommst du? Ja, gern. Wann? Um … Uhr: Wo? Zu Hause. In meinem Zimmer/im Garten/Partykeller/Park/Schwimmbad/in der Schule. Vielen Dank für die Einladung. Ich komme gern. Ich kann leider nicht kommen. Ich muss Hausaufgaben machen/mein Zimmer aufräumen/zu Hause helfen.	1a, 1b, 1c, 2a, 2b, 2c, 2d, 3e, 5a, 5c, 5f, 5i	1.3–4, 2.3–4, 3.3, 4.3–4

Pages	Objectives	Grammar	Pronunciation, Skill focus	Key language	PoS	AT level
64–65 **Ich muss aufräumen!**	Ask where things are Describe where things are	*auf, in, neben, unter* + dative	Identifying the meanings of unfamiliar words	*Ich muss mein Zimmer/das Wohnzimmer/den Partykeller aufräumen/sauber machen.* *Du musst … aufräumen/sauber machen.* *Wo ist der Luftballon/ Kassettenrecorder/Kartoffelsalat/ Apfelsaft/CD-Spieler?* *Wo ist die CD/Limonade/Cola?* *Wo ist das Buch?* *Wo sind die CDs/Luftballons/ Würstchen?* *Der Luftballon/die CD/das Buch ist im Schreibtisch/neben der Lampe/auf dem Regal/unter den CDs.*	1a, 1b, 1c, 2a, 2b, 2c, 2d, 3b, 3c, 3e, 5a, 5i	1.2, 1.4, 2.2–3, 3.2, 4.4
66–67 **Wie war die Party?**	Ask others which birthday presents they received Say what birthday presents you received Ask and give your opinion about parties or events	–	–	*Wie war die Party?* *Sie war toll/super.* *Was hast du zum Geburtstag bekommen?* *Ich habe … bekommen.* *einen Fußball/Gutschein/Pullover* *ein Buch/Computerspiel/Handy/ Skateboard/Stofftier* *Make-up/Geld/Schmuck/Inline-Skates* *Ich habe Pizza/Kartoffelsalat/ Würstchen/Chips gegessen.* *Ich habe Cola/Orangensaft/ Mineralwasser/Apfelsaft getrunken.* *Ich habe … gesehen.* *Ich habe … getroffen.* *Ich habe mit … getanzt.* *Ich habe Gitarre gespielt.*	1a, 1b, 1c, 2a, 2b, 2c, 2d, 3e, 5a, 5c, 5f, 5i	1.2, 1.3, 1.5, 2.3, 2.5, 3.2–3, 4.3, 4.5
68–69 **Thema im Fokus**	Encourage reading for pleasure Use language from Unit 5 creatively Encourage independent, pair- and groupwork	–	–	–	1c, 2e, 3b, 3e, 5a, 5c, 5d, 5f, 5g, 5i	2.4, 3.4, 4.3–4

5 | Wie war die Party?

Aims of the unit

- To be able to say when special events and celebrations are
- To be able to make, accept and decline invitations to a party
- To be able to describe the positions of objects in a room
- To be able to talk about presents you received
- To be able to describe parties or special events in the past

Die Klasse!-Clique
pages 58–59

Materials

- Students' Book pages 58–59
- Cassette 2 side A
- Workbook page 44

For general advice on exploiting the photo story, see pages 10–11 of the introduction to this book. In this episode, Atalay invites Annika, Jasmin and Sven to his birthday party. Annika and Jasmin are delighted, but Sven gives a lame excuse about doing homework. What is the real reason for his gloomy behaviour? At the party, Atalay, Annika and Jasmin have a great time – and have a big mess to clear up afterwards. Jasmin, however, is very concerned about Sven – what can the matter be?

AT 3.2 **1a** *Was meinst du? Vor dem Lesen: Rate!* This is a pre-reading activity. Pupils look at the photos without reading the text, and predict what the content of the photo story will be, choosing the sentence ending they consider more likely from each pair given. The only new vocabulary likely to present any difficulty is *durcheinander* – you could demonstrate this by muddling up a number of items on your desk.

Answers: 1 b; 2 b; 3 a; 4 a; 5 b

 2 *Hör gut zu und lies mit. Wie heißt das auf Deutsch?* Pupils listen to the recording and follow the text in their **AT 1.4** books. (Encourage them to listen/look out for the words **AT 3.4** from activity 1.) They then match the English sentences to their German equivalents in the text. This could be done as a whole-class activity. Encourage pupils to work out unfamiliar expressions from the context. For example, if they remember that *Geburtstag* is 'birthday' (*Klasse! 1* p. 18) but don't know how to say 'Happy birthday', then it's easy to work out which sentence in the text is the right one. T: *Wie heißt 'birthday' auf Deutsch?* P1: *Geburtstag.* T: *Richtig! Also, wie heißt 'Happy birthday'? Schauen wir den Text an: „Ich habe am Sonntag Geburtstag," „Herzlichen Glückwunsch zum Geburtstag" oder „Was hast du zum Geburtstag bekommen?"*, etc.

Answers:

1 Ich kann nicht kommen. 2 Herzlichen Glückwunsch zum Geburtstag! 3 Was hast du zum Geburtstag bekommen? 4 Ich muss den Partykeller aufräumen. 5 Der CD-Spieler ist unter dem Sofa. 6 Wo sind die Würstchen?

Transcript   p 59, activity 2

- He – ich habe am Sonntag Geburtstag und ich mache eine Party!
- Super! Wann? Und wo?
- Um 19 Uhr – zu Hause im Partykeller.
- Klasse! Ich komme gern!
- Ja, ich auch!
- Und du, Sven? Kommst du auch?
- Am Sonntag? Nein ... nein, ich kann leider nicht kommen. Ich – ich muss ... Hausaufgaben machen.
- Hausaufgaben machen? Am Sonntag?

- Hallo, Atalay! Herzlichen Glückwunsch zum Geburtstag!
- Hallo, Jasmin! Hallo, Annika!
- Und was hast du zum Geburtstag bekommen?
- Ein Skateboard! Ich habe ein Skateboard bekommen!

- Atalay, die Party war super! Aber ich habe zu viel gegessen – und ich habe zu viel getanzt!
- Oh nein – ich muss den Partykeller aufräumen! Schau mal – Cola auf den CDs, der CD-Spieler ist unter dem Sofa ... Was sagen Mutti und Vati?!
- Ich mache mit! Also, wo sind die Würstchen?
- Und der Apfelsaft? Wo ist er?
- Aber wo ist Sven?

AT 3.4 **3** *Beantworte die Fragen.* Pupils answer comprehension questions on the photo story. Pupils could work through the questions in pairs before you invite answers from the whole class. The answers can be derived from the text with the minimum of adaptation (transposing first person singular to third person singular in most instances).

Answers:

1 Er hat am Sonntag Geburtstag. 2 Die Party ist um 19 Uhr zu Hause im Partykeller. 3 Sven kann nicht kommen. 4 Er hat ein Skateboard bekommen. 5 Jasmin hat zu viel gegessen und getanzt. 6 Die Cola ist auf den CDs.

 ## Viel Spaß!

Party-Rap. The main aim is listening for pleasure, but the song also introduces vocabulary and structures for talking about birthdays and parties. For general advice on exploiting the songs in *Klasse! 2*, see page 7 of the introduction to this book.

Transcript

p 59, Viel Spaß!

Mein Geburtstag ist heute
Am 8. April!
Und ich mache eine Party
Hurra!
Kommst du?
Ja, ja, gern!

Wo ist die Party?
Im Partykeller!
Wie ist die Adresse?
Goldstraße 13!
Wann ist die Party?
Um 18 Uhr!

Herzlichen Glückwunsch!
Danke – vielen Dank!
Was hast du bekommen?
Einen Fußball
Einen Gutschein
Ein Rad und ein Buch

Wie war die Party?
Super – super und toll!
Was hast du gemacht?
Mit Tina getanzt
Pizza gegessen
und Cola getrunken

WB A, B Workbook activities A and B could be used at this point for exploitation of the song text.

For the next lesson

Ask pupils to bring in photos of parties, or any other visuals relating to celebrations which they can find. These can be used as additional/alternative visual stimuli for speaking and writing activities throughout this unit.

Wir feiern!
pages 60–61

Objectives

- Say when your birthday is
- Ask and say when special events/celebrations are

Key language

Wann hast du Geburtstag?
Mein Geburtstag ist am 8. April.
Ich habe am 8. April Geburtstag.
Weihnachten, Heiligabend, Silvester, Neujahr, Fasching, Ostern, Nikolaustag, Diwali, Id-ul-Fitr

National Curriculum PoS

statements 1a, 1b, 1c, 2a, 2b, 2c, 2d, 4c, 4d, 5a, 5f, 5i

Materials

- Students' Book pages 60–61
- Cassette 2 side A
- Workbook pages 45–47
- Copymasters 40, 41, 45

Preparatory work

Start by revising birthdays (from *Klasse! 1*, Unit 1). T: *Ich habe im [März] Geburtstag. Sean: Wann hast du Geburtstag?*, etc. If pupils have trouble with the months, get the whole class to recite them with you, then have individual pupils call out the names of the months in order round the class.

AT 1.2
AT 3.2
1 *Hör gut zu und lies mit.* Pupils listen to the recording and follow the text in the book. Play the recording, and ask questions to elicit the correct forms of the dates from pupils. T: *Wann hat Jasmin Geburtstag?* P1: *Dreizehn November.* T: *Sie hat **am** dreizehn**ten** November Geburtstag. Wann hat Atalay Geburtstag?*, etc. Ask the same two questions around the class until all pupils are confident about the ordinal forms.

Transcript

p 60, activity 1

– Wann hast du Geburtstag, Jasmin?
– Ich habe am 13. November Geburtstag. Und du, Atalay?
– Mein Geburtstag ist am 28. April.

WB C Workbook activity C could be used at this point for revision of the names of the months.

WB D Workbook activity D could be used at this point for work on recognition of ordinals.

AT 1.4
2 *Wann haben sie Geburtstag? Hör gut zu und finde die passenden Daten.* Pupils listen to the recording and match the dates to the speakers. In preparation, draw pupils' attention to the *Hilfe* box, which shows how to express dates in German. Elicit from the class that up to *zwanzig*, you add -*ten* to the cardinal number, and from *zwanzig* onwards you add -*sten*. Explain that *ersten*, *dritten* and *siebten* are the only irregular forms. Ask pupils to read out the dates a–g. T: *a: Wie sagt man das?* P1: *Am zehnten Juli*, etc. Then play the recording and complete the activity with the whole class.

Answers:

Miriam: c; Heiko: g; Jana: f; Torsten: a; Meike: e; Olaf: d; Kathi: b

Transcript

p 60, activity 2

– Miriam, wann hast du Geburtstag?
– Ich habe am 7. Mai Geburtstag.
– Und wann hast du Geburtstag, Heiko?
– Am 25. April – mein Geburtstag ist am 25. April.
– Und du, Jana? Wann hast du Geburtstag?
– Ich? Ich habe am 13. März Geburtstag.
– Torsten, wann hat du Geburtstag?
– Ich habe am 10. Juli Geburtstag – ja, mein Geburtstag ist am 10. Juli.
– Wann hast du Geburtstag, Meike?
– Am 1. Dezember – ich habe am 1. Dezember Geburtstag.
– Olaf, und du – wann hast du Geburtstag?
– Also, mein Geburtstag ist am 24. Februar.
– Kathi, und wann hast du Geburtstag?
– Ich – ich habe am 26. August Geburtstag.

C 40 Activity 1 on copymaster 40 provides further listening comprehension on dates, and could be used at this point.

T 2.2 **3a** *A zeigt auf eine Zahl und einen Monat in der Hilfe-Box, B antwortet.*

Pupils work together in pairs. They use the dates from the *Hilfe* box to create dialogues.

C 41 Activity 1 on copymaster 41 provides further speaking practice on dates (dialogues about birthdays) and could be used at this point.

T 2.3 **3b** *Du bist dran! Wann hast du Geburtstag? Macht Dialoge.* Still working in pairs, pupils now ask each other about their own birthdays.

WB E, F Workbook activities E and F could be used at this point for consolidation of dates.

WB G Workbook activity G provides an individual writing opportunity on birthdays.

Tipp

Briefe schreiben: Datum. This section focuses on writing the date as part of a letter heading. Explain that in German it is usual to begin a personal letter with just the town and the date, written in the top right-hand corner, not with the full postal address. However, it is usual to write the full address of the sender on the back of the envelope.

Explain also that the date in a letter heading is written in the accusative, i.e. *den 13. November*, etc., not *am 13. November*. The full stop after the number is important, because it makes it into an ordinal number. In other words, *13 November* would be *dreizehn November*, which does not make sense.

C 45 Copymaster 45 contains further advice on this topic; activity 1 could be used in preparation for activity 4 below.

4 *Dein Brieffreund/deine Brieffreundin fragt: „Wann hast du Geburtstag?" Schreib einen Antwortbrief.* Pupils write a short letter, focusing particularly on the date in the heading and the date of their birthday in the body of the letter. Ask the pupils for suggestions how to end the letter (e.g. *Dein/e*; *Viele Grüße*).

Background information

Carnival season takes place towards the end of February in the week before Lent. Typically, it is a time for fun and parties, for dressing up in fancy-dress costumes and for processions through towns and villages. *Rosenmontag*, *Faschingsdienstag* (Shrove Tuesday) and *Aschenmittwoch* (Ash Wednesday) are all marked by celebrations. Different regions have different names and customs. In Bavaria *Fasching* is celebrated, further north and particularly around the Rhineland they celebrate *Karneval*, and in the Black Forest and Basel they celebrate *Fastnacht*.

Diwali (the Hindu festival of lights) and Id-ul-Fitr (the end of Ramadan) are linked to the lunar calendar and, as such, take place on different dates each year. Searching for any of these terms on the Internet should

provide links to a number of sites containing pictures and further information.

5a *Hör gut zu und lies mit.* Pupils listen to the recording **AT 1.3** and follow the text in the book. Discuss with the class which of the celebrations are celebrated in Britain.
AT 3.2 T: *Feiern wir Fasching in England/Wales/Schottland/ Nordirland?*, etc. Draw pupils' attention to the fact that it is *im April* but *am ersten April*, etc., by writing up these forms on the board/OHT. Teachers will need to be sensitive to other religions which may be held by members of the class and be prepared to provide the German names for other festivals and celebrations.

Transcript   p 61, activity 5a

- Fasching (Karneval) ist im Februar – am Rosenmontag. Wir gehen in die Stadt.
- Ostern ist im März oder April. Es gibt Eier in vielen Farben.
- Martin, Martin! Du hast eine Maus in deiner Tasche!
- Eine Maus?? Aahh!!
- April, April!! Heute ist der 1. April!!
- Oh nein!
- Mein Geburtstag ist am 11. Juni. Ich bin dann 14 Jahre alt!
- Diwali ist im Oktober oder November. Es gibt Kerzen, Feuerwerke und Süßigkeiten!
- Ramadan beginnt dieses Jahr im November. Id-ul-Fitr ist das Ende von Ramadan und ist dieses Jahr im Dezember. Es gibt gutes Essen und neue Kleidung.
- Am 6. Dezember ist Nikolaustag! Der Nikolaus bringt Geschenke.
- Silvester ist am 31. Dezember. Frohes Neues Jahr!
- Weihnachten ist am 24. Dezember. Das ist Heiligabend.

Background information

Christmas celebrations in German-speaking countries are a little different from those in Britain. 6 December (*Nikolaustag*) and 24 December (*Heiligabend*) are important dates along with 25 December (*der Weihnachtstag*). On 6 December, *der Nikolaus* – a man with a long white beard, dressed in a long robe and a bishop's mitre (representing the 4th-century Bishop Nicholas of Myra, the original Santa Claus) - brings small presents (usually sweets and fruit) for children. However, as well as a sack full of presents for good children, he also carries a stick to punish bad children! Sometimes *der Nikolaus* is accompanied by an assistant, *der Knecht Ruprecht*.

The main distribution of presents (*die Bescherung*) takes place on the evening of 24 December round the Christmas tree (*Tannenbaum*). In Southern Germany, children believe these presents are brought by the Christ Child (*das Christkind*); elsewhere they believe in Father Christmas (*der Weihnachtsmann*).

German families also celebrate Christmas Day with a big dinner; unlike in Britain, however, the traditional dish is either carp (*Karpfen*, a large freshwater fish) or goose (*Gans*).

AT 2.2 **5b** *Wann ist … ? A fragt, B antwortet. Dann ist B dran.* Pupils work in pairs to create dialogues using *am* + date and *im* + month.

WB H. I Workbook activities H and I provide consolidation of cultural knowledge about the major festivals from activity 5a.

AT 4.2 *Noch mal! Zeichne einen Kalender und schreib die wichtigen Feiertage auf.* Pupils draw up a calendar showing important celebrations, taken from activity 5a. This could include drawings of the different celebrations and could form a classroom display. If pupils have access to the Internet, they should be able to find photos of *Fasching/Karneval* and other celebrations which they can incorporate into their calendars.

AT 4.3 *Extra! Schreib eine Liste von deinen wichtigen Feiertagen.* Pupils draw up their own personal list of important celebrations in sentences. (They will need help with this, e.g. Mother's Day, Father's Day.) The list could be illustrated with drawings or photos. The *Hilfe* box reminds pupils that it is *am* + date but *im* + month.

Gut gesagt!

Feiertagsgrüße. This section focuses on the pronunciation of various greetings.

6a *Hör gut zu und wiederhole.* Pupils listen to the greetings and then repeat them. Focus first of all on correct pronunciation, e.g long <o:> in *froh-*, short <ɒ> in *Ostern*, differentiation between *ü* and *u* in *Glückwunsch*. Then focus on intonation: stress on the last syllable in *April*, on the first syllable in *Herzlichen*, *Glückwunsch*, *Weihnachten* and *Ostern*. Break the long words down into individual syllables, chanting them with the class: *Herz-lich-en, Glück-wunsch, Ge-burts-tag, Weih-nach-ten*. Then concentrate on improving fluency (getting the rhythm of the whole utterance right will help here) and saying the greetings with appropriate enthusiasm.

Transcript	p 61, activity 6a

– Frohes Neues Jahr!
– April, April!
– Herzlichen Glückwunsch zum Geburtstag!
– Frohe Weihnachten!
– Frohe Ostern!

6b *Ratespiel: Schau die Bilder in Übung 5a an. Was sagst du wann? Schreib die Wörter auf.* Pupils match the greetings in activity 6a to the photos of the celebrations in activity 5a. Note that for several celebrations no special greeting is given.

Answers:

Ostern: Frohe Ostern!
1. April: April, April! (only when you've played a practical joke on someone)
Geburtstag: Herzlichen Glückwunsch zum Geburtstag!
Silvester: Frohes Neues Jahr!
Heligabend: Frohe Weihnachten!

6c *Ist alles richtig? Macht Dialoge.* As a follow-up to activity 6b, pupils work together in pairs to check each other's work orally.

Ich mache eine Party!
pages 62–63

Objectives
- Invite others to a party
- Accept invitations
- Make excuses

Key language
Ich habe am Wochenende/Samstag/Sonntag Geburtstag.
Ich mache eine Party.
Ich mache am Wochenende/Samstag/Sonntag eine Faschingsfete.
Wir machen am Sonntag ein Picknick.
Meine Schule macht am Freitag ein Schulfest.
Kommst du?
Ja, gern.
Wann? Um … Uhr.
Wo? Zu Hause. In meinem Zimmer/im Garten/ Partykeller/Park/Schwimmbad/in der Schule.
Vielen Dank für die Einladung.
Ich komme gern.
Ich kann leider nicht kommen.
Ich muss Hausaufgaben machen/mein Zimmer aufräumen/zu Hause helfen.

National Curriculum PoS
statements 1a, 1b, 1c, 2a, 2b, 2c, 2d, 3e, 5a, 5c, 5f, 5i

Materials
- Students' Book pages 62–63
- Cassette 2 side A
- Workbook pages 47–49
- Copymasters 40, 42, 43, 44, 45

Preparatory work
Briefly revise clock times (*Klasse!* 1 p. 95 and *Klasse!* 2 pp. 22–23) and addresses (*Klasse!* 1 pp. 50–51) with the class.

AT 1.3
AT 3.3

1a *Hör gut zu und lies mit.* Pupils listen to the recording and follow the text in their books. You could then ask pupils to close their books and see how much they have absorbed. T: *Wann ist die Party? Wie ist die Adresse? Wo ist die Party?*

Transcript	p 62, activity 1a

– Ich habe am Sonntag Geburtstag und ich mache eine Party. Kommst du?
– Vielen Dank für die Einladung! Ich komme gern. Und wann ist die Party?
– Am Sonntagabend um 19 Uhr.
– Okay – und wo?
– Zu Hause. Die Adresse ist …
– Kaiserstraße 74! Und wo ist die Party? Im Wohnzimmer?
– Nein, im Partykeller.

Background information
German houses are usually built with a cellar or basement. Often this will consist of several rooms, including a party room or games room, a workshop,

storage for bicycles, a laundry, etc. In most parts of western Germany, terraced houses are uncommon; in the suburbs and in villages, many people live in detached or semi-detached houses, larger on average than British homes; in cities, many people live in low-rise blocks of flats, often with a shared basement for washing machines, bicycles, etc.

AT 2.3 **1b** *A ist Atalay, B ist Britta. Spielt die Rollen.* Pupils work in pairs to read out the dialogue between Atalay and Britta. In preparation, go through the *Tipp* with the class.

Tipp

Sprechen: Rollenspiele. This panel gives advice on getting the most out of role-play dialogues. You could go through the advice with the class, giving examples of good and bad practice.

AT 1.4
AT 3.3 **2a** *Hör gut zu und finde die passenden Einladungen.* Pupils listen to the recording and match the printed invitations to the dialogues. Explain that they should read the invitations first and decide what key words to listen out for – one or two details will be sufficient to enable them to make the right match. For example, *Fasching* and *Goldstraße* are unique to invitation a, so as soon as they hear these they know that they have a match. Pupils could jot down the key words to listen out for.

As they listen to the recording, they should be scanning their key words. When they think they have made the right match, they should listen for a second key word to confirm it – they may have misheard the first time.

Answers: 1 b; 2 c; 3 a; 4 d

Transcript	p 62, activity 2a

1
– Hallo, Anke! Hier ist Tom!
– Hallo, Tom! Wie geht's?
– Gut. Du, Anke, ich mache am Samstag eine Geburtstagsparty. Kommst du?
– Vielen Dank! Ja, ich komme gern! Wo ist die Party?
– Zu Hause – zu Hause im Garten.
– Okay. Und wann?
– Abends um 20 Uhr.
2
– Sandra Fischer.
– Sandra, hier ist Verena. Meine Geschwister und ich – wir machen am Wochenende ein Picknick. Kommst du?
– Oh nein, am Samstag? Am Samstag fahre ich nach Bonn ...
– Nein, nein, am Sonntag – am Sonntagnachmittag.
– He, super – ich komme gern! Und wo?
– Das Picknick ist im Park – im Park am Stadtrand.
3
– Guten Tag, Heiko! Ich bin's – Melanie.
– Tag, Melanie!
– Du, was machst du am Montagabend? Ich mache eine Fete.
– Eine Faschingsfete?

– Ja. Kommst du?
– Ja, vielen Dank für die Einladung! Wo ist die Fete?
– Zu Hause im Partykeller. Um 18 Uhr.
– 18 Uhr. Und wie ist deine Adresse?
4
– Hallo, Andrea!
– Hallo, Uwe!
– Andrea, meine Schule macht am Freitag ein Schulfest. Kommst du?
– Ja, ich komme gern. Wann ist das Schulfest?
– Um 11 Uhr.
– Und wo?
– Die Schule ist in der Heimstraße.
– In der Heimstraße.

AT 2.4 **2b** *A wählt eine Einladung, B antwortet. Dann ist B dran.* Pupils use the invitations from activity 2a to create their own dialogues. In preparation, they could listen again to the recording and note down any useful expressions, e.g. for accepting an invitation.

C 40 Activity 2 on copymaster 40 provides further listening comprehension on party invitations (date, time and venue), and could be done at this point.

C 42 Activity 2 on copymaster 42 is a reading activity involving different types of party and could be done at this point.

C 45 Copymaster 45 contains further advice about conducting role-plays; activity 2 could be used for further role-play practice at this point.

AT 4.4
AT 2.4 **2c** *Zeichnet weitere Einladungen (z. B. mit dem Computer) und macht Dialoge.* Pupils collaborate in groups to write and design their own invitation cards, and then use them to create dialogues. In preparation, you could brainstorm occasions for a party with the whole class, e.g. end of term, Christmas, Easter. Pupils could include clip-art or original illustrations and photos with their invitations – encourage them to make the invitations look as inviting as possible, so that people will really want to go to the party. The invitations could form a classroom display, and pupils could vote for the most interesting one.

WB J Workbook activity J revises occasions for a celebration and could give pupils ideas for their illustrations.

WB K Workbook activity K offers additional listening practice on dates and party vocabulary.

WB L Workbook activity L offers an alternative, non-ICT format for the invitation.

Grammatik im Fokus

in + Dativ. This section focuses on the use of the dative after the preposition *in* and the elision of *in dem* to *im*. Pupils met *von* + dative in Unit 2, p. 26, so should be familiar with the concept of the dative case; however, this may be the first time they have been introduced formally to the dative forms of the definite article, although they have been exposed to them throughout *Klasse! 1* and *2*.

C 44   Copymaster 44 contains further information on *in* + dative. Activity 1 could be used here in preparation for activity 3 below.

3 *Wo ist die Party? Füll die Lücken mit im oder in der aus.* Pupils apply the information from *Grammatik im Fokus* by completing the phrases with *im* or *in der*. Explain that they need to decide whether the nouns are masculine/neuter or feminine. If they are not sure, they should consult the *Vokabular* at the back of the Students' Book, or their vocabulary books or dictionaries.

Answers:

1 im Partykeller; 2 im Wohnzimmer; 3 in der Schule; 4 im Park; 5 im Schwimmbad; 6 in der Disco

WB M   Workbook activity M could be used at this point to consolidate locations with *in* + dative.

AT 1.3
AT 3.3   **4a** *Tom macht eine Party – aber keine Freunde kommen! Hör gut zu und lies mit.* Pupils listen to the recording and follow the text in their books. Elicit from pupils that after *müssen* the infinitive of the main verb goes to the end of the sentence. For example, you could write on the board/OHT *Ich arbeite im Garten. → Ich muss im Garten …,* and invite pupils to complete the sentence.

Transcript   p 63, activity 4a

Freitag:
– Ich mache am Sonntag eine Party. Kommst du?
– Ich kann leider nicht kommen. Ich muss im Garten arbeiten.
– Ach nein! Ich kann nicht kommen! Ich muss Hausaufgaben machen.
– Nein, ich muss mein Zimmer aufräumen.
– Nein, ich muss zu Hause helfen.
– Nein, ich muss Zeitungen austragen.

Sonntag:
– Keine Freunde kommen zu meiner Party!
– Herzlichen Glückwunsch!

AT 2.4   **4b** *Nehmt den Cartoon auf Kassette auf.* Pupils collaborate in groups to make their own recording of the cartoon dialogues. Remind them about the advice given in the *Tipp* box on page 62 and encourage them to put as much feeling into the dialogue as possible.

C 43   Activity 1 on copymaster 43 could be used at this point for writing practice on invitations and accepting/declining them.

WB N   Workbook activity N could be used at this point for further practice of making excuses using *Ich muss …*

AT 4.3   *Noch mal! Schreib andere Ausreden für den Bildern.* Pupils use the picture cues to write other excuses for not going to the party. You could help less able pupils by eliciting the key expressions from the whole class and writing these up on the board/OHT. T: *Bild a: Was machen sie?* P1: *Sie spielen Fußball,* etc.

Answers:

a Ich muss Fußball spielen. b Ich muss abwaschen. c Ich muss um halb zehn ins Bett gehen. d Ich muss

lernen/Hausaufgaben machen. e Ich muss um sechs Uhr zu Hause sein.

AT 4.4   *Extra! Erfinde andere Ausreden und schreib einen Antwortbrief an Tom!* Pupils use their own knowledge of the language of daily routine, chores and leisure pursuits to write a letter giving excuses for not going to the party. Encourage them to recycle as many relevant expressions from Units 1–3 of *Klasse! 2* as possible.

Wiederholung

muss + Infinitiv. This panel reminds pupils about the word order of sentences which contain a modal auxiliary and a main verb (Unit 3, pp. 40–41).

Hilfe

This *Hilfe* box is an overview of the language for making invitations and accepting them or making excuses.

Follow-up activity. Pupils could write their own dialogues inviting people to a party, using the expressions from the *Hilfe* box. They could either record them on cassette or create a cartoon or photo story.

Ich muss aufräumen!
pages 64–65

Objectives
- Ask where things are
- Describe where things are

Key language
Ich muss mein Zimmer/das Wohnzimmer/den Partykeller aufräumen/sauber machen.
Du musst … sauber machen.
Wo ist der Luftballon/Kassettenrecorder/Kartoffelsalat/Apfelsaft/CD-Spieler?
Wo ist die CD/Limonade/Cola?
Wo ist das Buch?
Wo sind die CDs/Luftballons/Würstchen?
Der Luftballon/die CD/das Buch ist im Schreibtisch/neben der Lampe/auf dem Regal/unter den CDs.

National Curriculum PoS
statements 1a, 1b, 1c, 2a, 2b, 2c, 2d, 3b, 3c, 3e, 5a, 5i

Materials
- Students' Book pages 64–65
- Cassette 2 side A
- Workbook pages 49–51
- Copymasters 37, 41, 44

C 37   ## Preparatory work

Use the pictures from copymaster 37 copied onto an OHT or as flashcards to introduce the vocabulary for parties. (For general advice on using copymaster visuals, see page 12 of the introduction to this book.)

AT 1.4   **1a** *Atalay muss sein Zimmer aufräumen. Wo ist … ? Hör gut zu und finde die richtige Reihenfolge für die Bilder.* Pupils listen to the recording, look at the picture and put the items in the sequence in which they are mentioned.

In preparation, ask pupils to name as many of the objects in the picture as possible. T: *Was gibt es im Bild?* P1: *Es gibt ein Sofa.* P2: *Es gibt einen Computer,* etc. This revises the words for items of furniture as well as consolidating the new vocabulary you have just introduced.

Answers: f, h, a, e, b, d, g, c

Transcript   p 64, activity 1a

Atalay muss sein Zimmer aufräumen.
– Atalay, deine Party war super!
– Ja ... aber ich muss mein Zimmer aufräumen!
– Du musst dein Zimmer aufräumen? Kein Problem – ich mache mit! ... Oh, nein! Wo ist denn alles?
– Ja, wo ist der Kassettenrecorder?
– Und der CD-Spieler – wo ist der CD-Spieler?
– Die Luftballons – wo sind die Luftballons?
– Und meine Sascha-CD – wo ist die CD?
– Und Muttis Kartoffelsalat ... wo ist der Kartoffelsalat?
– Ja, und wo sind die Würstchen?
– Annika, wo ist der Apfelsaft?
– Und wo ist die Limonade?

AT 2.2
AT 1.2
1b *Wo ist alles? A fragt, B zeigt auf das passende Bild. Dann ist B dran.* Pupils work together in pairs. Partner A asks where one of the items listed in activity 1a is, B points to its position in the picture. In this way, pupils familiarize themselves with the key vocabulary without needing to form prepositional phrases at this stage. The *Hilfe* box will help pupils in formulating the questions.

WB O Workbook activity O could be used at this point to consolidate key vocabulary for parties.

Tipp

Neue Wörter. This section focuses on ways of identifying the meanings of unfamiliar words without recourse to a dictionary. In particular, it examines English cognates, word families (i.e. different parts of speech with the same root) and compounds containing familiar components.

2 *Lies noch einmal die Wörter in Übung 1a. Welche Wörter ...* Pupils return to the vocabulary in activity 1a and categorize it according to the three types described in the *Tipp.*

Answers:
(These are suggestions only:)
sehen englisch aus: die Limonade, die CDs, der Kassettenrecorder, die Luftballons
sehen bekannt aus: die Würstchen
enthalten bekannte Wörter: der Kartoffelsalat, der Apfelsaft, der CD-Spieler

AT 1.2
AT 3.2
3 *Wo ist alles? Hör gut zu und lies mit.* Pupils listen to the recording and follow the text in the book. You may prefer to do this activity after looking at the *Grammatik im Fokus* box with the class.

Transcript   p 65, activity 3

– Der Kassettenrecorder ist unter dem Schreibtisch.
– Die CD ist im Schreibtisch.
– Die Würstchen sind auf dem Schreibtisch.
– Die Limonade ist neben dem Schreibtisch.

WB P Workbook activity P provides additional listening comprehension on the four prepositions.

Grammatik im Fokus

auf, in, neben, unter. This section revises the term 'preposition', revises *in* + dative and introduces three further prepositions with the dative. Refer pupils to activity 3 above: the pictures clearly demonstrate the meanings of the prepositions. Now practise the four prepositions with the class using a variety of objects and the furniture in the classroom. T: (putting a pen on the desk) *Wo ist der Kuli?* P1: *(Der Kuli ist) auf dem Tisch,* etc. Then pupils could go on to ask each other questions P1: *Marc: Wo ist das Heft?* P2: *Das Heft ist unter dem Stuhl,* etc. Alternatively, pupils take it in turns to turn away or cover their eyes while a selected object is positioned. That pupil must locate the object and say where it is. Then someone else has a turn.

C 44 Copymaster 44 contains further information on the four prepositions *auf, in, neben, unter* + dative.

4a *Wo ist alles? Schau das Bild in Übung 1a an und finde die passenden Wörter.* Pupils compare the picture in activity 1a with the sentences and select the appropriate preposition from each pair. Pupils check each other's answers by doing activity 4b.

Answers: 1 auf; 2 im; 3 unter; 4 neben

4b *Ist alles richtig? A fragt, B antwortet. Dann ist B dran.* Pupils work together in pairs to check each other's answers to activity 4a orally.

WB Q Workbook activity Q consolidates the use of the four prepositions.

5 *dem, der oder den? Füll die Lücken aus.* Pupils fill in the correct form of the definite article. To reinforce the meanings of the prepositions, pupils could draw a simple picture next to each sentence.

Answers: 1 dem; 2 dem; 3 dem; 4 den; 5 der; 6 den

WB R Workbook activity R gives further practice of the dative forms of the definite article.

C 44 Activity 2 on copymaster 44 gives further practice of the dative forms of the definite article, followed by a written description of a picture.

WB S Workbook activity S is a speaking activity using the four prepositions in describing a picture.

C 41 Activity 2 on copymaster 41 is an information-gap speaking activity on the same topic.

AT 2.3 *Noch mal! Gedächtnisspiel: Schaut das Bild in Übung 1a an. Macht die Bücher zu. Wo ist alles?* Working in small groups, pupils study the picture in activity 1a, then close their books and try to remember where each item is in the picture.

AT 4.4 *Extra! Schau dein Klassenzimmer an. Was ist wo? Schreib fünf Sätze.* Pupils write sentences about where things are in the classroom. Encourage them to use each preposition at least once.

Follow-up activity. For homework, pupils find a suitable picture of an interior (e.g. from a glossy magazine) and write a description of it, using their dictionaries as necessary to research any new vocabulary they need.

Wie war die Party?
pages 66–67

Objectives

- Ask others which birthday presents they received
- Say what birthday presents you received
- Ask and give your opinion about parties or events

Key language

Wie war die Party?
Sie war toll/super.
Was hast du zum Geburtstag bekommen?
Ich habe … bekommen.
einen Fußball/Gutschein/Pullover
ein Buch/Computerspiel/Handy/Skateboard/Stofftier
Make-up/Geld/Schmuck/Inline-Skates
Ich habe Pizza/Kartoffelsalat/Würstchen/Chips gegessen.
Ich habe Cola/Orangensaft/Mineralwasser/Apfelsaft getrunken.
Ich habe … gesehen.
Ich habe … getroffen.
Ich habe mit … getanzt.
Ich habe Gitarre gespielt.

National Curriculum PoS

statements 1a, 1b, 1c, 2a, 2b, 2c, 2d, 3e, 5a, 5c, 5f, 5i

Materials

- Students' Book pages 66–67
- Cassette 2 side A
- Workbook pages 51–53
- Copymasters 38, 40, 42, 43

C 38 ## Preparatory work

To introduce *ich habe bekommen*, you could cut out the individual pictures on copymaster 38 (making enough copies for each pupil to receive one picture) and distribute them to the class. Also make a copy as an OHT and write the name of each object below the picture. Now you could go round the class asking *Was hast du bekommen?* At first, the pupil can just hold up his/her card. T: *Du hast ein Stofftier bekommen.* Gradually encourage them to start using *Ich habe … bekommen* in response to your questions. Explain that *ich habe … bekommen* is the perfect tense of the verb *bekommen* 'to receive or get', which is irregular because the past participle is exactly the same as the infinitive.

 1 *Was hat Atalay zum Geburtstag bekommen? Hör gut zu und lies mit.* Pupils listen to the recording and follow the text in the book.

AT 1.3
AT 3.3

Follow-up activity. Ask pupils to close their books, then ask comprehension questions. T: *Hat Atalay ein Buch bekommen? Hat er ein Handy bekommen?*, etc.

Transcript	p 66, activity 1

– Und was hast du zum Geburtstag bekommen?
– Ich habe ein Handy bekommen – und ein Skateboard!
– Hast du auch Geld bekommen?
– Nein, aber ich habe einen Gutschein bekommen – für 25 Euro!

 2a *Was haben Hanna und Bastian zum Geburtstag bekommen? Hör gut zu und finde die passenden Bilder.* Pupils listen to the recording and select the appropriate pictures for Hanna and Bastian. In preparation, ask the pupils to look at the pictures in pairs and to list as many of the German names for the items as possible. You could check the answers as a whole-class activity, by going through the pictures with the class and eliciting the name of each item (needed for activity 2b).

AT 1.5

Answers: Hanna: f, e, j, c, h; Bastian: d, a, i, b, g

Transcript	p 66, activity 2a

– Hallo, Hanna!
– Hallo, Svenja!
– Na, wie war deine Geburtstagsparty?
– Super! Sie war super!
– Und was hast du alles zum Geburtstag bekommen?
– Also, ich habe Inline-Skates bekommen, und ich habe einen roten Pullover bekommen.
– Rot ist meine Lieblingsfarbe!
– Ich habe auch ein Stofftier bekommen, einen blauen Hund!
– Hey, toll!
– Ja, und ich habe auch Make-up bekommen, von meiner Schwester. Ach ja, und Schmuck – ich habe auch Schmuck bekommen, von meinen Großeltern …

– Olivia – hi, Olivia!
– Hallo, Markus!
– Olivia, das ist mein Bruder Bastian. Er hat heute Geburtstag!
– Herzlichen Glückwunsch, Bastian! Wie alt bist du?
– Ich bin 15 Jahre alt.
– Und was hast du zum Geburtstag bekommen?
– Ein Handy – ich habe ein Handy bekommen.
– Von deinen Eltern?
– Ja, von meinen Eltern. Und ich habe Geld bekommen. Und einen Gutschein, von meiner Oma. Und ein Buch – ja, ich habe ein Wörterbuch bekommen, für die Schule. UND ich habe ein Computerspiel bekommen! ,Cyberskaters 2'!
– ,Cyberskaters 2'? Fantastisch!

AT 2.5 **2b** *Was hast du zum Geburtstag bekommen? Macht Dialoge mit den Bildern (Übung 2a).* Pupils now use the pictures from activity 2a to create their own dialogues, working in pairs. The *Hilfe* box contains a summary of the structures needed for this activity.

AT 2.3 **2c** *Gedächtnisspiel*. Pupils play the familiar memory game, this time listing items they received for their birthday (from activity 2a; more able pupils can introduce other items as well). Pupils might find it more fun to play this game in small groups rather than pairs.

C 40 Activity 3 on copymaster 40 provides further listening comprehension of a description of a party in the perfect tense and could be used at this point.

AT 4.5 **2d** *Dein Brieffreund/deine Brieffreundin fragt: „Was hast du zum Geburtstag bekommen?" Schreib einen Antwortbrief mit sechs Bildern von Übung 2a.* Pupils write letters about their birthday presents, choosing six items from activity 2a.

Follow-up activity. More able pupils can write about gifts they really have received, or would like to receive, using their dictionaries to research the relevant vocabulary.

WB T, U Workbook activities T and U consolidate the new vocabulary for presents introduced in activities 1 and 2 above.

AT 1.2 AT 3.2 **3** *Geburtstagsparty – was hat Atalay gemacht? Hör gut zu und lies mit.* Pupils listen to the recording and follow the text in the book. Write up the infinitives of the three participles on the board/OHT and elicit from the class which participle goes with which infinitive, and what its meaning is in English. T: *Ich habe … getroffen. Ist das von treffen, spielen oder sehen?* P1: *Treffen.* T: *Richtig. Wie heißt treffen auf Englisch?*, etc. You could add in a few more perfect tense forms from Units 1 and 4, e.g. *ich bin … gefahren, ich habe … gekauft, ich habe … gegessen.*

Transcript	p 67, activity 3

Meine Geburtstagsparty war super! Ich habe Susi getroffen. Ich habe Gitarre gespielt. Und ich habe Ina und Dominik gesehen.

AT 1.5 **4** *Schulfest – was hat Britta gemacht? Hör gut zu und finde die richtige Reihenfolge für die Bilder.* Pupils listen to the recording and put the pictures in the sequence in which they are mentioned in the dialogue. In preparation, pupils could discuss in pairs what vocabulary they expect to hear, judging by the pictures. To make this more focused, you could ask them specifically to make a list of perfect tense forms, e.g. *Bild a: ich habe getrunken; Bild b: ich habe gesehen/getroffen; Bild c: ich habe getanzt*, etc.

Answers: f, a, e, c, d, b

Transcript	p 67, activity 4

– Hallo, Britta!
– Hallo, Anne!
– Na, wie war die Fete am Donnerstag?
– Das Schulfest? Es war super, Anne – total toll!
– Und was hast du gemacht?
– Also, ich habe Kai getroffen – Kai aus der 8C ...

– Und was habt ihr gemacht?
– Wir haben Apfelsaft getrunken und wir haben Würstchen gegessen.
– Hast du auch getanzt?
– Ja, ich habe mit Kai getanzt – er ist super ... und ich habe Gitarre gespielt!
– Und hast du auch, ähm, Tim gesehen?
– Tim Meyer – aus der 8A?
– Ja, Tim Meyer ...
– Ja, ich habe Tim gesehen – Tim und seine Freundin Rita.
– Seine ... FREUNDIN???

WB V Workbook activity V reinforces the perfect tense forms of *spielen, treffen, trinken, tanzen* and *essen.*

C 42 Activity 1 on copymaster 42 is a general revision of party language, including invitations, question forms and statements in the perfect tense, and could be used at this point.

AT 2.5 **5** *Wie war die Party? Was hast du gemacht? A fragt, B wählt eine Einladung und antwortet.* Pupils work together in pairs to create a dialogue using one of the invitations. When they have finished their dialogue, they can swap roles and create another dialogue using the second invitation. In preparation, go through the *Hilfe* box with the class, and draw their attention to the *Wiederholung* panel, which contains a reminder of the imperfect *war.*

AT 4.3 *Noch mal! Dein Freund/deine Freundin fragt: „Wie war die Party? Was hast du gemacht?" Schreib eine E-Mail für eine Party von Übung 5.* Pupils write an e-mail about one of the two parties in activity 5, using the language they practised there.

AT 4.5 *Extra! Beschreib eine Party (deine Geburtstagsparty, ein Schulfest usw.): Was hast du gemacht? Was hast du gegessen/getrunken?* Pupils write imaginatively about another party they have been to, inventing different details. Encourage them to bring in other vocabulary they know and to research new vocabulary using their dictionaries. They could provide photos or drawings to accompany the text.

C 43 Activity 2 on copymaster 43 is a letter-writing activity which could be used in addition/as an alternative to *Noch mal!* or as preparation for *Extra!* above.

WB W Workbook activity W provides further speaking practice on the theme of this spread.

WB X Workbook activities X1 and X2 could be used as easier alternatives to *Noch mal!* and *Extra!* above, respectively.

Thema im Fokus
pages 68–69

National Curriculum PoS
statements 1c, 2e, 3b, 3e, 5a, 5c, 5d, 5f, 5g, 5i

Materials

- Students' Book pages 68–69
- Cassette 2 side A
- Copymaster 39

The final spread of each unit provides further reading practice, leading into a project outcome for the unit. See pages 8–9 of the introduction to this book for general notes on how to use these pages.

AT 3.4 **1** *Lies die Texte.* Pupils read the texts and look at the pictures. The main point of these texts is reading for personal interest. Remind pupils of the techniques for working out the meanings of unfamiliar words (page 64).

AT 2.4 **2** *Organisiert ein Schulfest!*
a *Macht eine Umfrage in der Klasse. Fragt:* Pupils conduct a class survey about the type of party they would like to have (occasion, date, venue).

AT 4.3–4 **b** *Schreibt Einladungen und zeichnet ein Einladungsposter.* On the basis of their survey, pupils choose the most popular party idea and write a poster advertising it. This could be done on computer, incorporating appropriate clip-art, a picture of the venue, etc.

AT 4.3 **c** *Essen und Trinken – was gibt es? Zeichnet und schreibt eine Speisekarte mit Preisen.* Pupils draw up a menu for the party. This could be decorated/illustrated with pictures of the food and drink on offer.

AT 4.4 **d** *Erfindet Ausreden für die Lehrer! Schreibt und zeichnet alles. Macht dann einen Wettbewerb: Was ist die Ausrede Nummer eins?* Pupils invent excuses for their teachers saying why they can't come to the party, accompanied by drawings. The more inventive (and wildly improbable) the excuses are, the better. You could brainstorm a few ideas with the class to get them started, e.g. for the least sporty teacher in the school: *Ich kann leider nicht kommen. Ich muss Fußball spielen.* The class then votes for the best excuse.

Kannst du ... ?

The end-of-unit summary is a checklist for pupils. See page 8 of the introduction to this book for ideas on how to use the checklist.

C 39 Copymaster 39 provides a useful reference for pupils revising the language of this unit.

Noch mal!-Seite Einheit 5
page 130

National Curriculum PoS
statements 1a, 1b, 1c, 2a, 2b, 2c, 2d, 5a, 5i

Materials

- Students' Book page 130
- Cassette 2 side A

This revision page is intended for less able pupils. It reinforces the basic vocabulary and structures from the

unit, and it can be used by pupils who experienced difficulty in completing some of the activities within the unit, or as alternative homework activities.

AT 2.2 **1** *Wann hast du Geburtstag? Macht Dialoge.* This activity relates to pages 60–61 and focuses on ordinal numbers. Pupils work together in pairs to create dialogues based on the picture cues.

AT 1.3 **2** *Tina macht eine Party, aber fünf Gäste kommen nicht. Hör gut zu und finde die passenden Notizen.* This activity relates to pages 62–63. Pupils listen to the recording to find out the names of the five guests who can't come to the party and match them to the excuses. Point out that they should familiarize themselves with the excuses before listening to the recording.

Follow-up activity. To check comprehension, pupils could draw a picture to accompany each of the excuses. They could write a caption for each using *Ich muss …*

Answers:

1 (Kathi) e; 2 (Ralf) c; 3 (Ina) d; 4 (Tobias) a; 5 (Susi) b

Transcript   p 130, activity 2

1
– Tina, guten Tag. Hier ist Kathi. Vielen Dank für die Einladung. Aber ich kann nicht kommen: Ich muss Hausaufgaben machen! Also, auf Wiederhören!

2
– Tina? Hier ist Ralf aus der 7A. Vielen Dank für die Einladung. Aber ich kann leider nicht kommen: Ich muss mein Zimmer aufräumen! Tschüs!

3
– Hallo, Tina. Ich bin's – Ina. Vielen Dank für die Einladung, Tina. Aber ich kann nicht kommen – leider: Ich muss im Garten arbeiten.

4
– Tag, Tina. Tobias hier. Also, danke für die Einladung. Ich kann leider nicht kommen, Tina – ich muss Zeitungen austragen ... Tschüs!

5
– Tag, Tina, ich bin's – Susi. Danke für die Einladung. Du, ich kann nicht kommen – ich muss zu Hause helfen!

AT 3.2 **3a** *Wo ist alles? Füll die Lücken aus.* Activity 3 relates to pages 64–65 and focuses on prepositions and party vocabulary. In activity 3a, pupils complete the sentences with the words from the box to match the picture.

Answers:

1 auf; 2 Schreibtisch; 3 Kassettenrecorder; 4 im; 5 neben; 6 Luftballons

AT 2.3 **3b** *Ist alles richtig? Macht Dialoge.* Pupils work together in pairs to check their answers to activity 3a orally.

AT 3.5 **4a** *Max hat Geburtstag. Was hat er gemacht? Finde die passenden Sätze.* Activity 4 relates to pages 66–67 and focuses on the perfect tense. In activity 4a, pupils select the appropriate past participle to complete each sentence.

Answers: 1 a; 2 b; 3 c; 4 b; 5 b; 6 b

T 4.5 **4b** *Du bist Max! Schreib einen Brief über deinen Geburtstag.* Pupils write letters based on their answers to activity 4a.

Extra!-Seite Einheit 5
page 131

National Curriculum PoS
statements 1a, 1b, 1c, 2a, 2i, 4c, 4d, 5f, 5i

Materials
- Students' Book page 131
- Cassette 2 side A

This extension page is intended for more able pupils. It contains slightly longer and more complex materials, and it can be used by pupils who have completed other activities quickly, or as alternative homework activities.

AT 3.4 **1** *Lies die Texte und finde die passenden Feste.* This activity relates to pages 60–61. Pupils read the four texts and then select the appropriate card for each.

Answers: 1 b; 2 c; 3 a; 4 d

 2a *Sara, Andi und Bea machen Partys. Kopiere den Zettel dreimal. Hör dann gut zu und mach Notizen.* Activity 2 relates to pages 62–63. In activity 2a pupils listen to the recording and note the details of each party. Explain to pupils that they should write down the day and the time, and the full address.

AT 1.4

Answers:

Sara: Geburtstag; Samstag um 20 Uhr; Kaiserstraße 106, im Partykeller.
Andi: Faschingsfete; Montag um 15.30 Uhr; Hagener Weg 39, im Zimmer.
Bea: Picknick; Sonntag um 11 Uhr; Schwimmbad Nord.

Transcript	p 131, activity 2a

– Hallo, hier ist Sara. Ich habe am Samstag Geburtstag, und ich mache eine Party. Kommst du? Die Geburtstagsparty ist zu Hause – im Partykeller. Jan und Viola kommen auch! Die Party ist um 20 Uhr. Meine Adresse ist Kaiserstraße – das schreibt man K – A – I – S – E – R – S – T – R – A – ß – E und meine Hausnummer ist 106. Tschüs!

– Guten Tag, ich bin's – Andi. Du, ich mache am Montag eine Fete – eine Faschingsfete. Kommst du? Die Fete ist zu Hause, in meinem Zimmer. Ja, und die Faschingsfete beginnt um 15 Uhr 30. Ach ja, und meine Adresse ist Hagener Weg – H – A – G – E – N – E – R W – E – G Nummer 39. Das ist neben dem Supermarkt.

– Hi, hier ist Bea aus der 7A. Also, wir machen am Sonntag ein Picknick – im Schwimmbad Nord. Kommst du? Karen und Sandro kommen auch! Es gibt Würstchen, Nudelsalat, Gemüseburger und Kuchen. Das Picknick ist um 11 Uhr. Das Schwimmbad ist am Stadtrand. Du fährst am besten mit dem Bus Linie 3. Die Bushaltestelle ist neben dem Schwimmbad.

AT 4.4 **2b** *Lies Toms E-Mail an Sara. Du bist dran! Schreib E-Mails an Andi und Bea so wie Tom.* Pupils write e-mails giving excuses, using Tom's e-mail as a model.

AT 3.5 **2c** *Lies Saras Brief und finde die passenden Antworten.* Pupils read the letter and then select the correct answer from each pair.

Answers: 1 b; 2 a; 3 a; 4 b; 5 a; 6 b

Workbook

Page 44
Use with page 59 in the Students' Book.

 A1 *Hör gut zu und sing mit!* Pupils listen to the rap-style song and then sing along. One group of pupils could sing the questions, another group could sing the responses. After playing the song through at normal volume while pupils sing along, you could try turning down the volume for the responses and the pupils can try to remember the correct words.

Transcript	W 44, activity A1

Mein Geburtstag ist heute
Am 8. April!
Und ich mache eine Party
Hurra!
Kommst du?
Ja, ja, gern!

Wo ist die Party?
Im Partykeller!
Wie ist die Adresse?
Goldstraße 13!
Wann ist die Party?
Um 18 Uhr!

Herzlichen Glückwunsch!
Danke – vielen Dank!
Was hast du bekommen?
Einen Fußball
Einen Gutschein
Ein Rad und ein Buch

Wie war die Party?
Super – super und toll!
Was hast du gemacht?
Mit Tina getanzt
Pizza gegessen
und Cola getrunken

AT 3.4 **A2** *Finde die passenden Antworten.* This activity consists of a few simple questions to increase pupils' comprehension of the song text and German culture. Pupils choose the appropriate answer from each pair.

Answers: 1 a; 2 a; 3 b

AT 3.4 **B** *Finde die passenden Bilder für jede Strophe (verse).* Pupils match the pictures to the verses of the song, again increasing their comprehension of the vocabulary used in the song.

Answers: 1 c; 2 d; 3 a; 4 b

Pages 45–46

Use with pages 60–61 in the Students' Book.

AT 3.1 **C** *Wann haben sie Geburtstag? Füll die Lücken aus.* Pupils complete the names of the months in this revision activity.

Follow-up activity. To check pronunciation, you could have the pupils call out the names of the months in order round the class. Correct any English pronunciations: as the names of the months are very similar to the English, there will be a tendency to pronounce them in the English way. To make the activity more interesting and challenging, you could ask for the months in reverse order, or every third or fifth month, etc.

Answers:

1 März; 2 August; 3 Juli; 4 Dezember; 5 Februar; 6 Oktober; 7 April; 8 Januar; 9 September; 10 Mai; 11 Juni; 12 November

AT 1.3 **D** *Familie Mai hat im Mai Geburtstag! Hör gut zu und finde die passenden Zahlen.* Pupils listen to the recording and note down the dates they hear.

Answers: 28, 7, 15, 22, 1, 30, 19, 26

Transcript   W 45, activity D

– Hallo, ich bin Herr Mai. Ich habe am 28. Mai Geburtstag, ja, am 28. Mai!

– Und ich bin Mutter Mai. Mein Geburtstag ist am 7. Mai – am 7. Mai.

– Ich heiße Markus – Markus Mai. Mein Geburtstag ist am 15. Mai. Ja, ich habe am 15. Mai Geburtstag.

– Ich bin Oma Mai. Ich bin 87 Jahre alt und ich habe am 22. Mai Geburtstag – juchu!

– Ich heiße Milli Mai. Mein Geburtstag ist am 1. Mai – dann bin ich 5 Jahre alt!

– Und ich bin Opa Mai. Mein Geburtstag ist am 30. Mai – am – 30. – Mai!

– Ich heiße Maria Mai. Ich bin die Tante. Mein Geburtstag? Mein Geburtstag ist am 19. Mai, am 19. Mai.

– Ich bin Onkel Manfred Mai. Und ich habe am 26. Mai Geburtstag – ja, am 26. Mai.

AT 1.3 **E1** *Wann haben Majas Freundinnen und Freunde Geburtstag? Sie schreibt ihr Tagebuch – aber sie macht Fehler. Hör gut zu und korrigiere die Fehler.* Pupils listen to the recording and correct the dates in the diary. (Suse's birthday is written correctly.) Remind pupils to put a full stop after the number to show that it is an ordinal number. Pupils check their own answers in activity E2.

Answers:

Simon: 29. April; Annika: 24. Januar; Michael: 11. November; Hanna: 8. Februar; Ralf: 13. Juli; Kathi: 27. März; Daniel: 16. September

---

Transcript   W 45, activity E1

Also, Nummer eins ist Suse – meine beste Freundin. Wann hat Suse Geburtstag? Das ist einfach. Sie hat am 3. August Geburtstag – am 3. August. Und Simon – wann hat er Geburtstag? Also, Simons Geburtstag ist am 29. April – ja, am 29. April. Und dann Annika – wann hat sie Geburtstag? Ach ja, sie hat am 24. Januar Geburtstag – 24. Januar. Und jetzt Michael – Michaels Geburtstag ist am 11. November – ja, am 11. November. Und Hanna – wann ist Hannas Geburtstag? Im Januar? Nein, im Februar – am 8. – Hanna: am 8. Februar. Und Ralf aus der 7C – wann hat Ralf Geburtstag? Im Juli – ja, Ralf hat am 13. Juli Geburtstag – am 13. Juli. Und Kathi – Kathis Geburtstag ist am … Moment … am 27. März – ja – am 27. März. Und dann noch Daniel – wann hat er Geburtstag? Ach ja – Daniels Geburtstag ist am 16. September.

AT 2.2 **E2** *Ist alles richtig? A fragt, B antwortet. Dann ist B dran.* Pupils work together in pairs to check their answers to activity E1 orally.

AT 2.3 **F** *Wann hast du Geburtstag? Macht Dialoge mit den Bildern.* Pupils use the cues to create dialogues, again working in pairs. This activity further consolidates ordinal numbers in dates.

AT 4.4 **G** *Du bist dran! Wann hast du Geburtstag? Wann hat deine Familie Geburtstag? Wann haben deine Freunde/Freundinnen Geburtstag?* Pupils write about the dates of their own birthdays and those of friends and family. This activity can form part of pupils' written records for continuous assessment purposes. See the general notes on pages 13–14 of the introduction to this book.

AT 3.1 **H** *Was ist das? Finde die passenden Bilder.* Pupils match the pictures to the names of the festivals. This activity helps to consolidate their cultural knowledge.

Answers: 1 c; 2 f; 3 b; 4 d; 5 g; 6 a; 7 e

Page 47

Use with pages 61–62 in the Students' Book.

AT 3.2 **I** *Sieh auch Lehrbuch, Seite 61, Übung 5a. Wann sind diese Feiertage? Lies die Sätze. Richtig oder falsch? Schreib ✔ oder ✘ und korrigiere dann die falschen Sätze.* Pupils look at the information about festivals in activity 5a on page 61 of the Students' Book and decide whether the statements in the Workbook are true or false, correcting the false ones.

Answers:

1 falsch: Heiligabend ist am 24. Dezember. 2 richtig; 3 falsch: Nikolaustag ist am 6. Dezember. 4 falsch: Diwali ist im Oktober oder im November. 5 falsch: Silvester ist am 31. Dezember. 6 falsch: Id-ul-Fitr ist im Dezember. 7 falsch: Fasching/Karneval ist im Februar.

AT 3.2 **J** *Finde die passenden Bilder.* Pupils match the pictures to the sentences about different types of celebration.

Answers: 1 b; 2 d; 3 a; 4 c

K *Luise macht eine Party und schreibt eine Einladung. Hör gut zu und füll die Lücken aus.* This activity practises listening for specific information. Pupils listen to the recording and then complete the invitation.

Answers:

> Einladung – Einladung – Einladung
> zur **Party**
> Ich habe am **Sonntag**
> Geburtstag und mache um **16** Uhr eine Fete!
> Wo: im **Partykeller**
> Adresse: **Gartenstraße 85**

> **Transcript**   W 47, activity K
>
> – Tom Meyer.
> – Hallo, Tom, hier ist Luise – Luise aus der 7B.
> – Hallo, Luise!
> – Du, Tom, ich habe am Sonntag Geburtstag und ich mache eine Party. Kommst du?
> – Ja, klar! Vielen Dank für die Einladung! Ich komme gern.
> – Super!
> – Und wann ist die Party?
> – Am Sonntagnachmittag um 16 Uhr.
> – Um 16 Uhr – okay. Und wo?
> – Zu Hause. Die Adresse ist Gartenstraße 85.
> – Gartenstraße 85 … Und wo ist die Party? Im Wohnzimmer?
> – Nein, im Partykeller.
> – Im Partykeller – klasse! Also, noch mal vielen Dank, Luise. Tschüs – bis Sonntag!

Page 48

Use with page 62 in the Students' Book.

L *Du bist dran! Schreib eine Einladung. Zeichne auch passende Bilder für die Party auf die Einladung.* Pupils write their own party invitation and decorate it with appropriate pictures. This activity can form part of pupils' written records for continuous assessment purposes.

M1 *Wo ist die Party? Schreib die Wörter richtig auf. Füll dann die Lücken rechts aus.* Pupils unjumble the letters to form the names of venues for a party, guided by the picture cues, adding *in* and the appropriate dative article. Pupils check their own answers by doing activity M2.

Answers:

a im Wohnzimmer; b in der Disco; c im Partykeller; d im Park; e im Schwimmbad; f in der Schule

M2 *Ist alles richtig? Macht Dialoge.* Pupils work together in pairs to create dialogues with their answers to activity M1.

Page 49

Use with pages 63–64 in the Students' Book.

N1 *Diese Freunde und Freundinnen kommen nicht zu Atalays Party. Was sagen sie? Finde die passenden Bilder.*

Activity N provides further practice of making excuses using *Ich muss …* In activity N1, pupils match the pictures to the excuses.

Answers: 1 b; 2 d; 3 a; 4 e; 5 c

N2 *Was sagst du? A wählt ein Bild von Übung N1, B antwortet. Dann ist B dran.* Pupils work together in pairs to check their answers to activity N1 orally.

O *Tom muss aufräumen. Wo ist … ? Finde 8 Wörter und schreib sie auf. Schreib auch den passenden Artikel (der, die, das) auf.* Pupils find the eight nouns in the wordsearch to describe the pictures and then add the appropriate form of the definite article for each noun. This activity helps to consolidate key vocabulary for parties.

Answers:

1 die CDs; 2 der Apfelsaft; 3 die Würstchen;
4 die Limonade; 5 der CD-Spieler; 6 der Kartoffelsalat;
7 die Luftballons; 8 der Kassettenrecorder

Page 50

Use with page 65 in the Students' Book.

P *Wo ist alles? Hör gut zu und finde die passenden Bilder.* Pupils listen to the recording and match the pictures to the sentences on the recording. This activity provides further listening comprehension involving the four prepositions *auf, in, neben, unter.*

Answers: 1 c; 2 a; 3 d; 4 b

> **Transcript**   W 50, activity P
>
> – Oh nein – ich muss aufräumen! Wo ist alles?
> 1 – Also, der Apfelsaft ist neben der Lampe.
> 2 – Und das Buch ist auf dem Bett.
> 3 – Die Würstchen sind im Kleiderschrank.
> 4 – Ja, und die Cola ist unter dem Stuhl.

Q *Füll die Lücken aus.* Pupils complete the sentences to describe the picture of the party room. This activity provides further practice with the prepositions *auf, in, neben* and *unter.*

Answers:

1 auf; 2 CD-Spieler; Kleiderschrank; 4 auf; 5 Apfelsaft;
6 Schreibtisch; 7 neben, Computer; 8 Limonade, auf

R *Wo ist alles? Füll die Lücken mit dem oder der aus.* Pupils complete the sentences with the correct dative form of the definite article.

Answers: 1 dem; 2 dem; 3 dem; 4 dem; 5 dem; 6 dem

Pages 51–52

Use with pages 65–67 in the Students' Book.

S *Dein Partner/Deine Partnerin muss aufräumen – und du auch! Wo ist alles? Macht Dialoge.* Pupils work together in pairs to create dialogues based on the picture. This activity provides pupils with an opportunity to use the four prepositions *auf, in, neben* and *unter* productively.

AT 4.1 **T1** *Was hast du zum Geburtstag bekommen? Schreib die passenden Wörter auf.* Pupils use the picture clues to complete the crossword. This activity helps to consolidate the vocabulary for various presents.

Answers:

AT 2.3 **T2** *Ist alles richtig? Was hast du zum Geburtstag bekommen? Macht Dialoge mit den Bildern in Übung T1.* Pupils work together in pairs to create dialogues with their answers to activity T1.

AT 1.5 **U** *Was haben Miriam und Thorsten zum Geburtstag bekommen? Hör gut zu und kreuz die passenden Bilder an.* Pupils listen to the recording for specific information and then fill in the table. Vocabulary for presents is the focus.

Miriam	x	x	x		x			
Thorsten				x		x	x	x

Transcript   W 52, activity U

– Hallo, Miriam! Herzlichen Glückwunsch zum Geburtstag!
– Hallo, Daniel! Danke!
– Na, was hast du zum Geburtstag bekommen?
– Oh, ich habe schon so viel bekommen! Schau mal: Ich habe einen Fußball bekommen!
– Super! Fußball ist dein Lieblingssport, ja?
– Ja, richtig! Und hier – ich habe einen Gutschein bekommen – von meinen Eltern. Einen Gutschein für 50 Euro!
– So viel Geld … toll! Und was hast du von deiner Oma bekommen?
– Ein Stofftier – ich habe auch ein Stofftier bekommen. Ein …
– … Pferd! Ein braunes Pferd!
– Ja, es heißt Polly. Und was habe ich noch bekommen? Ach ja, ich habe auch ein Buch bekommen – von Martin. Oh, was ist das denn?
– Hier, bitte – das ist mein Geschenk!
– Oh, Daniel – danke! Vielen Dank!

– Hallo, Thorsten!

– Oh, hallo, Verena!
– Na, wie war dein Geburtstag?
– Super! Wir haben ein Picknick im Park gemacht.
– Und was hast du zum Geburtstag bekommen?
– Ein Handy! Ich habe ein Handy bekommen – von meinem Vater in München.
– Oh, toll – ein Handy! Und was hast du von deiner Mutter bekommen?
– Ich habe Inline-Skates bekommen – hier! Das sind meine Inline-Skates! Ich fahre zum Park – zum Inline-Skating. Und was habe ich noch bekommen? Ach ja – ich habe auch Geld bekommen – 20 Euro.
– 20 Euro – klasse! Und was hast du noch bekommen?
– Ich habe auch einen Pullover bekommen – von meiner Tante.
– Ist das dieser Pullover?
– Ja, wie gefällt dir der Pullover?
– Er gefällt mir sehr gut.

AT 3.2 **V** *Finde die passenden Wörter.* Pupils select the appropriate past participle to complete each sentence. This activity revises the perfect tense forms of *spielen, treffen, trinken, tanzen* and *essen*.

Answers: 1 c; 2 d; 3 e; 4 a; 5 b

AT 2.5 **W** *Wie war deine Party – was hast du bekommen und gemacht? Macht Dialoge mit den Bildern.* Pupils work together in pairs to create dialogues using the picture cues. This activity provides further practice of the perfect tense and the imperfect of *sein*.

Page 53

Use with page 67 in the Students' Book.

AT 3.5 **X1** *Lies Lolas Brief und füll die Lücken aus.* Pupils read the letter and select appropriate words from the box to fill the gaps.

Answers:

Hallo Sarah!
Meine **Geburtstagsparty** am Samstag war super! Ich habe viele Geschenke **bekommen** und wir haben viel **gemacht**: Wir haben **Apfelsaft** getrunken und Kartoffelsalat **gegessen** – lecker! Ich habe auch **Gitarre** gespielt und ich habe mit Martin **getanzt**! Ich habe auch Marias Cousine **Monika** getroffen – sie ist sehr nett. Aber jetzt muss ich leider den Partykeller aufräumen …
Tschüs!
Lola

AT 4.5 **X2** *Du bist dran! Schreib einen Brief so wie Lola mit den Informationen unten.* Pupils write their own letter, using the picture cues and using Lola's letter in activity X1 as a model. This activity can form part of pupils' written records for continuous assessment purposes.

Can you ...?

The purpose of the checklist is to identify tasks in the Students' Book both by skill and by topic. Teachers may find this helpful in selecting specific tasks, as a record of pupils' achievements in an Attainment Target.

Einheit 5 Wie war die Party?	AT 1 Listening	AT 2 Speaking	AT 3 Reading	AT 4 Writing
60–61 Wir feiern!				
Say when your birthday is	1, 2	3a, 3b	1	4
Ask and say when special events/celebrations are	5a	5b, 6c	5a	Noch mal!, Extra!, 6b
62–63 Ich mache eine Party!				
Invite others to a party	1a, 2a, 4a	1b, 2b, 2c, 4b	1a, 2a, 4a	2c
Accept invitations	1a	1b, 2b, 2c	1a	–
Make excuses	4a	4b	4a	Noch mal!, Extra!
64–65 Ich muss aufräumen!				
Ask where things are	–	1b, 4b	–	–
Describe where things are	1a, 3	4b, Noch mal!	3, 4a	5, Extra!
66–67 Wie war die Party?				
Ask others which birthday presents they received	1, 2a	2b	1	–
Say what birthday presents you received	1, 2a	2b, 2c	1	2d
Ask and give your opinion about parties or events	3, 4	5	3	Noch mal!, Extra!

Copymasters

For general advice about using the copymasters, see page 7 of the introduction to this book.

Hören

1a *Wann haben sie Geburtstag? Hör gut zu und mach Kreise um die passenden Monate in Übung 1b.* Pupils listen to the recording and ring the months which they hear.

Answers:

1 Mai; 2 November; 3 Juli; 4 August; 5 Februar; 6 Oktober

Transcript C 40, activities 1a and 1b

1
– Hallo. Ich heiße Christian und ich habe am zweiten Mai Geburtstag.
2
– Tag! Ich bin Maria. Ich habe am dreizehnten November Geburtstag.
3
– Grüß dich! Ich bin die Steffi und ich habe am einundzwanzigsten Juli Geburtstag.
4
– Mein Name ist Torsten Beck. Mein Geburtstag ist am dreißigsten August.
5
– Hallo! Ich heiße Claudia und ich habe am dreiundzwanzigsten Februar Geburtstag.
6
– Guten Tag! Ich heiße Peter. Ich habe am siebzehnten Oktober Geburtstag.

1b *Hör noch einmal zu und füll die Lücken aus.* Pupils listen to the recording again and complete the sentences with the ordinal numbers. Remind pupils that they

should put a full stop after the number to make it an ordinal.

Answers:

1 Christian hat am **2.** Mai Geburtstag. 2 Maria hat am **13.** November Geburtstag. 3 Steffi hat am **21.** Juli Geburtstag. 4 Torsten hat am **30.** August Geburtstag. 5 Claudia hat am **23.** Februar Geburtstag. 6 Peter hat am **17.** Oktober Geburtstag.

2 *Wann und wo ist die Party? Hör gut zu und finde die passenden Informationen.* Pupils listen to the recording and match up the details of each party.

Answers:

2. Januar, 7 p.m., at school
12. März, 8 p.m., in teenager's room
6. Mai, 1 p.m., at swimming pool
26. Juni, 12.30 p.m., in garden
18. August, 12 noon, in park
3. November, 8.30 p.m., in Partykeller

Transcript C 40, activity 2

1
– Hallo! Angelika!
– Anja. Grüß dich!
– Angelika, meine Schule macht am 2. Januar ein Schulfest. Kommst du mit?
– Ja, gern. Wann ist es?
– Um sieben Uhr in der Schule. Alles klar?
– Ja, toll! Tschüs!
– Tschüs! Bis später!
2
– Hallo, Sandra! Hier spricht Andreas.
– Andreas! Hallo! Grüß dich!
– Du ... Ich mache am sechsundzwanzigsten Juni eine Party hier bei uns im Garten. Möchtest du kommen?

– Am sechsundzwanzigsten Juni? ... Ja ... Und wann?
– Um halb eins.
– Ja! Ich komme gern!
– Toll! Freut mich! Tschüs, Sandra!
– Tschüs, Andreas!

3
– Martina! Post für dich!
– Danke, Mutti. Eine Einladung! Super! ‚Wir machen eine Party ... um halb neun ... am dritten November ... im Partykeller. Markus und Stefan.'
– Sehr schön. Aber vergiss nicht deine Hausaufgaben!
– Oh, Mutti! ...

4
– Hallo. Hier ist die Veronika. Du, Paula, meine Schwester hat am achtzehnten August Geburtstag und wir machen um Mittag ein Picknick im Park. Kommst du mit? Ruf mich bitte an. Tschüs!

5
– Schwimmst du gern?
– Ja, sicher!
– Dann machen wir eine Party im Schwimmbad!
– Gute Idee. Wann denn?
– Nächste Woche, am Samstag ... das heißt ... am sechsten Mai.
– Ja, toll!
– Und ... sag mal ... um eins?
– Ja, okay! Am sechsten Mai um ein Uhr im Schwimmbad. Abgemacht!

6
– Tanja! Ich habe in zwei Wochen Geburtstag und ich mache eine Party. Kommst du?
– Wann ist das?
– Am Samstag den zwölften März – um acht Uhr in meinem Zimmer.
– Am zwölften, sagst du? Oh, nein! Ich kann leider nicht kommen! Ich muss meine Oma besuchen.
– Oh, schade!

3 *Hör gut zu und kreuz die passenden Bilder an.* Pupils listen to the recording and select the appropriate picture from each pair.

AT 1.4

Answers: 1 a; 2 a; 3 b; 4 a; 5 b

Transcript   C 40, activity 3

– Hallo. Tante Simone?
– Hallo, Liebling. Alles Gute zum Geburtstag! Hast du meine Karte bekommen?
– Ja, danke. Und danke auch für das Geld.
– Nichts zu danken! Und was hast du sonst zum Geburtstag bekommen?
– Ein Stofftier ... ein Computerspiel ... und Schmuck.
– Sehr schön! Und wie war deine Party?
– Es war fantastisch! Wirklich toll!
– Was hast du gemacht?
– Ich habe getanzt ... und Tobias hat seine Gitarre gespielt.
– Und was hast du gegessen und getrunken?
– Ich habe Chips gegessen und Orangensaft getrunken.
– Sehr schön! Na ... und wann kommst du zu mir?

– In sechs Wochen ... am vierzehnten Mai.
– Gut! ... Ich freue mich sehr! Bis dann! Tschüs, Liebling!
– Tschüs, Tante Simone!

C 41
AT 2.3

Sprechen

1a *Stell die Frage: „Wann hast du Geburtstag?" für die Schüler 1–4. Dein Partner/deine Partnerin antwortet. Schreib die Antworten auf.* Pupils work together in pairs to create dialogues based on an information-gap. Partner A asks *Wann hast du Geburtstag?* for each of the four people and writes down partner B's reply.

AT 2.3

1b *Dein Partner/deine Partnerin fragt: „Wann hast du Geburtstag?" Antworte für die Schüler 5–8 mit den Informationen unten.* This is the second part of the activity, with the roles reversed and a new set of four people's birthdays.

AT 2.4

2a *Frag deinen Partner/deine Partnerin: „Wo ist/sind ... ?" Ergänze das Bild in Übung 2b.* Pupils work together in pairs to create dialogues. This time the information-gap is pictorial: each partner has the same picture, but with different details omitted. Guided by the picture cues, partner A asks questions about the positions of various objects, and partner B answers by referring to his/her main picture. If necessary, partner B can refer to page 65 in the Students' Book, where the prepositions *auf, in, neben* and *unter* are shown together with the dative forms of the definite article.

AT 2.4

2b *Dein Partner/deine Partnerin stellt Fragen. Antworte mit den Informationen im Bild unten. Brauchst du Hilfe? Sieh Lehrbuch, Seite 65.* This is the second part of the activity, with the roles reversed and a new set of picture cues.

C 42
AT 3.3

Lesen

1 *Finde die passenden Antworten für die Fragen.* Pupils match the answers to the questions about the party.

Answers: 1 h; 2 b; 3 f; 4 a; 5 c; 6 i; 7 e; 8 d; 9 g

AT 3.4

2 *Finde die passenden Bilder für die Einladungen.* Pupils match the pictures to the invitations. *Grillparty* and *grillen* (no. 6) are new, but *Würstchen* is a clue.

Answers: 1 c; 2 e; 3 d; 4 a; 5 f; 6 b

C 43
AT 4.2

Schreiben

1 *Schreib die Sätze richtig auf.* Pupils put the words in the correct order to form sentences (expressions for making and accepting/refusing invitations).

Answers:

1 Ja, ich komme gern. 2 Ich habe am Samstag Geburtstag. 3 Wo ist die Party? 4 Meine Schule macht am Freitag ein Schulfest. 5 Ich kann leider nicht kommen. 6 Ich mache eine Party. 7 Vielen Dank für die Einladung. 8 Wir machen am Wochenende ein Picknick.

AT 4.5

2 *Lies Tanjas E-Mail und schau Monikas Partyfotos an. Schreib einen Antwortbrief an Tanja.* Pupils write a letter in response to the e-mail, using the pictures as prompts. Explain that they should aim to provide answers to all of

Tanja's questions, but not necessarily in the order in which they are asked.

C 44

Grammatik

This copymaster focuses on the dative case (of the definite article) after the prepositions *in, auf, neben* and *unter.*

1 *Ergänze die Sätze mit im oder in der.* Pupils read the 'Flashback' and then complete the sentences.

Answers: 1 im; 2 im; 3 in der; 4 im; 5 in der; 6 im

2a *Füll die Lücken aus.* Pupils read the 'Flashback' and then complete the sentences with the correct form of the definite article.

Answers: 1 dem; 2 dem; 3 dem; 4 dem; 5 der; 6 dem

2b *Schau das Bild an. Schreib Sätze für die Bilder a–i. Brauchst du Hilfe? Sieh Lehrbuch, Seite 64–65.* Pupils write sentences to describe the picture, referring to the Students' Book as necessary.

Answers:

a Die Limonade ist neben dem Computer. b Die Luftballons sind auf dem Fernseher. c Die CDs sind im Kleiderschrank. d Der Kartoffelsalat ist auf dem Tisch. e Der Apfelsaft ist unter dem Regal. f Die Würstchen sind unter dem Sofa. g Der Orangensaft ist neben dem CD-Spieler. h Die Chips sind im Schreibtisch. i Die Jacke ist unter dem Stuhl.

C 45

Tipp

This copymaster gives advice on letter writing, role-play tasks and working out the meanings of unfamiliar words.

1 *Wie beginnt man diese Briefe?* Pupils read the 'Flashback' and write the places and dates in letter format.

Answers:

1 Hannover, den. 1. Mai; 2 München, den 16. Juni; 3 London, den 3. März; 4 Paris, den 24. November; 5 Mannheim, den 30. Juli; 6 Berlin, den 12. August

2a *Schaut den Dialog im Lehrbuch, Seite 62, Übung 1a an. Schaut dann die Einladung unten an und macht einen Dialog.*

2b *Tauscht die Rollen.*

2c *Spielt den Dialog der Klasse vor!* Pupils read the 'Flashback' and then work together in pairs to create dialogues based on the party invitation and using the dialogue from activity 1a on page 62 of the Students' Book as a model.

Einheit 6 Wir gehen in die Stadt

National Curriculum

Pages	Objectives	Grammar	Pronunciation, Skill focus	Key language	PoS	AT level
70–71 **Die Klassel-Clique**	Reading and listening for pleasure. Familiarization with themes, structures and language of the unit	–	–	–	–	1.4, 3.2, 3.4
72–73 **Was kann man in Köln machen?**	Ask about what you can do in town. Say what you can do in town. Say what you want to do	*können* and *wollen*	–	*Was kann man in ... machen?* *Was können wir machen?* *Was willst du/wollt ihr machen?* *Man kann/Wir können ...* *Ich will/Wir wollen ...* einen Einkaufsbummel machen. in die Disco/Eisbahn/Eisdiele/Stadt gehen. ins Museum/Jugendzentrum/ Freizeitzentrum/Kino/Schwimmbad/ Popkonzert/Theater/Café/Fastfood-Restaurant gehen. ein Picknick machen.	1a, 1b, 1c, 2a, 2b, 2c, 2d, 3e, 5a, 5d, 5f, 5i	1.2–3, 2.3, 3.2–3, 4.2–3, 4.5
74–75 **Wo treffen wir uns?**	Talk about where you are going to meet	*in* + accusative and + dative *an* and *vor* + dative	Pronunciation: *ei* and *ie*	*Wo treffen wir uns?* *Wir treffen uns ...* *Treffen wir uns ...* neben dem Bahnhof/Café. vor dem Bahnhof/Jugendzentrum/ Museum. vor der Eisbahn. in der Eisdiele/Imbissstube. im Café/Kino. am Markt/Dom. an der Bushaltestelle/Post. Ich gehe ... in den Supermarkt. in die Stadt. ins Kino.	1a, 1b, 1c, 2a, 2b, 2c, 2d, 3e, 5a, 5d, 5f, 5i	1.2–3, 2.3–4, 3.3

Pages	Objectives	Grammar	Pronunciation, Skill focus	Key language	PoS	AT level
76–77 Was brauchst du?	Say what you do not have Say what you need Say which shops you need to go to	–	Adapting language for different contexts	Ich brauche … einen Fahrplan/Füller. eine Federmappe/Monatskarte/Postkarte/Telefonkarte. Asthmaspray/Duschgel/Make-up/Seife/Shampoo/Zahnpasta. Briefmarken/Buntstifte/Filzstifte/Halstabletten/Umschläge. Ich habe keinen/keine/kein/keine … Ich muss/Du musst/Wir müssen … zum Busbahnhof/Schreibwarenladen gehen. zur Apotheke/Drogerie/Post gehen.	1a, 1b, 1c, 2a, 2b, 2c, 2d, 2f, 3e, 5a, 5f, 5i	1.3–4, 2.3, 3.1, 3.3
78–79 Im Fundbüro	Ask if you can help someone Say what you have lost Ask and say what it is like Say you're sorry	Accusative of mein/meine/mein	–	Kann ich dir/Ihnen helfen? Ich habe … verloren. meinen Fotoapparat/Füller/Koffer/Rucksack/Schirm meine Brieftasche/Federmappe/Geldbörse/Schultasche/Tasche/Uhr mein Buch/T-Shirt Das tut mir Leid. Wie sieht er/sie/es aus? Er/Sie/Es ist rot/grün/blau/schwarz/weiß/silber/gold, etc. Er/Sie/Es ist aus Leder/Plastik/Stoff.	1a, 1b, 1c, 2a, 2b, 2c, 2d, 3e, 5a, 5f, 5i	1.2–3, 2.3, 2.5, 3.3, 4.3, 4.5
80–81 Thema im Fokus	Encourage reading for pleasure Use language from Unit 6 creatively Encourage independent, pair- and groupwork	–	–	–	1c, 2c, 2h, 3e, 5a 5d, 5e, 5f, 5g, 5i	2.4, 3.4–5, 4.5

133

6 Wir gehen in die Stadt

Aims of the unit
- To be able to talk about what you can do and want to do in town
- To be able to talk about where you are going to meet
- To be able to talk about what you need and what shops you need to go to
- To be able to describe objects you have lost

Die Klasse!-Clique
pages 70–71

Materials
- Students' Book pages 70–71
- Cassette 2 side B

For general advice on exploiting the photo story, see pages 10–11 of the introduction to this book.

In this episode, Annika meets an excited Jasmin in the street, dressed up for a date with her e-mail penfriend Sascha. However, they then see Sven, looking very depressed. At last Sven gets his problems off his chest, and tells Jasmin and Annika that he has to move back to Chemnitz with his parents. Jasmin phones Atalay to explain the situation, and the four of them hold a crisis meeting at the ice-cream café. Atalay comes up with a suggestion: Sven's grandmother lives in Wesel – couldn't Sven stay with her? Sven thinks that this might be worth a try. Suddenly, Jasmin realizes that she's very late for her date with Sascha …

AT 3.2 **1a** *Was meinst du? Vor dem Lesen: Rate!* This is a pre-reading activity. Pupils look at the photos without reading the text, and predict what the content of the photo story will be, choosing the sentence ending they consider more likely from each pair given. Ask if any of them remembers the meaning of *Fahrkarte* from *Klasse!* 1. Pupils could do this activity in pairs, and check their answers by listening to the recording and reading the text. Discuss the answers as a whole-class activity. You could ask pupils to volunteer answers and quote from the text to back them up.

Answers: 1 b; 2 a; 3 b; 4 a; 5 a

 2 *Hör gut zu und lies mit. Was ist das? Finde die passenden Wörter im Text.* Pupils listen to the recording
AT 1.4
AT 3.4 and follow the text in their books. They then find words in the text to match the definitions given. Encourage pupils to use their powers of deduction for questions 2 and 5, if they don't immediately know the answers: find a word with *Bus* in it; find a word with *Eis* in it.

Answers:

1 ein Café; 2 ein Busbahnhof; 3 Chemnitz; 4 Wesel; 5 Eisdiele

---

Transcript   p 71, activity 2

– Annika! Annika! Sascha und ich – wir wollen ins Café gehen!

– Dein E-Mail-Brieffreund? Er will ins Café gehen?

– Ja – heute Nachmittag! Wir treffen uns um 15 Uhr vor dem Busbahnhof – neben dem Café!

– Sven! Was ist los? Hast du Probleme?

– Oh, Jasmin! Ich muss wieder nach Chemnitz – meine Eltern wollen weg aus Wesel! Aber ich will hier bleiben!

– Atalay! Svens Eltern wollen wieder nach Chemnitz gehen – aber er will in Wesel bleiben! Komm schnell! Wir treffen uns vor der Eisdiele – in 15 Minuten!

– Wir sind deine Freunde – wir wollen helfen!
– Aber wie?
– Ich weiß: Deine Oma wohnt doch auch in Wesel?

– Ja, meine Oma hat eine Wohnung hier. Oma ist total super!

– Vielleicht kannst du in Wesel bleiben – bei deiner Oma!
– Ja, frag deine Eltern – und deine Oma!
– Ja – ja klar! Danke!

– Oh nein! Es ist Viertel vor vier! Sascha!!

AT 3.4 **3** *Wer ist das? Kopiere die Sätze und schreib die passenden Namen auf.* Pupils complete the sentences with the names of the characters. This activity requires them to have understood the gist of the photo story fairly clearly. Establish that *wollen* is the plural and *will* is the singular: elicit this from the class if possible.
T: *Was meint ihr? „Jasmin und Annika will" oder „Jasmin und Annika wollen"? Was ist richtig? „Jasmin will" oder „Jasmin wollen"?* Establish that *will/wollen* does not mean 'will' but 'want(s) to'. T: *Wie heißt „will" auf Englisch?* You could help less able pupils by writing all the possible names on the board/OHT: *Jasmin, Annika, Sven, Atalay, Sascha, Svens Eltern, Svens Oma.*

Answers:

1 Jasmin und Sascha wollen ins Café gehen. 2 Svens Eltern wollen nach Chemnitz fahren. 3 Sven will in Wesel bleiben. 4 Svens Oma wohnt auch in Wesel. 5 Annika, Sven, Jasmin und Atalay sind vor der Eisdiele.

For the next lesson

Ask pupils to collect any tourist brochures or adverts for things to do in and around their town or village. These can be used as additional/alternative visual stimuli for speaking and writing activities throughout this unit.

Was kann man in Köln machen?
pages 72–73

Objectives
- Ask about what you can do in town
- Say what you can do in town
- Say what you want to do

Key language

Was kann man in … machen?
Was können wir machen?
Was willst du/wollt ihr machen?
Man kann/Wir können …
Ich will/Wir wollen …
einen Einkaufsbummel machen.
in die Disco/Eisbahn/Eisdiele/Stadt gehen.
ins Museum/Jugendzentrum/Freizeitzentrum/Kino/
Schwimmbad/Popkonzert/Theater/Café/Fastfood-
Restaurant gehen.
ein Picknick machen.

National Curriculum PoS

statements 1a, 1b, 1c, 2a, 2b, 2c, 2d, 3e, 5a, 5d, 5f, 5i

Materials

- Students' Book pages 72–73
- Cassette 2 side B
- Workbook pages 54–56
- Copymasters 51A, 52, 53A

Preparatory work

Introduce the key public buildings/leisure vocabulary
for this spread. Write on the board/OHT the following
list of places:
das Fastfood-Restaurant
das Freizeitzentrum
das Jugendzentrum
das Museum
der Park
die Eisbahn
die Stadtmitte

Now write up the following sentences:
Man kann dort einen Einkaufsbummel machen.
Man kann dort alte Dinge sehen.
Man kann dort Schlittschuh fahren.
Man kann dort ein Picknick machen.
Man kann dort Squash, Fußball usw. spielen.
Man kann dort Hamburger essen.
Man kann dort Pool spielen, fernsehen, Freunde treffen
usw.

Elicit from the class what activities belong with which
places. T: *Man kann dort Hamburger essen. Was ist das?*
Das Museum? P1: *Nein, das Fastfood-Restaurant*, etc. *Die*
Eisbahn, einen Einkaufsbummel machen and *das*
Freizeitzentrum will be new to pupils, so you will need to
give clues to help them here, e.g. mime skating for
Eisbahn, write the names of shops next to
Einkaufsbummel, write '= *Sportzentrum*' next to
Freizeitzentrum.

 1a *Was kann man in Köln machen? Hör gut zu und*
finde die passenden Sätze für die Bilder. Pupils listen to
the recording and identify the correct sentences for the
photos. To consolidate the vocabulary, ask questions
about the pupils' own town. T: *Kann man hier ins*
Museum gehen? Kann man hier in die Eisbahn gehen?,
etc.

AT 1.2
AT 3.2

Answers: 1 d; 2 h; 3 g; 4 a; 5 c; 6 f; 7 b; 8 e

> **Transcript**   p 72, activity 1a
>
> 1 – Man kann ins Freizeitzentrum gehen.
> 2 – Man kann in die Eisbahn gehen.
> 3 – Man kann ein Picknick machen.
> 4 – Man kann ins Museum gehen.
> 5 – Man kann einen Einkaufsbummel machen.
> 6 – Man kann ins Popkonzert gehen.
> 7 – Man kann ins Jugendzentrum gehen.
> 8 – Man kann ins Fastfood-Restaurant gehen.

WB A Workbook activity A could be used here to consolidate
the names of buildings/places to go in town.

AT 1.3 **1b** *Was kann man in Köln machen? Was sagen Anke,*
Ralf, Heiko und Astrid? Hör gut zu und finde die
passenden Bilder von Übung 1a. Pupils listen to the
recording and then select the appropriate photos from
activity 1a for each speaker.

Follow-up activities. Pupils work together in pairs. Pupil
A says a number, and pupil B says the appropriate
sentence from activity 1a, e.g. P1: *Eins.* P2: *Man kann ins*
Freizeitzentrum gehen, etc. Alternatively, pupils could
play the memory game in pairs or groups. Each pupil in
turn repeats what the previous pupil has said and adds
another activity. P1: *Man kann ins Freizeitzentrum*
gehen. P2 : *Man kann ins Freizeitzentrum gehen und*
man kann einen Picknick machen, etc. They could add
any other leisure activities they have previously learned.

Answers: Anke: 2, 4; Ralf: 7, 8; Heiko: 6, 5; Astrid: 3, 1

> **Transcript**   p 72, activity 1b
>
> – Hallo, wie heißt du?
> – Ich heiße Anke.
> – Anke, was kann man in Köln machen?
> – Man kann sehr viel machen. Man kann in die Eisbahn
>   oder ins Museum gehen.
>
> – In die Eisbahn oder ins Museum … und was kann man
>   noch in Köln machen, Ralf?
> – Na ja, man kann ins Jugendzentrum gehen und man
>   kann auch ins Fastfood-Restaurant gehen.
>
> – Aha … Und du, Heiko? Was kann man in Köln machen?
> – Also, man kann ins Popkonzert gehen oder einen
>   Einkaufsbummel machen.
>
> – Astrid, du bist dran! Was kann man in Köln machen?
> – Viel! Man kann auch ein Picknick machen oder ins
>   Freizeitzentrum gehen.
>
> – Also, das ist Köln. Und jetzt zu Sabine in Essen …

C 51A Activity 2 on copymaster 51A provides additional, more
challenging reading comprehension on leisure activities
in a town and could be used at this point or as
preparation for activity 2 *Extra!* below.

C 52 Activity 1 on copymaster 52 consolidates the vocabulary
for buildings and leisure activities from activity 1 above.

AT 4.2 **2** *Was kann man in … machen? Schreib Sätze für die*
folgenden Städte. Pupils use the picture cues to write
sentences about what one can do in each of the towns.

This simply requires them to copy correctly the appropriate sentences from activity 1a. To help less able pupils, you could look at the picture cues with the class first and elicit from them the meaning of each cue.

Answers:

Bremen: Man kann ins Museum gehen und man kann ins Popkonzert gehen.
Stuttgart: Man kann in die Eisbahn gehen und man kann ins Jugendzentrum gehen.
Wien: Man kann ein Picknick machen und man kann ins Freizeitzentrum gehen.
Genf: Man kann ins Fastfood-Restaurant gehen und man kann einen Einkaufsbummel machen.

AT 2.3 — *Noch mal! Ratespiel: Wo kann man das machen?* Pupils work in pairs, using their answers to activity 2 to create dialogues with *Man kann …* The partner answering the questions could do so without reference to his/her answers to activity 2, or the activity could be done as a way for pupils to check each other's answers to activity 2.

AT 4.3 — *Extra! Mach ein Poster für deine Stadt. Was kann man dort machen? Finde Fotos und schreib Sätze.* Pupils create a poster for their own town, using the text from activity 1a as a model. Alternatively, this could be done as a web page, with digitized photos. You could restrict pupils to the vocabulary introduced above, and any other leisure vocabulary they already know. Alternatively, pupils could research suitable vocabulary using their dictionaries. Regional tourist office websites and other local websites will probably be a good source of appropriate images.

WB B — Workbook activity B provides additional listening comprehension on buildings and leisure activities, followed by speaking practice (pairwork) and an independent writing task, and could be used at this point.

🔊 / AT 1.3 / AT 3.3 — **3a** *Hör gut zu und lies mit.* Pupils listen to the recording and follow the text in the book. Elicit the forms of *wollen* and *können* from the class (they will find most of them in activity 3a and in the *Hilfe* box), and write up the paradigms on the board/OHT.

> **Transcript**   p 73, activity 3a
>
> – Also, was wollt ihr heute machen?
> – Ich will ins Freizeitzentrum gehen.
> – Und dann wollen wir ins Fastfood-Restaurant gehen! Willst du auch ins Kino gehen, Jasmin?

AT 2.3 — **3b** *Was wollt ihr heute machen? Macht Dialoge mit den Bildern in Übung 1a.* Pupils work together in pairs to create dialogues like the one in activity 3a, using the pictures from activity 1a. In preparation, demonstrate how *Ich will/Wir wollen* replaces *Man kann*, with the rest of the sentence remaining unchanged.

WB C — Workbook activity C could be used at this point for additional reading comprehension on making plans using *können* and *wollen*.

Grammatik im Fokus

können und wollen + Infinitiv. This section focuses on the modal verbs *können* and *wollen* and their use as auxiliaries. Before looking at this section with the class, remind them of *müssen* and *dürfen* (Unit 3, page 41): what happens to the main verb after *ich muss …* and *ich darf … ?*

After you have looked at the examples in the Students' Book with the class, you could construct some other examples as a whole-class activity, using the remaining examples from the *Hilfe* box. For example, write up:

Man geht in die Disco.
Ich gehe ins Kino.
Wir gehen ins Café.

For each sentence in turn, invite the class to suggest either *können* or *wollen* and then to call out the new sentence word by word. Do not correct incorrect suggestions immediately; let pupils discover them for themselves. Now introduce the full conjugations of *können* and *wollen* in the present tense.

4 *Schreib die Sätze richtig auf.* Pupils re-order the words to form sentences with *wollen* and *können*.

Answers:

1 Ich will ins Kino gehen. 2 Was willst du machen? 3 Wir können in die Disco gehen. 4 Man kann ins Jugendzentrum gehen. 5 Was wollt ihr heute machen? 6 Wir wollen einen Ausflug machen.

Follow-up activity. Working together in pairs, pupils write new sentences using *können* and *wollen*, bringing in other verbs they know such as *kaufen, trinken, essen, besuchen, besichtigen, fahren*. They then jumble these up and challenge other pairs to unjumble them.

C 53A — Activity 1 on copymaster 53A provides further practice of *können* and *wollen* and could be used at this point or after activity 5a.

5a *Kopiere Ahmids E-Mail und füll die Lücken aus.* Pupils complete Ahmid's e-mail with the correct forms of *können* and *wollen* from the box.

Answers:

Am Samstag gibt es keine Schule – was **können** wir machen? Also, ich **will** ins Schwimmbad oder vielleicht ins Freizeitzentrum gehen. Wir **können** auch ins Kino gehen. Wohin **willst** du gehen? Zum Essen **können** wir ins Fastfood-Restaurant oder ins Café gehen. Nachmittags **können** wir einen Einkaufsbummel machen oder in den Park gehen und Fußball spielen. Was **willst** du machen? Schreib bald wieder!

Ahmid

AT 4.5 — **5b** *Beantworte Ahmids E-Mail. Benutze die Informationen unten.* Pupils reply to Ahmid's e-mail using the picture cues. Suggest that they use *Ich will auch …* in responding to Ahmid's suggestions. More able pupils could also use *Ich will nicht …* for those of Ahmid's suggestions which are not covered by the picture cues.

5c *Du bist dran! Was kann man in deiner Stadt machen? Was willst du am Wochenende machen? Schreib eine E-Mail an Ahmid.* Pupils write their own e-mails, using the expressions they have learned on this spread. Encourage more able pupils to research new vocabulary for leisure activities in their area.

Workbook activity D could be set as homework to consolidate the forms of *können* and *wollen*.

Workbook activity E offers an alternative writing activity to 5c above.

Wo treffen wir uns?
pages 74–75

Objectives
• Talk about where you are going to meet

Key language
Wo treffen wir uns?
Wir treffen uns …
Treffen wir uns …
neben dem Bahnhof/Café.
vor dem Bahnhof/Jugendzentrum/Museum.
vor der Eisbahn.
in der Eisdiele/Imbissstube.
im Café/Kino.
am Markt/Dom.
an der Bushaltestelle/Post.
Ich gehe …
in den Supermarkt.
in die Stadt.
ins Kino.

National Curriculum PoS
statements 1a, 1b, 1c, 2a, 2b, 2c, 2d, 3e, 5a, 5d, 5f, 5i

Materials
• Students' Book pages 74–75
• Cassette 2 side B
• Workbook pages 56–58
• Copymasters 50, 51B, 52, 53A, 53B

1 *Hör gut zu und finde die passenden Hilfe-Wörter für die Bilder.* Pupils listen to the recording and select the appropriate expression from the *Hilfe* box for each picture. The recording in effect gives pupils the answers: all they need to do is find the phrase in the *Hilfe* box which is the closest match to what they hear. Completing this activity, and then studying the pictures and comparing them with the prepositional phrases, will help pupils to understand the difference between the spacial prepositions *an, neben* and *vor*. You could explain that *DB* stands for *Deutsche Bahn* and *H* in a circle stands for *Haltestelle*: these were first introduced in *Klasse! 1*, Unit 8.

Answers: 1 b; 2 c; 3 h; 4 f; 5 e; 6 d; 7 g; 8 a

Transcript p 74, activity 1
1 – Treffen wir uns vor dem Bahnhof?
2 – Nein, wir treffen uns am Markt.
3 – Treffen wir uns neben dem Café?
4 – Wir treffen uns in der Eisdiele.
5 – Treffen wir uns vor der Eisbahn?
6 – Nein. Wir treffen uns an der Bushaltestelle.
7 – Treffen wir uns in der Imbissstube?
8 – Oder treffen wir uns neben dem Bahnhof?

2a *„Wo treffen wir uns?" Was sagen sie? Hör gut zu und finde die passenden Bilder in Übung 1.* Pupils listen to the recording and then select the picture from activity 1 which matches the meeting place agreed upon in each conversation.

Answers: a 3; b 1; c 2; d 6; e 7

Transcript p 74, activity 2a
a
– Hallo, Richard!
– Hallo, Karl! Heute ist Alfredos Party. Wo treffen wir uns?
– Hmm … neben dem Café?
– Ja, treffen wir uns neben dem Café … In Ordnung, Karl.
b
– Hallo, Peter. Willst du Fußball spielen?
– Ja, super – aber wo treffen wir uns?
– Ich fahre mit dem Zug – also vor dem Bahnhof.
– Ja, Udo, vor dem Bahnhof, das geht.
c
– Hallo, Ute! Wollen wir heute ins Kino gehen?
– Ja, gerne! Und wo treffen wir uns?
– Am Markt.
– Am Markt, gut. Tschüs!
d
– Hallo, Jasmin. Anke hier. Jasmin, ich will einen Einkaufsbummel machen. Kommst du mit?
– Ja, okay. Also, wo treffen wir uns?
– An der Bushaltestelle?
– Okay, an der Bushaltestelle.
e
– Marietta? Wo treffen wir uns am Freitagabend?
– Ähm … wir treffen uns in der Imbissstube.
– Danke, Marietta. In der Imbissstube. Bis dann!

2b *Ist alles richtig? A fragt, B antwortet.* Pupils work in pairs to check their answers to activity 2a.

Workbook activity F could be used at this point to consolidate the prepositions *an, vor* and *in*.

Grammatik im Fokus
an und vor + Dativ. This section focuses on the use of the prepositions *an* and *vor* in a purely spacial sense. You could point out that this *an* is the same preposition as in *am 16. September*, etc. (Unit 5). Draw pupils' attention to the fact that *an + dem* contracts to *am* in the same way that *in + dem* contracts to *im*.

Activity 2 on copymaster 53A provides practice of *an/vor* + dative and could be used at this point.

3 *Füll die Lücken aus.* Pupils complete the sentences with the correct dative form of the definite article.

Answers: 1 dem; 2 der; 3 der; 4 der, am; 5 dem

WB G Workbook activity G is a writing task using *an* and *vor*, and could be used at this point.

C 50 Activity 2 on copymaster 50 provides a number of pairwork dialogues using *an*, *neben*, *vor* and *in* with places and *ich will* + leisure activities, and could be used at this point.

AT 1.3
AT 3.3 **4** *Hör gut zu und lies mit.* Pupils listen to the recording and follow the text in the book. This text illustrates the difference between *in* + accusative and *in* + dative, which is discussed below. You could point out the sentences *Treffen wir uns im Bahnhof?* and *Treffen wir uns um sieben Uhr im Café?* and explain that this is a way to make polite suggestions in German, like saying 'Shall we … ?' in English.

Transcript   p 75, activity 4

1 – Ich gehe morgens in den Supermarkt. Treffen wir uns im Bahnhof?

2 – Ich gehe heute in die Stadt. Wir treffen uns in der Eisdiele.

3 – Ich gehe am Freitag ins Kino. Treffen wir uns um sieben Uhr im Café?

Grammatik im Fokus

in + Akkusativ oder Dativ? This section focuses on the difference between *in* + accusative and *in* + dative. Before going through the explanation with the class, take another look at activity 4. Ask pupils what they notice about *in* and the words which follow it. If no pupils volunteer that *in* sometimes takes the dative and sometimes the accusative, write up examples on the board/OHT:

der Supermarkt, der Bahnhof	*Maskulinum*
Ich gehe in den Supermarkt.	*in den = ?*
Treffen wir uns im Bahnhof?	*im = Dativ*
die Stadt, die Eisdiele	*?*
Ich gehe in die Stadt.	*in die = ?*
Wir treffen uns in der Eisdiele.	*in der = ?*

Ask pupils for suggestions about what goes in the gaps marked by question marks. Once the table is complete (you could also do *Neutrum* with *Kino* and *Café*), ask the class if they can think of any reasons why *in* should sometimes be followed by the accusative, and sometimes by the dative. If they look blank, you could try giving hints, e.g. by walking into the classroom saying *Ich gehe in das Zimmer* and by standing still and saying *Ich bin im Zimmer.*

Now go through the explanation in the Students' Book. Point out that *in das* is usually contracted to *ins*. To consolidate this point of grammar, you could write up some more examples to complete as a whole-class activity, e.g.

Ich gehe _____ Eisdiele.
Ich gehe _____ Café.
Ich bin _____ Eisdiele.
Ich bin _____ Café.

5a *Schau die Sätze in Übung 4 an und finde die Sätze mit in + Akkusativ und in + Dativ. Schreib zwei Listen.* Pupils analyse the sentences in activity 4 and decide whether they are in the accusative or in the dative.

Answers:

Akkusativ: Ich gehe morgens in den Supermarkt. Ich gehe heute in die Stadt. Ich gehe am Freitag ins Kino.

Dativ: Treffen wir uns im Bahnhof? Wir treffen uns in der Eisdiele. Treffen wir uns um sieben Uhr im Café?

C 53B Activity 1 on copymaster 53B provides practice of *in* + accusative/dative and could be used at this point.

5b *in + Akkusativ oder in + Dativ? Finde die passenden Wörter.* Pupils select the correct forms of the definite article to complete the text.

Answers:

Heute gehe ich in **die** Stadt und dort esse ich **im** Fastfood-Restaurant. Ich kann auch **im** Café essen, aber das finde ich nicht so gut. Nachmittags gehe ich in **den** Park und auch **ins** Freizeitzentrum. Man kann Fußball **im** Park und Tennis **im** Freizeitzentrum spielen. Abends wollen meine Freundin und ich **ins** Kino gehen. Dann um elf Uhr gehe ich **ins** Bett.

WB H Workbook activity H provides further listening and written work on *in* + accusative/dative and could be used at this point.

WB I Workbook activity I is a pairwork speaking activity using picture cues and could be used as an alternative to, or in preparation for, activity 6 below.

WB J Workbook activity J is an independent writing task and could be used at this point or set as homework.

AT 2.4 **6** *Du bist dran! Was willst du am Samstag machen? A fragt und B antwortet. Dann ist B dran.* Pupils work together in pairs to create dialogues using *in* + accusative and *in* + dative.

Follow-up activity. If you want to set an independent writing activity as a homework, you could use the following activity:

Du willst deinen deutschen Freund/deine Freundin einladen. Schreib eine Einladung. Schreib:

- *Was? (Popkonzert, Party usw.)*
- *Wo? (am Markt, vor der Post usw.)*
- *Wann? (um sieben Uhr, um halb acht usw.)*

Beispiel:

Liebe Anje,

ich gehe am Samstag ins Popkonzert. Kommst du mit? Treffen wir uns vor der Post? Das Popkonzert beginnt um halb acht. Also, treffen wir uns um sieben Uhr? Bis dann Niki

51B Activity 1 on copymaster 51B is a reading comprehension based on the topics and language covered in this spread, and could be set as homework.

52 Activity 3 on copymaster 52 is a short guided writing task based on the topics and language covered in this spread, and could also be set as homework.

Gut gesagt!

ei, ie. This section focuses on the correct pronunciation of *ei* and *ie*, which are frequently confused by English speakers.

7a *Hör gut zu und lies mit.* Pupils listen to the recording and follow the text in their books.

> **Transcript** p 75, activities 7a and 7b
>
> In einer Eisdiele esse ich ein Eis, zwei Eis, drei Eis, schließlich vier Eis. Wie viele? Eins, zwei, drei, vier! Zu viel Eis ... Hilfe!

7b *Hör gut zu und wiederhole.* Pupils listen to the recording and then read the text aloud.

Was brauchst du?
pages 76–77

Objectives
- Say what you do not have
- Say what you need
- Say which shops you need to go to

Key language
Ich brauche …
einen Fahrplan/Füller.
eine Federmappe/Monatskarte/Postkarte/Telefonkarte.
Asthmaspray/Duschgel/Make-up/Seife/Shampoo/
Zahnpasta.
Briefmarken/Buntstifte/Filzstifte/Halstabletten/Umschläge.
Ich habe keinen/keine/kein/keine …
Ich muss/Du musst/Wir müssen …
zum Busbahnhof/Schreibwarenladen gehen.
zur Apotheke/Drogerie/Post gehen.

National Curriculum PoS
statements 1a, 1b, 1c, 2a, 2b, 2c, 2d, 2f, 3e, 5a, 5f, 5i

Materials
- Students' Book pages 76–77
- Cassette 2 side B
- Workbook pages 58–60
- Copymasters 46, 47, 49, 51A, 52, 54

Preparatory work
C 46
C 47 Use the pictures from copymasters 46 and 47 copied onto an OHT or as flashcards to introduce the vocabulary for shops and shopping. (For general advice on using copymaster visuals, see page 12 of the introduction to this book.)

1 *Hör gut zu und lies mit.* Pupils listen to the recording and follow the text in the book. Elicit from the class that *ich brauche* (introduced in *Klasse! 1*) means 'I need'.

> **Transcript** p 76, activity 1
>
> – Annika! Ich habe kein Shampoo! Ich muss in die Stadt gehen!
> – Ja, ich auch! Ich brauche eine Federmappe und einen Füller.
> – Also, du musst zum Schreibwarenladen gehen, und ich? Ich muss zur Drogerie gehen.

2a *Was kauft man wo? Verbinde die Bilder.* Pupils link the photos of the items to the appropriate shop signs. In preparation, explain to the class the difference between *eine Apotheke* and *eine Drogerie*. Point out the post horn, which is universally understood in Germany as the sign of a post office. Pupils check their own answers by doing activity 2b.

Answers: 1 d; 2 b; 3 a; 4 c; 5 e

Background information
In Germany, all medicines including headache tablets, etc. have to be bought from a pharmacist's (*Apotheke*) – you cannot buy them in other shops such as supermarkets. Drugstores (*Drogerien*) sell items such as cosmetics, skincare products, shampoo, etc. Pharmacists in Germany always display the red and white 'A' sign.

2b *Ist alles richtig? Hör gut zu.* Pupils listen to the recording to check their answers to activity 2a.

> **Transcript** p 76, activity 2b
>
> 1
> – Annika, ich brauche Zahnpasta, Shampoo, Duschgel und Seife.
> – Und ich brauche Make-up. Also, wir müssen zur Drogerie gehen!
> 2
> – Müssen wir auch zum Schreibwarenladen gehen?
> – Ja. Ich brauche Umschläge und Buntstifte. Du brauchst Filzstifte und eine Federmappe ... Oh, und mein Vater braucht einen Füller.
> 3
> – Ich brauche Briefmarken und eine Telefonkarte. Ich muss zur Post gehen.
> – Ich muss auch dorthin gehen. Ich brauche auch Postkarten.
> 4
> – Und wir müssen zur Apotheke gehen – ich brauche Asthmaspray.
> – Und ich brauche Halstabletten ...
> 5
> – Und dann brauche ich eine Monatskarte.
> – Ich brauche auch einen Fahrplan.
> – Hmm ... Fahrplan und Monatskarte, wir müssen zum Busbahnhof gehen.

Follow-up activity. For a speaking activity practising *Ich brauche* and *Ich habe keinen/keine/kein* with the vocabulary from activity 2, you could try the following game:

Pupils are divided up into groups of three or five. Each group receives two copies of copymaster 47 which are cut up into individual 'cards' and shuffled. The dealer gives each player an equal number of cards, face down. The object of the game is to get as many pairs of cards as possible. The player to the left of the dealer (player 1) starts the game by looking at his/her cards and saying *Ich brauche …* and the name of an item he/she needs to make a pair. In a clockwise direction, the other players respond by either saying *Ich habe keinen/keine/kein …* and the name of the item requested, or by handing over the card. They are allowed to lie. If nobody hands over the card requested, player 1 can challenge **one** other player: *Du hast …* The player challenged has to show his/her cards. If the challenge is incorrect, it is player 2's turn to play; if the challenge is correct, the player who lied has to hand over **two** cards. Players are out of the game when they have no cards left. The player who has most pairs at the end of the game wins.

WB K Workbook activity K consolidates the new vocabulary introduced in activity 2 above.

WB L Workbook activity L consolidates the names of shops from activity 2 and provides further written practice of *Ich muss zum/zur … gehen*.

C 51A Activity 1 on copymaster 51A is a reading comprehension activity using the language introduced in activities 1 and 2 above.

3a *Was sagen Paul, Guptal, Britta, Eli and Jenna? Kopiere die Tabelle. Hör gut zu und mach Notizen.* Pupils
AT 1.4 listen to the recording and complete the table. Explain that not all of the speakers will have items in all of the columns.

> – Gehst du in die Stadt, Mutti?
> – Ja, ich gehe in die Stadt, Jenna. Was brauchst du?
> – Ich habe keine Filzstifte und ich brauche eine Federmappe für die Schule.
> – Oh, Jenna! Dann muss ich zum Schreibwarenladen gehen.

AT 2.3 **3b** *Schaut die Tabelle an und macht Dialoge.* Pupils work together in pairs to create dialogues using their answers to activity 3a. In preparation, elicit from the class that *kein/keine/kein* takes the same endings as *ein/eine/ein*.

WB M Workbook activity M consolidates *ich brauche …/ich habe keinen/keine/kein* and the items of vocabulary introduced in activity 2 above, in listening, speaking and writing tasks. It could be used as preparation for, or a less complex alternative to, activity 3 above.

WB N Workbook activity N also consolidates *ich brauche …/ich habe keinen/keine/kein* and *du musst zum/zur … gehen*.

C 52 Activity 2 on copymaster 52 provides written practice of *keinen/keine/kein/keine* + item and *zum/zur* + shop, and could be used at this point.

C 49 Activity 2 on copymaster 49 provides further listening comprehension on the language introduced in this spread and could be used at this point.

Tipp

Bekannte Sprache ändern. This section focuses on adapting known language for different contexts.

C 54 Copymaster 54 is dedicated to adapting known language; its activities could be used in conjunction with the activities below.

Answers:

	Ich brauche …	Ich habe kein/keine …	Ich muss zum/zur … gehen.
Paul	Duschgel	Shampoo	Drogerie
Guptal	Postkarte	Briefmarken	Post
Britta		Asthmaspray	Drogerie
Eli	Monatskarte		Busbahnhof
Jenna	Federmappe	Filzstifte	Schreibwarenladen

Transcript   p 77, activity 3a

– Paul, was brauchst du in der Stadt?
– Ich brauche Duschgel und ich habe auch kein Shampoo. Ich muss zur Drogerie gehen.

– Ich muss zur Post gehen. Ich brauche eine Postkarte und ich habe keine Briefmarken.

– Hallo, Eli! Ich muss in die Stadt gehen.
– Ich gehe auch in die Stadt. Was brauchst du?
– Ich habe kein Asthmaspray mehr. Ich muss zur Drogerie gehen. Und du?
– Ich brauche eine Monatskarte. Also, ich muss zum Busbahnhof gehen.

4 *„Ich habe kein(e) …" Was hast du nicht? Schreib drei Listen.* Pupils apply the structure *Ich habe keinen/keine/kein* to the familiar contexts of school, family and pets. If you feel that *Welche Geschwister oder Familienmitglieder hast du nicht?* may be a sensitive issue in your class, ask pupils to choose two out of the three lists, or omit list 2 completely from the activity.

5 *Was musst du zu Hause machen? Schreib Sätze.* Pupils write some sentences about chores they have to do at home, thereby making the link between *müssen* in the contexts of shopping and of family life. The picture cues will help them to remember some of the relevant vocabulary from Unit 2.

6 *Du kochst für eine Party. Was kochst du und was brauchst du? Schreib eine Einkaufsliste.* Pupils write down dishes to cook for a party and the ingredients, recapping on the use of *brauchen* in recipes (*Klasse! 1*, pp. 68–69). For those who are not keen cooks, you could provide two or three simple suggestions on an OHT, perhaps with their ingredients jumbled.

7 *Wie kommst du am besten zum/zur … ? A wählt ein Bild, B fragt. Dann ist B dran.* Pupils work together in pairs to practise asking for directions. This activity makes the link between the present topic and directions (*Klasse! 1*, pp. 102–103). Make it clear to pupils that no answer is required for the purposes of this activity: they are just forming the questions.

Im Fundbüro
pages 78–79

Objectives
- Ask if you can help someone
- Say what you have lost
- Ask and say what it is like
- Say you're sorry

Key language
Kann ich dir/Ihnen helfen?
Ich habe … verloren.
meinen Fotoapparat/Füller/Koffer/Rucksack/Schirm
meine Brieftasche/Federmappe/Geldbörse/Schultasche/Tasche/Uhr
mein Buch/T-Shirt
Das tut mir Leid.
Wie sieht er/sie/es aus?
Er/Sie/Es ist rot/grün/blau/schwarz/weiß/silber/gold, etc.
Er/Sie/Es ist aus Leder/Plastik/Stoff.

National Curriculum PoS
statements 1a, 1b, 1c, 2a, 2b, 2c, 2d, 3e, 5a, 5f, 5i

Materials
- Students' Book pages 78–79
- Cassette 2 side B
- Workbook pages 60–63
- Copymasters 49, 50, 53B

Preparatory work
Bring in as many of the objects from activity 2a as possible, with a few other objects which pupils have learned the German names of, e.g. a shoe, a felt-tipped pen, etc. Introduce the names of the objects both verbally and in written form on the board/OHT, and place the objects on your desk. Now ask pupils what the objects are, giving support as necessary. T: (holding up camera) *Was ist das?* P1: *Ich weiß nicht.* T: *Ist das ein Fotoapparat oder ein Füller?* P1: *Ein Fotoapparat*, etc. Now ask a group of pupils to face the back of the class: can they remember what is on the desk? T: *Was ist auf dem Tisch?* P1: *Ein Füller.* T: *Sehr gut! Was noch?* P2: *Ein T-Shirt*, etc.

You could progress from here to describing the objects, introducing the use of pronouns where the opportunity arises. T: *Wie sieht das T-Shirt aus?* P1: *Das T-Shirt ist weiß.* T: *Richtig! Es ist weiß. Wie sieht die Uhr aus?*, etc.

1 *Thomas ist im Fundbüro. Hör gut zu und lies mit.* Pupils listen to the recording and follow the text in the book. Elicit from pupils the meaning of *ich habe … verloren.* T: *Wie sagt man 'I have lost …' auf Deutsch?* Give them the infinitive *verlieren* and explain that this is another irregular verb.

Transcript	p 78, activity 1

– Guten Morgen. Kann ich dir helfen?
– Ja, bitte. Ich habe meine Brieftasche verloren.
– Oh, das tut mir Leid. Wie sieht sie aus?
– Sie ist schwarz und aus Leder.

2a *Was haben sie verloren? Hör gut zu und finde die passenden Bilder.* Pupils listen to the recording and select the relevant picture for each speaker.

Answers:

1 g; 2 d; 3 j; 4 b; 5 h; 6 i; 7 k; 8 f; 9 a; 10 c; 11 e; 12 b

Transcript	p 78, activity 2a

1 – Ach nein! Wo ist mein Koffer?
2 – Mein Schirm, mein Schirm, wo ist mein Schirm?
3 – Ich habe mein Buch im Hotel verloren.
4 – Wo ist meine Geldbörse?
5 – Mutti, ich habe meine Schultasche verloren.
6 – Und wo ist mein Füller?
7 – Wo ist mein T-Shirt? Ich habe mein T-Shirt verloren.
8 – Und ich habe meinen Fotoapparat verloren.
9 – Ach nein! Ich habe meine Tasche verloren!
10 – Hilfe! Ich habe meine Uhr verloren.
11 – Können Sie mir bitte helfen? Ich habe meinen Rucksack verloren.
12 – Ich habe meine Brieftasche verloren!

WB O Workbook activity O consolidates the vocabulary from activity 2a above, including genders.

AT 2.3 **2b** *Was hast du verloren? A ist Beamter/Beamtin, B wählt ein Bild von Übung 2a.* Pupils work together in pairs to create dialogues, using the pictures from activity 2a as cues. More able pupils could be encouraged to continue the conversation with *Oh, das tut mir Leid. Wie sieht sie aus?*, etc.

Grammatik im Fokus

mein + Akkusativ. This section focuses on the accusative of *mein/meine/mein*. Point out (or elicit from pupils if possible) that the forms of *mein/meine/mein* are exactly the same as those of *ein/eine/ein*.

3 *Was hast du verloren? Füll die Lücken aus.* Pupils complete the sentences with the correct accusative forms of *mein/meine/mein*.

Answers:

1 meinen; 2 mein; 3 meinen; 4 meine; 5 mein; 6 meine

C 53B Activity 2 on copymaster 53B could be used for further practice of *meinen/meine/mein* at this point.

WB P Workbook activity P is another gap-fill task to practise *meinen/meine/mein*.

WB Q Workbook activity Q again practises *meinen/meine/mein*, in a gap-fill task followed by a listening comprehension.

AT 1.2 **4** *Hör gut zu und finde die passenden Fotos.* Pupils listen to the recording and match each photo to the appropriate description.

Answers: 1 b; 2 c; 3 a

Transcript   p 79, activity 4

1 – Wo ist meine … Ich habe meine … verloren! Sie ist grün und aus Leder.

2 – Ich kann mein … nicht finden. Ich habe mein … verloren. Es ist silber und aus Plastik.

3 – Ich habe meinen … verloren! Er ist blau und aus Stoff.

WB R Workbook activity R revises the pronouns *er/sie/es* in preparation for activity 5 below.

C 49 Activity 1 on copymaster 49 is a listening comprehension using dialogues similar to those in activity 5 below and could be used in preparation for that activity.

AT 2.5 **5** *Herr Hilflos hat alles verloren! Macht Dialoge. A ist der Beamte/die Beamtin im Fundbüro und B ist Herr Hilflos.* Pupils work together in pairs to create dialogues using the picture cues. Draw their attention to the *Hilfe* box which contains an overview of relevant language for this activity. Also, run through the examples in the *Wiederholung* box (pronouns). Help less able pupils by eliciting from the class which pronoun will be used with each item depicted. T: *Der Schirm: er, sie oder es?*, etc. To give further help, you could write up the example dialogue on the board/OHT, leaving gaps for the words which will change:

Guten Tag. Kann ich Ihnen helfen?
Ja, ich habe _____ _____ verloren.
Das tut mir Leid. Wie sieht _____ aus?, etc.

WB S Workbook activity S provides further practice of the language used in activity 5 above, in the form of an extensive listening comprehension followed by further pairwork dialogues.

C 50 Activity 1 on copymaster 50 provides further practice of pairwork dialogues.

AT 4.3 *Noch mal! Wie ist alles in deiner Schultasche? Schreib Sätze.* Pupils describe all the items in their school bags. Give them assistance with any items which they don't know the names for, or instruct them to restrict their description to terms they already know (e.g. *Klasse! 1* p. 37: *der Bleistift, der Filzstift, der Füller, der Kuli, der Radiergummi, der Rechner, der Spitzer, das Buch, das Heft, das Lineal*).

AT 4.5 *Extra! Du hast in den Ferien deinen Koffer verloren. Schreib einen Brief an das Fundbüro.* Pupils write a letter to a lost property office describing a missing suitcase and the items it contains. Encourage pupils to think of all the items they would take on holiday with them: clothes, reading/listening material, soap and shampoo, etc. This will involve some individual dictionary research.

Pupils have not previously written a formal letter in German. You could either ask them to write just the body of the letter, or you could supply them with the following information:

- full address top right
- date below this address
- address of the recipient (they can make this up) on the left
- open the letter *Sehr geehrte Damen und Herren,*
- remember to start the text with a small letter after the comma
- end the letter *Mit freundlichen Grüßen* (and name on next line)

WB T Workbook activity T provides an alternative/additional writing task to *Noch mal!* above.

Thema im Fokus
pages 80–81

National Curriculum PoS
statements 1c, 2c, 2h, 3e, 5a 5d, 5e, 5f, 5g, 5i

Materials
- Students' Book pages 80–81
- Cassette 2 side B
- Copymaster 48

The final spread of each unit provides further reading practice, leading into a project outcome for the unit. See pages 8–9 of the introduction to this book for general notes on how to use these pages.

AT 3.4 **1** *Lies die Salzburg-Broschüre.* The main aim of this activity is reading for personal interest, but the text will also provide ideas for the subsequent activities. Pupils will need to use their dictionaries or the *Vokabular* at the back of the Students' Book to identify unfamiliar vocabulary.

2 *Organisiert einen Ausflug für die Klasse!* Pupils work together in small groups throughout this activity. Try to ensure that at least one member of each group has access to the Internet at home, as this will greatly facilitate the research aspect of the project.

a *Wohin will die Klasse fahren? Wählt ein Land und eine Stadt.* Pupils select a destination for the imaginary class trip. Explain that they need not use one of the suggestions in the Students' Book, but encourage them to pick a large city – it will be easier to find information and provide an interesting range of activities.

AT 3.5 **b** *Was kann man dort machen? Lest Bücher und Broschüren oder surft im Internet. Schreibt eine Liste für die Klasse.* Pupils conduct research into their chosen destination, using authentic materials. The Internet is by far the best source of information for this kind of task. They then draw up a list of the venues and activities on offer. As the list needs to be both as clear and as enticing as possible, it would be good to incorporate photos, taken for example from tourism websites.

2.4 **c** *Macht eine Umfrage in der Klasse. Fragt:* Pupils conduct a class survey based on the list of activities they have drawn up in activity 2b. Explain that *Was brauchst du?* refers to the items the participants need to take with them. Discuss with pupils how best to present their list of activities so that the respondents to the survey can clearly see what is on offer.

4.5 **d** *Schreibt einen Plan für den Tag in dieser Stadt (z. B. mit dem Computer).* Pupils draw up a timetable and itinerary for the day, based on the most popular choices in the survey results. Accompanied by photos, this could become a classroom display and/or the basis for a presentation, and the class could vote for the most popular plan.

Kannst du ... ?

The end-of-unit summary is a checklist for pupils. See page 8 of the introduction to this book for ideas on how to use the checklist.

48 Copymaster 48 provides a useful reference for pupils revising the language of this unit.

Noch mal!-Seite Einheit 6
page 132

National Curriculum PoS
statements 1a, 1b, 1c, 2a, 2b, 2c, 2d, 5a

Materials
- Students' Book page 132
- Cassette 2 side B

This revision page is intended for less able pupils. It reinforces the basic vocabulary and structures from the unit, and it can be used by pupils who experienced difficulty in completing some of the activities within the unit, or as alternative homework activities.

1.4 **1a** *Karin ist mit ihrer Familie in Bonn. Was können sie machen? Hör gut zu und finde die richtige Reihenfolge für die Bilder.* Activity 1 relates to pages 72–73. In activity 1a, pupils listen to the recording and put the pictures in the order in which they hear the activities mentioned. In preparation, look at the pictures with the pupils and discuss what activities are depicted. They should then note down some key vocabulary they expect to hear in the recording, e.g. *Bild a: Park; Bild b: Konzert.*

Follow-up activity. Pupils listen again to the recording and write more detailed notes with whole expressions, e.g. *Bild a: in den Park gehen; Bild b: ins Konzert gehen.* These can then be used for activity 1b.

Answers: e, i, a, c, g, d, h, b, f

Transcript   p 132, activity 1a
- Vati, was können wir hier in Bonn machen?
- Na ja, man kann ins Museum gehen!
- Du kannst ins Museum gehen, Vati, aber ich? Nein, danke. Das Museum ist langweilig! Kann man nicht ins Freizeitzentrum gehen?
- Gute Idee, ich will auch nicht ins Museum gehen. Karin, willst du auch in den Park gehen?
- Ich? Oh, ja, gerne. Können wir ein Picknick im Park machen?
- Ja, natürlich. Und ins Schwimmbad! Willst du auch ins Schwimmbad gehen, Karin?
- Ähm ... ja, okay. Aber wo ist das Schwimmbad?
- Hier ist der Plan. Schau mal ... ja, hier ist das Schwimmbad – in der Stadtmitte, neben dem Kino. Wir können auch ins Kino gehen!
- Also, nachmittags können wir ins Schwimmbad oder ins Kino gehen und danach ins Café.
- Und abends will ich in die Disco gehen.
- Ja, und wir können ins Konzert gehen und dann natürlich ins Restaurant.
- Man kann viel in Bonn machen, nicht wahr?

AT 2.3 **1b** *Was kann man in Bonn machen? A fragt, B antwortet. Dann ist B dran.* Pupils work together in pairs to create dialogues using the pictures from activity 1a. See the suggestions above for preparation.

AT 3.4 **2a** *Lies den Text und finde das passende Bild.* Activity 2 relates to pages 78–79. In activity 2a, pupils read the text and then select the picture which matches the description.

Answer: c

AT 4.4 **2b** *Was hast du verloren? Schreib eine Karte wie Inge für die zwei anderen Bilder.* Pupils write their own cards for the two remaining pictures. In preparation, elicit from them what parts of the description will need changing.

AT 4.3 **3** *Was braucht Tom? Schreib seine Einkaufsliste.* This activity relates to pages 76–77. Pupils write sentences in response to the picture cues. Point out that *Ich brauche* and *Ich habe keinen/keine/kein* are interchangeable here: encourage pupils to use both. In preparation, you could elicit from pupils what each of the pictures depicts.

Answers:
(Accept any combination of *Ich brauche ...* / *Ich habe keinen/keine/kein* shown below.)
Ich brauche Shampoo. Ich brauche Seife. Ich brauche eine Federmappe. Ich brauche Umschläge. Ich brauche Briefmarken. Ich brauche Postkarten. Ich brauche eine Fahrkarte. Ich brauche einen Fahrplan.
Ich habe kein Shampoo. Ich habe keine Seife. Ich habe keine Federmappe. Ich habe keine Umschläge. Ich habe keine Briefmarken. Ich habe keine Postkarten. Ich habe keine Fahrkarte. Ich habe keinen Fahrplan.

Extra!-Seite Einheit 6
page 133

National Curriculum PoS
statements 1a, 1b, 1c, 2a, 2b, 2c, 2d, 2e, 3e, 5a, 5d, 5f, 5i

Materials
- Students' Book page 133
- Cassette 2 side B

This extension page is intended for more able pupils. It contains slightly longer and more complex materials, and it can be used by pupils who have completed other activities quickly, or as alternative homework activities.

AT 2.5 **1a** *Deine deutsche Partnerschule besucht am Wochenende deine Stadt. Was kann man machen? Diskutiere mit einem Partner/einer Partnerin.* Activity 1 relates to pages 72–75. In activity 1a, pupils work in pairs to create dialogues, using the vocabulary for leisure activities and public buildings from the unit.

AT 4.5 **1b** *Schreib den Plan für einen Tag:* Pupils draw up their own plan for a day out, which could be based on their dialogues in activity 1a above.

AT 1.4 **2** *Mark vom Mars muss in die Stadt gehen. Hör gut zu und schreib seine Einkaufsliste.* Activity 2 relates to pages 76–77. In activity 2a, pupils listen to the recording and write down the items that are mentioned.

Answers:

Seife, Zahnpasta, Umschläge, Briefmarken, Filzstifte, Füller, Make-up

---

Transcript p 133, activity 2a

Oh, meine liebe Verena ... Also was brauche ich? Ich brauche Seife. Ich habe sie verloren und ich kann auch die Zahnpasta nicht finden. Meine Zahnpasta ist rot und weiß – meine Lieblingsfarben. Rot und weiß sind auch Verenas Lieblingsfarben! Ich muss auch zur Post gehen und Umschläge und Briefmarken kaufen. Ich muss an meine Oma schreiben, aber ich habe die Adresse verloren. Ich habe auch meine Filzstifte verloren und ich habe keine für die Schule. Ach nein! Ich habe auch keinen Füller und heute habe ich Englisch mit Klasse 9B! Ach ja, und die Klasse will am Freitag ein Picknick im Park machen. Meine Freundin Verena vom Venus kommt mit. Sie ist so schön ... Hmmm! Ich brauche ein Geschenk für sie – Make-up! Ja, ich kaufe Make-up für sie!

AT 4.4 **2b** *Verena geht auch in die Stadt. Was braucht sie und wohin muss sie gehen? Schreib Sätze.* Pupils write sentences for Verena, using the pictures as cues.

Answers:

Ich brauche Shampoo. Ich muss zur Drogerie gehen. Ich brauche auch Duschgel. Ich brauche eine Monatskarte und einen Fahrplan. Ich muss zum Busbahnhof gehen. Ich brauche Halstabletten. Ich muss zur Apotheke gehen.

AT 3.5 **3a** *Helena schreibt an das Fundbüro in Köln. Lies den Brief und beantworte die Fragen in Sätzen.* Activity 3 relates to pages 78–79. In activity 3a, pupils read the letter and answer the comprehension questions.

Answers:

1 Sie hat ihre Schultasche verloren. 2 Sie hat sie am Montag(morgen) verloren. 3 Sie hat sie im Park verloren. 4 Die Tasche ist blau und weiß und aus Stoff und Leder. 5 Sie wohnt Hannoverstraße 46, 54000 Hagen.

AT 4.5 **3b** *Schreib einen Brief an das Fundbüro.* Pupils write their own letters to the lost property office, using Helena's letter as a model.

Workbook

Pages 54–55
Use with pages 72–73 in the Students' Book.

AT 4.1 **A** *Was kann man in der Stadt machen? Finde die Gebäude und schreib sie auf.* Pupils re-order the letters to form the names of buildings (all featured in the *Hilfe* box on page 73 of the Students' Book). If pupils get 'stuck' on a particular word, suggest that they do the easy ones first and then find the others by a process of elimination (for example: It's a long word with Z in it; it has a J so it can't be *Freizeitzentrum*, etc.). You could ask pupils to add the definite articles to help them to remember the genders of these words. More able pupils could do this activity without reference to the Students' Book; this has the benefit that it reactivates much more vocabulary as they search their memories for the solution, but it is also more challenging and time-consuming.

Answers:

1 (die) Eisdiele; 2 (das) Fastfood-Restaurant; 3 (das) Schwimmbad; 4 (die) Eisbahn; 5 (das) Freizeitzentrum; 6 (das) Jugendzentrum; 7 (das) Kino; 8 (das) Café; 9 (das) Museum; 10 (das) Theater

AT 1.4 **B1** *Was kann man in Basel machen? Hör gut zu und finde die richtige Reihenfolge für die Bilder.* Pupils listen to the recording and number the buildings in the order in which they are mentioned. As usual, pupils should examine the pictures first to get an idea of the likely content of the recording.

Answers:

1 Museum; 2 Eisbahn; 3 Schwimmbad; 4 Freizeitzentrum; 5 Theater; 6 Kino; 7 Café

Transcript W 54, activity B1

– Max, Max! Wo bist du?
– Ich bin hier, Andrea. Was denn?
– Max, alles ist langweilig! Was kann man in Basel machen?
– Wir können ins Museum gehen.
– Aber nein. Ich mag das Museum nicht. Es ist langweilig.
– Gehen wir dann in die Eisbahn?
– Eisbahn! Im Sommer! Das mag ich nicht.

– Wir können ins Schwimmbad gehen!
– Nein. Ich habe gerade Toast, Schinken, Käse und Jogurt zum Frühstück gegessen.
– Hmmm … Freizeitzentrum. Ja, wir können im Freizeitzentrum Tennis spielen.
– Aber Max, es regnet und es ist kalt.
– Gehen wir dann ins Theater?
– Nein, das kostet zu viel und ich habe nicht viel Geld.
– Also, man kann ins Kino gehen. Es gibt einen neuen Trickfilm – ‚Die intelligente Ente‘.
– Ein Trickfilm – nein, danke.
– Ins Café – man kann ins Café gehen.
– Ins Café. Eine gute Idee. Ich will eine Cola trinken.
– Endlich!

`2.3` **B2** *Was kann man in Basel machen? Macht Dialoge mit den Bildern in Übung B1.* Pupils work together to create dialogues using the pictures from activity B1 as cues.

`4.4` **B3** *Du bist dran! Was kann man in deiner Stadt machen?* Pupils write about the leisure opportunities in their own town or village. This activity can form part of pupils' written records for continuous assessment purposes. See the general notes on pages 13–14 of the introduction to this book.

`3.4` **C** *Lies Gabis E-Mail und die Sätze. Sind sie richtig oder falsch? Schreib ✔ oder ✘.* Pupils read the text and decide whether the statements are true or false. For additional writing practice, pupils could correct the false statements.

Answers: 1 ✘; 2 ✘; 3 ✘; 4 ✔; 5 ✘; 6 ✔

`3.2` **D1** *Füll die Lücken aus.* Pupils complete the sentences with the correct forms of *können* and *wollen* from the box.

Answers: 1 kann; 2 können; 3 will; 4 Willst; 5 will; 6 kann

`4.3` **D2** *Was will Familie Haab heute machen? Füll die Sprechblasen aus.* Pupils write sentences in response to the picture cues.

Answers:

1 Ich will ins Fastfood-Restaurant und in die Eisbahn gehen.
2 Wir wollen ins Museum und ins Theater gehen.
3 Ich will ins Kino und ins Jugendzentrum gehen.
4 Wir wollen in die Disco und ins Schwimmbad gehen.
5 Ich will ein Picknick machen und in die Eisdiele gehen.

Page 56

Use with pages 73–74 in the Students' Book.

`4.4–5` **E** *Du bist dran! Was willst du am Wochenende machen?* Pupils write a short paragraph about what they want to do at the weekend. This activity can form part of pupils' written records for continuous assessment purposes

`4.2` **F** *„Wo treffen wir uns?" Füll die Lücken aus.* Pupils complete the phrases with the correct combinations of preposition and definite article from the box.

Answers:

a am Busbahnhof. b in der Eisdiele. c vor dem Bahnhof. d in der Imbissstube. e am Markt. f an der Bushaltestelle. g vor der Eisbahn. h im Café.

`AT 4.4` **G** *„Wo treffen wir uns?" Schreib Sätze.* Pupils write sentences in response to the picture cues.

Answers:

a Wir treffen uns vor dem Café. b Wir treffen uns an der Eisbahn. c Wir treffen uns vor der Imbissstube. d Wir treffen uns am Bahnhof. e Wir treffen uns an der Bushaltestelle. f Wir treffen uns vor der Eisdiele.

Page 57

Use with page 75 in the Students' Book.

`AT 1.3` **H1** *Wohin gehen sie oder wo sind sie? Hör gut zu und finde die passenden Bilder.* Pupils listen to the recording and select the appropriate picture from each pair. This activity focuses on *in* + accusative = movement, *in* + dative = position.

Answers: 1 a; 2 b; 3 b; 4 b; 5 b

Transcript	W 57, activity H1

1 – Hallo, Katrin! Hier ist Ulli! Katrin, wir gehen in den Park, Gabi und ich. Kommst du mit? Treffen wir uns um 13.00 Uhr?
2 – Vati, ich bin im Supermarkt! Was für Obst willst du?
3 – Tag, Carsten! Wie geht's? Ich bin im Moment in der Eisdiele – mit der Susi. He, ich finde sie sehr nett!
4 – Kai, ich gehe heute Nachmittag ins Schwimmbad. Willst du auch kommen? Treffen wir uns um zwei Uhr an der Bushaltestelle?
5 – Hallo, Mutti! Ich bin im Freizeitzentrum! Um wie viel Uhr essen wir?

`AT 4.2` **H2** *in + Akkusativ oder Dativ? Ergänze die Sätze für die anderen Bilder in Übung H1.* Pupils complete the sentences with *in* and the correct form (accusative or dative) of the definite article (relating to the pictures which were not the answers in activity H1).

Answers: 1 im; 2 in den; 3 in die; 4 im; 5 ins

`AT 2.5` **I** *„Wohin gehen wir? Wo treffen wir uns?" Macht Dialoge mit den Informationen unten.* Pupils work in pairs to create dialogues using the picture cues.

Pages 58–59

Use with pages 75–77 in the Students' Book.

`AT 4.5` **J** *Du bist dran! Wohin gehst du am Wochenende? Wo triffst du deinen Freund/deine Freundin?* Pupils write a short paragraph about their own plans for the weekend. This activity can form part of pupils' written records for continuous assessment purposes.

`AT 4.1` **K** *Was ist das? Schreib die Wörter auf.* Pupils label the items shown in the pictures.

145

Answers:

a Shampoo; b Duschgel; c Seife; d Zahnpasta;
e Make-up;
f Federmappe; g Umschläge; h Buntstifte; i Füller;
j Filzstifte;
k Postkarten; l Telefonkarte; m Briefmarken;
n Monatskarte; o Fahrplan;
p Halstabletten; q Asthmaspray

AT 3.1 **L1** *Finde die passenden Wörter für die Geschäfte.* Pupils find the correct name for each shop or other building.

Answers:

a die Apotheke; b der Schreibwarenladen; c die Post;
d die Drogerie; e der Busbahnhof

AT 4.3–4 **L2** *Wohin musst du gehen? Schreib Sprechblasen für die Bilder in Übung L1.* Pupils write sentences with *Ich muss zur/zum … gehen*, using the pictures in activity L1 as cues.

Answers:

1 Ich muss zur Apotheke gehen. 2 Ich muss zum Schreibwarenladen gehen. 3 Ich muss zur Post gehen. 4 Ich muss zur Drogerie gehen. 5 Ich muss zum Busbahnhof gehen.

AT 1.4 **M1** *Was brauchen sie? Hör gut zu und kreuz die passenden Bilder an.* Pupils listen to the recording and complete the table.

Answers:

Kris: pen, pencil case;
Gabi: cough sweets, inhaler;
Anke: soap, shower gel;
Peter: postcards, envelopes;
Btitta: travel card

Transcript   W 59, activity M1

– Wo ist meine Federmappe? Wo ist mein Füller? Ich finde sie einfach nicht!
– Kris, was ist los?
– Mutti, ich habe keine Federmappe und keinen Füller für die Schule. Ich muss in die Stadt gehen!
– Ich gehe heute Nachmittag in die Stadt – die kaufe ich!

– Ich muss zur Drogerie gehen.
– Was brauchst du denn, Gabi?
– Schau mal, hier ist meine Liste. Ich habe kein Asthmaspray und ich habe keine Halstabletten.
– Also, gehen wir zur Drogerie!
– Brauchst du auch etwas, Anke?
– Ja, ich habe keine Seife, kein Duschgel und keine Zahnpasta.

– Wohin gehst du, Peter?
– Ich muss zum Schreibwarenladen gehen.
– Ich auch! Was brauchst du denn?
– Ähm … neue Buntstifte und auch Postkarten. Und ich habe keine Umschläge.
– Also, gehen wir los!

– Britta, warum fährst du heute mit dem Rad?
– Ich brauche eine neue Monatskarte – ich habe meine alte verloren.

– Ich brauche auch eine neue Monatskarte!
– Also, wir müssen beide zum Busbahnhof gehen!

AT 2.3 **M2** *Was brauchen sie? Macht Dialoge mit den Informationen in Übung M1.* Pupils work together in pairs to create dialogues using their answers to activity M1 and *Ich brauche …*

AT 4.3 **M3** *Schreib dann Sätze mit keinen/keine/kein/keine.* Pupils now write sentences using their answers to activity M1 and *kein/keine/kein*.

Answers:

Kris: Ich habe keinen Füller und keine Federmappe.
Gabi: Ich habe keine Halstabletten und kein Asthmaspray.
Anke: Ich habe keine Seife, kein Duschgel und keine Zahnpasta.
Peter: Ich habe keine Postkarten, keine Umschläge und keine Buntstifte.
Britta: Ich habe keine Monatskarte.

Page 60

Use with pages 77–78 in the Students' Book.

AT 2.3 **N** *Labyrinth-Spiel: A wählt einen Buchstaben, B beschreibt was er/sie braucht; A sagt wohin B gehen muss.* Pupils play the maze game together in pairs to practise *Ich brauche/Ich habe keinen/keine/kein …* and *Du musst …*

AT 4.1 **O** *Was gibt es im Fundbüro? Schreib die Wörter auf. Schreib auch der, die oder das auf.* Pupils label the items, each with the correct definite article.

Answers:

a der Koffer; b das T-Shirt; c der Schirm; d die Schultasche; e das Buch; f die Uhr; g die Geldbörse; h der Rucksack; i der Fotoapparat; j die Brieftasche

Pages 61–62

Use with pages 78–79 in the Students' Book.

P *Lies die Sätze und finde die passenden Wörter.* Pupils choose the correct form of *mein/meine/mein* to complete each sentence.

Answers:

1 Ich habe **meine** Tasche verloren. 2 Ich habe **mein** Buch verloren. 3 Ich habe **meinen** Schirm verloren. 4 Ich habe **meine** Uhr verloren. 5 Ich habe **meinen** Koffer verloren. 6 Ich habe **meinen** Rucksack verloren.

Q1 *Was haben Niki und Gerd verloren? Füll die Lücken aus.* Pupils supply the correct forms of *mein/meine/mein* to complete each sentence. They check their answers by doing activity Q2.

Answers:

Niki: Ich habe **meine** Tasche, **meine** Geldbörse, **mein** Buch und **meine** Uhr verloren.
Gerd: Ich habe **meinen** Rucksack, **mein** T-Shirt, **meinen** Schirm und **meine** Brieftasche verloren.

Q2 *Ist alles richtig? Hör gut zu.* Pupils listen to the recording to check their answers to activity Q1.

Transcript W 61, activity Q2

– Hallo, Niki, wie geht's?
– Nicht gut, Gerd! Ich habe meine Tasche verloren und in meiner Tasche sind meine Geldbörse, mein Buch und meine Uhr.
– Ach, nein! Mir geht es auch nicht gut.
– Wieso denn?
– Ich habe meinen Rucksack verloren.
– Hast du noch etwas verloren?
– Ich habe mein T-Shirt, meinen Schirm und auch meine Brieftasche verloren.

R1 *Wie ist er/sie/es? Finde die passenden Bilder.* Pupils match the pictures to the sentences. [T 3.2]

Answers: 1 c; 2 a; 3 b

R2 *Er, sie oder es? Füll die Lücken aus.* Pupils complete the sentences with the correct pronoun. [T 4.3]

Answers: 1 Sie; 2 Es; 3 sie; 4 Es; 5 er; 6 Es

S1 *Wie sieht er/sie/es aus? Hör gut zu und füll die Tabelle aus.* Pupils listen to the recording and complete the table. [T 1.4]

Answers:

	Farbe(n)	⬡	◼	◇
🧳	braun, schwarz	✗		
🧳	schwarz, silber		✗	
☂	rot, weiß			✗
👜	gelb, orange, rot, grün		✗	
👕	rot, grün		✗	
⌚	lila, weiß, blau			✗

Transcript W 62, activity S1

– Guten Tag! Kann ich Ihnen helfen?
– Ja, guten Tag! Ich habe meine Geldbörse verloren!
– Oh, das tut mir Leid! Wie sieht sie aus?
– Ähm … sie ist braun und schwarz, und aus Leder.
– Okay, schauen wir mal …

– Entschuldigung!
– Ja?

– Ich kann meine Schultasche nicht finden!
– Deine Schultasche? Wie sieht sie denn aus?
– Sie ist gelb und orange und rot … und grün!
– Und ist sie aus Plastik?
– Ähm … ja! Ja, aus Plastik! Nein, aus Stoff, ja, aus Stoff!

– Hallo!
– Ja, bitte?
– Ich habe mein T-Shirt verloren. Es ist rot und grün.
– Ein T-Shirt? Also, aus Stoff … Und wo haben sie es verloren?

– Guten Tag! Ich habe meinen Koffer verloren!
– Aha … und wie sieht er aus?
– Er ist schwarz. Schwarz und silber.
– Und aus Leder?
– Nein, aus Stoff!
– Aus Stoff …

– Hallo! Kann ich dir helfen?
– Ähm … ja … ja, bitte!
– Was hast du verloren?
– Meine Uhr!
– Oh, das tut mir Leid. Wie sieht deine Uhr aus?
– Wie sie aussieht?
– Ja, welche Farbe hat sie?
– Ähm … sie ist lila … und weiß … und blau.
– Okay, und ist sie aus Leder?
– Ähm … nein. Nein, sie ist aus Plastik.
– Okay, schauen wir mal …

– Guten Tag! Haben Sie einen Schirm?
– Ja, ich habe viele Schirme!
– Oh! Ich habe meinen Schirm verloren.
– Und wie sieht er aus?
– Er ist rot und weiß.
– Und aus Plastik?
– Ja! Natürlich!

S2 *Was hast du verloren? A ist Beamter/Beamtin, B hat etwas verloren. Macht Dialoge mit den Informationen in Übung S1.* Pupils work in pairs to create dialogues using their answers to activity S1. [AT 2.4]

Page 63
Use with page 79 in the Students' Book.

T *Was hast du verloren? Male die Bilder aus und schreib eine Karte.* Pupils write announcements for lost items using the pictures as cues. They choose the colour and material of the items and colour them in accordingly. [AT 4.4]

Can you …?
The purpose of the checklist is to identify tasks in the Students' Book both by skill and by topic. Teachers may find this helpful in selecting specific tasks, as a record of pupils' achievements in an Attainment Target.

Einheit 6 Wir gehen in die Stadt	AT 1 Listening	AT 2 Speaking	AT 3 Reading	AT 4 Writing
72–73 Was kann man in Köln machen?				
Ask about what you can do in town	1b	–	–	–
Say what you can do in town	1a, 1b	Noch mal!	1a	2, Extra!, 5c
Say what you want to do	3a	3b	3a	4, 5a, 5b, 5c
74–75 Wo treffen wir uns?				
Talk about where you are going to meet	1, 2a, 4	2b, 6	1, 3, 4	3, 5b
76–77 Was brauchst du?				
Say what you do not have	1, 3a	3b	1	4
Say what you need	1, 3a	3b	1	6
Say which shops you need to go to	2b, 3a	3b, 7	2a	–
78–79 Im Fundbüro				
Ask if you can help someone	1	2b, 5	1	–
Say what you have lost	1, 2a	2b, 5	1, 3	3, Extra!
Ask and say what it is like	1, 4	5	1, 4	Noch mal!, Extra!
Say you're sorry	1	2b, 5	1	–

Copymasters

For general advice about using the copymasters, see page 7 of the introduction to this book.

C 49

Hören

AT 1.3

1 *Hör gut zu und verbinde die passenden Bilder.* Pupils listen to the recording and then select the appropriate item in each column.

Answers:

1 rot, aus Plastik; 2 gelb, aus Leder; 3 schwarz, aus Plastik; 4 braun, aus Stoff; 5 grün, aus Leder

---

Transcript   C 49, activity 1

1
– Guten Morgen.
– Guten Morgen. Kann ich Ihnen helfen?
– Ich habe meine Geldbörse verloren. Sie ist rot und aus Plastik.
– Kein Problem! Wir haben die Geldbörse hier.
2
– Wo ist dein Füller Max?
– Ich habe keinen Füller. Ich habe meine Federmappe verloren.
– Oh, schade. Wie sieht sie aus?
– Sie ist gelb und aus Leder.
– Gehen wir zum Klassenzimmer? Vielleicht ist deine Federmappe dort.
3
– Guten Tag. Kann ich Ihnen helfen?
– Guten Tag. Ja, bitte. Ich habe meine Uhr verloren. Sie ist schwarz und aus Plastik.
– Das tut mir Leid. Wir haben hier keine Uhr.
4
– Hallo, Monika. Was ist los?
– Hallo, Anke. Ich kann meinen Koffer nicht finden.
– Das tut mir Leid. Wie sieht er aus?
– Er ist braun und aus Stoff.
– Gehen wir zum Fundbüro?
– Eine gute Idee.

5
– Wohin gehst du Paul?
– Ich gehe zum Fundbüro. Ich habe meinen Rucksack verloren.
– Wie sieht er aus?
– Er ist grün und aus Leder.

AT 1.4

2a *Wohin gehen Peter und Jana? Hör gut zu und schreib zwei Listen.* Pupils listen to the recording and then fill in *zum/zur* and the name of the shop or other place that Peter and Jana need to visit.

Answers:

Peter: zur Drogerie; zum Busbahnhof; zum Schreibwarenladen
Jana: zur Post; zum Schreibwarenladen; zur Eisdiele

Transcript   C 49, activities 2a and 2b

– Machst du einen Einkaufsbummel, Peter?
– Einkaufsbummel? Ich muss einkaufen gehen!
– Also, was ist auf deiner Einkaufsliste?
– Erstens habe ich kein Shampoo und ich brauche auch Seife.
– Kein Problem, du musst zur Drogerie gehen. Und dann?
– Ich habe Umschläge und Briefmarken, aber ich habe keine neue Monatskarte und keinen Fahrplan für die Sommerferien.
– Kein Problem, Peter. Wir können auch zum Busbahnhof gehen. Sonst noch etwas?
– Ja, ich muss zum Schreibwarenladen. Ich habe Buntstifte, aber ich habe keine Filzstifte. Ich brauche auch eine schöne Federmappe für meine Schwester. Sie hat morgen Geburtstag. Und du? Hast du auch eine Einkaufsliste, Jana?
– Ja, ich habe meine Geburtstagsliste. Gestern bin ich fünfzehn geworden und jetzt habe ich viel Geld!
– Wohin willst du denn gehen?

> – Ich will zur Post gehen. Ich brauche Briefmarken und auch Umschläge. Ich muss viele Briefe schreiben. Ich habe auch keine Telefonkarte.
> – Und dann?
> – Ich muss auch zum Schreibwarenladen gehen. Ich habe keinen Füller für die Schule und ich habe nur eine alte Federmappe. Ich brauche auch neue Buntstifte.
> – Und dann?
> – Und dann gehen wir zur Eisdiele.
> – Zur Eisdiele?
> – Ja, wir brauchen beide ein Eis!

2b *Hör noch einmal gut zu. Was sagen Peter und Jana? Füll die Kästchen aus.* Pupils listen to the recording again and mark each picture according to whether the speakers say *Ich habe ein …* (H), *Ich brauche ein …* (B), or *Ich habe kein …* (K).

Answers:

Peter: shampoo K, soap B, envelopes H, stamps H, season ticket K, timetable K, crayons H, felt tips K, pencil case B.
Jana: stamps B, envelopes B, phone card K, fountain pen K, pencil case H, crayons B, ice-cream sundaes B.

Sprechen

1a *Dein Partner/deine Partnerin stellt Fragen. Beantworte die Fragen.* Pupils work together in pairs to create dialogues based on an information-gap. In answer to Partner B's questions, A describes one of the four objects depicted.

1b *Stell die Fragen unten. Dein Partner/deine Partnerin antwortet.* This is the second part of the activity, with the roles reversed.

2a *Dein Partner/deine Partnerin fragt: „Was willst du machen?" und „Wo treffen wir uns?" Beantworte die Fragen.* In answer to B's questions, A describes an activity and a meeting place, using the picture cues.

2b *Stell die Fragen unten. Dein Partner/deine Partnerin antwortet.* This is the second part of the activity with the roles reversed.

Lesen 1

1 *Was brauchen sie? Finde die passenden Bilder.* Pupils read the speech bubbles and select the appropriate set of items for each character.

Answers: Chan: c; Anke: b; Gerd: a

2 *Eine Stadttour von Küchl. Lies den Text und finde die richtige Reihenfolge für die Bilder.* Pupils read the leaflet and put the pictures in the correct sequence.

Answers: d, g, c, b, i, e, a, h

Lesen 2

1 *Sara schreibt eine E-Mail an ihre Freundinnen. Lies den Text und die Fragen. Kreuz die richtigen Antworten an.* Pupils read the e-mail and select the correct answers to the questions.

Answers: 1 b; 2 c; 3 a; 4 c; 5 c; 6 b; 7 a

Schreiben

1 *Was kann man in Wesel machen? Schreib die Wörter richtig auf.* Pupils re-order the letters to form the names of places to go and things to do in town.

Answers:

1 Freizeitzentrum; 2 Fastfood-Restaurant; 3 Eisbahn; 4 Café; 5 Einkaufsbummel; 6 Stadt

2 *Was brauchen sie und wohin müssen sie gehen? Füll die Lücken aus.* Pupils complete the sentences with *keinen/keine/kein/keine* + noun and *zum/zur* + noun in response to the picture cues.

Answers:

1 Ich habe **kein Shampoo** und ich muss **zur Drogerie** gehen.
2 Ich habe **keinen Füller** und ich muss **zum Schreibwarenladen** gehen.
3 Ich habe **keine Briefmarken** und ich muss **zur Post** gehen.
4 Ich habe **keine Halstabletten** und ich muss **zur Apotheke** gehen.
5 Ich habe **keinen Fahrplan** und ich muss **zum Bahnhof** gehen.

3 *Du bist auf Urlaub in Deutschland und willst deinen Freund/deine Freundin einladen. Schreib eine Einladung:* Pupils complete the sentences according to the picture cues.

Answers:

Ich will **ins Kino (gehen) und ins Fastfood-Restaurant gehen.**
Wir treffen uns **neben der Post am Markt.**
Wir treffen uns um **zwei Uhr.**
Was willst du machen?

Grammatik 1

This copymaster focuses on *können* and *wollen* and *an* and *vor* + dative.

1 *Schreib diese Sätze auf Deutsch.* Pupils read the 'Flashback' and complete the translations of the English sentences, putting the modal auxiliary and the infinitive in their correct positions.

Answers:

1 **Man kann** ins Kino **gehen.**
2 **Wir können** in die Disco **gehen.**
3 **Wir wollen** in die Stadt **fahren.**
4 **Ich will** ins Schwimmbad **gehen.**
5 **Wir können** einen Einkaufsbummel **machen.**
6 **Ich will** ins Freizeitzentrum **gehen.**

2 *Schreib Sätze auf Deutsch.* Pupils read the 'Flashback' and write sentences using the picture cues and prepositions provided.

Answers:

Any grammatically correct and meaningful sentences with the following adverbial phrases: am Bahnhof; vor dem Dom; am Markt; vor der Eisbahn; an der Bushaltestelle; am Café

C 53B **Grammatik 2**

This copymaster focuses on *in* + accusative/dative and the possessive adjective *mein/meine/mein* in the nominative and accusative.

1 *Finde die passenden Wörter.* Pupils read the 'Flashback' and select the correct combination of *in* + accusative/dative definite article.

Answers:

1 Er geht **ins** Schwimmbad. 2 Er ist **im** Kino. 3 Er geht **in die** Schule. 4 Er geht **in den** Bahnhof. 5 Er ist **im** Café. 6 Er ist **in der** Eisdiele.

2 *Füll die Lücken aus.* Pupils read the 'Flashback' and then complete the sentences with the correct accusative form of *mein/meine/mein/meine*.

Answers:

1 meine; 2 meinen; 3 mein; 4 meinen; 5 meine; 6 mein

C 54 **Tipp**

This copymaster gives advice on adapting language to different contexts.

1 *Jetzt bist du dran! Schreib so viele Sätze wie möglich mit:* Pupils read the 'Flashback' and then write as many sentences as possible with the four diverse noun phrases: *eine schwarze Katze, Briefmarken, Shampoo* and *die Schule.* Encourage them to look over Units 1–6 in the Students' Book and select as many diverse structures as possible, in the perfect and present tenses, with modal auxiliaries, prepositions, etc. You may wish to set a time limit, or a limit to the number of sentences. Pupils could then read out their sentences to the class.

2a *Lies die Texte von Frau Neumann und Herrn Althaus.* Pupils read the two texts and examine the pictures.

2b *Was sind die Unterschiede zwischen Frau Neumann und Herrn Althaus? Schreib eine Liste.* Pupils write sentences contrasting Frau Neumann and Herr Althaus.

3 *Du bist dran! Beschreib Frau Maus und Herrn Sicher.* Pupils write their own descriptions of Frau Maus and Herr Sicher, in either the first or the third person singular.

4-6 Wiederholung

Materials
- Students' Book pages 82–83
- Cassette 2 side B

This revision spread provides consolidation and further practice of language from Units 4–6. You can either take pupils through the activities as a whole class, or they can work independently or in pairs. The activities should help pupils prepare for the assessment for Units 4–6.

3.3 **1a** *Luise macht eine Party. Was tragen ihre Gäste? Finde die passenden Bilder.* Activity 1 revises the material from Unit 4, pages 52–53. In activity 1a, pupils read the descriptions of clothes (*ich trage einen/eine/ein* + mixed-declension adjective + noun; *ich trage* + strong-declension adjective + plural noun) and match the pictures to the speech bubbles (there are eight pictures but only four speech bubbles).

Answers: 1 d; 2 g; 3 b; 4 e

4.4 **1b** *Was tragen die anderen Gäste? Schreib Sprechblasen für die anderen Bilder (Übung 1a).* Pupils now write descriptions (in the first person) for the remaining four characters in activity 1a, using the speech bubbles in activity 1a as a model.

Answers:

a Ich trage eine blaue Jeans, eine gelbe Jacke und ein braunes Hemd. Ich trage auch grüne Schuhe.

c Ich trage einen blauen Rock, eine schwarze Bluse und graue Schuhe. Und ich trage eine schwarze Strumpfhose.

f Ich trage ein schwarzes Sweatshirt, eine grüne Hose, eine blaue Mütze und rote Turnschuhe.

h Ich trage ein rotes Kleid, einen blauen Pullover und eine weiße Jacke. Und ich trage weiße Schuhe.

AT 4.4 **2a** *Ina muss ihr Zimmer aufräumen! Wo ist alles? Schreib Sätze.* Activity 2 revises the material from Unit 5, pages 64–65. In activity 2a, pupils write sentences to describe the position of the objects in the room shown in the picture (*in/unter/neben/auf/vor* + dative). Pupils check each other's answers by doing activity 2b.

Answers:

(Accept any alternatives which are justified by the picture.)
Der Pullover ist unter dem Bett.
Das Stofftier ist im Kleiderschrank.
Das Handy ist auf dem Stuhl.
Die Schulmappe ist unter dem Schreibtisch.
Die Inline-Skates sind auf dem Schreibtisch/neben dem Computer.
Die Bluse/Das Hemd ist auf dem Bett.

AT 2.3 **2b** *Ist alles richtig? Macht Dialoge.* Pupils work together in pairs to create dialogues describing the picture, in the process checking each other's answers to activity 2a.

AT 3.5 **3a** *Lies Saras E-Mail und beantworte die Fragen.* Activity 3 revises the material from Unit 5, pages 66–67, and also

Unit 4, pages 54–55; activity 3b offers the scope for a wider revision of language covered so far. In activity 3a, pupils read the text and answer the comprehension questions (perfect tense + *haben/sein; weil* + subordinate clause; *müssen*).

Answers:

1 Gestern war Saras Geburtstag.
2 Sie hat einen schwarzen Minirock, ein grünes T-Shirt und 40 Euro bekommen.
3 Der Rock gefällt ihr, weil sie am liebsten Röcke trägt.
4 Das T-Shirt gefällt ihr nicht, weil es zu lang und zu groß ist.
5 Sie ist in die Stadt gefahren. Sie hat Turnschuhe gekauft. Sie hat eine Geburtstagsparty gemacht. Sie hat Pizza gegessen, sie hat Cola getrunken und sie hat getanzt. Sie hat Katrin und Daniel getroffen.
6 Sie muss den Partykeller aufräumen.

AT 4.5 **3b** *Du bist dran! Was hast du zum Geburtstag bekommen? Wie gefallen dir die Geschenke? Was hast du gemacht? Schreib eine E-Mail so wie Sara.* Pupils write their own texts on the model of Sara's e-mail. Encourage them to use adjectives to describe the presents and to describe a diverse range of activities.

 4a *Was wollen sie machen? Hör gut zu. Kopiere den Zettel und mach Notizen.* Activity 4 revises the material **AT 1.4** from Unit 6, pages 72–77. In activity 4a, pupils listen to the answerphone messages and note the key points: who is calling, what he/she wants to do, when to meet, where to meet. Remind pupils that they only have time to write brief notes, not whole sentences. You could help pupils by writing up the names of the callers on the board/OHT.

Answers:

(Accept variations)
Wer: Lisa
Was: Jugendzentrum
Wann: (heute Nachmittag,) 15 Uhr
Wo: vor dem Freizeitzentrum

Wer: Philipp
Was: Schreibwarenladen, Kino
Wann: 14 Uhr
Wo: am Markt

Wer: Meike Kaiser, Laura
Was: (neue) Disco
Wann: 20 Uhr
Wo: am Busbahnhof

Wer: Nick
Was: Einkaufsbummel
Wann: morgen, 15.30 Uhr
Wo: in der Eisdiele

Wer: Hanna
Was: Computerspiel (kaufen)
Wann: morgen, 16 Uhr
Wo: vor dem Einkaufszentrum

Transcript p 83, activity 4a

– Hallo, Martin! Hier ist Lisa. Hast du heute Nachmittag Zeit? Ich will ins Jugendzentrum gehen. Susi und Uwe kommen auch! Also, wir treffen uns um 15 Uhr vor dem Freizeitzentrum. Tschüs!

– Martin, ich bin's – Philipp. Ich muss nach der Schule in die Stadt gehen – also, ich muss zum Schreibwarenladen gehen. Ich brauche einen neuen Füller. Und danach will ich ins Kino gehen. Treffen wir uns am Markt – um 14 Uhr?

– Tag, Martin! Meike hier – Meike Kaiser. Laura und ich – wir wollen heute abend in die neue Disco fahren. Wir wollen mit dem Bus fahren – Linie 3. Wir treffen uns um 20 Uhr am Busbahnhof. Bis dann!

– Hallo, Martin! Hier ist Nick. Ich will morgen einen Einkaufsbummel machen. Meine Mutter hat am Wochenende Geburtstag und ich habe kein Geschenk. Hast du Zeit? Dann treffen wir uns um 15 Uhr 30 in der Eisdiele. Tschüs!

– Martin? Guten Tag, hier ist Hanna aus der 6A. Du interessierst dich für Computer, nicht wahr? Also, ich will ein Computerspiel für meinen Bruder kaufen ... aber welches? Hast du morgen Zeit? Treffen wir uns um 16 Uhr vor dem Einkaufszentrum? Vielen Dank!

AT 2.4 **4b** *Du bist dran! Nimm weitere Telefon-Nachrichten auf Kassette auf (mit den Informationen unten).* Pupils use the picture cues as the basis for further answerphone messages, which they record on tape. Point out or elicit from the pupils that as well as the message content (what they want to do, time and meeting place) they should also think about a greeting, giving their name (a different name for each message) and how to end the message. Listening to the recording for activity 4a again should help them to formulate their messages. Encourage them to record their messages several times, improving their fluency with each one. They could also try to vary their tone of voice according to how interesting they find the different activities.

AT 4.4 **5** *Mark vom Mars muss einkaufen. Wohin muss er gehen? Lies seine Einkaufsliste und schreib einen Zettel für ihn.* This activity revises the material from Unit 6, pages 76–77. Pupils write sentences using *du hast keinen/keine/kein …* and *du musst zum/zur … gehen*. This requires them to think of the appropriate shop in which to buy each item. As a follow-up activity, pupils could rewrite their sentences using *du brauchst …*

Answers:

(Accept any sensible variations.)
Du hast keine Briefmarken – du musst zur Post gehen.
Du hast kein Duschgel – du musst zur Drogerie gehen.
Du hast keine Filzstifte – du musst zum Schreibwarenladen gehen.
Du hast keine Halstabletten – du musst zur Apotheke gehen.
Du hast keine Monatskarte – du musst zum Busbahnhof/Bahnhof gehen.

4-6 Kontrolle

Materials
- Copymasters 86–89
- Cassette 2 side B

C 86

Hören

1 *Was tragen Turabi und Güyal nicht gern, gern und am liebsten? Hör gut zu und füll die Tabelle aus – schreib ✗ (nicht gern), ✔ (gern) und ✔✔ (am liebsten).* Pupils listen to the recording and complete the table with Turabi's and Güyal's likes, dislikes and favourites.

AT 1.3

Answers:

Turabi	✔	✗		
Güyal			✔	✗

Turabi			✗	✔✔
Güyal	✔✔	✗		

Mark scheme:
1 mark for each correct detail completed (total 8 marks)

Assessment criteria:
Pupils who complete 6 or more details correctly show evidence of performance at AT1 level 3.

> **Transcript** C 86, activity 1
> – Turabi, wie gefallen dir Jacken?
> – Jacken? Hmm, ich trage sie nicht gern. Ich trage Sweatshirts am liebsten. Sweatshirts gefallen mir sehr gut.
> – Und Krawatten?
> – Ich muss eine Krawatte zur Schule tragen - das mag ich gar nicht. Nein, Krawatten trage ich nicht gern – aber T-Shirts, die trage ich gern.
> – Also, T-Shirts gefallen dir gut?
> – Ja, stimmt.
> – Und du Güyal, was gefällt dir gut?
> – Hosen! Ich trage gern Hosen, aber Mützen gefallen mir gar nicht. Ich trage sie nicht gern, weil sie sehr altmodisch sind.
> – Und was gefällt dir sehr gut, Güyal?
> – Das ist einfach - Hemden. Ich trage Hemden am liebsten, aber ich trage Schuhe nicht sehr gern. Mir gefallen Schuhe nicht sehr gut. Ich trage gern Turnschuhe.

2 *Guptal, Kathi, Michael und Alex bekommen Einladungen. Hör gut zu und füll die Tabelle aus.* Pupils listen to the recording and complete the table with the details of the invitations.

AT 1.4

Answers:

	Datum der Einladung?	Wofür ist die Einladung?	Warum kann er/sie nicht hingehen?
Guptal	12. Mai	ein Schulfest	Er muss seinen Großeltern im Haus und Garten helfen.
Kathi	4. April	eine Geburtstagsparty	Sie muss Zeitungen austragen.
Michael	23. Februar	Fashingsfete	Er muss seine Oma besuchen.
Alex	15. Juni	ein Picknick	Er muss seine Hausaufgaben machen.

Mark scheme:
1 mark for each correct detail completed (total 9 marks)

Assessment criteria:
Pupils gaining 6 or more marks show evidence of performance at AT 1 level 4. As this is a listening comprehension task, minor errors in the accuracy of the German are acceptable provided that communication is not impaired.

> **Transcript** C 86, activity 2
> – Ja, hallo, Mohammed, hier ist Guptal.
> – Hallo, Guptal. Was ist los?
> – Ich habe eine Einladung von meinem Freund Paul. Seine Schule macht am zwölften Mai ein Schulfest.
> – Ah, toll!
> – Ja, aber ich kann leider nicht gehen.
> – Aber warum nicht?
> – Ich muss meinen Großeltern im Garten helfen. Sie sind sehr alt und ich helfe am Wochenende im Garten und im Haus.
>
> – Hast du einen Brief bekommen, Kathi?
> – Ja, Mutti. Eine Einladung von Helena für den vierten April. Sie hat am vierten April Geburtstag und sie macht eine Party zu Hause.
> – Das ist aber toll, Kathi. Was ist das Problem?
> – Ich kann leider nicht gehen.
> – Warum nicht?
> – Ich muss am Freitagabend Zeitungen austragen.
> – Oh, schade.
>
> – Hallo, Michael. Karla hier. Bist du am dreiundzwanzigsten Februar frei? Wir machen eine Faschingsfete in der Schule – kommst du? Ruf mich bitte an. Tschüs, Karla.
> – He, toll! Vati, es gibt am dreiundzwanzigsten Februar eine Faschingsfete in Karlas Schule – sie hat mich eingeladen!

– Hmm ... aber leider kannst du nicht gehen, Michael.
– Aber warum nicht, Vati?
– Wir müssen am dreiundzwanzigsten Oma besuchen.

– Was hast du da, Alex? Ist das eine Einladung?
– Ja, Klasse 9B macht ein Picknick im Park – ich bin eingeladen.
– Toll! Und wann ist das Picknick?
– Am Wochenende – am fünfzehnten Juni! Ach, nein! Ich kann leider nicht gehen!
– Aber warum nicht?
– Mein Vater sagt, ich muss jedes Wochenende meine Hausaufgaben machen. Er ist gemein, finde ich!
– Deine Hausaufgaben machen?!! Das ist total unfair.

3 *Hör gut zu und beantworte die Fragen.* Pupils listen to the recording and answer the comprehension questions.

Answers:

1 Er trägt eine schwarze Mütze und ein rotes T-Shirt. (Manchmal trägt er auch blaue Jeans und einen gelben Pullover.)
2 Es war am 19. Juli.
3 eine Tasche, einen Rucksack, eine Jacke
4 die Tasche: grün und aus Stoff; der Rucksack: groß, braun, neu und aus Leder; Die Jacke: gelb, ganz neu und sehr teuer

Mark scheme:
Award 1 mark for each detail correctly communicated up to a total of 13 marks.

Assessment criteria:
Pupils gaining 10 or more marks show evidence of performance at AT 1 level 5. As this is a listening comprehension task, minor errors in the accuracy of the German are acceptable provided that communication is not impaired.

Transcript   C 86, activity 3

Liebe Zuhörer. Können Sie uns bitte helfen? Wir suchen Dieter Meyer. Herr Meyer ist siebenunddreißig Jahre alt und wohnt in Duisburg. Er hat lange schwaze Haare und trägt gern eine schwarze Mütze und ein rotes T-Shirt. Manchmal trägt er auch blaue Jeans und einen gelben Pullover.

Am neunzehnten Juli war ein Schulfest in der Friedrichs-Schule und Herr Meyer war auch auf dem Schulfest! Eine Frau hat ihre Tasche verloren. Die Tasche war grün und aus Stoff. Ein Kind hat seinen Rucksack verloren. Der Rucksack war groß, braun, neu und aus Leder. Eine andere Frau hat eine gelbe Jacke verloren. Die Jacke war ganz neu und war sehr teuer.

Haben Sie Herrn Meyer gesehen? Können Sie uns helfen? Rufen Sie die Polizei an. Die Nummer ist 00 76 45 36. Vielen Dank.

C 87   **Sprechen**

AT 2.5   **1a** *Frag deinen Partner/deine Partnerin: „Was hast du verloren? Wo hast du das verloren?"* Pupils work together

in pairs to create dialogues about items of lost property (*Was hast du verloren? Ich habe ... verloren. Wo hast du das verloren? Ich habe das im/in der ... verloren.*) using the questions and picture cues provided. Partner A asks the questions, partner B responds.

AT 2.5   **1b** *Dein Partner/deine Partnerin stellt Fragen. Du antwortest.* This is the second half of the activity with the roles reversed.

Mark scheme:
2 marks for each correct answer communicated. If the answer is partially communicated, or if the answer contains a significant grammatical error, 1 mark may be awarded. Up to 3 additional marks may be awarded for pronunciation (total 15).

Assessment criteria:
Pupils who communicate 8 answers correctly without significant error, show evidence of performance at AT2 level 4 or 5 depending on the length and quality of their response. If the answers are partially communicated or contain significant grammatical errors, 1 mark per answer may be awarded and the performance would show evidence of AT2 level 2 or 3.

AT 2.5   **2a** *Frag deinen Partner/deine Partnerin:* Pupils work together in pairs to create dialogues about a birthday party (*Wann war die Party? Die Party war am ... Wo war die Party? Die Party war ... Was hast du bekommen? Ich habe ... bekommen. Was hast du gegessen und getrunken? Ich habe ... gegessen und ... getrunken.*) using the questions and picture cues provided. Partner A asks the questions, partner B responds.

AT 2.5   **2b** *Dein Partner/deine Partnerin stellt Fragen. Antworte mit den Informationen rechts.* This is the second half of the activity with the roles reversed.

Mark scheme:
2 marks for each correct answer fully and unambiguously communicated, including the correct appropriate tense. If the answer is partially communicated, or if the answer contains significant grammatical error, 1 mark may be awarded. Up to 3 additional marks may be awarded for pronunciation (total 15).

Assessment criteria:
Pupils who communicate 8 answers correctly without significant error, show evidence of performance at AT2 level 4 or 5 depending on the length and quality of their response. If the answers are partially communicated or contain significant grammatical errors, 1 mark per answer may be awarded and the performance would show evidence of AT2 level 2 or 3.

C 88A   **Lesen 1**

AT 3.3   **1** *Was trägt Gabi und wohin geht sie? Finde die passenden Bilder für die Sätze.* Pupils read the speech bubbles and choose the two appropriate pictures (clothing and event) for each one.

Answers: 1 c, i; 2 e, h; 3 d, g; 4 a, f; 5 b, j

Mark scheme:
1 mark for each correct answer (total 10)

Assessment criteria:
Pupils gaining 8 or more marks show evidence of performance at AT3 level 3.

Lesen 2

C 88B

AT 3.3 **1** *Wo treffen sie sich? Finde die passenden Bilder.* Pupils read the four notes and select the appropriate picture for each (there are four pictures left over).

Answers: 1 f; 2 a; 3 c; 4 h

Mark scheme:
1 mark for each correct answer (total 4).

Assessment criteria:
Pupils with 3 or more correct answers show evidence of performance at AT3 level 3.

AT 3.5 **2** *Lies die E-Mail und beantworte die Fragen.* Pupils read the text and answer the comprehension questions.

Answers:

1 Er war in Bonn.
2 Er ist mit dem Zug dorthin gefahren.
3 Er hat seine Freundin Anna getroffen.
4 Er hat seine Brieftasche verloren.
5 Sie war ganz neu, braun und silber und aus Leder.
6 Sie war im Fundbüro.
7 Er hat Hamburger gegessen und Limonade getrunken.
8 Er geht ins Schwimmbad, weil er dort seine Schwester trifft.

Mark scheme:
2 marks for each answer accurately communicated. 1 mark may be awarded for answers containing significant error, or for accurate communication of the answer in the form of a phrase or single words (total 16).

Assessment criteria:
Pupils gaining 12 or more marks show evidence of performance at AT3 level 5. Teachers may award level 4 to pupils whose performance narrowly misses 12 marks.

Note that Copymasters 88A and 88B (*Lesen 1* and *Lesen 2*) should be treated as one assessment, totalling 30 marks.

C 89

Schreiben

AT 4.3 **1** *Wo sind die Kleidungsstücke? Schreib Sätze.* Pupils write sentences with *auf/unter/neben/vor/in* + dative to describe the position of the items of clothing in the picture.

Answers:

a (Das T-Shirt ist im Kleiderschrank.)
b Die Hose ist auf dem Regal.
c Die Jeans ist vor dem Computer.
d Das Sweatshirt ist vor dem Kleiderschrank.
e Das/Ein Hemd ist neben der Lampe.
f Die Krawatte ist auf dem Stuhl.
g Der Pullover ist neben dem Fernseher.
h Die Schuhe sind unter dem Bett.
i Das/Ein Hemd ist unter dem Bett.

Mark scheme:
1 mark for each complete description accurately communicated, including correct use of the preposition. Half a mark may be awarded for each complete description containing significant error, or for accurate communication of part of the message (total 8).

Assessment criteria:
Pupils gaining 6 or more marks show evidence of performance at AT4 level 3.

AT 4.4 **2** *Beschreib Thomas' ,Schuluniform'.* Pupils write a short paragraph to describe Thomas' clothes and give their opinion of them.

Answers:

(Some suggestions)
Er trägt eine Jeans, ein T-Shirt und eine Jacke. Seine Uniform sieht teuer aus. Ich mag die Jeans gern.

Mark scheme:
2 marks for each complete detail accurately communicated. 1 mark may be awarded for each detail communicated containing significant error, or for accurate communication of part of the message (total 6).

Assessment criteria:
Pupils gaining 3 or more marks show evidence of performance at AT4 level 4. Teachers may award level 3 for pupils whose performance narrowly misses 3 marks.

AT 4.5 **3** *Sofia macht eine Faschingsfete. Lies den Zeitplan und beschreib Sofias Tag.* Pupils write a paragraph about Sophia's plans (from Sophia's point of view), using the schedule and the picture cues.

Answers:

Pupils' answers will vary in their formulation, but should contain the following information:
Montag 2. Feb., 19.30 Uhr
im Jugendzentrum
Umschläge, Würstchen: Schreibwarenladen, Supermarkt
kein Make-up, keine CDs: Drogerie, Kaufhaus

Mark scheme:
2 marks for each complete detail accurately communicated. 1 mark may be awarded for each detail communicated containing significant error, or for accurate communication of part of the message (total 16).

Assessment criteria:
Pupils gaining 12 or more marks show evidence of performance at AT4 level 5. Teachers may award level 3 or 4 for pupils whose performance narrowly misses 12 marks, depending on the quality of the response.

Einheit 7 Meine Umgebung

Pages	Objectives	Grammar	Pronunciation, Skill focus	Key language	PoS	AT level
					National curriculum	
84–85 Die Klasse!-Clique	Reading and listening for pleasure Familiarization with themes, structures and language of the unit	–	–	–	–	1.4, 3.2, 3.4
86–87 Ich wohne gern in der Stadt	Describe your town Give your opinion about living in a town	Adjective endings, accusative, mixed declension, strong declension plural *weil*	–	*Ich wohne gern/nicht gern in der Stadt, weil es … gibt.* *einen schönen Park/einen tollen Zoo* *eine Sparkasse/eine Tankstelle* *ein Krankenhaus/ein großes Einkaufszentrum/ein modernes Fußballstadion/ein neues Hotel* *alte Gebäude/viele Geschäfte* *viel zu tun* *zu viele Autos* *zu viel Lärm/Umweltverschmutzung/Verkehr* *keine Natur*	1a, 1b, 1c, 2a, 2b, 2c, 2d, 3e, 4c, 4d, 5a, 5c, 5f, 5i	1.2–4, 2.3, 3.2, 3.4, 4, 4.2, 4.4
88–89 Ich wohne gern auf dem Land	Describe the countryside Give your opinion about living in the country	–	Expressing opinions Summarizing a spoken or written text	*Es gibt viele …* *Bäume/Blumen/Eichhörnchen/Frösche/Igel/Schmetterlinge/Schnecken/Seen/Spinnen/Vögel* *Ich wohne gern/lieber auf dem Land, weil es …* *Ich wohne nicht gern auf dem Land weil es …* *sehr ruhig ist.* *viel Natur/viele Tiere gibt.* *keinen Lärm/keinen Verkehr gibt.* *keine Umweltverschmutzung/keine Autos gibt.* *keine Disco/Jugendzentrum/kein Kino gibt.*	1a, 1b, 1c, 2a, 2b, 2c, 2d, 2e, 2h, 2i, 3d, 3e, 5a, 5c, 5d, 5f, 5i	1.3–4, 2.2–4, 3.1, 3.3, 4.1, 4.4

Pages	Objectives	Grammar	Pronunciation, Skill focus	Key language	PoS	AT level
90–91 Was ist Umwelt?	Identify names and items linked to the environment Talk about the most serious problems for the environment	Comparative and superlative of adjectives	–	*Was ist das größte Problem?* *Ich finde/glaube/denke …* *ist/sind das größte Problem.* *… ist gefährlicher/schlimmer/* *umweltfeindlicher als …* *… ist am gefährlichsten/schlimmsten/* *umweltfeindlichsten.* *der Müll/Wald/Verkehr/Lärm* *die Erde/Luft* *das Wasser* *die Fabriken/Zigaretten/Pflanzen/* *Kraftwerke/Menschen/Pestizide*	1a, 1b, 1c, 2a, 2b, 2c, 2d, 3e, 5a, 5c, 5d, 5f, 5i	1.3–4, 2.4, 3.3, 4.3–4
92–93 Ich bin umweltfreundlich!	Talk about actions that help or damage the environment	–	Pronunciation of long words	*Ich kaufe Recyclingpapier.* *Ich kaufe Cola in Dosen.* *Ich fahre mit dem Rad.* *Ich nehme Plastiktüten.* *Ich bringe Flaschen zum* *Altglascontainer.* *Ich trenne meinen Müll.* *Ich bringe Altpapier zum* *Altpapiercontainer.* *Ich bade jeden Tag.* *Ich fahre mit dem Auto.* *Ich trenne meinen Müll nicht.*	1a, 1b, 1c, 2a, 2b, 2c, 2d, 3e, 5a, 5c, 5d, 5f, 5i	1.3–4, 2.4, 3.3–4, 4.3–4
94–95 Thema im Fokus	Encourage reading for pleasure Use language from Unit 7 creatively Encourage independent, pair- and groupwork	–	–	–	1c, 2c, 2d, 3d, 3e, 4c, 4d, 5a, 5c, 5d, 5f, 5g, 5h, 5i	2.3–4, 4.1–5

7 Meine Umgebung

Aims of the unit

- To be able to talk about living in a town
- To be able to talk about living in the country
- To be able to talk about serious problems for the environment
- To be able to talk about actions that help or damage the environment

Die Klasse!-Clique
pages 84–85

Materials

- Students' Book pages 84–85
- Cassette 3 side A
- Workbook page 64

For general advice on exploiting the photo story, see pages 10–11 of the introduction to this book.

In this episode, Annika, Jasmin and Atalay are in the park. Jasmin is depressed because she has missed her meeting with Sascha. Meanwhile, Atalay is keen to try out his brand-new skateboard, but two older boys on the skateboard ramp say he is too young to join in. Atalay defiantly leaps on his skateboard – and promptly falls off. Jasmin and Annika look on in dismay: is Atalay badly hurt?

AT 3.2 **1a** *Was meinst du? Vor dem Lesen: Rate!* This is a prereading activity. Pupils look at the photos without reading the text, and predict what the content of the photo story will be, choosing the sentence ending they consider more likely from each pair given. Pupils could do this activity in pairs, and check their answers by listening to the recording and reading the text (activity 2). Discuss the answers as a whole-class activity. You could ask pupils to volunteer answers and quote from the text to back them up.

Answers: 1 a; 2 a; 3 a; 4 b; 5 b

AT 1.4
AT 3.4

2 *Hör gut zu und lies mit. Wie heißt das auf Deutsch?* Pupils listen to the recording and follow the text in the book. They then match the English expressions to their German equivalents in the text. This could be done as a whole-class activity.

Answers:

1 Weil es langweilig ist. 2 Heute Abend gibt es ein Konzert. 3 Kann ich auch mal fahren?
4 Skateboardfahren ist zu gefährlich. 5 Na wartet!

> **Transcript** p 85, activity 2
>
> – Wo ist Sascha?
> – Alles ist langweilig! Ich wohne nicht gern in Wesel, weil es langweilig ist!
> – Oh, Jasmin ... Wesel ist langweilig – ohne Sascha! Aber hier – schau mal: Heute Abend gibt es ein Konzert im

> Jugendzentrum – mit der Gruppe ‚Morgenstern‘. Kommst du mit? Alexander kommt auch!
> – Ja, super! ‚Morgenstern‘ ist meine Lieblingsgruppe!
>
> – Das ist mein neues Skateboard – kann ich auch mal fahren?
> – Nein! Du bist viel zu klein!
> – Ja, Skateboardfahren ist zu gefährlich für Kinder!
> – Zu klein? Na wartet ...
>
> – Hilfe – nein!!
> – Atalay!!
> – Nein – Atalay!!

AT 3.4 **3** *Wer ist das? Schreib die passenden Namen auf.* Pupils decide who each sentence applies to.

Answers:

1 Jasmin; 2 Annika und Jasmin; 3 ‚Morgenstern‘;
4 Atalay; 5 Sascha

Viel Spaß!

Stadt und Land. The main aim is listening for pleasure, but the song also introduces vocabulary for talking about town and country and the environment. For general advice on exploiting the songs in *Klasse! 2*, see page 7 of the introduction to this book.

> **Transcript** p 85, Viel Spaß!
>
> Busse und Gebäude
> Lärm und viele Leute
> Straßenbahnen, Motorräder
> Altpapier und Müll
>
> Blumen, Tiere, Bäume
> Lämmer in der Scheune
> Schmetterlinge, Seen, Wälder
> Erde, Wasser, Luft

WB A Workbook activity A could be used at this point for exploitation of the song text.

Ich wohne gern in der Stadt
pages 86–87

Objectives

- Describe your town
- Give your opinion about living in a town

Key language

Ich wohne gern/nicht gern in der Stadt, weil es ... gibt.
einen schönen Park/einen tollen Zoo
eine Sparkasse/eine Tankstelle
ein Krankenhaus/ein großes Einkaufszentrum/
ein modernes Fußballstadion/ein neues Hotel
alte Gebäude/viele Geschäfte
viel zu tun

zu viele Autos
zu viel Lärm/Umweltverschmutzung/Verkehr
keine Natur

National Curriculum PoS
statements 1a, 1b, 1c, 2a, 2b, 2c, 2d, 3e, 4c, 4d, 5a, 5c, 5f, 5i

Materials
- Students' Book pages 86–87
- Cassette 3 side A
- Workbook pages 65–67
- Copymasters 56, 58, 60, 61, 62A

Preparatory work
At this point you could revise *ich wohne in* and (*nicht*) *gern*. T: *Ich wohne in ... Wo wohnt ihr? Maria?* P1: *Ich wohne in ...*, etc. T: *Wer wohnt in ... ?* (show of hands) *Wer wohnt gern in ... ? Wer wohnt nicht gern in ... ?*

You could also revise public buildings and *es gibt* (introduced in *Klasse! 1* p. 57). In *Klasse! 1*, words for various public buildings were introduced (e.g. p.100), including: d*er Bahnhof, der Dom, der Markt, der Park; die Bank, die Disco, die Kirche, die Post; das Hallenbad, das Kino, das Rathaus, das Schloss, das Sportzentrum, das Theater.* In Unit 6 of *Klasse! 2*, pupils revised some of these and learned other words for buildings or facilities, e.g. *die Eisdiele, die Eisbahn; das Freizeitzentrum, das Jugendzentrum, das Museum, das Schwimmbad, das Theater.* All of this vocabulary is relevant for the new language context of this unit. Pupils should also know various means of transport which are relevant here: *der Bus, der Zug, die U-Bahn, die Straßenbahn, das Auto.* You could revise some of this vocabulary now, e.g. by asking *Gibt es in [Stadt] ein Schwimmbad? Gibt es hier ein Theater?*, etc. Asking questions of this kind will not only refresh relevant vocabulary in the pupils' minds, but also encourage them to start to reflect on the facilities available in their town in a more mature and critical way than they may be used to.

C 56 Use the relevant pictures from copymaster 56 copied onto an OHT, or as flashcards, to introduce the vocabulary for public buildings and other urban features. (For general advice on using copymaster visuals, see page 12 of the introduction to this book.)

AT 1.3 / AT 3.2 **1a** *Annika wohnt in Wesel. Was gibt es in der Stadt? Hör gut zu und lies mit.* Pupils listen to the recording and look at the photos and text in the book. Establish that the plural of *das Gebäude* is *die Gebäude*, e.g. by drawing rough outlines of one, then several buildings on the board/OHT.

Transcript   p 86, activity 1a

- Annika, du wohnst in der Stadt - in Wesel. Was gibt es in Wesel?
- Also, es gibt ein großes Einkaufszentrum und es gibt viele Geschäfte. Und ein Fußballstadion - ja, es gibt ein modernes Fußballstadion ... und auch ein neues hotel. Man kann auch Sehenswürdigkeiten besichtigen - es gibt alte Gebäude ...
- Welche Gebäude?

- Es gibt ein Museum und einen Dom. Ja, und eine Tankstelle, ein Krankenhaus ...
- Gibt es auch einen Park?
- Ja, es gibt einen schönen Park - man kann dort Fußball spielen oder man kann ein Picknick machen. Es gibt auch eine Sparkasse und einen tollen Zoo.

AT 2.3 **1b** *Du wohnst in Wesel. Was gibt es in der Stadt? B wählt drei Bilder, A fragt. Dann ist A dran.* Pupils work together in pairs to create dialogues using the photos from activity 1a.

WB B Workbook activity B could be used here to consolidate the new vocabulary.

C 61 Activity 1 on copymaster 61 could also be used here to consolidate the new vocabulary.

Wiederholung
Adjektive + Akkusativ. This section revises adjective endings in the accusative after *einen/eine/ein* (i.e. mixed declension) and in the plural with no determiner (i.e. strong declension). Try to elicit the endings from the class with closed books before looking at this section.

2 *Sara beschreibt ihre Stadt. Kopiere ihren Brief und füll die Lücken aus.* Pupils copy out the letter and complete the adjectives with the correct accusative endings. Before they attempt the activity, elicit from the class that the pattern is *einen ...en, eine ...e, ein ...es*, and in the plural *...e*. Point out that the indefinite article (or the lack of an article because the word is plural) gives them all the information they need to select the right ending – they don't even need to understand the text!

Answers:

Ich wohne in Bocholt. Es gibt einen **interessanten** Park, ein **modernes** Krankenhaus und ein **neues** Einkaufszentrum. Es gibt auch **viele** Geschäfte und ein **großes** Hotel. Und es gibt einen **kleinen** Zoo, **alte** Gebäude und ein **schönes** Fußballstadion!

Follow-up activity. Pupils work together in pairs. Partner A writes five nouns from activity 1a on individual pieces of paper, e.g. *Einkaufszentrum, Geschäfte, Tankstelle, Sparkasse, Zoo.* Partner B writes five adjectives to describe buildings on individual pieces of paper, e.g. *groß, interessant, langweilig, schön, toll.* The pieces of paper are turned over (keeping the two sets separate). Partner A asks *Was gibt es in Wesel?* Partner B turns over one piece of paper from each pile and gives the appropriate answer, e.g. *Es gibt moderne Geschäfte.* Then partner B asks, and partner A answers. This is quite a challenging activity because it requires pupils to recognize the gender of each noun and apply the appropriate accusative ending to the adjective.

WB C Workbook activity C could be used here for revision of adjective endings.

C 61 Activity 2 on copymaster 61 could be used here for writing practice with adjective endings.

C 62A Copymaster 62A contains further information in English about adjective endings. Activity 1 can be used here for further practice of this point of grammar.

⊙♂
AT 1.2
AT 3.2
3 *Sven wohnt nicht gern in Wesel. Warum nicht? Hör gut zu und lies mit.* Pupils listen to the recording and look at the pictures and read the text in the book. Introduce the uncountable nouns *der Lärm, die Umweltverschmutzung, die Natur, der Verkehr,* asking, for example: *Gibt es in [Stadt] zu viel Lärm? Gibt es hier zu viel Umwelt-verschmutzung?*, etc.

> **Transcript**   p 87, activity 3
>
> – Und du, Sven? Wohnst du auch gern in Wesel?
> – Nein, ich wohne nicht gern in Wesel. Es gibt zu viele Autos und es gibt zu viel Lärm. Und es gibt zu viel Umweltverschmutzung. Es gibt keine Natur und es gibt auch zu viel Verkehr.

WB D Workbook activity D consolidates the vocabulary introduced in activity 3 above.

⊙♂
AT 1.4
AT 3.4
4a *Wie finden Uwe und Katja ihre Stadt Bremen? Hör gut zu. Kopiere die Sprechblasen und füll die Lücken aus.* Pupils listen to the recording and then complete the speech bubbles for Uwe and Katja. Point out to pupils that they should leave generous gaps when they copy out the speech bubbles, as some gaps are for more than one word. Check the answers with the class before pupils go on to activity 4b.

Answers:

Ich wohne nicht gern in Bremen, weil es **keine Natur** gibt. Und ich wohne nicht gern hier, weil es viele **Autos** und **viel Verkehr** gibt. Aber ich wohne gern hier, weil es **viel zu tun** gibt.

Ich wohne gern hier, weil es **alte Gebäude** gibt. Aber ich wohne nicht gern in Bremen, weil es viel **Umweltverschmutzung** gibt. Und ich wohne nicht gern hier, weil es **viel Lärm** gibt.

> **Transcript**   p 87, activity 4a
>
> Uwe
> – Ich wohne nicht gern in Bremen, weil es keine Natur gibt. Und ich wohne nicht gern hier, weil es viele Autos und viel Verkehr gibt. Aber ich wohne gern hier, weil es viel zu tun gibt.
>
> Katja
> – Ich wohne gern hier, weil es alte Gebäude gibt. Aber ich wohne nicht gern in Bremen, weil es viel Umweltverschmutzung gibt. Und ich wohne nicht gern hier, weil es viel Lärm gibt.

AT 2.3 **4b** *Ratespiel: Wer sagt was? A beginnt, dann ist B dran.* Pupils work together in pairs. Partner A reads out a statement from activity 4a. (Pupils will need the correct answers to activity 4a for this.) Partner B, without looking at his/her book, has to decide whether the statement is made by Uwe or Katja. Then partner B chooses a statement and partner A has to decide who says it.

WB E Workbook activity E could be used here for further consolidation of the language for discussing urban problems.

WB F Workbook activity F focuses on the advantages and disadvantages of living in town, and can form part of pupils' written records for continuous assessment purposes.

C 58 Activity 2 on copymaster 58 provides further listening practice on the advantages and disadvantages of town life, and could be used at this point.

Wiederholung

weil. This panel contains a reminder of how to join two statements together with *weil.* Before looking at the panel, you could ask pupils to underline or highlight all the verbs in activity 4a as a reminder that verbs go to the end after *weil.*

AT 4.2 *Noch mal! Schreib zwei Listen: Was findest du gut und schlecht in deiner Stadt?* Pupils write lists of the good and bad points of their town in note form, using language from the spread and other vocabulary for public buildings, etc. which they already know. If they don't live in a town, ask them to write about a town they know well.

AT 4.4 *Extra! Deine Stadt hat eine neue Website und macht dort eine Umfrage: „Wohnst du gern hier? Warum (nicht)?"* *Schreib eine E-Mail an deine Stadt.* This is an independent writing activity: pupils write an e-mail explaining why they like/don't like living in their town. Encourage them to use *Ich wohne (nicht) gern in [Stadt], weil ...* + verb to the end. If they don't live in a town, ask them to write about a town they know well.

C 62A Copymaster 62A contains information in English about subordinate clauses with *weil.* Activity 2 can be used here for further writing practice with *weil.*

C 60 Activity 1 on copymaster 60 provides further reading practice on the advantages and disadvantages of town life (using *weil*), and could be set for homework.

Ich wohne gern auf dem Land
pages 88–89

Objectives
• Describe the countryside
• Give your opinion about living in the country

Key language
Es gibt viele Bäume/Blumen/Eichhörnchen/Frösche/Igel/ Schmetterlinge/Schnecken/Seen/Spinnen/Vögel
Ich wohne gern/lieber auf dem Land weil es ...
Ich wohne nicht gern auf dem Land weil es ...
... sehr ruhig ist.
... viel Natur/viele Tiere gibt.
... keinen Lärm/keinen Verkehr gibt.
... keine Umweltverschmutzung/keine Autos gibt.
... keine Disco/kein Jugendzentrum/kein Kino gibt.
... langweilig ist

National Curriculum PoS
statements 1a, 1b, 1c, 2a, 2b, 2c, 2d, 2e, 2h, 2i, 3d, 3e, 5a, 5c, 5d, 5f, 5i

Materials
- Students' Book pages 88–89
- Cassette 3 side A
- Workbook pages 67–69
- Copymasters 55, 58, 59, 61, 63

C 55

Preparatory work
Use the pictures from copymasters 55 copied onto an OHT, or as flashcards, to introduce the vocabulary for nature and wildlife. (For general advice on using copymaster visuals, see page 12 of the introduction to this book.) Once the vocabulary has been introduced, you could ask for personal reactions, as establishing an emotional connection will help to make the vocabulary more memorable. T: *Wer mag Eichhörnchen? Wer mag Blumen? Wer mag Schnecken?*, etc.

AT 1.3
AT 3.1

1 *Was gibt es auf dem Land? Hör gut zu und finde die richtige Reihenfolge für die Fotos.* Pupils listen to the recording and look at the photos and captions, before putting the photos in the sequence in which the nature items are mentioned on the recording.

Answers: a, b, h, j, d, e, g, f, c, i

> **Transcript**   p 88, activity 1
>
> Ich wohne in einem kleinen Dorf auf dem Land. Es gibt viele Bäume. Es gibt viele Blumen – hmmm. Es gibt auch viele Seen. Ja, und es gibt viele Tiere: Es gibt viele Vögel, es gibt viele Frösche und es gibt viele Igel. Es gibt auch viele Schnecken, viele Schmetterlinge und viele Eichhörnchen. Und es gibt viele Spinnen – iih!

AT 2.2

Noch mal! Macht 10 Karten mit den Bildern von Übung 1a. A nimmt eine Karte und fragt, B antwortet. Dann ist B dran. Working in pairs, pupils draw a picture of each of the items from activity 1a onto individual pieces of card or paper. Alternatively, they can use copymaster 55. The pupils then take it in turns to pick up a card and ask their partner what it shows. Draw pupils' attention to the form of the question and the answer: *Was sind das? Das sind Frösche*, etc. Contrast this with the singular: *Was ist das? Das ist ein Frosch.*

AT 2.4

Extra! Macht 10 Karten mit den Bildern von Übung 1a. A nimmt eine Karte und beschreibt das Wort, B rät. Dann ist B dran. Working in pairs, pupils draw a picture of each of the items from activity 1a onto individual pieces of card or paper. Alternatively, they can use copymaster 55. The 'cards' are shuffled and laid face down. Partner A takes a card and describes the picture on it. Pupil B has to guess what it is. Draw pupils' attention to the form of the answer: *Das sind Frösche*, etc. Contrast this with the singular: *Das ist ein Frosch.*

C 58

Activity 1 on copymaster 58 can be used at this point for consolidation of some of the new vocabulary introduced above, and also for revision of some 'urban' vocabulary from the previous spread.

AT 2.3

2 *Warum wohnst du gern auf dem Land? Benutzt die 10 Karten von Noch mal!/Extra! A fragt, B nimmt eine Karte und antwortet. Dann ist B dran.* Pupils work together in pairs to create dialogues. Partner A asks *Warum wohnst du gern auf dem Land?* Partner B answers with a sentence including *weil*, using one of the cards from *Noch mal!/Extra!* above as a prompt. Then the roles are reversed.

C 59

Activity 1 on copymaster 59 provides further dialogue practice on the advantages and disadvantages of country and town life, and could be used at this point.

C 61

Activity 3 on copymaster 61 provides further writing practice on the same topic.

AT 4.1

3 *Was ist der Singular für die Pluralwörter? Schreib die Wörter auf. (Schreib auch der, die, das auf.)* Pupils use their dictionaries to find the singular forms and genders of the plural nouns in the box (key vocabulary from activity 1 above).

Answers:

Bäume – der Baum; Blumen – die Blume; Eichhörnchen – das Eichhörnchen; Igel – der Igel; Vögel – der Vogel; Seen – der See; Schmetterlinge – der Schmetterling; Frösche – der Frosch; Schnecken – die Schnecke; Spinnen – die Spinne

WB G

Workbook activity G consolidates the wildlife/nature vocabulary (plural nouns) introduced above, and provides another opportunity to create dialogues with *warum?* and *weil*.

AT 3.3

4a *Lies die Sätze – sind sie positiv oder negativ?* Pupils read the sentences and categorize them as positive or negative.

Answers:

Positive: 2, 3, 5, 7   Negative: 1, 4, 6, 8

AT 4.4

4b *„Ich wohne gern/nicht gern auf dem Land, weil ..."* *Schreib neue Sätze mit den Sätzen von Übung 4a.* Pupils write sentences with *weil* incorporating the sentences from activity 4a. Elicit from the class what changes in word order will be necessary when *weil* is inserted before each of the sentences.

Answers:

(Suggestions only.)
Ich wohne gern auf dem Land, weil es viel Natur und viele Tiere gibt./weil es sehr ruhig ist/keinen Lärm gibt./weil es keine Umweltverschmutzung gibt./weil es keinen Verkehr gibt.

Ich wohne nicht gern auf dem Land, weil es kein Jugendzentrum gibt./weil es keine Disco gibt./weil es sehr langweilig ist./weil es kein Schwimmbad gibt.

WB H

Workbook activity H consolidates the language for discussing advantages and disadvantages of living in the country.

Tipp
Deine Meinung mit Takt sagen. In this section, pupils are shown ways in which they can express their opinion

tactfully and politely, even when they disagree with someone. Go through the *positiv* and *negativ* speech bubbles individually:

Positiv. Point out that it is often best to avoid outright contradiction – nobody likes to be told he/she is wrong! Pupils can agree with what their conversation partner says, and then go on to introduce a counter-argument.

Negativ. Point out that sometimes an outright contradiction is called for – but it should be made in a polite tone of voice.

As a first step in practising the structures shown here, make a simple statement, e.g. *Ich finde Wesel langweilig,* and invite individual pupils to agree or disagree with it, each using a different expression.

AT 2.4 **5** *Warum wohnst du lieber/nicht gern auf dem Land? Macht Dialoge mit den Informationen von Übung 4a.* Pupils work together to create dialogues using the sentences from activity 4 above. Partner A reads out one of his/her *weil*-sentences from activity 4b, and partner B responds with agreement/polite disagreement and a counter-argument. Less able pupils could prepare by arranging their sentences into argument and counter-argument before starting the speaking activity, e.g.

Ich wohne gern auf dem Land, weil es viel Natur und viele Tiere gibt.
Ich wohne nicht gern auf dem Land, weil es kein Jugendzentrum gibt.

Ich wohne gern auf dem Land, weil es sehr ruhig ist/keinen Lärm gibt.
Ich wohne nicht gern auf dem Land, weil es keine Disco gibt.

Ich wohne gern auf dem Land, weil es keine Umweltverschmutzung gibt.
Ich wohne nicht gern auf dem Land, weil es kein Schwimmbad gibt.

Ich wohne gern auf dem Land, weil es keinen Verkehr gibt.
Ich wohne nicht gern auf dem Land, weil es sehr langweilig ist.

C 63 Copymaster 63 contains further advice in English on giving opinions, and activity 2 provides further dialogue practice on this topic.

🔊 **6a** *Lea und Daniel wohnen auf dem Land. Wer sagt was? Hör gut zu und finde die passenden Sätze von Übung 4a.* Pupils listen to the recording and note which speaker gives which reasons from activity 4a above.

AT 1.4

Answers:

Lea: 6, 1, 4, 8   Daniel: 3, 2, 5, 7

Transcript   p 89, activities 6a and 6b

– Lea, du wohnst auf dem Land. Wohnst du gern hier?
– Nein! Ich wohne nicht gern hier, weil es langweilig ist. Es gibt nichts zu tun.
– Und du, Daniel?

– Also, ich wohne lieber auf dem Land, weil es keinen Lärm gibt – es ist sehr ruhig hier! Das finde ich gut. Und ich wohne gerne hier, weil es viele Tiere gibt – und weil es viel Natur gibt.
– Ja, aber was gibt es für die Jugend?
– Nichts! Ich wohne nicht gern hier, weil es kein Jugendzentrum gibt – und weil es keine Disco gibt.
– Aber ich wohne lieber hier, weil es keine Umweltverschmutzung gibt. Es gibt viele schöne Seen hier.
– Ja, es gibt viele schöne Seen – aber was ist im Winter? Ich wohne nicht gern auf dem Land, weil es kein Hallenbad gibt!
– Also, ich wohne gern auf dem Land, weil es keine Autos und keinen Verkehr gibt.

Tipp

Eine Zusammenfassung schreiben. This section focuses on how to write a summary of a spoken or written text.

🔊 **6b** *Warum wohnt Lea nicht gern auf dem Land? Hör noch einmal zu und schreib eine kurze Zusammenfassung.* Pupils listen to the recording again and write a summary of Lea's opinions. Break the task down into stages as described in the *Tipp* panel:

1 Write down key words. Stop the tape after each of Lea's utterances for pupils to do this, then elicit key words from the whole class and write them on the board/OHT.

2 Combine several sentences/phrases/words into one shorter, summarizing sentence. Pupils do this from their notes. More able pupils can do this individually; with less able pupils, do this as a whole-class activity. Now play the recording again so that pupils can check that they have got all the essential points.

3 Write the summary. Pupils can do this as an individual activity.

C 63 Copymaster 63 contains further advice in English about writing a summary, and activity 1 provides further practice of summarizing a written text.

AT 4.4 **7** *Schreib ein Werbeplakat für ein Jugendzentrum auf dem Land oder in der Stadt: „Ich wohne gern auf dem Land/in der Stadt, weil ..." Wie viele Sätze kannst du schreiben?* Pupils write and design a poster advertising the virtues of living in town/in the country. The *Hilfe* box contains a basic list of sentences to get them started. Encourage pupils to think of as many reasons as possible. The poster could be drawn by hand or designed on computer, and illustrated with photos or drawings.

WB I Workbook activity I consolidates language for discussing advantages and disadvantages of living in the country and can form part of pupils' written records for continuous assessment purposes.

Was ist Umwelt?
pages 90–91

Objectives
- Identify names and items linked to the environment
- Talk about the most serious problems for the environment

Key language
Was ist das größte Problem?
Ich finde/glaube/denke …
… ist/sind das größte Problem.
… ist gefährlicher/schlimmer/umweltfeindlicher als …
… ist am gefährlichsten/schlimmsten/ umweltfeindlichsten.
der Müll/Wald/Verkehr/Lärm
die Erde/Luft
das Wasser
die Fabriken/Zigaretten/Pflanzen/Kraftwerke/ Pestizide

National Curriculum PoS
statements 1a, 1b, 1c, 2a, 2b, 2c, 2d, 3e, 5a, 5c, 5d, 5f, 5i

Materials
- Students' Book pages 90–91
- Cassette 3 side A
- Workbook pages 69–71
- Copymasters 56, 62B

Preparatory work
C 56

Explain that the word *Umwelt* is made up of two parts: *um* = 'around' and *Welt* = 'world'. Ask pupils what they think the word might mean in English.

Use the relevant pictures from copymaster 56 copied onto an OHT, or as flashcards, to introduce the vocabulary for environmental problems. (For general advice on using copymaster visuals, see page 12 of the introduction to this book.)

AT 1.3

1 *Was ist Umwelt? Hör gut zu und finde die richtige Reihenfolge für die Bilder.* Pupils listen to the recording and look at the pictures and captions in the book. They then put the pictures into the sequence in which they are mentioned on the recording. Point out the word *Kraftwerk*. This is made up of two parts: *Kraft* = 'power' and *Werk* = 'works' or 'industrial site'; so what is the equivalent term in English?

Follow-up activities. Ask pupils for translations of the individual terms to check comprehension: T: *Wie heißt „Wald" auf Englisch? Wie heißt „Kraftwerke" auf Englisch?*, etc.

Ask the class to close their books, then pose the question: *Was ist Umwelt?* Elicit as many answers as possible from the class. (Pupils could also answer with nouns from the previous spread, e.g. *Seen, Bäume, Schnecken, Vögel.*) Alternatively, do this as a pairwork activity.

Answers: n, c, e, j, b, i, g, l, m, h, d, a, f, k

Transcript   p 90, activity 1

Umwelt ist … Erde, Fabriken, Kraftwerke, Lärm, Luft, Menschen, Müll, Pestizide, Pflanzen, Tiere, Verkehr, Wald, Wasser, Zigaretten.

WB J, K
WB L, M
Workbook activities J–M consolidate the vocabulary introduced in activity 1 above.

2 *Probleme für die Umwelt. Hör gut zu und lies mit.*
AT 1.3
AT 3.3
Pupils listen to the recording and follow the text in the book. This text introduces comparatives and superlatives of adjectives. Point out *umweltfeindlich-*: pupils already know that *Umwelt* means 'environment'; *ein Feind* is an enemy, and *-lich* is just an ending to make a noun into an adjective. Ask pupils for suggestions as to what the adjective might mean. Establish the meaning of *gefährlich*, reminding pupils of its use in the photo story (p. 84): *Skateboardfahren ist zu gefährlich für Kinder.*

Transcript   p 90, activity 2

– Ich finde, Müll ist schlimmer als Verkehr. Kraftwerke sind am schlimmsten - sie sind sehr gefährlich für die Umwelt!
Marieke (15)

– Fabriken sind umweltfeindlicher als Müll, denke ich. Aber Pestizide sind am umweltfeindlichsten - für Menschen, Tiere und Pflanzen.
Thomas (16)

– Ich glaube, Zigaretten sind gefährlicher als Lärm. Und was ist am gefährlichsten? Fabriken - sie sind das größte Problem!
Anne (14)

WB N
Workbook activity N consolidates the vocabulary for discussing environmental problems and could be used at this point.

Grammatik im Fokus
Komparative und Superlative. This section focuses on the formation and use of the comparative and superlative forms of adjectives. The comparative and the attributive form of the superlative (*der/die/das -ste*) should present little difficulty, being very similiar to the English '-er' comparative and '-est' superlative respectively. Explain that *groß* is one of a small number of adjectives which take an *Umlaut* in the comparative and superlative forms – this is not a general feature.

For the predicative form of the superlative (*am -sten*), you could explain that Germans always say that something is 'at the biggest/worst', etc.

To establish the patterns of the comparative and superlative firmly in pupils' minds, practise each form in turn with familiar short adjectives, e.g. *schön, klein, schlimm, toll*, avoiding those with irregularities (e.g. *gut, kurz*, etc.).

Only if the question arises, point out that there is no comparative with *mehr* in German, analogous to 'more dangerous', etc. in English – no matter how long the adjective, German adds *-er* to the end.

3a *Schau die Texte in Übung 2 an. Finde alle Sätze mit -er als und am -sten und schreib zwei Listen.* Pupils analyse the text in activity 2 for comparative and superlative forms.

Answers:

schlimmer als; umweltfeindlicher als; gefährlicher als am schlimmsten; am umweltfeindlichsten; am gefährlichsten

3b *Was denken diese Schüler? Was ist -er als ...? Was ist am ...-sten? Schreib Sätze.* Pupils use the key words to construct sentences using comparative and superlative adjectives. Point out that *schlecht(e)sten* usually has an extra -e- to help pronunciation.

Answers:

1 Verkehr ist schlimmer als Müll. Aber Lärm ist am schlimmsten.
2 Zigaretten sind gefährlicher als Fabriken. Aber Kraftwerke sind am gefährlichsten.
3 Müll ist umweltfeindlicher als Lärm. Aber Verkehr ist am umweltfeindlichsten.
4 Zigaretten sind schlechter als Pestizide. Aber Fabriken sind am schlecht(e)sten.

WB 0 Workbook activity O provides further practice of comparative and superlative forms.

C 62B Copymaster 62B contains further information in English about the comparative and superlative, and activity 1 provides further practice of these forms.

4 *Hör gut zu. Was glauben Jasmin, Atalay, Annika und Sven? Wer sagt was?* Pupils listen to the recording and identify which of the speakers says each of the sentences. This activity introduces ways of putting forward an idea as one's opinion, not as fact, using *Ich finde/glaube/denke, ...* or *..., finde/glaube/denke ich.* Referring back to page 89, you could point out that this is a good way of 'softening' a difference of opinion.

AT 1.4

Answers: Jasmin: 1, 8; Atalay: 5, 3; Annika: 4, 6; Sven: 2, 7

Transcript   p 91, activity 4

– Jasmin, was ist das größte Problem für die Umwelt?
– Also, ich finde, Verkehr ist das größte Problem. Verkehr ist schlimmer als Müll. Autos sind am schlimmsten – sie sind am gefährlichsten für Menschen und Tiere!
– Was glaubst du, Atalay – was ist das größte Problem für die Umwelt?
– Ich denke, Fabriken sind viel umweltfeindlicher als Verkehr – Verkehr ist nicht so schlimm. Aber Kraftwerke sind am gefährlichsten, glaube ich.
– Und du, Annika? Was denkst du – was ist das größte Problem?
– Pestizide sind das schlimmste Problem – ja, Pestizide. Und Zigaretten – Zigaretten sind schlimmer als ... als Lärm oder Müll. Zigaretten sind total ungesund!
– Was ist das größte Problem für die Umwelt, Sven – was glaubst du?
– Also, ich finde, Lärm ist am umweltfeindlichsten. Kraftwerke sind auch schlimm – sie sind gefährlicher als Zigaretten, denke ich.

AT 4.3   **5a** *Du bist dran! Was ist das größte Problem für die Umwelt? Was ist nicht so gefährlich – und was ist schlimmer? Was glaubst du? Mach Notizen.* Pupils make notes about their own views on the environmental problems introduced on this spread, using the comparative and superlative.

AT 2.4   **5b** *Macht Dialoge mit deinen Notizen von Übung 5a.* Pupils work together in pairs to create dialogues using their notes from activity 5a.

AT 4.4   **5c** *Eine Jugend-Umweltgruppe fragt auf ihrer Website: „Was ist das größte Problem für die Umwelt?" Schreib eine E-Mail mit deinen Notizen (Übung 5a).* Pupils now use their notes from activity 5a as the basis for an e-mail.

Ich bin umweltfreundlich!
pages 92–93

Objectives
* Talk about actions that help or damage the environment

Key language
Ich kaufe Recyclingpapier.
Ich kaufe Cola in Dosen.
Ich fahre mit dem Rad.
Ich nehme Plastiktüten.
Ich bringe Flaschen zum Altglascontainer.
Ich trenne meinen Müll.
Ich bringe Altpapier zum Altpapiercontainer.
Ich bade jeden Tag.
Ich fahre mit dem Auto.
Ich trenne meinen Müll nicht.

National Curriculum PoS
statements 1a, 1b, 1c, 2a, 2b, 2c, 2d, 3e, 5a, 5c, 5d, 5f, 5i

Materials
* Students' Book pages 92–93
* Cassette 3 side A
* Workbook pages 71–73
* Copymasters 58, 59, 60

AT 1.3
AT 3.3

1a *Hör gut zu und finde die passenden Fotos.* Pupils listen to the recording and match the pictures to the speakers.

Follow-up activity. Pupils work together in pairs to decide how they would translate each of the sentences into English. Although there are several new items of vocabulary, the photo should make the meaning clear in each case.

Answers: 1 c; 2 i; 3 d; 4 e; 5 f; 6 h; 7 g; 8 b; 9 a; 10 j

Transcript   p 92, activity 1a

1 – Ich fahre mit dem Rad.
2 – Ich fahre mit dem Auto.
3 – Ich nehme Plastiktüten.
4 – Ich bringe Flaschen zum Altglascontainer.

> 5 – Ich trenne meinen Müll.
> 6 – Ich bade jeden Tag.
> 7 – Ich bringe Altpapier zum Altpapiercontainer.
> 8 – Ich kaufe Cola in Dosen.
> 9 – Ich kaufe Recyclingpapier.
> 10 – Ich trenne meinen Müll nicht.

T3.3 **1b** *Was ist umweltfreundlich* ✔ *und was ist umweltfeindlich* ✘*? Was glaubst du? Lies noch einmal die Sätze in Übung 1a und schreib zwei Listen.* Pupils categorize the actions described in activity 1a as environmentally friendly or harmful to the environment. To familiarize pupils with the new expressions, ask them to write out the sentences in full, rather than just writing down the appropriate letter for each. (They check each other's answers in activity 1c.)

Answers:

umweltfreundlich:
Ich kaufe Recyclingpapier.
Ich fahre mit dem Rad.
Ich bringe Flaschen zum Altglascontainer.
Ich trenne meinen Müll.
Ich bringe Altpapier zum Altpapiercontainer.

umweltfeindlich:
Ich kaufe Cola in Dosen.
Ich nehme Plastiktüten.
Ich bade jeden Tag.
Ich fahre mit dem Auto.
Ich trenne meinen Müll nicht.

AT 2.4 **1c** *Ist alles richtig? Macht Dialoge.* Pupils work together in pairs to create dialogues using their lists for activity 1b.

C 58 Activity 3 on copymaster 58 contains further listening practice to consolidate the new vocabulary from activity 1 above.

Background information

In Germany, almost everyone sorts household rubbish. Paper and cardboard go in the *blaue Tonne*; raw kitchen waste such as vegetable peelings, and other compostable material such as teabags, coffee filter papers, etc. go into the *grüne Tonne* or *Biotonne*; plastic packaging, plastic bottles, cans and aluminium foil go into the *gelbe Tonne* or *gelbe Sack*, and of course non-returnable glass bottles go into the *Altglascontainer*. Many bottles are taken back to the shops, as refundable deposits on bottles are very common in Germany. The remaining rubbish, *der Restmüll*, is disposed of in the normal way. Even in public places like railway stations there are different bins for different kinds of rubbish – it is becoming less and less acceptable just to throw everything into one bin.

AT 4.4 **2a** *Schreib ein Umwelttagebuch: Was machst du immer, oft, manchmal, selten oder nie?* Pupils combine the adverbs of frequency with the sentences from activity 1a to state how much or how little they do to protect the environment.

C 59 Activity 2 on copymaster 59 provides dialogue practice on *Was machst du für die Umwelt?* and could be used at this point in preparation for activity 2b below.

AT 2.4 **AT 4.3** **2b** *Mach eine Umfrage: „Was machst du wie oft?" Schreib die Resultate auf (z. B. mit dem Computer).* Pupils conduct a class survey based on their work in activity 2a. They then display the results of their survey in a visually attractive and clear way, e.g. as a pie chart or bar graph. They could draw graphics to represent each of the environmentally friendly/harmful activities.

WB P Workbook activity P consolidates the vocabulary for describing environmentally friendly/harmful behaviour, and could be used at this point.

3a *Hör gut zu und lies mit.* Pupils listen to the recording and follow the cartoon strip in the book.

AT 1.4

AT 3.4

> **Transcript** p 93, activity 3a
>
> – So viele Autos ... so viel Lärm! Und so viel Müll – das ist umweltfeindlich!
> – Diese Schule ist umweltfreundlich! Wir räumen den Schulhof auf!
> – Wir bringen Flaschen zum Altglascontainer!
> – Wir fahren mit dem Rad zur Schule!
> – Und was machst du für die Umwelt, Tom?
> – Ich? Ich bringe Altpapier zum Altpapiercontainer!
> – Tom!! Oh nein!!

AT 2.4 **3b** *Nehmt den Cartoon auf Kassette auf.* Pupils work together in groups to record their own version of the cartoon. Encourage them to rehearse first, and put as much expression into the recording as possible. The three speech bubbles with *wir* could be spoken in chorus by three or more pupils. Pupils might also like to include sound effects, e.g. traffic noises for the first scene, glass clinking for the third, bicycle bells for the fourth and a dull thud as Tom throws his school books into the recycling container in the final scene.

AT 3.3 **4a** *Hier sind weitere Sätze. Was glaubst du – was ist umweltfreundlich* ✔ *und was ist umweltfeindlich* ✘*?* Pupils read the statements and decide which of the actions described are environmentally friendly and which are harmful to the environment. They then do activity 4b to see whether their answers are correct or not.

Answers: 1 ✔; 2 ✔; 3 ✘; 4 ✘; 5 ✔; 6 ✔

4b *Ist alles richtig? Hör gut zu.* Pupils listen to the recording to find out whether their answers to activity 4a are correct.

AT 1.3

> **Transcript** p 93, activity 4b
>
> 1 – Ich kaufe Limonade in Recyclingflaschen. Das ist umweltfreundlich!
> 2 – Ich dusche jeden Morgen. Das ist umweltfreundlich!
> 3 – Ich bringe Flaschen zum Müll. Das ist umweltfeindlich!
> 4 – Ich kaufe neues weißes Papier. Das ist umweltfeindlich!
> 5 – Ich gehe immer zu Fuß. Das ist umweltfreundlich!
> 6 – Ich nehme Tüten aus Stoff. Das ist umweltfreundlich!

WB Q Workbook activity Q extends the theme 'Müll' to items not covered above.

WB R   In Workbook activity R, pupils write two or three sentences about what they do to help protect the environment. This activity can form part of pupils' written records for continuous assessment purposes.

C 60   Activity 2 on copymaster 60 provides more extensive reading comprehension on environmentally friendly behaviour and the urban and rural environments, and could be set as homework.

AT 4.3   *Noch mal! Macht ein Umweltplakat. Was ist umweltfreundlich – und was ist umweltfeindlich? Zeichnet Bilder und schreibt die Wörter auf.* Pupils work together in pairs to design an eco-poster with lists of environmentally friendly and environmentally harmful behaviour. They should draw pictures or find photos to illustrate each point. The poster could be designed on computer; alternatively, pupils might prefer to design an A4 leaflet or a web page. They could invent a symbol for '*umweltfreundlich*' (e.g. a smiley face or flower head) and a symbol for '*umweltfeindlich*' (e.g. skull-and-crossbones).

AT 4.4   *Extra! Was ist umweltfreundlich – und was ist umweltfeindlich? Schreib eine Broschüre für die Jugend-Umweltgruppe ‚Grüne Jugend'.* Pupils work together in pairs to design an eco-leaflet with statements about environmentally friendly and environmentally harmful behaviour. This could be illustrated: see *Noch mal!* above for ideas.

Gut gesagt!

Lange Wörter. This section focuses on the pronunciation of long words in German. Point out that almost all long words in German are in fact just short words joined together. So, when pupils come across long words, they should look for parts of the word that they recognize. This will help them to break up the word into manageable (and pronounceable!) chunks, rather than getting lost in a bewildering mass of letters. For example, how many smaller words can they recognize in *umweltfreundlich* or *Altpapiercontainer*?

Explain that once they have done this, they can start to break down the word into syllables – basic units of sound with one vowel and probably one or more consonants. These are the 'building blocks' that all words are made up from. Can they break up *umweltfreundlich* and *Altpapiercontainer* into syllables? How many are there?

Having understood how the word is put together, the final step is to learn the rhythm of how it is pronounced: in all words, some syllables are stressed – spoken more loudly than others. Now play the recording for activity 5. Where does the stress lie in each word? Can they tap out the rhythm on their desks?

[cassette icon]   **5** *Hör gut zu und wiederhole.* Pupils listen to the recording and then repeat the words. They could chant them chorally and then you could ask individual pupils to pronounce each word, paying particular attention to the stress. Encourage pupils to practise these words at home by themselves.

Transcript   p 93, activity 5

umweltfreundlich
Limonade
Umweltverschmutzung
Recyclingflaschen
Plastiktüten
umweltfeindlich
Altpapiercontainer
Zigaretten

Thema im Fokus
pages 94–95

National Curriculum PoS
statements 1c, 2c, 2d, 3d, 3e, 4c, 4d, 5a, 5c, 5d, 5f, 5g, 5h, 5i

Materials
- Students' Book pages 94–95
- Cassette 3 side A
- Copymaster 57

The final spread of each unit provides further reading practice, leading into a project outcome for the unit. See pages 8–9 of the introduction to this book for general notes on how to use these pages. The text '*Schule im Garten*' is provided for pupils to read for personal interest, but will also provide useful ideas and vocabulary for the subsequent activities. Key words are provided in the box, but pupils will also need to use their dictionaries or the *Vokabular* at the back of the Students' Book to identify other unfamiliar vocabulary.

1 *Macht eine Umweltschutz-Aktion in der Schule!* Pupils work together in groups to plan an environmental campaign for their school. The aim could be to produce a useful plan on a realistic scale which can be put into practice. However, you may prefer to make the campaign a purely theoretical exercise. If the aim is to carry out the plan, the simplest and most manageable form is probably the litter-gathering exercise given as an example. Instead of being a 'one-off' action, the campaign could be spread over a longer period of time, e.g. providing separate containers for different kinds of rubbish for a week and recording how much rubbish is gathered each day in each container. The text '*Schule im Garten*' contains further ideas.

AT 4.3–4   **a** *Was wollt ihr machen? Was ist wichtig? Schreibt einen Plan.* Pupils draw up an action plan of things they are going to do.

AT 4.2   **b** *Was braucht ihr für die Aktion? Schreibt eine Liste.* Pupils draw up a list of things they need for the campaign. This may involve some dictionary work or vocabulary help from the teacher or language assistant.

AT 4.4–5   **c** *Wann macht ihr die Aktion? Fragt euren Lehrer/eure Lehrerin und schreibt ein Einladungsposter.* Pupils agree a time for the campaign to take place (if the campaign is not to be put into practice, pupils can choose any time) and work in pairs to design a poster inviting their fellow pupils to take part.

2 *Nach der Aktion: Macht ein Umweltschutz-Poster für die Schule.* After the (real or imaginary) campaign, pupils work together in groups to design a poster to foster on-going environmental awareness in the school. All of the activities 2a–2d can form part of the poster. Alternatively, pupils could create a web page. If pupils have sufficient expertise to set this up, it could have hyperlinks from a main menu to the various sections, external links to environmental websites such as Friends of the Earth, and simple animations as well as still graphics and photos.

AT 4.2 **a** *Trennt den Müll und notiert die Resultate. Schreibt die Resultate mit dem Computer auf.* Pupils record what was achieved (or invent results if the campaign is imaginary), in tabular form as shown, or in another format, such as a pie chart or bar chart. Different groups of pupils could compete to find the most interesting/clearest way of presenting the results (e.g. as a graphic of a rubbish bin with layers of the various kinds of rubbish).

AT 4.1 **b** *Was ist alles Umwelt? Schreibt ein Umweltschutz-ABC und zeichnet Bilder.* Pupils create their own illustrated conservation/environment ABC.

AT 4.3 **c** *Was ist umweltfreundlich – und was ist umweltfeindlich? Findet oder zeichnet Bilder und schreibt Sätze.* Pupils write sentences to show environmentally friendly and environmentally harmful behaviour, and illustrate these with drawings or photos. More able pupils could research new language (e.g. *das Licht ausschalten*); less able pupils could confine themselves to the language introduced in this unit.

AT 2.3–4
AT 4.2 **d** *Macht eine Schulumfrage. Fragt: „Was ist das größte Problem für die Umwelt?" und schreibt die Resultate auf (z. B. mit dem Computer).* Pupils conduct a survey asking their fellow pupils (in the class, year, or school as a whole) what they think are the most serious environmental problems. If the whole year or school is to participate, then the survey will need to be in English, and the results translated into German.

Other possibilities would be for pupils to e-mail any German contacts they have, or their German partner school, or post their questions on an appropriate German-language bulletin board/newsgroup.

For the sake of simplicity, you may wish to restrict the options offered in the questionnaire to the vocabulary introduced in this unit. However, to get a more representative set of options (and to stretch more able pupils with more challenging vocabulary work) pupils could ask a small 'test group' of individuals *Was ist das größte Problem für die Umwelt?* **without** providing a list of options to choose from. Their replies could then form the basis for the list of options offered in the full survey.

Kannst du ... ?

The end-of-unit summary is a checklist for pupils. See page 8 of the introduction to this book for ideas on how to use the checklist.

C 57 Copymaster 57 provides a useful reference for pupils revising the language of this unit.

Noch mal!-Seite Einheit 7
page 134

National Curriculum PoS
statements 1a, 1b, 1c, 2a, 2b, 2c, 2d, 5a, 5i

Materials
- Students' Book page 134
- Cassette 3 side A

This revision page is intended for less able pupils. It reinforces the basic vocabulary and structures from the unit, and it can be used by pupils who experienced difficulty in completing some of the activities within the unit, or as alternative homework activities.

AT 3.2 **1a** *Was gibt es in deiner Stadt? Finde die passenden Bilder für die Sätze.* This activity relates to pages 86–87. Pupils match the pictures of public buildings and other urban features to the phrases.

Answers: 1 f; 2 c; 3 e; 4 d; 5 b; 6 a

AT 2.2 **1b** *B wählt drei Bilder, A fragt. Dann ist A dran.* Pupils work together in pairs to create dialogues with *Was gibt es ... ? Es gibt ...* , using the pictures from activity 1a as cues.

AT 1.4 **2a** *Meike und Stefan wohnen auf dem Land. Warum wohnen sie gern/nicht gern auf dem Land? Hör gut zu und mach Notizen.* Activity 2 relates to pages 88–89. In activity 2a, pupils listen to the recording and take notes about the (dis)advantages of living in the country.

Answers:

Meike: viel Natur, viele Tiere, keinen Lärm/ruhig, keine Umweltverschmutzung, kein Verkehr/keine Autos

Stefan: langweilig, keine Disco, kein Jugendzentrum, kein Schwimmbad

---

Transcript   p 134, activity 2a

– Meike, du wohnst auf dem Land. Wohnst du gern auf dem Land?
– Ja, ich wohne gern auf dem Land, weil es hier viel Natur gibt. Und es gibt auch viele Tiere: Vögel, Frösche, Eichhörnchen ...
– Und du, Stefan? Wohnst du auch gern auf dem Land?
– Nein! Ich wohne nicht gern hier, weil es langweilig ist. Es gibt zum Beispiel keine Disco – das ist schlecht.
– Ja, aber es gibt hier keinen Lärm – es ist sehr ruhig hier! Das ist doch gut, oder?
– Also, ich wohne nicht gern hier, weil es kein Jugendzentrum gibt.
– Und ich wohne lieber auf dem Land, weil es keine Umweltverschmutzung gibt. Und es gibt keine Autos und keinen Verkehr.
– Ja, aber es gibt hier auf dem Land kein Schwimmbad. Das finde ich blöd.

AT 2.4 **2b** *Warum wohnen Meike und Stefan gern/nicht gern auf dem Land? A fragt, B antwortet. Dann ist B dran.*

Pupils work in pairs to create dialogues using their notes from activity 2a.

AT 3.3 **3a** *Lies die Website-Homepage der Jugend-Umweltgruppe 'Grüne Jugend'.* Activity 3 relates to pages 90–91. In activity 3a, pupils read the short web page text.

AT 4.3 **3b** *Schreib Sätze für die Homepage-Seite 2 (mit den Informationen von Übung 3a).* Pupils write sentences with the comparative and superlative forms of *schlimm* and *gefährlich* and the key words provided in the e-mail text.

Answers:

Müll ist am schlimmsten.
Verkehr ist schlimmer als Lärm.
Kraftwerke sind am gefährlichsten.
Pestizide sind gefährlicher als Zigaretten.

AT 2.4 **4** *Was machst du für die Umwelt? Macht Dialoge.* This activity relates to pages 92–93. Pupils work together in pairs to create dialogues using the picture cues. Ask pupils what each of the pictures signifies, or elicit/suggest key words, before they attempt the activity, e.g.

Ich kaufe Recyclingpapier.
Ich fahre nicht mit dem Auto.
Ich dusche.
Ich bringe Altpapier zum Altpapiercontainer.
Ich fahre Rad.
Ich bringe Flaschen zum Altglascontainer.
Ich nehme Tüten aus Stoff.
Ich trenne meinen Müll.

Extra!-Seite Einheit 7
page 135

National Curriculum PoS
statements 1a, 1b, 1c, 2a, 2b, 2c, 2d, 3e, 5a, 5c, 5i

Materials
- Students' Book page 135
- Cassette 3 side A

This extension page is intended for more able pupils. It contains slightly longer and more complex materials, and it can be used by pupils who have completed other activities quickly or as alternative homework activities.

AT 2.4 **1** *Warum wohnst du gern/nicht gern in der Stadt? Macht Dialoge mit den Informationen.* This activity relates to pages 86–87. Pupils work together in pairs to create dialogues about the advantages and disadvantages of living in town with *Ich wohne (nicht) gern in der Stadt, weil …* using the picture cues. You may want to elicit key words/*weil*-clauses from pupils before they attempt the activity, e.g.

weil es viele Geschäfte gibt
weil es ein Fußballstadion gibt
weil es einen Zoo gibt
weil es viele Gebäude gibt
weil es viel Verkehr gibt

weil es kein Jugendzentrum gibt
weil es viel Lärm gibt
weil es keine Natur gibt

AT 3.4 **2a** *Lies Anjas Brief und beantworte die Fragen.* Activity 2 relates to pages 88–89. Pupils read the text and answer the comprehension questions. To avoid unnecessary repetition on the one hand and potential sentence structure problems on the other, ask pupils to write a separate *weil*-clause for each reason (questions 2 and 3).

Answers:

1 Sie wohnt in einem kleinen Dorf auf dem Land.
2 Sie wohnt gern hier, weil es keinen Verkehr gibt, weil es viel Natur gibt und weil es keinen Lärm gibt.
3 Sie wohnt nicht gern hier, weil es manchmal langweilig ist, weil es keine Disco gibt und weil es kein Hallenbad gibt.

AT 4.4 **2b** *Warum wohnst du lieber/nicht gern auf dem Land? Schreib einen Antwortbrief mit den Informationen unten.* Pupils write a letter in response to Anja's letter using the picture cues. Before they attempt the activity, you could elicit key words or *weil*-clauses, e.g.:

weil es viel Natur gibt
weil es keine Autos/keinen Verkehr gibt
weil es kein Kino gibt
weil es kein Jugendzentrum gibt
weil es keine Geschäfte gibt
weil es keine Fabriken gibt

AT 3.3 **3a** *Finde die passenden Wörter für die Sätze.* Activity 3 relates to pages 90–91. In activity 3a, pupils match the environment nouns in the box to the definitions. You could also ask them to supply the appropriate definite article.

Answers:

1 (das) Wasser; 2 (die – pl.) Pflanzen; 3 (der) Müll; 4 (die – pl.) Tiere; 5 (der) Verkehr; 6 (der) Lärm

AT 2.3 **3b** *A wählt ein Wort von Übung 3a und fragt: „Was ist das?", B sagt drei passende Wörter. Dann ist B dran.* Pupils work together in pairs to create dialogues using the nouns and definitions from activity 3a.

Follow-up activity. Pupils could go on to write their own definitions for other 'environment' nouns and challenge each other to find the correct noun to match each definition.

AT 1.4 **4a** *Was machen Annika und Sven für die Umwelt? Hör gut zu und mach Notizen.* Activity 4 relates to pages 92–93. In activity 4a, pupils listen to the recording and make notes. Point out to pupils that *nehmen* is irregular: *ich nehme – du nimmst, er/sie nimmt.*

Suggested answers:

Annika: fährt nicht mit dem Auto, fährt mit dem Rad, geht zu Fuß, nimmt Tüten aus Stoff, kauft Recyclingpapier, duscht

Sven: trennt seinen Müll, bringt Flaschen zum Altglascontainer, kauft Cola in Recyclingflaschen

> **Transcript** p 135, activity 4a
>
> – Annika, was machst du für die Umwelt?
> – Also, ich mache viel für die Umwelt. Ich fahre nie mit dem Auto: Ich fahre mit dem Rad, oder ich gehe zu Fuß.
> – Und du, Sven? Was machst du für die Umwelt?
> – Ich? Ich trenne meinen Müll zu Hause ...
> – Macht deine Familie das auch?
> – Ja klar! Wir trennen alle unseren Müll und wir bringen Flaschen zum Altglascontainer. Ja, und ich kaufe keine Cola in Dosen – ich kaufe Cola in Recyclingflaschen.
> – Das ist super! Und was machst du für die Umwelt beim Einkaufen, Annika?
> – Ich nehme keine Plastiktüten. Ich nehme Tüten aus Stoff. Ja, und für die Schule kaufe ich Recyclingpapier. Und was mache ich noch für die Umwelt? Ach ja: Ich bade nie – ich dusche lieber.

AT 4.4 **4b** *Die Jugend-Umweltorganisation der Stadt Wesel hat eine neue Website – das Thema der Homepage ist: ,Was tust du für die Umwelt?' Schreib mit deinen Notizen einen Artikel für Annika oder Sven.* Pupils use their notes for activity 4a to write a paragraph for Annika or Sven about what she/he does for the environment.

Workbook

Page 64

Use with page 85 in the Students' Book.

A1 *Hör gut zu und sing mit!* Pupils listen to the song and then sing along. This song is particularly good for pronunciation, as the words are chanted rather than sung. It may also encourage reluctant singers to take part!

> **Transcript** W 64, activity A1
>
> Busse und Gebäude
> Lärm und viele Leute
> Straßenbahnen, Motorräder
> Altpapier und Müll
>
> Blumen, Tiere, Bäume
> Lämmer in der Scheune
> Schmetterlinge, Seen, Wälder
> Erde, Wasser, Luft

AT 3.2 **A2** *Finde die passenden Bilder für jede Wortreihe.* Pupils write the number of the relevant line of the song next to each picture. The song contains a large proportion of new vocabulary, so this activity will need careful preparation. Ask the class which verse describes the town and which the country (the large pictures make this quite clear). T: *Zeilen eins bis vier: Ist das die Stadt oder das Land?*, etc. Now look at the vocabulary in more detail, asking pupils to pick out any words they recognize and say what they mean in English. They should recognize *Busse, Straßenbahnen* and *Wasser*, although they may need help to recognize that *Busse* is the plural of *Bus*. They should also be able to work out

Motorräder (if you give them *das Motorrad*), *Altpapier*, *Tiere* (if you remind them of *Haustiere* and *der/die Tierfreund/in*) and *Lämmer* (if you give them *das Lamm*).

This should be enough vocabulary to enable most pupils to complete the activity. Pupils should match the easiest lines first (those with vocabulary they can recognize) and then complete the others by a process of elimination. They could complete the activity in pairs before you elicit the correct answers from the whole class.

If you think that pupils require more support, look at pictures a–h with them and ask whether each picture is of the town or the country. T: *Zeilen eins bis vier: Ist das die Stadt oder das Land? ... Bild a: Ist das die Stadt oder das Land?*, etc. Once this has been established, pupils only have four lines to choose from for each picture.

Follow-up activity. You could now ask pupils what they think the new vocabulary in the song text means in English: *Gebäude, Lärm, Müll, Blumen, Bäume, Scheune, Schmetterlinge, Seen, Wälder, Erde* and *Luft* will all be unfamiliar, but most can be worked out by comparing the pictures a–h with the relevant lines of the song and discounting known vocabulary.

Answers: a 7; b 3; c 5; d 4; e 8; f 2; g 6; h 1

Pages 65–66

Use with pages 86–87 in the Students' Book.

AT 3.1 **B1** *Was gibt es in deiner Stadt? Schreib die Wörter richtig auf.* Activity B helps pupils to assimilate new vocabulary from activity 1 on page 86 of the Students' Book. In activity B1, pupils re-order the letters to form the words for various urban features, all of which are introduced in activity 1. As usual, they should do the easiest ones first. They may need to refer to the Students' Book for the more difficult ones, or look at the pictures in B2 below for clues. More able pupils could do this activity without reference to the Students' Book; this has the benefit that it reactivates much more vocabulary, as they search their memories for the solution, but it is also much more challenging and time-consuming.

Answers:

1 Krankenhaus; 2 Sparkasse; 3 Hotel; 4 Fußballstadion; 5 Geschäfte; 6 Zoo; 7 Gebäude; 8 Einkaufszentrum; 9 Tankstelle; 10 Park

AT 3.1 **B2** *Finde die passenden Bilder für die Wörter in Übung B1.* Pupils match the words from activity B1 to the pictures.

Answers: a 2; b 7; c 4; d 1; e 3; f 5; g 9; h 8; i 6; j 10

 B3 *Was gibt es alles in Münster? Hör gut zu und finde die richtige Reihenfolge für die Bilder in Übung B2.* Pupils
AT 1.4 listen to the recording and put the pictures in activity B2 into the sequence in which the items are mentioned.

Answers: c, f, h, b, e, g, j, i, d, a

Transcript   W 65, activity B3

– Markus, wohnst du in der Stadt?
– Ja, ich wohne in der Stadt – in Münster.
– Was gibt es in Münster?
– Also, Münster ist eine tolle Stadt! Es gibt ein
  Fußballstadion. Ich gehe jedes Wochenende ins
  Fußballstadion. Und man kann in Münster einkaufen –
  es gibt viele Geschäfte.
– Gibt es auch ein Einkaufszentrum?
– Ja, es gibt auch ein Einkaufszentrum am Stadtrand.
  Und man kann auch Sehenswürdigkeiten besichtigen –
  also, es gibt alte Gebäude …
– Aha … und was gibt es noch in Münster?
– Ein Hotel – es gibt ein Hotel am Bahnhof und es gibt
  auch eine Tankstelle. Ja, die Tankstelle ist neben der
  Schule. Ach ja, und es gibt einen Park – der Park ist
  super! Dort kann man Skateboard fahren. Tja, was gibt
  es noch in der Stadt? Oh, und es gibt einen Zoo im
  Park! Der Zoo ist sehr interessant. Ja, und es gibt auch
  ein Krankenhaus. Das Krankenhaus ist in der
  Stadtmitte. Und es gibt auch eine Sparkasse. Ja, das
  gibt es alles in Münster.

Transcript   W 66, activity C1

– Herzlich willkommen in Potsdam! Potsdam ist super –
  Potsdam ist toll! Und: Potsdam ist ganz in der Nähe
  von Berlin! Also: Kommen auch Sie nach Potsdam!
  Susi, du wohnst in der Stadt. Was gibt es alles in
  Potsdam?
– Also, Potsdam ist eine kleine Stadt, aber es gibt hier
  sehr viel: Man kann Sehenswürdigkeiten besichtigen,
  zum Beispiel alte Gebäude – ja, es gibt viele alte
  Gebäude. Und es gibt einen Park.
– Ja, das gibt es alles in Potsdam! Und der Park – ist
  das ein kleiner Park?
– Nein, der Park ist groß – es gibt einen sehr großen
  Park. Und es gibt ein neues Fußballstadion …
– Gibt es auch ein Einkaufszentrum?
– Ja, es gibt ein kleines Einkaufszentrum und es gibt
  schöne Geschäfte neben dem Einkaufszentrum.
– Und was gibt es noch in Potsdam?
– Ach, es gibt so viel … es gibt auch ein Hotel – ein
  modernes Hotel …
– Gibt es auch einen Zoo?
– Oh ja, es gibt einen interessanten Zoo. Ja, der Zoo ist
  super!
– Also, meine Damen und Herren, liebe Jugendlichen:
  Kommen auch Sie nach Potsdam

AT 2.3 **B4** *Was gibt es in Münster? A fragt und zeigt auf ein Bild von Übung B2, B antwortet. Dann ist B dran.* Pupils work together in pairs to create dialogues with *es gibt …,* using the pictures in activity B2 as cues.

 C1 *Potsdam ist eine tolle Stadt! Was gibt es dort – und wie ist alles? Hör gut zu und kreuz die passenden Wörter an.* Activity C focuses on the adjectives used to describe buildings and other urban features. In activity C1, pupils listen to the recording and put a cross against the adjectives which are used to describe each of the locations depicted in the table.

AT 1.4

Answers:

AT 2.3 **C2** *Ist alles richtig? A fragt, B antwortet.* Pupils work together in pairs to check their answers to activity C1 orally, at the same time practising the adjective endings (accusative after *ein* and accusative plural).

AT 3.2 **D** *Warum wohnt Tim nicht gern in Potsdam? Finde die passenden Bilder.* This activity consolidates vocabulary for urban problems (mostly uncountable nouns). Pupils match the pictures to the speech bubbles.

Answers: 1 c; 2 e; 3 b; 4 a; 5 d

	alt	groß	klein	modern	neu	interessant	schön
	✗						
			✗				
					✗		
							✗
				✗			
			✗				
		✗					

Page 67

Use with pages 87–88 in the Students' Book.

E *Warum wohnen Daniel und Kathi nicht gern in Rostock? Hör gut zu und füll die Tabelle aus.* This activity consolidates vocabulary for urban problems. Pupils listen to the recording and then put a cross against each of the problems mentioned by Daniel and Kathi.

Answers:

Daniel	✗	✗			
Kathi			✗	✗	✗

> **Transcript** W 67, activity E
>
> – Daniel, wohnst du gern in Rostock?
> – Nein, ich wohne nicht gern in Rostock, weil es keine Natur gibt.
> – Und du, Kathi? Warum wohnst du nicht gern in Rostock?
> – Also, ich wohne nicht gern hier, weil es viele Autos gibt. Das finde ich doof.
> – Ja, und ich wohne auch nicht gern hier, weil es viel Verkehr gibt. Das ist schlecht, finde ich.
> – Ich wohne auch nicht gern in Rostock, weil es viel Umweltverschmutzung gibt. Und ich wohne nicht gern hier, weil es viel Lärm gibt.

AT 4.4 **F** *Du bist dran! Wohnst du gern/nicht gern in der Stadt? Warum (nicht)?* Pupils use the picture prompts to give opinions about the advantages and disadvantages of living in town. This activity can form part of pupils' written records for continuous assessment purposes. See the general notes on pages 13–14 of the introduction to this book.

AT 4.1 **G1** *Was gibt es auf dem Land? Schreib die Wörter auf.* Activity G consolidates the wildlife/nature vocabulary (plural nouns) introduced in activity 1 on page 88 of the Students' Book. In activity G1, pupils label the pictures. Remind them not to forget *Umlauts* where they are required.

Answers:

a Vögel; b Frösche; c Schnecken; d Bäume;
e Schmetterlinge; f Igel; g Spinnen; h Blumen; i Seen;
j Eichhörnchen

AT 2.3 **G2** *Ist alles richtig? A wählt ein Bild, B antwortet. Dann ist B dran.* Pupils work together in pairs to check each other's answers to activity G1 orally, using *Was gibt es … ? Es gibt …*

Page 68

Use with pages 88–89 in the Students' Book.

AT 2.4 **G3** *Warum wohnst du gern auf dem Land? A fragt, B wählt ein Bild und antwortet mit Ich wohne gern hier, weil es … gibt. Dann ist B dran.* Pupils work together in

pairs to create dialogues with *warum?* and *weil*, using the pictures from activity G1 as cues.

H *„Ich wohne gern/nicht gern auf dem Land, weil …"* *Wer sagt was? Hör gut zu und schreib E (Erdal) oder A (Anna) auf.* This activity consolidates the language for discussing the advantages and disadvantages of living in the country. Pupils listen to the recording and decide which speaker mentions each advantage/disadvantage.

Answers: Erdal: c, f, g, d; Anna: a, e, b

> **Transcript** W 68, activity H
>
> – Erdal, du wohnst auf dem Land. Wohnst du gern hier?
> – Ja, ich wohne gern auf dem Land, weil es keinen Lärm gibt – es ist sehr ruhig hier! Das finde ich gut.
> – Und du, Anna? Wohnst du auch gern auf dem Land?
> – Nein, ich wohne nicht gern hier, weil es kein Jugendzentrum gibt. Das ist doof!
> – Na ja, das stimmt. Und ich wohne nicht gern hier, weil es keine Disco gibt. Aber Tanzen ist mein Lieblingssport!
> – Aber ich wohne gern auf dem Land, weil es viele Tiere gibt – und weil es viel Natur gibt. Das ist sehr schön.
> – Ja, und ich wohne gern hier, weil es keine Umweltverschmutzung gibt.
> – Ja, und keinen Verkehr! Ich wohne gern hier, weil es keinen Verkehr gibt.
> – Ja, okay, aber hier ist es oft langweilig! Also, ich wohne nicht gern auf dem Land, weil es kein Kino gibt!

AT 3.4 **I1** *Lies Inas Brief und die Sätze. Sind sie richtig oder falsch?* Activity I consolidates language for discussing advantages and disadvantages of living in the country. In activity I1, pupils read the letter and then decide whether the statements are true or false.

Answers:

1 falsch; 2 richtig; 3 richtig; 4 richtig; 5 falsch; 6 falsch

Page 69

Use with pages 89–90 in the Students' Book.

AT 4.4 **I2** *Du bist dran! Warum wohnst du gern/nicht gern auf dem Land? Schreib einen Brief so wie Ina mit den Informationen unten.* Pupils use the picture prompts to give opinions about the advantages and disadvantages of living in the country. This activity can form part of pupils' written records for continuous assessment purposes.

AT 3.1 **J1** *Was ist Umwelt? Finde die passenden Wörter für die Bilder.* Activity J consolidates the vocabulary introduced in activity 1 on page 90 of the Students' Book. In activity

J1, pupils find the appropriate noun 1–14 to label each of the items a–n in the picture.

a 7; b 3; c 5; d 4; e 10; f 2; g 6; h 14; i 1; j 13; k 11; l 12; m 9; n 8

AT 2.2 **J2** *Ratespiel: A wählt ein Wort und buchstabiert es, B rät das Wort. Dann ist B dran.* Pupils work together in pairs. Partner A chooses a word from activity J1 and spells it out, pausing after each letter for partner B to try to guess the word. After partner B guesses correctly, the roles are reversed.

Page 70

Use with page 90 in the Students' Book.

AT 3.1 **K** *Lies die Wörter in Übung J1. Welche Wörter sind im Plural – und welche sind im Singular? Schreib zwei Listen.* Pupils categorize the words from activity J1 into singular and plural, using their dictionaries as necessary.

Answers:

Singular: Wasser, Luft, Verkehr, Müll, Wald, Erde, Lärm; Plural: Menschen, Fabriken, Pflanzen, Kraftwerke, Zigaretten, Pestizide

AT 4.1 **L** *Finde den Singular für die Plural-Wörter in Übung K. Schau im Wörterbuch nach und schreib sie auf.* Pupils use their dictionaries to look up the singular forms of the plural nouns from activity K. You could also ask pupils to write the definite article for each noun.

Answers:

Menschen: (der) Mensch; Fabriken: (die) Fabrik; Pflanzen: (die) Pflanze; Kraftwerke: (das) Kraftwerk; Zigaretten: (die) Zigarette; Pestizide: (das) Pestizid

AT 3.1 **M1** *Welche Wörter sind was? Ordne sie unter die passenden Überschriften.* Activity M consolidates 'environmental' vocabulary and revises some general vocabulary. In M1, pupils put each word into the appropriate category.

Answers:

Lärm:	Kassettenrecorder, Verkehr, Autos
Menschen:	Kinder, Erwachsene, Jugendliche
Müll:	Papier, Chipstüten, Coladosen
Pflanzen:	Bäume, Gemüse, Blumen
Tiere:	Vögel, Pferde, Frösche
Wasser:	Mineralwasser, Seen, Schwimmbad

Page 71

Use with pages 90–92 in the Students' Book.

AT 2.2 **M2** *Ist alles richtig? A fragt, B antwortet. Dann ist B dran.* Pupils work in pairs to check each other's answers to activity M1 orally.

AT 1.4 **N** *Was ist das größte Problem für die Umwelt – was sagen Uwe, Klara, Heiko und Vanessa? Hör gut zu und finde die passenden Bilder für jede Person.* This activity consolidates vocabulary for discussing environmental problems. Pupils listen to the recording and write the appropriate name next to each item.

Answers: a Heiko; b Uwe; c Vanessa; d Klara

Transcript   W 71, activity N

- Uwe, was ist das größte Problem für die Umwelt? Müll?
- Nein, Müll ist nicht so schlimm. Also, ich finde, Verkehr ist am schlimmsten – ja, Verkehr ist das größte Problem.
- Und du, Klara? Was meinst du: Was ist das größte Problem für die Umwelt?
- Ich finde, Verkehr ist nicht so umweltfeindlich. Nein, Kraftwerke sind am gefährlichsten für Menschen und Tiere!
- Was ist das größte Problem für die Umwelt, Heiko?
- Lärm ist schlimmer als Kraftwerke, glaube ich. Lärm ist am umweltfeindlichsten – ja, Lärm ist das größte Problem.
- Was glaubst du, Vanessa – was ist das größte Problem für die Umwelt?
- Ich denke, Pestizide sind viel umweltfeindlicher als Lärm – Lärm ist nicht so schlimm. Nein, Pestizide sind am gefährlichsten, glaube ich.

AT 4.3 **O** *Was sagen sie? Füll die Lücken aus.* Pupils complete the comparative and superlative forms.

Answers:

1 Lärm ist schlimm. Aber Verkehr ist schlimm**er** als Lärm. Und Fabriken sind am schlimm**sten**!
2 Zigaretten sind gefährlich. Und Pestizide sind gefährlich**er als** Zigaretten. Aber Kraftwerke sind **am gefährlichsten**!
3 Müll ist umweltfeindlich. Aber Fabriken sind **umweltfeindlicher als** Müll. Und Pestizide sind **am umweltfeindlichsten**!

AT 3.2 **P1** *„Ich bin umweltfreundlich!" Finde die passenden Bilder.* Activity P consolidates the vocabulary for describing environmentally friendly/harmful behaviour. In activity P1, pupils match the pictures to the sentences.

Answers: 1 c; 2 d; 3 e; 4 b; 5 a

Pages 72-73

Use with pages 92–93 in the Students' Book.

AT 3.2 **P2** *Das ist nicht umweltfreundlich! Finde die passenden Wörter und schreib die Sätze richtig auf.* Pupils join the sentence halves together and write out the correct sentences in full.

Answers:

1 Ich nehme Plastiktüten. 2 Ich fahre mit dem Auto. 3 Ich trenne meinen Müll nicht. 4 Ich bade jeden Tag. 5 Ich kaufe Cola in Dosen.

AT 2.3 **P3** *Wie bist du? A sagt: „Du bist umweltfreundlich/ umweltfeindlich", B wählt einen Satz und antwortet. Dann ist B dran.* Pupils work in pairs to create dialogues using their answers to activities P1 and P2.

3.1–2 **Q1** *Müll in der Schule – was ist das alles? Finde die passenden Wörter.* Activity Q extends the theme '*Müll*' to items not covered in this unit of the Students' Book, although most, if not all, should be familiar from earlier units. In activity Q1, pupils find the picture to match each description.

Answers: 1 c; 2 g; 3 e; 4 h; 5 a; 6 b; 7 f; 8 i; 9 j; 10 d

3.1–2 **Q2** *Was kommt wohin? Schreib die Wörter von Übung Q1 in die passenden Container.* Pupils sort the objects from activity Q1 into appropriate categories.

Answers:

Altpapiercontainer: eine Postkarte, ein Buch, eine Jugendzeitschrift, ein altes Schulheft

Müll: eine Chipstüte, ein halbes Brötchen, eine Coladose

Altglascontainer: eine Flasche Apfelsaft, ein Glas Jogurt, eine Mineralwasserflasche

Q3 *Ist alles richtig? Hör gut zu.* Pupils listen to the recording to check their answers to activity Q2.

AT 1.3

> **Transcript**   W 73, activity Q3
>
> – Puuhhh … so viel Müll!
> – Also – was kommt wohin?
> – Hier ist eine Chipstüte. Die Chipstüte kommt in den Müll.
> – Und diese Postkarte. Sie kommt in den Altpapiercontainer.

> – Und hier ist eine Flasche Apfelsaft. Sie kommt in den Altglascontainer.
> – Oh, schau mal – ein Buch – ein altes Buch! Das Buch kommt in den Altpapiercontainer.
> – Was ist das? Eine Coladose. Die Coladose kommt in den Müll.
> – Und ich habe ein Glas Jogurt – hmm … Erdbeerjogurt – lecker! Das Glas kommt in den Altglascontainer.
> – Oh, und hier ist eine Jugendzeitschrift. Aber sie ist sehr alt … die Zeitschrift kommt in den Altpapiercontainer.
> – Iih! Ein halbes Brötchen!! Bähh!! Also, das Brötchen kommt in den Müll!
> – Und hier ist eine Mineralwasserflasche. Die Flasche kommt in den Altglascontainer.
> – Ist das alles?
> – Nein, was ist das? Ein altes Schulheft …
> – … Mathe – langweilig! Das Schulheft kommt in den Altpapiercontainer.

AT 4.4 **R** *Du bist dran! Was machst du für die Umwelt?* Pupils write two or three sentences about what they do to help protect the environment. This activity can form part of pupils' written records for continuous assessment purposes.

Can you …?

The purpose of the checklist is to identify tasks in the Students' Book both by skill and by topic. Teachers may find this helpful in selecting specific tasks, as a record of pupils' achievements in an Attainment Target.

Einheit 7 Meine Umgebung	AT 1 Listening	AT 2 Speaking	AT 3 Reading	AT 4 Writing
86–87 Ich wohne gern in der Stadt				
Describe your town	1a	1b	1a	2
Give your opinion about living in a town	3, 4a	4b	3, 4a	4a, Noch mal!, Extra!
88–89 Ich wohne gern auf dem Land				
Describe the countryside	1	Noch mal!, Extra!	1, 3	–
Give your opinion about living in the country	6a, 6b	2, 5	4a	4b, 6b, 7
90–91 Was ist Umwelt?				
Identify names and items linked to the environment	1	–	–	–
Talk about the most serious problems for the environment	2, 4	5b	2	3b, 5a, 5c
92–93 Ich bin umweltfreundlich!				
Talk about actions that help or damage the environment	1a, 3a, 4b	1c, 2b, 3b	1a, 1b, 3a, 4a	2a, 2b, Noch mal! Extra!

Copymasters

For general advice about using the copymasters, see page 7 of the introduction to this book.

C 58 ### Hören

1a *Was ist das? Hör gut zu und finde die richtige Reihenfolge für die Wörter.* Pupils listen to the recording and identify each sound effect. They then find the key word to describe the sound effect.

Answers:

Bäume: 7; Disco: 4; Freizeitzentrum: 8; Frösche: 6; Kino: 1; Verkehr: 5; Vögel: 3; Wasser: 2

> **Transcript** C 58, activities 1a and 1b
>
> 1
> – Sag mir, dass du mich liebst! ... Bitte!
> – Nein. Ich kann nicht ... Ich liebe Beatrice ...
> – Oh, nein ...
> 2
> [Sound of water]
> 3
> [Sound of birdsong]
> 4
> [In a disco]
> 5
> [Sound of cars in a congested road]
> 6
> [Sound of a frog croaking]
> 7
> [Sound of trees in the wind]
> 8
> [Sound of people swimming]

1b *Ist man in der Stadt oder auf dem Land? Hör noch einmal zu und schreib die Nummern auf.* Pupils listen again to the recording and categorize the sound effects as urban or rural sounds.

Answers:

Man ist in der Stadt: 1, 4, 5, 8
Man ist auf dem Land: 2, 3, 6, 7

2 *Wohnen sie gern oder nicht gern in der Stadt? Warum (nicht)? Hör gut zu und finde die passenden Bilder.* Pupils listen to the speakers describing why they like/dislike living in town, and find the picture to match each one.

Answers: a 5; b 2; c 4; d 1; e 6; f 3

> **Transcript** C 58, activity 2
>
> 1 – Ich wohne nicht gern in der Stadt, weil es viel Verkehr gibt.
> 2 – Ich wohne sehr gern in der Stadt, weil es ein modernes Fußballstadion gibt.
> 3 – Ich wohne nicht gern in der Stadt, weil es keine Natur gibt.
> 4 – Ich wohne gern in der Stadt, weil es einen schönen Park gibt.
> 5 – Ich wohne gern in der Stadt, weil es ein großes Einkaufszentrum gibt.
> 6 – Ich wohne nicht gern in der Stadt, weil es viel Lärm gibt.

3 *Martin ist sehr umweltfreundlich! Was macht er? Hör gut zu und kreuz die passenden Bilder an.* Pupils listen to the recording and select from each pair the picture which corresponds to what Martin says about his 'eco-friendly' daily routine.

Answers: 1 a; 2 b; 3 b; 4 a; 5 b

> **Transcript** C 58, activity 3
>
> Hallo! Ich wohne sehr gern hier in unserer Stadt. Und weil ich gern hier wohne, mache ich auch viel für unsere Umwelt. Wie? Hier ist ein typischer Tag ...
>
> Ich stehe um sieben Uhr auf und gehe in die Dusche - das verbraucht nicht so viel Wasser wie ein Bad. Dann fahre ich mit dem Rad in die Stadt. Ich fahre nie mit dem Auto. Zu viel Verkehr in der Stadt ist schlecht für die Luft – und auch schlecht für uns und unsere Kinder.
>
> Unsere Umwelt hier ist schön. Unser Müll aber nicht. Ich esse gern zu Mittag im Park. Ich trage meine Mittagsbrote in einer Tasche aus Stoff und ich kaufe keine Dosen. Nach dem Essen trenne ich meinen Müll. Ich bringe Altpapier zum Altpapiercontainer und Flaschen zum Altglascontainer. Dann gehe ich wieder ins Büro – wo ich nur auf Recyclingpapier schreibe.
>
> Ich mache viel für die Umwelt. Was machst du?

C 59 Sprechen

AT 2.4 1a *Frag deinen Partner/deine Partnerin:* Pupils work together in pairs to create dialogues. Partner A asks Partner B whether he/she likes living in the town and in the country, and B responds according to the picture cues, giving reasons with *weil.*

AT 2.4 1b *Dein Partner/deine Partnerin fragt. Du antwortest.* This is the second part of the activity, with the roles reversed.

AT 2.4 2a *Frag deinen Partner/deine Partnerin: „Was machst du für die Umwelt?"* Partner A asks partner B what he/she does to help protect the environment. Partner B responds according to the picture cues.

AT 2.4 2b *Dein Partner/deine Partnerin fragt. Du antwortest.* This is the second part of the activity, with the roles reversed.

C 60 Lesen

AT 3.3 1 *Wer sagt was? Finde die passenden Bilder für die Sätze.* Pupils read the speech bubbles (reasons to like/dislike living in town) and select the appropriate picture for each one.

Answers: 1 c; 2 f; 3 a; 4 e; 5 d; 6 b

AT 3.4 2 *Lies den Artikel. Sind die Sätze richtig oder falsch?* Pupils read the text about Anja's attitude to the environment and town and country life and decide whether the statements are true or false.

Answers:

1 falsch; 2 falsch; 3 falsch; 4 richtig; 5 falsch; 6 richtig

C 61 Schreiben

AT 4.1 1 *Schreib die Wörter richtig auf und finde die passenden Bilder.* Pupils re-order the letters to form words for public buildings and other urban features, and select the appropriate picture for each one.

Answers:

1c Geschäfte; 2a Fußballstadion; 3g Sparkasse;
4h Krankenhaus; 5e Hotel; 6b Einkaufszentrum;
7d Gebäude; 8f Tankstelle

T4.3 **2** *Schau die Bilder und Wörter an und schreib Sätze.*
Pupils write sentences with *Es gibt …* in response to the
picture cues, choosing an appropriate adjective to
describe each building or other feature.

Answers:

(Accept any other reasonable permutations of adjective
and noun.)

a Es gibt ein großes Fußballstadion.
b Es gibt schöne Geschäfte.
c Es gibt ein altes Hotel.
d Es gibt einen interessanten Zoo.
e Es gibt einen kleinen Park.
f Es gibt ein modernes Krankenhaus.

T4.4 **3** *Was sagen sie? Schreib Sprechblasen.* Pupils write
sentences with *Ich wohne gern/nicht gern in der
Stadt/auf dem Land, weil …*, in response to the picture
cues.

Answers:

a Ich wohne gern in der Stadt, weil es ein
  Jugendzentrum gibt.
b Ich wohne nicht gern auf dem Land, weil es keine
  Disco gibt.
c Ich wohne nicht gern in der Stadt, weil es (zu) viel
  Verkehr gibt.
d Ich wohne gern auf dem Land, weil es viele Bäume
  gibt.
e Ich wohne gern in der Stadt, weil es ein
  Freizeitzentrum/Sportzentrum gibt.
f Ich wohne nicht gern auf dem Land, weil es kein Kino
  gibt.

C 62A **Grammatik 1**

This copymaster focuses on es *gibt* + accusative;
adjective endings in the accusative after *einen/eine/ein*
and in the accusative plural; *weil* + subordinate word
order.

1 *Füll die Lücken aus.* Pupils read the 'Flashback' and
complete the sentence with the adjectives in an
appropriate order and with the correct endings for the
nouns that follow.

Answers:

(Accept other combinations of adjective and noun, as
long as the endings are correct.)
Es gibt ein sehr **interessantes** Museum, einen **großen**
Dom, ein **neues** Fußballstadion, einen **tollen** Zoo, viele
alte Gebäude und ein **schönes** Café!

2 *Verbinde die Sätze mit weil.* Pupils read the
'Flashback' and combine each pair of sentences into one
sentence with *weil*.

Answers:

1 Ich wohne gern in der Stadt, weil es viel zu tun gibt.
2 Ich wohne gern hier, weil es viele Geschäfte gibt.
3 Ich wohne gern in meiner Stadt, weil es ein großes
  Fußballstadion gibt.
4 Ich wohne nicht gern in der Stadt, weil es viel Verkehr
  gibt.
5 Ich wohne nicht gern hier, weil es zu viel Lärm gibt.
6 Ich wohne nicht gern in meiner Stadt, weil es viel
  Umweltverschmutzung gibt.

C 62B **Grammatik 2**

This copymaster focuses on comparative and
superlative forms of adjectives.

1 *Ergänze die Sätze.* Pupils read the 'Flashback' and
complete each sentence with the appropriate
comparative or superlative form.

Answers:

1 schlimmsten; 2 gefährlicher; 3 größte; 4 schlechter;
5 schönsten; 6 umweltfeindlicher; 7 schlimmste;
8 ruhiger

C 63 **Tipp**

This copymaster gives advice on writing summaries and
agreeing/disagreeing with an opinion.

1a *Lies den Brief.* Pupils read the 'Flashback' and then
read the letter, making sure they understand all of it.

1b *Was sind die Schlüsselwörter? Schreib eine Liste.*
Pupils note what they consider to be the key words in
the text.

1c *Schreib eine kurze Zusammenfassung (nicht mehr als
50 Wörter).* Pupils write a short summary of the letter.

Possible answer:

Thomas wohnt nicht gern in der Stadt, weil es zu viel
Lärm und Umweltverschmutzung gibt.
Er geht aber gern ins Kino und ins Freizeitzentrum und
alle seine Freunde und seine Familie wohnen in der
Stadt.

1d *Hier sind einige Schlüsselwörter aus Andreas' Brief.
Was hat Andreas an Thomas geschrieben?* Pupils read the
key words and use them to 'reconstruct' Andreas's letter.

2 *Wohnt ihr gern in der Stadt? Macht Dialoge.* Pupils
read the 'Flashback' and then work together in pairs to
create dialogues in which they state opinions and agree
and disagree with each other. Note that more
expressions are given here than in the Students' Book.

Einheit 8 Gesundes Leben | National Curriculum

Pages	Objectives	Grammar	Pronunciation, Skill focus	Key language	PoS	AT level
96–97 Die Klasse!-Clique	Reading and listening for pleasure Familiarization with themes, structures and language of the unit	–	–	–	–	1.4, 3.2, 3.4
98–99 Mein Bauch tut weh!	Name parts of your body Say where it hurts Ask what's wrong and since when Say how long you've been ill Understand the doctor's instructions	*seit* + present tense	–	*Wo tut es weh?* *... tut/tun weh.* *mein Arm/Bauch/Fuß/Hals/Kopf/ Rücken* *meine Nase/Hand* *mein Bein/Knie* *meine Ohren/Zähne* *Ich habe Bauch-/Hals-/ Kopfschmerzen.* *Ich habe Fieber/Grippe/Heuschnupfen/ Husten/Schnupfen.* *Seit wann?* *Seit gestern/zwei Tagen/Montag/einer Woche.* *Nimm diese Tabletten/Tropfen/Lotion* *…* *Nimm dieses Medikament …* *einmal/zweimal/dreimal täglich* *vor/nach dem Essen* *mit Wasser*	1a, 1b, 1c, 2a, 2b, 2c, 2d, 5a, 5c, 5d, 5i	1.2–4, 2.1–4, 3.2–3, 4.4
100–101 Iss dich fit!	Discuss what's good and bad for your health	–	Meanings and genders of compound nouns Pronunciation of compound nouns	*Ich esse jeden Tag …* *Fastfood/Fleisch/Gemüse/Obst/ Süßigkeiten* *Äpfel/Chips/Cornflakes/Currywurst/ Eis/Hähnchen/Hamburger/Kartoffeln/ Kekse/Kuchen/Orangen/ Paprika/Pizza/Pommes frites/Salat/Schinken/Schokolade/ Toast/Würstchen* *Ich trinke jeden Tag …* *Apfelsaft/Cola/Kaffee/Limonade/Milch/ Mineralwasser/Orangensaft/Tee* *Das ist (ziemlich) gesund/ungesund, finde ich.*	1a, 1b, 1c, 2a, 2b, 2c, 2d, 3d, 3e, 5a, 5c, 5d, 5f, 5i	1.4, 2.3, 3.4, 4.1, 4.3, 4.5

Pages	Objectives	Grammar	Pronunciation, Skill focus	Key language	PoS	AT level
102–103 **Meine Gesundheit**	Say what you do for your health Give advice on healthy eating	Imperative	–	*Was für Sport machst du?* *Ich spiele seit zwei Jahren Tennis/Fußball/Golf/Basketball/Volleyball.* *Iss viel Obst und Gemüse!* *Mach viel Sport!* *Trink viel Wasser!* *Geh viel zu Fuß!* *Rauch nicht!* *Iss kein Fastfood!* *Iss keine Süßigkeiten!* *Trink keinen Alkohol!*	1a, 1b, 1c, 2a, 2b, 2c, 2d, 2e, 3e, 5a, 5c, 5d, 5f, 5i	1.3, 2.4, 3.3–4, 4.4
104–105 **Was soll man für die Gesundheit tun?**	Say what you should do for a healthy lifestyle Say what you shouldn't do for a healthy lifestyle Say what you're going to do for your health	*sollen* Future tense	Making a short presentation	*Man soll …* *Ich werde …* *viel Obst und Gemüse essen.* *kein Fastfood essen.* *wenig Fleisch essen.* *keine Süßigkeiten essen.* *viel Mineralwasser trinken.* *Sport treiben.* *nicht rauchen.* *zu Fuß zur Schule gehen.*	1a, 1b, 1c, 2a, 2b, 2c, 2d, 3e, 5a, 5c, 5d, 5f, 5i	1.3–4, 2.4, 3.2–3, 3.5, 4.4–5
106–107 **Thema im Fokus**	Encourage reading for pleasure Use language from Unit 8 creatively Encourage independent, pair- and groupwork	–	–	–	1b, 1c, 2c, 2d, 2e, 2h, 3b, 3d, 3e, 5a, 5c, 5d, 5g, 5i	2.4, 4.2–4

8 Gesundes Leben

Aims of the unit

- To be able to describe pains and ailments and understand the doctor's instructions
- To be able to discuss what's good and bad for your health
- To be able to give advice on healthy eating and a healthy lifestyle
- To be able to say what you're going to do for your health

Die Klasse!-Clique
pages 96–97

Materials

- Students' Book pages 96–97
- Cassette 3 side A
- Workbook page 74

For general advice on exploiting the photo story, see pages 10–11 of the introduction to this book.

In this episode, we rejoin Atalay after his skateboard accident. He has had a heavy fall, but has no serious injuries – other than to his pride! At Jasmin's house, Jasmin's mother puts him to rights with tablets, lotion and a sling for his arm. The two older boys are now rather sheepish and contrite after their earlier arrogance towards Atalay, and invite him to use their skateboard ramp any time he likes. Meanwhile, Jasmin is overjoyed to find a message from Sascha on her mobile phone, inviting her to go out with him that evening.

AT 3.2   **1** *Was meinst du? Vor dem Lesen: Rate!* This is a pre-reading activity. Pupils look at the photos without reading the text, and predict what the content of the photo story will be, choosing the sentence ending they consider more likely from each pair given. Pupils could do this activity in pairs, and check their answers by listening to the recording and reading the text (activity 2). Once you have played the text, discuss the answers as a whole-class activity. You could ask pupils to volunteer answers and quote from the text to back them up.

Answers: 1 a; 2 b; 3 b; 4 a; 5 b

 2 *Hör gut zu und lies mit. Wie heißt das auf Deutsch?*
AT 1.4
AT 3.4 Pupils listen to the recording and follow the text in the book. They then match the English expressions to their German equivalents in the text. This could be done as a whole-class activity. Although the expressions are new, or contain unfamiliar words, pupils should try to work them out using cognates (*Tabletten, Lotion*), similar words/phrases which are known (*Fußball, zu Fuß, so Fuß* means 'foot') or context and a process of elimination ('Which picture seems to match the English expressions best? Which sentences for that picture definitely don't have the meaning I'm looking for?'). Give them hints if they get 'stuck', e.g. the literal meaning of *Was fehlt dir?* is 'What is missing to you?'; *Kopf* means

'head', etc. Less able pupils could be given the German expressions in the wrong order (maybe with one or two additional ones) to match to the English.

Answers:

1 Was fehlt dir? 2 Wo tut es weh? 3 Mein Fuß tut weh!
4 Ich habe Kopfschmerzen. 5 Nimm diese Tabletten.
6 Nimm diese Lotion.

Transcript   p 97, activity 2

- Atalay, was fehlt dir?
- Wo tut es weh?
- Au! Mein Fuß tut weh – und mein Arm! Und ich habe Kopfschmerzen!
- Du musst nach Hause gehen! Komm! Meine Mutter ist zu Hause!
- Ja – wir kommen mit!

- Hier – nimm diese Tabletten – mit Wasser. Und nimm auch diese Lotion – für deinen Fuß.
- Danke, Frau Meyer!

- Atalay – es tut mir Leid.
- Ja – Entschuldigung, Atalay!
- Kann ich dir helfen? Hier ist dein Skateboard!
- Du kannst jeden Tag auf unserer Skateboardbahn fahren, Atalay!
- Ja? Vielen Dank!

- Ich habe eine Nachricht – von Sascha!! „Hallo Jasmin! Wo warst du gestern? Treffen wir uns heute Abend im Jugendzentrum um 19 Uhr 30 – vor der Imbissstube? Es gibt ein Konzert – mit der Gruppe ‚Morgenstern‘. Ich trage eine weiße Jeans und ein schwarzes T-Shirt. Bitte komm – Sascha!"

AT 3.4   **3** *Sind die Sätze richtig oder falsch?* Pupils answer true/false comprehension questions on the text. They will need to be told that *Bein* (question 1) means 'leg'.

Answers:

1 richtig; 2 richtig; 3 falsch; 4 falsch; 5 richtig; 6 falsch

Viel Spaß!

Au, au, au! The main aim is listening for pleasure, but the song also introduces parts of the body and … *tut weh.* For general advice on exploiting the songs in *Klasse! 2*, see page 7 of the introduction to this book.

Transcript   p 97, Viel Spaß!

Wo tut es weh?
Wo tut es weh?
Was fehlt dir?
Wo tut es weh?

Mein Arm tut weh!
Au, au, au!

Refrain

Mein Bein tut weh!
Mein Arm tut weh!
Au, au, au!

Refrain

Mein Knie tut weh!
Mein Bein tut weh!
Mein Arm tut weh!
Au, au, au!

Refrain

Mein Fuß tut weh!
Mein Knie tut weh!
Mein Bein tut weh!
Mein Arm tut weh!
Au, au, au!

Refrain

Mein Kopf tut weh!
Mein Fuß tut weh!
Mein Knie tut weh!
Mein Bein tut weh!
Mein Arm tut weh!
Au, au, au!

Refrain

B A, B Workbook activities A and B could be used at this point for exploitation of the song text.

Mein Bauch tut weh!
pages 98–99

Objectives
- Name parts of your body
- Say where it hurts
- Ask what's wrong and since when
- Say how long you've been ill
- Understand the doctor's instructions

Key language
Wo tut es weh?
… tut/tun weh.
mein Arm/Bauch/Fuß/Hals/Kopf/Rücken
meine Nase/Hand
mein Bein/Knie
meine Ohren/Zähne
Ich habe Bauch-/Hals-/Kopfschmerzen.
Ich habe Fieber/Grippe/Heuschnupfen/Husten/Schnupfen.
Seit wann?
Seit gestern/zwei Tagen/Montag/einer Woche.
Nimm diese Tabletten/Tropfen/Lotion …
Nimm dieses Medikament …
einmal/zweimal/dreimal täglich.
vor/nach dem Essen.
mit Wasser.

National Curriculum PoS
statements 1a, 1b, 1c, 2a, 2b, 2c, 2d, 5a, 5c, 5d, 5i

Materials
- Students' Book pages 98–99
- Cassette 3 side A
- Workbook pages 75–77
- Copymasters 64, 65, 67, 68, 69, 70, 71A

C 64 ## Preparatory work
Use the pictures from copymaster 64 copied onto an OHT, or as flashcards, to introduce the vocabulary for parts of the body. (For general advice on using copymaster visuals, see page 12 of the introduction to this book.)

Now use this vocabulary with the possessive adjectives. To start with, you could ask 'yes/no' questions: T: (pointing to ear) *Ist das mein Arm?*, etc. Then use *dein* and ask pupils to point to the relevant parts of their bodies. T: *Dani, wo ist dein Fuß?*, etc. Now elicit the parts of the body and the possessive adjectives from the class. T: (pointing to head) *Was ist das?* P1: *Das ist dein Kopf.* T: *Richtig! Das ist mein Kopf*, etc.

At this point, you could introduce *weh tun* by saying for example: *Au! Mein Kopf tut weh!* and miming a headache. Then go on to mime other aches and pains, asking *Wo tut es weh?* to elicit from the class *Dein Arm tut weh, dein Fuß tut weh*, etc.

AT 1.2 **AT 3.2** **1a** *Hör gut zu und lies mit.* Pupils listen to the recording and look at the diagram in the book, which introduces the parts of the human body. As they listen, ask pupils to point to the relevant part of the body on the diagram. On a second playing, ask them to point to the relevant part of their own body. Ask the class to close their books, and play the recording a third time, with pupils pointing again to the relevant part of their own body.

Transcript	p 98, activity 1a

– Au! Mein Kopf tut weh!
– Meine Nase tut weh!
– Oooh! Meine Ohren tun weh!
– Mein Hals tut weh!
– Au, Au, Au! Meine Zähne tun weh!
– Mein Rücken tut weh!
– Mein Arm tut weh!
– Bääh! Mein Bauch tut weh!
– Meine Hand tut weh!
– Uuhh! Mein Knie tut weh!
– Mein Bein tut weh!
– Oooh! Mein Fuß tut weh!

WB C Workbook activity C consolidates the terms for the parts of the body.

AT 2.1–2 **1b** *Was tut weh? A macht eine Pantomime, B rät. Dann ist B dran.* Pupils work together in pairs. Partner A mimes having a pain in a part of his/her body and partner B tries to guess. Then the roles are reversed. Mime one or two examples for the whole class by way of preparation.

AT 1.2
AT 3.2

2 *Hör gut zu und finde die passenden Bilder für die Sätze.* This activity introduces *Ich habe ...schmerzen.* Pupils listen to the recording and read the speech bubbles, and find the relevant picture to illustrate each complaint. Establish that *Zahn* is the singular of *Zähne*.

Answers: 1 c; 2 d; 3 a; 4 b

> **Transcript**   p 98, activity 2
>
> 1 – Ich habe Kopfschmerzen.
> 2 – Ich habe Zahnschmerzen.
> 3 – Ich habe Bauchschmerzen.
> 4 – Ich habe Halsschmerzen.

AT 2.3

3 *Was tut weh? Macht Dialoge – von Kopf bis Fuß!* Pupils work together in small groups. They take it in turns to complain about aches and pains, using ... *tut/tun weh* and *ich habe ...schmerzen*, working from head to foot.

WB D Workbook activity D provides further practice on *ich habe ...schmerzen.*

C 65 In preparation for activity 4 below, use the pictures from copymaster 65 copied onto an OHT, or as flashcards, to introduce the vocabulary for ailments and remedies.

AT 1.3
AT 3.3

4 *Sven und Annika sind beim Arzt. Hör gut zu und lies mit.* Pupils listen to the recording and follow the text in the book. This activity introduces *seit*, various words for ailments (*Husten, Fieber, Grippe, Heuschnupfen*) and the adverb of frequency *zweimal täglich*. Ask pupils what they think each of the ailments might be, acting out the symptoms to help them as necessary.

> **Transcript**   p 99, activity 4
>
> – Wo tut es weh, Sven?
> – Mein Kopf tut weh und ich habe Halsschmerzen. Und ich habe auch Husten.
> – Seit wann hast du Husten?
> – Seit zwei Tagen.
> – Hmm ... Du hast auch Fieber. Also, du hast Grippe, Sven!
>
> – Hallo, Annika! Was fehlt dir?
> – Ich habe Heuschnupfen!
> – Hier – nimm diese Tabletten zweimal täglich.
> – Vor dem Essen?
> – Nein, nach dem Essen.

WB E Workbook activity E provides further practice on dialogues at the doctor's surgery.

C 69 Activity 1 on copymaster 69 could be used here for basic reading comprehension on ailments.

C 70 Activity 1 on copymaster 70 could be used here for basic writing practice with ailments.

C 67 Activity 1 on copymaster 67 could be used for listening comprehension on dialogues at the doctor's surgery in preparation for activity 5a below.

AT 1.4

5a *Hör gut zu. Wo tut es weh – und seit wann? Und was müssen sie nehmen? Kopiere den Zettel dreimal und mach Notizen.* Pupils listen to the recording and make notes.

Answers:

Name:	Atalay
Wo tut es weh?	Kopf, Bauch
Seit wann?	seit 2 Tagen
Nimm:	Medikament, einmal täglich, mit Wasser
Name:	Jasmin
Wo tut es weh?	Hals, Nase
Seit wann?	seit Montag
Nimm:	Tropfen, dreimal täglich
Name:	Daniel
Wo tut es weh?	Fuß
Seit wann?	seit gestern
Nimm:	Lotion, zweimal täglich

> **Transcript**   p 99, activity 5a
>
> – Tag, Atalay! Na, wo tut es weh?
> – Ich habe Kopfschmerzen – und mein Bauch tut weh! Aua-aua-aua!
> – Seit wann tut dein Bauch weh?
> – Mein Bauch tut seit zwei Tagen weh.
> – Bauchschmerzen ... Nimm dieses Medikament einmal täglich – mit Wasser.
>
> – Und was fehlt dir, Jasmin?
> – Ich habe Halsschmerzen – und meine Nase tut weh!
> – Seit wann?
> – Seit Montag.
> – Hmm ... Schauen wir mal ...
> – Autsch!
> – Du hast Heuschnupfen, Jasmin. Nimm diese Tropfen dreimal täglich.
>
> – Hallo, Daniel! Wo tut es weh?
> – Mein Fuß tut weh – au!
> – Seit wann tut dein Fuß weh?
> – Seit gestern – mein Fuß tut seit gestern weh.
> – Hier – nimm diese Lotion zweimal täglich.

AT 2.4 **5b** *A ist Arzt/Ärztin, B ist Jasmin, Atalay oder Daniel. Macht Dialoge mit den Notizen von Übung 5a.* Pupils work together in pairs to create dialogues using their notes from activity 5a. Draw pupils' attention to the *Hilfe* box which contains a summary of structures and vocabulary which can be used in this activity.

WB F Workbook activity F provides further comprehension practice on the vocabulary for ailments.

WB G Workbook activity G provides further comprehension practice on the vocabulary for remedies.

C 68 Activities 1 and 2 on copymaster 68 provide more doctor's surgery role plays, and could be used at this point.

Grammatik im Fokus

seit. This section focuses on the use of *seit* as a temporal preposition. Make sure that pupils understand that *seit* is used with the present tense where 'since' is used with the perfect tense (or as here, the perfect continuous) in English. To practise this point of grammar, you could provide some more English sentences for the class to translate into German, such as: 'My knee has been hurting for three days'; 'I've had a headache since yesterday', etc.

Explain that *seit* is a preposition (but it places things in time rather than space), and that it takes the dative. This means that *zwei Tage* becomes *seit zwei Tagen*, with the dative plural ending *-n*, and *eine Woche* becomes *einer Woche*.

C 70 Activity 2 on copymaster 70 could be used here for basic writing practice with *seit* as well as other doctor's surgery expressions.

6 *Schreib Sätze mit den Notizen unten.* Pupils use the key words to write appropriate sentences with *seit* and the present tense.

Answers:

1 Ich habe seit gestern Grippe. 2 Mein Arm tut seit zwei Tagen weh. 3 Ich habe seit Dienstag Schnupfen. 4 Mein Bauch tut seit drei Tagen weh./Ich habe seit drei Tagen Bauchschmerzen. 5 Ich habe seit Mittwoch Husten. 6 Mein Bein tut seit einer Woche weh.

C 71A Copymaster 71A contains information in English about *seit*. Activity 1 could be used at this point for further writing practice with *seit*.

WB H Workbook activity H provides further practice of dialogues at the doctor's surgery.

AT 4.4 **7** *Uwe war beim Arzt und kann nicht zur Schule gehen. Wo tut es weh – und seit wann? Und was muss er nehmen? Kopiere seinen Entschuldigungsbrief und füll die Lücken aus.* Pupils read the letter and fill in the gaps according to the picture cues.

Answers:

Lieber Herr Jung,
ich kann heute leider nicht in die Schule gehen. Ich habe seit **gestern Grippe/Fieber**. Ich habe **Kopfschmerzen** und meine **Ohren** tun weh. Ich muss **zweimal täglich Tabletten** nehmen – **nach dem Essen**.

WB I Workbook activity I provides further practice of writing a letter of excuse describing ailments.

Follow-up activity. Ask pupils to write their own excuse letter for homework, using activity 7 as a model.

Iss dich fit!
pages 100–101

Objectives
- Discuss what's good and bad for your health

Key language
Ich esse jeden Tag …
Fastfood/Fleisch/Gemüse/Obst/Süßigkeiten
Äpfel/Chips/Cornflakes/Currywurst/Eis/Hähnchen/
Hamburger/Kartoffeln/Kekse/Kuchen/Orangen/
Paprika/Pizza/
Pommes frites/Salat/Schinken/ Schokolade/Toast/
Würstchen
Ich trinke jeden Tag …
Apfelsaft/Cola/Kaffee/Limonade/Milch/Mineralwasser/
Orangensaft/Tee
Das ist (ziemlich) gesund/ungesund, finde ich.

National Curriculum PoS
statements 1a, 1b, 1c, 2a, 2b, 2c, 2d, 3d, 3e, 5a, 5c, 5d, 5f, 5i

Materials
- Students' Book pages 100–101
- Cassette 3 side A
- Workbook pages 78-80
- Copymaster 72A

Preparatory work
Revise basic food and drink from *Klasse! 1* (Unit 5) by asking *Was isst du gern? Was trinkst du gern?* Write up the foodstuffs on the board/OHT, eliciting if possible, or otherwise supplying the gender of each item. If pupils initially have difficulty remembering much relevant vocabulary, start off by asking yes/no questions, e.g. *Isst du gern Schokolade? Trinkst du gern Limonade?*, etc.

Now introduce *gesund* and *ungesund*, perhaps as '*gut für dich*' and '*schlecht für dich*' respectively, and ask pupils which of the foodstuffs mentioned are healthy or unhealthy. T: *Ist Schokolade gesund? Was meint ihr?*, etc.

AT 3.4 **1a** *Mach das Quiz.* Pupils read and answer the healthy-eating quiz. Most of the food vocabulary should be familiar to pupils from *Klasse! 1*, but *Kekse* is new.

Answers:

1 Fastfood: Currywurst, Hamburger, Pizza, Pommes frites, (Hähnchen)
  Gemüse: Kartoffeln, Salat, Paprika
  Süßigkeiten: Schokolade, Eis, Kekse, Kuchen
  Obst: Äpfel, Bananen, Orangen, Tomaten
  Fleisch: Hähnchen, Schinken, Würstchen, (Currywurst, Hamburger)
2 1/2: Gemüse, Obst
  3: Fleisch
  4/5: Fastfood, Süßigkeiten
3 Sehr gesund: Mineralwasser, Apfelsaft, Orangensaft
  Ziemlich gesund: Tee
  Ungesund: Cola, Limonade, Kaffee
4 Frühstück
5 1b, 2b, 3a, 4b, 5b

AT 1.4 **1b** *Ist alles richtig? Hör gut zu.* Pupils listen to the recording and compare their answers to the quiz with the answers given on the recording. Discuss with them any answers which differ from those on the recording, but which they feel to be right. You could point out (or elicit from the class) that most things are healthy in moderation, and a balanced, varied diet is probably the healthiest option overall, whereas a diet consisting solely of fruit and mineral water wouldn't be healthy at all!

Transcript   p 100, activity 1b

Herzlich willkommen zum Klasse! 2-Quiz: Gesund essen und trinken! Hier ist Frage Nummer 1: Lebensmittel – was ist was?

Also, Fastfood: Das sind Currywurst, Hamburger, Pizza, Pommes frites.

Gemüse: Das sind Kartoffeln, Paprika, Salat.

Süßigkeiten: Das sind Eis, Kekse, Kuchen, Schokolade.

Obst: Das sind Äpfel, Bananen, Orangen, Tomaten.

Und Fleisch: Das sind Hähnchen, Schinken, Würstchen.

Und jetzt Frage Nummer 2: Man isst es jeden Tag – was ist gesund oder ungesund?

1 und 2 – Sehr gesund sind Gemüse und Obst.

3 – Fleisch ist manchmal gesund – aber nicht jeden Tag!

4 und 5 – Ungesund sind jeden Tag Fastfood und Süßigkeiten.

Frage Nummer 3: Trinken – was ist gesund?

Sehr gesund sind jeden Tag Mineralwasser, Orangensaft und Milch.

Ziemlich gesund ist Tee.

Ungesund ist jeden Tag Cola, Kaffee und Limonade.

Frage Nummer 4: Welche Mahlzeit ist die Nummer eins für die Gesundheit? Die Antwort ist Frühstück: Cornflakes, Toast und Tee – Frühstück ist sehr wichtig für die Gesundheit! Süßigkeiten und Fastfood zum Mittagessen und Abendessen sind nicht so gut.

Und hier ist die Frage Nummer 5: Welches Essen ist gesund?

1 – b ist gesund: Müsli mit Jogurt und Erdbeeren. a – Müsli mit Zucker und Sahne – ist ungesund.

2 – b ist auch gesund: Nudeln mit Pilzen und Tomaten. Aber a – Nudeln mit Käse und Ei – ist ungesund.

Und 3 – a – Pizza mit Spinat und Thunfisch – ist gesund. b ist aber ungesund: Pizza mit Wurst und Käse.

4 – a ist auch ungesund: Reissalat mit Majonäse. Aber b ist gesund: Grüner Salat mit Zwiebeln.

Und 5 – b ist gesund: Brot mit Tomate und ohne Butter. Aber a – Brötchen mit Butter und Marmelade – ist ungesund.

Ja, das war unser Quiz: ‚Gesund essen und trinken'!

WB J, K, L Workbook activities J–L consolidate food and drink vocabulary, and could be used at this point.

AT 4.1 **2** *Du bist dran! Was hast du gestern gegessen und getrunken? Schreib eine Liste.* In this vocabulary extension exercise, pupils write a list of what they ate yesterday, using their dictionaries as necessary. Bear in mind when doing this activity and the following ones, that diet may well be a sensitive issue with some members of the class.

AT 4.1 **3a** *Lies deine Wörter von Übung 2 und die Wörter vom Quiz. Was isst und trinkst du: jeden Tag, manchmal, selten und nie? Schreib vier Listen.* Pupils categorize the food items from activities 1 and 2 in terms of how often they consume them. Less able pupils may benefit from a brief revision of the adverbs of time before attempting this task.

AT 2.3 **3b** *Diskutiere deine Liste mit deinem Partner/deiner Partnerin: Ist das gesund oder ungesund?* Pupils work together in pairs to discuss their answers to activity 3a.

WB M Workbook activity M provides the opportunity for pupils to review the food vocabulary from activities J–L and create further dialogues using *gesund* and *ungesund*.

AT 4.3 *Noch mal! Schreib einen ‚Gesund essen und trinken-Speiseplan' für deine Familie – für eine Woche.* Pupils draw up a menu for their family for a week, using the vocabulary from activities 1 and 2. The menu could be illustrated with drawings or photos.

AT 4.5 *Extra! Was hast du letzte Woche gegessen und getrunken? Schreib ein Tagebuch: Wie ist alles? Sehr gesund, ziemlich gesund, nicht so gesund oder ungesund?* Pupils write a 'food diary' for the last week, using the perfect tense where appropriate: *ich habe … gegessen/getrunken.*

Tipp

Zusammengesetzte Nomen. This section focuses on compound nouns and will help pupils gain confidence in recognizing and working with longer, multi-componented words.

4a *Einige Nomen bestehen aus mehreren Wörtern. Was bedeuten diese Wörter? Rate!* Pupils try to work out the meanings of the compound nouns without the use of reference materials. The components of each noun should be known to them. If they experience difficulty with any of the items, remind them of the importance of breaking down each noun into its component words.

Answers:

1 football match/game of football; 2 table tennis; 3 cheesecake; 4 taxi driver; 5 washing machine; 6 drinking water

4b *Ist alles richtig? Schau im Wörterbuch nach.* Pupils use their dictionaries to check their answers to activity 4a.

5a *der, die oder das? Finde die passenden Artikel für die Wörter in Übung 4a.* Pupils use their dictionaries to find out the gender of each of the compound nouns in activity 4a. Draw their attention to the advice that it is always the last component of the compound which determines the gender.

Answers:

1 das Fußballspiel; 2 das Tischtennis; 3 der Käsekuchen; 4 der Taxifahrer; 5 die Waschmaschine; 6 das Trinkwasser

5b *Finde fünf andere zusammengesetzte Nomen in Einheit 8. Was bedeuten sie? Und sind sie der, die oder das?* Pupils find five more compound nouns and establish their meaning and gender. Examples from pages 100–101 include: *das Lebensmittel, die Überschrift, das Fastfood, die Currywurst, das Mineralwasser, der Apfelsaft, der Orangensaft, der Speiseplan, das Tagebuch.*

C 72A Copymaster 72A contains further information in English about compound nouns. Activity 1 provides more extensive dictionary practice with compound nouns from Units 1–8 of *Klasse! 2.*

Gut gesagt!

Zusammengesetzte Nomen. This section focuses on the pronunciation of compound nouns.

6 *Hör gut zu und wiederhole.* Pupils listen to the recording and repeat the words. Establish that the main stress in each of the words lies on the first component (though not necessarily on the first syllable): *HEUschnupfen, MineRALwasser, BAUCHschmerzen, ORANgensaft, CUrrywurst, THUNfisch, VOLLeyball, PAUsenbrot.* You could ask the class to write out the words and underline the syllables which they think carry the main stress.

Transcript	p 101, activity 6
Heuschnupfen	
Mineralwasser	
Bauchschmerzen	
Orangensaft	
Currywurst	
Thunfisch	
Volleyball	
Pausenbrot	

Meine Gesundheit
pages 102–103

Objectives
- Say what you do for your health
- Give advice on healthy eating

Key language
Was für Sport machst du?
Ich spiele seit zwei Jahren
Tennis/Fußball/Golf/Basketball/Volleyball.
Iss viel Obst und Gemüse!
Mach viel Sport!
Trink viel Wasser!
Geh viel zu Fuß!
Rauch nicht!
Iss kein Fastfood!
Iss keine Süßigkeiten!
Trink keinen Alkohol!

National Curriculum PoS
statements 1a, 1b, 1c, 2a, 2b, 2c, 2d, 2e, 3e, 5a, 5c, 5d, 5f, 5i

Materials
- Students' Book pages 102–103
- Cassette 3 side A
- Workbook pages 80–81
- Copymasters 67, 69, 71A

Preparatory work
Revise sports and leisure activities (*Klasse! 1* Unit 7, *Klasse! 2* Unit 6), by asking *Machst/Treibst du Sport? Was für Sport treibst/machst du? Wie oft machst du das?*, etc.

`AT 3.4` **1a** *Lies die Texte.* Pupils read the texts, in which three teenagers describe what they do to keep fit and healthy.

`AT 3.4` **1b** *Wer macht was? Finde die passenden Bilder.* Pupils match each picture of an activity to the appropriate text.

Answers: Jakob: b, f, h, c; Nadine: d; Torsten: a, e, g

`AT 3.4` **1c** *Lies die Texte noch einmal. Wer macht was seit wann/wie oft? Mach Notizen.* Pupils match each of the adverbials of time (phrases with *seit*, and adverbs of frequency) to a character and a leisure activity in activity 1a. They write their answers in note form.

Answers:
(Accept variations in wording.)
1 seit fünf Jahren: Nadine – Fußball; 2 seit zwei Jahren: Torsten – Hund; 3 seit sechs Monaten: Jakob – Golf; 4 seit zehn Jahren: Jakob – Ski; 5 jeden Morgen: Torsten – Park; 6 jeden Winter: Jakob – Ski (Österreich); 7 zweimal pro Woche: Nadine – Fußball; 8 jeden Tag: Jakob – Mountainbike/Rad

`AT 4.4` **1d** *Was machen Jakob, Nadine und Torsten für ihre Gesundheit – und seit wann und wie oft? Schreib drei kurze Artikel mit deinen Notizen von Übung 1c.* Pupils use their notes from activity 1c to write short articles about Jakob, Nadine and Torsten in the third person. Ask more able pupils to attempt this activity with the Students' Book closed.

`C 67` Activity 3 on copymaster 67 provides listening practice on healthy lifestyles.

`C 69` Activity 3 on copymaster 69 provides further reading practice on healthy lifestyles.

`AT 2.4` **2a** *Du bist dran! Was für Sport machst du für deine Gesundheit? Seit wann und wie oft machst du das? A ist Reporter und fragt, B antwortet.* Pupils work together in pairs to create dialogues about what sports they take part in, how often they do them and how long they have been doing them for. In preparation, you could ask the whole class what sports they do, providing the German terms for any new sports and writing these up on the board/OHT. Less able pupils could make detailed notes to support them in the speaking activity. Alternatively, pupils could prepare by looking up the German terms for their favourite sports in their dictionaries. One partner takes the role of the interviewer, and the other takes the role of the interviewee. Then the roles are reversed. The interviews could be recorded on cassette.

`AT 4.4` **2b** *Machst du Sport? Seit wann und wie oft? Schreib einen Artikel so wie in Übung 1a.* Pupils write about the sports they do, using the articles in activity 1a as models. Alternatively, pupils could write about their interview partners from activity 2a, using the third person.

`WB N` Workbook activity N provides consolidation of sports vocabulary and adverbs of time/frequency through listening comprehension, speaking and writing tasks.

`AT 1.3`
`AT 3.3` **3** *Hör gut zu und lies mit.* Pupils listen to the recording and follow the text in the book. This text draws pupils' attention to the imperative.

Transcript	p 103, activity 3

- Iss viel Obst und Gemüse! Das ist gesund.
- Rauch nicht! Das ist ungesund.
- Iss keine Süßigkeiten! Süßigkeiten sind nicht gesund.
- Trink viel Wasser! Wasser ist sehr gesund.
- Mach viel Sport! Sport ist gesund und macht fit.
- Iss kein Fastfood! Fastfood ist ungesund.
- Trink keinen Alkohol! Alkohol ist ungesund.
- Geh viel zu Fuß! Das ist gesund – und macht fit.

Grammatik im Fokus

Der Imperativ. This section focuses on the imperative. Pupils have been exposed to the *du* and *ihr* forms of the imperative since the beginning of *Klasse! 1*, and were introduced to imperatives in directions in Unit 8 of *Klasse! 1* (pp. 102–103), where they also practised the polite *Sie* form. However, this is the first time they have looked at the formation of imperatives in any detail.

4a *Schreib die Sätze richtig auf.* Pupils put the words in the correct sequence to form instructions with the imperative (all in the *du* form). Pupils check each other's answers by doing activity 4b.

Answers:

1 Iss keine Chips! 2 Kauf keine Schokolade! 3 Trink jeden Tag Mineralwasser! 4 Geh nicht in Fastfood-Restaurants! 5 Mach zweimal pro Woche Sport! 6 Iss viel Obst und Salat!

4b *Ist alles richtig? A fragt, B antwortet.* Pupils work together in pairs to check each other's answers to activity 4a.

`C 71A` Copymaster 71A contains information in English about the imperative. Activity 2 is a transformation activity of the same kind as activity 5 below, and could be used for additional practice.

5 *Schreib neue Imperativ-Sätze.* Pupils transform the statements into commands (*du* and *Sie* forms).

Answers:

1 Nimm diese Tabletten! 2 Gehen Sie zu Fuß in die Stadt! 3 Koch ohne Fleisch! 4 Spielen Sie jeden Tag Fußball! 5 Geh um 20 Uhr ins Bett! 6 Nehmen Sie diese Tropfen!

`AT 4.4` **6a** *Schreib eine 'Tipps für die Gesundheit'-Broschüre: Erfinde weitere Tipps für die Gesundheit und finde oder zeichne Bilder.* Pupils design and write a leaflet giving health advice, illustrating it with drawings or photos. Alternatively, this activity could be done as a web page. Pupils should re-use some of the language introduced in this spread, but also develop their own ideas, using their dictionaries as necessary. The advice should be phrased as instructions in the imperative.

`AT 2.4` **6b** *Diskutiere deine Broschüre mit deinem Partner/ deiner Partnerin.* Pupils work together in pairs to compare their leaflets from activity 6a.

`WB O, P` Workbook activities O and P provide further practice of health advice with imperatives, in tasks using all four skills.

Was soll man für die Gesundheit tun?
pages 104–105

Objectives
- Say what you should do for a healthy lifestyle
- Say what you shouldn't do for a healthy lifestyle
- Say what you're going to do for your health

Key language

Man soll …
Ich werde …
viel Obst und Gemüse essen.
kein Fastfood essen.
wenig Fleisch essen.
keine Süßigkeiten essen.
viel Mineralwasser trinken.
Sport treiben.
nicht rauchen.
zu Fuß zur Schule gehen.

National Curriculum PoS
statements 1a, 1b, 1c, 2a, 2b, 2c, 2d, 3e, 5a, 5c, 5d, 5f, 5i

Materials
- Students' Book pages 104–105
- Cassette 3 side A
- Workbook pages 82–83
- Copymasters 67, 69, 70, 71B, 72B

Preparatory work
Revise the 'health issues' (healthy and unhealthy activities and eating/drinking habits) which have been introduced in the unit so far, perhaps as a brainstorming exercise: *Was ist gesund? Was ist ungesund?*

`AT 1.4` `AT 3.2` **1** *Was soll man für die Gesundheit tun? Hör gut zu und lies mit.* Pupils listen to the recording and follow the text in the book. Ask them what they think *man soll* might mean from the context in which it is used: confirm that it means 'one/you should'.

Transcript	p 104, activity 1

Was soll man für die Gesundheit tun? Man soll viel Obst und Gemüse essen – VIEL Obst und Gemüse – hmm – lecker! Und man soll kein Fastfood essen – bähh!! Man soll wenig Fleisch essen. Und man soll keine Süßigkeiten essen – ja, leider – keine Süßigkeiten! Ja, und man soll viel Mineralwasser trinken, sehr – viel – Mineralwasser! Und man soll … Sport … treiben … am besten … jeden … Tag … Und man soll nicht rauchen – iih!! Und man soll auch zu Fuß zur Schule gehen – das ist gesund!

`WB Q` Workbook activity Q provides further listening comprehension on health advice using *man soll.*

`AT 1.4` **2** *Was sagen Jana und Marius – was soll man für die Gesundheit tun? Hör gut zu und finde die passenden Bilder in Übung 1.* Pupils listen to the recording and decide which pictures from activity 1 match what each speaker says.

Answers: Jana: d, f, b, g; Marius: a, e, h, c

Transcript p 104, activity 2

– Hallo, wir machen eine Umfrage zum Thema Gesundheit. Macht ihr mit?
– Ja, gern!
– Ja, okay, jetzt geht's los. Wie heißt du?
– Jana – ich heiße Jana.
– Also, Jana, was soll man für die Gesundheit tun – was meinst du?
– Für die Gesundheit? Also, man soll zum Beispiel keine Schokolade und keine Kekse essen – das ist ungesund.
– Keine Schokolade und keine Kekse ... Und was soll man sonst noch tun?
– Tja ... Ach ja, man soll jeden Tag Sport machen – also, zum Beispiel in der Schule, nachmittags oder abends ... Das macht fit. Und man soll auch keine Hamburger oder Pommes frites essen – das ist auch nicht gesund. Ja, und keine Currywurst – leider!
– Und was soll man sonst noch für die Gesundheit tun?
– Also, man soll auch nicht rauchen – das ist sehr ungesund!
– Vielen Dank, Jana. Und wie heißt du?
– Mein Name ist Marius.
– Ja, Marius, was soll man für die Gesundheit tun?
– Hhmmm ... Man soll viele Bananen, Äpfel und Orangen essen – am besten jeden Tag – und man soll auch viel Salat essen – viel Salat, Kartoffeln, Tomaten usw.
– Ja, und was soll man sonst noch tun?
– Man soll viel Wasser trinken – viel Wasser und keine Cola und keine Limonade. Ja, das ist auch gesund.
– Was soll man sonst für die Gesundheit tun, Marius?
– Also, man soll immer zu Fuß gehen – zum Beispiel in die Stadt oder zur Schule. Ja, und man soll wenig Wurst und Schinken essen. Das ist ungesund.
– Wenig Wurst und Schinken. Vielen Dank, Jana und Marius!

Grammatik im Fokus

ich/man soll ... This section focuses on the modal verb *sollen.* Before going through the information with the class, ask them what modal verbs they can think of. So far they have had: *müssen* and *dürfen,* introduced in Unit 3 (p. 41); *können* and *wollen,* introduced in Unit 6 (p. 73). Ask them what happens to a main verb when it is used with a modal auxiliary, i.e. establish that it goes to the end of the clause/sentence, in the infinitive form. To revise the syntax further, you could take a simple sentence and then add a modal verb by way of demonstration, for example:

Ich esse viel Obst. + *müssen* = *Ich muss viel Obst essen.*

Now ask pupils to do the same with each of the other modal verbs in turn, before turning to the grammar explanation of *sollen* in the Students' Book.

3 *Schreib neue Sätze mit Man soll ...* Pupils transform the sentences using *man soll.*

Answers:

1 Man soll keinen Kuchen essen. 2 Man soll jeden Tag Obst essen. 3 Man soll viel zu Fuß gehen. 4 Man soll keine Pizza essen. 5 Man soll viel Wasser trinken. 6 Man soll jeden Tag schwimmen.

C 71B Copymaster 71B contains further information in English about *sollen.* Activity 1 is a transformation task of the same kind as activity 3 above and could be used here for further practice.

WB R Workbook activity R provides further writing practice with *man soll.*

AT 4.4 **4** *Was soll man in der Schule für die Gesundheit tun? Mach ein Poster für das Klassenzimmer.* Pupils write and design a poster giving advice about health at school, using *man soll.* Point out that pupils can use the healthy eating vocabulary from pages 102–103, as well as the vocabulary from the current spread. The poster can be illustrated with cartoons, drawings or photos. This is also an ideal opportunity for IT work.

AT 2.4 *Noch mal! Wie findet dein Partner/deine Partnerin deine Tipps? Macht Dialoge.* Pupils work together in pairs to discuss their ideas for the poster. This could be done at an intermediate stage in activity 4, when pupils have written the first draft of their advice but have not yet drawn up the poster in its finished form.

AT 4.5 *Extra! Lies deine Tipps noch einmal. Warum soll man das tun? Schreib Sätze mit weil.* Pupils add reasons to their advice, using *weil.* Check that pupils remember that *weil* sends the verb to the end.

5 *Es ist Neujahr. Jasmin will im neuen Jahr viel für ihre Gesundheit tun. Hör gut zu und lies mit.* This activity introduces the future tense. Pupils listen to the recording and follow the text in the book. Before going on to look at the grammar explanation, ask them what they think *ich werde* means in English, judging by the context. Confirm that it means 'I will' or 'I'm going to'.

AT 1.3 **AT 3.3**

Transcript p 105, activity 5

Also, was will ich im neuen Jahr für meine Gesundheit tun? Nummer 1: Ich werde viel Sport treiben. Ja, und Nummer 2: Ich werde kein Fastfood essen. Nummer 3: Ich werde jeden Tag Obst essen. Und jetzt Nummer 4: Ich werde zu Fuß zur Schule gehen. Nummer 5: Ich werde viel Mineralwasser trinken. Und Nummer 6: Ich werde keine Süßigkeiten essen. Puh! Das ist doch schwierig!

WB S Workbook activity S provides writing practice with the future tense, for use in conjunction with *Grammatik im Fokus.*

Grammatik im Fokus

ich werde ... This section introduces the future tense. You could point out that pupils have already referred to **future time** many times in *Klasse! 2* – using the **present tense**: this is quite usual and correct in German, but the future tense is used when you are making resolutions, i.e. saying emphatically what you **will** do.

You could now practise syntax with *werden* in the same way as described above for *sollen*.

C 67 Activity 2 on copymaster 67 provides listening practice on resolutions with the future tense and could be used in preparation for activity 6 below.

C 69 Activity 2 on copymaster 69 provides reading practice on resolutions with the future tense and could be used in preparation for activity 6 below.

6 *Schreib Neujahrs-Sätze mit Ich werde …* Pupils transform the statements using *werden*.

Answers:

1 Ich werde keine Chips essen. 2 Ich werde jeden Tag Tennis spielen. 3 Ich werde viel Obst und Gemüse essen. 4 Ich werde keinen Alkohol trinken. 5 Ich werde mit dem Rad zur Schule fahren. 6 Ich werde kein Fleisch essen.

C 71B Copymaster 71B contains information in English about the future tense. Activity 2a is a transformation task similar to activity 6 above and could be used here for further practice.

7 *Was willst du für deine Gesundheit tun? Macht Dialoge mit den Informationen unten.* Pupils work together in pairs to create dialogues with *Ich werde …*, using the picture cues.

WB T, U Workbook activities T and U provide further writing and speaking practice on resolutions in the future tense.

C 70 Activity 3 on copymaster 70 provides further writing practice on resolutions in the future tense and could be used to prepare for activity 8 below.

AT 3.5 **8a** *Du bist dran! Lies Ulrikes Brief. Schreib dann einen*
AT 4.5 *Antwortbrief mit deinen Neujahrs-Sätzen.* Pupils read Ulrike's letter and then write a reply describing their own resolutions. Make sure that they understand that they should think of new resolutions, not use those from activities 6 and 7 above.

AT 2.5 **8b** *Lies deine ‚Neujahrs-Hitparade‘ vor. Die Klasse hört zu. Welche ‚Neujahrs-Hitparade‘ ist die Nummer eins?* Pupils present their list of New Year's resolutions to the class. Discuss the *Tipp* with pupils in preparation for the presentation.

C 72B Copymaster 72B contains further advice in English about making a presentation. Activities 1–4 could be used as an alternative to activity 8 above or for further practice.

Thema im Fokus
pages 106–107

National Curriculum PoS
statements 1b, 1c, 2c, 2d, 2e, 2h, 3b, 3d, 3e, 5a, 5c, 5d, 5g, 5i

Materials
• Students' Book pages 106–107
• Copymaster 66

The final spread of each unit provides further reading practice, leading into a project outcome for the unit. See pages 8–9 of the introduction to this book for general notes on how to use these pages. The text '*Ein Herz für die Gesundheit*' is provided for pupils to read for personal interest, but will also provide useful ideas and vocabulary for the subsequent activities. Pupils may need to use their dictionaries or the *Vokabular* at the back of the Students' Book to look up unfamiliar vocabulary. Most of the activities on this page can be completed by hand or on computer.

AT 4.3–4 **1a** *Macht eine Sport-Umfrage in der Schule. Fragt: „Wie oft machst du Sport?" und schreibt die Resultate auf.* Pupils conduct a survey in the school (in English, or perhaps confined to the classes that do German) about how often their fellow pupils do sport, and record the results. They can use the first part of the text on page 106 as a model. More able pupils could conduct a more detailed survey including the type of sport (*Welche Sportarten machst du?*) and the duration (*Wie lange?/Wie viele Stunden pro Woche?*). Pupils could present the results in written form, or in the form of a graph or chart, maybe comparing boys and girls or the different years of the school. They could also ask the teachers how much sport they do!

AT 4.3 **1b** *Was für Sport kann man in der Schule machen? Schreibt und zeichnet einen Sport-Stundenplan.* Pupils find out what sports are available in their school and draw up a sports timetable in German (similar to the *Sport-AGs* timetable on page 106), illustrated with appropriate symbols.

AT 4.3–4 **2a** *Macht eine Schulumfrage: „Was isst du jeden Tag, manchmal oder nie?" Schreibt die Resultate auf. Fragt auch: „Was meinst du – ist dein Essen und Trinken sehr gesund, ziemlich gesund, nicht so gesund oder ungesund?" und schreibt die Resultate auf.* Pupils conduct a survey in the school (in English, or perhaps confined to the classes that do German) about eating habits and record the results. Again, pupils could present the results in written form, as in the example on page 106 (*Essen und Trinken*), or in the form of a graph or chart.

AT 4.2–3 **2b** *Macht einen ‚Gesund essen und trinken‘-Speiseplan für: a Pausenbrote; b die Kantine.* Pupils draw up 'healthy eating and drinking' menus for break and lunchtime. These can be illustrated with drawings or photos. As in the example, these could be contrasted with 'unhealthy eating and drinking' menus.

AT 2.4 **3** *Macht einen Radiospot für das Schulradio – nehmt alle Informationen auf Kassette auf.* Pupils practise their presentation skills by recording their findings and their menu proposal on cassette. Encourage them to deliver their presentation in an appropriately journalistic style, as in the example, making their findings sound as dramatic as possible.

Kannst du … ?
The end-of-unit summary is a checklist for pupils. See page 8 of the introduction to this book for ideas on how to use the checklist.

C 66 Copymaster 66 provides a useful reference for pupils revising the language of this unit.

Noch mal!-Seite Einheit 8
page 136

National Curriculum PoS
statements 1a, 1b, 1c, 2a, 2b, 3e, 5a, 5i

Materials
- Students' Book page 136
- Cassette 3 side B

This revision page is intended for less able pupils. It reinforces the basic vocabulary and structures from the unit, and it can be used by pupils who experienced difficulty in completing some of the activities within the unit, or as alternative homework activities.

AT 1.2   **1** *Hör gut zu und finde die passenden Bilder.* This activity relates to pages 98–99. Pupils listen to the recording and find the cartoon to match each speaker's complaint.

Answers: 1 c; 2 d; 3 e; 4 b; 5 f; 6 a

```
Transcript                          p 136, activity 1

1 – Ich habe Bauchschmerzen.
2 – Mein Arm tut weh.
3 – Ich habe Kopfschmerzen.
4 – Ich habe Fieber.
5 – Ich habe Heuschnupfen.
6 – Meine Ohren tun weh.
```

AT 3.3   **2a** *Lies die Sätze. Was ist gut für die Gesundheit – und was ist nicht gut?* Activity 2 relates to pages 100–102. In activity 2a, pupils read the statements and categorize them as healthy or unhealthy behaviour. Pupils check their own answers by doing activity 2b.

Answers:

1 ungesund; 2 gesund; 3 gesund; 4 ungesund; 5 ungesund; 6 gesund

AT 2.4   **2b** *Welche Sätze sind nicht gut für die Gesundheit? Macht neue Sätze – jetzt sind sie gut für die Gesundheit!* Pupils work together in pairs to discuss their answers to activity 2a and suggest healthy alternatives to the examples of unhealthy behaviour. You may prefer pupils to prepare written notes before attempting this activity, for example:

1: Ich esse jeden Tag Schokolade – ungesund. Obst – gesund.

AT 4.4   **3** *Du bist sehr sportlich – was machst du seit wann/wie oft? Schreib Sätze mit den Informationen.* Activity 3 relates to pages 102–103. Pupils write sentences with *seit* or adverbs of frequency and the present tense, using the word and picture cues.

Answers:

a Ich spiele seit zwei Jahren Tennis. b Ich schwimme seit acht Monaten. c Ich spiele seit sechs Jahren Basketball. d Ich spiele jedes Wochenende Volleyball. e Ich fahre zweimal pro Woche Rad. f Ich tanze abends.

AT 4.3   **4a** *Sven will im neuen Jahr viel für seine Gesundheit tun. Lies seine Neujahrs-Sätze und finde die passenden Wörter.* Activity 4 relates to pages 104–105. In activity 4a, pupils consolidate their understanding of the future tense by reading Sven's New Year's resolutions and selecting the appropriate word from each pair of alternatives to make the resolutions healthy ones.

Answers:

1 Ich werde **keine** Süßigkeiten essen.
2 Ich werde **nicht** rauchen.
3 Ich werde **viel** Sport treiben.
4 Ich werde **kein** Fastfood essen.
5 Ich werde viel **Mineralwasser** trinken.
6 Ich werde **viel** Obst essen.

AT 2.5   **4b** *A ist Frau Ungesund, B ist Herr Ungesund. Sie wollen nichts für ihre Gesundheit tun! Macht Dialoge mit den Sätzen in Übung 4a.* Pupils work together in pairs to create dialogues using the unhealthy alternatives from activity 4a, practising using the future tense.

Extra!-Seite Einheit 8
page 137

National Curriculum PoS
statements 1a, 1b, 1c, 2a, 2b, 3e, 5a, 5c, 5d, 5f, 5i

Materials
- Students' Book page 137
- Cassette 3 side B

This extension page is intended for more able pupils. It contains slightly longer and more complex materials, and it can be used by pupils who have completed other activities quickly or as alternative homework activities.

AT 1.4   **1a** *Hör gut zu. Was essen und trinken Tobias, Miriam und Heino? Mach Notizen für (F) Frühstück, (M) Mittagessen und (A) Abendessen.* Activity 1 relates to pages 100–104. In activity 1a, pupils listen to the recording and make notes about who eats and drinks what, and when. This is an extensive and challenging listening activity. After playing the whole recording through once, ask pupils what foods and drinks they can remember hearing. Then play the recording again, stopping after each question-answer exchange for pupils to make notes. Play the recording a third time for pupils to complete and check their notes, pausing the cassette when the interviewer thanks each interviewee and addresses the next one. At this point, pupils could compare notes in pairs to check that they have the same answers, and request a fourth playing if necessary. If time is short, only use one or two of the interviews.

Answers:

Tobias: F: Müsli, Banane, Milch, Tee
         M: Currywurst, Hamburger, Pommes frites, Limonade
         A: Kartoffelsalat, Majonäse, Würstchen, Kaffee

Miriam: F: Brötchen, Butter, Honig, Marmelade, Kaffee (mit Zucker und Sahne)
         M: Brötchen, Käse, grünen Salat, Jogurt, Apfel, Mineralwasser
         A: Nudeln, Tomaten, Pilze, Obstsalat, Milch

Heino: F: Schokolade, Kakao
         M: Gemüsepizza (ohne Käse), Orangensaft, Orange, Banane
         A: Chips, Kekse, Cola

Transcript   p 137, activity 1a

- Hallo – guten Tag! Ich bin von Radio 1 Live. Ich mache eine Umfrage – das Thema ist ‚Gesund essen und trinken‘.
- He, super! Kann ich mitmachen? Ich heiße Tobias.
- Ja, gern. Also, Tobias, was isst du zum Frühstück?
- Zum Frühstück esse ich meistens Müsli mit Banane und Milch und ich trinke Tee.
- Und was isst du zum Mittagessen?
- Also, mittags gehe ich zur Imbissbude. Dort esse ich Currywurst oder Hamburger mit Pommes frites.
- Und was trinkst du mittags?
- Limonade – ich trinke zum Mittagessen Limonade.
- Und abends? Was isst du zum Abendessen?
- Abends esse ich am liebsten Kartoffelsalat mit Majonäse und zwei oder drei Würstchen. Und ich trinke Kaffee.
- Vielen Dank, Tobias. Und wie heißt du?
- Mein Name ist Miriam.
- Und was isst du morgens, Miriam?
- Also, zum Frühstück esse ich zwei Brötchen mit Butter, Honig und Marmelade. Und ich trinke Kaffee mit Zucker und Sahne.
- Und was isst du zum Mittagessen? Hähnchen oder Fisch?
- Nein, ich bin Vegetarierin. Ich esse mittages meistens ein Brötchen mit Käse und einen grünen Salat und ich esse einen Jogurt und einen Apfel. Ich trinke normalerweise Mineralwasser.
- Und was isst du zum Abendessen?
- Abends esse ich mit meinen Eltern. Wir essen oft Nudeln mit Tomaten und Pilzen und einen Obstsalat.
- Und was trinkst du abends?
- Milch – ich trinke zum Abendessen Milch.
- Danke, Miriam. So, und wie ist dein Name?
- Ich heiße Heino.
- Heino, was isst du zum Frühstück?
- Ich esse morgens meistens Schokolade – ich mag kein Müsli und keine Cornflakes – und ich trinke Kakao.
- Und mittags? Was isst du zum Mittagessen?
- Ich esse mittags Gemüsepizza ohne Käse – Käse mag ich nicht – und ich trinke Orangensaft. Ach ja, und ich esse auch eine Orange oder eine Banane.
- Und was isst du abends?
- Zum Abendessen esse ich nicht viel – eine Tüte Chips oder eine Packung Kekse. Und ich trinke Cola.

AT 4.2 **1b** *Lies deine Notizen von Übung 1a. Welche Mahlzeiten sind sehr gesund, ziemlich/manchmal gesund oder ungesund?* Pupils read their notes for activity 1a and categorize each of the meals (not each of the foods individually) as very healthy, quite healthy or unhealthy. They could then discuss their answers in pairs.

AT 4.4 **1c** *Welche Mahlzeiten sind ungesund? Schreib neue gesunde Mahlzeiten für Tobias, Miriam und Heino.* Pupils now make recommendations using *man soll*, saying which of the meals from activity 1a are unhealthy, and recommending healthy alternatives.

AT 2.4 **1d** *Macht weitere Tipps für die Gesundheit.* Pupils work together in pairs to create dialogues in which they give further advice about healthy living. You may wish them to make some notes in preparation, for example a list of tips 1–5 in note form.

AT 3.5 **2a** *Lies Annes E-Mail und beantworte die Fragen.* Activity 2 relates to pages 98–99 and pages 104–105. In activity 2a, pupils read Anne's e-mail and answer the comprehension questions. For question 6, pupils can answer in the present tense – or the future if you supply them with the third person form *wird* + infinitive.

Answers:

1 Sie kann nicht zu Olivers Party kommen.
2 Sie hat seit drei Tagen Grippe.
3 Ihr Kopf und ihr Hals tun weh.
4 Sie soll die Tabletten dreimal täglich nehmen und viel Wasser trinken und Obst essen.
5 Sie soll keinen Sport machen, weil das zu anstrengend ist.
6 Sie geht um 19 Uhr ins Bett./Sie wird um 19 Uhr ins Bett gehen.

AT 4.5 **2b** *Du bist dran! Schreib eine E-Mail so wie Anne mit den Informationen unten.* Pupils write an e-mail using the picture cues and using the text from activity 2a as a model.

Workbook

Page 74

Use with page 97 in the Students' Book.

A1 *Hör gut zu und sing mit!* Pupils listen to the song and then sing along. Singing this song will help pupils to memorize the key vocabulary for parts of the body and the structures … *tut weh* and *Was fehlt dir?* Pupils might like to 'act out' the various pains while listening/singing. You could divide the class into singers on the one hand, and 'actors' on the other, perhaps with pupils volunteering for each group. Alternatively, you could mime the various pains yourself and gradually reduce the volume of the recording with each playing, until pupils are singing the verses in response to your mime prompts.

Transcript   W 74, activity A1

Wo tut es weh?
Wo tut es weh?
Was fehlt dir?
Wo tut es weh?

Mein Arm tut weh!
Au, au, au!

Refrain

Mein Bein tut weh!
Mein Arm tut weh!
Au, au, au!

Refrain

Mein Knie tut weh!
Mein Bein tut weh!
Mein Arm tut weh!
Au, au, au!

Refrain

Mein Fuß tut weh!
Mein Knie tut weh!
Mein Bein tut weh!
Mein Arm tut weh!
Au, au, au!

Refrain

Mein Kopf tut weh!
Mein Fuß tut weh!
Mein Knie tut weh!
Mein Bein tut weh!
Mein Arm tut weh!
Au, au, au!

Refrain

AT 3.3 | **A2** *Wo tut es weh? Finde die passenden Bilder für die Sätze 1–5.* Pupils find the appropriate body part (with a box next to it) in the picture for each of the numbered song lines. This will require them to look up the nouns in their dictionaries or in the *Vokabular* at the back of the Students' Book.

Answers: 1 arm; 2 leg; 3 knee; 4 foot; 5 head

AT 4.2 | **B** *Du bist dran! Schreib weitere Sätze mit den Bildern a–f.* Pupils write sentences using … *tut/tun weh* for each of the body parts labelled a-f. They will need to use their dictionaries or the *Vokabular* at the back of the Students' Book for this task. Draw their attention to singular noun + *tut*, plural noun + *tun*.

Answers:

a Meine Augen tun weh. b Meine Nase tut weh. c Meine Zähne tun weh. d Meine Ohren tun weh. e Mein Hals tut weh. f Mein Bauch tut weh.

Pages 75–76

Use with pages 98-99 in the Students' Book.

AT 4.2 | **C1** *Wo tut es weh? Schreib die Wörter auf.* Pupils complete the diagram with the words for the parts of the body (with the possessive adjective *mein* in the correct

nominative form). Pupils check their own answers by doing activity C2.

Answers:

1 mein Kopf; 2 meine Nase; 3 meine Ohren; 4 meine Zähne; 5 mein Hals; 6 mein Arm; 7 mein Bauch; 8 mein Rücken; 9 meine Hand; 10 mein Knie; 11 mein Bein; 12 mein Fuß

AT 2.3 | **C2** *Ist alles richtig? A sagt eine Zahl (ein Bild) von Übung C1, B antwortet.* Pupils work together in pairs to create dialogues with *Wo tut es weh? – Mein(e) … tut/tun weh*, thereby checking each other's answers to activity C1.

AT 4.3 | **D** *„Ich habe …schmerzen!" Was sagen sie? Schreib Sprechblasen.* Pupils write speech bubbles, forming compounds with the relevant part of the body + *schmerzen*. Point out that Germans say 'ears ache' (i.e. plural of *Ohr*).

Answers:

a Ich habe Kopfschmerzen! b Ich habe Ohrenschmerzen! c Ich habe Rückenschmerzen! d Ich habe Zahnschmerzen!

AT 3.3 | **E1** *Beim Arzt – finde die richtige Reihenfolge für den Dialog.* Pupils put the speech bubbles into the correct order to make a dialogue between doctor and patient. Pupils check their own answers by doing activity E2.

Answers: a 4; b 6; c 2; d 1; e 5; f 3

AT 1.3 | **E2** *Ist alles richtig? Hör gut zu.* Pupils listen to the recording to check their answers to activity E1.

Transcript   W 76, activity E2

– Guten Morgen! Was fehlt dir?
– Ich habe Fieber.
– Seit wann hast du Fieber?
– Seit gestern.
– Hast du auch Husten?
– Ja, ich habe auch Husten.

AT 3.2 | **F** *„Was fehlt dir?" Finde die passenden Bilder.* Pupils find the correct picture to match each speech bubble (various ailments).

Answers: 1 b; 2 d; 3 c; 4 e; 5 a

Page 77

Use with page 99 in the Students' Book.

AT 1.3 | **G** *Was sagt der Arzt? Hör gut zu und finde die passenden Bilder.* Pupils listen to the recording and then select the picture which shows the treatment prescribed for each patient. You may want to point out the form of address *Herr/Frau Doktor*, which is the usual way of addressing a doctor, even though 'doctor' in German is *Arzt/Ärztin*. By way of advance preparation for the imperative on page 103 of the Students' Book, you could also draw pupils' attention to the imperative forms, which are different according to whether the doctor is talking to an adult or a child.

Answers: a 4; b 1; c 2; d 5; e 3

Transcript   W 77, activity G

1 – Ja, Herr Meyer, Sie haben eine Grippe. Nehmen Sie
    diese Tabletten zweimal täglich.
2 – So, Martin, nimm diese Tropfen einmal täglich.
    – Vor dem Essen?
    – Nein, nach dem Essen.
3 – Frau Weiß, hier ist ist Ihre Lotion.
    – Danke, Herr Doktor.
    – Nehmen Sie die Lotion dreimal täglich.
4 – Also, Susanne, du hast Fieber. Nimm dieses
    Medikament jeden Tag.
    – Mit Wasser?
    – Ja, mit Wasser.
5 – Ich habe Tabletten für Sie, Herr Sauer.
    – Vielen Dank.
    – Nehmen Sie diese Tabletten dreimal täglich – vor dem
    Essen.

AT 2.4   **H** *Beim Arzt – macht Dialoge mit den Informationen unten.* Pupils work together in pairs to create dialogues using the notes provided, using the vocabulary for pains (*ich habe …schmerzen or … tut/tun weh*) and ailments (*ich habe Grippe/Fieber/Husten/Schnupfen/ Heuschnupfen*) and *seit* with the present tense.

AT 3.3
AT 4.3   **I1** *Tina muss am Samstag zu Hause bleiben. Lies die Nachricht an Tinas Freundin und füll die Lücken aus.* Pupils read the note and complete it with the help of the picture cues.

Answers:

Ich kann heute leider nicht **ins Kino** gehen. Ich habe seit **zwei Tagen** Husten und ich habe seit **gestern Fieber**. Und mein **Rücken** tut weh!

AT 4.4   **I2** *Schreib eine weitere Nachricht mit den Informationen unten.* Pupils write their own note according to the picture cues and using the note from activity I1 as a model.

Suggested answer:

Ich kann heute leider nicht in die Disco gehen. Ich habe seit einer Woche Schnupfen. Ich habe auch seit Donnerstag Kopfschmerzen und Ohrenschmerzen.

Pages 78–79

Use with pages 100–101 in the Students' Book.

AT 4.1   **J** *Was isst du zum Frühstück? Schreib die Wörter auf.* Pupils complete the crossword puzzle according to the picture clues (breakfast food and drink).

Answers:

1 Kaffee; 2 Tee; 3 Honig; 4 Marmelade; 5 Cornflakes; 6 Müsli; 7 Milch; 8 Butter; 9 Brötchen; 10 Zucker

AT 3.1   **K1** *Finde 14 Essen- und Trinken-Wörter und schreib sie auf.* Pupils divide up the wordsnake to form nouns for food and drink and write out the words.

Answers:

1 Nudeln; 2 Salat; 3 Käse; 4 Orangensaft; 5 Fisch; 6 Brot; 7 Mineralwasser; 8 Banane; 9 Kartoffeln; 10 Apfel; 11 Cola; 12 Jogurt; 13 Reis; 14 Limonade

AT 3.1   **K2** *Finde dann die passenden Bilder für die Wörter in Übung K1.* Pupils now match the nouns from activity K1 to the pictures.

Answers:

a 10; b 14; c 11; d 9; e 3; f 2; g 4; h 5; i 1; j 7; k 8; l 12; m 6; n 13

AT 4.1   **L1** *Was isst Sven gern? Füll die Lücken aus.* Pupils complete the nouns (fast food items) with the help of the picture clues.

Answers:

1 Pizza; 2 Hähnchen; 3 Schokolade; 4 Pommes frites; 5 Currywurst; 6 Hamburger; 7 Eis mit Sahne; 8 Kartoffelsalat; 9 Chips

AT 2.3   **L2** *Was isst du gern? Macht Dialoge mit den Bildern von Übung L1.* Pupils work together in pairs to create dialogues using their answers to activity L1.

AT 3.1   **M1** *Lies noch einmal die Essen- und Trinken-Wörter in Übung J–L. Was meinst du – was ist sehr gesund, ziemlich gesund oder ungesund? Schreib die Wörter auf.* Pupils review the food and drink vocabulary from activities J–L and categorize each item according to its healthiness. They check their answers by doing activity M2.

Pages 80–81

Use with pages 101–103 in the Students' Book.

AT 2.4   **M2** *Was sagt dein Partner/deine Partnerin? Macht Dialoge.* Pupils work together in pairs to discuss their answers to activity M1. At this point you could remind them that the *Tipp* on page 89 of the Students' Book gave a range of expressions for agreeing and disagreeing with an opinion.

AT 1.4   **N1** *Was machen Anne und Thomas für ihre Gesundheit? Hör gut zu und schreib A (Anne) oder T (Thomas) auf.* Pupils listen to the recording and then decide whether each of the picture cues applies to Anne or Thomas.

Answers: a A; b T; c T; d A; e T; f A; g A; h T

Transcript   W 80, activity N1

– Ich heiße Anne und ich bin 15 Jahre alt. Ich mache ziemlich viel für meine Gesundheit. Ich spiele zweimal pro Woche Basketball – Basketball ist anstrengend, aber es macht Spaß. Und ich spiele seit drei Jahren Tennis. Ich spiele jedes Wochenende mit meiner Mutter Tennis. Aber mein Lieblingssport ist Schwimmen: Ich schwimme jeden Morgen – im Sommer und im Winter. Was mache ich noch für meine Gesundheit? Also, ich gehe immer zu Fuß: Zur Schule, in die Stadt … das ist gesund und macht fit.

– Mein Name ist Thomas. Ich bin 14 Jahre alt. Was mache ich für meine Gesundheit? Ich mache gern Sport – ja, ich bin ziemlich sportlich. Mein Lieblingssport ist Volleyball. Ich spiele dreimal pro Woche: Ich spiele mittwochs in der Schule und am Montag und am Samstag spiele ich im Sportzentrum. Und ich fahre seit sechs Monaten Rollschuh – ich habe zum Geburtstag Inline-Skates bekommen. Ja, und ich fahre auch sehr gern Rad: Ich fahre jeden Tag mit dem Rad zur Schule. Und ich mache jeden Morgen und jeden Abend einen Spaziergang mit Otto – das ist mein Hund.

T2.4 **N2** *„Was machst du für die Gesundheit?" Macht Dialoge.* Pupils work together in pairs to create dialogues about what they do to keep fit and healthy.

T4.4 **N3** *Du bist dran! Wie oft/seit wann machst du das? Schreib Sätze mit den Wörtern.* Pupils write sentences about what they do to keep fit, using the adverbs of frequency and phrases with *seit* provided. This activity can form part of pupils' written records for continuous assessment purposes.

T4.2 **O1** *Schreib die Sätze richtig auf.* Pupils re-order the words to form instructions about healthy living using the imperative.

Answers:

1 Trink viel Wasser! 2 Rauch nicht! 3 Iss viel Gemüse! 4 Geh viel zu Fuß! 5 Iss keine Süßigkeiten! 6 Trink keinen Alkohol! 7 Mach viel Sport! 8 Iss kein Fastfood!

T3.2 **O2** *Finde die passenden Bilder für die Sätze in Übung O1.* Pupils match the instructions from activity O1 to the pictures. They check their answers by doing activity O3.

Answers: a 3; b 2; c 5; d 1; e 7; f 8; g 6; h 4

T1.3 **O3** *Ist alles richtig? Hör gut zu.* Pupils listen to the recording to check their answers to activity O2.

> **Transcript**   W 81, activity O3
>
> a – Iss viel Gemüse! Gemüse ist sehr gesund.
> b – Rauch nicht! Das ist nicht gesund.
> c – Iss keine Süßigkeiten! Süßigkeiten sind ungesund.
> d – Trink viel Wasser! Das ist gesund.
> e – Mach viel Sport! Sport ist gesund und macht fit.
> f – Iss kein Fastfood! Das ist nicht gesund.
> g – Trink keinen Alkohol! Alkohol ist ungesund.
> h – Geh viel zu Fuß! Das ist gesund – und macht fit.

AT 4.3 **O4** *Schreib weitere Tipps für die Gesundheit.* Pupils write four more health tips in the imperative, in response to the picture cues.

Suggested answers:

a Iss kein/nicht (zu) viel/wenig Fleisch!
b Iss (viel) Fisch!
c Fahr (viel/oft/immer) mit dem Rad!
d Trink keinen/nicht (zu) viel/wenig Kaffee!

AT 2.4 **P** *Welche Tipps in Übung O findest du gut/wichtig? Warum? Macht Dialoge mit deinem Partner/deiner Partnerin.* Pupils work together in pairs to discuss the health tips in activity O.

Pages 82-83

Use with pages 104-105 in the Students' Book.

AT 1.3 **Q** *Was soll man für die Gesundheit tun? Hör gut zu und finde die passenden Bilder.* Pupils listen to the recording and put the pictures into the sequence in which the corresponding pieces of advice occur on the recording.

Answers: a 3; b 4; c 8; d 1; e 6; f 5; g 7; h 2

> **Transcript**   W 82, activity Q
>
> 1 – Was soll man für die Gesundheit tun? Man soll wenig Fleisch essen.
> 2 – Man soll auch zu Fuß zur Schule gehen.
> 3 – Man soll keine Süßigkeiten essen.
> 4 – Man soll viel Obst und Gemüse essen.
> 5 – Und man soll Sport treiben.
> 6 – Ja, und man soll viel Mineralwasser trinken.
> 7 – Man soll auch nicht rauchen.
> 8 – Und man soll kein Fastfood essen.

AT 4.3 **R** *Schreib Sprechblasen für die Bilder.* Pupils write speech bubbles with *man soll* to match the picture cues.

Suggested answers:

a Man soll keine Cola trinken.
b Man soll (viel) Milch trinken.
c Man soll keine Chips essen.
d Man soll (viel) Rad fahren.
e Man soll keine Schokolade essen.
f Man soll (viel) (grünen) Salat essen.

AT 4.3 **S** *Matthias will im neuen Jahr viel für die Gesundheit tun. Füll die Lücken aus.* Pupils complete the captions for the pictures illustrating Matthias's New Year's resolutions.

Answers:

a Ich werde viel zu Fuß gehen. b Ich werde kein Fastfood essen. c Ich werde viel Sport treiben/machen. d Ich werde keine Süßigkeiten essen. e Ich werde viel Mineralwasser trinken. f Ich werde nicht rauchen.

AT 4.5 **T1** *Was willst du im neuen Jahr für die Gesundheit tun? Schreib Sätze für dein Tagebuch.* Pupils write New Year's resolutions with *Ich werde …* according to the picture cues. Pupils check their own answers by doing activity T2.

Suggested answers:

(Accept slight differences in phrasing.)
1 Ich werde viel Obst und Gemüse essen.
2 Ich werde keine Limonade trinken.
3 Ich werde viel Fußball spielen.
4 Ich werde keine Pommes frites essen.
5 Ich werde viel Jogurt essen.
6 Ich werde keinen Alkohol trinken.

AT 2.5 **T2** *Ist alles richtig? A fragt, B antwortet. Dann ist B dran.* Pupils work together in pairs to check their answers to activity T1 orally.

AT 4.5 **U** *Du bist dran! Was willst du im neuen Jahr für die Gesundheit tun?* Pupils now write their own New Year's resolutions using the future tense. This activity can form part of pupils' written records for continuous assessment purposes.

Can you …?

The purpose of the checklist is to identify tasks in the Students' Book both by skill and by topic. Teachers may find this helpful in selecting specific tasks, as a record of pupils' achievements in an Attainment Target.

Einheit 8 Gesundes Leben	AT 1 Listening	AT 2 Speaking	AT 3 Reading	AT 4 Writing
98–99 Mein Bauch tut weh!				
Name parts of your body	1a	–	1a	–
Say where it hurts	2, 4, 5a	1b, 3, 5b	2, 4	6, 7
Ask what's wrong and since when	4, 5a	5b	4	–
Say how long you've been ill	4, 5a	5b	4	6, 7
Understand the doctor's instructions	5a	5b	–	7
100–101 Iss dich fit!				
Discuss what's good and bad for your health	1b	3b	1a	2, 3a, Noch mal!, Extra!
102–103 Meine Gesundheit				
Say what you do for your health	–	2a	1a, 1b, 1c	1d, 2b
Give advice on healthy eating	3	4b, 6b	3	4a, 5, 6a
104–105 Was soll man für die Gesundheit tun?				
Say what you should do for a healthy lifestyle	1, 2	Noch mal!, Extra!	1	3, 4
Say what you shouldn't do for a healthy lifestyle	1, 2	Noch mal!, Extra!	1	3, 4
Say what you're going to do for your health	5	7, 8b	5, 8a	6, 8a

Copymasters

For general advice about using the copymasters, see page 7 of the introduction to this book.

C 67 Hören

1 *Hör gut zu und finde die passenden Bilder.* Pupils listen to the recording and select the appropriate pictures (1–6 and a–f) for the ailment and treatment mentioned for each patient.

AT 1.3

Answers: 1 a; 2 f; 3 c; 4 d; 5 e; 6 b

Transcript C 67, activity 1

1
– Was fehlt dir?
– Ich habe seit zwei Tagen Kopfschmerzen.
– Dann nimm diese Tabletten zweimal täglich.
– Danke.
2
– Wo tut's weh?
– Ich habe seit gestern Bauchschmerzen.
– Nimm dieses Medikament dreimal täglich nach dem Essen.
3
– Ich habe seit zwei Wochen Heuschnupfen.
– Nimm diese Tabletten zweimal täglich mit Wasser.
4
– Was fehlt dir?
– Ich habe seit drei Tagen Husten.
– Nimm dieses Medikament dreimal täglich vor dem Essen.

5
– Wo tut es weh?
– Ich habe seit zwei Tagen Halsschmerzen.
– Nimm diese Tropfen zweimal täglich.
6
– Ich habe seit gestern Fieber.
– Nimm diese Tabletten dreimal täglich nach dem Essen.

2 *Was machen sie im Neuen Jahr? Hör gut zu und finde die passenden Bilder.* Pupils listen to the recording (New Year's resolutions for a healthier lifestyle) and match the pictures to the speakers.

AT 1.3

Answers: Markus: h, c, a; Ralf: d, i, e; Michael: f, g, b

Transcript C 67, activity 2

1
– Hallo! Ich heiße Markus. Was soll ich denn im neuen Jahr machen? Ich soll zu Fuß zur Schule gehen - das macht fit! Und ich soll viel Obst und Gemüse essen und kein Fastfood mehr!
2
– Hallo! Ich bin der Ralf. Ich mache schon viel Sport, aber ich werde auch zweimal pro Woche schwimmen gehen. Ich soll keinen Kuchen essen – das ist nicht so gesund – aber viel Mineralwasser trinken. Ich trinke im Moment zu viel Cola.
3
– Ich heiße Michael und ich bin fünfzehn. Ich werde jeden Tag mit dem Rad zur Schule fahren und keine Süßigkeiten essen. Und ich will fit bleiben – also, ich soll nicht rauchen. Das ist ja klar!

3 *Hör gut zu. Wer ist das – Claudia oder Renate? Schreib C oder R in die Kästchen.* Pupils listen to the recording and then decide which of the speakers the statements about lifestyle apply to.

Answers: 1 C; 2 R; 3 R; 4 C; 5 C; 6 R

Transcript   C 67, activity 3

– Claudia, was machst du für deine Gesundheit?
– Also, ich mache ziemlich viel für meine Gesundheit. Ich gehe jeden Tag zu Fuß zur Schule und dreimal pro Woche mache ich Sport nach der Schule. Am Montag spiele ich Basketball. Am Mittwoch gehe ich schwimmen. Und am Freitag spiele ich Tennis.
– Das ist ja sehr gesund! Und du, Renate? Was für Sport machst du?
– Ich mache nicht sehr gern Sport – das finde ich langweilig und zu anstrengend. Aber ich bin auch ziemlich aktiv! Jeden Freitag gehe ich gern in die Disco und ich tanze den ganzen Abend. Das macht bestimmt fit. Ich fahre auch ziemlich gern Rad und ich gehe auch mit meinem Hund in den Park.
– Das ist auch gut! Und beim Essen? Isst du gesund, Renate?
– Hmmm ... am liebsten esse ich Fastfood und Eis! Aber ich esse auch gern Obst. Obst ist sehr gesund, finde ich.
– Und du, Claudia?
– Ich esse meistens sehr gesund. Ich esse viel Obst und Gemüse und kein Fastfood. Ich trinke auch nur Mineralwasser oder Milch – und manchmal auch Orangensaft.
– Und was machst du in deiner Freizeit, Claudia?
– Abends nach dem Essen sehe ich gern fern. Das ist leider nicht so gut für die Gesundheit.
– Und du, Renate?
– Also, am Wochenende fahre ich oft Skateboard mit meinem Bruder. Das macht Spaß!

C 68 **Sprechen**

1a *Frag deinen Partner/deine Partnerin: „Was fehlt dir? Seit wann hast du ... ?"*

1b *Was soll er/sie machen? Schau die Bilder an und antworte. (Sieh Lehrbuch, Seite 99, wenn du Hilfe brauchst.)* Pupils work in pairs to create dialogues. Partner A is the doctor, partner B is the patient. A asks B what the problem is and how long it has been going on, B answers according to his/her cues and A prescribes a treatment according to his/her cues. There is material for four possible dialogues.

2 *Dein Partner/deine Partnerin fragt: „Was fehlt dir? Seit wann hast du ... ?" Schau die Bilder unten an und antworte.* This is the second part of the activity with the roles reversed and with different cues, providing material for four more dialogues.

C 69 **Lesen**

1 *Wo tut es weh? Finde die passenden Bilder.* Pupils read the sentences and select the appropriate picture for each ailment.

Answers: 1 f; 2 b; 3 a; 4 e; 5 d; 6 c

2 *Finde die passenden Bilder für die Sprechblasen.* Pupils read the resolutions with *ich werde ...* and select the appropriate picture for each.

Answers: 1 c; 2 f; 3 d; 4 a; 5 b; 6 e

3 *Lies Astrids E-Mail. Sind die Sätze richtig oder falsch? Füll die Tabelle aus.* Pupils read the e-mail about Astrid's healthy lifestyle and then answer the comprehension questions.

Answers:

1 falsch; 2 richtig; 3 falsch; 4 richtig; 5 falsch; 6 [doesn't say]

C 70 **Schreiben**

1 *Kreuzworträtsel. Schreib die Wörter auf.* Pupils complete the crossword puzzle in accordance with the picture clues.

Answers:

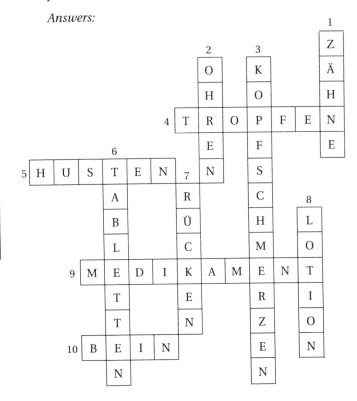

2 *Schreib die Sätze richtig auf.* Pupils re-order the words to make sentences relevant to a visit to the doctor's (*seit* + present tense; imperative of *nehmen*).

Answers:

1 Ich habe seit zwei Tagen Fieber. 2 Nimm dieses Medikament zweimal täglich. 3 Nimm diese Tabletten nach dem Essen. 4 Mein Hals tut seit zwei Tagen weh. 5 Seit wann hast du Grippe? 6 Ich habe seit einer Woche Heuschnupfen.

3a *Schau die Bilder an und schreib eine ‚Neujahrs-Hitparade'.* Pupils write New Year's resolutions using the future tense, in response to the picture cues.

Answers:

1 Ich werde mit dem Rad zur Schule fahren.
2 Ich werde keinen Kuchen essen.
3 Ich werde (oft) schwimmen/ins Schwimmbad gehen.
4 Ich werde kein Fastfood essen.
5 Ich werde keinen Kaffee trinken.
6 Ich werde (oft) Tennis spielen.

AT 4.5 **3b** *Du bist dran! Schreib deine eigene ‚Neujahrs-Hitparade'.* Pupils write their own list of New Year's resolutions.

C 71A **Grammatik 1**

This copymaster focuses on *seit* + present tense and the imperative.

1 *Schau die Bilder an und schreib Sätze.* Pupils read the 'Flashback' and write sentences about ailments with *seit* and the present tense, using the word and picture cues provided.

Answers:

1 Mein Fuß tut seit einer Woche weh.
2 Mein Hals tut seit gestern weh./Ich habe seit gestern Halsschmerzen.
3 Ich habe seit zwei Tagen Fieber.
4 Ich habe seit zwei Wochen Heuschnupfen.
5 Ich habe seit Mittag Kopfschmerzen./Mein Kopf tut seit Mittag weh.
6 Ich habe seit Mittwoch Bauchschmerzen./Mein Bauch tut seit Mittwoch weh.

2 *Schreib neue Sätze mit dem Imperativ.* Pupils read the 'Flashback' and then transform the statements into instructions in the imperative (*du* and *Sie* forms).

Answers:

1 Geh zu Fuß zur Schule! 2 Fahren Sie mit dem Rad in die Stadt! 3 Iss keinen Kuchen mehr! 4 Trinken Sie keinen Alkohol! 5 Spiel jeden Tag Tennis! 6 Nehmen Sie dieses Medikament!

C 71B **Grammatik 2**

This copymaster focuses on *sollen* and the future tense.

1 *Das macht fit! Schreib neue Sätze mit sollen für das Poster.* Pupils read the 'Flashback' and then transform the sentences using *man soll …*

Answers:

1 Man soll jede Woche schwimmen. 2 Man soll zu Fuß zur Schule gehen. 3 Man soll sehr oft Rad fahren. 4 Man soll oft Tennis spielen. 5 Man soll jeden Winter Ski fahren. 6 Man soll jeden Tag Sport machen.

2a *Gesund im Neuen Jahr! Schreib neue Sätze mit werden für die Liste.* Pupils turn the statements about unhealthy behaviour into resolutions about healthy behaviour, using the future tense.

Answers:

1 Ich werde keine Süßigkeiten essen. 2 Ich werde viel Mineralwasser trinken. 3 Ich werde nie Fastfood essen. 4 Ich werde wenig Fleisch essen. 5 Ich werde keinen Alkohol trinken. 6 Ich werde keine Chips essen.

2b *Du bist dran! Schreib deine eigene Neujahrs-Sätze auf der Liste in Übung 2a.* Pupils add some New Year's resolutions of their own, using *Ich werde … + infinitive.*

C 72A **Tipp 1**

This copymaster gives advice on compound nouns.

1 *Hier ist eine Liste von zusammengesetzten Nomen aus dem Lehrbuch, Einheiten 1–8. Finde die einzelnen Wörter für jedes Beispiel und auch die Bedeutung (meaning). Brauchst du Hilfe? Schau im Wörterbuch nach!* Pupils read the 'Flashback', then break down the compound nouns into their components and write their definitions, using their dictionaries as necessary. Point out to them that not all of the components will be nouns: it is also possible to use a verb as the first part of a compound noun, by taking off the *-en* ending.

Answers:

der Altglascontainer	das Altglas	+	der Container	= bottle bank
der Brieffreund	der Brief	+	der Freund	= penfriend (male)
die Ferienwohnung	die Ferien (pl.)	+	die Wohnung	= holiday flat/apartment
das Freizeitzentrum	die Freizeit	+	das Zentrum	= leisure centre
das Fußballstadion	der Fußball	+	das Stadion	= football stadium
die Halstablette	der Hals	+	die Tablette	= throat sweet
das Haustier	das Haus	+	das Tier	= pet
die Jugendherberge	die Jugend	+	die Herberge	= youth hostel
der Kartoffelsalat	die Kartoffel	+	der Salat	= potato salad
die Postkarte	die Post	+	die Karte	= postcard
die Radiosendung	das Radio	+	die Sendung	= radio programme
die Schuluniform	die Schule	+	die Uniform	= school uniform
das Schlüsselwort	der Schlüssel	+	das Wort	= key word
das Schulfest	die Schule	+	das Fest	= school function
das Taschengeld	die Tasche + n	+	das Geld	= pocket money
die Tierfreundin	das Tier	+	die Freundin	= animal lover (female)
der Wetterbericht	das Wetter	+	der Bericht	= weather report/forecast
das Wochenende	die Woche + n	+	das Ende	= weekend
das Wörterbuch	die Wörter (pl.)	+	das Buch	= dictionary

72B **Tipp 2**

This copymaster focuses on giving a presentation.

1 *Mach Notizen zum Thema: ‚Was ich für meine Gesundheit mache‘. Brauchst du Hilfe? Sieh Lehrbuch, Seite 104–105.* Pupils read the 'Flashback' and then make brief notes on their own lifestyle, detailing the types of healthy food and drink they normally consume and what else they do for their health. More able pupils should be encouraged to do this without reference to the Students' Book.

2 *Schreib den Text (50 Wörter) für deine Präsentation.* Pupils write full sentences in preparation for their oral presentation.

3 *Schreib dann Schlüsselwörter für deinen Text.* Pupils reduce their written text to brief key words to act as prompts.

4 *Übe deine Präsentation und führ sie der Klasse vor! Viel Glück!* Encourage pupils to practise their presentation using their prompts, before speaking in front of the class or a partner.

Einheit 9 Zukunft

Pages	Objectives	Grammar	Pronunciation, Skill focus	Key language	PoS	AT level
108–109 Die Klassel-Clique	Reading and listening for pleasure Familiarization with themes, structures and language of the unit	–	–	–	–	1.5, 3.2–3, 3.5
110–111 Was machst du in den Sommerferien?	Ask others about their plans for the holidays Talk about your plans for the holidays Talk about other people's plans for the holidays	Future tense	Reading comprehension Pronunciation of ch and sch	Was machst du in den Sommerferien? Ich werde/will … Er/Sie wird/will … Wir werden/wollen … Sie werden/wollen … … besuchen. nach … fahren/fliegen. Urlaub in … machen. eine Radtour machen. zu Hause bleiben. lange schlafen. faulenzen. ins Popkonzert/Schwimmbad gehen. Fußball spielen.	1a, 1b, 1c, 2a, 2b, 2c, 2d, 2i, 5a, 5i	2.5, 3.5, 4.5
112–113 Ich werde Hausaufgaben machen!	Talk about resolutions for the new academic year Compare this year and next year	Review of perfect, present and future tenses	–	Ich werde … jeden Tag Hausaufgaben machen. um 7 Uhr aufstehen. um 20 Uhr ins Bett gehen. mit meinen Freunden Deutsch sprechen. mein Taschengeld für einen Computer sparen. Briefe an meinen Brieffreund/meine Brieffreundin in … schreiben. E-Mails an meinen Austauschschüler/meine Austauschschülerin in … schreiben. Dieses Jahr habe ich … gemacht/gewählt/gelernt. Nächstes Jahr werde ich … machen/wählen/lernen. einen Computerkurs/Kochkurs eine Theater-AG/Umwelt-AG Basketball/Fußball/Tennis/Volleyball Geige/Gitarre/Klavier Nähen/Werken	1a, 1b, 1c, 2a, 2b, 2c, 2d, 5a, 5f, 5i	1.3, 1.5–6, 2.5–6, 3.3, 3.5, 4.3, 4.5–6

Pages	Objectives	Grammar	Pronunciation, Skill focus	Key language	PoS	AT level
114–115 Berufe	Say what jobs your parents do Ask what someone else's parents do Talk about your future job plans	Masculine and feminine forms of job titles *Ich möchte … werden*	–	Was ist dein Vater/deine Mutter von Beruf? Was möchtest du später werden? Mein Vater ist … Meine Mutter ist … Ich möchte … werden. Arzt/Büroarbeiter/Feuerwehrmann/Geschäftsmann/Hausmann/Informatiker/Kellner/Krankenpfleger/ Lehrer/Mechaniker/Polizist/Postbote/Fahrer/Sekretär/Tierarzt/Verkäufer Ärztin/Büroarbeiterin/Feuerwehrfrau/Geschäftsfrau/Hausfrau/Informatikerin/Kellnerin/Krankenschwester/Lehrerin/LKW-Fahrerin/Mechanikerin/Polizistin/Postbotin/Sekretärin/Tierärztin/Verkäuferin	1a, 1b, 1c, 2a, 2b, 2c, 2d, 3e, 5a, 5c, 5f, 5i	1.2–3, 1.5, 2.2–3, 2.5, 3.3, 4.2, 4.5
116–117 Ich möchte gern Popstar werden!	Talk about what you would like to do in the future	Review: *ich möchte*	Recording a longer text	Ich möchte später/gern … ein Auto haben. viel Geld verdienen. eine große Wohnung/ein schönes Haus haben. um die Welt reisen. jeden Tag im Restaurant essen. Designermode tragen. viele Geschenke für meine Familie/Freunde kaufen. viele Popstars treffen. jedes Wochenende eine Party machen.	1a, 1b, 1c, 2a, 2b, 2c, 2d, 3e, 5a, 5c, 5f, 5i	1.3, 1.5, 2.3, 2.5, 3.3, 3.5, 4.5
118–119 Thema im Fokus	Use language from Unit 9 creatively Encourage independent, pair- and groupwork	–	–	–	1c, 2c, 2d, 3e, 5a, 5c, 5d, 5f, 5i	2.5, 4.5

9 Zukunft

Aims of the unit

- To be able to talk about plans for the holidays
- To be able to talk about resolutions for the future
- To be able to talk about jobs and your future job plans
- To be able to talk about your other aspirations for the future

Die Klasse!-Clique
pages 108–109

Materials

- Students' Book pages 108–109
- Cassette 3 side B

For general advice on exploiting the photo story, see pages 10–11 of the introduction to this book.

In this episode, it is half past seven, and a nervous Jasmin is waiting in front of the fast food stall for her e-mail penfriend Sascha, whom she has never seen. Alexander is there too, waiting for someone. When the two notice each other, the realization dawns on Jasmin that Alexander is wearing what 'Sascha' said he would wear: white jeans and a black T-shirt. Alexander is 'Sascha'! (Explain to pupils that Sascha is the shortened form of Alexander, just as Sandy is short for Alexander in English.) A month later, Jasmin, Atalay, Sven and Annika are discussing their plans for the coming summer holidays. Atalay is going to learn to skateboard properly, Sven is going to visit his parents in Chemnitz, Annika is off to Bavaria and Berlin – and Jasmin plans to stay in Wesel to enjoy Alexander's company.

As pupils will need to remember the previous episodes of the photo story to 'get the point' of this final episode and understand the surprise, you could begin by running through the previous episodes very briefly, asking pupils to summarize what happens in each, and gently drawing attention to Jasmin's two potential romantic attachments, Sascha and Alexander. You could divide the class into eight groups and ask each group to recount one episode of the photo story in one sentence.

AT 3.2 **1a** *Was meinst du? Vor dem Lesen: Beantworte die Fragen.* This is a pre-reading activity. Pupils look at the photos without reading the text, and predict what the content of the photo story will be, answering the questions. They check their answers by listening to the recording and reading the text (activity 1b).

Answers:

1 Jasmin ist vor der Imbissstube. 2 Sie will Sascha treffen. 3 Sascha trägt eine weiße Jeans und ein schwarzes T-Shirt. 4 Sascha ist Alexander.

AT 1.5 **1b** *Ist alles richtig? Hör gut zu und lies mit.* Pupils check **AT 3.5** their answers to activity 1a by listening to the recording and reading the text. Once you have played the text, discuss the answers as a whole-class activity.

Transcript	p 109, activity 1b

– Es ist 19 Uhr 30! Wo ist Sascha??

– Moment ... weiße Jeans, schwarzes T-Shirt ...

– Alexander? Sascha?! ...

– Aber ... Jasmin??!

– Einen Monat später ...

– Was machst du in den Sommerferien, Atalay?

– Ich werde einen Skateboardkurs machen!

– Ich werde meine Eltern in Chemnitz besuchen – aber im September bin ich wieder in Wesel!

– Und du, Jasmin? Was machst du in den Sommerferien?

– Ich werde zu Hause bleiben. Ich werde lange schlafen und faulenzen! Und ich werde mit Alexander ins Schwimmbad gehen – jeden Tag!

– Und was machst du, Annika?

– Ich? Ich werde eine Radtour machen – nach Bayern! Und ich werde meinen Cousin in Berlin besuchen.

AT 3.3 **2** *Nach dem Lesen: Lies die Texte. Welcher Text ist richtig?* Pupils read the two summaries and decide which one matches the photo story.

Answer: 2

AT 3.3 **3** *Wer macht was? Kopiere die Tabelle und kreuz die passenden Namen an.* This activity focuses pupils on the future tense, one of the main grammatical emphases of this final unit. Pupils decide which statement in the future tense applies to which character.

Answers:

	Jasmin	Annika	Atalay	Sven
1 Ich werde nach Berlin fahren.		✗		
2 Ich werde in Wesel bleiben.	✗			
3 Ich werde nach Chemnitz fahren.				✗
4 Ich werde mit dem Rad nach Bayern fahren.		✗		
5 Ich werde Skateboardfahren lernen.			✗	
6 Ich werde jeden Tag ins Schwimmbad gehen.	✗			

Was machst du in den Sommerferien?
pages 110–111

Objectives

- Ask others about their plans for the holidays
- Talk about your plans for the holidays
- Talk about other people's plans for the holidays

Key language

Was machst du in den Sommerferien?
Ich werde/will …
Er/Sie wird/will …
Wir werden/wollen …
Sie werden/wollen …
… besuchen.
nach … fahren/fliegen.
Urlaub in … machen.
eine Radtour machen.
zu Hause bleiben.
lange schlafen.
faulenzen.
ins Popkonzert/Schwimmbad gehen.
Fußball spielen.

National Curriculum PoS

statements 1a, 1b, 1c, 2a, 2b, 2c, 2d, 2i, 5a, 5i

Materials

- Students' Book pages 110–111
- Cassette 3 side B
- Workbook pages 84–86
- Copymasters 76, 77, 78A, 79, 80A, 81

Preparatory work

Revise *nach* + town/country (and *in* + country if appropriate) by talking about your own plans for the summer holidays, using a photo, a brochure or another visual. T: *Ich werde im Sommer nach [Stadt/Land] fahren.* Ask two or three pupils where they are planning to go. T: *Wohin fährst du in den Sommerferien?* Supply the German place names as necessary. You could also revise holiday activities from Unit 1, now in the future tense instead of in the perfect tense. T: *Ich werde im Sommer nach … fahren/in … Urlaub machen. Ich werde die Stadt besichtigen. Ich werde auch meine Freunde besuchen. Ich werde … essen. Ich werde … trinken.*

AT 3.5 | **1a** *Lies die Texte.* Pupils read the three texts, in which teenagers describe their holiday plans using the future tense. In Unit 8, pupils met only the first person singular of the future tense: here they are introduced to other forms.

You could provide a little geographical information in conjunction with this text. Point out that *Nizza* is an important resort city on the French Riviera (Mediterranean). Can pupils guess what its English/French name might be? (Answer: Nice.) Monaco is the second smallest state in the world (the smallest is the Vatican); it is in the south east of France, on the Mediterranean, and is famous for its casinos at Monte Carlo. Flensburg is the northernmost town in Germany, almost on the Danish border, and Kiel is further south and east on the Baltic Sea. This is a great area for cycling, as there is lots of nature, countryside and seaside to enjoy – and there are no big hills.

AT 3.5 | **1b** *Finde die passenden Futur-Sätze (Übung 1a) für die Bilder.* Pupils find the sentences in the texts to match the pictures. The pictures are in the same sequence in which the sentences occur in the text.

Answers:

a Ich werde eine Radtour machen. (Mark)
b Wir werden viel faulenzen. (Anne)
c Wir werden auch einen Ausflug nach Monaco machen. (Anne)
d Ich werde im Sommer zu Hause bleiben. (Hannes)
e Aber mein Bruder wird nach Amerika fahren! (Hannes)
f Er wird mit seiner Schulklasse fahren! (Hannes)
g Sie werden Disneyworld besuchen. (Hannes)
h Sie werden auch nach New York fahren. (Hannes)

C 79 | Activity 1 on copymaster 79 could be used here for basic writing practice with the future tense.

AT 2.5 | **1c** *Was sind deine Traumsommerferien? B wählt fünf Bilder von Übung 1b, A fragt. Dann ist B dran.* Pupils work together in pairs to create dialogues using the pictures from activity 1b as cues for sentences with *Ich werde …*

WB A | Workbook activity A practises the word order of sentences in the future tense.

WB B, C | Workbook activities B and C provide reading, listening and speaking practice of plans for the summer holidays.

C 76 | Activity 3 on copymaster 76 provides further listening comprehension on plans for the summer holidays.

C 77 | Activity 1 on copymaster 77 provides further speaking practice on plans for the summer holidays.

C 78A | Activity 2 on copymaster 78A provides further reading practice on plans for the summer holidays.

Grammatik im Fokus

Futur + werden. This section focuses on the formation of the future tense, including the conjugation of *werden* in all its present tense forms. (Only the first person singular was introduced in Unit 8.)

Point out that *Futur* means 'future' only in the grammatical sense of 'future tense', i.e. *werden* + infinitive. The normal word for the future is *die Zukunft* – the title of this unit.

With a more able group, you may wish to discuss further the idea of 'futurity' at this point. Pupils may have realized that it is often possible to talk about the future in the present tense (*Präsens*; e.g. Unit 5 *Ich mache eine Party*, etc.), just as we say, for example: 'I'm having a party next week' in English, instead of saying 'I will have a party next week'. This is particularly the case when an adverb of time (e.g. *nächste Woche*) makes it obvious that the future is meant.

Now look at the *Hilfe* box on page 110. Make sure that pupils understand that *ich will* means 'I want to', not 'I will', which is *ich werde*. Ask pupils *Was machst du in den Sommerferien?* and then questions which elicit other forms of the verb, such as *Was macht Tim in den Sommerferien? Was machen Alice und ihre Familie in den Sommerferien?*, etc.

2a *Schreib deine Sätze von Übung 1b in vier Listen auf: ich, er, wir und sie (Plural).* Pupils now categorize the sentences from activity 1b in terms of person and number.

199

2b *Finde dann andere Futur-Sätze in den Texten von Übung 1a und schreib sie in die Listen auf. Wie viele kannst du finden?* Pupils analyse the remaining sentences in the three texts.

2c *Füll die Lücken aus.* Pupils complete the sentences with the correct forms of *werden*. They could then complete the same task with *wollen*, if you are confident that they have grasped the difference between the two verbs.

Answers:

1 werden; 2 werde; 3 wird; 4 wirst; 5 werde; 6 werden

WB D   Workbook activity D is a gap-fill task practising the forms of auxiliary *werden*.

WB E   Workbook activity E is a gap-fill task on plans expressed in the future tense.

C 80A   Copymaster 80A contains information in English about the future tense. Activity 1 practises the future tense in all persons.

Tipp

Lesen … und verstehen! This section gives advice on doing reading comprehension activities. Discuss the advice with the class and then do activity 3 (or just the first question) as a whole-class activity, going through each of the steps described, eliciting the answers at each stage from pupils.

You could then give pupils the following checklist, as a final stage:

Lies noch einmal alle Antworten gut durch:
- *Hast du alle Wörter richtig geschrieben (buchstabiert)?*
- *Sind die Zeitformen richtig (Präsens, Perfekt/Imperfekt oder Futur)?*
- *Sind alle Verb-Endungen richtig?*
- *Sind alle Plural-Endungen richtig?*
- *Sind alle Adjektiv-Endungen richtig?*

3 *Lies noch einmal die Texte in Übung 1a und beantworte die Fragen.* Pupils answer the comprehension questions on the texts in activity 1a, going through the steps described in the *Tipp*.

Answers:

1 Sie werden in Norddeutschland Urlaub machen.
2 Er will jeden Tag 30 Kilometer fahren.
3 Sie wird in Nizza Urlaub machen.
4 Sie will im Urlaub faulenzen, weil das Schuljahr sehr anstrengend war.
5 Er wird zu Hause in Potsdam bleiben.

C 81   Copymaster 81 contains further advice on reading and understanding longer texts. Activity 1 puts the advice into practice, and could be used here.

AT 4.5   **4** *Du bist dran! Schreib einen Text (so wie in Übung 1a) mit den Informationen unten.* Pupils write their own texts in the future tense, using the picture cues.

WB F   Workbook activity F is an opportunity for independent writing on the subject of plans for the summer holidays.

Gut gesagt!

ch, sch. This section focuses on the pronunciation of *ch* and *sch*.

 5a *Hör gut zu und wiederhole.* Pupils listen to the recording and repeat the words.

Transcript	p 111, activity 5a
besuchen	
machen	
Wochenende	
schlafen	
Schwimmbad	
Schottland	

 5b *Hör gut zu und wiederhole.* Pupils listen to the recording and repeat the sentences. Draw pupils' attention to the distinction between *ch* as in *ich* and as in *nach*.

Transcript	p 111, activity 5b
Ich werde nach Frankreich fahren,	
Mascha wird nach Süddeutschland fliegen,	
Michi wird in die Schweiz fahren	
Und Sascha wird nach Österreich fliegen!	

Ich werde Hausaufgaben machen!
pages 112–113

Objectives
- Talk about resolutions for the new academic year
- Compare this year and next year

Key language
Ich werde …
jeden Tag Hausaufgaben machen.
um 7 Uhr aufstehen.
um 20 Uhr ins Bett gehen.
mit meinen Freunden Deutsch sprechen.
mein Taschengeld für einen Computer sparen.
Briefe an meinen Brieffreund/meine Brieffreundin in … schreiben.
E-Mails an meinen Austauschschüler/meine Austauschschülerin in … schreiben.
Dieses Jahr habe ich … gemacht/gewählt/gelernt.
Nächstes Jahr werde ich … machen/wählen/lernen.
einen Computerkurs/Kochkurs
eine Theater-AG/Umwelt-AG
Basketball/Fußball/Tennis/Volleyball
Geige/Gitarre/Klavier
Nähen/Werken

National Curriculum PoS
statements 1a, 1b, 1c, 2a, 2b, 2c, 2d, 5a, 5f, 5i

Materials
- Students' Book pages 112–113
- Cassette 3 side B
- Workbook pages 87–89
- Copymasters 76, 80A

1a *Atalay will im neuen Schuljahr viel für die Schule tun. Hör gut zu und finde die passenden Bilder für die Sätze.* Pupils listen to the recording and follow the text in the book, before matching each of the pictures to the appropriate resolution.

Answers: 1 d; 2 f; 3 e; 4 a; 5 c; 6 g; 7 b

> **Transcript** p 112, activity 1a
>
> Also, nächste Woche beginnt das neue Schuljahr – und ich will dieses Jahr viel für die Schule tun! Was werde ich machen – was ist wichtig? Also, ich werde jeden Tag Hausaufgaben machen – das ist wichtig – leider! Ja, und ich werde mein Taschengeld für einen neuen Computer sparen. Ich kann dann meinen Hausaufgaben mit meinem Computer machen! Und ich werde morgens früh aufstehen – ja, ich werde um 7 Uhr aufstehen – dann kann ich vor der Schule Frühstück essen! Und abends – abends werde ich um 21 Uhr ins Bett gehen! Das ist langweilig – aber das ist gut für die Schule. Und was werde ich auch machen? Hmmm ... also, ich bin in Englisch nicht gut ... Ich werde mit meinen Freunden Englisch sprechen – jeden Tag: Vor der Schule, nach der Schule. Und ich werde auch Briefe an meine Brieffreundin in England schreiben – in Englisch. Und ich werde viele E-Mails an meinen Austauschschüler in Amerika schreiben – auch in Englisch. Gute Idee!

1b *„Was werde ich für die Schule tun?" B wählt Bilder für A (von Übung 1a), A antwortet. Dann ist B dran.* Pupils work together in pairs to create dialogues with *ich werde*, using the pictures from activity 1a as cues.

Workbook activities G–J provide listening, writing and speaking practice of the future tense in the context of resolutions for the next academic year.

Noch mal! Was willst du im neuen Schuljahr für die Schule tun? Schreib Sätze mit Ich werde. Benutze die Hilfe-Sätze rechts. Pupils write their own resolutions for the new academic year with *ich werde*, using the expressions provided in the *Hilfe* box.

Extra! Erfinde weitere Sätze. Pupils write their own resolutions for the new academic year without the aid of prompts, using language they already know.

2 *Hör gut zu und lies mit.* Pupils listen to the recording and follow the text in the book. In this activity, pupils can start to see how references to the past and future can be combined, with the appropriate choice of tenses. Explain that 'AG' is the abbreviation for *Arbeitsgemeinschaft*; in the narrow sense, this means a study group, in the wider sense, it means any organized extra-curricular activity at school.

> **Transcript** p 113, activity 2
>
> – Dieses Jahr habe ich Geige gelernt. Nächstes Jahr werde ich Klavier lernen.
> – Dieses Jahr habe ich einen Kochkurs gemacht. Nächstes Jahr werde ich eine Theater-AG machen.
> – Dieses Jahr habe ich Werken gewählt. Nächstes Jahr werde ich Nähen wählen.

Workbook activity K is a reading comprehension on sentences similiar to those in activity 2 above, and can be used in preparation for activity 3.

3 *Was haben sie dieses Jahr gemacht? Was werden sie nächstes Jahr machen? Hör gut zu und finde die passenden Hilfe-Wörter.* Pupils listen to the recording and select the appropriate expressions from the *Hilfe* box for the activities mentioned by each speaker.

Answers:

Atalay: dieses Jahr: Kochkurs, Werken
nächstes Jahr: Theater-AG, Nähen
Annika: dieses Jahr: Klavier, Basketball
nächstes Jahr: Geige, Fußball
Sven: dieses Jahr: Umwelt-AG, Geige
nächstes Jahr: Kochkurs, Gitarre
Jasmin: dieses Jahr: Theater-AG, Fußball
nächstes Jahr: Computerkurs, Tennis

> **Transcript** p 113, activity 4
>
> – Also, was machen wir nächstes Jahr? Wer hat eine Idee? Atalay?
> – Hmm ... dieses Jahr habe ich einen Kochkurs gemacht. Aber nächstes Jahr werde ich eine Theater-AG machen. Ich interessiere mich sehr für Theater! Was machst du, Annika?
> – Also, dieses Jahr habe ich Klavier gelernt – leider! Klavier ist total schwer! Nächstes Jahr werde ich Geige lernen. Und du, Sven?
> – Na ja, dieses Jahr habe ich eine Umwelt-AG gewählt. Aber nächstes Jahr werde ich einen Kochkurs wählen – ich koche gern!
> – Und machst du einen Computerkurs, Jasmin?
> – Ja. Dieses Jahr habe ich eine Theater-AG gewählt – aber das war langweilig! Also, nächstes Jahr werde ich einen Computerkurs wählen – ich spare für einen Computer! Und du, Atalay? Was hast du noch gemacht?
> – Also, dieses Jahr habe ich Werken gewählt. Aber Werken ist langweilig, finde ich! Nächstes Jahr werde ich Nähen wählen – ich finde Mode toll! Wie findest du Nähen, Jasmin?
> – Nähen? Ich weiß nicht ... Vielleicht Tennis ...
> – Oder Fußball? Dieses Jahr habe ich Basketball gemacht. Aber ich mag die Lehrerin nicht. Also, nächstes Jahr werde ich Fußball wählen – der Lehrer ist super!
> – Fußball?? Dieses Jahr habe ich Fußball gemacht – und Fußball war total anstrengend! Nein, nächstes Jahr werde ich Tennis machen. Und du, Sven?
> – Keinen Sport!! Also, dieses Jahr habe ich Geige gelernt. Aber nächstes Jahr werde ich Gitarre wählen – dann kann ich in einer Gruppe spielen!

Workbook activities L and M provide writing and speaking practice respectively of the perfect and future tenses in the context of extra-curricular activities.

Activity 2 on copymaster 76 provides further listening practice on resolutions for the next academic year, and could be used at this point.

201

AT 2.6
AT 4.6
4 *Was hast du dieses Jahr gemacht? Was willst du nächstes Jahr machen? Schreib einen Plan. Mach dann Dialoge mit deinem Partner/deiner Partnerin.* Pupils work together in pairs to create dialogues about their after-school clubs and activities, comparing what they did this year with what they plan to do next year. They should select from the choices in the *Hilfe* box.

Grammatik im Fokus

Perfekt, Präsens und Futur. This section reviews the three main tenses that pupils have met so far.

5 *Lies Daniels E-Mail und finde vier Sätze im Perfekt, Präsens und Futur.* Pupils analyse the tenses used in the text.

Answers:

Perfekt:

Was hast du am Wochenende gemacht?
Wir sind zum Schwimmbad im Park gefahren.
Gestern habe ich Mathe und Englisch gemacht.
Gestern habe ich bis um 22 Uhr ferngesehen.
Danach bin ich ins Bett gegangen – um 22 Uhr 30!

Präsens:

sie wohnt in Köln.
Ich mache auch viel für die Schule
ich mache jeden Tag Hausaufgaben!
und heute lerne ich Französisch.
Biologie ist mein Lieblingsfach!

Futur:

Ich werde am Sonntag meine Schwester besuchen.
Morgen werde ich Biologie machen.
Ich werde auch abends früh ins Bett gehen.
Und heute werde ich auch spät ins Bett gehen
ich werde mit Kathi in die neue Disco am Bahnhof gehen!

WB N
Workbook activity N briefly revises the formation of the perfect and future tenses.

AT 4.5
6a *Was hat Hanna letzte Woche gemacht? Schreib einen Brief – im Perfekt.* Pupils transform the sentences from the present tense into the perfect tense.

Answers:

Ich habe um 7 Uhr Müsli gegessen.
Ich bin mit dem Bus zur Schule gefahren.
Ich habe Deutsch, Mathe und Geschichte gelernt.
Ich habe Pizza gegessen und ich habe Cola getrunken.
Ich habe nachmittags Hausaufgaben gemacht.
Ich bin um 22 Uhr ins Bett gegangen.

AT 4.5
6b *Was wird Hanna nächste Woche machen? Schreib Sätze im Futur.* Pupils now transform the sentences in activity 6a into the future tense.

Answers:

Ich werde um 7 Uhr Müsli essen.
Ich werde mit dem Bus zur Schule fahren.
Ich werde Deutsch, Mathe und Geschichte lernen.
Ich werde Pizza essen und ich werde Cola trinken.
Ich werde nachmittags Hausaufgaben machen.
Ich werde um 22 Uhr ins Bett gehen.

Follow-up activity. Pupils could write diary entries for their favourite celebrity, describing what he/she did last week (perfect tense), is doing now (present tense) and plans to do next week (future tense).

WB O
Workbook activity O provides writing and speaking practice combining the perfect, present and future tenses.

C 80A
Copymaster 80A contains information in English about the perfect, present and future tenses. Activity 2 provides practice in forming these tenses and translating them into English.

Berufe
pages 114–115

Objectives
- Say what jobs your parents do
- Ask what someone else's parents do
- Talk about your future job plans

Key language
Was ist dein Vater/deine Mutter von Beruf?
Was möchtest du später werden?
Mein Vater ist …
Meine Mutter ist …
Ich möchte … werden.
*Arzt/Büroarbeiter/Feuerwehrmann/Geschäftsmann/
Hausmann/Informatiker/Kellner/Krankenpfleger/
Lehrer/LKW-Fahrer/Mechaniker/Polizist/Postbote/
Sekretär/Tierarzt/Verkäufer
Ärztin/Büroarbeiterin/Feuerwehrfrau/Geschäftsfrau/
Hausfrau/Informatikerin/Kellnerin/ Krankenschwester/
Lehrerin/LKW-Fahrerin/Mechanikerin/Polizistin/
Postbotin/Sekretärin/Tierärztin/ Verkäuferin*

National Curriculum PoS
statements 1a, 1b, 1c, 2a, 2b, 2c, 2d, 3e, 5a, 5c, 5f, 5i

Materials
- Students' Book pages 114–115
- Cassette 3 side B
- Workbook pages 90–92
- Copymasters 73, 76, 78A, 79, 80B

C 73
Preparatory work
Introduce professions using the pictures from copymaster 73 copied onto an OHT, or as flashcards. (For general advice on using copymaster visuals, see page 12 of the introduction to this book.) Introduce the form *Mein Vater ist Arzt./Meine Mutter ist Ärztin*, etc., pointing out that no indefinite article is used.

As this could be a sensitive topic, due to unemployment, family break-up, loss of a parent or disparity in families' economic situations, there should be no requirement for pupils to give information about their parents' real jobs.

AT 1.2
1a *Was ist dein Vater/deine Mutter von Beruf? Hör gut zu und finde die richtige Reihenfolge für die Bilder.* Pupils listen to the recording and then put the jobs into the sequence in which they are mentioned.

Answers: g, c, e, h, b, d, f, a

Transcript   p 114, activity 1a

– Mein Vater ist Arzt.
– Meine Mutter ist Ärztin.
– Mein Vater ist Kellner.
– Meine Mutter ist Kellnerin.
– Mein Vater ist Lehrer.
– Meine Mutter ist Lehrerin.
– Mein Vater ist Polizist.
– Meine Mutter ist Polizistin.
– Mein Vater ist Sekretär.
– Meine Mutter ist Sekretärin.
– Mein Vater ist Postbote.
– Meine Mutter ist Postbotin.
– Mein Vater ist Hausmann.
– Meine Mutter ist Hausfrau.
– Mein Vater ist Krankenpfleger.
– Meine Mutter ist Krankenschwester.

AT 2.2 **1b** *A zeigt auf ein Bild und fragt: „Was ist dein Vater/deine Mutter von Beruf?", B antwortet. Dann ist B dran.* Pupils work together in pairs to create dialogues with job titles, using the pictures from activity 1a as cues.

WB P Workbook activity P provides consolidation of the job titles introduced in activity 1 above.

C 76 Activity 1 on copymaster 76 provides further listening practice on professions.

C 78A Activity 1 on copymaster 78A provides reading practice on professions.

Grammatik im Fokus

Berufe. This section focuses on masculine and feminine forms of job titles and the fact that no article is required when talking about professions. Point out that most feminine forms are of the type which adds *-in* to the masculine, occasionally with an *Umlaut.*

AT 4.2 **2a** *Lies die Berufe und schreib die passenden Maskulinum- oder Femininum-Formen für die Wörter auf.* Pupils provide the missing masculine or feminine forms of the job titles. They check their own answers by doing activity 2b.

Answers:

1 Tierärztin; 2 Verkäufer; 3 Informatiker; 4 LKW-Fahrer; 5 Mechanikerin; 6 Geschäftsmann; 7 Büroarbeiterin; 8 Feuerwehrfrau

AT 1.3 **2b** *Ist alles richtig? Hör gut zu.* Pupils listen to the recording to check their answers to activity 2a.

Transcript   p 115, activity 2b

1
– Was ist deine Mutter von Beruf?
– Meine Mutter ist Tierärztin.
2
– Was ist dein Vater?
– Mein Vater? Er ist Verkäufer.

3
– Und was ist dein Vater von Beruf?
– Mein Vater ist Informatiker.
4
– Und dein Vater?
– Mein Vater ist LKW-Fahrer.
5
– Und was ist deine Mutter?
– Meine Mutter ist Mechanikerin.
6
– Und du? Was ist dein Vater?
– Mein Vater ist Geschäftsmann.
7
– Und deine Mutter? Was ist sie von Beruf?
– Meine Mutter ist Büroarbeiterin.
8
– Und deine Mutter?
– Meine Mutter ist Feuerwehrfrau.

WB Q Workbook activity Q provides further listening comprehension on career aspirations.

AT 2.3 **3** *A ‚spielt' einen Beruf von Übung 2a und sagt: „Mein Vater/meine Mutter ist ...", B rät den Beruf. Dann ist B dran.* Pupils play charades in pairs, using the job titles from activity 2a. The partner who is miming supplies the gender by saying *Mein Vater ist .../Meine Mutter ist ...*

AT 1.3 **AT 3.3** **4** *Was sind Jasmins, Annikas und Atalays Pläne für die Zukunft? Hör gut zu und lies mit.* Pupils listen to the recording and follow the text in the book. In preparation, ask pupils in what context they have met *ich möchte* before (*Klasse! 1*, pp. 76–79, buying food). Can they remember a sentence using *ich möchte*? If not, provide one or two examples, e.g. *Ich möchte ein Kilo Äpfel. Ich möchte ein Eis.* Ask what *ich möchte* means; confirm that it means 'I would like …'

After playing the recording, explain to the class that the verb *werden* here is the same verb which is used to form the future tense, but here it is used in a completely different sense: can they suggest what this might be? Confirm that *werden* here means 'to become'.

Transcript   p 115, activity 4

– Jasmin, was möchtest du später werden?
– Ich möchte Tierärztin werden.
– Und du, Atalay? Was möchtest du später werden?
– Ich? Ich möchte Informatiker werden!
– Und was möchtest du später werden, Annika?
– Polizistin! Ich möchte Polizistin werden.

Grammatik im Fokus

Ich möchte ... werden. This section revises *ich möchte* in this new context of jobs, and introduces *werden* in the sense of 'to become'. To a more able group, you could explain at this point that *ich möchte* can be combined with any infinitive to mean 'I would like to' + verb.

AT 2.5 **5a** *Was möchtest du später werden? A und B wählen Bilder von Übung 1a und 2a. A fragt, B antwortet.* Pupils work together to create dialogues with *ich möchte ...*

werden, using the pictures from activities 1a and 2a above as cues.

C 79 Activity 2 on copymaster 79 provides writing practice of *er/sie möchte … werden.*

C 80B Copymaster 80B contains information in English about using *ich möchte*. Activity 2 provides further writing practice of *ich möchte* + noun/infinitive.

AT 2.5
AT 4.5 **5b** *Mach eine Umfrage. Frag: „Was möchtest du später werden?" und schreib die Resultate auf (z. B. mit dem Computer).* Pupils conduct a class survey of career aspirations and write up the results, perhaps in the form of a pie chart or other graphical form of presentation, or using photographs or drawings to illustrate the results. Encourage pupils to use their dictionaries to research the names of jobs they really want to do, rather than restricting themselves to the job titles introduced above. This task is ideal for IT work.

WB R, S Workbook activities R and S provide writing practice of career aspirations.

Ich möchte gern Popstar werden! ■
pages 116–117

Objectives
• Talk about what you would like to do in the future

Key language
Ich möchte später/gern …
ein Auto haben.
viel Geld verdienen.
eine große Wohnung/ein schönes Haus haben.
um die Welt reisen.
jeden Tag im Restaurant essen.
Designermode tragen.
viele Geschenke für meine Familie/Freunde kaufen.
viele Popstars treffen.
jedes Wochenende eine Party machen.

National Curriculum PoS
statements 1a, 1b, 1c, 2a, 2b, 2c, 2d, 3e, 5a, 5c, 5f, 5i

Materials
• Students' Book pages 116–117
• Cassette 3 side B
• Workbook pages 92–93
• Copymasters 74, 77, 78B, 79

C 74 **Preparatory work**

Introduce vocabulary to describe aspirations using the pictures from copymaster 74 copied onto an OHT, or as flashcards. (For general advice on using copymaster visuals, see page 12 of the introduction to this book.)

AT 1.5
AT 3.3 **1a** *Was möchte Sven später gern machen? Hör gut zu und finde die passende Reihenfolge für die Sätze.* Pupils listen to the recording and put Sven's aspirations in the sequence in which they are mentioned.

Answers: 5, 4, 2, 1, 6, 3

– Was möchtest du später gern machen, Sven?
– Ich möchte später gern ein schönes Auto haben. Ich möchte auch eine große Wohnung kaufen – ja, eine schöne große Wohnung! Und ich möchte gern jeden Tag im Restaurant essen – ja, jeden Tag Spaghetti – oder Pizza oder Hähnchen! Ja, und ich möchte Filmstar werden – Filmstar in Amerika! Ich möchte später auch viele Geschenke für meine Freunde kaufen. Und ich möchte gern jedes Wochenende eine Party machen!

WB T Workbook activity T provides reading comprehension on aspirations, and could be used here or after activity 1b.

AT 2.3 **1b** *Was möchtest du später gern machen? A fragt, B wählt einen Satz von Übung 1a. Dann ist B dran.* Pupils work together in pairs to create dialogues with *ich möchte* + infinitive, using the sentences from activity 1a. In preparation, you could go through the conjugation of *möchte* for all persons singular and plural. Point out that *gern* is an 'optional extra' here, whose function is to emphasize that this is a wish.

AT 1.3
AT 3.3 **2a** *Was möchte Tom später gern machen? Hör gut zu und lies mit.* Pupils listen to the recording and follow the cartoon strip in the book. This activity introduces further ideas for dreams and aspirations with *ich möchte (gern).*

Transcript p 116, activity 2a

Ich möchte gern Designermode tragen!
Ich möchte viele Popstars treffen!
Ich möchte später gern viel Geld verdienen!
Ich möchte später um die Welt reisen!
Ich möchte später gern im Lotto gewinnen!
Ich möchte gern im Ausland arbeiten!

AT 2.3 **2b** *Nimm den Cartoon auf Kassette auf.* Pupils record their own version of the cartoon on cassette. This could be done as an individual activity (giving you the opportunity to check pronunciation, e.g. of *ch* in *möchte*), or as a collaborative activity in pairs or groups: instead of one speaker, there could be two or three speakers, who could bring in ideas from activity 1a as well as those in the cartoon.

WB U Workbook activity U provides listening comprehension and speaking practice of aspirations.

AT 3.5 **3a** *Lies den Artikel und beantworte die Fragen in Sätzen.* Pupils read the text and then answer the comprehension questions.

Answers:
1 Sie möchte ein Kino kaufen.
2 Sie möchte Popstar oder Geschäftsfrau werden.
3 Sie möchte ein schönes Haus/viel Geld haben.
4 Sie möchte jeden Tag im Fastfood-Restaurant essen.
5 Sie möchte dort Hamburger mit Pommes frites und Currywurst essen.
6 Sie möchte nach New York fahren.

4.5   **3b** *Schreib einen Artikel an das Jugendmagazin mit den Informationen unten.* Pupils write a text with *ich möchte* on the model of activity 3a, using the picture cues provided.

WB V   Workbook activity V is an opportunity for independent writing on the subject of aspirations.

C 77   Activity 2 on copymaster 77 provides speaking practice on the subjects of professions and aspirations, and could be used at this point.

78B   Activity 1 on copymaster 78B provides further reading practice on the subjects of professions and aspirations, and could also be used here.

C 79   Activity 3 on copymaster 79 could be used here for writing practice on aspirations.

Tipp

Lange Texte aufnehmen. This section gives advice on making an extended recording. Discuss the advice with pupils, showing how it can be applied to activity 4. Ask pupils why they think each of the pieces of advice is important. Do they have any further advice to add? (e.g. Make the recording in a quiet room. Remember to smile while you are speaking – it makes your voice sound more friendly and enthusiastic. Make several versions and choose the best one.)

AT 4.5   **4** *Du bist dran! Ein deutscher Radiosender für*
AT 2.5   *Jugendliche fragt: „Was möchtest du später gern machen?" Schreib einen Text und nimm alles auf Kassette auf.* Pupils put the advice from the *Tipp* into practice in making a recording about their aspirations.

Thema im Fokus
pages 118–119

National Curriculum PoS
statements 1c, 2c, 2d, 3e, 5a, 5c, 5d, 5f, 5i

Materials
- Students' Book pages 118–119
- Cassette 3 side B
- Copymaster 75

As in previous units, the final spread of each unit provides a project outcome for the unit. However, in this unit the reading text is replaced by a board game to act as the stimulus for the project.

AT 2.5   Pupils play the game in groups. A throw of the die decides which square they land on; the colour of the square determines which of the four questions they must answer, and the picture cue determines what answer they should give. All four questions have to do with the future, and need to be answered with the future tense (red or blue squares), with *ich will …* (option for blue squares) or with *ich möchte … werden* (yellow or green squares). If the player makes a mistake in his/her answer (either of content or grammar), he/she moves back two spaces. You may wish to give a set of answers to each group, to be referred to only in the event of a dispute.

Answers:

1 Ich werde nach Amerika/in die USA fliegen.
2 Ich will/werde (jeden Tag) Hausaufgaben machen.
3 Ich möchte Lehrer/in werden.
4 Ich möchte (gern) viel Geld verdienen/haben.
5 Ich werde (viel) faulenzen.
6 Ich will/werde um sieben Uhr aufstehen.
7 Ich möchte Informatiker/in werden.
8 Ich möchte (gern) ein schönes/neues Auto haben.
9 Ich werde meinen Brieffreund/meine Brieffreundin besuchen.
10 Ich will/werde mit meinen Freunden Deutsch sprechen.
11 Ich möchte Kellner/in werden.
12 Ich möchte (gern) Popstar werden.
13 Ich werde eine Radtour machen.
14 Ich will/werde mein Taschengeld für einen Computer sparen/einen Computer kaufen.
15 Ich möchte Tierarzt/Tierärztin werden.
16 Ich möchte (gern) um die Welt fliegen/reisen.
17 Ich werde zu Hause bleiben.
18 Ich will/werde an meinen deutschen Brieffreund/Austauschschüler/meine deutsche Brieffreundin/Austauschschülerin schreiben.
19 Ich möchte Sekretär/Sekretärin werden.
20 Ich möchte (gern) ein schönes/großes Haus/ein Schloss haben.
21 Ich werde (jeden Tag) ins Schwimmbad gehen.
22 Ich will/werde um 21.30 Uhr/halb zehn ins Bett gehen.
23 Ich möchte Geschäftsmann/Gsschäftsfrau werden.
24 Ich möchte (gern) viele Geschenke (für meine Familie/Freunde) kaufen.

AT 2.5   **1** *Macht weitere Spiele!* Pupils work together in groups
AT 4.5   to devise other board games on the model of the one on page 118. The format of the game should be the same (24 squares of four different colours, each containing a picture cue), the same rules should apply, and the game should revise points of grammar covered in this unit.

a *Findet 4 Fragen-Themen (so wie die Fragen im Spiel auf Seite 118) und schreibt sie auf (z. B. mit dem Computer).* Pupils devise four questions (one for each colour). As in the examples given, each of the questions should elicit a different structure in the answer.

b *Findet 6 Antworten für jedes Fragen-Thema und schreibt sie auf (z. B. mit dem Computer).* Pupils devise six answers for each of the four questions. Remind them that it must be possible to suggest each answer clearly with a picture cue.

c *Findet oder zeichnet Bilder für die Antworten (z. B. mit dem Computer).* Pupils find a photograph or draw a picture to illustrate each of the answers. The Web and clip-art libraries are excellent electronic resources for this task.

d *Macht das Spiel: zeichnet die Felder in ☐, ☐, ☐ und ☐ (z. B. mit dem Computer) und klebt die Bilder auf.* Pupils draw and colour the playing board and place the picture cues. This is an ideal task for completion on computer, using DTP or paint/draw software or even a sophisticated word-processing package.

e *Schreibt die Fragen mit den passenden Farben auf, so wie auf Seite 118.* Pupils write and colour the key to the questions.

f *Tauscht das Spiel mit einer anderen Gruppe (deine Gruppe nimmt das andere Spiel, die andere Gruppe nimmt euer Spiel) – und los geht's! Viel Spaß!* Groups of pupils exchange games and play the other group's game.

Kannst du ... ?

The end-of-unit summary is a checklist for pupils. See page 8 of the introduction to this book for ideas on how to use the checklist.

`C 75` Copymaster 75 provides a useful reference for pupils revising the language of this unit.

Noch mal!-Seite Einheit 9
page 138

National Curriculum PoS
statements 1a, 1b, 1c, 2a, 2b, 2c, 2d, 5a, 5i

Materials
- Students' Book page 138
- Cassette 3 side B

This revision page is intended for less able pupils. It reinforces the basic vocabulary and structures from the unit, and it can be used by pupils who experienced difficulty in completing some of the activities within the unit, or as alternative homework activities.

`AT 1.3` **1** *Was machen sie in den Sommerferien? Hör gut zu und finde die passenden Bilder.* This activity relates to pages 110–111. Pupils listen to the recording and match the pictures to the holiday plans described by the speakers.

Answers: 1 c; 2 d; 3 a; 4 b; 5 f; 6 e

> **Transcript**   p 138, activity 1
> 1 – Ich werde nach Amerika fliegen – nach Disneyworld in Florida!
> 2 – Ich werde zu Hause bleiben. Da ist es nie langweilig!
> 3 – Ich? Ich werde meine Großeltern besuchen.
> 4 – Ich werde faulenzen – den ganzen Tag!
> 5 – Ich werde jeden Tag ins Schwimmbad gehen.
> 6 – Ich werde am Wochenende einen Ausflug machen.

`AT 2.4` **2** *Was ist dein Vater/deine Mutter von Beruf? Macht Dialoge.* This activity relates to pages 114–115. Pupils work together in pairs to create dialogues about their parents' professions, using the picture cues.

`AT 3.3` **3** *Finde die passenden Wörter rechts für die Wörter links.* This activity relates to pages 116–117. Pupils find the appropriate infinitive to complete each sentence beginning *Ich möchte ...*

Answers: 1 g; 2 f; 3 b; 4 c; 5 a; 6 d

`AT 3.5` **4a** *Kopiere Daniels Brief und füll die Lücken aus.* Activity 4 relates to structures and vocabulary throughout the unit. In activity 4a, pupils complete Daniel's letter about his plans and aspirations in accordance with the picture cues.

Answers:

Was machst du in den Sommerferien? Ich werde mit **dem Zug** nach **Frankreich fahren**. Ich werde dort meinen **französischen Brieffreund/Austauschschüler/Freund besuchen**. Ich freue mich schon sehr! Und was machst du nächstes Jahr in der Schule? Dieses Jahr habe ich **Sport/eine Sport-AG gewählt/gemacht**. Nächstes Jahr werde ich **einen Computerkurs machen**. Ich werde auch viel für die Schule tun: Ich werde **Hausaufgaben machen** und ich werde **um halb neun ins Bett gehen**! Was möchtest du später werden? Ich möchte **Arzt/Krankenpfleger** oder **Lehrer werden**. Und ich möchte **ein (schönes) Auto haben** und **eine (schöne) Wohnung haben**.

`AT 4.5` **4b** *Schreib einen Antwortbrief an Daniel mit den Informationen unten.* Pupils write their own letter about plans and aspirations using *ich werde ...* and *ich möchte* + infinitive, in response to the picture cues.

Extra!-Seite Einheit 9
page 139

National Curriculum PoS
statements 1a, 1b, 1c, 2a, 2b, 2c, 2d, 3e, 5a, 5c, 5d, 5f, 5i

Materials
- Students' Book page 139
- Cassette 3 side B

This extension page is intended for more able pupils. It contains slightly longer and more complex materials, and it can be used by pupils who have completed other activities quickly, or as alternative homework activities.

`AT 3.4` **1a** *Lies die Texte und finde die passenden Berufe.* Activity 1 relates to pages 114–115. Pupils match the pictures of professions to the job descriptions.

Answers: 1 d; 2 b; 3 e; 4 a; 5 c

Follow-up activity. Pupils write further job descriptions to challenge their classmates with.

`AT 2.5` **1b** *Was möchtest du gern werden – und warum? Wählt Berufe und macht Dialoge mit den Informationen von Übung 1a.* Pupils work together in pairs to create dialogues based on the material from activity 1a with *ich möchte ... werden*. More able pupils could be encouraged to give their reasons in a *weil* clause.

`AT 4.5` **2** *Herr Hilflos hat im Lotto gewonnen! Was möchte er machen? Schreib ein Tagebuch für Herrn Hilflos mit den Informationen.* This activity relates to pages 116–117. Pupils write sentences with *ich möchte gern* in response to the picture cues.

Answers:

(Any order.)
Ich möchte gern Designermode tragen.
Ich möchte gern um die Welt reisen.
Ich möchte gern Partys machen.
Ich möchte gern Geschenke kaufen.
Ich möchte gern ein großes/schönes Haus haben.
Ich möchte gern ein schönes Auto haben.

3a *Carola beschreibt ihre Pläne für die Zukunft. Hör gut zu und mach Notizen.* Activity 3 uses vocabulary and structures from the whole unit. In activity 3a, pupils listen to the recording and make notes about Carola's plans and aspirations. As there is a lot of information to note down, pupils will need to hear the recording a number of times.

Answers:

Sommerferien:	Urlaub in Österreich/Wien, Cousine besuchen, Radtour (Wienerwald)
Schule:	Nähen, Kochkurs, mit Freundinnen Englisch sprechen, Briefe an Austauschschülerin in Amerika schreiben
Berufe:	Ärztin, Geschäftsfrau
möchte später gern:	im Lotto gewinnen, Filmstar werden, im Ausland arbeiten (England, Frankreich)

Transcript   p 139, activity 3a

– Hallo! Ich bin von Radio Bremen 4. Wir machen eine Umfrage – das Thema ist: ‚Pläne für die Zukunft'.
– He, super – kann ich mitmachen?
– Ja, gern. Wie heißt du und wie alt bist du?
– Ich heiße Carola und ich bin 15 Jahre alt.
– Also, die erste Frage ist „Pläne für die Sommerferien". Was machst du dieses Jahr in den Sommerferien, Carola?
– Also, ich werde Urlaub in Österreich machen – in Wien. Ich werde dort meine Cousine besuchen. Ja, und ich werde auch dort eine Radtour im Wienerwald machen.
– Okay, und jetzt die Schule: Was machst du nächstes Jahr in der Schule?
– Na ja, dieses Jahr habe ich Werken und Fußball gemacht. Aber Werken ist schwer und Fußball ist anstrengend! Nächstes Jahr werde ich Nähen wählen und ich werde einen Kochkurs machen. Nähen ist interessant und ich koche sehr gern. Ich werde auch sonst viel für die Schule tun: Ich werde mit meinen Freundinnen Englisch sprechen und ich werde Briefe an meine Austauschschülerin in Amerika schreiben.
– Und was möchtest du später werden, Carola?
– Ich möchte gerne Ärztin werden – mein Vater ist auch Arzt, meine Mutter ist Krankenschwester. Oder ich möchte Geschäftsfrau werden.
– Ja, und was möchtest du später gern machen?
– Ich möchte später gern im Lotto gewinnen – und ich möchte Filmstar werden! Also, ich möchte gern im Ausland arbeiten – am liebsten in England oder in Frankreich.
– Vielen Dank, Carola.

3b *Ein Jugendmagazin fragt: „Was sind deine Pläne für die Zukunft?" Schreib einen Artikel für Carola mit deinen Notizen von Übung 3a.* Pupils write an article (first person singular) for Carola from their notes for activity 3a, using *ich werde …* and *ich möchte (gern).*

3c *Du bist dran! Macht eine Radioumfrage so wie in Übung 3a – A ist Reporter, B antwortet. Dann ist B dran.* Pupils work together in pairs to create interviews about their plans and aspirations, taking it in turns to be the reporter and the interviewee. The reporter should take notes on the interviewee's responses, as these will be needed for activity 3d.

3d *Schreib einen kurzen Artikel für deinen Partner/deine Partnerin mit den Antworten von Übung 3c.* Pupils write an article for their partner (third person singular) from their notes for activity 3c.

Workbook

Pages 84–86

Use with pages 110–111 in the Students' Book.

A *Schreib die Sätze richtig auf.* Pupils put the words in the correct sequence to form statements in the future tense about plans for the summer holidays.

Answers:

1 Ich werde viel faulenzen.
2 Katja wird einen Ausflug machen.
3 Wir werden ins Kino gehen.
4 Martin wird Tennis spielen.
5 Wir werden nach Italien fahren.
6 Ich werde meine Oma besuchen.

B1 *Was machst du in den Sommerferien? Finde die passenden Sätze für die Bilder.* Pupils match the sentences (future tense, first and third person singular and plural) to the pictures.

Answers: a 5; b 3; c 6; d 2; e 1; f 4

B2 *Ratespiel: A spielt ein Bild von Übung B1 und fragt, B antwortet. Dann ist B dran.* Pupils work together in pairs to create dialogues about plans for the summer. Partner A picks a picture from activity B1 and mimes the activity. Partner B has to guess the activity and provide the appropriate sentence in the future tense.

C1 *Was machen Sarah und Carsten in den Sommerferien? Hör gut zu und schreib S (Sarah) oder C (Carsten) auf.* Pupils listen to the recording about Sarah's and Carsten's plans for the summer holidays and match each of the pictures to one of the two speakers.

Answers: Sarah: g, d, b, f; Carsten: c, a, e

Transcript   W 85, activity C1

– Mein Name ist Sarah und ich bin 15 Jahre alt. Meine Mutter kommt aus Österreich. Wir werden also Urlaub in Österreich machen. Wir werden nach St. Wolfgang fahren – das ist eine kleine Stadt im Westen. Ich werde

---

morgens faulenzen – super! Und nachmittags? Wir werden einen Ausflug machen – in St. Wolfgang gibt es viele Sehenswürdigkeiten. Und es gibt dort viel für junge Leute: Wir werden abends in die Disco gehen.

– Hallo! Ich heiße Carsten und ich wohne in Köln. Ich werde Urlaub in England machen – Ich werde nach Newcastle fliegen. Ich werde dort meinen Brieffreund Matthew besuchen. Matthew ist sehr nett! Er war im Winter in Köln. Ja, was werde ich in Newcastle machen? Also, Matthew und ich – wir werden in ein Popkonzert gehen. Super! Ich freue mich schon sehr. Ja, und ich werde Golf spielen – jeden Tag. Golf ist Matthews Lieblingssport.

AT 2.4 **C2** *„Was machst du in den Sommerferien?" Macht Dialoge mit den Bildern in Übung C1.* Pupils work together in pairs to create dialogues about their plans for the summer holidays (future tense), using the pictures from activity C1 as cues.

AT 4.5 **D** *Was machen Sven, Atalay, Jasmin und Annika in den Ferien? Lies Svens Postkarte und füll die Lücken aus.* Pupils complete the text, using the correct forms of *werden* from the box to complete the future tense forms.

Answers:

Was **wirst** du in den Sommerferien machen? Ich **werde** meine Eltern in Chemnitz besuchen. Meine Schwester und ich – wir **werden** dort viel faulenzen. Und Jasmin? Jasmin **wird** zu Hause bleiben – und Atalay auch. Sie **werden** einen Skateboardkurs machen! Und Annika **wird** eine Radtour machen.

AT 4.5 **E1** *Lies Susis E-Mail und füll die Lücken aus.* Pupils complete the future tense forms in the text with the appropriate infinitives.

Answers:

Was machst du in den Sommerferien? Ich werde Urlaub in Spanien **machen** – zwei Wochen lang! Ich werde nach Valencia **fliegen** und ich werde dort meine Brieffreundin Pilar **besuchen**. Wir werden auch einen Ausflug nach Madrid **machen**. Ach ja, und wir werden auch ins Popkonzert **gehen** – super! Und am Wochenende werde ich mit Pilar Volleyball **spielen** – am Strand!

AT 4.5 **E2** *Was macht Tobias in den Sommerferien? Schreib eine E-Mail-Nachricht (so wie Susi) mit den Bildern.* Pupils use the picture prompts to write an e-mail about holiday plans, using the text from activity E1 as a model.

AT 4.5 **F** *Du bist dran! Was machst du in den Sommerferien?* Pupils now write their own text about summer holiday plans, using the future tense. This activity can form part of pupils' written records for continuous assessment purposes. See the general notes on pages 13–14 of the introduction to this book.

Pages 87–89

Use with pages 112–113 in the Students' Book.

AT 1.5 **G** *Jasmin und Sven wollen im neuen Schuljahr viel für die Schule tun. Hör gut zu und schreib J (Jasmin) oder S*

(Sven) auf. Pupils listen to the recording and match each of the pictures to one of the two speakers.

Answers: Jasmin: g, e, d, c; Sven: f, b, a

Transcript W 87, activity G

– Also, Jasmin, ich werde im neuen Schuljahr viel für die Schule tun!
– Ja, ich auch! Ich werde mit meinen Freundinnen Französisch sprechen – jeden Tag
– Gute Idee! Und ich werde jeden Tag Hausaufgaben machen!
– Langweilig! Aber ich werde E-Mails an meine Austauschschülerin in England schreiben!
– Und was will ich tun? Ich weiß: Ich werde um 7 Uhr 30 aufstehen!
– Um 7 Uhr 30?? Puh, und was werde ich tun? Ah ja – ich werde mein Taschengeld für einen Computer sparen!
– He, super! Und ich werde Briefe an meinen Brieffreund in Amerika schreiben! Einmal pro Woche!
– Dein Brieffreund in Amerika? Er ist super, finde ich … Also, und was werde ich tun? Ich werde um 21 Uhr ins Bett gehen!

AT 4.3 **H** *Was will Daniel im neuen Schuljahr tun? Schreib Sprechblasen.* Pupils write a speech bubble with *Ich werde …* for each of the activities shown in the pictures.

Answers:

a Ich werde um 7 Uhr aufstehen.
b Ich werde mit meinen Freunden Deutsch sprechen.
c Ich werde jeden Tag Hausaufgaben machen.
d Ich werde an meine Brieffreundin in Frankreich schreiben.
e Ich werde um 21.30 Uhr ins Bett gehen.
f Ich werde E-Mails an meinen Austauschschüler in Amerika schreiben.

AT 2.5 **I** *„Was willst du im neuen Schuljahr für die Schule tun?" Macht Dialoge mit den Bildern von Übung G und H.* Pupils work together in pairs to create dialogues about what they are going to do next academic year, using the pictures from activities G and H as cues.

AT 4.5 **J** *Du bist dran! Was willst du im neuen Schuljahr für die Schule tun?* In this independent writing activity, pupils write about their 'resolutions' for the next academic year. This activity can form part of pupils' written records for continuous assessment purposes.

AT 3.3 **K** *Finde die passenden Bilder.* Pupils find the picture which matches each pair of statements (perfect tense and future tense) about extra-curricular activities.

Answers: 1 b; 2 c; 3 a

AT 4.6 **L** *Was haben sie dieses Jahr gemacht? Was wollen sie nächstes Jahr machen? Füll die Sprechblasen aus.* Pupils complete the speech bubbles (statements in the perfect tense and the future tense) in response to the picture cues.

Answers:

a Dieses Jahr habe ich Tennis gewählt. Nächstes Jahr werde ich Fußball wählen.

b Dieses Jahr habe ich einen Kochkurs gemacht. Nächstes Jahr werde ich eine Theater-AG machen.

c Dieses Jahr habe ich Volleyball gemacht. Nächstes Jahr werde ich Geige lernen.

AT 2.6 **M** *Was hast du dieses Jahr gemacht? Was willst du nächstes Jahr machen? Macht Dialoge mit den Informationen.* Pupils work together in pairs to create dialogues about extra-curricular activities in the perfect and future tenses, using the key words provided.

N *Sieh auch Lehrbuch, Seite 113. Lies die Sätze und füll die Lücken aus.* Pupils complete the perfect and future tense forms, referring to the Students' Book as necessary.

Answers:

Ich habe Hausaufgaben gemacht. Ich bin in die Disco gegangen.
Ich werde Hausaufgaben machen. Ich werde in die Disco gehen.

AT 4.6 **O1** *Was hast du am Wochenende gemacht? Was machst du heute? Und was wirst du nächste Woche machen? Schreib eine Postkarte mit den Bildern.* Pupils write sentences in the perfect, present and future tenses, in response to the picture cues.

Answers:

Am Wochenende bin ich ins Kino gegangen und (ich) habe einen Picknick gemacht.
Heute esse ich Pizza und (ich) mache meine Hausaufgaben.
Nächste Woche werde ich Tennis spielen und (ich werde) um 7 Uhr aufstehen.

AT 2.6 **O2** *Du bist dran! Was hast du am Wochenende gemacht? Was machst du heute? Und was wirst du nächste Woche machen? Mach eine Kassette mit deinen Informationen.* Pupils record a presentation about what they did at the weekend, are doing today and will do next week, using the perfect, present and future tenses.

Pages 90–91

Use with pages 114–115 in the Students' Book.

AT 4.1 **P1** *Was ist er/sie von Beruf? Schreib die passenden Wörter auf.* Pupils supply captions for the photos, remembering to use the correct masculine or feminine forms of the job titles.

Answers:

a Krankenpfleger; b Sekretärin; c Kellnerin; d Postbote; e Arzt; f Lehrer; g Hausfrau; h Polizistin

AT 4.1 **P2** *Schreib die passenden Maskulinum- und Femininum-Formen für die Wörter in Übung P1 auf.* Pupils now supply the missing masculine or feminine forms of the job titles from activity P1, consulting their dictionaries or the *Vokabular* at the back of the Students' Book, as necessary.

Answers:

a	Krankenpfleger	Krankenschwester
b	Sekretär	Sekretärin
c	Kellner	Kellnerin
d	Postbote	Postbotin
e	Arzt	Ärztin
f	Lehrer	Lehrerin
g	Hausmann	Hausfrau
h	Polizist	Polizistin

AT 2.2 **P3** *Ratespiel: „Was ist dein Vater/deine Mutter von Beruf?" A buchstabiert einen Beruf, B antwortet. Dann ist B dran.* Pupils work together in pairs to practise job titles. Partner A spells out a job title, and partner B tries to guess the answer after every letter. Then the roles are reversed.

AT 1.3 **Q** *Was möchten sie werden? Hör gut zu und finde die richtige Reihenfolge für die Berufe.* Pupils listen to the recording and put the professions into the sequence in which they are mentioned.

Answers: b, d, f, c, e, a, h, g

> **Transcript** W 91, activity Q
>
> 1 – Ich möchte Geschäftsfrau werden – das finde ich toll!
> 2 – Und ich – ich mag Tiere. Ich möchte Tierarzt werden.
> 3 – Ich möchte LKW-Fahrerin werden. Ja, LKW-Fahrerin.
> 4 – Also, ich – ich möchte Feuerwehrmann werden!
> 5 – Und ich möchte Verkäuferin werden – in einem Supermarkt oder in einem Kaufhaus.
> 6 – Ich finde Autos interessant. Ich möchte Mechaniker werden.
> 7 – Ja, und ich mag Computer. Ich möchte Informatikerin werden.
> 8 – Also, ich möchte Büroarbeiter werden. Das ist interessant, finde ich!

AT 4.3 **R** *„Ich möchte … werden" – was sagen diese Schüler/Schülerinnen? Schreib Sätze für sie.* Pupils write a sentence with *ich möchte … werden* and the appropriate job title for each of the pictures.

Answers:

Ute:	Ich möchte Ärztin werden.
Tim:	Ich möchte Hausmann werden.
Ina:	Ich möchte Krankenschwester werden.
Heiko:	Ich möchte Polizist werden.
Sandra:	Ich möchte Geschäftsfrau werden.
Anne:	Ich möchte Lehrerin werden.
Olli:	Ich möchte Informatiker werden.
Jens:	Ich möchte Kellner werden.

Page 92

Use with pages 115–116 in the Students' Book.

AT 4.5 **S** *Du bist dran! Was möchtest du später werden?* Pupils now write about their own career aspirations. This activity can form part of pupils' written records for continuous assessment purposes.

AT 3.3 **T** *Was möchte Leah später gern machen? Finde die passenden Bilder.* Pupils match the pictures to the

sentences describing Leah's aspirations (*möchte +
infinitive*).

Answers: 1 b; 2 f; 3 d; 4 a; 5 c; 6 e

Page 93

AT 1.3 Use with pages 116–117 in the Students' Book.

U1 *Was möchten Svenja und Tobias später gern machen?
Hör gut zu und schreib S (Svenja) oder T (Tobias) auf.*
Pupils listen to the recording and decide which
aspirations depicted in the pictures apply to Svenja and
which to Tobias.

Answers: Svenja: e, b, d; Tobias: c, f, a

Transcript	W 93, activity U1

– Svenja, was möchtest du später gern machen?
– Ich? Ich möchte gern Designermode tragen! Prada,
   Gucci, Versace … Und du, Tobias?
– Also, ich möchte viele Filmstars treffen! Zum Beispiel in
   Hollywood …
– Ja, super! Und ich möchte später gern viel Geld
   verdienen! Das ist wichtig, finde ich!

– Ja, und ich möchte später gern um die Welt reisen! Von
   Afrika nach Asien – oder Australien … oder Amerika …
– Oh, ja, super! Und was möchte ich später noch gern
   machen? Ich weiß: Ich möchte gern im Lotto gewinnen!
– He, tolle Idee! Und ich – ich möchte gern im Ausland
   arbeiten! In New York zum Beispiel – oder Paris …
– Oh, ja, klasse!

AT 2.3 **U2** *Was möchtest du später gern machen? A fragt und
wählt ein Bild, B antwortet. Dann ist B dran.* Pupils work
together in pairs to create dialogues about aspirations
with *ich möchte +* infinitive, using the pictures from
activity U1 as cues.

AT 4.5 **V** *Du bist dran! Was möchtest du später gern machen?*
Pupils write about their own aspirations, using *ich
möchte +* infinitive. This activity can form part of pupils'
written records for continuous assessment purposes.

Can you …?

The purpose of the checklist is to identify tasks in the
Students' Book both by skill and by topic. Teachers may
find this helpful in selecting specific tasks, as a record of
pupils' achievements in an Attainment Target.

Einheit 9 Zukunft	AT 1 Listening	AT 2 Speaking	AT 3 Reading	AT 4 Writing
110–111 Was machst du in den Sommerferien?				
Ask others about their plans for the holidays	–	1c	–	–
Talk about your plans for the holidays	–	1c	1a, 1b	2a, 2b, 2c, 4
Talk about other people's plans for the holidays	–	–	3	2a, 2b, 2c
112–113 Ich werde Hausaufgaben machen!				
Talk about resolutions for the new academic year	1a	1b	1a	Noch mal!, Extra!
Compare this year and next year	2, 3	4	2, 5	4, 6a, 6b
114–115 Berufe				
Say what jobs your parents do	1a, 2b	1b, 3	–	2a
Ask what someone else's parents do	–	1b	–	–
Talk about your future job plans	4	5a, 5b	4	5b
116–117 Ich möchte gern Popstar werden!				
Talk about what you would like to do in the future	1a, 2a	1b, 2b, 4	1a, 2a, 3a	3b, 4

Copymasters

For general advice about using the copymasters, see
page 7 of the introduction to this book.

C 76 Hören

AT 1.2 **1** *Was möchten sie später werden? Hör gut zu und finde
die passenden Bilder.* Pupils listen to the recording about
job aspirations and select the appropriate picture for
each speaker.

Answers: 1 c; 2 e; 3 h; 4 g; 5 a; 6 f; 7 b; 8 d

Transcript	C 76, activity 1

Was möchtest du später werden?
1
– Ich möchte Tierarzt werden.
2
– Ich möchte Lehrer werden.

3
– Ich möchte Polizistin werden.
4
– Ich möchte Informatikerin werden.
5
– Ich möchte Kellner werden.
6
– Ich möchte Mechanikerin werden.
7
– Ich möchte Krankenschwester werden.
8
– Ich möchte Popstar werden.

AT 1.4 **2** *Rosa schreibt ihre ‚Neujahrs-Hitparade‘. Hör gut zu
und finde die richtige Reihenfolge für die Bilder.* Pupils
listen to the recording of Rosa's New Year's resolutions
and put the pictures into the sequence in which the
activities are mentioned.

Answers: d, i, e, f, a, b, g, j, c, h

Transcript C 76, activity 2

Also ... das neue Jahr beginnt. Und hier ist meine ‚Neujahrs-Hitparade'.
Okay ...
Nummer eins. Ich werde montags bis freitags um Viertel vor sieben aufstehen.
Nummer zwei. Ich werde jeden Tag zu Fuß zur Schule gehen.
Nummer drei. Ich werde nur gesund essen. Keine Chips und Süßigkeiten!
Nummer vier. Ich werde viel Sport machen. Das macht fit!
Nummer fünf. Ich werde jeden Tag meine Hausaufgaben vor dem Abendessen machen.
Nummer sechs. Ich werde an meine Brieffreundin in Amerika schreiben.
Nummer sieben. Ich werde mein Taschengeld für ein neues Fahrrad sparen.
Nummer acht. Ich werde einen Computerkurs machen.
Nummer neun. Ich werde nur Recyclingpapier kaufen.
Nummer zehn. Ich werde meinen Eltern zu Hause helfen.

---

3 *Hör gut zu und kreuz die passenden Bilder an.* Pupils listen to the recording of teenagers' summer holiday plans, and select the appropriate picture from each pair.

Answers: 1 b; 2 b; 3 b; 4 b

Transcript C 76, activity 3

1
– Was machst du in den Sommerferien, Timo?
– Das weiß ich nicht. Ich glaube, ich werde Freunde besuchen und ins Schwimmbad gehen. Und auch Basketball spielen. Das ist mein Lieblingssport!
2
– Und du, Steffi? Was machst du in den Sommerferien?
– Ja. Meine Familie und ich – wir werden nächste Woche nach Paris fliegen!
– Toll!
– Ja, und wir werden jeden Tag im Restaurant essen und auch ins Hotelschwimmbad gehen.
– Viel Spaß!
3
– Ahmed! Was machst du in den Sommerferien?
– Mein Vater und ich werden am Wochenende eine Radtour machen. Meine Mutter und meine Schwester werden aber zu Hause bleiben – sie fahren nicht so gern Rad.
– Und hast du noch einige Pläne?
– Ja. Ich werde lange schlafen! Und in zwei Wochen gehe ich mit meinen Freunden in ein Popkonzert. Das finde ich toll!
4
– Und was machst du, Lara?
– Das weiß ich noch nicht ... aber ich werde sicher einige Ausflüge mit meiner Familie machen. Und wir werden auch ins Schwimmbad gehen und viel Tennis spielen. Das macht immer Spaß!

C 77 Sprechen
AT 2.5

1a *Frag deinen Partner/deine Partnerin: „Was machst du in den Sommerferien?" Mach Notizen.* Pupils work in pairs to create dialogues. Partner A asks partner B about his/her plans for the summer holidays; partner B answers according to the picture cues, using *ich werde …*, while partner A makes notes.

AT 2.5

1b *Dein Partner/deine Partnerin fragt: „Was machst du in den Sommerferien?" Antworte mit den Informationen unten.* This is the second part of the activity with the roles reversed and with different cues.

AT 2.5

2a *Frag deinen Partner/deine Partnerin:* Pupils work in pairs to create dialogues. Partner A asks partner B about his/her parents' professions, own career plans and other aspirations; partner B answers according to the picture cues.

AT 2.5

2b *Dein Partner/deine Partnerin stellt Fragen. Antworte mit den Informationen unten.* This is the second part of the activity with the roles reversed and with different cues.

C 78A Lesen 1
AT 3.2

1 *Wo arbeiten sie? Finde die passenden Antworten.* Pupils join the sentence halves together to form sentences describing the professions.

Answers: 1 c; 2 a; 3 d; 4 f; 5 b; 6 e

AT 3.4

2 *Lies Mariekes E-Mail und die Tagebuchseiten. Welches Tagebuch ist Mariekes?* Pupils read Marieke's description of her summer holiday plans and decide which diary belongs to her.

Answer: 2

C 78B Lesen 2
AT 3.5

1 *Lies das Interview mit Xenia Zukunftskind und finde die passenden Antworten.* Pupils read the text, in which Xenia talks about her parents' professions and her own aspirations, and then select the correct answer from each pair.

Answers: 1 b; 2 b; 3 b; 4 b; 5 a

C 79 Schreiben
AT 4.1

1 *Was machst du in den Sommerferien? Füll die Lücken aus.* Pupils complete the sentences (plans for the summer holidays) with the appropriate words from the box.

Answers:

1 Ich werde **Tennis** spielen.
2 Ich werde **meine Oma** besuchen.
3 Ich werde **lange** schlafen.
4 Ich werde **nach Amerika** fliegen.
5 Ich werde **eine Radtour** machen.
6 Ich werde **ins Schwimmbad** gehen.

AT 4.3 **2** *Was möchten sie später werden? Schreib Sätze.* Pupils write sentences with *möchte … werden* and the correct masculine/feminine forms of job titles in response to the picture cues.

Answers:

1 Thomas möchte Kellner werden.
2 Silke möchte Mechanikerin werden.
3 Michael möchte Krankenpfleger werden.
4 Maria möchte Feuerwehrfrau werden.
5 Rudi möchte Polizist werden.
6 Johanna möchte Postbotin werden.
7 Karl möchte Lehrer werden.
8 Angelika möchte Geschäftsfrau werden.

AT 4.5 **3** *Was möchte Heike später machen? Schreib den Brief weiter.* Pupils complete the letter with sentences using *ich möchte* + infinitive, in response to the picture cues.

Answers:

(The letter should contain the following sentences)
Ich möchte um die Welt reisen.
Ich möchte viele Geschenke (für meine Familie) kaufen.
Ich möchte einen Kochkurs machen.
Ich möchte Klavier lernen.
Ich möchte nach Paris/Frankreich fliegen.
Ich möchte Popstar werden.

C 80A **Grammatik 1**

This copymaster focuses on the future tense (full conjugation of *werden* in the present tense) and use of the perfect, present and future tenses.

1 *Schreib neue Sätze mit werden.* Pupils read the 'Flashback' and then transform the statements into the future tense.

Answers:

1 Ich werde eine Theater-AG machen.
2 Er wird zu Fuß zur Schule gehen.
3 Du wirst Badminton spielen.
4 Sie werden für einen Kassettenrecorder sparen.
5 Wir werden meine Oma besuchen.
6 Ich werde Designermode tragen.

2a *Was hast du gestern gemacht? Was wirst du morgen machen? Schreib Sätze.* Pupils read the 'Flashback' and then write new sentences in the perfect and the future tense, using the present tense sentences and the key words given.

Answers:

1 Gestern bin ich nach Paris gefahren. Morgen werde ich nach Berlin fahren.
2 Gestern bin ich nach Deutschland gereist. Morgen werde ich nach Hause reisen.
3 Gestern habe ich Obst und Gemüse gekauft. Morgen werde ich Souvenirs kaufen.
4 Gestern habe ich im Park gegessen. Morgen werde ich im Hotel essen.

5 Gestern bin ich ins Theater gegangen. Morgen werde ich in die Disco gehen.
6 Gestern habe ich Geige gelernt. Morgen werde ich Klavier lernen.

2b *Übersetze dann die Sätze in Übung 2a.* Pupils translate their sentences from activity 2a into English. For more able pupils, this is an excellent opportunity to compare tense usage in English and German (e.g. the perfect tense with a reference to a definite time in the past is not possible in English, but it is in German; there is no continuous form in German).

Answers:

(Accept the present continuous for the 'tomorrow' sentences as well.)

1 Today I'm going to Italy. Yesterday I went to Paris. Tomorrow I'll go to Berlin.
2 Today I'm travelling around the world. Yesterday I travelled to Germany. Tomorrow I'll travel home.
3 Today I'm buying a lot of presents. Yesterday I bought fruit and vegetables. Tomorrow I'll buy souvenirs.
4 Today I'm eating in the restaurant. Yesterday I ate in the park. Tomorrow I'll eat in the hotel.
5 Today I'm going to the cinema. Yesterday I went to the theatre. Tomorrow I'll go to the disco.
6 Today I'm learning the guitar. Yesterday I learned the violin. Tomorrow I'll learn the piano.

C 80B **Grammatik 2**

This copymaster focuses on *ich möchte* + noun and *ich möchte* + infinitive.

1 *Was sind sie von Beruf? Füll die Lücken aus.* Pupils read the 'Flashback' which details how feminines of occupations are formed, and reminds pupils that occupations never need *ein* or *eine*. They then fill in the masculine or feminine forms of the occupations listed.

Answers:

1 Polizistin; 2 Lehrerin; 3 Krankenpfleger; 4 Geschäftsfrau; 5 Arzt; 6 Verkäuferin; 7 Hausmann

2 *Schreib die Sätze auf Deutsch.* Pupils first read the 'Flashback' which details different usages of *ich möchte* + a noun, + an infinitive, or + *werden*. Pupils then translate the sentences into German, using *möchte*.

Answers:

1 Ich möchte eine Tasse Tee, bitte.
2 Ich möchte (gern) um die Welt reisen.
3 Ich möchte (gern) eine Radtour machen.
4 Ich möchte (gern) Filmstar werden.
5 Sie möchte (gern) Lehrerin werden.
6 Er möchte (gern) Arzt werden.
7 Ich möchte ein Kilo Bananen.
8 Ich möchte ins Kino gehen.

Tipp

This copymaster gives advice on reading longer texts.

1 *Lies den Artikel rechts und beantworte die Fragen.*
After reading the 'Flashback' advice, pupils read the text
and answer the comprehension questions.

Answers:

(Accept variations in phrasing and content.)

1 Sie beginnen morgen.
2 Julia freut sich auf die Ferien, weil sie ihre
  Brieffreundin in Frankreich besuchen wird.
3 Nadine und Markus freuen sich nicht auf die Ferien.
  Nadine muss viel zu Hause helfen. Markus muss zu
  Hause bleiben.
4 Sie möchte nach Italien oder Spanien fliegen und am
  Strand in der Sonne liegen.
5 Ihre Mutter arbeitet in einem Geschäft.
6 Er surft im Internet und er hört Musik.

7-9 Wiederholung

Materials

- Students' Book pages 120–121
- Cassette 3 side B

This revision spread provides consolidation and further practice of language from Units 7–9. You can either take pupils through the activities as a whole class, or they can work independently or in pairs. The activities should help pupils prepare for the assessment for Units 7–9.

AT 1.4

1a *Andi wohnt in der Stadt. Warum wohnt er gern in der Stadt – und warum wohnt er nicht gern dort? Hör gut zu und mach Notizen.* Activity 1 revises the material from Unit 7, pages 86–87. In activity 1a, pupils listen to the recording and make notes about what Andi likes and dislikes about living in a city. Pupils should listen to the recording at least three times: a first time to understand the gist; a second time to make notes; and a third time to complete and check their notes.

Answers:

gern: nie langweilig, viele Geschäfte, großes Einkaufszentrum, modernes Fußballstadion, Jugendzentrum, viele Discos
nicht gern: zu viele Autos und Verkehr, keine Natur, zu viel Umweltverschmutzung, zu viel Lärm

---

Transcript   p 120, activity 1a

– Andi, du wohnst in der Stadt – in Dresden. Wohnst du gern in der Stadt?
– Ja und nein. Ich wohne gern in der Stadt, weil es hier nie langweilig ist – es gibt viel zu machen: Es gibt viele Geschäfte, es gibt ein großes Einkaufszentrum, es gibt ein modernes Fußballstadion ... Aber ich wohne nicht gern in der Stadt, weil es zu viele Autos und Verkehr gibt.
– Gibt es viel Natur in Dresden?
– Nein, es gibt hier keine Natur – das finde ich schlecht. Es gibt zu viel Umweltverschmutzung! Aber ich wohne auch gern in der Stadt, weil es ein Jugendzentrum und viele Discos gibt – das ist super.
– Und ist es sehr ruhig in Dresden?
– Oh nein! Ich wohne nicht gern in der Stadt, weil es zu viel Lärm gibt – morgens, mittags und abends!

AT 4.4   **1b** *Was sagt Andi? Schreib eine Zusammenfassung mit deinen Notizen von Übung 1a.* Pupils use their notes from activity 1a to write sentences with *weil*.

AT 3.1   **2a** *Lies die Wörter. Was ist umweltfeindlich? Finde sieben Wörter und schreib eine Liste.* Activity 2 revises the material from Unit 7, pages 90–93. In activity 2a, pupils select the seven nouns from the box which represent things which are harmful to the environment in some way.

Answers:

Fabriken, Kraftwerke, Lärm, Pestizide, Müll, Verkehr, Zigaretten

---

AT 2.4   **2b** *Lies die Wörter auf deiner Liste (Übung 2a). Was glaubst du – was ist das größte Problem für die Umwelt? Macht Dialoge.* Pupils work together in pairs to create dialogues with superlatives (*... ist das größte Problem*), using their list of words from activity 2a. Elicit from the class that a plural noun requires *sind* rather than *ist*: *Fabriken sind das größte Problem*, etc. You could ask more able pupils to construct more complex dialogues, by disagreeing with each other using comparatives as well as superlatives, for example:

A: *Ich finde, Lärm ist das größte Problem.*
B: *Nein, Müll ist gefährlicher/umweltfeindlicher als Lärm.*
A: *Ja, aber Pestizide sind gefährlicher/umweltfeindlicher als Müll.*

AT 1.5

3 *Andi macht ein Picknick – aber viele Freunde und Freundinnen kommen nicht! Was haben sie – und seit wann? Hör gut zu und mach Notizen.* This activity revises the material from Unit 8, pages 98–99. Pupils listen to the recording and make notes about who has what problem, and how long he/she has been suffering from it. Pupils will need to listen at least three times to extract all the details required.

Answers:

Wer:	Vera
Probleme:	Grippe, Kopfschmerzen, Hals tut weh
Seit wann:	seit Samstag
Er/Sie muss:	zweimal pro Tag Halstabletten nehmen
Wer:	Thomas
Probleme:	Husten
Seit wann:	seit gestern
Er/Sie muss:	Tropfen nehmen
Wer:	Susi
Probleme:	Fuß tut weh
Seit wann:	seit zwei Tagen
Er/Sie muss:	eine Lotion nehmen
Wer:	Matthias
Probleme:	Bauchschmerzen
Seit wann:	seit Montag
Er/Sie muss:	Tabletten nehmen, dreimal pro Tag
Wer:	Anne
Probleme:	Heuschnupfen
Seit wann:	seit gestern
Er/Sie muss:	(zur Apotheke fahren und ein) Medikament kaufen

Transcript   p 120, activity 3

– Hallo, Andi! Hier ist Vera. Du, ich kann leider nicht zum Picknick kommen. Ich habe Grippe! Ich habe seit Samstag Kopfschmerzen und mein Hals tut weh. Ich muss zweimal pro Tag Halstabletten nehmen. Also, tschüs!

– Andi? ich bin's – Thomas. Ich kann heute Nachmittag nicht kommen. Ich habe Husten – ich habe seit gestern Husten! Ich muss Tropfen nehmen. Viel Spaß beim Picknick!

– Tag, Andi! Susi hier. Ich kann heute nicht zum Picknick kommen – leider! Mein Fuß tut seit zwei Tagen weh – ich kann nicht zu Fuß gehen! Ich war beim Arzt und ich muss eine Lotion nehmen. Tschüs!

– Hallo, Andi! Hier ist Matthias. Andi, ich kann nicht zum Picknick kommen! Ich habe seit Montag Bauchschmerzen und ich kann nichts essen! Ich muss auch Tabletten nehmen – dreimal pro Tag. Auf Wiederhören!

– Guten Tag, Andi. Ich bin's – Anne. Du, Andi, ich kann heute Nachmittag nicht zum Picknick kommen – leider! Ich habe seit gestern Heuschnupfen. Ich muss zur Apotheke fahren und ein Medikament kaufen. Also, viel Spaß heute nachmittag!

AT 3.2 **4a** *Tipps für die Gesundheit – finde die passenden Sätze für die Bilder.* Activity 4 revises the material from Unit 8, pages 100–105. In activity 4a, pupils match the speech bubbles (instructions for healthy living, in the imperative) to the pictures.

Answers: 1 f; 2 h; 3 c; 4 g; 5 d; 6 b; 7 e; 8 a

4b *Schreib die passenden Infinitive für die Imperative in Übung 4a auf.* Pupils supply the infinitive for each of the imperatives from activity 4a. Make sure that all pupils understand the term *Imperativ*.

Answers:

a machen; b essen; c rauchen; d essen; e trinken; f gehen; g trinken; h essen

AT 2.3 **4c** *Was soll man für die Gesundheit tun? A wählt ein Bild von Übung 4a, B antwortet mit Man soll ... Dann ist B dran.* Pupils work together in pairs to create dialogues with *man soll* + infinitive, using the pictures from activity 4a as cues.

AT 4.3 **4d** *Lies noch einmal die Sätze in Übung 4a – das willst du alles im neuen Jahr für die Gesundheit tun! Schreib Sätze für dein Tagebuch mit Ich werde ...* Pupils now transform the imperative instructions in activity 4a into resolutions in the future tense.

Answers:

(Any order.)
Ich werde viel zu Fuß gehen. Ich werde kein Fastfood essen. Ich werde nicht rauchen. Ich werde viel Wasser trinken. Ich werde viel Obst und Gemüse essen. Ich werde keine Süßigkeiten essen. Ich werde keinen Alkohol trinken. Ich werde viel Sport machen.

AT 3.5 **5a** *Michael sucht einen Brieffreund/eine Brieffreundin. Lies seine E-Mail und beantworte die Fragen.* Activity 5 revises the material from Unit 8 and Unit 9. In activity 5a, pupils read the text and answer the comprehension questions. Pupils should answer the questions in full sentences.

Answers:

1 Er wohnt gern auf dem Land, weil es viel Natur und viele Tiere gibt.
2 Er wohnt nicht gern dort, weil es ziemlich langweilig ist und weil es keine Disco, kein Kino und kein Schwimmbad gibt.
3 Er geht jeden Tag zu Fuß zur Schule. Er spielt jeden Tag Tennis. Er fährt im Sommer Skateboard und er fährt im Winter Ski. Er ist Vegetarier.
4 Er wird jeden Tag Hausaufgaben machen und er wird sein Taschengeld für einen Computer sparen.
5 Er möchte gern Geschäftsmann werden.
6 Er möchte auch viel Geld verdienen und er möchte im Ausland arbeiten.

AT 4.5 **5b** *Du bist dran! Schreib einen Antwort-E-Mail an Michael. (Tipp: Beantworte alle die Fragen in Übung 5a für dich!)* Pupils now write their own text, using Michael's e-mail from activity 5a as a model. Less able pupils could use this as an adaptation exercise; more able pupils could produce more independent pieces of writing. As a starting point, they should establish what questions Michael could have been asked before he wrote his e-mail, and then set out to answer the same questions for themselves.

7-9 Kontrolle

Materials

- Copymasters 90–93
- Cassette 3 side B

 Hören

1 *Was für Berufe haben sie? Hör gut zu und finde die passenden Bilder.* Pupils listen to the recording and find the picture which illustrates each profession mentioned.

Answers: 1 a; 2 f; 3 h; 4 e; 5 j

Mark scheme:
1 mark for each picture identified correctly (total 5 marks)

Assessment criteria:
Pupils who identify 4 or more pictures correctly show evidence of performance at AT1 level 3.

> **Transcript** C 90, activity 1
>
> 1– Mein Vater arbeitet zu Hause. Er ist Hausmann.
> 2– Meine Mutter arbeitet in einem Krankenhaus. Sie ist Ärztin.
> 3– Meine Mutter arbeitet mit Computern. Sie ist Informatikerin.
> 4– Mein Vater arbeitet mit Katzen und Hunden. Er ist Tierarzt.
> 5– Mein Vater arbeitet in einem Hotel. Er ist Kellner.

2 *Was tut Herrn Hilflos weh? Hör gut zu und schreib* ✔ *oder* ✗ *in die passenden Kästchen.* Pupils listen to the recording and then indicate on the picture which parts of Herr Hilflos' body are still troubling him and which have improved.

Answers:

✔ = stomach, throat, nose, hay fever, leg, back
✗ = temperature, ears, arm, foot

Mark scheme:
1 mark for each correct answer (total 10 marks)

Assessment criteria:
Pupils with 8 or more correct answers show evidence of performance at AT1 level 4.

> **Transcript** C 90, activity 2
>
> – Also, Herr Hilflos, wie geht es Ihnen heute?
> – Nicht sehr gut, Frau Doktor.
> – Aber Sie haben kein Fieber und die Ohren sind viel besser.
> – Ja, aber der Bauch tut weh und ich habe Halsschmerzen.
> – Und wie ist die Nase?
> – Sie ist nicht sehr gut. Sie ist immer rot und ich habe Heuschnupfen.
> – Der Arm und der Fuß sind jetzt viel besser. Wie ist das Bein?

> – Ja, das Bein tut schrecklich weh und auch der Rücken.
> – Na ja, Herr Hilflos. Sie müssen noch drei Wochen im Krankenhaus bleiben, aber dann geht es Ihnen wieder besser!

3a *Philipp macht eine Umfrage in seiner Klasse. Was sind für seine Freunde die schlimmsten Umweltprobleme? Hör gut zu und füll die Tabelle aus.*

 3b *Was soll man für die Umwelt tun? Was sagen Philipps Freunde? Hör noch einmal zu und füll die Tabelle aus.* Pupils listen to the recording and then complete the table with the problems and remedies mentioned.

Answers:

	Die schlimmsten Umweltprobleme	Was soll man machen?
Monika	Müll – Papier und alte Dosen überall	Müll sortieren, Recycling
Thomas	Kraftwerke – gefährlich für Wasser und Luft	Energie sparen
Annette	Verkehr – Autos und Lärm	zu Fuß gehen, Auto zu Hause lassen
Jessica	Pestizide – gefährlich für die Erde, Tiere, Menschen	weniger Pestizide benutzen
Gerd	große Städte – viele Fabriken und Geschäfte	mehr Natur haben – Parks, Bäume

Mark scheme:
Award 1 mark for each detail correctly communicated with 8 marks available for *Die schlimmsten Umweltprobleme* and 4 marks for *Was soll man machen?* up to a total of 12 marks.

Assessment criteria:
Pupils with 9 or more marks show evidence of performance at AT1 level 5. As this is a listening comprehension task, minor errors in the accuracy of the German are acceptable provided that communication is not impaired.

> **Transcript** C 90, activities 3a and 3b
>
> – Monika, was ist für dich das größte Umweltproblem und warum?
> – Ich finde, Müll ist das größte Problem, weil es überall Papier und alte Dosen gibt.
> – Aber was soll man machen?
> – Man soll den Müll sortieren und auch Recycling machen.
> – Und du, Thomas?

- Ich glaube, Kraftwerke sind am schlimmsten, weil sie sehr gefährlich sind. Sie sind gefährlich für das Wasser und die Luft.
- Aber was soll man machen?
- Man soll Energie sparen – dann brauchen wir nicht so viele Kraftwerke.

- Findest du Kraftwerke auch am schlimmsten, Annette?
- Nein. Ich finde Verkehr am umweltfeindlichsten, weil es so viele Autos und Lärm gibt.
- Ich weiß, was man machen soll.
- Was denn?
- Man soll zu Fuß gehen und das Auto zu Hause lassen.

- Und du, Jessica?
- Ich denke, Pestizide sind das schlimmste Problem, weil sie sehr gefährlich für die Erde, Tiere und Menschen sind.
- Hmm ... das ist ein großes Problem. Was soll man denn machen?
- Das ist einfach! Man soll weniger Pestizide benutzen.

- Ich finde, große Städte sind das größte Problem.
- Warum, Gerd?
- Weil es so viele Fabriken und Geschäfte gibt.
- Und was soll man machen?
- Man soll mehr Natur in der Stadt haben – Parks, Bäume usw.

Sprechen

C 91

AT 2.5

1a *Zukunftsspiel – die Ferien. A sagt einen Satz, dann ist B dran usw. Ihr müsst fünf Sätze sagen.* Pupils work together in pairs to describe their plans for the holidays using the future tense. Each partner has to construct five sentences. No cues are provided.

Mark scheme:
2 marks for each correct answer communicated. If the answer is partially communicated, or if the answer contains significant grammatical error, 1 mark may be awarded (total 10).

Assessment criteria:
Pupils who communicate 4 answers correctly without significant error, show evidence of performance at AT2 level 4 or 5 depending on the length and quality of their response. If the answers are partially communicated or contain significant grammatical errors, 1 mark may be awarded and the performance would show evidence of AT2 levels 2 or 3.

AT 2.5

1b *Sagt weitere Sätze über Berufe und Zukunftspläne. Ihr müsst fünf Sätze sagen.* Pupils describe their plans and aspirations for the future using the future tense. Each partner again has to construct five sentences. No cues are provided.

Mark scheme:
2 marks for each correct answer communicated. If the answer is partially communicated, or if the answer contains a significant grammatical error, 1 mark may be awarded (total 10).

Assessment criteria:
Pupils who communicate 4 answers correctly without significant error show evidence of performance at AT2 level 4 or 5 depending on the length and quality of their response. If the answers are partially communicated or contain significant grammatical errors, 1 mark may be awarded and the performance would show evidence of AT2 levels 2 or 3.

AT 2.4

2a *Du wohnst lieber auf dem Land. Dein Partner/deine Partnerin wohnt lieber in der Stadt. Was findest du gut? A sagt einen Satz, dann ist B dran usw.* Pupils give the reasons why they like living in town or country (*Ich wohne lieber auf dem Land, weil es … gibt*), using the picture cues provided.

AT 2.4

2b *Und was findest du nicht gut? A sagt einen Satz, dann ist B dran usw.* Pupils give the reasons why they dislike living in the town or country (*Ich wohne nicht gern auf dem Land, weil es … gibt*), using the picture cues provided.

Mark scheme:
1 mark for each correct answer fully and unambiguously communicated, including correct use of *weil*. If the answer is partially communicated, or if the answer contains significant grammatical error, 1 mark may be awarded. Up to 2 marks may be awarded for pronunciation (total 10).

Assessment criteria:
Pupils with 6 or more correct answers show evidence of performance at AT2 level 4.

Lesen 1

C 92A

AT 3.2

1 *Was ist gesund und was ist ungesund? Lies die Sätze und schreib ✔ (gesund) oder ✘ (ungesund) in die Kästchen.* Pupils read the sentences and decide whether they show a healthy or an unhealthy lifestyle.

Answers: gesund: 1, 2, 5, 7, 10; ungesund: 3, 4, 6, 8, 9

Mark scheme:
1 mark for each correct answer (total 10)

Assessment criteria:
Pupils with 8 or more correct answers show evidence of performance at AT3 level 2.

AT 3.3

2 *Was macht Klasse 9H in den Sommerferien? Finde die passenden Bilder für die Sprechblasen.* Pupils read the speech bubbles about plans for the summer holidays and then select the appropriate pictures for each speaker.

Answers:
Hans: f, i; Jasmin: a, h; Ahmid: g, d; Kai: j, c; Silke: e, b

Mark scheme:
1 mark for each correct answer (total 10)

Assessment criteria:
Pupils with 8 or more marks show evidence of performance at AT3 level 3.

| C 92B | **Lesen 2**

| AT 3.4 | **1** *Wie hilft Guptal der Umwelt? Lies den Text und finde die richtige Reihenfolge für die Bilder.* Pupils read the text and then put the pictures into the order that they are mentioned in the text.

Answers: b, e, a, c, d

Mark scheme:

1 mark for each correct answer (total 5)

Assessment criteria:

Pupils with 4 or more correct answers show evidence of performance at AT3 level 4.

| AT 3.4 | **1b** *Sind die Sätze richtig oder falsch? Schreib ✔ oder ✗ in die Kästchen.* Pupils read the text again, and decide whether the sentences are true or false.

Answers:

1 ✗ 2 ✗ 3 ✔ 4 ✔ 5 ✗

Mark scheme:

1 mark for each correct answer (total 5)

Assessment criteria:

Pupils who mark 4 or more answers correctly show evidence of performance at AT3 level 4.

Note that Copymasters 92A and 92B (*Lesen 1* and *Lesen 2*) should be treated as one assessment, totalling 30 marks.

| C 93 | **Schreiben**

| AT 4.4 | **1** *Was gibt es in dieser Stadt? Beschreib die Stadt.* Pupils write sentences to describe the town depicted in the picture.

Possible answers:

In dieser Stadt gibt es …
eine Tankstelle/ein (großes, modernes) Hotel/ein (modernes) Krankenhaus
Fabriken/ein Kraftwerk/viel Verkehr/viele Autos
einen (kleinen) Park/viel Müll
Blumen/Vögel/einen See/Frösche/Eichhörnchen

Mark scheme:

1 mark for each complete description accurately communicated. Half a mark may be awarded for each complete description containing significant error, or for accurate communication of part of the message (total 8).

Assessment criteria:

Pupils gaining 6 or more marks show evidence of performance at AT4 level 4.

| AT 4.5 | **2** *Was hast du letzte Woche gemacht? Was wirst du nächste Woche machen? Schreib Sätze.* Pupils write sentences in the perfect tense and the future tense in response to the picture cues.

Answers:

a Ich habe ein Picknick gemacht.
  Ich werde ein Picknick machen.
b Ich habe Fußball gespielt.
  Ich werde Fußball spielen.
c Ich bin in die Disco gegangen.

Ich werde in die Disco gehen.
d Ich habe einen Einkaufsbummel gemacht.
  Ich werde einen Einkaufsbummel machen.
e Ich bin ins Schwimmbad gegangen.
  Ich werde ins Schwimmbad gehen.
f Ich habe meinen Freund/meine Freundin besucht.
  Ich werde meinen Freund/meine Freundin besuchen.

Mark scheme:

1 mark for each complete sentence accurately communicated. Sentences which contain significant error but which nevertheless communicate the meaning effectively (including the time frame) may be awarded half a mark (total 10).

Assessment criteria:

Pupils gaining 8 or more marks show evidence of performance at AT4 level 5. Teachers may award level 3 or 4 to pupils whose performance narrowly misses 8 marks.

| AT 4.5 | **3a** *Was sind ihre Zukunftspläne für die nächste Woche, die Sommerferien und später? Schreib Sätze mit Ich werde … und Ich möchte …* Pupils write sentences in the future tense (plans for next week and the summer holidays) and with *ich möchte …* + infinitive (aspirations for the future).

Answers:

Nächste Woche: Ich werde eine E-Mail an meinen Freund/meine Freundin schreiben. Ich werde auch ins Schwimmbad gehen.

Die Sommerferien: Ich werde nach Griechenland fahren/fliegen und ich werde im Restaurant essen.

Später: Ich möchte Mechanikerin werden. Und ich möchte viel Geld verdienen.

Mark scheme:

1 mark for each complete sentence accurately communicated. Sentences which contain significant error but which nevertheless communicate the meaning effectively may be awarded half a mark (total 6).

Assessment criteria:

Pupils gaining 4 or more marks show evidence of performance at AT4 level 5. Teachers may award level 3 or 4 to pupils whose performance narrowly misses 4 marks.

| AT 4.5 | **3b** *Du bist dran! Beschreib deine Zukunftspläne für die nächste Woche, die Sommerferien und später.* Pupils now write their own plans and aspirations for the future, using the future tense and *ich möchte* + infinitive.

Mark scheme:

1 mark for each complete sentence accurately communicated. Sentences which contain significant error but which nevertheless communicate the meaning effectively may be awarded half a mark (total 6).

Assessment criteria:

Pupils gaining 4 or more marks show evidence of performance at AT4 level 5. Teachers may award level 3 or 4 to pupils whose performance narrowly misses 4 marks.